Chapter R

Review of Basic Algebra

Exercise Set R.1

In Exercises 1-5, consider the following numbers: $-6, 0, 1,$ $-\frac{1}{2}, -4, \frac{7}{9}, 12, -\frac{6}{5}, 3.45, 5\frac{1}{2}, \sqrt{3}, \sqrt{25}, -\frac{12}{3},$ $0.131331333133331\ldots.$

1. The natural numbers are numbers used for counting. The natural numbers in the list above are 1, 12, and $\sqrt{25}$ ($\sqrt{25} = 5$).

3. The rational numbers can be named as quotients of integers with nonzero divisors. The rational numbers in the list above are $-6, 0, 1, -\frac{1}{2}, -4, \frac{7}{9}, 12, -\frac{6}{5}, 3.45$ ($3.45 = \frac{345}{100}$), $5\frac{1}{2}$ ($5\frac{1}{2} = \frac{11}{2}$), $\sqrt{25}$ ($\sqrt{25} = 5$), and $-\frac{12}{3}$.

5. The real numbers consist of the rational numbers and the irrational numbers. All of the numbers in the list are real numbers.

In Exercises 7-11, consider the following numbers: $-\sqrt{5}, -3.43,$ $-11, 12, 0, \frac{11}{34}, -\frac{7}{13}, \pi, -3.565665666566665\ldots$

7. The whole numbers consist of the natural numbers and 0. The whole numbers in the list above are 12 and 0.

9. The integers consist of the whole numbers and their opposites. The integers in the list above are -11, 12, and 0.

11. The irrational numbers are the numbers that are not rational. The irrational numbers in the list above are $-\sqrt{5}$, π, and $-3.565665666566665\ldots.$

13. We list the members of the set.
    $\{m, a, t, h\}$

15. We list the members of the set.
    $\{1, 2, 3, 4, 5, 6, 7, 8, 9, 10, 11, 12\}$

17. We list the members of the set.
    $\{2, 4, 6, 8, \ldots\}$

19. We specify conditions by which we know whether a number is in the set.
    $\{x | x$ is a whole number less than or equal to $5\}$

21. We specify conditions by which we know whether a number is in the set.
    $\left\{\frac{a}{b} \middle| a \text{ and } b \text{ are integers and } b \neq 0\right\}$

23. We specify conditions by which we know whether a number is in the set.
    $\{x | x$ is a real number and $x > -3\}$, or $\{x | x > -3\}$

25. Since 13 is to the right of 0 on the number line, we have $13 > 0$.

27. Since -8 is to the left of 2 on the number line, we have $-8 < 2$.

29. Since -8 is to the left of 8, we have $-8 < 8$.

31. Since -8 is to the left of -3, we have $-8 < -3$.

33. Since -2 is to the right of -12, we have $-2 > -12$.

35. Since -9.9 is to the left of -2.2, we have $-9.9 < -2.2$.

37. Since $37\frac{1}{5}$ is to the right of $-1\frac{67}{100}$, we have $37\frac{1}{5} > -1\frac{67}{100}$.

39. We convert to decimal notation: $\frac{6}{13} = 0.461538\ldots$ and $\frac{13}{25} = 0.52$. Thus $\frac{6}{13} < \frac{13}{25}$.

41. $-8 > x$
    The inequality $x < -8$ has the same meaning.

43. $-12.7 \leq y$
    The inequality $y \geq -12.7$ has the same meaning.

45. $6 \leq -6$ False since neither $6 < -6$ nor $6 = -6$ is true.

47. $5 \geq -8.4$ True since $5 > -8.4$ is true.

49. $x < -2$
    We shade all numbers less than -2. We indicate that -2 is not a solution by using an open circle at -2.

51. $x \leq -2$
    We shade all the numbers to the left of -2 and use a solid circle at -2 to indicate that it is also a solution.

53. $x > -3.3$
    We shade all the numbers to the right of -3.3 and use an open circle at -3.3 to indicate that it is not a solution.

S0-AXN-337

55. $x \geq 2$

We shade all the numbers to the right of 2 and use a solid circle at 2 to indicate that it is also a solution.

57. The distance of -6 from 0 is 6, so $|-6| = 6$.

59. The distance of 28 from 0 is 28, so $|28| = 28$.

61. The distance of -35 from 0 is 35, so $|-35| = 35$.

63. The distance of $-\frac{2}{3}$ from 0 is $\frac{2}{3}$, so $\left|-\frac{2}{3}\right| = \frac{2}{3}$.

65. The distance of $\frac{0}{7}$, or 0, from 0 is 0, so $\left|\frac{0}{7}\right| = 0$.

67. Discussion and Writing Exercise

69. $|-3| = 3$, so $|-3| \leq 5$.

71. $|-7| = 7$, so $|4| \leq |-7|$.

73. For comparison, we first write each number in decimal notation.

$\frac{1}{11} = 0.090909\ldots$

$1.1\% = 0.011$

$\frac{2}{7} = 0.285714285714\ldots$

$0.3\% = 0.003$

$0.11 = 0.11$

$\frac{1}{8}\% = 0.00125$ $\left(\frac{1}{8} = 0.125\right)$

$0.009 = 0.009$

$\frac{99}{1000} = 0.099$

$0.286 = 0.286$

$\frac{1}{8} = 0.125$

$1\% = 0.01$

$\frac{9}{100} = 0.09$

Then these rational numbers listed from least to greatest are $\frac{1}{8}\%$, 0.3%, 0.009, 1%, 1.1%, $\frac{9}{100}$, $\frac{1}{11}$, $\frac{99}{1000}$, 0.11, $\frac{1}{8}$, $\frac{2}{7}$, and 0.286.

Exercise Set R.2

1. $-10 + (-18)$

The sum of two negative numbers is negative. We add their absolute values, $10 + 18 = 28$, and make the answer negative.

$-10 + (-18) = -28$

3. $7 + (-2)$

We find the difference of their absolute values, $7 - 2 = 5$. Since the positive number has the larger absolute value, the answer is positive.

$7 + (-2) = 5$

5. $-8 + (-8)$

The sum of two negative numbers is negative. We add the absolute values, $8 + 8 = 16$, and make the answer negative.

$-8 + (-8) = -16$

7. $7 + (-11)$

We find the difference of their absolute values, $11 - 7 = 4$. Since the negative number has the larger absolute value, the answer is negative.

$7 + (-11) = -4$

9. $-16 + 6$

We find the difference of their absolute values, $16 - 6 = 10$. Since the negative number has the larger absolute value, the answer is negative.

$-16 + 6 = -10$

11. $-26 + 0$

One number is 0. The sum is -26.

$-26 + 0 = -26$

13. $-8.4 + 9.6$

We find the difference of their absolute values, $9.6 - 8.4 = 1.2$. Since the positive number has the larger absolute value, the answer is positive.

$-8.4 + 9.6 = 1.2$

15. $-2.62 + (-6.24)$

The sum of two negative numbers is negative. We add the absolute values, $2.62 + 6.24 = 8.86$, and make the answer negative.

$-2.62 + (-6.24) = -8.86$

17. $-\frac{5}{9} + \frac{2}{9}$

We find the difference of their absolute values, $\frac{5}{9} - \frac{2}{9} = \frac{3}{9} = \frac{1}{3}$. Since the negative number has the larger absolute value, the answer is negative.

$-\frac{5}{9} + \frac{2}{9} = -\frac{1}{3}$

19. $-\frac{11}{12} + \left(-\frac{5}{12}\right)$

The sum of two negative numbers is negative. We add their absolute values, $\frac{11}{12} + \frac{5}{12} = \frac{16}{12}$, or $\frac{4}{3}$, and make the answer negative.

$-\frac{11}{12} + \left(-\frac{5}{12}\right) = -\frac{4}{3}$

STUDENT'S SOLUTIONS MANUAL
JUDITH A. PENNA

INTERMEDIATE ALGEBRA
NINTH EDITION

Marvin L. Bittinger

Indiana University Purdue University at Indianapolis

Addison
Wesley

Boston San Francisco New York
London Toronto Sydney Tokyo Singapore Madrid
Mexico City Munich Paris Cape Town Hong Kong Montreal

Reproduced by Addison-Wesley from camera-ready copy supplied by the author.

Copyright © 2003 Pearson Education, Inc.

All rights reserved. No part of this publication may be reproduced, stored in a retrieval system, or transmitted, in any form or by any means, electronic, mechanical, photocopying, recording, or otherwise, without the prior written permission of the publisher. Printed in the United States of America.

ISBN   0-201-79702-X

1 2 3 4 5 6 7 8 9 10 VG 05 04 03 02

Contents

21. $\dfrac{2}{5} + \left(-\dfrac{3}{10}\right)$

We find the difference of their absolute values.

$\dfrac{2}{5} - \dfrac{3}{10} = \dfrac{2}{5} \cdot \dfrac{2}{2} - \dfrac{3}{10} = \dfrac{4}{10} - \dfrac{3}{10} = \dfrac{1}{10}$

Since the positive number has the larger absolute value, the answer is positive.

$\dfrac{2}{5} + \left(-\dfrac{3}{10}\right) = \dfrac{1}{10}$

23. $-\dfrac{2}{5} + \dfrac{3}{4}$

We find the difference of their absolute values.

$\dfrac{3}{4} - \dfrac{2}{5} = \dfrac{3}{4} \cdot \dfrac{5}{5} - \dfrac{2}{5} \cdot \dfrac{4}{4} = \dfrac{15}{20} - \dfrac{8}{20} = \dfrac{7}{20}$

Since the positive number has the larger absolute value, the answer is positive.

$-\dfrac{2}{5} + \dfrac{3}{4} = \dfrac{7}{20}$

25. When $a = -4$, then $-a = -(-4) = 4$.

(The opposite, or additive inverse, of -4 is 4.)

27. When $a = 3.7$, then $-a = -3.7$.

(The opposite, or additive inverse, of 3.7 is -3.7.)

29. The opposite, or additive inverse, of 10 is -10, because $10 + (-10) = 0$.

31. The opposite, or additive inverse, of 0 is 0, because $0 + 0 = 0$.

33. $3 - 7 = 3 + (-7) = -4$

35. $-5 - 9 = -5 + (-9) = -14$

37. $23 - 23 = 23 + (-23) = 0$

39. $-23 - 23 = -23 + (-23) = -46$

41. $-6 - (-11) = -6 + 11 = 5$

43. $10 - (-5) = 10 + 5 = 15$

45. $15.8 - 27.4 = 15.8 + (-27.4) = -11.6$

47. $-18.01 - 11.24 = -18.01 + (-11.24) = -29.25$

49. $-\dfrac{21}{4} - \left(-\dfrac{7}{4}\right) = -\dfrac{21}{4} + \dfrac{7}{4} = -\dfrac{14}{4} = -\dfrac{7}{2}$

51. $-\dfrac{1}{3} - \left(-\dfrac{1}{12}\right) = -\dfrac{1}{3} + \dfrac{1}{12} = -\dfrac{4}{12} + \dfrac{1}{12} = -\dfrac{3}{12} = -\dfrac{1}{4}$

53. $-\dfrac{3}{4} - \dfrac{5}{6} = -\dfrac{3}{4} + \left(-\dfrac{5}{6}\right) = -\dfrac{9}{12} + \left(-\dfrac{10}{12}\right) = -\dfrac{19}{12}$

55. $\dfrac{1}{3} - \dfrac{4}{5} = \dfrac{1}{3} + \left(-\dfrac{4}{5}\right) = \dfrac{5}{15} + \left(-\dfrac{12}{15}\right) = -\dfrac{7}{15}$

57. $3(-7)$

The product of a positive number and a negative number is negative. We multiply their absolute values, $3 \cdot 7 = 21$, and make the answer negative.

$3(-7) = -21$

59. $-2 \cdot 4$

The product of a negative number and a positive number is negative. We multiply their absolute values, $2 \cdot 4 = 8$, and make the answer negative.

$-2 \cdot 4 = -8$

61. $-8(-3)$

The product of two negative numbers is positive. We multiply their absolute values, $8 \cdot 3 = 24$, and make the answer positive.

$-8(-3) = 24$

63. $-7 \cdot 16$

The product of a negative number and a positive number is negative. We multiply their absolute values, $7 \cdot 16 = 112$, and make the answer negative.

$-7 \cdot 16 = -112$

65. $-6(-5.7)$

The product of two negative numbers is positive. We multiply their absolute values, $6(5.7) = 34.2$, and make the answer positive.

$-6(-5.7) = 34.2$

67. $-\dfrac{3}{5} \cdot \dfrac{4}{7}$

The product of a negative number and a positive number is negative. We multiply their absolute values, $\dfrac{3}{5} \cdot \dfrac{4}{7} = \dfrac{12}{35}$, and make the answer negative.

$-\dfrac{3}{5} \cdot \dfrac{4}{7} = -\dfrac{12}{35}$

69. $-3\left(-\dfrac{2}{3}\right)$

The product of two negative numbers is positive. We multiply their absolute values, $3 \cdot \dfrac{2}{3} = \dfrac{6}{3} = 2$, and make the answer positive.

$-3\left(-\dfrac{2}{3}\right) = 2$

71. $\quad -3(-4)(5)$

$= 12(5)$ The product of two negative numbers is positive.

$= 60$ The product of two positive numbers is positive.

73. $-4.2(-6.3)$

The product of two negative numbers is positive. We multiply the absolute values, $4.2(6.3) = 26.46$, and make the answer positive.

$-4.2(-6.3) = 26.46$

75. $-\dfrac{9}{11} \cdot \left(-\dfrac{11}{9}\right)$

The product of two negative numbers is positive. We multiply their absolute values, $\dfrac{9}{11} \cdot \dfrac{11}{9} = \dfrac{99}{99} = 1$, and make the answer positive.

$-\dfrac{9}{11} \cdot \left(-\dfrac{11}{9}\right) = 1$

77.
$$-\frac{2}{3} \cdot \left(-\frac{2}{3}\right) \cdot \left(-\frac{2}{3}\right)$$

$$= \frac{4}{9} \cdot \left(-\frac{2}{3}\right) \qquad \text{The product of two negative numbers is positive.}$$

$$= -\frac{8}{27} \qquad \text{The product of a positive number and a negative number is negative.}$$

79. When a negative number is divided by a positive number, the answer is negative.
$$\frac{-8}{4} = -2$$

81. When a positive number is divided by a negative number, the answer is negative.
$$\frac{56}{-8} = -7$$

83. When a negative number is divided by a negative number, the answer is positive.
$$-77 \div (-11) = \frac{-77}{-11} = 7$$

85. When a negative number is divided by a negative number, the answer is positive.
$$\frac{-5.4}{-18} = \frac{5.4}{18} = 0.3$$

87. $\frac{5}{0}$ Not defined: Division by 0.

89. $\frac{0}{32} = 0$ because $0 \cdot 32 = 0$.

91. $\frac{9}{y-y}$ Not defined: $y - y = 0$ for any y.

93. The reciprocal of $\frac{3}{4}$ is $\frac{4}{3}$, because $\frac{3}{4} \cdot \frac{4}{3} = 1$.

95. The reciprocal of $-\frac{7}{8}$ is $-\frac{8}{7}$, because $-\frac{7}{8} \cdot \left(-\frac{8}{7}\right) = 1$.

97. The reciprocal of 25 is $\frac{1}{25}$, because $25 \cdot \frac{1}{25} = 1$.

99. The reciprocal of 0.2 is $\frac{1}{0.2}$.
This can also be expressed as follows:
$$\frac{1}{0.2} = \frac{1}{0.2} \cdot \frac{10}{10} = \frac{10}{2} = 5.$$

101. The reciprocal of $-\frac{a}{b}$ is $-\frac{b}{a}$, because $-\frac{a}{b} \cdot \left(-\frac{b}{a}\right) = 1$.

103. $\frac{2}{7} \div \left(-\frac{11}{3}\right) = \frac{2}{7} \cdot \left(-\frac{3}{11}\right) = -\frac{6}{77}$

105. $-\frac{10}{3} \div -\frac{2}{15} = -\frac{10}{3} \cdot \left(-\frac{15}{2}\right) = \frac{150}{6}$, or 25

107. $18.6 \div (-3.1) = \frac{18.6}{-3.1} = -\frac{18.6}{3.1} = -6$

109. $(-75.5) \div (-15.1) = \frac{-75.5}{-15.1} = \frac{75.5}{15.1} = 5$

111. $-48 \div 0.4 = \frac{-48}{0.4} = -\frac{48}{0.4} = -120$

113. $\frac{3}{4} \div \left(-\frac{2}{3}\right) = \frac{3}{4} \cdot \left(-\frac{3}{2}\right) = -\frac{9}{8}$

115. $-\frac{5}{4} \div \left(-\frac{3}{4}\right) = -\frac{5}{4} \cdot \left(-\frac{4}{3}\right) = \frac{20}{12} = \frac{5}{3}$

117. $-\frac{2}{3} \div \left(-\frac{4}{9}\right) = -\frac{2}{3} \cdot \left(-\frac{9}{4}\right) = \frac{18}{12} = \frac{3}{2}$

119. $-\frac{3}{8} \div \left(-\frac{8}{3}\right) = -\frac{3}{8} \cdot \left(-\frac{3}{8}\right) = \frac{9}{64}$

121. $-6.6 \div 3.3 = \frac{-6.6}{3.3} = -2$

123. $\frac{-12}{-13} = \frac{12}{13}$, or $0.\overline{923076}$

125. $\frac{48.6}{-30} = \frac{16.2}{-10} = -1.62$

127. $\frac{-9}{17-17}$ Not defined: $17 - 17 = 0$

129. $\frac{2}{3}$:   The opposite of $\frac{2}{3}$ is $-\frac{2}{3}$, because
$$\frac{2}{3} + \left(-\frac{2}{3}\right) = 0.$$
The reciprocal of $\frac{2}{3}$ is $\frac{3}{2}$, because
$$\frac{2}{3} \cdot \frac{3}{2} = 1.$$

$-\frac{5}{4}$:   The opposite of $-\frac{5}{4}$ is $\frac{5}{4}$, because $-\frac{5}{4} + \frac{5}{4} = 0$.

The reciprocal of $-\frac{5}{4}$ is $-\frac{4}{5}$, because
$$-\frac{5}{4} \cdot \left(-\frac{4}{5}\right) = 1.$$

0:   The opposite of 0 is 0, because $0 + 0 = 0$.
The reciprocal of 0 does not exist. (Only nonzero numbers have reciprocals.)

1:   The opposite of 1 is -1, because $1 + (-1) = 0$.
The reciprocal of 1 is 1, because $1 \cdot 1 = 1$.

-4.5:   The opposite of -4.5 is 4.5, because $-4.5 + 4.5 = 0$.

The reciprocal of -4.5 is $-\frac{1}{4.5}$, because
$$-4.5 \cdot \left(-\frac{1}{4.5}\right) = 1. \text{ (Note that}$$
$$-\frac{1}{4.5} = -\frac{1}{4.5} \cdot \frac{10}{10} = -\frac{10}{45}, \text{ or } -\frac{2}{9}.\text{)}$$

$x, x \neq 0$:   The opposite of x is $-x$, because $x + (-x) = 0$.

The reciprocal of x, $x \neq 0$, is $\frac{1}{x}$, because $x \cdot \frac{1}{x} = 1$.

131. Discussion and Writing Exercise

133. The set of whole numbers is $\{0, 1, 2, 3, \ldots\}$. The whole numbers in the given list are 26 and 0.

135. The set of integers is $\{\ldots, -3, -2, -1, 0, 1, 2, 3, \ldots\}$. The integers in the given list are -13, 26 and 0.

137. The set of rational numbers is
$$\left\{ \frac{p}{q} \,\middle|\, p \text{ is an integer, } q \text{ is an integer, and } q \neq 0 \right\}.$$
Decimal notation for rational numbers either terminates or has a repeating block of digits. The integers in the given list are -12.47, -13, 26, 0, $-\dfrac{23}{32}$, and $\dfrac{7}{11}$.

139. Since -7 is to the left of 8 on the number line, we have $-7 < 8$.

141. Since -45.6 is to the left of -23.8 on the number line, we have $-45.6 < -23.8$.

143.
$$\frac{1}{r_1} + \frac{1}{r_2}$$
$$= \frac{1}{12} + \frac{1}{6} \quad \text{Substituting 12 for } r_1 \text{ and 6 for } r_2$$
$$= \frac{1}{12} + \frac{2}{12}$$
$$= \frac{3}{12}, \text{ or } \frac{1}{4}$$

The conductance is $\dfrac{1}{4}$.

145. We want to find a number c such that $-625 = -0.02 \cdot c$. From the definition of division we know that $c = \dfrac{-625}{-0.02} = 31{,}250$

Exercise Set R.3

1. $\underbrace{4 \cdot 4 \cdot 4 \cdot 4 \cdot 4}_{5 \text{ factors}} = 4^5$

3. $\underbrace{5 \cdot 5 \cdot 5 \cdot 5 \cdot 5 \cdot 5}_{6 \text{ factors}} = 5^6$

5. $\underbrace{m \cdot m \cdot m}_{3 \text{ factors}} = m^3$

7. $\underbrace{\frac{7}{12} \cdot \frac{7}{12} \cdot \frac{7}{12} \cdot \frac{7}{12}}_{4 \text{ factors}} = \left(\frac{7}{12}\right)^4$

9. $\underbrace{(123.7)(123.7)}_{2 \text{ factors}} = (123.7)^2$

11. $2^7 = \underbrace{2 \cdot 2 \cdot 2 \cdot 2 \cdot 2 \cdot 2 \cdot 2}_{7 \text{ factors}} = 128$

13. $(-2)^5 = \underbrace{(-2) \cdot (-2) \cdot (-2) \cdot (-2) \cdot (-2)}_{5 \text{ factors}} = -32$

15. $\left(\frac{1}{3}\right)^4 = \underbrace{\frac{1}{3} \cdot \frac{1}{3} \cdot \frac{1}{3} \cdot \frac{1}{3}}_{4 \text{ factors}} = \frac{1}{81}$

17. $(-4)^3 = \underbrace{(-4) \cdot (-4) \cdot (-4)}_{3 \text{ factors}} = -64$

19. $(-5.6)^2 = \underbrace{(-5.6)(-5.6)}_{2 \text{ factors}} = 31.36$

21. $5^1 = 5 \qquad$ (For any number a, $a^1 = a$.)

23. $34^0 = 1 \qquad$ (For any nonzero number a, $a^0 = 1$.)

25. $(\sqrt{6})^0 = 1 \qquad$ (For any nonzero number a, $a^0 = 1$.)

27. $\left(\frac{7}{8}\right)^1 = \frac{7}{8} \qquad$ (For any number a, $a^1 = a$.)

29. $\left(\frac{1}{4}\right)^{-2} = \frac{1}{\left(\frac{1}{4}\right)^2} = \frac{1}{\frac{1}{16}} = 1 \cdot \frac{16}{1} = 16$

31. $\left(\frac{2}{3}\right)^{-3} = \frac{1}{\left(\frac{2}{3}\right)^3} = \frac{1}{\frac{8}{27}} = 1 \cdot \frac{27}{8} = \frac{27}{8}$

33. $y^{-5} = \dfrac{1}{y^5}$

35. $\dfrac{1}{a^{-2}} = a^2$

37. $(-11)^{-1} = \dfrac{1}{(-11)^1} = \dfrac{1}{-11} = -\dfrac{1}{11}$

39. $\dfrac{1}{3^4} = 3^{-4}$

41. $\dfrac{1}{b^3} = b^{-3}$

43. $\dfrac{1}{(-16)^2} = (-16)^{-2}$

45. $[12 - 4(5 - 1)] = [12 - 4(4)]$
$$= [12 - 16]$$
$$= -4$$

47. $9[8 - 7(5 - 2)] = 9[8 - 7 \cdot 3]$
$$= 9[8 - 21]$$
$$= 9[-13]$$
$$= -117$$

49. $[5(8 - 6) + 12] - [24 - (8 - 4)] = [5 \cdot 2 + 12] - [24 - 4]$
$$= [10 + 12] - [24 - 4]$$
$$= 22 - 20$$
$$= 2$$

51. $[64 \div (-4)] \div (-2) = -16 \div (-2)$
$= 8$

53. $19(-22) + 60 = -418 + 60$
$= -358$

55. $(5 + 7)^2 = 12^2 = 144$
$5^2 + 7^2 = 25 + 49 = 74$

57. $2^3 + 2^4 - 20 \cdot 30 = 8 + 16 - 600$
$= 24 - 600$
$= -576$

59. $5^3 + 36 \cdot 72 - (18 + 25 \cdot 4)$
$= 5^3 + 36 \cdot 72 - (18 + 100)$
$= 5^3 + 36 \cdot 72 - 118$
$= 125 + 36 \cdot 72 - 118$
$= 125 + 2592 - 118$
$= 2717 - 118$
$= 2599$

61. $(13 \cdot 2 - 8 \cdot 4)^2 = (26 - 32)^2$
$= (-6)^2$
$= 36$

63. $4000 \cdot (1 + 0.12)^3 = 4000(1.12)^3$
$= 4000(1.404928)$
$= 5619.712$

65. $(20 \cdot 4 + 13 \cdot 8)^2 - (39 \cdot 15)^3$
$= (80 + 104)^2 - (585)^3$
$= 184^2 - 585^3$
$= 33,856 - 200,201,625$
$= -200,167,769$

67. $18 - 2 \cdot 3 - 9 = 18 - 6 - 9$
$= 12 - 9$
$= 3$

69. $(18 - 2 \cdot 3) - 9 = (18 - 6) - 9$
$= 12 - 9$
$= 3$

71. $[24 \div (-3)] \div \left(-\frac{1}{2}\right)$
$= -8 \div \left(-\frac{1}{2}\right)$
$= -8 \cdot (-2)$
$= 16$

73. $15 \cdot (-24) + 50 = -360 + 50$
$= -310$

75. $4 \div (8 - 10)^2 + 1 = 4 \div (-2)^2 + 1$
$= 4 \div 4 + 1$
$= 1 + 1$
$= 2$

77. $6^3 + 25 \cdot 71 - (16 + 25 \cdot 4)$
$= 6^3 + 25 \cdot 71 - (16 + 100)$
$= 6^3 + 25 \cdot 71 - 116$
$= 216 + 25 \cdot 71 - 116$
$= 216 + 1775 - 116$
$= 1991 - 116$
$= 1875$

79. $5000 \cdot (1 + 0.16)^3 = 5000 \cdot (1.16)^3$
$= 5000(1.560896)$
$= 7804.48$

81. $4 \cdot 5 - 2 \cdot 6 + 4 = 20 - 12 + 4$
$= 8 + 4$
$= 12$

83. $4 \cdot (6 + 8)/(4 + 3) = 4 \cdot 14/7$
$= 56/7$
$= 8$

85. $[2 \cdot (5 - 3)]^2 = [2 \cdot 2]^2$
$= 4^2$
$= 16$

87. $8(-7) + 6(-5) = -56 - 30$
$= -86$

89. $19 - 5(-3) + 3 = 19 + 15 + 3$
$= 34 + 3$
$= 37$

91. $9 \div (-3) + 16 \div 8 = -3 + 2$
$= -1$

93. $7 + 10 - (-10 \div 2) = 7 + 10 - (-5)$
$= 7 + 10 + 5$
$= 17 + 5$
$= 22$

95. $5^2 - 8^2 = 25 - 64$
$= -39$

97. $20 + 4^3 \div (-8) = 20 + 64 \div (-8)$
$= 20 + (-8)$
$= 12$

99. $-7(3^4) + 18 = -7 \cdot 81 + 18$
$= -567 + 18$
$= -549$

101. $9[(8-11)-13] = 9[-3-13]$
$$= 9[-16]$$
$$= -144$$

103. $256 \div (-32) \div (-4) = -8 \div (-4)$
$$= 2$$

105. $\dfrac{5^2 - |4^3 - 8|}{9^2 - 2^2 - 1^5} = \dfrac{5^2 - |64 - 8|}{81 - 4 - 1}$
$$= \dfrac{5^2 - |56|}{77 - 1}$$
$$= \dfrac{5^2 - 56}{77 - 1}$$
$$= \dfrac{25 - 56}{76}$$
$$= \dfrac{-31}{76}$$
$$= -\dfrac{31}{76}$$

107. $\dfrac{30(8-3) - 4(10-3)}{10|2-6| - 2(5+2)} = \dfrac{30 \cdot 5 - 4 \cdot 7}{10|-4| - 2 \cdot 7}$
$$= \dfrac{150 - 28}{10 \cdot 4 - 2 \cdot 7}$$
$$= \dfrac{122}{40 - 14}$$
$$= \dfrac{122}{26}$$
$$= \dfrac{61}{13}$$

109. Discussion and Writing Exercise

111. The distance of $-\dfrac{9}{7}$ from 0 is $\dfrac{9}{7}$, so $\left|-\dfrac{9}{7}\right| = \dfrac{9}{7}$.

113. The distance of 0 from 0 is 0, so $|0| = 0$.

115. $23 - 56 = 23 + (-56) = -33$

117. $-23 - (-56) = -23 + 56 = 33$

119. $(-10)(2.3) = -23$

(The product of a negative number and a positive number is negative.)

121. $10(-2.3) = -23$

(The product of a positive number and a negative number is negative.)

123. $(-2)^0 - (-2)^3 - (-2)^{-1} + (-2)^4 - (-2)^{-2}$
$$= 1 - (-8) - \left(-\dfrac{1}{2}\right) + 16 - \dfrac{1}{(-2)^2}$$
$$= 1 - (-8) - \left(-\dfrac{1}{2}\right) + 16 - \dfrac{1}{4}$$
$$= 1 + 8 + \dfrac{1}{2} + 16 - \dfrac{1}{4}$$
$$= 25\dfrac{1}{4}$$

125. $9 \cdot 5 + 2 - (8 \cdot 3 + 1) = 22$

127. $(0.2)^{(-0.2)^{-1}} = (0.2)^{1/-0.2} = (0.2)^{-5} =$
$$\dfrac{1}{(0.2)^5} = \dfrac{1}{0.00032} = 3125$$

Exercise Set R.4

1. 8 more than b

We have $b + 8$, or $8 + b$.

3. 13.4 less than c

We have $c - 13.4$.

5. 5 increased by q

We have $5 + q$, or $q + 5$.

7. b more than a

We have $a + b$, or $b + a$.

9. x divided by y

We have $x \div y$, or $\dfrac{x}{y}$

11. x plus w

We have $x + w$, or $w + x$.

13. m subtracted from n

We have $n - m$.

15. The sum of p and q

We have $p + q$, or $q + p$.

17. Three times q

We have $3q$.

19. -18 multiplied by m

We have $-18m$.

21. The product of 17% and your salary

Let s represent your salary. We have $17\%s$, or $0.17s$.

23. We have $75t$.

25. We have $\$40 - x$.

27. Substitute -4 for z and carry out the multiplication.
$$23z = 23(-4) = -92$$

29. Substitute -24 for a and -8 for b and carry out the division.
$$\dfrac{a}{b} = \dfrac{-24}{-8} = 3$$

31. Substitute 36 for m and 4 for n and carry out the calculations.
$$\dfrac{m-n}{8} = \dfrac{36-4}{8} = \dfrac{32}{8} = 4$$

33. Substitute 9 for z and 2 for y and carry out the calculations.

$$\frac{5z}{y} = \frac{5 \cdot 9}{2} = \frac{45}{2}, \text{ or } 22\frac{1}{2}, \text{ or } 22.5$$

35. Substitute 4 for b and 6 for c and carry out the calculations.

$$2c \div 3b = 2 \cdot 6 \div 3 \cdot 4$$
$$= 12 \div 3 \cdot 4$$
$$= 4 \cdot 4$$
$$= 16$$

37. Substitute 3 for r and 27 for s and carry out the calculations.

$$25 - r^2 + s \div r^2 = 25 - 3^2 + 27 \div 3^2$$
$$= 25 - 9 + 27 \div 9$$
$$= 25 - 9 + 3$$
$$= 16 + 3$$
$$= 19$$

39. Substitute 15 for m and 3 for n and carry out the calculations.

$$m + n(5 + n^2) = 15 + 3(5 + 3^2)$$
$$= 15 + 3(5 + 9)$$
$$= 15 + 3 \cdot 14$$
$$= 15 + 42$$
$$= 57$$

41. Substitute \$7345 for P, 6% or 0.06 for r, and 1 for t and carry out the calculations.

$$I = Prt$$
$$I = \$7345(0.06)(1)$$
$$I = \$440.70$$

43. Substitute 3.14 for π and 6 for r in each formula and carry out the calculations.

$$A = \pi r^2$$
$$= 3.14(6)^2$$
$$= 3.14(36)$$
$$= 113.04 \text{ cm}^2$$

$$C = 2\pi r$$
$$= 2(3.14)(6)$$
$$= 37.68 \text{ cm}$$

45. Discussion and Writing Exercise

47. $3^5 = 3 \cdot 3 \cdot 3 \cdot 3 \cdot 3 = 243$

49. $(-10)^2 = (-10)(-10) = 100$

51. $(-5.3)^2 = (-5.3)(-5.3) = 28.09$

53. $(4.5)^0 = 1$ (For any nonzero number a, $a^0 = 1$.)

55. $(3x)^1 = 3x$ (For any number a, $a^1 = a$.)

57. Distance = speed × time

$$d = r \cdot t$$

59. Substitute 2 for x and 4 for y and carry out the calculations.

$$\frac{y+x}{2} + \frac{3y}{x} = \frac{4+2}{2} + \frac{3 \cdot 4}{2} = \frac{6}{2} + \frac{12}{2} = 3 + 6 = 9$$

Exercise Set R.5

1. Substitute and find the value of each expression. For example, for $x = -2$, $2x + 3x = 2(-2) + 3(-2) = -4 - 6 = -10$.

	$2x+3x$	$5x$	$2x-3x$
$x = -2$	-10	-10	2
$x = 5$	25	25	-5
$x = 0$	0	0	0

The values of $2x + 3x$ and $5x$ are the same for the given values of x and, indeed, for any allowable replacement for x. Thus, they are equivalent.

The values of $2x + 3x$ and $2x - 3x$ do not agree for $x = -2$ and for $x = 5$. Since one disagreement is sufficient to show that two expressions are not equivalent, we know that these expressions are not equivalent. Similarly, $5x$ and $2x - 3x$ are not equivalent.

3. Substitute and find the value of each expression. For example, for $x = -1$, $4x + 8x = 4(-1) + 8(-1) = -4 - 8 = -12$.

	$4x+8x$	$4(x+3x)$	$4(x+2x)$
$x = -1$	-12	-16	-12
$x = 3.2$	38.4	51.2	38.4
$x = 0$	0	0	0

The values of $4x + 8x$ and $4(x + 2x)$ are the same for the given values of x and, indeed, for any allowable replacement for x. Thus, they are equivalent.

The values of $4x + 8x$ and $4(x + 3x)$ do not agree for $x = -1$ and for $x = 3.2$. Since one disagreement is sufficient to show that two expressions are not equivalent, we know that these expressions are not equivalent. Similarly, $4(x + 3x)$ and $4(x + 2x)$ are not equivalent.

5. Since $8x = 8 \cdot x$, we multiply by 1 using x/x as a name for 1.

$$\frac{7}{8} = \frac{7}{8} \cdot 1 = \frac{7}{8} \cdot \frac{x}{x} = \frac{7x}{8x}$$

7. Since $8a = 4 \cdot 2a$, we multiply by 1 using $\frac{2a}{2a}$ as a name for 1.

$$\frac{3}{4} = \frac{3}{4} \cdot 1 = \frac{3}{4} \cdot \frac{2a}{2a} = \frac{6a}{8a}$$

9. $\dfrac{25x}{15x} = \dfrac{5 \cdot 5x}{3 \cdot 5x}$ We look for the largest common factor of the numerator and denominator and factor each.

$= \dfrac{5}{3} \cdot \dfrac{5x}{5x}$ Factoring the expression

$= \dfrac{5}{3} \cdot 1$ $\left(\dfrac{5x}{5x} = 1\right)$

$= \dfrac{5}{3}$

11. $-\dfrac{100a}{25a}$

$= -\dfrac{25a \cdot 4}{25a \cdot 1}$ Factoring numerator and denominator

$= -\dfrac{25a}{25a} \cdot \dfrac{4}{1}$ Factoring the expression

$= -1 \cdot \dfrac{4}{1}$ $\left(\dfrac{25a}{25a} = 1\right)$

$= -\dfrac{4}{1}$

$= -4$

13. $w + 3 = 3 + w$ Commutative law of addition

15. $rt = tr$ Commutative law of multiplication

17. $4 + cd = cd + 4$ Commutative law of addition

or

$4 + cd = cd + 4 = dc + 4$ Commutative laws of addition and multiplication

or

$4 + cd = 4 + dc$ Commutative law of multiplication

19. $yz + x = x + yz$ Commutative law of addition

or

$yz + x = x + yz = x + zy$ Commutative laws of addition and multiplication

or

$yz + x = zy + x$ Commutative law of multiplication

21. $m + (n + 2) = (m + n) + 2$ Associative law of addition

23. $(7 \cdot x) \cdot y = 7 \cdot (x \cdot y)$ Associative law of multiplication

25. $(a + b) + 8 = a + (b + 8)$ Associative law

$= a + (8 + b)$ Commutative law

$(a + b) + 8 = a + (b + 8)$ Associative law

$= a + (8 + b)$ Commutative law

$= (a + 8) + b$ Associative law

$(a + b) + 8 = (b + a) + 8$ Commutative law

$= b + (a + 8)$ Associative law

Other answers are possible.

27. $7 \cdot (a \cdot b) = 7 \cdot (b \cdot a)$ Commutative law

$= (7 \cdot b) \cdot a$ Associative law

$7 \cdot (a \cdot b) = (7 \cdot a) \cdot b$ Associative law

$= b \cdot (7 \cdot a)$ Commutative law

$= b \cdot (a \cdot 7)$ Commutative law

$7 \cdot (a \cdot b) = 7 \cdot (b \cdot a)$ Commutative law

$= (b \cdot a) \cdot 7$ Commutative law

Other answers are possible.

29. $4(a + 1) = 4 \cdot a + 4 \cdot 1$

$= 4a + 4$

31. $8(x - y) = 8 \cdot x - 8 \cdot y$

$= 8x - 8y$

33. $-5(2a + 3b) = -5 \cdot 2a + (-5) \cdot 3b$

$= -10a - 15b$

35. $2a(b - c + d) = 2a \cdot b - 2a \cdot c + 2a \cdot d$

$= 2ab - 2ac + 2ad$

37. $2\pi r(h + 1) = 2\pi r \cdot h + 2\pi r \cdot 1$

$= 2\pi rh + 2\pi r$

39. $\dfrac{1}{2}h(a + b) = \dfrac{1}{2}h \cdot a + \dfrac{1}{2}h \cdot b$

$= \dfrac{1}{2}ha + \dfrac{1}{2}hb$

41. $4a - 5b + 6 = 4a + (-5b) + 6$

The terms are $4a$, $-5b$, and 6.

43. $2x - 3y - 2z = 2x + (-3y) + (-2z)$

The terms are $2x$, $-3y$, and $-2z$.

45. $24x + 24y = 24 \cdot x + 24 \cdot y$

$= 24(x + y)$

47. $7p - 7 = 7 \cdot p - 7 \cdot 1$

$= 7(p - 1)$

49. $7x - 21 = 7 \cdot x - 7 \cdot 3$

$= 7(x - 3)$

51. $xy + x = x \cdot y + x \cdot 1$

$= x(y + 1)$

53. $2x - 2y + 2z = 2 \cdot x - 2 \cdot y + 2 \cdot z$

$= 2(x - y + z)$

55. $3x + 6y - 3 = 3 \cdot x + 3 \cdot 2y - 3 \cdot 1$

$= 3(x + 2y - 1)$

57. $ab + ac - ad = a \cdot b + a \cdot c - a \cdot d$

$= a(b + c - d)$

59. $\dfrac{1}{4}\pi rr + \dfrac{1}{4}\pi rs = \dfrac{1}{4}\pi r \cdot r + \dfrac{1}{4}\pi r \cdot s$

$\qquad\qquad = \dfrac{1}{4}\pi r(r + s)$

61. Discussion and Writing Exercise

63. Let x and y represent the numbers. Then we have

$\qquad (x + y)^2.$

65. $-34.2 + -67.8 = -34.2 + (-67.8) = -102$

67. $-\dfrac{1}{4}\left(-\dfrac{1}{2}\right) = \dfrac{1 \cdot 1}{4 \cdot 2} = \dfrac{1}{8}$

69. Let $x = 1$ and $y = -1$.

$\qquad x^2 + y^2 = 1^2 + (-1)^2 = 1 + 1 = 2$

$\qquad (x + y)^2 = (1 + (-1))^2 = 0^2 = 0$

Since the expressions have different values, they are not equivalent.

71. For $x = -2$, $x^2 \cdot x^3 = (-2)^2 \cdot (-2)^3 = 4(-8) = -32$ and $x^5 = (-2)^5 = -32$.

For $x = 0$, $x^2 \cdot x^3 = 0^2 \cdot 0^3 = 0 \cdot 0 = 0$ and $x^5 = 0^5 = 0$.

For $x = 1$, $x^2 \cdot x^3 = 1^2 \cdot 1^3 = 1 \cdot 1 = 1$ and $x^5 = 1^5 = 1$.

Indeed, the expressions have the same value for all values of x, so they are equivalent.

Exercise Set R.6

1. $7x + 5x = (7 + 5)x$

$\qquad\quad = 12x$

3. $8b - 11b = (8 - 11)b$

$\qquad\qquad = -3b$

5. $14y + y = 14y + 1y$

$\qquad\qquad = (14 + 1)y$

$\qquad\qquad = 15y$

7. $12a - a = 12a - 1a$

$\qquad\qquad = (12 - 1)a$

$\qquad\qquad = 11a$

9. $t - 9t = 1t - 9t$

$\qquad\quad = (1 - 9)t$

$\qquad\quad = -8t$

11. $5x - 3x + 8x = (5 - 3 + 8)x$

$\qquad\qquad\qquad = 10x$

13. $3x - 5y + 8x = (3 + 8)x - 5y$

$\qquad\qquad\qquad = 11x - 5y$

15. $3c + 8d - 7c + 4d = (3 - 7)c + (8 + 4)d$

$\qquad\qquad\qquad\qquad = -4c + 12d$

17. $4x - 7 + 18x + 25 = (4 + 18)x + (-7 + 25)$

$\qquad\qquad\qquad\qquad = 22x + 18$

19. $\quad 1.3x + 1.4y - 0.11x - 0.47y$

$\quad = (1.3 - 0.11)x + (1.4 - 0.47)y$

$\quad = 1.19x + 0.93y$

21. $\quad \dfrac{2}{3}a + \dfrac{5}{6}b - 27 - \dfrac{4}{5}a - \dfrac{7}{6}b$

$\quad = \left(\dfrac{2}{3} - \dfrac{4}{5}\right)a + \left(\dfrac{5}{6} - \dfrac{7}{6}\right)b - 27$

$\quad = \left(\dfrac{10}{15} - \dfrac{12}{15}\right)a + \left(-\dfrac{2}{6}\right)b - 27$

$\quad = -\dfrac{2}{15}a - \dfrac{1}{3}b - 27$

23. $P = 2l + 2w$

$\quad P = 2 \cdot l + 2 \cdot w$

$\quad P = 2(l + w)$

25. $-(-2c) = -1(-2c)$

$\qquad\qquad = [-1(-2)]c$

$\qquad\qquad = 2c$

27. $-(b + 4) = -1(b + 4)$

$\qquad\qquad = -1 \cdot b + (-1)4$

$\qquad\qquad = -b - 4$

29. $-(b - 3) = -1(b - 3)$

$\qquad\qquad = -1 \cdot b - (-1) \cdot 3$

$\qquad\qquad = -b + [-(-1)3]$

$\qquad\qquad = -b + 3$, or $3 - b$

31. $-(t - y) = -1(t - y)$

$\qquad\qquad = -1 \cdot t - (-1) \cdot y$

$\qquad\qquad = -t + [-(-1)y]$

$\qquad\qquad = -t + y$, or $y - t$

33. $-(x + y + z) = -1(x + y + z)$

$\qquad\qquad\qquad = -1 \cdot x + (-1) \cdot y + (-1) \cdot z$

$\qquad\qquad\qquad = -x - y - z$

35. $\quad -(8x - 6y + 13)$

$\quad = -8x + 6y - 13 \qquad$ Changing the sign of every term inside parentheses

37. $\quad -(-2c + 5d - 3e + 4f)$

$\quad = 2c - 5d + 3e - 4f \qquad$ Changing the sign of every term inside parentheses

39. $\quad -\left(-1.2x + 56.7y - 34z - \dfrac{1}{4}\right)$

$\quad = 1.2x - 56.7y + 34z + \dfrac{1}{4} \qquad$ Changing the sign of every term inside parentheses

41. $a + (2a + 5) = a + 2a + 5$
$$= 3a + 5$$

43. $4m - (3m - 1) = 4m - 3m + 1$
$$= m + 1$$

45. $5d - 9 - (7 - 4d) = 5d - 9 - 7 + 4d$
$$= 9d - 16$$

47. $-2(x + 3) - 5(x - 4)$
$$= -2(x + 3) + [-5(x - 4)]$$
$$= -2x - 6 + [-5x + 20]$$
$$= -2x - 6 - 5x + 20$$
$$= -7x + 14$$

49. $5x - 7(2x - 3) - 4$
$$= 5x + [-7(2x - 3)] - 4$$
$$= 5x + [-14x + 21] - 4$$
$$= 5x - 14x + 21 - 4$$
$$= -9x + 17$$

51. $8x - (-3y + 7) + (9x - 11)$
$$= 8x + 3y - 7 + 9x - 11$$
$$= 17x + 3y - 18$$

53. $\frac{1}{4}(24x - 8) - \frac{1}{2}(-8x + 6) - 14$
$$= \frac{1}{4}(24x - 8) + \left[-\frac{1}{2}(-8x + 6)\right] - 14$$
$$= 6x - 2 + [4x - 3] - 14$$
$$= 6x - 2 + 4x - 3 - 14$$
$$= 10x - 19$$

55. $7a - [9 - 3(5a - 2)] = 7a - [9 - 15a + 6]$
$$= 7a - [15 - 15a]$$
$$= 7a - 15 + 15a$$
$$= 22a - 15$$

57. $5\{-2 + 3[4 - 2(3 + 5)]\} = 5\{-2 + 3[4 - 2(8)]\}$
$$= 5\{-2 + 3[4 - 16]\}$$
$$= 5\{-2 + 3[-12]\}$$
$$= 5\{-2 - 36\}$$
$$= 5\{-38\}$$
$$= -190$$

59. $[10(x + 3) - 4] + [2(x - 1) + 6]$
$$= [10x + 30 - 4] + [2x - 2 + 6]$$
$$= 10x + 26 + 2x + 4$$
$$= 12x + 30$$

61. $[7(x + 5) - 19] - [4(x - 6) + 10]$
$$= [7x + 35 - 19] - [4x - 24 + 10]$$
$$= [7x + 16] - [4x - 14]$$
$$= 7x + 16 - 4x + 14$$
$$= 3x + 30$$

63. $3\{[7(x - 2) + 4] - [2(2x - 5) + 6]\}$
$$= 3\{[7x - 14 + 4] - [4x - 10 + 6]\}$$
$$= 3\{[7x - 10] - [4x - 4]\}$$
$$= 3\{7x - 10 - 4x + 4\}$$
$$= 3\{3x - 6\}$$
$$= 9x - 18$$

65. $4\{[5(x - 3) + 2^2] - 3[2(x + 5) - 9^2]\}$
$$= 4\{[5(x - 3) + 4] - 3[2(x + 5) - 81]\}$$
$$= 4\{[5x - 15 + 4] - 3[2x + 10 - 81]\}$$
$$= 4\{[5x - 11] - 3[2x - 71]\}$$
$$= 4\{5x - 11 - 6x + 213\}$$
$$= 4\{-x + 202\}$$
$$= -4x + 808$$

67. $2y + \{8[3(2y - 5) - (8y + 9)] + 6\}$
$$= 2y + \{8[6y - 15 - 8y - 9] + 6\}$$
$$= 2y + \{8[-2y - 24] + 6\}$$
$$= 2y + \{-16y - 192 + 6\}$$
$$= 2y + \{-16y - 186\}$$
$$= 2y - 16y - 186$$
$$= -14y - 186$$

69. Discussion and Writing Exercise

71. $17 + (-54)$

We find the difference of the absolute values: $54 - 17 = 37$. Since the negative number has the larger absolute value, the answer is negative.

$17 + (-54) = -37$

73. $-13.78 + (-9.32)$

The sum of two negative numbers is negative. We add their absolute values, $13.78 + 9.32 = 23.1$, and make the answer negative.

$-13.78 + (-9.32) = -23.1$

75. When a negative number is divided by a positive number, the answer is negative.

$-256 \div 16 = -16$

77. When a positive number is divided by a negative number, the answer is negative.

$256 \div (-16) = -16$

79. $8(a - b) = 8 \cdot a - 8 \cdot b = 8a - 8b$

81. $6x(a - b + 2c) = 6x \cdot a - 6x \cdot b + 6x \cdot 2c =$
$6ax - 6bx + 12cx$

83. $24a - 24 = 24 \cdot a - 24 \cdot 1 = 24(a - 1)$

85. $ab - ac + a = a \cdot b - a \cdot c + a \cdot 1 = a(b - c + 1)$

87. $(3 - 8)^2 + 9 = 34$

89. $5 \cdot 2^3 \div (3 - 4)^4 = 40$

91.
$$[11(a - 3) + 12a] - \{6[4(3b - 7) - (9b + 10)] + 11\}$$
$$= [11a - 33 + 12a] - \{6[12b - 28 - 9b - 10] + 11\}$$
$$= [23a - 33] - \{6[3b - 38] + 11\}$$
$$= 23a - 33 - \{18b - 228 + 11\}$$
$$= 23a - 33 - \{18b - 217\}$$
$$= 23a - 33 - 18b + 217$$
$$= 23a - 18b + 184$$

93.
$$z - \{2z + [3z - (4z + 5x) - 6z] + 7z\} - 8z$$
$$= z - \{2z + [3z - 4z - 5x - 6z] + 7z\} - 8z$$
$$= z - \{2z - 7z - 5x + 7z\} - 8z$$
$$= z - \{2z - 5x\} - 8z$$
$$= z - 2z + 5x - 8z$$
$$= -9z + 5x$$

95.
$$x - \{x + 1 - [x + 2 - (x - 3 - \{x + 4 -$$
$$[x - 5 + (x - 6)]\})]\}$$
$$= x - \{x + 1 - [x + 2 - (x - 3 - \{x + 4 - [2x - 11]\})]\}$$
$$= x - \{x + 1 - [x + 2 - (x - 3 - \{x + 4 - 2x + 11\})]\}$$
$$= x - \{x + 1 - [x + 2 - (x - 3 - \{-x + 15\})]\}$$
$$= x - \{x + 1 - [x + 2 - (x - 3 + x - 15)]\}$$
$$= x - \{x + 1 - [x + 2 - (2x - 18)]\}$$
$$= x - \{x + 1 - [x + 2 - 2x + 18]\}$$
$$= x - \{x + 1 - [-x + 20]\}$$
$$= x - \{x + 1 + x - 20\}$$
$$= x - \{2x - 19\}$$
$$= x - 2x + 19$$
$$= -x + 19$$

Exercise Set R.7

1. $3^6 \cdot 3^3 = 3^{6+3} = 3^9$

3. $6^{-6} \cdot 6^2 = 6^{-6+2} = 6^{-4} = \dfrac{1}{6^4}$

5. $8^{-2} \cdot 8^{-4} = 8^{-2+(-4)} = 8^{-6} = \dfrac{1}{8^6}$

7. $b^2 \cdot b^{-5} = b^{2+(-5)} = b^{-3} = \dfrac{1}{b^3}$

9. $a^{-3} \cdot a^4 \cdot a^2 = a^{-3+4+2} = a^3$

11. $(2x)^3(3x)^2 = 8x^3 \cdot 9x^2$
$$= 8 \cdot 9 \cdot x^3 \cdot x^2$$
$$= 72x^{3+2}$$
$$= 72x^5$$

13. $(14m^2n^3)(-2m^3n^2) = 14 \cdot (-2) \cdot m^2 \cdot m^3 \cdot n^3 \cdot n^2$
$$= -28m^{2+3}n^{3+2}$$
$$= -28m^5n^5$$

15. $(-2x^{-3})(7x^{-8}) = -2 \cdot 7 \cdot x^{-3} \cdot x^{-8}$
$$= -14x^{-3+(-8)}$$
$$= -14x^{-11} = -\dfrac{14}{x^{11}}$$

17. $(15x^{4t})(7x^{-6t}) = 15 \cdot 7 \cdot x^{4t} \cdot x^{-6t}$
$$= 105x^{4t+(-6t)}$$
$$= 105x^{-2t}$$
$$= \dfrac{105}{x^{2t}}$$

19. $\dfrac{8^9}{8^2} = 8^{9-2} = 8^7$

21. $\dfrac{6^3}{6^{-2}} = 6^{3-(-2)} = 6^{3+2} = 6^5$

23. $\dfrac{10^{-3}}{10^6} = 10^{-3-6} = 10^{-3+(-6)} = 10^{-9} = \dfrac{1}{10^9}$

25. $\dfrac{9^{-4}}{9^{-6}} = 9^{-4-(-6)} = 9^{-4+6} = 9^2$

27. $\dfrac{x^{-4n}}{x^{6n}} = x^{-4n-6n} = x^{-10n} = \dfrac{1}{x^{10n}}$

29. $\dfrac{w^{-11q}}{w^{-6q}} = w^{-11q-(-6q)} = w^{-11q+6q} = w^{-5q} =$
$$\dfrac{1}{w^{5q}}$$

31. $\dfrac{a^3}{a^{-2}} = a^{3-(-2)} = a^{3+2} = a^5$

33. $\dfrac{2yx^7y^5}{-9x^2y} = \dfrac{27}{-9}x^{7-2}y^{5-1} = -3x^5y^4$

35. $\dfrac{-24x^6y^7}{18x^{-3}y^9} = \dfrac{-24}{18}x^{6-(-3)}y^{7-9}$
$$= -\dfrac{24}{18}x^{6+3}y^{-2}$$
$$= -\dfrac{4}{3}x^9y^{-2} = -\dfrac{4x^9}{3y^2}$$

37. $\dfrac{-18x^{-2}y^3}{-12x^{-5}y^5} = \dfrac{-18}{-12}x^{-2-(-5)}y^{3-5}$
$$= \dfrac{18}{12}x^{-2+5}y^{-2}$$
$$= \dfrac{3}{2}x^3y^{-2} = \dfrac{3x^3}{2y^2}$$

39. $(4^3)^2 = 4^{3 \cdot 2} = 4^6$

41. $(8^4)^{-3} = 8^{4(-3)} = 8^{-12} = \dfrac{1}{8^{12}}$

43. $(6^{-4})^{-3} = 6^{-4(-3)} = 6^{12}$

45. $(5a^2b^2)^3 = 5^3(a^2)^3(b^2)^3$
$ = 125a^{2 \cdot 3}b^{2 \cdot 3}$
$ = 125a^6b^6$

47. $(-3x^3y^{-6})^{-2} = (-3)^{-2}(x^3)^{-2}(y^{-6})^{-2}$
$\phantom{(-3x^3y^{-6})^{-2}} = \dfrac{1}{(-3)^2}x^{3(-2)}y^{-6(-2)}$
$\phantom{(-3x^3y^{-6})^{-2}} = \dfrac{1}{9}x^{-6}y^{12}$
$\phantom{(-3x^3y^{-6})^{-2}} = \dfrac{y^{12}}{9x^6}$

49. $(-6a^{-2}b^3c)^{-2} = (-6)^{-2}(a^{-2})^{-2}(b^3)^{-2}c^{-2}$
$\phantom{(-6a^{-2}b^3c)^{-2}} = \dfrac{1}{(-6)^2}a^{-2(-2)}b^{3(-2)}c^{-2}$
$\phantom{(-6a^{-2}b^3c)^{-2}} = \dfrac{1}{36}a^4b^{-6}c^{-2} = \dfrac{a^4}{36b^6c^2}$

51. $\left(\dfrac{4^{-3}}{3^4}\right)^3 = \dfrac{(4^{-3})^3}{(3^4)^3} = \dfrac{4^{-3 \cdot 3}}{3^{4 \cdot 3}} = \dfrac{4^{-9}}{3^{12}} = \dfrac{1}{4^9 \cdot 3^{12}}$

53. $\left(\dfrac{2x^3y^{-2}}{3y^{-3}}\right)^3 = \dfrac{(2x^3y^{-2})^3}{(3y^{-3})^3}$
$\phantom{\left(\dfrac{2x^3y^{-2}}{3y^{-3}}\right)^3} = \dfrac{2^3(x^3)^3(y^{-2})^3}{3^3(y^{-3})^3}$
$\phantom{\left(\dfrac{2x^3y^{-2}}{3y^{-3}}\right)^3} = \dfrac{8x^9y^{-6}}{27y^{-9}}$
$\phantom{\left(\dfrac{2x^3y^{-2}}{3y^{-3}}\right)^3} = \dfrac{8x^9y^{6-(-9)}}{27}$
$\phantom{\left(\dfrac{2x^3y^{-2}}{3y^{-3}}\right)^3} = \dfrac{8x^9y^3}{27}$

55. $\left(\dfrac{125a^2b^{-3}}{5a^4b^{-2}}\right)^{-5} = \left(\dfrac{5a^4b^{-2}}{125a^2b^{-3}}\right)^5$
$\phantom{\left(\dfrac{125a^2b^{-3}}{5a^4b^{-2}}\right)^{-5}} = \left(\dfrac{a^{4-2}b^{-2-(-3)}}{25}\right)^5$
$\phantom{\left(\dfrac{125a^2b^{-3}}{5a^4b^{-2}}\right)^{-5}} = \left(\dfrac{a^2b}{25}\right)^5$
$\phantom{\left(\dfrac{125a^2b^{-3}}{5a^4b^{-2}}\right)^{-5}} = \dfrac{(a^2)^5(b)^5}{(25)^5} = \dfrac{a^{2 \cdot 5}b^{1 \cdot 5}}{25^{1 \cdot 5}}$
$\phantom{\left(\dfrac{125a^2b^{-3}}{5a^4b^{-2}}\right)^{-5}} = \dfrac{a^{10}b^5}{25^5}, \text{ or } \dfrac{a^{10}b^5}{5^{10}}$
$\phantom{\left(\dfrac{125a^2b^{-3}}{5a^4b^{-2}}\right)^{-5} = } [25^5 = (5^2)^5 = 5^{10}]$

57. $\left(\dfrac{-6^5y^4z^{-5}}{2^{-2}y^{-2}z^3}\right)^6 = (-1 \cdot 6^5 \cdot 2^2 y^{4-(-2)}z^{-5-3})^6$
$\phantom{\left(\dfrac{-6^5y^4z^{-5}}{2^{-2}y^{-2}z^3}\right)^6} = (-1 \cdot 6^5 \cdot 2^2 y^6 z^{-8})^6$
$\phantom{\left(\dfrac{-6^5y^4z^{-5}}{2^{-2}y^{-2}z^3}\right)^6} = (-1)^6(6^5)^6(2^2)^6(y^6)^6(z^{-8})^6$
$\phantom{\left(\dfrac{-6^5y^4z^{-5}}{2^{-2}y^{-2}z^3}\right)^6} = 1 \cdot 6^{5 \cdot 6}2^{2 \cdot 6}y^{6 \cdot 6}z^{-8 \cdot 6}$
$\phantom{\left(\dfrac{-6^5y^4z^{-5}}{2^{-2}y^{-2}z^3}\right)^6} = 6^{30}2^{12}y^{36}z^{-48}$
$\phantom{\left(\dfrac{-6^5y^4z^{-5}}{2^{-2}y^{-2}z^3}\right)^6} = \dfrac{6^{30}2^{12}y^{36}}{z^{48}}$

59. $[(-2x^{-4}y^{-2})^{-3}]^{-2} = [(-2)^{-3}(x^{-4})^{-3}(y^{-2})^{-3}]^{-2}$
$\phantom{[(-2x^{-4}y^{-2})^{-3}]^{-2}} = [(-2)^{-3}x^{12}y^6]^{-2}$
$\phantom{[(-2x^{-4}y^{-2})^{-3}]^{-2}} = [(-2)^{-3}]^{-2}(x^{12})^{-2}(y^6)^{-2}$
$\phantom{[(-2x^{-4}y^{-2})^{-3}]^{-2}} = (-2)^6x^{-24}y^{-12}$
$\phantom{[(-2x^{-4}y^{-2})^{-3}]^{-2}} = \dfrac{64}{x^{24}y^{12}}$

61. $\left(\dfrac{3a^{-2}b}{5a^{-7}b^5}\right)^{-7} = \left(\dfrac{5a^{-7}b^5}{3a^{-2}b}\right)^7$
$\phantom{\left(\dfrac{3a^{-2}b}{5a^{-7}b^5}\right)^{-7}} = \left(\dfrac{5a^{-7-(-2)}b^{5-1}}{3}\right)^7$
$\phantom{\left(\dfrac{3a^{-2}b}{5a^{-7}b^5}\right)^{-7}} = \left(\dfrac{5a^{-5}b^4}{3}\right)^7$
$\phantom{\left(\dfrac{3a^{-2}b}{5a^{-7}b^5}\right)^{-7}} = \dfrac{5^7(a^{-5})^7(b^4)^7}{3^7}$
$\phantom{\left(\dfrac{3a^{-2}b}{5a^{-7}b^5}\right)^{-7}} = \dfrac{5^7a^{-35}b^{28}}{3^7}$
$\phantom{\left(\dfrac{3a^{-2}b}{5a^{-7}b^5}\right)^{-7}} = \dfrac{5^7b^{28}}{3^7a^{35}}$

63. $\dfrac{10^{2a+1}}{10^{a+1}} = 10^{2a+1-(a+1)} = 10^{2a+1-a-1} = 10^a$

65. $\dfrac{9a^{x-2}}{3a^{2x+2}} = \dfrac{9}{3} \cdot \dfrac{a^{x-2}}{a^{2x+2}} = 3a^{x-2-(2x+2)} =$
$3a^{x-2-2x-2} = 3a^{-x-4}$

67. $\dfrac{45x^{2a+4}y^{b+1}}{-9x^{a+3}y^{2+b}} = \dfrac{45}{-9} \cdot \dfrac{x^{2a+4}y^{b+1}}{x^{a+3}y^{2+b}} =$
$-5x^{2a+4-(a+3)}y^{b+1-(2+b)} = -5x^{2a+4-a-3}y^{b+1-2-b} =$
$-5x^{a+1}y^{-1}, \text{ or } \dfrac{-5x^{a+1}}{y}$

69. $(8^x)^{4y} = 8^{x \cdot 4y} = 8^{4xy}$

71. $(12^{3-a})^{2b} = 12^{(3-a)(2b)} = 12^{6b-2ab}$

73. $(5x^{a-1}y^{b+1})^{2c} = 5^{2c}x^{(a-1)(2c)}y^{(b+1)(2c)} =$
$5^{2c}x^{2ac-2c}y^{2bc+2c}, \text{ or } (5^2)^c x^{2ac-2c}y^{2bc+2c} =$
$25^c x^{2ac-2c}y^{2bc+2c}$

75. $\dfrac{4x^{2a+3}y^{2b-1}}{2x^{a+1}y^{b+1}} = \dfrac{4}{2} \cdot \dfrac{x^{2a+3}y^{2b-1}}{x^{a+1}y^{b+1}} =$
$2x^{2a+3-(a+1)}y^{2b-1-(b+1)} = 2x^{2a+3-a-1}y^{2b-1-b-1} =$
$2x^{a+2}y^{b-2}$

77. 4.7,000,000,000.

    ↑_____

      10 places

Large number, so the exponent is positive.

$47,000,000,000 = 4.7 \times 10^{10}$

79. 0.00000001.6

    └_____↑

     8 places

Small number, so the exponent is negative.

$0.000000016 = 1.6 \times 10^{-8}$

81. 6.832,000,000.

    ↑_____

      9 places

Large number, so the exponent is positive.

$6,832,000,000 = 6.832 \times 10^9$

83. $\dfrac{135.2}{1000} = 0.1352$

   0.1 . 352

   └↑

   1 place

Small number, so the exponent is negative.

$\dfrac{135.2}{1000} = 1.352 \times 10^{-1}$

85. 6.73000000.

    └_____↑

     8 places

Positive exponent so the number is large.

$6.73 \times 10^8 = 673,000,000$

87. 0.00006.6 cm

    ↑____┘

    5 places

Negative exponent, so the number is small.

6.6×10^{-5} cm $= 0.000066$ cm

89. $10^{14} = 1 \times 10^{14}$

   1.00000000000000.

   └_____↑

     14 places

Positive exponent, so the number is large.

$10^{14} = 100,000,000,000,000$

91. $(2.3 \times 10^6)(4.2 \times 10^{-11})$

$= (2.3 \times 4.2)(10^6 \times 10^{-11})$

$= 9.66 \times 10^{-5}$

93. $(2.34 \times 10^{-8})(5.7 \times 10^{-4})$

$= (2.34 \times 5.7)(10^{-8} \times 10^{-4})$

$= 13.338 \times 10^{-12}$

$= (1.3338 \times 10^1) \times 10^{-12}$

$= 1.3338 \times (10^1 \times 10^{-12})$

$= 1.3338 \times 10^{-11}$

95. $\dfrac{8.5 \times 10^8}{3.4 \times 10^5} = \dfrac{8.5}{3.4} \times \dfrac{10^8}{10^5}$

$= 2.5 \times 10^3$

97. $\dfrac{4.0 \times 10^{-6}}{8.0 \times 10^{-3}} = \dfrac{4.0}{8.0} \times \dfrac{10^{-6}}{10^{-3}}$

$= 0.5 \times 10^{-3}$

$= (5 \times 10^{-1}) \times 10^{-3}$

$= 5 \times (10^{-1} \times 10^{-3})$

$= 5 \times 10^{-4}$

99. We convert 500 to scientific notation and divide.

$\dfrac{4.961}{5 \times 10^2} = \dfrac{4.961}{5} \times \dfrac{1}{10^2}$

$= 0.9922 \times 10^{-2}$

$= (9.922 \times 10^{-1}) \times 10^{-2}$

$= 9.922 \times 10^{-3}$ lb

101.   2000 yr

$= 2000 \text{ yr} \times \dfrac{365 \text{ days}}{1 \text{ yr}} \times \dfrac{24 \text{ hr}}{1 \text{ day}} \times \dfrac{60 \text{ min}}{1 \text{ hr}} \times \dfrac{60 \text{ sec}}{1 \text{ min}}$

$= 63,072,000,000$ sec

$= 6.3072 \times 10^{10}$ sec

103. 13 wk $= 13 \text{ wk} \times \dfrac{1 \text{ yr}}{52 \text{ wk}} = \dfrac{13}{52} \text{ yr} = 0.25$ yr

Now light travels 5.87×10^{14} mi in 100 yr, or

$\dfrac{5.87 \times 10^{14} \text{ mi}}{100 \text{ yr}}$, so the distance traveled in 13 weeks, or 0.25 yr is given by:

$\dfrac{5.87 \times 10^{14} \text{ mi}}{100 \text{ yr}} \times 0.25 \text{ yr}$

$= \dfrac{5.87 \times 10^{14} \text{ mi}}{10^2 \text{ yr}} \times 2.5 \times 10^{-1} \text{ yr}$

$= (5.87 \times 2.5) \times \left(\dfrac{10^{14} \times 10^{-1}}{10^2}\right)$ mi

$= 14.675 \times 10^{11}$ mi

$= (1.4675 \times 10) \times 10^{11}$ mi

$= 1.4675 \times 10^{12}$ mi

105. We divide.

$\dfrac{2.4 \times 10^{13}}{5.88 \times 10^{12}} = \dfrac{2.4}{5.88} \times \dfrac{10^{13}}{10^{12}}$

$\approx 0.408 \times 10$

$\approx (4.08 \times 10^{-1}) \times 10$

≈ 4.08 light-years

107. $\dfrac{10,000}{300,000} = \dfrac{10^4}{3 \times 10^5}$

$\approx 0.333 \times 10^{-1}$

$\approx (3.33 \times 10^{-1}) \times 10^{-1}$

$\approx 3.33 \times 10^{-2}$

The part of the total number of words in the English language that an average person knows is about 3.33×10^{-2}.

109. First we divide to find the number of \$5 bills in \$4,540,000.

$\dfrac{\$4,540,000}{\$5} = \dfrac{4.54 \times 10^6}{5} = 0.908 \times 10^6 =$

$(9.08 \times 10^{-1}) \times 10^6 = 9.08 \times 10^5$

Then we divide 1 ton, or 2000 lb, by the number of bills to find the weight of a single bill.

$\dfrac{2000}{9.08 \times 10^5} = \dfrac{2 \times 10^3}{9.08 \times 10^5} = \dfrac{2}{9.08} \times \dfrac{10^3}{10^5} \approx$

$0.220 \times 10^{-2} \approx (2.2 \times 10^{-1}) \times 10^{-2} \approx 2.2 \times 10^{-3}$

A five-dollar bill weighs about 2.2×10^{-3} lb.

111. Discussion and Writing Exercise

113. $9x - (-4y + 8) + (10x - 12)$

$= 9x + 4y - 8 + 10x - 12$

$= 19x + 4y - 20$

115. $4^2 + 30 \cdot 10 - 7^3 + 16 = 16 + 30 \cdot 10 - 343 + 16$

$= 16 + 300 - 343 + 16$

$= 316 - 343 + 16$

$= -27 + 16$

$= -11$

117. $20 - 5 \cdot 4 - 8 = 20 - 20 - 8$

$= 0 - 8$

$= -8$

119. $\dfrac{(2^{-2})^{-4} \times (2^3)^{-2}}{(2^{-2})^2 \cdot (2^5)^{-3}} = \dfrac{2^8 \times 2^{-6}}{2^{-4} \cdot 2^{-15}}$

$= \dfrac{2^{8+(-6)}}{2^{-4+(-15)}}$

$= \dfrac{2^2}{2^{-19}}$

$= 2^{2-(-19)}$

$= 2^{21}$

121. $\left[\left(\dfrac{a^{-2}}{b^7} \right)^{-3} \cdot \left(\dfrac{a^4}{b^{-3}} \right)^2 \right]^{-1} = \left[\dfrac{(a^{-2})^{-3}}{(b^7)^{-3}} \cdot \dfrac{(a^4)^2}{(b^{-3})^2} \right]^{-1}$

$= \left[\dfrac{a^6}{b^{-21}} \cdot \dfrac{a^8}{b^{-6}} \right]^{-1}$

$= \left[\dfrac{a^{6+8}}{b^{-21+(-6)}} \right]^{-1}$

$= \left[\dfrac{a^{14}}{b^{-27}} \right]^{-1}$

$= \dfrac{a^{-14}}{b^{27}}$

$= \dfrac{1}{a^{14}b^{27}}$

123. $\left[\dfrac{(2x^a y^b)^3}{(-2x^a y^b)^2} \right]^2 = \left[\dfrac{(2x^a y^b)^3}{(2x^a y^b)^2} \right]^2 \quad [(-2x^a y^b)^2 = (2x^a y^b)^2]$

$= [(2x^a y^b)^{3-2}]^2$

$= (2x^a y^b)^2$

$= 2^2 (x^a)^2 (y^b)^2$

$= 4x^{2a} y^{2b}$

Chapter 1

Solving Linear Equations and Inequalities

Exercise Set 1.1

1. $x + 23 = 40$ Writing the equation

$17 + 23 \;?\; 40$ Substituting 17 for x

$\qquad 40 \;\Big|\;$ TRUE

Since the left-hand and the right-hand sides are the same, 17 is a solution of the equation.

3. $2x - 3 = -18$ Writing the equation

$2(-8) - 3 \;?\; -18$ Substituting -8 for x

$-16 - 3 \;\Big|\;$

$\qquad -19 \;\Big|\;$ FALSE

Since the left-hand and the right-hand sides are not the same, -8 is not a solution of the equation.

5. $\dfrac{-x}{9} = -2$ Writing the equation

$\dfrac{-45}{9} \;?\; -2$ Substituting

$\qquad -5 \;\Big|\;$ FALSE

Since the left-hand and the right-hand sides are not the same, 45 is not a solution of the equation.

7. $2 - 3x = 21$

$2 - 3 \cdot 10 \;?\; 21$ Substituting

$2 - 30 \;\Big|\;$

$\qquad -28 \;\Big|\;$ FALSE

Since the left-hand and the right-hand sides are not the same, 10 is not a solution of the equation.

9. $5x + 7 = 102$

$5 \cdot 19 + 7 \;?\; 102$

$95 + 7 \;\Big|\;$

$\qquad 102 \;\Big|\;$ TRUE

Since the left-hand and the right-hand sides are the same, 19 is a solution of the equation.

11. $7(y - 1) = 84$

$7(-11 - 1) \;?\; 84$

$7(-12) \;\Big|\;$

$\qquad -84 \;\Big|\;$ FALSE

Since the left-hand and the right-hand sides are not the same, -11 is not a solution of the equation.

13. $y + 6 = 13$

$y + 6 - 6 = 13 - 6$ Subtracting 6 on both sides

$y + 0 = 7$ Simplifying

$y = 7$ Using the identity property of 0

Check: $y + 6 = 13$

$7 + 6 \;?\; 13$

$\qquad 13 \;\Big|\;$ TRUE

The solution is 7.

15. $-20 = x - 12$

$-20 + 12 = x - 12 + 12$ Adding 12 on both sides

$-8 = x + 0$ Simplifying

$-8 = x$ Using the identity property of 0

Check: $-20 = x - 12$

$-20 \;?\; -8 - 12$

$\Big|\; -20$ TRUE

The solution is -8.

17. $-8 + x = 19$

$8 - 8 + x = 8 + 19$ Adding 8

$0 + x = 27$

$x = 27$ Using the identity property of 0

Check: $-8 + x = 19$

$-8 + 27 \;?\; 19$

$\qquad 19 \;\Big|\;$ TRUE

The solution is 27.

19. $-12 + z = -51$

$12 + (-12) + z = 12 + (-51)$ Adding 12

$0 + z = -39$

$z = -39$

The number -39 checks, so it is the solution.

21. $p - 2.96 = 83.9$

$p - 2.96 + 2.96 = 83.9 + 2.96$

$p + 0 = 86.86$

$p = 86.86$

The number 86.86 checks, so it is the solution.

23.
$$-\frac{3}{8} + x = -\frac{5}{24}$$
$$\frac{3}{8} + \left(-\frac{3}{8}\right) + x = \frac{3}{8} + \left(-\frac{5}{24}\right)$$
$$0 + x = \frac{3}{8} \cdot \frac{3}{3} + \left(-\frac{5}{24}\right)$$
$$x = \frac{9}{24} + \left(-\frac{5}{24}\right)$$
$$x = \frac{4}{24}$$
$$x = \frac{1}{6}$$

The number $\frac{1}{6}$ checks, so it is the solution.

25.
$$3x = 18$$
$$\frac{3x}{3} = \frac{18}{3} \quad \text{Dividing by 3 on both sides}$$
$$1 \cdot x = \frac{18}{3} \quad \text{Simplifying}$$
$$x = 6$$

Check:
$$\begin{array}{c} 3x = 18 \\ \hline 3 \cdot 6 \ ? \ 18 \\ 18 \ \big| \end{array} \quad \text{TRUE}$$

The solution is 6.

27.
$$-11y = 44$$
$$\frac{-11y}{-11} = \frac{44}{-11}$$
$$1 \cdot y = \frac{44}{-11}$$
$$y = -4$$

Check:
$$\begin{array}{c} -11y = 44 \\ \hline -11(-4) \ ? \ 44 \\ 44 \ \big| \end{array} \quad \text{TRUE}$$

The solution is -4.

29.
$$-\frac{x}{7} = 21$$
$$-\frac{1}{7}x = 21$$
$$-7\left(-\frac{1}{7}\right)x = -7 \cdot 21 \quad \text{Multiplying by } -7$$
$$\text{on both sides}$$
$$1 \cdot x = -147$$
$$x = -147$$

Check:
$$\begin{array}{c} -\dfrac{x}{7} = 21 \\ \hline -\dfrac{-147}{7} \ ? \ 21 \\ -(-21) \ \big| \\ 21 \ \big| \end{array} \quad \text{TRUE}$$

The solution is -147.

31.
$$-96 = -3z$$
$$\frac{-96}{-3} = \frac{-3z}{-3} \quad \text{Dividing by } -3$$
$$\frac{-96}{-3} = 1 \cdot z$$
$$32 = z$$

Check:
$$\begin{array}{c} -96 = -3z \\ \hline -96 \ ? \ -3 \cdot 32 \\ -96 \ \big| \end{array} \quad \text{TRUE}$$

The solution is 32.

33.
$$4.8y = -28.8$$
$$\frac{4.8y}{4.8} = \frac{-28.8}{4.8}$$
$$1 \cdot y = -\frac{28.8}{4.8}$$
$$y = -6$$

The number -6 checks, so it is the solution.

35.
$$\frac{3}{2}t = -\frac{1}{4}$$
$$\frac{2}{3} \cdot \frac{3}{2}t = \frac{2}{3} \cdot \left(-\frac{1}{4}\right)$$
$$1 \cdot t = -\frac{2}{12}$$
$$t = -\frac{1}{6}$$

The number $-\frac{1}{6}$ checks, so it is the solution.

37.
$$6x - 15 = 45$$
$$6x - 15 + 15 = 45 + 15 \quad \text{Adding 15}$$
$$6x = 60$$
$$\frac{6x}{6} = \frac{60}{6} \quad \text{Dividing by 6}$$
$$x = 10$$

Check:
$$\begin{array}{c} 6x - 15 = 45 \\ \hline 6 \cdot 10 - 15 \ ? \ 45 \\ 60 - 15 \ \big| \\ 45 \ \big| \end{array} \quad \text{TRUE}$$

The solution is 10.

39.
$$5x - 10 = 45$$
$$5x - 10 + 10 = 45 + 10$$
$$5x = 55$$
$$\frac{5x}{5} = \frac{55}{5}$$
$$x = 11$$

Check:
$$\begin{array}{c} 5x - 10 = 45 \\ \hline 5 \cdot 11 - 10 \ ? \ 45 \\ 55 - 10 \ \big| \\ 45 \ \big| \end{array} \quad \text{TRUE}$$

The solution is 11.

41.
$$9t + 4 = -104$$
$$9t + 4 - 4 = -104 - 4$$
$$9t = -108$$
$$\frac{9t}{9} = \frac{-108}{9}$$
$$t = -12$$

Check:
$$\frac{9t + 4 = -104}{9(-12) + 4 \ ? \ -104}$$
$$-108 + 4 \ \Big|$$
$$-104 \ \Big| \qquad \text{TRUE}$$

The solution is -12.

43.
$$-\frac{7}{3}x + \frac{2}{3} = -18, \quad \text{LCM is 3}$$
$$3\left(-\frac{7}{3}x + \frac{2}{3}\right) = 3(-18) \qquad \begin{array}{l}\text{Multiplying by 3 to}\\ \text{clear fractions}\end{array}$$
$$-7x + 2 = -54$$
$$-7x = -56 \qquad \text{Subtracting 2}$$
$$x = \frac{-56}{-7} \qquad \text{Dividing by } -7$$
$$x = 8$$

The number 8 checks. It is the solution.

45.
$$\frac{6}{5}x + \frac{4}{10}x = \frac{32}{10}, \quad \text{LCM is 10}$$
$$10\left(\frac{6}{5}x + \frac{4}{10}x\right) = 10 \cdot \frac{32}{10} \qquad \begin{array}{l}\text{Multiplying by 10 to}\\ \text{clear fractions}\end{array}$$
$$12x + 4x = 32$$
$$16x = 32 \qquad \text{Collecting like terms}$$
$$x = \frac{32}{16} \qquad \text{Dividing by 16}$$
$$x = 2$$

The number 2 checks. It is the solution.

47.
$$0.9y - 0.7y = 4.2$$
$$10(0.9y - 0.7y) = 10(4.2) \qquad \begin{array}{l}\text{Multiplying by 10 to clear}\\ \text{fractions}\end{array}$$
$$9y - 7y = 42$$
$$2y = 42 \qquad \text{Collecting like terms}$$
$$y = \frac{42}{2}$$
$$y = 21$$

The number 21 checks, so it is the solution.

49.
$$8x + 48 = 3x - 12$$
$$5x + 48 = -12 \qquad \text{Subtracting } 3x$$
$$5x = -60 \qquad \text{Subtracting 48}$$
$$x = \frac{-60}{5} \qquad \text{Dividing by 5}$$
$$x = -12$$

The number -12 checks, so it is the solution.

51.
$$7y - 1 = 23 - 5y$$
$$12y - 1 = 23 \qquad \text{Adding } 5y$$
$$12y = 24 \qquad \text{Adding 1}$$
$$y = \frac{24}{12} \qquad \text{Dividing by 12}$$
$$y = 2$$

The number 2 checks, so it is the solution.

53.
$$3x - 4 = 5 + 12x$$
$$-4 = 5 + 9x \qquad \text{Subtracting } 3x$$
$$-9 = 9x \qquad \text{Subtracting 5}$$
$$-1 = x \qquad \text{Dividing by 9}$$

The number -1 checks, so it is the solution.

55.
$$5 - 4a = a - 13$$
$$5 = 5a - 13 \qquad \text{Adding } 4a$$
$$18 = 5a \qquad \text{Adding 13}$$
$$\frac{18}{5} = a \qquad \text{Dividing by 5}$$

The number $\frac{18}{5}$ checks. It is the solution.

57.
$$3m - 7 = -7 - 4m - m$$
$$3m - 7 = -7 - 5m \qquad \text{Collecting like terms}$$
$$3m = -5m \qquad \text{Adding 7}$$
$$8m = 0 \qquad \text{Adding } 5m$$
$$m = \frac{0}{8} \qquad \text{Dividing by 8}$$
$$m = 0$$

The number 0 checks, so it is the solution.

59.
$$5x + 3 = 11 - 4x + x$$
$$5x + 3 = 11 - 3x \qquad \text{Collecting like terms}$$
$$8x + 3 = 11 \qquad \text{Adding } 3x$$
$$8x = 8 \qquad \text{Subtracting 3}$$
$$x = \frac{8}{8} \qquad \text{Dividing by 8}$$
$$x = 1$$

The number 1 checks, so it is the solution.

61.
$$-7 + 9x = 9x - 7$$
$$-7 = -7 \qquad \text{Subtracting } 9x$$

The equation $-7 = -7$ is true. Replacing x by **any real** number gives a true sentence. Thus, all real numbers **are** solutions.

63.
$$6y - 8 = 9 + 6y$$
$$-8 = 9 \qquad \text{Subtracting } 6y$$

The equation $-8 = 9$ is false. No matter what number we try for x we get a false sentence. Thus, the equation **has** no solution.

65. $2(x + 7) = 4x$

     $2x + 14 = 4x$ Multiplying to remove parentheses

         $14 = 2x$ Subtracting $2x$

          $7 = x$ Dividing by 2

Check: $\dfrac{2(x+7) = 4x}{}$

$$2(7 + 7) \; ? \; 4 \cdot 7$$
$$2 \cdot 14 \;\big|\; 28$$
$$28 \;\big|\; \quad\text{TRUE}$$

The solution is 7.

67. $80 = 10(3t + 2)$

     $80 = 30t + 20$

     $60 = 30t$

      $2 = t$

Check: $\dfrac{80 = 10(3t + 2)}{}$

$$80 \; ? \; 10(3 \cdot 2 + 2)$$
$$\big|\; 10(6 + 2)$$
$$\big|\; 10 \cdot 8$$
$$\big|\; 80 \quad\text{TRUE}$$

The solution is 2.

69. $180(n - 2) = 900$

     $180n - 360 = 900$

         $180n = 1260$

           $n = 7$

Check: $\dfrac{180(n - 2) = 900}{}$

$$180(7 - 2) \; ? \; 900$$
$$180 \cdot 5 \;\big|$$
$$900 \;\big|\; \quad\text{TRUE}$$

The solution is 7.

71. $5y - (2y - 10) = 25$

     $5y - 2y + 10 = 25$

        $3y + 10 = 25$

           $3y = 15$

            $y = 5$

Check: $\dfrac{5y - (2y - 10) = 25}{}$

$$5 \cdot 5 - (2 \cdot 5 - 10) \; ? \; 25$$
$$25 - (10 - 10) \;\big|$$
$$25 - 0 \;\big|$$
$$25 \;\big|\; \quad\text{TRUE}$$

The solution is 5.

73. $7(3x + 6) = 11 - (x + 2)$

     $21x + 42 = 11 - x - 2$

     $21x + 42 = 9 - x$

     $22x + 42 = 9$

         $22x = -33$

            $x = \dfrac{-33}{22}$

            $x = -\dfrac{3}{2}$

The number $-\dfrac{3}{2}$ checks, so it is the solution.

75. $2[9 - 3(-2x - 4)] = 12x + 42$

     $2[9 + 6x + 12] = 12x + 42$

        $2[6x + 21] = 12x + 42$

      $12x + 42 = 12x + 42$

            $42 = 42$

We get a true equation. Replacing x with any real number gives a true sentence. Thus, all real numbers are solutions.

77. $\dfrac{1}{8}(16y + 8) - 17 = -\dfrac{1}{4}(8y - 16)$

     $2y + 1 - 17 = -2y + 4$

        $2y - 16 = -2y + 4$

        $4y - 16 = 4$

            $4y = 20$

             $y = 5$

The number 5 checks, so it is the solution.

79. $3[5 - 3(4 - t)] - 2 = 5[3(5t - 4) + 8] - 26$

     $3[5 - 12 + 3t] - 2 = 5[15t - 12 + 8] - 26$

       $3[-7 + 3t] - 2 = 5[15t - 4] - 26$

       $-21 + 9t - 2 = 75t - 20 - 26$

          $9t - 23 = 75t - 46$

             $-23 = 66t - 46$

              $23 = 66t$

            $\dfrac{23}{66} = t$

The number $\dfrac{23}{66}$ checks, so it is the solution.

81. $\dfrac{2}{3}\left(\dfrac{7}{8}+4x\right)-\dfrac{5}{8}=\dfrac{3}{8}$

$\dfrac{2}{3}\left(\dfrac{7}{8}+4x\right)=1$

$\dfrac{7}{12}+\dfrac{8}{3}x=1$

$12\left(\dfrac{7}{12}+\dfrac{8}{3}x\right)=12\cdot 1$

$7+32x=12$

$32x=5$

$x=\dfrac{5}{32}$

The number $\dfrac{5}{32}$ checks, so it is the solution.

83. $5(4x-3)-2(6-8x)+10(-2x+7)=-4(9-12x)$

$20x-15-12+16x-20x+70=-36+48x$

$16x+43=-36+48x$

$43=-36+32x$

$79=32x$

$\dfrac{79}{32}=x$

The number $\dfrac{79}{32}$ checks, so it is the solution.

85. Discussion and Writing Exercise

87. $a^{-9}\cdot a^{23}=a^{-9+23}=a^{14}$

89. $\quad(6x^5y^{-4})(-3x^{-3}y^{-7})$

$=6\cdot(-3)\cdot x^5\cdot x^{-3}\cdot y^{-4}\cdot y^{-7}$

$=-18x^{5+(-3)}y^{-4+(-7)}$

$=-18x^2y^{-11}$

$=-\dfrac{18x^2}{y^{11}}$

91. $2(6-10x)=2\cdot 6-2\cdot 10x=12-20x$

93. $-4(3x-2y+z)=-4\cdot 3x-4(-2y)-4\cdot z$

$=-12x+8y-4z$

95. $2x-6y=2\cdot x-2\cdot 3y$

$=2(x-3y)$

97. $4x-10y+2=2\cdot 2x-2\cdot 5y+2\cdot 1$

$=2(2x-5y+1)$

99. $\{1,2,3,4,5,6,7,8,9\}$;

$\{x|x$ is a positive integer less than $10\}$

101. $4.23x-17.898=-1.65x-42.454$

$5.88x-17.898=-42.454$

$5.88x=-24.556$

$x\approx-4.176$

103. $\quad\dfrac{3x}{2}+\dfrac{5x}{3}-\dfrac{13x}{6}-\dfrac{2}{3}=\dfrac{5}{6}$, LCM is 6

$6\left(\dfrac{3x}{2}+\dfrac{5x}{3}-\dfrac{13x}{6}-\dfrac{2}{3}\right)=6\cdot\dfrac{5}{6}$

Multiplying by 6 to clear fractions

$3\cdot 3x+2\cdot 5x-1\cdot 13x-2\cdot 2=1\cdot 5$

$9x+10x-13x-4=5$

$6x-4=5\quad$ Collecting like terms

$6x=9\quad$ Adding 4

$x=\dfrac{9}{6}\quad$ Dividing by 6

$x=\dfrac{3}{2}$

The number $\dfrac{3}{2}$ checks, so it is the solution.

105. $\quad x-\{3x-[2x-(5x-(7x-1))]\}=x+7$

$x-\{3x-[2x-(5x-7x+1)]\}=x+7$

$x-\{3x-[2x-(-2x+1)]\}=x+7$

$x-\{3x-[2x+2x-1]\}=x+7$

$x-\{3x-[4x-1]\}=x+7$

$x-\{3x-4x+1\}=x+7$

$x-\{-x+1\}=x+7$

$x+x-1=x+7$

$2x-1=x+7$

$x-1=7$

$x=8$

The number 8 checks, so it is the solution.

Exercise Set 1.2

1. $\quad d=rt$

$\dfrac{d}{t}=r\quad$ Dividing by t

3. $\quad A=bh$

$\dfrac{A}{b}=h\quad$ Dividing by b

5. $\quad P=2l+2w$

$P-2l=2w\quad$ Subtracting $2l$

$\dfrac{P-2l}{2}=w\quad$ Dividing by 2

or $\dfrac{P}{2}-l=w$

7. $\quad A=\dfrac{1}{2}bh$

$2A=bh\quad$ Multiplying by 2

$\dfrac{2A}{h}=b\quad$ Dividing by h

9. $\quad A=\dfrac{a+b}{2}$

$2A=a+b\quad$ Multiplying by 2

$2A-b=a\quad$ Subtracting b

11. $F = ma$

$\dfrac{F}{a} = m$ Dividing by a

13. $I = Prt$

$\dfrac{I}{Pr} = t$ Dividing by Pr

15. $E = mc^2$

$\dfrac{E}{m} = c^2$ Dividing by m

17. $Q = \dfrac{p - q}{2}$

$2Q = p - q$ Multiplying by 2

$2Q + q = p$ Adding q

19. $Ax + By = c$

$By = c - Ax$ Subtracting Ax

$y = \dfrac{c - Ax}{B}$ Dividing by B

21. $I = 1.08 \dfrac{T}{N}$

$IN = 1.08T$ Multiplying by N

$N = \dfrac{1.08T}{I}$ Dividing by I

23. $T = B + Bqt$

$T = B(1 + qt)$ Factoring

$\dfrac{T}{1 + qt} = B$ Dividing by $1 + qt$

25. a) We substitute 8.5 for d and 24.1 for a and calculate P.

$P = 9.337da - 299$

$P = 9.337(8.5)(24.1) - 299$

$P = 1912.68445 - 299$

$P = 1613.68445$

The projected birth weight is about 1614 g.

b) $P = 9.337da - 299$

$P + 299 = 9.337da$

$\dfrac{P + 299}{9.337d} = a$

27. a) We substitute 3 for a and 250 for d and calculate c.

$c = \dfrac{ad}{a + 12}$

$c = \dfrac{3 \cdot 250}{3 + 12}$

$c = \dfrac{750}{15}$

$c = 50$

The child's dosage is 50 mg.

b) $c = \dfrac{ad}{a + 12}$

$c(a + 12) = ad$

$\dfrac{c(a + 12)}{a} = d$

This result can also be expressed as follows:

$$d = \dfrac{c(a + 12)}{a} = \dfrac{ac + 12c}{a} = c + \dfrac{12c}{a}$$

29. a) We substitute 87 for w, 185 for h, and 60 for a and calculate K.

$K = 19.18w + 7h - 9.52a + 92.4$

$K = 19.18(87) + 7(185) - 9.52(60) + 92.4$

$K = 2484.86$

Marv needs about 2485 calories per day.

b) Solve for a:

$K = 19.18w + 7h - 9.52a + 92.4$

$K + 9.52a = 19.18w + 7h + 92.4$

$9.52a = 19.18w + 7h + 92.4 - K$

$a = \dfrac{19.18w + 7h + 92.4 - K}{9.52}$

Solve for h:

$K = 19.18w + 7h - 9.52a + 92.4$

$K - 19.18w + 9.52a - 92.4 = 7h$

$\dfrac{K - 19.18w + 9.52a - 92.4}{7} = h$

Solve for w:

$K = 19.18w + 7h - 9.52a + 92.4$

$K - 7h + 9.52a - 92.4 = 19.18w$

$\dfrac{K - 7h + 9.52a - 92.4}{19.18} = w$

31. Discussion and Writing Exercise

33. $\dfrac{80}{-16} = -\dfrac{80}{16} = -5$

35. $-\dfrac{1}{2} \div \dfrac{1}{4} = -\dfrac{1}{2} \cdot \dfrac{4}{1} = -\dfrac{4}{2} = -2$

37. $-\dfrac{2}{3} \div \left(-\dfrac{5}{6} \right) = -\dfrac{2}{3} \cdot \left(-\dfrac{6}{5} \right) = \dfrac{2 \cdot 6}{3 \cdot 5} = \dfrac{2 \cdot 2 \cdot 3}{3 \cdot 5} =$

$\dfrac{2 \cdot 2 \cdot \cancel{3}}{\cancel{3} \cdot 5} = \dfrac{4}{5}$

39. $\dfrac{-90}{15} = -\dfrac{90}{15} = -6$

41. $A = \pi rs + \pi r^2$

$A - \pi r^2 = \pi rs$

$\dfrac{A - \pi r^2}{\pi r} = s$

43. Solve for V_1:

$\dfrac{P_1 V_1}{T_1} = \dfrac{P_2 V_2}{T_2}$

$V_1 = \dfrac{T_1 P_2 V_2}{P_1 T_2}$ Multiplying by $\dfrac{T_1}{P_1}$

Solve for P_2:

$$\frac{P_1 V_1}{T_1} = \frac{P_2 V_2}{T_2}$$

$$\frac{P_1 V_1 T_2}{T_1 V_2} = P_2 \quad \text{Multiplying by } \frac{T_2}{V_2}$$

45. We substitute \$75 for P, \$3 for I, and 5%, or 0.05, for r in the formula $t = \frac{I}{Pr}$.

$$t = \frac{I}{Pr}$$

$$t = \frac{\$3}{\$75(0.05)} \quad \text{Substituting}$$

$$t = 0.8$$

It will take 0.8 yr.

47. $H = W\left(\dfrac{v}{234}\right)^3$

a) $H = 2700\left(\dfrac{83}{234}\right)^3$

$H \approx 120.5$ horsepower

b) $H = 3100\left(\dfrac{73}{234}\right)^3$

$H \approx 94.1$ horsepower

Exercise Set 1.3

1. *Familiarize*. Let d = Armstrong's distance from Montiucon. Then $2d$ = his distance from Brive-la-Gaillarde. The total distance from Brive-la-Gaillarde to Montiucon is 194 km.

Translate.

Distance from Montiucon	plus	Distance from Brive-la-Gaillarde	is	Total distance
d	$+$	$2d$	$=$	194

Solve. We solve the equation.

$$d + 2d = 194$$
$$3d = 194$$
$$d = \frac{194}{3}$$

If $d = \dfrac{194}{3}$, then $2d = 2 \cdot \dfrac{194}{3} = \dfrac{388}{3}$, or $129\frac{1}{3}$.

Check. The distance from Brive-la-Gaillarde, $\dfrac{388}{3}$ km, is twice $\dfrac{194}{3}$, the distance from Montiucon. Also,

$$\frac{194}{3} + \frac{388}{3} = \frac{582}{3} = 194 \text{ km, the total distance. The}$$
answer checks.

State. Armstrong has completed $129\frac{1}{3}$ km of the stage.

3. *Familiarize*. Let x = the first angle. Then $5x$ = the second angle and $x - 2$ = the third angle. The sum of the measures of the angles is $180°$.

Translate.

First angle	+	Second angle	+	Third angle	is	180°.
x	$+$	$5x$	$+$	$(x-2)$	$=$	180

Solve. We solve the equation.

$$x + 5x + (x - 2) = 180$$
$$7x - 2 = 180$$
$$7x = 182$$
$$x = 26$$

If $x = 26$, then $5x = 5 \cdot 26 = 130$ and $x - 2 = 26 - 2 = 24$.

Check. The second angle, $130°$, is five times the first and the third angle, $24°$, is $2°$ less than the first. Also, $26° + 130° + 24° = 180°$. The numbers check.

State. The first angle is $26°$, the second is $130°$, and the third is $24°$.

5. *Familiarize*. Let p = the price of the computer before the sales tax is added. Then the sales tax is 6% of p, or $0.06p$.

Translate.

Cost of computer	+	Sales tax	is	Total price
p	$+$	$0.06p$	$=$	1187.20

Solve. We solve the equation.

$$p + 0.06p = 1187.20$$
$$1p + 0.06p = 1187.20$$
$$1.06p = 1187.20$$
$$p = 1120$$

Check. 6% of \$1120 is \$67.20 and $\$1120 + \$67.20 = \$1187.20$. The answer checks.

State. The price of the computer is \$1120.

7. *Familiarize*. Let w = the width of the court. Then $w + 44$ = the length. Recall that the perimeter of a rectangle with length l and width w is $2l + 2w$.

Translate.

Perimeter	is	288 ft.
$2(w + 44) + 2w$	$=$	288

Solve. We solve the equation.

$$2(w + 44) + 2w = 288$$
$$2w + 88 + 2w = 288$$
$$4w + 88 = 288$$
$$4w = 200$$
$$w = 50$$

If $w = 50$, then $w + 44 = 50 + 44 = 94$.

Check. The length, 94 ft, is 44 ft longer than the width. Also $2 \cdot 94 + 2 \cdot 50 = 188 + 100 = 288$. The numbers check.

State. The length of the court is 94 ft and the width is 50 ft.

9. *Familiarize*. Recall that the perimeter of a square is 4 times the length of a side. Let s = the length of a side of the smaller square. Then $2s$ = the length of a side of the larger square. The sum of the two perimeters is 100 cm.

***Translate*.**

$$4s \quad + \quad 4 \cdot 2s \quad = \quad 100$$

***Solve*.** We solve the equation.

$$4s + 4 \cdot 2s = 100$$
$$4s + 8s = 100$$
$$12s = 100$$
$$s = \frac{100}{12} = \frac{25}{3}$$

If $s = \frac{25}{3}$, then $4s = 4 \cdot \frac{25}{3} = \frac{100}{3}$, or $33\frac{1}{3}$;

$2s = 2 \cdot \frac{25}{3} = \frac{50}{3}$ and $4 \cdot \frac{50}{3} = \frac{200}{3}$, or $66\frac{2}{3}$.

***Check*.** The length of a side of the larger square, $\frac{50}{3}$, is twice the length of a side of the smaller square, $\frac{25}{3}$. Also $33\frac{1}{3} + 66\frac{2}{3} = 100$. The numbers check.

***State*.** The wire should be cut so that one piece is $33\frac{1}{3}$ cm long. Then the other piece will be $66\frac{2}{3}$ cm long.

11. *Familiarize*. Let p = the selling price of the house. Then $p - 100,000$ is the amount that exceeds \$100,000. Also 7% of \$100,000 is \$7000.

***Translate*.**

$$\underbrace{7\% \text{ of } \$100,000}_{} \quad + \quad 5\% \text{ of } \underbrace{\text{the amount that exceeds } \$100,000}_{} \quad \text{is } \$15,250.$$

$$7000 \quad + \quad 0.05 \cdot \quad (p - 100,000) \quad = \quad 15,250$$

***Solve*.** We solve the equation.

$$7000 + 0.05 \cdot (p - 100,000) = 15,250$$
$$7000 + 0.05p - 5000 = 15,250$$
$$0.05p + 2000 = 15,250$$
$$0.05p = 13,250$$
$$p = 265,000$$

***Check*.** If the selling price is \$265,000, then the amount that exceeds \$100,000 is \$265,000 − \$100,000, or \$165,000. Then the commission would be \$7000 + 0.05(\$165,000), or \$15,250. The answer checks.

***State*.** The selling price of the house was \$265,000.

13. *Familiarize*. Let x = the first odd integer. Then $x + 2$ and $x + 4$ are the next two odd integers.

***Translate*.**

$$\underbrace{\text{First integer}}_{} \quad + \text{ 2 times } \underbrace{\text{Second integer}}_{} +$$

$$x \quad + 2 \quad \cdot \quad (x + 2) \quad +$$

$$\text{3 times } \underbrace{\text{Third integer}}_{} \text{ is 70.}$$

$$3 \quad \cdot \quad (x + 4) \quad = 70$$

***Solve*.** We solve the equation.

$$x + 2 \cdot (x + 2) + 3 \cdot (x + 4) = 70$$
$$x + 2x + 4 + 3x + 12 = 70$$
$$6x + 16 = 70$$
$$6x = 54$$
$$x = 9$$

If $x = 9$, then $x + 2 = 9 + 2$, or 11, and $x + 4 = 9 + 4$, or 13.

***Check*.** The numbers 9, 11, and 13 are consecutive odd integers. Also $9 + 2 \cdot 11 + 3 \cdot 13 = 9 + 22 + 39 = 70$. The numbers check.

***State*.** The numbers are 9, 11, and 13.

15. *Familiarize*. Let x = the first number. Then $x + 1$ = the second number. The sum of the numbers is 697.

***Translate*.**

$$\underbrace{\text{First number}}_{} \quad + \quad \underbrace{\text{Second number}}_{} \quad \text{is } 697.$$

$$x \quad + \quad (x + 1) \quad = \quad 697$$

***Solve*.** We solve the equation.

$$x + (x + 1) = 697$$
$$2x + 1 = 697$$
$$2x = 696$$
$$x = 348$$

If $x = 348$, then $x + 1 = 348 + 1 = 349$.

***Check*.** The numbers 348 and 349 are consecutive integers. Also, $348 + 349 = 697$. The numbers check.

***State*.** The numbers are 348 and 349.

17. *Familiarize*. Let c = the number of square feet of carpet the customer had cleaned. Then the square footage that exceeds 200 sq ft is $c - 200$. The cost for cleaning the stairs is \$1.40(13), or \$18.20.

***Translate*.**

$$\$75 + \$0.25 \text{ times } \underbrace{\text{footage that exceeds 200 sq ft}}_{} + \underbrace{\text{cost of cleaning stairs}}_{} = \$253.95$$

$$75 + 0.25 \quad \cdot \quad (c - 200) \quad + \quad 18.20 \quad = 253.95$$

Solve. We solve the equation.

$$75 + 0.25 \cdot (c - 200) + 18.20 = 253.95$$
$$75 + 0.25c - 50 + 18.20 = 253.95$$
$$0.25c + 43.20 = 253.95$$
$$0.25c = 210.75$$
$$c = 843$$

Check. If the total square footage is 843 sq ft, then the area in excess of 200 sq ft is $843 - 200$, or 643 sq ft. The cost of cleaning this excess area is \$160.75. Then the total cost is \$75 + \$160.75 + \$18.20, or \$253.95. The answer checks.

State. The customer had 843 sq ft of carpet cleaned.

19. *Familiarize*. Let s = the original salary. Then the amount of the raise is 8% of s, or $0.08s$.

Translate.

$$\underbrace{\text{Original salary}}_{s} \quad \underset{+}{\text{plus}} \quad \underset{0.08s}{\text{Raise}} \quad \underset{=}{\text{is}} \quad \underset{42,066}{\$42,066.}$$

Solve. We solve the equation.

$$s + 0.08s = 42,066$$
$$1s + 0.08s = 42,066$$
$$1.08s = 42,066$$
$$s = 38,950$$

Check. 8% of \$38,950 is \$3116, and \$38,950 + \$3116 is \$42,066. The answer checks.

State. The salary before the raise was \$38,950.

21. a) In 2008, $x = 2008 - 2000 = 8$. We substitute 8 for x in the equation and compute y.

$$y = -1777x + 27,153$$
$$y = -1777(8) + 27,153$$
$$y = -14,216 + 27,153$$
$$y = 12,937$$

We predict that there will be 12,937 gun deaths in 2008.

In 2015, $x = 2015 - 2000 = 15$. We substitute 15 for x in the equation and compute y.

$$y = -1777x + 27,153$$
$$y = -1777(15) + 27,153$$
$$y = -26,655 + 27,153$$
$$y = 498$$

We predict that there will be 498 gun deaths in 2015.

b) We substitute 11,157 for y in the equation and solve for x.

$$y = -1777x + 27,153$$
$$11,157 = -1777x + 27,153$$
$$-15,996 = -1777x \quad \text{Subtracting 27,153}$$
$$9 \approx x \quad \text{Dividing by } -1777$$

The number of gun deaths will be 11,157 nine years after 2000, or in 2009.

23. *Familiarize*. We will use the formula $d = rt$. Let t = the time, in hours, it takes the Delta Queen to cruise 2 mi upstream. The speed of the boat traveling upstream is $7 - 3$, or 4 mph.

Translate. We substitute in the formula.

$$d = rt$$
$$2 = 4t$$

Solve. We solve the equation.

$$2 = 4t$$
$$\frac{1}{2} = t$$

Check. If the boat travels at a speed of 4 mph for $\frac{1}{2}$ hr, it travels $4 \cdot \frac{1}{2}$, or 2 mi. The answer checks.

State. It will take the boat $\frac{1}{2}$ hr to cruise 2 mi upstream.

25. *Familiarize*. Let t = the number of minutes it will take the plane to reach the cruising altitude. The plane needs to travel a distance of $29,000 - 8000$, or 21,000 ft.

Translate. We use the motion formula.

$$d = rt$$
$$21,000 = 3500t$$

Solve. We solve the equation.

$$21,000 = 3500t$$
$$\frac{21,000}{3500} = t$$
$$6 = t$$

Check. The distance the plane travels at a speed of 3500 ft/min for 6 min is $3500 \cdot 6$, or 21,000 ft. The answer checks.

State. It will take 6 min for the plane to reach the cruising altitude.

27. Discussion and Writing Exercise

29.
$$-44 \cdot 55 - 22 = -2420 - 22$$
$$= -2442$$

31.
$$(5 - 12)^2 = (-7)^2$$
$$= 49$$

33.
$$5^2 - 2 \cdot 5 \cdot 12 + 12^2 = 25 - 2 \cdot 5 \cdot 12 + 144$$
$$= 25 - 10 \cdot 12 + 144$$
$$= 25 - 120 + 144$$
$$= -95 + 144$$
$$= 49$$

35.
$$\frac{12|8 - 10| + 9 \cdot 6}{5^4 + 4^5} = \frac{12|-2| + 9 \cdot 6}{625 + 1024}$$
$$= \frac{12 \cdot 2 + 9 \cdot 6}{1649}$$
$$= \frac{24 + 54}{1649}$$
$$= \frac{78}{1649}$$

37. $[-64 \div (-4)] \div (-16) = 16 \div -16$
$$= -1$$

39. $2^{13} \div 2^5 \div 2^3 = 2^8 \div 2^3$
$$= 2^5, \text{ or } 32$$

41. *Familiarize.* Let p = the price of the house in 1994. In 1995 real estate prices increased 6%, so the house was worth $p + 0.06p$, or $1.06p$. In 1996 prices increased 2%, so the house was then worth $1.06p + 0.02(1.06p)$, or $1.02(1.06p)$. In 1997 prices dropped 1%, so the value of the house became $1.02(1.06p) - 0.01(1.02)(1.06p)$, or $0.99(1.02)(1.06p)$.

Translate.

The price of the house in 1997 was $117,743.

$$0.99(1.02)(1.06p) = 117,743$$

Solve. We carry out some algebraic manipulation.
$$0.99(1.02)(1.06p) = 117,743$$
$$p = \frac{117,743}{0.99(1.02)(1.06)}$$
$$p \approx 110,000$$

Check. If the price of the house in 1994 was $110,000, then in 1995 it was worth $1.06(\$110,000)$, or $\$116,600$. In 1996 it was worth $1.02(\$116,600)$, or $\$118,932$, and in 1997 it was worth $0.99(\$118,932)$, or $\$117,743$. Our answer checks.

State. The house was worth $110,000 in 1994.

43. *Familiarize.* Let n represent the number of romance novels. Then 65%n, or $0.65n$, represents the number of science fiction novels; 46%$(0.65n)$, or $(0.46)(0.65n)$, or $0.299n$, represents the number of horror novels; and 17%$(0.299n)$, or $0.17(0.299n)$, or $0.05083n$, represents the number of mystery novels.

Translate.

Romance novels + Science fiction novels + Horror novels + Mystery novels is 400.

$$n + 0.65n + 0.299n + 0.05083n = 400$$

Solve.
$$n + 0.65n + 0.299n + 0.05083n = 400$$
$$1.99983n = 400$$
$$n \approx 200$$

Check. If the number of romance novels is 200, then the other novels are:

Science fiction: $0.65(200) = 130$

Horror: $0.299(200) \approx 60$

Mystery: $0.05083(200) \approx 10$

The total number of novels is $200 + 130 + 60 + 10$, or 400. The numbers check.

State. The professor has 130 science fiction novels.

45. *Familiarize.* Let p = the total percent change, represented in decimal notation. We represent the original population as 1 (100% of the population). After a 20% increase the population is $1 + 0.2 \cdot 1$, or 1.2. When this new population is increased by 30%, we have $1.2 + 0.3(1.2)$, or $1.3(1.2)$. When this population is decreased by 20% we have $1.3(1.2) - 0.2[1.3(1.2)]$, or $0.8(1.3)(1.2)$.

Translate.

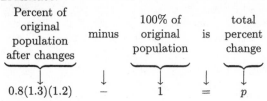

Percent of original population after changes minus 100% of original population is total percent change

$$0.8(1.3)(1.2) \quad - \quad 1 \quad = \quad p$$

Solve.
$$0.8(1.3)(1.2) - 1 = p$$
$$1.248 - 1 = p \qquad \text{Multiplying}$$
$$0.248 = p$$
$$0.25 \approx p \qquad \text{Rounding}$$

Since p is a positive number, it represents an increase in population.

Check. We repeat the computations. The result checks.

State. The total percent change is a 25% increase.

47. *Familiarize.* Let s = the number of seconds after which the watches will show the same time again. The difference in time between the two watches is
$$2.5\frac{\text{sec}}{\text{hr}} = 2.5\frac{\text{sec}}{\text{hr}} \times \frac{1 \text{ hr}}{60 \text{ min}} \times \frac{1 \text{ min}}{60 \text{ sec}} = \frac{2.5 \text{ sec}}{3600 \text{ sec}}.$$
The watches will show the same time again when the difference in time between them is
$$12 \text{ hr} = 12 \text{ hr} \times \frac{60 \text{ min}}{1 \text{ hr}} \times \frac{60 \text{ sec}}{1 \text{ min}} = 43,200 \text{ sec}.$$

Translate.

Difference in time, per 3600 sec times how many seconds is 43,200 sec

$$\frac{2.5}{3600} \quad \cdot \quad s \quad = \quad 43,200$$

Solve.
$$\frac{2.5}{3600}s = 43,200$$
$$\frac{3600}{2.5} \cdot \frac{2.5}{3600}s = \frac{3600}{2.5} \cdot 43,200$$
$$s = 62,208,000$$

Check. At a rate of $\frac{2.5 \text{ sec}}{3600 \text{ sec}}$, in 62,208,000 sec the difference in time will be $\frac{2.5}{3600} \cdot 62,208,000$, or 43,200 sec, or 12 hr. The result checks.

State. The watches will show the same time again after 62,208,000 sec.

49. Answers may vary. One possibility is: A piece of material 75 cm long is to be cut into two pieces, one of them $\frac{2}{3}$ as long as the other. How should the material be cut?

51. *Familiarize*. Using the properties of parallel lines intersected by a transversal, we know that $m\angle 8 = m\angle 4$. Also $m\angle 4 + m\angle 2 = 180°$ and $m\angle 4 = m\angle 1$.

Translate. First we find x and use it to find $m\angle 4$.
$$\begin{array}{ccc} m\angle 8 & = & m\angle 4 \\ \downarrow & \downarrow & \downarrow \\ 5x + 25 & = & 8x + 4 \end{array}$$

Solve.
$$5x + 25 = 8x + 4$$
$$21 = 3x \qquad \text{Subtracting } 5x \text{ and } 4$$
$$7 = x$$

If $x = 7$, we have $m\angle 4 = 8 \cdot 7 + 4 = 60°$.

Then $m\angle 4 + m\angle 2 = 180°$, so
$$60° + m\angle 2 = 180°$$
$$m\angle 2 = 120°. \qquad \text{Subtracting } 60°$$

Also, $m\angle 4 = m\angle 1 = 60°$.

Check. We go over the computations. The results check.

State. $m\angle 2 = 120°$ and $m\angle 1 = 60°$.

Exercise Set 1.4

1. $x - 2 \geq 6$

-4 : We substitute and get $-4 - 2 \geq 6$, or $-6 \geq 6$, a false sentence. Therefore, -4 is not a solution.

0 : We substitute and get $0 - 2 \geq 6$, or $-2 \geq 6$, a false sentence. Therefore, 0 is not a solution.

4 : We substitute and get $4 - 2 \geq 6$, or $2 \geq 6$, a false sentence. Therefore, 4 is not a solution.

8 : We substitute and get $8 - 2 \geq 6$, or $6 \geq 6$, a true sentence. Therefore, 8 is a solution.

3. $t - 8 > 2t - 3$

0 : We substitute and get $0 - 8 > 2 \cdot 0 - 3$, or $-8 > -3$, a false sentence. Therefore, 0 is not a solution.

-8 : We substitute and get $-8 - 8 > 2(-8) - 3$, or $-16 > -19$, a true sentence. Therefore, -8 is a solution.

-9 : We substitute and get $-9 - 8 > 2(-9) - 3$, or $-17 > -21$, a true sentence. Therefore, -9 is a solution.

-3 : We substitute and get $-3 - 8 > 2(-3) - 3$, or $-11 > -9$, a false sentence. Therefore, -3 is not a solution.

$-\frac{7}{8}$: We substitute and get $-\frac{7}{8} - 8 > 2\left(-\frac{7}{8}\right) - 3$, or $-\frac{71}{8} > -\frac{38}{8}$, a false sentence. Therefore, $-\frac{7}{8}$ is not a solution.

5. Interval notation for $\{x | x < 5\}$ is $(-\infty, 5)$.

7. Interval notation for $\{x | -3 \leq x \leq 3\}$ is $[-3, 3]$.

9. Interval notation for the given graph is $(-2, 5)$.

11. Interval notation for the given graph is $(-\sqrt{2}, \infty)$.

13.
$$x + 2 > 1$$
$$x + 2 - 2 > 1 - 2 \qquad \text{Subtracting } 2$$
$$x > -1$$
The solution set is $\{x | x > -1\}$, or $(-1, \infty)$.

15.
$$y + 3 < 9$$
$$y + 3 - 3 < 9 - 3 \qquad \text{Subtracting } 3$$
$$y < 6$$
The solution set is $\{y | y < 6\}$, or $(-\infty, 6)$.

17.
$$a - 9 \leq -31$$
$$a - 9 + 9 \leq -31 + 9 \qquad \text{Adding } 9$$
$$a \leq -22$$
The solution set is $\{a | a \leq -22\}$, or $(-\infty, -22]$.

19.
$$t + 13 \geq 9$$
$$t + 13 - 13 \geq 9 - 13 \qquad \text{Subtracting } 13$$
$$t \geq -4$$
The solution set is $\{t | t \geq -4\}$, or $[-4, \infty)$.

21.
$$y - 8 > -14$$
$$y - 8 + 8 > -14 + 8 \qquad \text{Adding } 8$$
$$y > -6$$
The solution set is $\{y | y > -6\}$, or $(-6, \infty)$.

23.
$$x - 11 \leq -2$$
$$x - 11 + 11 \leq -2 + 11 \qquad \text{Adding } 11$$
$$x \leq 9$$
The solution set is $\{x | x \leq 9\}$, or $(-\infty, 9]$.

25.
$$8x \geq 24$$
$$\frac{8x}{8} \geq \frac{24}{8} \qquad \text{Dividing by } 8$$
$$x \geq 3$$
The solution set is $\{x | x \geq 3\}$, or $[3, \infty)$.

27. $0.3x < -18$

$$\frac{0.3x}{0.3} < \frac{-18}{0.3} \qquad \text{Dividing by } 0.3$$

$$x < -60$$

The solution set is $\{x|x < -60\}$, or $(-\infty, -60)$.

29. $-9x \geq -8.1$

$$\frac{-9x}{-9} \leq \frac{-8.1}{-9} \qquad \text{Dividing by } -9 \text{ and reversing the inequality symbol}$$

$$x \leq 0.9$$

The solution set is $\{x|x \leq 0.9\}$, or $(-\infty, 0.9]$.

31.
$$-\frac{3}{4}x \geq -\frac{5}{8}$$

$$-\frac{4}{3}\left(-\frac{3}{4}x\right) \leq -\frac{4}{3}\left(-\frac{5}{8}\right) \qquad \text{Multiplying by } -\frac{4}{3} \text{ and reversing the inequality symbol}$$

$$x \leq \frac{20}{24}$$

$$x \leq \frac{5}{6}$$

The solution set is $\left\{x\middle|x \leq \frac{5}{6}\right\}$, or $\left(-\infty, \frac{5}{6}\right]$.

33. $2x + 7 < 19$

$$2x + 7 - 7 < 19 - 7 \qquad \text{Subtracting } 7$$

$$2x < 12$$

$$\frac{2x}{2} < \frac{12}{2} \qquad \text{Dividing by } 2$$

$$x < 6$$

The solution set is $\{x|x < 6\}$, or $(-\infty, 6)$.

35. $5y + 2y \leq -21$

$$7y \leq -21 \qquad \text{Collecting like terms}$$

$$\frac{7y}{7} \leq \frac{-21}{7} \qquad \text{Dividing by } 7$$

$$y \leq -3$$

The solution set is $\{y|y \leq -3\}$, or $(-\infty, -3]$.

37. $2y - 7 < 5y - 9$

$$-5y + 2y - 7 < -5y + 5y - 9 \qquad \text{Adding } -5y$$

$$-3y - 7 < -9$$

$$-3y - 7 + 7 < -9 + 7 \qquad \text{Adding } 7$$

$$-3y < -2$$

$$\frac{-3y}{-3} > \frac{-2}{-3} \qquad \text{Dividing by } -3 \text{ and reversing the inequality symbol}$$

$$y > \frac{2}{3}$$

The solution set is $\left\{y\middle|y > \frac{2}{3}\right\}$, or $\left(\frac{2}{3}, \infty\right)$.

39.
$$0.4x + 5 \leq 1.2x - 4$$

$$-1.2x + 0.4x + 5 \leq -1.2x + 1.2x - 4 \qquad \text{Adding } -1.2x$$

$$-0.8x + 5 \leq -4$$

$$-0.8x + 5 - 5 \leq -4 - 5 \qquad \text{Subtracting } 5$$

$$-0.8x \leq -9$$

$$\frac{-0.8x}{-0.8} \geq \frac{-9}{-0.8} \qquad \text{Dividing by } -0.8 \text{ and reversing the inequality symbol}$$

$$x \geq 11.25$$

The solution set is $\{x|x \geq 11.25\}$, or $[11.25, \infty)$.

41.
$$5x - \frac{1}{12} \leq \frac{5}{12} + 4x$$

$$12\left(5x - \frac{1}{12}\right) \leq 12\left(\frac{5}{12} + 4x\right) \qquad \text{Clearing fractions}$$

$$60x - 1 \leq 5 + 48x$$

$$60x - 1 - 48x \leq 5 + 48x - 48x \qquad \text{Subtracting } 48x$$

$$12x - 1 \leq 5$$

$$12x - 1 + 1 \leq 5 + 1 \qquad \text{Adding } 1$$

$$12x \leq 6$$

$$\frac{12x}{12} \leq \frac{6}{12} \qquad \text{Dividing by } 12$$

$$x \leq \frac{1}{2}$$

The solution set is $\left\{x\middle|x \leq \frac{1}{2}\right\}$, or $\left(-\infty, \frac{1}{2}\right]$.

43.
$$4(4y - 3) \geq 9(2y + 7)$$

$$16y - 12 \geq 18y + 63 \qquad \text{Removing parentheses}$$

$$16y - 12 - 18y \geq 18y + 63 - 18y \qquad \text{Subtracting } 18y$$

$$-2y - 12 \geq 63$$

$$-2y - 12 + 12 \geq 63 + 12 \qquad \text{Adding } 12$$

$$-2y \geq 75$$

$$\frac{-2y}{-2} \leq \frac{75}{-2} \qquad \text{Dividing by } -2 \text{ and reversing the inequality symbol}$$

$$y \leq -\frac{75}{2}$$

The solution set is $\left\{y\middle|y \leq -\frac{75}{2}\right\}$, or $\left(-\infty, -\frac{75}{2}\right]$.

45. $3(2 - 5x) + 2x < 2(4 + 2x)$

$$6 - 15x + 2x < 8 + 4x$$

$$6 - 13x < 8 + 4x \qquad \text{Collecting like terms}$$

$$6 - 17x < 8 \qquad \text{Subtracting } 4x$$

$$-17x < 2 \qquad \text{Subtracting } 6$$

$$x > -\frac{2}{17} \qquad \text{Dividing by } -17 \text{ and reversing the inequality symbol}$$

The solution set is $\left\{x\middle|x > -\frac{2}{17}\right\}$, or $\left(-\frac{2}{17}, \infty\right)$.

47. $5[3m - (m + 4)] > -2(m - 4)$

$5(3m - m - 4) > -2(m - 4)$

$5(2m - 4) > -2(m - 4)$

$10m - 20 > -2m + 8$

$12m - 20 > 8$ Adding $2m$

$12m > 28$ Adding 20

$m > \dfrac{28}{12}$

$m > \dfrac{7}{3}$

The solution set is $\left\{ m \middle| m > \dfrac{7}{3} \right\}$, or $\left(\dfrac{7}{3}, \infty \right)$.

49. $3(r - 6) + 2 > 4(r + 2) - 21$

$3r - 18 + 2 > 4r + 8 - 21$

$3r - 16 > 4r - 13$ Collecting like terms

$-r - 16 > -13$ Subtracting $4r$

$-r > 3$ Adding 16

$r < -3$ Multiplying by -1 and reversing the inequality symbol

The solution set is $\{r | r < -3\}$, or $(-\infty, -3)$.

51. $19 - (2x + 3) \leq 2(x + 3) + x$

$19 - 2x - 3 \leq 2x + 6 + x$

$16 - 2x \leq 3x + 6$ Collecting like terms

$16 - 5x \leq 6$ Subtracting $3x$

$-5x \leq -10$ Subtracting 16

$x \geq 2$ Dividing by -5 and reversing the inequality symbol

The solution set is $\{x | x \geq 2\}$, or $[2, \infty)$.

53. $\dfrac{1}{4}(8y + 4) - 17 < -\dfrac{1}{2}(4y - 8)$

$2y + 1 - 17 < -2y + 4$

$2y - 16 < -2y + 4$ Collecting like terms

$4y - 16 < 4$ Adding $2y$

$4y < 20$ Adding 16

$y < 5$

The solution set is $\{y | y < 5\}$, or $(-\infty, 5)$.

55. $2[4 - 2(3 - x)] - 1 \geq 4[2(4x - 3) + 7] - 25$

$2[4 - 6 + 2x] - 1 \geq 4[8x - 6 + 7] - 25$

$2[-2 + 2x] - 1 \geq 4[8x + 1] - 25$

$-4 + 4x - 1 \geq 32x + 4 - 25$

$4x - 5 \geq 32x - 21$

$-28x - 5 \geq -21$

$-28x \geq -16$

$x \leq \dfrac{-16}{-28}$ Dividing by -28 and reversing the inequality symbol

$x \leq \dfrac{4}{7}$

The solution set is $\left\{ x \middle| x \leq \dfrac{4}{7} \right\}$, or $\left(-\infty, \dfrac{4}{7} \right]$.

57. $\dfrac{4}{5}(7x - 6) < 40$

$5 \cdot \dfrac{4}{5}(7x - 6) < 5 \cdot 40$ Clearing the fraction

$4(7x - 6) < 200$

$28x - 24 < 200$

$28x < 224$

$x < 8$

The solution set is $\{x | x < 8\}$, or $(-\infty, 8)$.

59. $\dfrac{3}{4}(3 + 2x) + 1 \geq 13$

$4\left[\dfrac{3}{4}(3 + 2x) + 1 \right] \geq 4 \cdot 13$ Clearing the fraction

$3(3 + 2x) + 4 \geq 52$

$9 + 6x + 4 \geq 52$

$6x + 13 \geq 52$

$6x \geq 39$

$x \geq \dfrac{39}{6}$, or $\dfrac{13}{2}$

The solution set is $\left\{ x \middle| x \geq \dfrac{13}{2} \right\}$, or $\left[\dfrac{13}{2}, \infty \right)$.

61. $\dfrac{3}{4}\left(3x - \dfrac{1}{2} \right) - \dfrac{2}{3} < \dfrac{1}{3}$

$\dfrac{9x}{4} - \dfrac{3}{8} - \dfrac{2}{3} < \dfrac{1}{3}$

$24\left(\dfrac{9x}{4} - \dfrac{3}{8} - \dfrac{2}{3} \right) < 24 \cdot \dfrac{1}{3}$ Clearing fractions

$54x - 9 - 16 < 8$

$54x - 25 < 8$

$54x < 33$

$x < \dfrac{33}{54}$, or $\dfrac{11}{18}$

The solution set is $\left\{ x \middle| x < \dfrac{11}{18} \right\}$, or $\left(-\infty, \dfrac{11}{18} \right)$.

63.
$$0.7(3x+6) \geq 1.1 - (x+2)$$
$$10[0.7(3x+6)] \geq 10[1.1 - (x+2)] \quad \text{Clearing decimals}$$
$$7(3x+6) \geq 11 - 10(x+2)$$
$$21x + 42 \geq 11 - 10x - 20$$
$$21x + 42 \geq -9 - 10x$$
$$31x + 42 \geq -9$$
$$31x \geq -51$$
$$x \geq -\frac{51}{31}$$

The solution set is $\left\{ x \mid x \geq -\dfrac{51}{31} \right\}$, or $\left[-\dfrac{51}{31}, \infty \right)$.

65.
$$a + (a-3) \leq (a+2) - (a+1)$$
$$a + a - 3 \leq a + 2 - a - 1$$
$$2a - 3 \leq 1$$
$$2a \leq 4$$
$$a \leq 2$$

The solution set is $\{a \mid a \leq 2\}$, or $(-\infty, 2]$.

67. a) We substitute 214 for W and 73 for H and calculate I.
$$I = \frac{704.5W}{H^2}$$
$$I = \frac{704.5(192)}{73^2}$$
$$I \approx 25.38$$

b) *Familiarize.* We will use the formula $I = \dfrac{704.5W}{H^2}$. Recall that $H = 73$ in.

Translate. An index I less than 25 indicates the lowest risk category, so we have
$$I < 25, \text{ or } \frac{704.5W}{H^2} < 25.$$

Now we replace H with 73.
$$\frac{704.5W}{73^2} < 25$$

Solve. We solve the inequality.
$$\frac{704.5W}{73^2} < 25$$
$$\frac{704.5W}{5329} < 25$$
$$704.5W < 133,225$$
$$W < 189.1 \quad \text{Rounding}$$

Check. As a partial check we can substitute a value of W less than 189.1 and a value greater than 189.1 in the formula.

For $W = 189$: $I = \dfrac{704.5(189)}{73^2} \approx 24.97$

For $W = 190$: $I = \dfrac{704.5(190)}{73^2} \approx 25.12$

Since a value of W less than 189.1 gives a body mass index less than 25 and a value of W greater than 189.1 gives an index greater than 25, we have a partial check.

State. Weights of approximately 189.1 lb or less will keep Marv in the lowest risk category. In terms of an inequality we write
$$\{W \mid W < \text{ (approximately) } 189.1 \text{ lb}\}.$$

69. *Familiarize.* List the information in a table. Let $x =$ the score on the fourth test.

Test	Score
Test 1	89
Test 2	92
Test 3	95
Test 4	x
Total	360 or more

Translate. We can easily get an inequality from the table.
$$89 + 92 + 95 + x \geq 360$$

Solve.
$$276 + x \geq 360 \quad \text{Collecting like terms}$$
$$x \geq 84 \quad \text{Adding } -276$$

Check. If you get 84 on the fourth test, your total score will be $89 + 92 + 95 + 84$, or 360. Any higher score will also give you an A.

State. A score of 84 or better will give you an A. In terms of an inequality we write $\{x \mid x \geq 84\}$.

71. *Familiarize.* Let $v =$ the blue book value of the car. Since the car was not replaced, we know that $9200 does not exceed 80% of the blue book value.

Translate. We write an inequality stating that $9200 does not exceed 80% of the blue book value.
$$9200 \leq 0.8v$$

Solve.
$$9200 \leq 0.8v$$
$$11,500 \leq v \quad \text{Multiplying by } \frac{1}{0.8}$$

Check. We can do a partial check by substituting a value for v greater than 11,500. When $v = 11,525$, then 80% of v is $0.8(11,525)$, or $9220. This is greater than $9200; that is, $9200 does not exceed this amount. We cannot check all possible values for v, so we stop here.

State. The blue book value of the car is $11,500 or more. In terms of an inequality we write $\{v \mid v \geq \$11,500\}$.

73. *Familiarize.* We make a table of information.

Plan A: Monthly Income	Plan B: Monthly Income
$400 salary	$610 salary
8% of sales	5% of sales
Total: 400 + 8% of sales	Total: 610 + 5% of sales

Translate. We write an inequality stating that the income from Plan A is greater than the income from Plan B. We let $S =$ gross sales.
$$400 + 8\%S > 610 + 5\%S$$

Solve.

$$400 + 0.08S > 610 + 0.05S$$
$$400 + 0.03S > 610$$
$$0.03S > 210$$
$$S > 7000$$

Check. We calculate for $S = \$7000$ and for some amount greater than $7000 and some amount less than $7000.

Plan A:	Plan B:
$400 + 8\%(7000)$	$610 + 5\%(7000)$
$400 + 0.08(7000)$	$610 + 0.05(7000)$
$400 + 560$	$610 + 350$
$960	$960

When $S = \$7000$, the income from Plan A is equal to the income from Plan B.

Plan A:	Plan B:
$400 + 8\%(8000)$	$610 + 5\%(8000)$
$400 + 0.08(8000)$	$610 + 0.05(8000)$
$400 + 640$	$610 + 400$
$1040	$1010

When $S = \$8000$, the income from Plan A is greater than the income from Plan B.

Plan A:	Plan B:
$400 + 8\%(6000)$	$610 + 5\%(6000)$
$400 + 0.08(6000)$	$610 + 0.05(6000)$
$400 + 480$	$610 + 300$
$880	$910

When $S = \$6000$, the income from Plan A is less than the income from Plan B.

State. Plan A is better than Plan B when gross sales are greater than $7000. In terms of an inequality we write $\{S | S > \$7000\}$.

75. Familiarize. Let $c = $ the number of checks per month. Then the Anywhere plan will cost $0.20c$ per month and the Acu-checking plan will cost $2 + \$0.12c$ per month.

Translate. We write an inequality stating that the Acu-checking plan costs less than the Anywhere plan.

$$2 + 0.12c < 0.20c$$

Solve.

$$2 + 0.12c < 0.20c$$
$$2 < 0.08c$$
$$25 < c$$

Check. We can do a partial check by substituting a value for c less than 25 and a value for c greater than 25. When $c = 24$, the Acu-checking plan costs $2 + \$0.12(24)$, or $4.88, and the Anywhere plan costs $0.20(24)$, or $4.80, so the Anywhere plan is less expensive. When $c = 26$, the Acu-checking plan costs $2 + \$0.12(26)$, or $5.12, and the Anywhere plan costs $0.20(26)$, or $5.20, so Acu-checking is less expensive. We cannot check all possible values for c, so we stop here.

State. The Acu-checking plan costs less for more than 25 checks per month. In terms of an inequality we write $\{c | c > 25\}$.

77. Familiarize. Let $p = $ the number of guests at the wedding party. Then the number of guests in excess of 25 is $p - 25$. The cost under plan A is $30p$, and the cost under plan B is $1300 + 20(p - 25)$.

Translate. We write an inequality stating that plan B costs less than plan A.

$$1300 + 20(p - 25) < 30p$$

Solve. We solve the inequality.

$$1300 + 20(p - 25) < 30p$$
$$1300 + 20p - 500 < 30p$$
$$800 + 20p < 30p$$
$$800 < 10p$$
$$80 < p$$

Check. We calculate for $p = 80$ and for some number less than 80 and some number greater than 80.

Plan A:	Plan B:
$30 \cdot 80$	$1300 + 20(80 - 25)$
$2400	$2400

When 80 people attend, plan B costs the same as plan A.

Plan A:	Plan B:
$30 \cdot 79$	$1300 + 20(79 - 25)$
$2370	$2380

When fewer than 80 people attend, plan B costs more than plan A.

Plan A:	Plan B:
$30 \cdot 81$	$1300 + 20(81 - 25)$
$2430	$2420

When more than 80 people attend, plan B costs less than plan A.

State. For parties of more than 80 people, plan B will cost less. In terms of an inequality we write $\{p | p > 80\}$.

79. Familiarize. We want to find the values of s for which $I > 36$.

Translate. $2(s + 10) > 36$

Solve.

$$2s + 20 > 36$$
$$2s > 16$$
$$s > 8$$

Check. For $s = 8$, $I = 2(8 + 10) = 2 \cdot 18 = 36$. Then any U.S. size larger than 8 will give a size larger than 36 in Italy.

State. For U.S. dress sizes larger than 8, dress sizes in Italy will be larger than 36. In terms of an inequality we write $\{s | s > 8\}$.

81. a) Substitute 0 for t and carry out the calculation.

$$N = 0.733(0) + 8.398$$
$$N = 0 + 8.398$$
$$N = 8.398$$

Each person drank 8.398 gal of bottled water in 1990.

Substitute 5 for t and carry out the calculation.

$$N = 0.733(5) + 8.398$$
$$N = 3.665 + 8.398$$
$$N = 12.063$$

Each person drank 12.063 gal of bottled water in 1995.

In 2000, $t = 2000 - 1990 = 10$. Substitute 10 for t and carry out the calculation.

$$N = 0.733(10) + 8.398$$
$$N = 7.33 + 8.398$$
$$N = 15.728$$

Each person will drink 15.728 gal of bottled water in 2000.

b) *Familiarize*. The amount of bottled water that each person drinks t years after 1990 is given by $0.733t + 8.398$.

Translate.

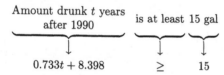

Amount drunk t years after 1990	is at least	15 gal
$0.733t + 8.398$	$\geq$	15

Solve. We solve the inequality.

$$0.733t + 8.398 \geq 15$$
$$0.733t \geq 6.602 \quad \text{Subtracting 8.398}$$
$$t \geq 9 \quad \text{Rounding}$$

Check. We calculate for 9, for some number less than 9, and for some number greater than 9.

For $t = 9$: $0.733(9) + 8.398 \approx 15$.

For $t = 8$: $0.733(8) + 8.398 \approx 14.3$.

For $t = 10$: $0.733(10) + 8.398 \approx 15.7$.

For a value of t greater than or equal to 9, the number of gallons of bottled water each person drinks is at 15. We cannot check all the possible values of t, so we stop here.

State. Each person will drink at least 15 gal of bottled water 9 or more years after 1990, or for all years after 1999.

83. Discussion and Writing Exercise

85. $3a - 6(2a - 5b) = 3a - 12a + 30b$
$$= -9a + 30b$$

87. $4(a - 2b) - 6(2a - 5b)$
$$= 4a - 8b - 12a + 30b$$
$$= -8a + 22b$$

89. $30x - 70y - 40 = 10 \cdot 3x - 10 \cdot 7y - 10 \cdot 4$
$$= 10(3x - 7y - 4)$$

91. $-8x + 24y - 4 = -4 \cdot 2x - 4(-6y) - 4 \cdot 1$
$$= -4(2x - 6y + 1)$$

93. $-2.3 - 8.9 = -2.3 + (-8.9) = -11.2$

95. $-2.3 + (-8.9) = -11.2$

97. a) *Familiarize*. We will use

$$S = 460 + 94p \quad \text{and} \quad D = 2000 - 60p.$$

Translate. Supply is to exceed demand, so we have

$$S > D, \text{ or}$$
$$460 + 94p > 2000 - 60p.$$

Solve. We solve the inequality.

$$460 + 94p > 2000 - 60p$$

$460 + 154p > 2000$	Adding $60p$
$154p > 1540$	Subtracting 460
$p > 10$	Dividing by 154

Check. We calculate for $p = 10$, for some value of p less than 10, and for some value of p greater than 10.

For $p = 10$: $S = 460 + 94 \cdot 10 = 1400$
                $D = 2000 - 60 \cdot 10 = 1400$

For $p = 9$: $S = 460 + 94 \cdot 9 = 1306$
                $D = 2000 - 60 \cdot 9 = 1460$

For $p = 11$: $S = 460 + 94 \cdot 11 = 1494$
                $D = 2000 - 60 \cdot 11 = 1340$

For a value of p greater than 10, supply exceeds demand. We cannot check all possible values of p, so we stop here.

State. Supply exceeds demand for values of p greater than 10. In terms of an inequality we write $\{p | p > 10\}$.

b) We have seen in part (a) that $D = S$ for $p = 10$, $S < D$ for a value of p less than 10, and $S > D$ for a value of p greater than 10. Since we cannot check all possible values of p, we stop here. Supply is less than demand for values of p less than 10. In terms of an inequality we write $\{p | p < 10\}$.

99. True

101. $x + 5 \leq 5 + x$
$$5 \leq 5 \quad \text{Subtracting } x$$

We get a true inequality, so all real numbers are solutions.

103. $x^2 + 1 > 0$

$x^2 \geq 0$ for all real numbers, so $x^2 + 1 \geq 1 > 0$ for all real numbers.

Exercise Set 1.5

1. $\{9, 10, 11\} \cap \{9, 11, 13\}$

The numbers 9 and 11 are common to the two sets, so the intersection is $\{9, 11\}$.

3. $\{a, b, c, d\} \cap \{b, f, g\}$

Only the letter b is common to the two sets. The intersection is $\{b\}$.

5. $\{9, 10, 11\} \cup \{9, 11, 13\}$

The numbers in either or both sets are 9, 10, 11, and 13, so the union is $\{9, 10, 11, 13\}$.

7. $\{a, b, c, d\} \cup \{b, f, g\}$

The letters in either or both sets are a, b, c, d, f, and g, so the union is $\{a, b, c, d, f, g\}$.

9. $\{2, 5, 7, 9\} \cap \{1, 3, 4\}$

There are no numbers common to the two sets. The intersection is the empty set, $\emptyset$.

11. $\{3, 5, 7\} \cup \emptyset$

The numbers in either or both sets are 3, 5, and 7, so the union is $\{3, 5, 7\}$.

13. $-4 < a$ *and* $a \leq 1$ can be written $-4 < a \leq 1$. In interval notation we have $(-4, 1]$.

The graph is the intersection of the graphs of $a > -4$ and $a \leq 1$.

15. We can write $1 < x < 6$ in interval notation as $(1, 6)$.

The graph is the intersection of the graphs of $x > 1$ and $x < 6$.

17. $-10 \leq 3x + 2$ *and* $3x + 2 < 17$

$\quad -12 \leq 3x \quad$ *and* $\quad 3x < 15$

$\quad \ -4 \leq x \quad$ *and* $\quad \ \ x < 5$

The solution set is the intersection of the solution sets of the individual inequalities. The numbers common to both sets are those that are greater than or equal to -4 *and* less than 5. Thus the solution set is $\{x| -4 \leq x < 5\}$, or $[-4, 5)$.

19. $3x + 7 \geq 4 \quad$ *and* $\quad 2x - 5 \geq -1$

$\quad 3x \geq -3 \ $ *and* $\quad \ \ 2x \geq 4$

$\quad \ \ x \geq -1 \ $ *and* $\quad \ \ \ x \geq 2$

The solution set is $\{x|x \geq -1\} \cap \{x|x \geq 2\} = \{x|x \geq 2\}$, or $[2, \infty)$.

21. $4 - 3x \geq 10 \quad$ *and* $\quad 5x - 2 > 13$

$\quad -3x \geq 6 \quad$ *and* $\quad \ \ 5x > 15$

$\quad \ \ x \leq -2 \ $ *and* $\quad \ \ \ \ x > 3$

The solution set is $\{x|x \leq -2\} \cap \{x|x > 3\} = \emptyset$.

23. $\qquad -4 < x + 4 < 10$

$\quad -4 - 4 < x + 4 - 4 < 10 - 4 \qquad$ Subtracting 4

$\qquad \ \ -8 < x < 6$

The solution set is $\{x| -8 < x < 6\}$, or $(-8, 6)$.

25. $\quad 6 > -x \geq -2$

$\ -6 < x \leq 2 \qquad$ Multiplying by -1

The solution set is $\{x| -6 < x \leq 2\}$, or $(-6, 2]$.

27. $\qquad 1 < 3y + 4 \leq 19$

$\quad 1 - 4 < 3y + 4 - 4 \leq 19 - 4 \quad$ Subtracting 4

$\qquad \ -3 < 3y \leq 15$

$\qquad \ \dfrac{-3}{3} < \dfrac{3y}{3} \leq \dfrac{15}{3} \quad$ Dividing by 3

$\qquad \ -1 < y \leq 5$

The solution set is $\{y| -1 < y \leq 5\}$, or $(-1, 5]$.

29. $\qquad -10 \leq 3x - 5 \leq -1$

$\quad -10 + 5 \leq 3x - 5 + 5 \leq -1 + 5 \quad$ Adding 5

$\qquad \quad -5 \leq 3x \leq 4$

$\qquad \quad \dfrac{-5}{3} \leq \dfrac{3x}{3} \leq \dfrac{4}{3} \quad$ Dividing by 3

$\qquad \quad -\dfrac{5}{3} \leq x \leq \dfrac{4}{3}$

The solution set is $\left\{x| -\dfrac{5}{3} \leq x \leq \dfrac{4}{3}\right\}$, or $\left[-\dfrac{5}{3}, \dfrac{4}{3}\right]$.

31. $\qquad 2 < x + 3 \leq 9$

$\quad 2 - 3 < x + 3 - 3 \leq 9 - 3 \quad$ Subtracting 3

$\qquad \ -1 < x \leq 6$

The solution set is $\{x| -1 < x \leq 6\}$, or $(-1, 6]$.

33. $\qquad -6 \leq 2x - 3 < 6$

$\quad -6 + 3 \leq 2x - 3 + 3 < 6 + 3$

$\qquad \ -3 \leq 2x < 9$

$\qquad \ \dfrac{-3}{2} \leq \dfrac{2x}{2} < \dfrac{9}{2}$

$\qquad \ -\dfrac{3}{2} \leq x < \dfrac{9}{2}$

The solution set is $\left\{x| -\dfrac{3}{2} \leq x < \dfrac{9}{2}\right\}$, or $\left[-\dfrac{3}{2}, \dfrac{9}{2}\right)$.

35. $\quad -\dfrac{1}{2} < \dfrac{1}{4}x - 3 \le \dfrac{1}{2}$

$$-\dfrac{1}{2} + 3 < \dfrac{1}{4}x - 3 + 3 \le \dfrac{1}{2} + 3$$

$$\dfrac{5}{2} < \dfrac{1}{4}x \le \dfrac{7}{2}$$

$$4 \cdot \dfrac{5}{2} < 4 \cdot \dfrac{1}{4}x \le 4 \cdot \dfrac{7}{2}$$

$$10 < x \le 14$$

The solution set is $\{x | 10 < x \le 14\}$, or $(10, 14]$.

37. $\quad -3 < \dfrac{2x - 5}{4} < 8$

$$4(-3) < 4\left(\dfrac{2x-5}{4}\right) < 4 \cdot 8$$

$$-12 < 2x - 5 < 32$$

$$-12 + 5 < 2x - 5 + 5 < 32 + 5$$

$$-7 < 2x < 37$$

$$\dfrac{-7}{2} < \dfrac{2x}{2} < \dfrac{37}{2}$$

$$-\dfrac{7}{2} < x < \dfrac{37}{2}$$

The solution set is $\left\{x \,\middle|\, -\dfrac{7}{2} < x < \dfrac{37}{2}\right\}$, or $\left(-\dfrac{7}{2}, \dfrac{37}{2}\right)$.

39. $x < -2$ or $x > 1$ can be written in interval notation as $(-\infty, -2) \cup (1, \infty)$.

The graph is the union of the graphs of $x < -2$ and $x > 1$.

41. $x \le -3$ or $x > 1$ can be written in interval notation as $(-\infty, -3] \cup (1, \infty)$.

The graph is the union of the graphs of $x \le -3$ and $x > 1$.

43. $\quad x + 3 < -2 \qquad or \qquad x + 3 > 2$

$$x + 3 - 3 < -2 - 3 \quad or \quad x + 3 - 3 > 2 - 3$$

$$x < -5 \qquad or \qquad x > -1$$

The solution set is $\{x | x < -5$ or $x > -1\}$, or $(-\infty, -5) \cup (-1, \infty)$.

45. $\quad 2x - 8 \le -3 \qquad or \qquad x - 1 \ge 3$

$$2x - 8 + 8 \le -3 + 8 \quad or \quad x - 1 + 1 \ge 3 + 1$$

$$2x \le 5 \qquad or \qquad x \ge 4$$

$$\dfrac{2x}{2} \le \dfrac{5}{2} \qquad or \qquad x \ge 4$$

$$x \le \dfrac{5}{2} \qquad or \qquad x \ge 4$$

The solution set is $\left\{x \,\middle|\, x \le \dfrac{5}{2}$ or $x \ge 4\right\}$, or

$\left(-\infty, \dfrac{5}{2}\right] \cup [4, \infty)$.

47. $\quad 7x + 4 \ge -17 \quad or \quad 6x + 5 \ge -7$

$$7x \ge -21 \quad or \qquad 6x \ge -12$$

$$x \ge -3 \quad or \qquad x \ge -2$$

The solution set is $\{x | x \ge -3\}$, or $[-3, \infty)$.

49. $\quad 7 > -4x + 5 \qquad or \qquad 10 \le -4x + 5$

$$7 - 5 > -4x + 5 - 5 \quad or \quad 10 - 5 \le -4x + 5 - 5$$

$$2 > -4x \qquad or \qquad 5 \le -4x$$

$$\dfrac{2}{-4} < \dfrac{-4x}{-4} \qquad or \qquad \dfrac{5}{-4} \ge \dfrac{-4x}{-4}$$

$$-\dfrac{1}{2} < x \qquad or \qquad -\dfrac{5}{4} \ge x$$

The solution set is $\left\{x \,\middle|\, x \le -\dfrac{5}{4}$ or $x > -\dfrac{1}{2}\right\}$, or

$\left(-\infty, -\dfrac{5}{4}\right] \cup \left(-\dfrac{1}{2}, \infty\right)$.

51. $\quad 3x - 7 > -10 \quad or \quad 5x + 2 \le 22$

$$3x > -3 \quad or \qquad 5x \le 20$$

$$x > -1 \quad or \qquad x \le 4$$

All real numbers are solutions. In interval notation, the solution set is $(-\infty, \infty)$.

53. $\quad -2x - 2 < -6 \qquad or \qquad -2x - 2 > 6$

$$-2x - 2 + 2 < -6 + 2 \quad or \quad -2x - 2 + 2 > 6 + 2$$

$$-2x < -4 \qquad or \qquad -2x > 8$$

$$\dfrac{-2x}{-2} > \dfrac{-4}{-2} \qquad or \qquad \dfrac{-2x}{-2} < \dfrac{8}{-2}$$

$$x > 2 \qquad or \qquad x < -4$$

The solution set is $\{x | x < -4$ or $x > 2\}$, or $(-\infty, -4) \cup (2, \infty)$.

55. $\quad \dfrac{2}{3}x - 14 < -\dfrac{5}{6} \qquad or \qquad \dfrac{2}{3}x - 14 > \dfrac{5}{6}$

$$6\left(\dfrac{2}{3}x - 14\right) < 6\left(-\dfrac{5}{6}\right) \quad or \quad 6\left(\dfrac{2}{3}x - 14\right) > 6 \cdot \dfrac{5}{6}$$

$$4x - 84 < -5 \qquad or \qquad 4x - 84 > 5$$

$$4x - 84 + 84 < -5 + 84 \quad or \quad 4x - 84 + 84 > 5 + 84$$

$$4x < 79 \qquad or \qquad 4x > 89$$

$$\dfrac{4x}{4} < \dfrac{79}{4} \qquad or \qquad \dfrac{4x}{4} > \dfrac{89}{4}$$

$$x < \dfrac{79}{4} \qquad or \qquad x > \dfrac{89}{4}$$

The solution set is $\left\{x \,\middle|\, x < \dfrac{79}{4}$ or $x > \dfrac{89}{4}\right\}$, or

$\left(-\infty, \dfrac{79}{4}\right) \cup \left(\dfrac{89}{4}, \infty\right)$.

57.
$$\frac{2x-5}{6} \le -3 \quad or \quad \frac{2x-5}{6} \ge 4$$

$$6\left(\frac{2x-5}{6}\right) \le 6(-3) \quad or \quad 6\left(\frac{2x-5}{6}\right) \ge 6 \cdot 4$$

$$2x - 5 \le -18 \quad or \quad 2x - 5 \ge 24$$

$$2x - 5 + 5 \le -18 + 5 \quad or \quad 2x - 5 + 5 \ge 24 + 5$$

$$2x \le -13 \quad or \quad 2x \ge 29$$

$$\frac{2x}{2} \le \frac{-13}{2} \quad or \quad \frac{2x}{2} \ge \frac{29}{2}$$

$$x \le -\frac{13}{2} \quad or \quad x \ge \frac{29}{2}$$

The solution set is $\left\{x \middle| x \le -\frac{13}{2} \ or \ x \ge \frac{29}{2}\right\}$, or

$$\left(-\infty, -\frac{13}{2}\right] \cup \left[\frac{29}{2}, \infty\right).$$

59. *Familiarize.* We will use the formula $P = 1 + \frac{d}{33}$.

Translate. We want to find those values of P for which

$$1 \le P \le 7$$

or

$$1 \le 1 + \frac{d}{33} \le 7.$$

Solve. We solve the inequality.

$$1 \le 1 + \frac{d}{33} \le 7$$

$$0 \le \frac{d}{33} \le 6$$

$$0 \le d \le 198$$

Check. We could do a partial check by substituting some values for d in the formula. The result checks.

State. The pressure is at least 1 atm and at most 7 atm for depths d in the set $\{d|0 \text{ ft} \le d \le 198 \text{ ft}\}$.

61. *Familiarize.* Let b = the number of beats per minute. Note that $10 \text{ sec} = 10 \text{ sec} \times \frac{1 \text{ min}}{60 \text{ sec}} = \frac{10}{60} \times \frac{\text{sec}}{\text{sec}} \times 1 \text{ min} = \frac{1}{6}$ min. Then in 10 sec, or $\frac{1}{6}$ min, the woman should have between $\frac{1}{6} \cdot 138$ and $\frac{1}{6} \cdot 162$ beats.

Translate. We want to find the value of b for which

$$\frac{1}{6} \cdot 138 < b < \frac{1}{6} \cdot 162$$

Solve. We solve the inequality.

$$\frac{1}{6} \cdot 138 < b < \frac{1}{6} \cdot 162$$

$$23 < b < 27$$

Check. If the number of beats in 10 sec, or $\frac{1}{6}$ min, is between 23 and 27, then the number of beats per minute is between $6 \cdot 23$ and $6 \cdot 27$, or between 138 and 162. The answer checks.

State. The number of beats should be between 23 and 27.

63. *Familiarize.* We will use the formula $I = \frac{704.5W}{H^2}$, where $H = 73$. That is, $I = \frac{704.5W}{73^2}$.

Translate. We want to find those values of I for which

$$20 < I < 30$$

or

$$20 < \frac{704.5W}{73^2} < 30.$$

Solve. We solve the inequality.

$$20 < \frac{704.5W}{73^2} < 30$$

$$20 < \frac{704.5W}{5329} < 30$$

$$106,580 < 704.5W < 159,870$$

$$151 < W < 227 \quad \text{Rounding}$$

Check. We could do a partial check by substituting some values for W in the formula. The result checks.

State. Weights between approximately 151 lb and 227 lb will allow Marv to keep his body mass index between 20 and 30. These weights are the values of W in the set $\{W|151 \text{ lb} < W < 227 \text{ lb}\}$.

65. *Familiarize.* We will use the equation $C = 0.25(t-600) + 89.95$.

Translate. We want to find the values of C for which

$$333.95 < C < 439.95$$

or

$$333.95 < 0.25(t - 600) + 89.95 < 439.95.$$

Solve. We solve the inequality.

$$333.95 < 0.25(t - 600) + 89.95 < 439.95$$

$$244 < 0.25(t - 600) < 350$$

$$976 < t - 600 < 1400$$

$$1576 < t < 2000$$

Check. We could do a partial check by substituting some values for t in the formula. The answer checks.

State. Times between 1576 min and 2000 min will keep the cost between \$333.95 and \$439.95. The times are values of t in the set $\{t|1576 \text{ min} < t < 2000 \text{ min}\}$.

67. Discussion and Writing Exercise

69. $|-3.2| = 3.2$

(The distance of -3.2 from 0 is 3.2.)

71. $|-5 + 7| = |2| = 2$

73.
$$(-2x^{-4}y^6)^5 = (-2)^5(x^{-4})^5(y^6)^5$$
$$= -32x^{-20}y^{30}$$
$$= -\frac{32y^{30}}{x^{20}}$$

75.
$$\frac{-4a^5b^{-7}}{5a^{-12}b^8} = -\frac{4a^{5-(-12)}b^{-7-8}}{5}$$
$$= -\frac{4a^{17}b^{-15}}{5}$$
$$= -\frac{4a^{17}}{5b^{15}}$$

77. $\left(\dfrac{56a^5b^{-6}}{28a^7b^{-8}}\right)^{-3} = (2a^{-2}b^2)^{-3}$

$\qquad\qquad\qquad = 2^{-3}a^{-2(-3)}b^{2(-3)}$

$\qquad\qquad\qquad = \dfrac{1}{2^3}a^6b^{-6}$

$\qquad\qquad\qquad = \dfrac{a^6}{8b^6}$

79. $x - 10 < 5x + 6 \le x + 10$

$\qquad -10 < 4x + 6 \le 10 \qquad$ Subtracting x

$\qquad -16 < 4x \le 4$

$\qquad -4 < x \le 1$

The solution set is $\{x \mid -4 < x \le 1\}$, or $(-4, 1]$.

81. $\qquad -\dfrac{2}{15} \le \dfrac{2}{3}x - \dfrac{2}{5} \le \dfrac{2}{15}$

$\qquad -\dfrac{2}{15} \le \dfrac{2}{3}x - \dfrac{6}{15} \le \dfrac{2}{15}$

$\qquad \dfrac{4}{15} \le \dfrac{2}{3}x \le \dfrac{8}{15}$

$\qquad \dfrac{3}{2} \cdot \dfrac{4}{15} \le \dfrac{3}{2} \cdot \dfrac{2}{3}x \le \dfrac{3}{2} \cdot \dfrac{8}{15}$

$\qquad \dfrac{2}{5} \le x \le \dfrac{4}{5}$

The solution set is $\left\{x \mid \dfrac{2}{5} \le x \le \dfrac{4}{5}\right\}$, or $\left[\dfrac{2}{5}, \dfrac{4}{5}\right]$.

83. $3x < 4 - 5x < 5 + 3x$

$\qquad 0 < 4 - 8x < 5 \qquad$ Subtracting $3x$

$\qquad -4 < -8x < 1$

$\qquad \dfrac{1}{2} > x > -\dfrac{1}{8}$

The solution set is $\left\{x \mid -\dfrac{1}{8} < x < \dfrac{1}{2}\right\}$, or $\left(-\dfrac{1}{8}, \dfrac{1}{2}\right)$.

85. $x + 4 < 2x - 6 \le x + 12$

$\qquad 4 < x - 6 \le 12 \qquad$ Subtracting x

$\qquad 10 < x \le 18$

The solution set is $\{x \mid 10 < x \le 18\}$, or $(10, 18]$.

87. If $-b < -a$, then $-1(-b) > -1(-a)$, or $b > a$, or $a < b$. The statement is true.

89. Let $a = 5$, $c = 12$, and $b = 2$. Then $a < c$ and $b < c$, but $a \not< b$. The given statement is false.

91. The numbers in either the set of all rational numbers or the set of all irrational numbers are all real numbers, so the union is all real numbers.

There are no numbers common to the set of all rational numbers and the set of all irrational numbers, so the intersection is $\emptyset$.

Exercise Set 1.6

1. $|9x| = |9| \cdot |x| = 9|x|$

3. $|2x^2| = |2| \cdot |x^2|$

$\qquad = 2|x^2|$

$\qquad = 2x^2 \qquad$ Since x^2 is never negative

5. $|-2x^2| = |-2| \cdot |x^2|$

$\qquad = 2|x^2|$

$\qquad = 2x^2 \qquad$ Since x^2 is never negative

7. $|-6y| = |-6| \cdot |y| = 6|y|$

9. $\left|\dfrac{-2}{x}\right| = \dfrac{|-2|}{|x|} = \dfrac{2}{|x|}$

11. $\left|\dfrac{x^2}{-y}\right| = \dfrac{|x^2|}{|-y|}$

$\qquad = \dfrac{x^2}{|-y|}$

$\qquad = \dfrac{x^2}{|y|} \qquad$ The absolute value of the opposite of a number is the same as the absolute value of the number.

13. $\left|\dfrac{-8x^2}{2x}\right| = |-4x| = |-4| \cdot |x| = 4|x|$

15. $|-8 - (-46)| = |38| = 38$, or

$\qquad |-46 - (-8)| = |-38| = 38$

17. $|36 - 17| = |19| = 19$, or

$\qquad |17 - 36| = |-19| = 19$

19. $|-3.9 - 2.4| = |-6.3| = 6.3$, or

$\qquad |2.4 - (-3.9)| = |6.3| = 6.3$

21. $|-5 - 0| = |-5| = 5$, or

$\qquad |0 - (-5)| = |5| = 5$

23. $|x| = 3$

$\qquad x = -3 \ \text{ or } \ x = 3 \quad$ Absolute-value principle

The solution set is $\{-3, 3\}$.

25. $|x| = -3$

The absolute value of a number is always nonnegative. Therefore, the solution set is $\emptyset$.

27. $|q| = 0$

The only number whose absolute value is 0 is 0. The solution set is $\{0\}$.

29. $|x - 3| = 12$

$\qquad x - 3 = -12 \ \text{ or } \ x - 3 = 12 \quad$ Absolute-value principle

$\qquad\qquad\qquad\qquad\qquad\qquad\qquad$ principle

$\qquad x = -9 \quad \text{or} \qquad x = 15$

The solution set is $\{-9, 15\}$.

31. $|2x - 3| = 4$

$2x - 3 = -4$ or $2x - 3 = 4$ Absolute-value principle

$2x = -1$ or $2x = 7$

$x = -\dfrac{1}{2}$ or $x = \dfrac{7}{2}$

The solution set is $\left\{ -\dfrac{1}{2}, \dfrac{7}{2} \right\}$.

33. $|4x - 9| = 14$

$4x - 9 = -14$ or $4x - 9 = 14$

$4x = -5$ or $4x = 23$

$x = -\dfrac{5}{4}$ or $x = \dfrac{23}{4}$

The solution set is $\left\{ -\dfrac{5}{4}, \dfrac{23}{4} \right\}$.

35. $|x| + 7 = 18$

$|x| + 7 - 7 = 18 - 7$ Subtracting 7

$|x| = 11$

$x = -11$ or $x = 11$ Absolute-value principle

The solution set is $\{-11, 11\}$.

37. $574 = 283 + |t|$

$291 = |t|$ Subtracting 283

$t = -291$ or $t = 291$ Absolute-value principle

The solution set is $\{-291, 291\}$.

39. $|5x| = 40$

$5x = -40$ or $5x = 40$

$x = -8$ or $x = 8$

The solution set is $\{-8, 8\}$.

41. $|3x| - 4 = 17$

$|3x| = 21$ Adding 4

$3x = -21$ or $3x = 21$

$x = -7$ or $x = 7$

The solution set is $\{-7, 7\}$.

43. $7|w| - 3 = 11$

$7|w| = 14$ Adding 3

$|w| = 2$ Dividing by 7

$w = -2$ or $w = 2$ Absolute-value principle

The solution set is $\{-2, 2\}$.

45. $\left| \dfrac{2x - 1}{3} \right| = 5$

$\dfrac{2x - 1}{3} = -5$ or $\dfrac{2x - 1}{3} = 5$

$2x - 1 = -15$ or $2x - 1 = 15$

$2x = -14$ or $2x = 16$

$x = -7$ or $x = 8$

The solution set is $\{-7, 8\}$.

47. $|m + 5| + 9 = 16$

$|m + 5| = 7$ Subtracting 9

$m + 5 = -7$ or $m + 5 = 7$

$m = -12$ or $m = 2$

The solution set is $\{-12, 2\}$.

49. $10 - |2x - 1| = 4$

$-|2x - 1| = -6$ Subtracting 10

$|2x - 1| = 6$ Multiplying by -1

$2x - 1 = -6$ or $2x - 1 = 6$

$2x = -5$ or $2x = 7$

$x = -\dfrac{5}{2}$ or $x = \dfrac{7}{2}$

The solution set is $\left\{ -\dfrac{5}{2}, \dfrac{7}{2} \right\}$.

51. $|3x - 4| = -2$

The absolute value of a number is always nonnegative. The solution set is $\emptyset$.

53. $\left| \dfrac{5}{9} + 3x \right| = \dfrac{1}{6}$

$\dfrac{5}{9} + 3x = -\dfrac{1}{6}$ or $\dfrac{5}{9} + 3x = \dfrac{1}{6}$

$3x = -\dfrac{13}{18}$ or $3x = -\dfrac{7}{18}$

$x = -\dfrac{13}{54}$ or $x = -\dfrac{7}{54}$

The solution set is $\left\{ -\dfrac{13}{54}, -\dfrac{7}{54} \right\}$.

55. $|3x + 4| = |x - 7|$

$3x + 4 = x - 7$ or $3x + 4 = -(x - 7)$

$2x + 4 = -7$ or $3x + 4 = -x + 7$

$2x = -11$ or $4x + 4 = 7$

$x = -\dfrac{11}{2}$ or $4x = 3$

$x = -\dfrac{11}{2}$ or $x = \dfrac{3}{4}$

The solution set is $\left\{ -\dfrac{11}{2}, \dfrac{3}{4} \right\}$.

57. $|x + 3| = |x - 6|$

$x + 3 = x - 6$ or $x + 3 = -(x - 6)$

$3 = -6$ or $x + 3 = -x + 6$

$3 = -6$ or $2x = 3$

$3 = -6$ or $x = \dfrac{3}{2}$

The first equation has no solution. The second equation has $\dfrac{3}{2}$ as a solution. There is only one solution of the original equation. The solution set is $\left\{ \dfrac{3}{2} \right\}$.

59. $|2a + 4| = |3a - 1|$

$\quad 2a + 4 = 3a - 1 \quad or \quad 2a + 4 = -(3a - 1)$

$\quad -a + 4 = -1 \quad or \quad 2a + 4 = -3a + 1$

$\quad\quad -a = -5 \quad or \quad 5a + 4 = 1$

$\quad\quad\quad a = 5 \quad or \quad\quad 5a = -3$

$\quad\quad\quad a = 5 \quad or \quad\quad\quad a = -\dfrac{3}{5}$

The solution set is $\left\{5, -\dfrac{3}{5}\right\}$.

61. $|y - 3| = |3 - y|$

$\quad y - 3 = 3 - y \quad or \quad y - 3 = -(3 - y)$

$\quad 2y - 3 = 3 \quad\quad or \quad y - 3 = -3 + y$

$\quad\quad 2y = 6 \quad\quad or \quad\quad -3 = -3$

$\quad\quad\quad y = 3 \quad\quad\quad\quad$ True for all real values of y

All real numbers are solutions.

63. $|5 - p| = |p + 8|$

$\quad 5 - p = p + 8 \quad or \quad 5 - p = -(p + 8)$

$\quad 5 - 2p = 8 \quad\quad or \quad 5 - p = -p - 8$

$\quad\quad -2p = 3 \quad\quad or \quad\quad 5 = -8$

$\quad\quad\quad p = -\dfrac{3}{2} \quad\quad\quad$ False

The solution set is $\left\{-\dfrac{3}{2}\right\}$.

65. $\left|\dfrac{2x - 3}{6}\right| = \left|\dfrac{4 - 5x}{8}\right|$

$\quad \dfrac{2x-3}{6} = \dfrac{4-5x}{8} \quad or \quad \dfrac{2x-3}{6} = -\left(\dfrac{4-5x}{8}\right)$

$\quad 24\left(\dfrac{2x-3}{6}\right) = 24\left(\dfrac{4-5x}{8}\right) or \quad \dfrac{2x-3}{6} = \dfrac{-4+5x}{8}$

$\quad 8x - 12 = 12 - 15x \quad or \; 24\left(\dfrac{2x-3}{6}\right) = 24\left(\dfrac{-4+5x}{8}\right)$

$\quad 23x - 12 = 12 \quad\quad or \quad 8x - 12 = -12 + 15x$

$\quad\quad 23x = 24 \quad\quad or \quad -7x - 12 = -12$

$\quad\quad\quad x = \dfrac{24}{23} \quad\quad or \quad\quad\quad -7x = 0$

$\quad\quad\quad\quad\quad\quad\quad\quad\quad\quad\quad\quad\quad x = 0$

The solution set is $\left\{\dfrac{24}{23}, 0\right\}$.

67. $\left|\dfrac{1}{2}x - 5\right| = \left|\dfrac{1}{4}x + 3\right|$

$\quad \dfrac{1}{2}x - 5 = \dfrac{1}{4}x + 3 \quad or \quad \dfrac{1}{2}x - 5 = -\left(\dfrac{1}{4}x + 3\right)$

$\quad \dfrac{1}{4}x - 5 = 3 \quad\quad or \quad \dfrac{1}{2}x - 5 = -\dfrac{1}{4}x - 3$

$\quad\quad \dfrac{1}{4}x = 8 \quad\quad or \quad \dfrac{3}{4}x - 5 = -3$

$\quad\quad\quad x = 32 \quad\quad or \quad\quad \dfrac{3}{4}x = 2$

$\quad\quad\quad x = 32 \quad\quad or \quad\quad\quad x = \dfrac{8}{3}$

The solution set is $\left\{32, \dfrac{8}{3}\right\}$.

69. $|x| < 3$

$\quad -3 < x < 3$

The solution set is $\{x| -3 < x < 3\}$, or $(-3, 3)$.

71. $|x| \geq 2$

$\quad x \leq -2 \text{ or } x \geq 2$

The solution set is $\{x|x \leq -2 \text{ or } x \geq 2\}$, or $(-\infty, -2] \cup [2, \infty)$.

73. $|x - 1| < 1$

$\quad -1 < x - 1 < 1$

$\quad\quad 0 < x < 2$

The solution set is $\{x|0 < x < 2\}$, or $(0, 2)$.

75. $5|x + 4| \leq 10$

$\quad |x + 4| \leq 2 \quad\quad\quad\quad\quad$ Dividing by 5

$\quad -2 \leq x + 4 \leq 2$

$\quad -6 \leq x \leq -2 \quad\quad$ Subtracting 4

The solution set is $\{x| -6 \leq x \leq -2\}$, or $[-6, -2]$.

77. $|2x - 3| \leq 4$

$\quad -4 \leq 2x - 3 \leq 4$

$\quad -1 \leq 2x \leq 7 \quad\quad\quad$ Adding 3

$\quad -\dfrac{1}{2} \leq x \leq \dfrac{7}{2} \quad\quad$ Dividing by 2

The solution set is $\left\{x\left| -\dfrac{1}{2} \leq x \leq \dfrac{7}{2}\right.\right\}$, or $\left[-\dfrac{1}{2}, \dfrac{7}{2}\right]$.

79. $|2y - 7| > 10$

$\quad 2y - 7 < -10 \quad or \quad 2y - 7 > 10$

$\quad 2y < -3 \quad\quad or \quad\quad 2y > 17 \quad$ Adding 7

$\quad y < -\dfrac{3}{2} \quad\quad or \quad\quad y > \dfrac{17}{2} \quad$ Dividing by 2

The solution set is $\left\{y\left|y < -\dfrac{3}{2} \text{ or } y > \dfrac{17}{2}\right.\right\}$, or

$\left(-\infty, -\dfrac{3}{2}\right) \cup \left(\dfrac{17}{2}, \infty\right)$.

81. $|4x - 9| \geq 14$

$\qquad 4x - 9 \leq -14 \quad or \quad 4x - 9 \geq 14$

$\qquad\quad 4x \leq -5 \quad or \qquad 4x \geq 23$

$\qquad\quad x \leq -\dfrac{5}{4} \quad or \qquad x \geq \dfrac{23}{4}$

The solution set is $\left\{ x \Big| x \leq -\dfrac{5}{4} \text{ or } x \geq \dfrac{23}{4} \right\}$, or

$\left(-\infty, -\dfrac{5}{4} \right] \cup \left[\dfrac{23}{4}, \infty \right)$.

83. $|y - 3| < 12$

$\qquad -12 < y - 3 < 12$

$\qquad\quad -9 < y < 15 \qquad\qquad \text{Adding 3}$

The solution set is $\{ y | -9 < y < 15 \}$, or $(-9, 15)$.

85. $|2x + 3| \leq 4$

$\qquad -4 \leq 2x + 3 \leq 4$

$\qquad -7 \leq 2x \leq 1 \qquad\qquad \text{Subtracting 3}$

$\qquad -\dfrac{7}{2} \leq x \leq \dfrac{1}{2} \qquad\qquad \text{Dividing by 2}$

The solution set is $\left\{ x \Big| -\dfrac{7}{2} \leq x \leq \dfrac{1}{2} \right\}$, or $\left[-\dfrac{7}{2}, \dfrac{1}{2} \right]$.

87. $|4 - 3y| > 8$

$\qquad 4 - 3y < -8 \quad or \quad 4 - 3y > 8$

$\qquad\quad -3y < -12 \quad or \qquad -3y > 4 \qquad \text{Subtracting 4}$

$\qquad\qquad y > 4 \quad or \qquad y < -\dfrac{4}{3} \quad \text{Dividing by } -3$

The solution set is $\left\{ y \Big| y < -\dfrac{4}{3} \text{ or } y > 4 \right\}$, or

$\left(-\infty, -\dfrac{4}{3} \right) \cup (4, \infty)$.

89. $|9 - 4x| \geq 14$

$\qquad 9 - 4x \leq -14 \quad or \quad 9 - 4x \geq 14$

$\qquad\quad -4x \leq -23 \quad or \qquad -4x \geq 5 \qquad \text{Subtracting 9}$

$\qquad\quad x \geq \dfrac{23}{4} \quad or \qquad x \leq -\dfrac{5}{4} \quad \text{Dividing by } -4$

The solution set is $\left\{ x \Big| x \leq -\dfrac{5}{4} \text{ or } x \geq \dfrac{23}{4} \right\}$ or

$\left(-\infty, -\dfrac{5}{4} \right] \cup \left[\dfrac{23}{4}, \infty \right)$.

91. $|3 - 4x| < 21$

$\qquad -21 < 3 - 4x < 21$

$\qquad -24 < -4x < 18 \qquad \text{Subtracting 3}$

$\qquad\quad 6 > x > -\dfrac{9}{2} \qquad \text{Dividing by } -4 \text{ and}$
$\qquad\qquad\qquad\qquad\qquad\quad \text{simplifying}$

The solution set is $\left\{ x \Big| 6 > x > -\dfrac{9}{2} \right\}$, or

$\left\{ x \Big| -\dfrac{9}{2} < x < 6 \right\}$, or $\left(-\dfrac{9}{2}, 6 \right)$.

93. $\left| \dfrac{1}{2} + 3x \right| \geq 12$

$\qquad \dfrac{1}{2} + 3x \leq -12 \quad or \quad \dfrac{1}{2} + 3x \geq 12$

$\qquad\quad 3x \leq -\dfrac{25}{2} \quad or \qquad 3x \geq \dfrac{23}{2} \qquad \text{Subtracting } \dfrac{1}{2}$

$\qquad\quad x \leq -\dfrac{25}{6} \quad or \qquad x \geq \dfrac{23}{6} \qquad \text{Dividing by 3}$

The solution set is $\left\{ x \Big| x \leq -\dfrac{25}{6} \text{ or } x \geq \dfrac{23}{6} \right\}$, or

$\left(-\infty, -\dfrac{25}{6} \right] \cup \left[\dfrac{23}{6}, \infty \right)$.

95. $\left| \dfrac{x - 7}{3} \right| < 4$

$\qquad -4 < \dfrac{x - 7}{3} < 4$

$\qquad -12 < x - 7 < 12 \qquad \text{Multiplying by 3}$

$\qquad\quad -5 < x < 19 \qquad\quad \text{Adding 7}$

The solution set is $\{ x | -5 < x < 19 \}$, or $(-5, 19)$.

97. $\left| \dfrac{2 - 5x}{4} \right| \geq \dfrac{2}{3}$

$\qquad \dfrac{2 - 5x}{4} \leq -\dfrac{2}{3} \quad or \quad \dfrac{2 - 5x}{4} \geq \dfrac{2}{3}$

$\qquad 2 - 5x \leq -\dfrac{8}{3} \quad or \quad 2 - 5x \geq \dfrac{8}{3} \qquad \text{Multiplying by 4}$

$\qquad -5x \leq -\dfrac{14}{3} \quad or \qquad -5x \geq \dfrac{2}{3} \qquad \text{Subtracting 2}$

$\qquad\quad x \geq \dfrac{14}{15} \quad or \qquad x \leq -\dfrac{2}{15} \quad \text{Dividing by } -5$

The solution set is $\left\{ x \Big| x \leq -\dfrac{2}{15} \text{ or } x \geq \dfrac{14}{15} \right\}$, or

$\left(-\infty, -\dfrac{2}{15} \right] \cup \left[\dfrac{14}{15}, \infty \right)$.

99. $|m + 5| + 9 \leq 16$

$\qquad |m + 5| \leq 7 \qquad\qquad \text{Subtracting 9}$

$\qquad -7 \leq m + 5 \leq 7$

$\qquad -12 \leq m \leq 2$

The solution set is $\{ m | -12 \leq m \leq 2 \}$, or $[-12, 2]$.

101. $7 - |3 - 2x| \geq 5$

$\qquad -|3 - 2x| \geq -2 \qquad\qquad \text{Subtracting 7}$

$\qquad |3 - 2x| \leq 2 \qquad\qquad \text{Multiplying by } -1$

$\qquad -2 \leq 3 - 2x \leq 2$

$\qquad -5 \leq -2x \leq -1 \qquad \text{Subtracting 3}$

$\qquad \dfrac{5}{2} \geq x \geq \dfrac{1}{2} \qquad\qquad \text{Dividing by } -2$

The solution set is $\left\{ x \Big| \dfrac{5}{2} \geq x \geq \dfrac{1}{2} \right\}$, or $\left\{ x \Big| \dfrac{1}{2} \leq x \leq \dfrac{5}{2} \right\}$, or

$\left[\dfrac{1}{2}, \dfrac{5}{2} \right]$.

103. $\left|\dfrac{2x-1}{0.0059}\right| \le 1$

$$-1 \le \dfrac{2x-1}{0.0059} \le 1$$
$$-0.0059 \le 2x - 1 \le 0.0059$$
$$0.9941 \le 2x \le 1.0059$$
$$0.49705 \le x \le 0.50295$$

The solution set is $\{x | 0.49705 \le x \le 0.50295\}$, or $[0.49705, 0.50295]$.

105. Discussion and Writing Exercise

107. Let $x =$ the number; $49\% x$, or $0.49x$

109. Let x and y represent the numbers; $\dfrac{x}{y} - 50$

111. $-43.5 + (-5.8) = -49.3$

(Add absolute values and make the result negative.)

113. $-43.5(-5.8) = 252.3$

(Multiply absolute values and make the result positive.)

115. $-\dfrac{7}{8} \div \dfrac{3}{4} = -\dfrac{7}{8} \cdot \dfrac{4}{3}$

$$= -\dfrac{7 \cdot 4}{8 \cdot 3}$$
$$= -\dfrac{7 \cdot 4}{2 \cdot 4 \cdot 3}$$
$$= -\dfrac{7 \cdot \cancel{4}}{2 \cdot \cancel{4} \cdot 3}$$
$$= -\dfrac{7}{6}$$

117. $-\dfrac{7}{8} - \dfrac{3}{4} = -\dfrac{7}{8} - \dfrac{3}{4} \cdot \dfrac{2}{2}$

$$= -\dfrac{7}{8} - \dfrac{6}{8}$$
$$= -\dfrac{13}{8}$$

119. $|d - 6 \text{ ft}| \le \dfrac{1}{2} \text{ ft}$

$$-\dfrac{1}{2} \text{ ft} \le d - 6 \text{ ft} \le \dfrac{1}{2} \text{ ft}$$
$$5\dfrac{1}{2} \text{ ft} \le d \le 6\dfrac{1}{2} \text{ ft}$$

The solution set is $\left\{d \middle| 5\dfrac{1}{2} \text{ ft} \le d \le 6\dfrac{1}{2} \text{ ft}\right\}$.

121. $|x + 5| = x + 5$

From the definition of absolute value, $|x + 5| = x + 5$ only when $x + 5 \ge 0$, or $x \ge -5$. The solution set is $\{x | x \ge -5\}$, or $[-5, \infty)$.

123. $|7x - 2| = x + 4$

From the definition of absolute value, we know $x + 4 \ge 0$, or $x \ge -4$. So we have $x \ge -4$ and

$$7x - 2 = x + 4 \quad or \quad 7x - 2 = -(x + 4)$$
$$6x = 6 \qquad or \quad 7x - 2 = -x - 4$$
$$x = 1 \qquad or \qquad 8x = -2$$
$$x = 1 \qquad or \qquad x = -\dfrac{1}{4}$$

The solution set is $\left\{x \middle| x \ge -4 \; and \; x = 1 \; or \; x = -\dfrac{1}{4}\right\}$, or $\left\{1, -\dfrac{1}{4}\right\}$.

125. $|x - 6| \le -8$

From the definition of absolute value we know that $|x - 6| \ge 0$. Thus $|x - 6| \le -8$ is false for all x. The solution set is $\emptyset$.

127. $|x + 5| > x$

The inequality is true for all $x < 0$ (because absolute value must be nonnegative). The solution set in this case is $\{x | x < 0\}$. If $x = 0$, we have $|0 + 5| > 0$, which is true. The solution set in this case is $\{0\}$. If $x > 0$, we have the following:

$$x + 5 < -x \quad or \quad x + 5 > x$$
$$2x < -5 \qquad or \qquad 5 > 0$$
$$x < -\dfrac{5}{2} \qquad or \qquad 5 > 0$$

Although $x > 0$ and $x < -\dfrac{5}{2}$ yields no solution, $x > 0$ and $5 > 0$ (true for all x) yield the solution set $\{x | x > 0\}$ in this case. The solution set for the inequality is $\{x | x < 0\} \cup \{0\} \cup \{x | x > 0\}$, or all real numbers.

129. $|x| \ge 0$

Since the absolute value of a number is always nonnegative, all real numbers are solutions.

131. $-3 < x < 3$ is equivalent to $|x| < 3$.

133. $x \le -6$ or or $x \ge 6$ is equivalent to $|x| \ge 6$.

135. $\quad x < -8 \quad or \qquad x > 2$

$\quad x + 3 < -5 \quad or \quad x + 3 > 5 \quad$ Adding 3

$\quad |x + 3| > 5$

Chapter 2

Graphs, Functions, and Applications

1. $A(4,1)$ is 4 units right and 1 unit up.

   $B(2,5)$ is 2 units right and 5 units up.

   $C(0,3)$ is 0 units left or right and 3 units up.

   $D(0,-5)$ is 0 units left or right and 5 units down.

   $E(6,0)$ is 6 units right and 0 units up or down.

   $F(-3,0)$ is 3 units left and 0 units up or down.

   $G(-2,-4)$ is 2 units left and 4 units down.

   $H(-5,1)$ is 5 units left and 1 unit up.

   $J(-6,6)$ is 6 units left and 6 units up.

3.

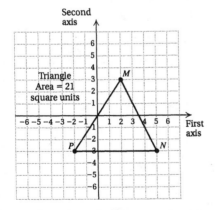

   A triangle is formed. The area of a triangle is found by using the formula $A = \frac{1}{2}bh$. In this triangle the base and height are respectively 7 units and 6 units.

   $$A = \frac{1}{2}bh = \frac{1}{2} \cdot 7 \cdot 6 = \frac{42}{2} = 21 \text{ square units}$$

5. We substitute 1 for x and -1 for y (alphabetical order of variables).

   $$\frac{y = 2x - 3}{\begin{array}{c|c} -1 \ ? \ 2 \cdot 1 - 3 \\ \quad | \quad -1 \qquad \text{TRUE} \end{array}}$$

   Thus, $(1,-1)$ is a solution of the equation.

7. We substitute 3 for x and 5 for y (alphabetical order of variables).

   $$\frac{4x - y = 7}{\begin{array}{c|c} 4 \cdot 3 - 5 \ ? \ 7 \\ 12 - 5 \quad | \\ 7 \quad | \quad \text{TRUE} \end{array}}$$

   Thus, $(3,5)$ is a solution of the equation.

9. We substitute 0 for a and $\frac{3}{5}$ for b (alphabetical order of variables).

   $$\frac{2a + 5b = 7}{\begin{array}{c|c} 2 \cdot 0 + 5 \cdot \frac{3}{5} \ ? \ 7 \\ 0 + 3 \quad | \\ 3 \quad | \quad \text{FALSE} \end{array}}$$

   Thus, $\left(0, \frac{3}{5}\right)$ is not a solution of the equation.

11. To show that a pair is a solution, we substitute, replacing x with the first coordinate and y with the second coordinate in each pair.

   $$\frac{y = 4 - x}{\begin{array}{c|c} 5 \ ? \ 4 - (-1) \\ 4 + 1 \\ 5 \quad \text{TRUE} \end{array}} \qquad \frac{y = 4 - x}{\begin{array}{c|c} 1 \ ? \ 4 - 3 \\ 1 \quad \text{TRUE} \end{array}}$$

   In each case the substitution results in a true equation. Thus, $(-1,5)$ and $(3,1)$ are both solutions of $y = 4 - x$. We plot these points and sketch the line passing through them.

   The line appears to pass through $(1,3)$ also. We check to determine if $(1,3)$ is a solution.

$$\frac{y = 4 - x}{3 \; ? \; 4 - 1}$$
$$\left| \; 3 \quad \text{TRUE} \right.$$

Thus, $(1,3)$ is another solution. There are other correct answers, including $(-2,6)$, $(0,4)$, $(2,2)$, $(4,0)$, and $(5,-1)$.

13. To show that a pair is a solution, we substitute, replacing x with the first coordinate and y with the second coordinate in each pair.

$$\frac{3x + y = 7}{3 \cdot 2 + 1 \; ? \; 7}$$
$$\begin{array}{c|c} 6 + 1 & \\ 7 & \text{TRUE} \end{array}$$

$$\frac{3x + y = 7}{3 \cdot 4 - 5 \; ? \; 7}$$
$$\begin{array}{c|c} 12 - 5 & \\ 7 & \text{TRUE} \end{array}$$

In each case the substitution results in a true equation. Thus, $(2,1)$ and $(4,-5)$ are both solutions of $3x + y = 7$. We plot these points and sketch the line passing through them.

The line appears to pass through $(1,4)$ also. We check to determine if $(1,4)$ is a solution of $3x + y = 7$.

$$\frac{3x + y = 7}{3 \cdot 1 + 4 \; ? \; 7}$$
$$\begin{array}{c|c} 3 + 4 & \\ 7 & \text{TRUE} \end{array}$$

Thus, $(1,4)$ is another solution. There are other correct answers, including $(3,-2)$.

15. To show that a pair is a solution, we substitute, replacing x with the first coordinate and y with the second coordinate in each pair.

$$\frac{6x - 3y = 3}{6 \cdot 1 - 3 \cdot 1 \; ? \; 3}$$
$$\begin{array}{c|c} 6 - 3 & \\ 3 & \text{TRUE} \end{array}$$

$$\frac{6x - 3y = 3}{6(-1) - 3(-3) \; ? \; 3}$$
$$\begin{array}{c|c} -6 + 9 & \\ 3 & \text{TRUE} \end{array}$$

In each case the substitution results in a true equation. Thus, $(1,1)$ and $(-1,-3)$ are both solutions of $6x - 3y = 3$. We plot these points and sketch the line passing through them.

The line appears to pass through $(0,-1)$ also. We check to determine if $(0,-1)$ is a solution of $6x - 3y = 3$.

$$\frac{6x - 3y = 3}{6 \cdot 0 - 3(-1) \; ? \; 3}$$
$$\begin{array}{c|c} 0 + 3 & \\ 3 & \text{TRUE} \end{array}$$

Thus, $(0,-1)$ is another solution. There are other correct answers including $(-2,-5)$, $(2,3)$, and $(3,5)$.

17. $y = x - 1$

We find some ordered pairs that are solutions.

When $x = -2$, $y = -2 - 1 = -3$.

When $x = -1$, $y = -1 - 1 = -2$.

When $x = 0$, $y = 0 - 1 = -1$.

When $x = 1$, $y = 1 - 1 = 0$.

When $x = 2$, $y = 2 - 1 = 1$.

When $x = 3$, $y = 3 - 1 = 2$.

x	y
-2	-3
-1	-2
0	-1
1	0
2	1
3	2

Plot these points, draw the line they determine, and label it $y = x - 1$.

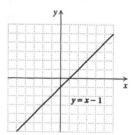

19. $y = x$

We find some ordered pairs that are solutions, plot them, and draw and label the line.

When $x = -2$, $y = -2$.

When $x = -1$, $y = -1$.

When $x = 0$, $y = 0$.

When $x = 1$, $y = 1$.

When $x = 2$, $y = 2$.

When $x = 3$, $y = 3$.

x	y
-2	-2
-1	-1
0	0
1	1
2	2
3	3

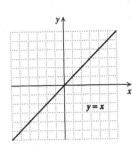

21. $y = \dfrac{1}{4}x$

We find some ordered pairs that are solutions, using multiples of 4 for x to avoid fractions. Then we plot these points and draw and label the line.

When $x = -4$, $y = \dfrac{1}{4}(-4) = -1$.

When $x = 0$, $y = \dfrac{1}{4} \cdot 0 = 0$.

When $x = 4$, $y = \dfrac{1}{4} \cdot 4 = 1$.

x	y	(x, y)
-4	-1	$(-4, -1)$
0	0	$(0, 0)$
4	1	$(4, 1)$

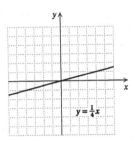

23. $y = 3 - x$

We find some ordered pairs that are solutions, plot them, and draw and label the line.

When $x = -2$, $y = 3 - (-2) = 3 + 2 = 5$.

When $x = 1$, $y = 3 - 1 = 2$.

When $x = 5$, $y = 3 - 5 = -2$.

x	y	(x, y)
-2	5	$(-2, 5)$
1	2	$(1, 2)$
5	-2	$(5, -2)$

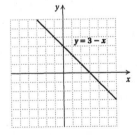

25. $y = 5x - 2$

We find some ordered pairs that are solutions, plot them, and draw and label the line.

When $x = -1$, $y = 5(-1) - 2 = -5 - 2 = -7$.

When $x = 0$, $y = 5 \cdot 0 - 2 = -2$.

When $x = 1$, $y = 5 \cdot 1 - 2 = 5 - 2 = 3$.

x	y	(x, y)
-1	-7	$(-1, -7)$
0	-2	$(0, -2)$
1	3	$(1, 3)$

27. $y = \dfrac{1}{2}x + 1$

We find some ordered pairs that are solutions, using even numbers for x to avoid fractions. Then we plot these points and draw and label the line.

When $x = -4$, $y = \dfrac{1}{2}(-4) + 1 = -2 + 1 = -1$.

When $x = 0$, $y = \dfrac{1}{2} \cdot 0 + 1 = 1$.

When $x = 4$, $y = \dfrac{1}{2} \cdot 4 + 1 = 2 + 1 = 3$.

x	y	(x, y)
-4	-1	$(-4, -1)$
0	1	$(0, 1)$
4	3	$(4, 3)$

29. $x + y = 5$

First we solve for y.

$$x + y = 5$$
$$y = 5 - x$$

Now we find some ordered pairs that are solutions, plot them, and draw and label the line.

When $x = 0$, $y = 5 - 0 = 5$.

When $x = 2$, $y = 5 - 2 = 3$.

When $x = 5$, $y = 5 - 5 = 0$.

x	y	(x, y)
0	5	$(0, 5)$
2	3	$(2, 3)$
5	0	$(5, 0)$

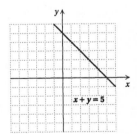

31. $y = -\dfrac{5}{3}x - 2$

We find some ordered pairs that are solutions, using multiples of 3 for x to avoid fractions. Then we plot these points and draw and label the line.

When $x = -3$, $y = -\dfrac{5}{3}(-3) - 2 = 5 - 2 = 3$.

When $x = 0$, $y = -\dfrac{5}{3} \cdot 0 - 2 = -2$.

When $x = 3$, $y = -\dfrac{5}{3} \cdot 3 - 2 = -5 - 2 = -7$.

x	y	(x, y)
-3	3	$(-3, 3)$
0	-2	$(0, -2)$
3	-7	$(3, -7)$

33. $x + 2y = 8$

First we solve for y.

$$x + 2y = 8$$
$$2y = 8 - x$$
$$\frac{1}{2} \cdot 2y = \frac{1}{2}(8 - x)$$
$$y = \frac{1}{2} \cdot 8 - \frac{1}{2} \cdot x$$
$$y = 4 - \frac{1}{2}x$$
$$y = -\frac{1}{2}x + 4$$

Now we find some ordered pairs that are solutions, using even numbers for x to avoid fractions. Then we plot these points and draw and label the line.

When $x = -2$, $y = -\dfrac{1}{2}(-2) + 4 = 1 + 4 = 5$.

When $x = 2$, $y = -\dfrac{1}{2} \cdot 2 + 4 = -1 + 4 = 3$.

When $x = 4$, $y = -\dfrac{1}{2} \cdot 4 + 4 = -2 + 4 = 2$.

x	y	(x, y)
-2	5	$(-2, 5)$
2	3	$(2, 3)$
4	2	$(4, 2)$

35. $y = \dfrac{3}{2}x + 1$

We find some ordered pairs that are solutions, using even numbers for x to avoid fractions. Then we plot these points and draw and label the line.

When $x = -4$, $y = \dfrac{3}{2}(-4) + 1 = -6 + 1 = -5$.

When $x = 0$, $y = \dfrac{3}{2} \cdot 0 + 1 = 1$.

When $x = 2$, $y = \dfrac{3}{2} \cdot 2 + 1 = 3 + 1 = 4$.

x	y	(x, y)
-4	-5	$(-4, -5)$
0	1	$(0, 1)$
2	4	$(2, 4)$

37. $8y + 2x = 4$

First we solve for y.

$$8y + 2x = 4$$
$$8y = 4 - 2x$$
$$\frac{1}{8} \cdot 8y = \frac{1}{8}(4 - 2x)$$
$$y = \frac{1}{8} \cdot 4 - \frac{1}{8} \cdot 2x$$
$$y = \frac{1}{2} - \frac{1}{4}x$$
$$y = -\frac{1}{4}x + \frac{1}{2}$$

Now we find some ordered pairs that are solutions, plot them, and draw and label the line.

When $x = -4$, $y = -\dfrac{1}{4}(-4) + \dfrac{1}{2} = 1 + \dfrac{1}{2} = \dfrac{3}{2}$.

When $x = 0$, $y = -\dfrac{1}{4} \cdot 0 + \dfrac{1}{2} = \dfrac{1}{2}$.

When $x = 4$, $y = -\dfrac{1}{4} \cdot 4 + \dfrac{1}{2} = -1 + \dfrac{1}{2} = -\dfrac{1}{2}$.

x	y	(x, y)
-4	$\dfrac{3}{2}$	$\left(-4, \dfrac{3}{2}\right)$
0	$\dfrac{1}{2}$	$\left(0, \dfrac{1}{2}\right)$
4	$-\dfrac{1}{2}$	$\left(4, -\dfrac{1}{2}\right)$

39. $8y + 2x = -4$

First we solve for y.

$$8y + 2x = -4$$
$$8y = -4 - 2x$$
$$\frac{1}{8} \cdot 8y = \frac{1}{8}(-4 - 2x)$$
$$y = \frac{1}{8}(-4) - \frac{1}{8} \cdot 2x$$
$$y = -\frac{1}{2} - \frac{1}{4}x$$
$$y = -\frac{1}{4}x - \frac{1}{2}$$

Now we find some ordered pairs that are solutions, plot them, and draw and label the line.

When $x = -4$, $y = -\dfrac{1}{4}(-4) - \dfrac{1}{2} = 1 - \dfrac{1}{2} = \dfrac{1}{2}$.

When $x = 0$, $y = -\dfrac{1}{4} \cdot 0 - \dfrac{1}{2} = -\dfrac{1}{2}$.

When $x = 4$, $y = -\dfrac{1}{4} \cdot 4 - \dfrac{1}{2} = -1 - \dfrac{1}{2} = -\dfrac{3}{2}$.

x	y	(x, y)
-4	$\dfrac{1}{2}$	$\left(-4, \dfrac{1}{2}\right)$
0	$-\dfrac{1}{2}$	$\left(0, -\dfrac{1}{2}\right)$
4	$-\dfrac{3}{2}$	$\left(4, -\dfrac{3}{2}\right)$

41. $y = x^2$

To find an ordered pair, we choose any number for x and then determine y. For example, if $x = 2$, then $y = 2^2 = 4$. We find several ordered pairs, plot them, and connect them with a smooth curve.

x	y
-2	4
-1	1
0	0
1	1
2	4

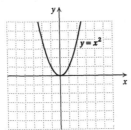

43. $y = x^2 + 2$

To find an ordered pair, we choose any number for x and then determine y. For example, if $x = 2$, then $y = 2^2 + 2 = 4 + 2 = 6$. We find several ordered pairs, plot them, and connect them with a smooth curve.

x	y
-2	6
-1	3
0	2
1	3
2	6

45. $y = x^2 - 3$

To find an ordered pair, we choose any number for x and then determine y. For example, if $x = 2$, then $y = 2^2 - 3 = 4 - 3 = 1$. We find several ordered pairs, plot them, and connect them with a smooth curve.

x	y
-2	1
-1	-2
0	-3
1	-2
2	1
3	6

47. $y = -\dfrac{1}{x}$

To find an ordered pair, we choose any number for x and then determine y. For example, if $x = -4$, then $y = \dfrac{1}{4}$. We find several ordered pairs, plot them, and connect them with a smooth curve.

x	y
-4	$\dfrac{1}{4}$
-2	$\dfrac{1}{2}$
$-\dfrac{1}{2}$	2
$\dfrac{1}{2}$	-2
2	$-\dfrac{1}{2}$
4	$-\dfrac{1}{4}$

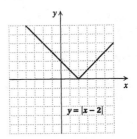

Note that we cannot use 0 as a first-coordinate, since $-1/0$ is undefined. Thus, the graph has two branches, one on each side of the y-axis.

49. $y = |x - 2|$

To find an ordered pair, we choose any number for x and then determine y. For example, if $x = 5$, then $y = |5-2| = |3| = 3$. We find several ordered pairs, plot them, and connect them with a smooth curve.

x	y
5	3
3	1
2	0
-1	3
-2	4
-3	5

51. $y = x^3$

To find an ordered pair, we choose any number for x and then determine y. For example, if $x = -1$, then $y = (-1)^3 = -1$. We find several ordered pairs, plot them, and connect them with a smooth curve.

x	y
-2	-8
-1	-1
0	0
1	1
2	8

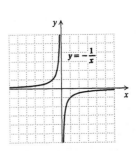

53. Discussion and Writing Exercise

55. $-3 < 2x - 5 \le 10$

$\qquad 2 < 2x \le 15 \qquad$ Adding 5

$\qquad 1 < x \le \dfrac{15}{2} \qquad$ Dividing by 2

The solution set is $\left\{ x \middle| 1 < x \le \dfrac{15}{2} \right\}$, or $\left(1, \dfrac{15}{2} \right]$.

57. $3x - 5 \le -12 \ \ or \ \ 3x - 5 \ge 12$

$\qquad 3x \le -7 \quad or \qquad 3x \ge 17$

$\qquad x \le -\dfrac{7}{3} \quad or \qquad x \ge \dfrac{17}{3}$

The solution set is $\left\{ x \middle| x \le -\dfrac{7}{3} \ or \ x \ge \dfrac{17}{3} \right\}$, or

$\left(-\infty, -\dfrac{7}{3} \right] \cup \left[\dfrac{17}{3}, \infty \right)$.

59. *Familiarize*. The formula for the area of a triangle with base b and height h is $A = \dfrac{1}{2}bh$.

Translate. Substitute 200 for A and 16 for b in the formula.

$$A = \dfrac{1}{2}bh$$

$$200 = \dfrac{1}{2} \cdot 16 \cdot h$$

Carry out. We solve the equation.

$$200 = \dfrac{1}{2} \cdot 16 \cdot h$$

$$200 = 8h \qquad \text{Multiplying}$$

$$25 = h \qquad \text{Dividing by 8 on both sides}$$

Check. The area of a triangle with base 16 ft and height 25 ft is $\dfrac{1}{2} \cdot 16 \cdot 25$, or 200 ft². The answer checks.

State. The seed can fill a triangle that is 25 ft tall.

61. *Familiarize*. Let $m =$ the distance after the first $\dfrac{1}{2}$ mile, in units of $\dfrac{1}{4}$ miles. Then the taxi ride costs $\$1.00 + \$0.30m$ and the total distance is $\dfrac{1}{2} + \dfrac{m}{4}$ miles.

Translate. The taxi ride costs $\$5.20$, so we have

$$1.00 + 0.30m = 5.20.$$

Solve. We solve the equation.

$$1.00 + 0.30m = 5.20$$

$$10 + 3m = 52 \qquad \text{Multiplying by 10}$$

$$3m = 42$$

$$m = 14$$

When $m = 14$, the total distance is $\dfrac{1}{2} + \dfrac{14}{4} = \dfrac{16}{4} = 4$ mi.

Check. If the distance is $\dfrac{1}{2}$ mi plus 14 additional $\dfrac{1}{4}$ mi segments, then the fare is $\$1.00 + \$0.30(14) = \$1.00 + \$4.20 = \$5.20$.

State. It is 4 mi from Johnson Street to Elm Street.

63. $y = x^3 - 3x + 2$

65. We use DOT mode when graphing $y = \dfrac{1}{x - 2}$.

67. Note that the sum of the coordinates of each point on the graph is 4. Thus, we have $x + y = 4$, or $y = -x + 4$.

69. This is the graph of $y = |x|$ (see Example 9) with 3 subtracted from each x-coordinate. Thus, we have $y = |x| - 3$.

Exercise Set 2.2

1. Yes; each member of the domain is matched to only one member of the range.

3. Yes; each member of the domain is matched to only one member of the range.

5. Yes; each member of the domain is matched to only one member of the range.

7. No; a member of the domain is matched to more than one member of the range. In fact, each member of the domain is matched to 3 members of the range.

9. This correspondence is a function, because each person in the family has only one height.

11. The correspondence is not a function, since it is reasonable to assume that at least one avenue is intersected by more than one road.

13. This correspondence is a function, because each number in the domain, when squared and then increased by 4, corresponds to only one number in the range.

15. $f(x) = x + 5$

a) $f(4) = 4 + 5 = 9$

b) $f(7) = 7 + 5 = 12$

c) $f(-3) = -3 + 5 = 2$

d) $f(0) = 0 + 5 = 5$

e) $f(2.4) = 2.4 + 5 = 7.4$

f) $f\left(\dfrac{2}{3} \right) = \dfrac{2}{3} + 5 = 5\dfrac{2}{3}$

17. $h(p) = 3p$

   a) $h(-7) = 3(-7) = -21$

   b) $h(5) = 3 \cdot 5 = 15$

   c) $h(14) = 3 \cdot 14 = 42$

   d) $h(0) = 3 \cdot 0 = 0$

   e) $h\left(\dfrac{2}{3}\right) = 3 \cdot \dfrac{2}{3} = \dfrac{6}{3} = 2$

   f) $h(a+1) = 3(a+1) = 3a + 3$

19. $g(s) = 3s + 4$

   a) $g(1) = 3 \cdot 1 + 4 = 3 + 4 = 7$

   b) $g(-7) = 3(-7) + 4 = -21 + 4 = -17$

   c) $g(6.7) = 3(6.7) + 4 = 20.1 + 4 = 24.1$

   d) $g(0) = 3 \cdot 0 + 4 = 0 + 4 = 4$

   e) $g(-10) = 3(-10) + 4 = -30 + 4 = -26$

   f) $g\left(\dfrac{2}{3}\right) = 3 \cdot \dfrac{2}{3} + 4 = 2 + 4 = 6$

21. $f(x) = 2x^2 - 3x$

   a) $f(0) = 2 \cdot 0^2 - 3 \cdot 0 = 0 - 0 = 0$

   b) $f(-1) = 2(-1)^2 - 3(-1) = 2 + 3 = 5$

   c) $f(2) = 2 \cdot 2^2 - 3 \cdot 2 = 8 - 6 = 2$

   d) $f(10) = 2 \cdot 10^2 - 3 \cdot 10 = 200 - 30 = 170$

   e) $f(-5) = 2(-5)^2 - 3(-5) = 50 + 15 = 65$

   f) $f(4a) = 2(4a)^2 - 3(4a) = 32a^2 - 12a$

23. $f(x) = |x| + 1$

   a) $f(0) = |0| + 1 = 0 + 1 = 1$

   b) $f(-2) = |-2| + 1 = 2 + 1 = 3$

   c) $f(2) = |2| + 1 = 2 + 1 = 3$

   d) $f(-3) = |-3| + 1 = 3 + 1 = 4$

   e) $f(-10) = |-10| + 1 = 10 + 1 = 11$

   f) $f(a-1) = |a-1| + 1$

25. $f(x) = x^3$

   a) $f(0) = 0^3 = 0$

   b) $f(-1) = (-1)^3 = -1$

   c) $f(2) = 2^3 = 8$

   d) $f(10) = 10^3 = 1000$

   e) $f(-5) = (-5)^3 = -125$

   f) $f(-10) = (-10)^3 = -1000$

27. $F(x) = 2.75x + 71.48$

   a) $F(32) = 2.75(32) + 71.48$

       $= 88 + 71.48$

       $= 159.48 \text{ cm}$

   b) $F(35) = 2.75(35) + 71.48$

       $= 96.25 + 71.48$

       $= 167.73 \text{ cm}$

29. $\quad P(d) = 1 + \dfrac{d}{33}$

$$P(20) = 1 + \frac{20}{33} = 1\frac{20}{33} \text{ atm}$$

$$P(30) = 1 + \frac{30}{33} = 1\frac{10}{11} \text{ atm}$$

$$P(100) = 1 + \frac{100}{33} = 1 + 3\frac{1}{33} = 4\frac{1}{33} \text{ atm}$$

31. $\quad W(d) = 0.112d$

$\quad W(16) = 0.112(16) = 1.792 \text{ cm}$

$\quad W(25) = 0.112(25) = 2.8 \text{ cm}$

$\quad W(100) = 0.112(100) = 11.2 \text{ cm}$

33. Graph $f(x) = 3x - 1$

Make a list of function values in a table.

$\quad f(-1) = 3(-1) - 1 = -3 - 1 = -4$

$\quad f(0) = 3 \cdot 0 - 1 = 0 - 1 = -1$

$\quad f(1) = 3 \cdot 1 - 1 = 3 - 1 = 2$

$\quad f(2) = 3 \cdot 2 - 1 = 6 - 1 = 5$

x	$f(x)$
-1	-4
0	-1
1	2
2	5

Plot these points and connect them.

35. Graph $g(x) = -2x + 3$

Make a list of function values in a table.

$\quad g(-1) = -2(-1) + 3 = 2 + 3 = 5$

$\quad g(0) = -2 \cdot 0 + 3 = 0 + 3 = 3$

$\quad g(3) = -2 \cdot 3 + 3 = -6 + 3 = -3$

x	$g(x)$
-1	5
0	3
3	-3

Plot these points and connect them.

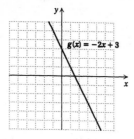

37. Graph $f(x) = \dfrac{1}{2}x + 1$.

Make a list of function values in a table.

$f(-2) = \dfrac{1}{2}(-2) + 1 = -1 + 1 = 0$

$f(0) = \dfrac{1}{2} \cdot 0 + 1 = 0 + 1 = 1$

$f(4) = \dfrac{1}{2} \cdot 4 + 1 = 2 + 1 = 3$

x	$f(x)$
-2	0
0	1
4	3

Plot these points and connect them.

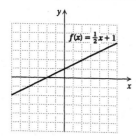

39. Graph $f(x) = 2 - |x|$.

Make a list of function values in a table.

$f(-3) = 2 - |-3| = 2 - 3 = -1$

$f(-2) = 2 - |-2| = 2 - 2 = 0$

$f(-1) = 2 - |-1| = 2 - 1 = 1$

$f(0) = 2 - |0| = 2 - 0 = 2$

$f(1) = 2 - |1| = 2 - 1 = 1$

$f(2) = 2 - |2| = 2 - 2 = 0$

$f(3) = 2 - |3| = 2 - 3 = -1$

x	$f(x)$
-3	-1
-2	0
-1	1
0	2
1	1
2	0
3	-1

Plot these points and connect them.

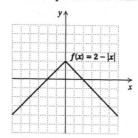

41. Graph $f(x) = x^2$.

Make a list of function values in a table.

$f(-3) = (-3)^2 = 9$

$f(-2) = (-2)^2 = 4$

$f(-1) = (-1)^2 = 1$

$f(0) = 0^2 = 0$

$f(1) = 1^2 = 1$

$f(2) = 2^2 = 4$

$f(3) = 3^2 = 9$

x	$f(x)$
-3	9
-2	4
-1	1
0	0
1	1
2	4
3	9

Plot these points and connect them.

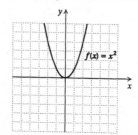

43. Graph $f(x) = x^2 - x - 2$.

Make a list of function values in a table.

$f(-3) = (-3)^2 - (-3) - 2 = 9 + 3 - 2 = 10$

$f(-2) = (-2)^2 - (-2) - 2 = 4 + 2 - 2 = 4$

$f(-1) = (-1)^2 - (-1) - 2 = 1 + 1 - 2 = 0$

$f(0) = 0^2 - 0 - 2 = -2$

$f(1) = 1^2 - 1 - 2 = 1 - 1 - 2 = -2$

$f(2) = 2^2 - 2 - 2 = 4 - 2 - 2 = 0$

$f(3) = 3^2 - 3 - 2 = 9 - 3 - 2 = 4$

x	$f(x)$
-3	10
-2	4
-1	0
0	-2
1	-2
2	0
3	4

Plot these points and connect them.

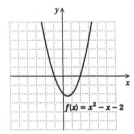

45. We can use the vertical line test:

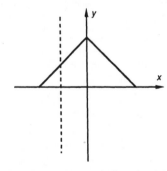

Visualize moving this vertical line across the graph. No vertical line will intersect the graph more than once. Thus, the graph is a graph of a function.

47. We can use the vertical line test:

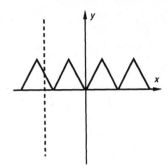

Visualize moving this vertical line across the graph. No vertical line will intersect the graph more than once. Thus, the graph is a graph of a function.

49. We can use the vertical line test.

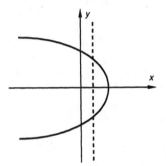

It is possible for a vertical line to intersect the graph more than once. Thus this is not the graph of a function.

51. We can use the vertical line test.

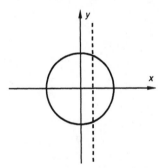

It is possible for a vertical line to intersect the graph more than once. Thus this is not a graph of a function.

53. Locate the point that is directly above 225. Then estimate its second coordinate by moving horizontally from the point to the vertical axis. The rate is about 75 per 10,000 men.

55. Locate 2 on the horizontal axis and move directly up to the graph. Then move across to the vertical axis and read the revenue. The movie revenue for week 2 was about $25 million.

57. Discussion and Writing Exercise

59. Discussion and Writing Exercise

61. *Familiarize*. If x represents the first integer, then $x + 2$ represents the second integer, and $x + 4$ represents the third.

Translate. We write an equation.

First integer plus two times the second plus three times the third is 124.

$$x + 2(x + 2) + 3(x + 4) = 124$$

Carry out. Solve the equation.

$$x + 2(x + 2) + 3(x + 4) = 124$$
$$x + 2x + 4 + 3x + 12 = 124$$
$$6x + 16 = 124$$
$$6x = 108$$
$$x = 18$$

If $x = 18$, then $x + 2 = 18 + 2$, or 20, and $x + 4 = 18 + 4$, or 22.

Check. 18, 20, and 22 are consecutive even integers. Also, $18 + 2 \cdot 20 + 3 \cdot 22 = 18 + 40 + 66 = 124$. The numbers check.

State. The integers are 18, 20, and 22.

63.
$$S = 2lh + 2lw + 2wh$$
$$S - 2wh = 2lh + 2lw$$
$$S - 2wh = l(2h + 2w)$$
$$\frac{S - 2wh}{2h + 2w} = l$$

65. $4x - 2 \le 5x + 7$

$\quad -2 \le x + 7$ Subtracting $4x$

$\quad -9 \le x$ Subtracting 7

The solution set is $\{x | -9 \le x\}$, or $\{x | x \ge -9\}$, or $[-9, \infty)$.

67. $-6x + 2x - 32 < 64$

$\quad -4x - 32 < 64$ Collecting like terms

$\quad -4x < 96$ Adding 32

$\quad x > -24$ Dividing by -4 and reversing the inequality symbol

The solution set is $\{x | x > -24\}$, or $(-24, \infty)$.

69. $|5x + 7| = 10$

$5x + 7 = 10 \quad or \quad 5x + 7 = -10$

$5x = 3 \quad or \qquad 5x = -17$

$x = \dfrac{3}{5} \quad or \qquad x = -\dfrac{17}{5}$

The solution set is $\left\{ -\dfrac{17}{5}, \dfrac{3}{5} \right\}$.

71. $|3x - 7| \ge 24$

$3x - 7 \le -24 \quad or \quad 3x - 7 \ge 24$

$3x \le -17 \quad or \qquad 3x \ge 31$

$x \le -\dfrac{17}{3} \quad or \qquad x \ge \dfrac{31}{3}$

The solution set is $\left\{ x \middle| x \le -\dfrac{17}{3} \ or \ x \ge \dfrac{31}{3} \right\}$, or $\left(-\infty, -\dfrac{17}{3} \right] \cup \left[\dfrac{31}{3}, \infty \right)$.

73. To find $f(g(-4))$, we first find $g(-4)$:

$g(-4) = 2(-4) + 5 = -8 + 5 = -3$.

Then $f(g(-4)) = f(-3) = 3(-3)^2 - 1 = 3 \cdot 9 - 1 = 27 - 1 = 26$.

To find $g(f(-4))$, we first find $f(-4)$:

$f(-4) = 3(-4)^2 - 1 = 3 \cdot 16 - 1 = 48 - 1 = 47$.

Then $g(f(-4)) = g(47) = 2 \cdot 47 + 5 = 94 + 5 = 99$.

75. We know that $(-1, -7)$ and $(3, 8)$ are both solutions of $g(x) = mx + b$. Substituting, we have

$$-7 = m(-1) + b, \quad or \quad -7 = -m + b,$$
$$and \quad 8 = m(3) + b, \quad or \quad 8 = 3m + b.$$

Solve the first equation for b and substitute that expression into the second equation.

$-7 = -m + b$	First equation
$m - 7 = b$	Solving for b
$8 = 3m + b$	Second equation
$8 = 3m + (m - 7)$	Substituting
$8 = 3m + m - 7$	
$8 = 4m - 7$	
$15 = 4m$	
$\dfrac{15}{4} = m$	

We know that $m - 7 = b$, so $\dfrac{15}{4} - 7 = b$, or $-\dfrac{13}{4} = b$.

We have $m = \dfrac{15}{4}$ and $b = -\dfrac{13}{4}$, so $g(x) = \dfrac{15}{4}x - \dfrac{13}{4}$.

Exercise Set 2.3

1. a) Locate 1 on the horizontal axis and then find the point on the graph for which 1 is the first coordinate. From that point, look to the vertical axis to find the corresponding y-coordinate, 3. Thus, $f(1) = 3$.

   b) The domain is the set of all x-values in the graph. It is $\{-4, -3, -2, -1, 0, 1, 2\}$.

   c) To determine which member(s) of the domain are paired with 2, locate 2 on the vertical axis. From there look left and right to the graph to find any points for which 2 is the second coordinate. Two such points exist, $(-2, 2)$ and $(0, 2)$. Thus, the x-values for which $f(x) = 2$ are -2 and 0.

   d) The range is the set of all y-values in the graph. It is $\{1, 2, 3, 4\}$.

3. a) Locate 1 on the horizontal axis and then find the point on the graph for which 1 is the first coordinate. From that point, look to the vertical axis to find the corresponding y-coordinate, 2. Thus, $f(1) = 2$.

b) The domain is the set of all x-values in the graph. It is $\{-6, -4, -2, 0, 1, 3, 4\}$.

c) To determine which member(s) of the domain are paired with 2, locate 2 on the vertical axis. From there look left and right to the graph to find any points for which 2 is the second coordinate. Two such points exist, $(1, 2)$ and $(3, 2)$. Thus, the x-values for which $f(x) = 2$ are 1 and 3.

d) The range is the set of all y-values in the graph. It is $\{-5, -2, 0, 2, 5\}$.

5. a) Locate 1 on the horizontal axis and then find the point on the graph for which 1 is the first coordinate. From that point, look to the vertical axis to find the corresponding y-coordinate, about 2.5 or $\frac{5}{2}$.

Thus, $f(1) \approx \frac{5}{2}$.

b) The set of all x-values in the graph extends from -3 to 5, so the domain is $\{x| -3 \leq x \leq 5\}$, or $[-3, 5]$.

c) To determine which member(s) of the domain are paired with 2, locate 2 on the vertical axis. From there look left and right to the graph to find any points for which 2 is the second coordinate. One such point exists. Its first coordinate appears to be about $2\frac{1}{4}$ or $\frac{9}{4}$. Thus, the x-value

for which $f(x) = 2$ is about $\frac{9}{4}$.

d) The set of all y-values in the graph extends from 1 to 4, so the range is $\{y|1 \leq y \leq 4\}$, or $[1, 4]$.

7. a) Locate 1 on the horizontal axis and the find the point on the graph for which 1 is the first coordinate. From that point, look to the vertical axis to find the corresponding y-coordinate. It

appears to be about $2\frac{1}{4}$, or $\frac{9}{4}$. Thus, $f(1) \approx \frac{9}{4}$.

b) The set of all x-values in the graph extends from -4 to 3, so the domain is $\{x| -4 \leq x \leq 3\}$, or $[-4, 3]$.

c) To determine which member(s) of the domain are paired with 2, locate 2 on the vertical axis. From there look left and right to the graph to find any points for which 2 is the second coordinate. One such point exists. Its first coordinate is about 0, so the x-value for which $f(x) = 2$ is about 0.

d) The set of all y-values in the graph extends from -5 to 4, so the range is $\{y| -5 \leq y \leq 4\}$, or $[-5, 4]$.

9. a) Locate 1 on the horizontal axis and then find the point on the graph for which 1 is the first coordinate. From that point, look to the vertical axis to find the corresponding y-coordinate, 2. Thus, $f(1) = 2$.

b) The set of all x-values in the graph extends from -5 to 4, so the domain is $\{x| -5 \leq x \leq 4\}$, or $[-5, 4]$.

c) To determine which member(s) of the domain are paired with 2, locate 2 on the vertical axis. From there look left and right to the graph to find any points for which 2 is the second coordinate. All points in the set $\{x|1 \leq x \leq 4\}$, or $[1, 4]$ satisfy this condition. These are the x-values for which $f(x) = 2$.

d) The set of all y-values in the graph extends from -3 to 2, so the range is $\{y| -3 \leq y \leq 2\}$, or $[-3, 2]$.

11. a) Locate 1 on the horizontal axis and then find the point on the graph for which 1 is the first coordinate. From that point, look to the vertical axis to find the corresponding y-coordinate, -1. Thus, $f(1) = -1$.

b) The set of all x-values in the graph extends from -6 to 5, so the domain is $\{x| -6 \leq x \leq 5\}$, or $[-6, 5]$.

c) To determine which member(s) of the domain are paired with 2, locate 2 on the vertical axis. From there look left and right to the graph to find any points for which 2 is the second coordinate. Three such points exist, $(-4, 2)$, $(0, 2)$ and $(3, 2)$. Thus, the x-values for which $f(x) = 2$ are -4, 0, and 3.

d) The set of all y-values in the graph extends from -2 to 2, so the range is $\{y| -2 \leq y \leq 2\}$, or $[-2, 2]$.

13. $f(x) = \dfrac{2}{x + 3}$

Since $\dfrac{2}{x + 3}$ cannot be calculated when the denominator is 0, we find the x-value that causes $x + 3$ to be 0:

$x + 3 = 0$

$\quad x = -3 \quad$ Subtracting 3 on both sides

Thus, -3 is not in the domain of f, while all other real numbers are. The domain of f is

$\{x|x \text{ is a real number } and \ x \neq -3\}$, or

$(-\infty, -3) \cup (-3, \infty)$.

15. $f(x) = 2x + 1$

Since we can calculate $2x + 1$ for any real number x, the domain is the set of all real numbers.

17. $f(x) = x^2 + 3$

Since we can calculate $x^2 + 3$ for any real number x, the domain is the set of all real numbers.

19. $f(x) = \dfrac{8}{5x - 14}$

Since $\dfrac{8}{5x - 14}$ cannot be calculated when the denominator is 0, we find the x-value that causes $5x - 14$ to be 0:

$5x - 14 = 0$

$5x = 14$

$x = \dfrac{14}{5}$

Thus, $\dfrac{14}{5}$ is not in the domain of f, while all other real numbers are. The domain of f is

$\left\{x \middle| x \text{ is a real number } and \ x \neq \dfrac{14}{5}\right\}$, or

$\left(\infty, \dfrac{14}{5}\right) \cup \left(\dfrac{14}{5}, \infty\right)$.

21. $f(x) = |x| - 4$

Since we can calculate $|x| - 4$ for any real number x, the domain is the set of all real numbers.

23. $f(x) = \dfrac{4}{|2x - 3|}$

Since $\dfrac{4}{|2x - 3|}$ cannot be calculated when the denominator is 0, we find the x-values that causes $|2x - 3|$ to be 0:

$$|2x - 3| = 0$$
$$2x - 3 = 0$$
$$2x = 3$$
$$x = \frac{3}{2}$$

Thus, $\dfrac{3}{2}$ is not in the domain of f, while all other real numbers are. The domain of f is

$$\left\{ x \middle| x \text{ is a real number } and \text{ } x \neq \frac{3}{2} \right\}, \text{ or}$$

$$\left(-\infty, \frac{3}{2} \right) \cup \left(\frac{3}{2}, \infty \right).$$

25. $g(x) = \dfrac{1}{x - 1}$

Since $\dfrac{1}{x - 1}$ cannot be calculated when the denominator is 0, we find the x-value that causes $x - 1$ to be 0:

$$x - 1 = 0$$
$$x = 1$$

Thus, 1 is not in the domain of g, while all other real numbers are. The domain of g is

$\{x | x \text{ is a real number } and \text{ } x \neq 1\}$, or $(-\infty, 1) \cup (1, \infty)$.

27. $g(x) = x^2 - 2x + 1$

Since we can calculate $x^2 - 2x + 1$ for any real number x, the domain is the set of all real numbers.

29. $g(x) = x^3 - 1$

Since we can calculate $x^3 - 1$ for any real number x, the domain is the set of all real numbers.

31. $g(x) = \dfrac{7}{20 - 8x}$

Since $\dfrac{7}{20 - 8x}$ cannot be calculated when the denominator is 0, we find the x-values that cause $20 - 8x$ to be 0:

$$20 - 8x = 0$$
$$-8x = -20$$
$$x = \frac{5}{2}$$

Thus, $\dfrac{5}{2}$ is not in the domain of g, while all other real numbers are. The domain of g is

$$\left\{ x \middle| x \text{ is a real number } and \text{ } x \neq \frac{5}{2} \right\}, \text{ or}$$

$$\left(-\infty, \frac{5}{2} \right) \cup \left(\frac{5}{2}, \infty \right).$$

33. $g(x) = |x + 7|$

Since we can calculate $|x + 7|$ for any real number x, the domain is the set of all real numbers.

35. $g(x) = \dfrac{-2}{|4x + 5|}$

Since $\dfrac{-2}{|4x + 5|}$ cannot be calculated when the denominator is 0, we find the x-value that causes $|4x + 5|$ to be 0:

$$|4x + 5| = 0$$
$$4x + 5 = 0$$
$$4x = -5$$
$$x = -\frac{5}{4}$$

Thus, $-\dfrac{5}{4}$ is not in the domain of g, while all other real numbers are. The domain of g is

$$\left\{ x \middle| x \text{ is a real number } and \text{ } x \neq -\frac{5}{4} \right\}, \text{ or}$$

$$\left(-\infty, -\frac{5}{4} \right) \cup \left(-\frac{5}{4}, \infty \right).$$

37. The input -1 has the output -8, so $f(-1) = -8$; the input 0 has the output 0, so $f(0) = 0$; the input 1 has the output -2, so $f(1) = -2$.

39. Discussion and Writing Exercise

41. *Familiarize.* We list the given information in a table.

Plan A: Monthly Income	Plan B: Monthly Income
$800 salary	$1000 salary
5% of sales	7% of sales over $15,000
Total: 800 + 5% of sales	Total: 1000 + 7% of sales over 15,000

Translate. We write an inequality stating that the income from Plan B is greater than the income from Plan A. We let s = sales Then $s - 15,000$ = sales over 15,000.

$$1000 + 7\%(s - 15,000) > 800 + 5\%s$$

Solve.

$$1000 + 0.07(s - 15,000) > 800 + 0.05s$$
$$1000 + 0.07s - 1050 > 800 + 0.05s$$
$$0.07s - 50 > 800 + 0.05s$$
$$0.02s - 50 > 800$$
$$0.02s > 850$$
$$s > 42,500$$

Check. We can do a partial check by computing the income from each plan for an amount less than 42,500 and for an amount greater than 42,500. We conclude that the answer checks.

State. Plan B is better than Plan A for sales of more than $42,500. Expressed as an inequality the result is $\{s | s > \$42,500\}$.

43. $|x| = 8$

$x = -8 \text{ or } x = 8$

The solution set is $\{-8, 8\}$.

45. $|x - 7| = 11$

$\qquad x - 7 = -11 \quad or \quad x - 7 = 11$

$\qquad\qquad x = -4 \quad or \qquad x = 18$

The solution set is $\{-4, 18\}$.

47. $|3x - 4| = |x + 2|$

$\quad 3x - 4 = x + 2 \quad or \quad 3x - 4 = -(x + 2)$

$\quad 2x - 4 = 2 \qquad or \quad 3x - 4 = -x - 2$

$\qquad 2x = 6 \qquad or \qquad 4x - 4 = -2$

$\qquad\; x = 3 \qquad or \qquad\quad 4x = 2$

$\qquad\; x = 3 \qquad or \qquad\quad x = \dfrac{1}{2}$

The solution set is $\left\{\dfrac{1}{2}, 3\right\}$.

49. $|3x - 8| = -11$

Since the absolute value of a number must be nonnegative, the equation has no solution. The solution is $\emptyset$.

51. We graph each function and determine the range.

The range of $f(x) = \dfrac{2}{x + 3}$ is $(-\infty, 0) \cup (0, \infty)$; the range of $f(x) = x^2 - 2x + 3$ is $[2, \infty)$; the range of $f(x) = |x| - 4$ is $[-4, \infty)$; the range of $f(x) = |x - 4|$ is $[0, \infty)$.

Exercise Set 2.4

1. $y = 4x + 5$

$\qquad\;\uparrow\qquad\uparrow$

$\;\; y = mx + b$

The slope is 4, and the y-intercept is $(0, 5)$.

3. $f(x) = -2x - 6$

$\qquad\qquad\uparrow\qquad\;\uparrow$

$\;\; f(x) = mx + b$

The slope is -2, and the y-intercept is $(0, -6)$.

5. $y = -\dfrac{3}{8}x - \dfrac{1}{5}$

$\qquad\quad\uparrow\qquad\;\uparrow$

$\;\; y = mx + b$

The slope is $-\dfrac{3}{8}$, and the y-intercept is $\left(0, -\dfrac{1}{5}\right)$.

7. $g(x) = 0.5x - 9$

$\qquad\qquad\uparrow\qquad\uparrow$

$\;\; g(x) = mx + b$

The slope is 0.5, and the y-intercept is $(0, -9)$.

9. First we find the slope-intercept form of the equation by solving for y. This allows us to determine the slope and y-intercept easily.

$$2x - 3y = 8$$

$$-3y = -2x + 8$$

$$\dfrac{-3y}{-3} = \dfrac{-2x + 8}{-3}$$

$$y = \dfrac{2}{3}x - \dfrac{8}{3}$$

The slope is $\dfrac{2}{3}$, and the y-intercept is $\left(0, -\dfrac{8}{3}\right)$.

11. First we find the slope-intercept form of the equation by solving for y. This allows us to determine the slope and y-intercept easily.

$$9x = 3y + 6$$

$$9x - 6 = 3y$$

$$\dfrac{9x - 6}{3} = \dfrac{3y}{y}$$

$$3x - 2 = y, \text{ or}$$

$$y = 3x - 2$$

The slope is 3, and the y-intercept is $(0, -2)$.

13. First we find the slope-intercept form of the equation by solving for y. This allows us to determine the slope and y-intercept easily.

$$3 - \dfrac{1}{4}y = 2x$$

$$-\dfrac{1}{4}y = 2x - 3$$

$$-4\left(-\dfrac{1}{4}y\right) = -4(2x - 3)$$

$$y = -8x + 12$$

The slope is -8, and the y-intercept is $(0, 12)$.

15. First we find the slope-intercept form of the equation by solving for y. This allows us to determine the slope and y-intercept easily.

$$17y + 4x + 3 = 7 + 4x$$

$$17y + 3 = 7$$

$$17y = 4$$

$$y = \dfrac{4}{17}, \text{ or}$$

$$y = 0 \cdot x + \dfrac{4}{17}$$

The slope is 0, and the y-intercept is $\left(0, \dfrac{4}{17}\right)$.

17. We can use any two points on the line, such as $(0, 3)$ and $(4, 1)$.

$$\text{Slope} = \dfrac{\text{change in } y}{\text{change in } x}$$

$$= \dfrac{1 - 3}{4 - 0} = \dfrac{-2}{4} = -\dfrac{1}{2}$$

19. We can use any two points on the line, such as $(-3, 1)$ and $(3, 3)$.

$$\text{Slope} = \dfrac{\text{change in } y}{\text{change in } x}$$

$$= \dfrac{3 - 1}{3 - (-3)} = \dfrac{2}{6} = \dfrac{1}{3}$$

21. $\text{Slope} = \dfrac{\text{change in } y}{\text{change in } x} = \dfrac{5 - 9}{4 - 6} = \dfrac{-4}{-2} = 2$

23. $\text{Slope} = \dfrac{\text{change in } y}{\text{change in } x} = \dfrac{-8 - (-4)}{3 - 9} = \dfrac{-4}{-6} = \dfrac{2}{3}$

25. Slope $= \dfrac{\text{change in } y}{\text{change in } x} = \dfrac{8.7 - 12.4}{-5.2 - (-16.3)} = \dfrac{-3.7}{11.1} =$

$-\dfrac{37}{111} = -\dfrac{1}{3}$

27. Slope $= \dfrac{0.4}{5} = 0.08 = 8\%$; this can also be expressed as $\dfrac{2}{25}$.

29. Slope $= \dfrac{43.33}{1238} = 0.035 = 3.5\%$

31. The rate of change can be found using the coordinates of any two points on the line. We use $(2000, 9.7)$ and $(2005, 35)$.

$\text{Rate} = \dfrac{\text{change in volume of e-mail}}{\text{corresponding change in time}}$

$= \dfrac{35 - 9.7}{2005 - 2000}$

$= \dfrac{25.3}{5}$

$= 5.06$ billion messages daily per year

33. We can use the coordinates of any two points on the line. We'll use $(0, 30)$ and $(3, 3)$.

Slope $= \dfrac{\text{change in } y}{\text{change in } x} = \dfrac{3 - 30}{3 - 0} = \dfrac{-27}{3} = -9$

The rate of change is $-\$900$ per year. That is, the value is decreasing at a rate of $\$900$ per year.

35. We can use the coordinates of any two points on the line. We'll use $(15, 470)$ and $(55, 510)$:

Slope $= \dfrac{\text{change in } y}{\text{change in } x} = \dfrac{510 - 470}{55 - 15} = \dfrac{40}{40} = 1$

The average SAT math score is increasing at a rate of 1 point per thousand dollars of family income.

37. Discussion and Writing Exercise

39. $3^2 - 24 \cdot 56 + 144 \div 12$

$= 9 - 24 \cdot 56 + 144 \div 12$

$= 9 - 1344 + 144 \div 12$

$= 9 - 1344 + 12$

$= -1335 + 12$

$= -1323$

41. $10\{2x + 3[5x - 2(-3x + y^1 - 2)]\}$

$= 10\{2x + 3[5x - 2(-3x + y - 2)]\}$

$= 10\{2x + 3[5x + 6x - 2y + 4]\}$

$= 10\{2x + 3[11x - 2y + 4]\}$

$= 10\{2x + 33x - 6y + 12\}$

$= 10\{35x - 6y + 12\}$

$= 350x - 60y + 120$

43. *Familiarize*. Let t represent the length of a side of the triangle. Then $t - 5$ represents the length of a side of the square.

Translate.

Perimeter of the square	is the same as	perimeter of the triangle
$4(t - 5)$	$=$	$3t$

Solve.

$4(t - 5) = 3t$

$4t - 20 = 3t$

$t - 20 = 0$

$t = 20$

Check. If 20 is the length of a side of the triangle, then the length of a side of the square is $20 - 5$, or 15. The perimeter of the square is $4 \cdot 15$, or 60, and the perimeter of the triangle is $3 \cdot 20$, or 60. The numbers check.

State. The square and triangle have sides of length 15 yd and 20 yd, respectively.

45. $|5x - 8| < 32$

$-32 < 5x - 8 < 32$

$-24 < 5x < 40 \qquad$ Adding 8

$-\dfrac{24}{5} < x < 8 \qquad$ Dividing by 5

The solution set is $\left\{ x \mid -\dfrac{24}{5} < x < 8 \right\}$, or $\left(-\dfrac{24}{5}, 8 \right)$.

47. $|5x - 8| = -32$

Since the absolute value of a number is nonnegative the equation has no solution. The solution is $\{\ \}$, or $\emptyset$.

Exercise Set 2.5

1. $x - 2 = y$

To find the x-intercept we let $y = 0$ and solve for x. We have $x - 2 = 0$, or $x = 2$. The x-intercept is $(2, 0)$.

To find the y-intercept we let $x = 0$ and solve for y.

$x - 2 = y$

$0 - 2 = y$

$-2 = y$

The y-intercept is $(0, -2)$. We plot these points and draw the line.

We use a third point as a check. We choose $x = 5$ and solve for y.

$5 - 2 = y$

$3 = y$

We plot $(5, 3)$ and note that it is on the line.

3. $x + 3y = 6$

To find the x-intercept we let $y = 0$ and solve for x.

$$x + 3y = 6$$
$$x + 3 \cdot 0 = 6$$
$$x = 6$$

The x-intercept is $(6, 0)$.

To find the y-intercept we let $x = 0$ and solve for y.

$$x + 3y = 6$$
$$0 + 3y = 6$$
$$3y = 6$$
$$y = 2$$

The y-intercept is $(0, 2)$.

We plot these points and draw the line.

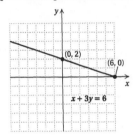

We use a third point as a check. We choose $x = 3$ and solve for y.

$$3 + 3y = 6$$
$$3y = 3$$
$$y = 1$$

We plot $(3, 1)$ and note that it is on the line.

5. $2x + 3y = 6$

To find the x-intercept we let $y = 0$ and solve for x.

$$2x + 3y = 6$$
$$2x + 3 \cdot 0 = 6$$
$$2x = 6$$
$$x = 3$$

The x-intercept is $(3, 0)$.

To find the y-intercept we let $x = 0$ and solve for y.

$$2x + 3y = 6$$
$$2 \cdot 0 + 3y = 6$$
$$3y = 6$$
$$y = 2$$

The y-intercept is $(0, 2)$.

We plot these points and draw the line.

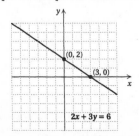

We use a third point as a check. We choose $x = -3$ and solve for y.

$$2(-3) + 3y = 6$$
$$-6 + 3y = 6$$
$$3y = 12$$
$$y = 4$$

We plot $(-3, 4)$ and note that it is on the line.

7. $f(x) = -2 - 2x$

We can think of this equation as $y = -2 - 2x$.

To find the x-intercept we let $f(x) = 0$ and solve for x. We have $0 = -2 - 2x$, or $2x = -2$, or $x = -1$. The x-intercept is $(-1, 0)$.

To find the y-intercept we let $x = 0$ and solve for $f(x)$, or y.

$$y = -2 - 2x$$
$$y = -2 - 2 \cdot 0$$
$$y = -2$$

The y-intercept is $(0, -2)$.

We plot these points and draw the line.

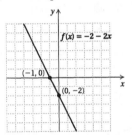

We use a third point as a check. We choose $x = -3$ and calculate y.

$$y = -2 - 2(-3) = -2 + 6 = 4$$

We plot $(-3, 4)$ and note that it is on the line.

9. $5y = -15 + 3x$

To find the x-intercept we let $y = 0$ and solve for x. We have $0 = -15 + 3x$, or $15 = 3x$, or $5 = x$. The x-intercept is $(5, 0)$.

To find the y-intercept we let $x = 0$ and solve for y.

$$5y = -15 + 3x$$
$$5y = -15 + 3 \cdot 0$$
$$5y = -15$$
$$y = -3$$

The y-intercept is $(0, -3)$.

We plot these points and draw the line.

We use a third point as a check. We choose $x = -5$ and solve for y.

$$5y = -15 + 3(-5)$$
$$5y = -15 - 15$$
$$5y = -30$$
$$y = -6$$

We plot $(-5, -6)$ and note that it is on the line.

11. $2x - 3y = 6$

To find the x-intercept we let $y = 0$ and solve for x.

$$2x - 3y = 6$$
$$2x - 3 \cdot 0 = 6$$
$$2x = 6$$
$$x = 3$$

The x-intercept is $(3, 0)$.

To find the y-intercept we let $x = 0$ and solve for y.

$$2x - 3y = 6$$
$$2 \cdot 0 - 3y = 6$$
$$-3y = 6$$
$$y = -2$$

The y-intercept is $(0, -2)$.

We plot these points and draw the line.

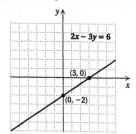

We use a third point as a check. We choose $x = -3$ and solve for y.

$$2(-3) - 3y = 6$$
$$-6 - 3y = 6$$
$$-3y = 12$$
$$y = -4$$

We plot $(-3, -4)$ and note that it is on the line.

13. $2.8y - 3.5x = -9.8$

To find the x-intercept we let $y = 0$ and solve for x.

$$2.8y - 3.5x = -9.8$$
$$2.8(0) - 3.5x = -9.8$$
$$-3.5x = -9.8$$
$$x = 2.8$$

The x-intercept is $(2.8, 0)$.

To find the y-intercept we let $x = 0$ and solve for y.

$$2.8y - 3.5x = -9.8$$
$$2.8y - 3.5(0) = -9.8$$
$$2.8y = -9.8$$
$$y = -3.5$$

The y-intercept is $(0, -3.5)$.

We plot these points and draw the line.

We use a third point as a check. We choose $x = 5$ and solve for y.

$$2.8y - 3.5(5) = -9.8$$
$$2.8y - 17.5 = -9.8$$
$$2.8y = 7.7$$
$$y = 2.75$$

We plot $(5, 2.75)$ and note that it is on the line.

15. $5x + 2y = 7$

To find the x-intercept we let $y = 0$ and solve for x.

$$5x + 2y = 7$$
$$5x + 2 \cdot 0 = 7$$
$$5x = 7$$
$$x = \frac{7}{5}$$

The x-intercept is $\left(\frac{7}{5}, 0\right)$.

To find the y-intercept we let $x = 0$ and solve for y.

$$5x + 2y = 7$$
$$5 \cdot 0 + 2y = 7$$
$$2y = 7$$
$$y = \frac{7}{2}$$

The y-intercept is $\left(0, \frac{7}{2}\right)$.

We plot these points and draw the line.

We use a third point as a check. We choose $x = 3$ and solve for y.

$$5 \cdot 3 + 2y = 7$$
$$15 + 2y = 7$$
$$2y = -8$$
$$y = -4$$

We plot $(3, -4)$ and note that it is on the line.

17. $y = \dfrac{5}{2}x + 1$

First we plot the y-intercept $(0,1)$. Then we consider the slope $\dfrac{5}{2}$. Starting at the y-intercept and using the slope, we find another point by moving 5 units up and 2 units to the right. We get to a new point $(2,6)$.

We can also think of the slope as $\dfrac{-5}{-2}$. We again start at the y-intercept $(0,1)$. We move 5 units down and 2 units to the left. We get to another new point $(-2,-4)$. We plot the points and draw the line.

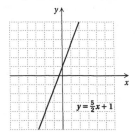

19. $f(x) = -\dfrac{5}{2}x - 4$

First we plot the y-intercept $(0,-4)$. We can think of the slope as $\dfrac{-5}{2}$. Starting at the y-intercept and using the slope, we find another point by moving 5 units down and 2 units to the right. We get to a new point $(2,-9)$.

We can also think of the slope as $\dfrac{5}{-2}$. We again start at the y-intercept $(0,-4)$. We move 5 units up and 2 units to the left. We get to another new point $(-2,1)$. We plot the points and draw the line.

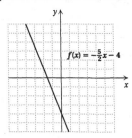

21. $x + 2y = 4$

First we write the equation in slope-intercept form by solving for y.

$$x + 2y = 4$$
$$2y = -x + 4$$
$$\frac{2y}{2} = \frac{-x+4}{2}$$
$$y = -\frac{1}{2}x + 2$$

Now we plot the y-intercept $(0,2)$. We can think of the slope as $\dfrac{-1}{2}$. Starting at the y-intercept and using the slope, we find another point by moving 1 unit down and 2 units to the right. We get to a new point $(2,1)$.

We can also think of the slope as $\dfrac{1}{-2}$. We again start at the y-intercept $(0,2)$. We move 1 unit up and 2 units to

the left. We get to another new point $(-2,3)$. We plot the points and draw the line.

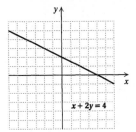

23. $4x - 3y = 12$

First we write the equation in slope-intercept form by solving for y.

$$4x - 3y = 12$$
$$-3y = -4x + 12$$
$$\frac{-3y}{-3} = \frac{-4x+12}{-3}$$
$$y = \frac{4}{3}x - 4$$

Now we plot the y-intercept $(0,-4)$ and consider the slope $\dfrac{4}{3}$. Starting at the y-intercept and using the slope, we find another point by moving 4 units up and 3 units to the right. We get to a new point $(3,0)$. In a similar manner we can move from the point $(3,0)$ to find another point $(6,4)$. We plot these points and draw the line.

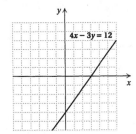

25. $f(x) = \dfrac{1}{3}x - 4$

First we plot the y-intercept $(0,-4)$. Then we consider the slope $\dfrac{1}{3}$. Starting at the y-intercept and using the slope, we find another point by moving 1 unit up and 3 units to the right. We get to a new point $(3,-3)$.

We can also think of the slope as $\dfrac{-1}{-3}$. We again start at the y-intercept $(0,-4)$. We move 1 unit down and 3 units to the left. We get to another new point $(-3,-5)$. We plot these points and draw the line.

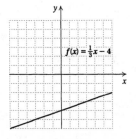

27. $5x + 4 \cdot f(x) = 4$

First we solve for $f(x)$.

$$5x + 4 \cdot f(x) = 4$$
$$4 \cdot f(x) = -5x + 4$$
$$\frac{4 \cdot f(x)}{4} = \frac{-5x + 4}{4}$$
$$f(x) = -\frac{5}{4}x + 1$$

Now we plot the y-intercept $(0, 1)$. We can think of the slope as $\dfrac{-5}{4}$. Starting at the y-intercept and using the slope, we find another point by moving 5 units down and 4 units to the right. We get to a new point $(4, -4)$.

We can also think of the slope as $\dfrac{5}{-4}$. We again start at the y-intercept $(0, 1)$. We move 5 units up and 4 units to the left. We get to another new point $(-4, 6)$. We plot these points and draw the line.

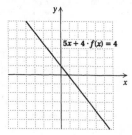

29. $x = 1$

Since y is missing, any number for y will do. Thus all ordered pairs $(1, y)$ are solutions. The graph is parallel to the y-axis.

x	y
1	-2
1	0	⟵ x-intercept
1	3

↑   ⌐— Choose any
x must   number for y.
be 1.

This is a vertical line, so the slope is not defined.

31. $y = -1$

Since x is missing, any number for x will do. Thus all ordered pairs $(x, -1)$ are solutions. The graph is parallel to the x-axis.

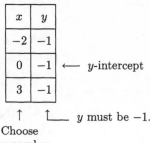

x	y
-2	-1
0	-1	⟵ y-intercept
3	-1

↑   ⌐— y must be -1.
Choose
any number
for x.

This is a horizontal line, so the slope is 0.

33. $f(x) = -6$

Since x is missing all ordered pairs $(x, 6)$ are solutions. The graph is parallel to the x-axis.

This is a horizontal line, so the slope is 0.

35. $y = 0$

Since x is missing, all ordered pairs $(x, 0)$ are solutions. The graph is the x-axis.

This is a horizontal line, so the slope is 0.

37. $2 \cdot f(x) + 5 = 0$

$$2 \cdot f(x) = -5$$
$$f(x) = -\frac{5}{2}$$

Since x is missing, all ordered pairs $\left(x, -\dfrac{5}{2}\right)$ are solutions. The graph is parallel to the x-axis.

This is a horizontal line, so the slope is 0.

39. $7 - 3x = 4 + 2x$

$7 - 5x = 4$

$-5x = -3$

$x = \dfrac{3}{5}$

Since y is missing, all ordered pairs $\left(\dfrac{3}{5}, y\right)$ are solutions.
The graph is parallel to the y-axis.

This is a vertical line, so the slope is not defined.

41. We first solve for y and determine the slope of each line.

$x + 6 = y$

$y = x + 6$ Reversing the order

The slope of $y = x + 6$ is 1.

$y - x = -2$

$y = x - 2$

The slope of $y = x - 2$ is 1.

The slopes are the same, and the y-intercepts are different. The lines are parallel.

43. We first solve for y and determine the slope of each line.

$y + 3 = 5x$

$y = 5x - 3$

The slope of $y = 5x - 3$ is 5.

$3x - y = -2$

$3x + 2 = y$

$y = 3x + 2$ Reversing the order

The slope of $y = 3x + 2$ is 3.

The slopes are not the same; the lines are not parallel.

45. We determine the slope of each line.

The slope of $y = 3x + 9$ is 3.

$2y = 6x - 2$

$y = 3x - 1$

The slope of $y = 3x - 1$ is 3.

The slopes are the same, and the y-intercepts are different. The lines are parallel.

47. We solve each equation for x.

$12x = 3 \qquad\qquad -7x = 10$

$x = \dfrac{1}{4} \qquad\qquad x = -\dfrac{10}{7}$

We have two vertical lines, so they are parallel.

49. We determine the slope of each line.

The slope of $y = 4x - 5$ is 4.

$4y = 8 - x$

$4y = -x + 8$

$y = -\dfrac{1}{4}x + 2$

The slope of $4y = 8 - x$ is $-\dfrac{1}{4}$.

The product of their slopes is $4\left(-\dfrac{1}{4}\right)$, or -1; the lines are perpendicular.

51. We determine the slope of each line.

$x + 2y = 5$

$2y = -x + 5$

$y = -\dfrac{1}{2}x + \dfrac{5}{2}$

The slope of $x + 2y = 5$ is $-\dfrac{1}{2}$.

$2x + 4y = 8$

$4y = -2x + 8$

$y = -\dfrac{1}{2}x + 2$

The slope of $2x + 4y = 8$ is $-\dfrac{1}{2}$.

The product of their slopes is $\left(-\dfrac{1}{2}\right)\left(-\dfrac{1}{2}\right)$, or $\dfrac{1}{4}$; the lines are not perpendicular. For the lines to be perpendicular, the product must be -1.

53. We determine the slope of each line.

$2x - 3y = 7$

$-3y = -2x + 7$

$y = \dfrac{2}{3}x - \dfrac{7}{3}$

The slope of $2x - 3y = 7$ is $\dfrac{2}{3}$.

$2y - 3x = 10$

$2y = 3x + 10$

$y = \dfrac{3}{2}x + 5$

The slope of $2y - 3x = 10$ is $\dfrac{3}{2}$.

The product of their slopes is $\dfrac{2}{3} \cdot \dfrac{3}{2} = 1$; the lines are not perpendicular. For the lines to be perpendicular, the product must be -1.

55. Solving the first equation for x and the second for y, we have $x = \dfrac{3}{2}$ and $y = -2$. The graph of $x = \dfrac{3}{2}$ is a vertical line, and the graph of $y = -2$ is a horizontal line. Since one line is vertical and the other is horizontal, the lines are perpendicular.

57. Discussion and Writing Exercise

59. $5.\underset{\underbrace{\qquad\qquad}_{\text{10 places}}}{\overset{\uparrow}{3,000,000,000.}}$

Large number, so the exponent is positive.

$53,000,000,000 = 5.3 \times 10^{10}$

61. $\underset{\underset{\text{2 places}}{\underbrace{\;\;}}}{0.01.\,8}$

Small number, so the exponent is negative.

$0.018 = 1.8 \times 10^{-2}$

63. Negative exponent, so the number is small.

$\underset{\underset{\text{5 places}}{\underbrace{\qquad\;}}}{0.00002.\,13}$

$2.13 \times 10^{-5} = 0.0000213$

65. Positive exponent, so the number is large.

$\underset{\underset{\text{4 places}}{\underbrace{\qquad}}}{2.0000.}$

$2 \times 10^4 = 20,000$

67. $9x - 15y = 3 \cdot 3x - 3 \cdot 5y = 3(3x - 5y)$

69. $21p - 7pq + 14p = 7p \cdot 3 - 7p \cdot q + 7p \cdot 2$
$$= 7p(3 - q + 2)$$

71. The equation will be of the form $y = b$. Since the line passes through $(-2, 3)$, b must be 3. Thus, we have $y = 3$.

73. Find the slope of each line.
$$5y = ax + 5$$
$$y = \frac{a}{5}x + 1$$

The slope of $5y = ax + 5$ is $\dfrac{a}{5}$.
$$\frac{1}{4}y = \frac{1}{10}x - 1$$
$$4 \cdot \frac{1}{4}y = 4\left(\frac{1}{10}x - 1\right)$$
$$y = \frac{2}{5}x - 4$$

The slope of $\dfrac{1}{4}y = \dfrac{1}{10}x - 1$ is $\dfrac{2}{5}$.

In order for the graphs to be parallel, their slopes must be the same. (Note that the y-intercepts are different.)
$$\frac{a}{5} = \frac{2}{5}$$
$$a = 2 \qquad \text{Multiplying by 5}$$

75. The y-intercept is $\left(0, \dfrac{2}{5}\right)$, so the equation is of the form $y = mx + \dfrac{2}{5}$. We substitute -3 for x and 0 for y in this equation to find m.

$$y = mx + \frac{2}{5}$$
$$0 = m(-3) + \frac{2}{5} \qquad \text{Substituting}$$
$$0 = -3m + \frac{2}{5}$$
$$3m = \frac{2}{5} \qquad \text{Adding } 3m$$
$$m = \frac{2}{15} \qquad \text{Multiplying by } \frac{1}{3}$$

The equation is $y = \dfrac{2}{15}x + \dfrac{2}{5}$.

(We could also have found the slope as follows:
$$m = \frac{\dfrac{2}{5} - 0}{0 - (-3)} = \frac{\dfrac{2}{5}}{3} = \frac{2}{15})$$

77. All points on the x-axis are pairs of the form $(x, 0)$. Thus any number for x will do and y must be 0. The equation is $y = 0$. This equation is a function because its graph passes the vertical-line test.

79. We substitute 4 for x and 0 for y.
$$y = mx + 3$$
$$0 = m(4) + 3$$
$$-3 = 4m$$
$$-\frac{3}{4} = m$$

81. a) Graph II indicates that 200 mL of fluid was dripped in the first 3 hr, a rate of 200/3 mL/hr. It also indicates that 400 mL of fluid was dripped in the next 3 hr, a rate of 400/3 mL/hr, and that this rate continues until the end of the time period shown. Since the rate of 400/3 mL/hr is double the rate of 200/3 mL/hr, this graph is appropriate for the given situation.

b) Graph IV indicates that 300 mL of fluid was dripped in the first 2 hr, a rate of 300/2, or 150 mL/hr. In the next 2 hr, 200 mL was dripped. This is a rate of 200/2, or 100 mL/hr. Then 100 mL was dripped in the next 3 hr, a rate of 100/3, or $33\dfrac{1}{3}$ mL/hr. Finally, in the remaining 2 hr, 0 mL of fluid was dripped, a rate of 0/2, or 0 mL/hr. Since the rate at which the fluid was given decreased as time progressed and eventually became 0, this graph is appropriate for the given situation.

c) Graph I is the only graph that shows a constant rate for 5 hours, in this case from 3 PM to 8 PM. Thus, it is appropriate for the given situation.

d) Graph III indicates that 100 mL of fluid was dripped in the first 4 hr, a rate of 100/4, or 25 mL/hr. In the next 3 hr, 200 mL was dripped. This is a rate of 200/3, or $66\frac{2}{3}$ mL/hr. Then 100 mL was dripped in the next hour, a rate of 100 mL/hr. In the last hour 200 mL was dripped, a rate of 200 mL/hr. Since the rate at which the fluid was given gradually increased, this graph is appropriate for the given situation.

Exercise Set 2.6

1. We use the slope-intercept equation and substitute -8 for m and 4 for b.
$$y = mx + b$$
$$y = -8x + 4$$

3. We use the slope-intercept equation and substitute 2.3 for m and -1 for b.
$$y = mx + b$$
$$y = 2.3x - 1$$

5. We use the slope-intercept equation and substitute $-\frac{7}{3}$ for m and -5 for b.
$$y = mx + b$$
$$y = -\frac{7}{3}x - 5$$

7. We use the slope-intercept equation and substitute $\frac{2}{3}$ for m and $\frac{5}{8}$ for b.
$$y = mx + b$$
$$y = \frac{2}{3}x + \frac{5}{8}$$

9. Using the point-slope equation:

Substitute 4 for x_1, 3 for y_1, and 5 for m.
$$y - y_1 = m(x - x_1)$$
$$y - 3 = 5(x - 4)$$
$$y - 3 = 5x - 20$$
$$y = 5x - 17$$

Using the slope-intercept equation:

Substitute 4 for x, 3 for y, and 5 for m in $y = mx + b$ and solve for b.
$$y = mx + b$$
$$3 = 5 \cdot 4 + b$$
$$3 = 20 + b$$
$$-17 = b$$

Then we use the equation $y = mx + b$ and substitute 5 for m and -17 for b.
$$y = 5x - 17$$

11. Using the point-slope equation:

Substitute 9 for x_1, 6 for y_1, and -3 for m.
$$y - y_1 = m(x - x_1)$$
$$y - 6 = -3(x - 9)$$
$$y - 6 = -3x + 27$$
$$y = -3x + 33$$

Using the slope-intercept equation:

Substitute 9 for x, 6 for y, and -3 for m in $y = mx + b$ and solve for b.
$$y = mx + b$$
$$6 = -3 \cdot 9 + b$$
$$6 = -27 + b$$
$$33 = b$$

Then we use the equation $y = mx + b$ and substitute -3 for m and 33 for b.
$$y = -3x + 33$$

13. Using the point-slope equation:

Substitute -1 for x_1, -7 for y_1, and 1 for m.
$$y - y_1 = m(x - x_1)$$
$$y - (-7) = 1(x - (-1))$$
$$y + 7 = 1(x + 1)$$
$$y + 7 = x + 1$$
$$y = x - 6$$

Using the slope-intercept equation:

Substitute -1 for x, -7 for y, and 1 for m in $y = mx + b$ and solve for b.
$$y = mx + b$$
$$-7 = 1(-1) + b$$
$$-7 = -1 + b$$
$$-6 = b$$

Then we use the equation $y = mx + b$ and substitute 1 for m and -6 for b.
$$y = 1x - 6, \text{ or } y = x - 6$$

15. Using the point-slope equation:

Substitute 8 for x_1, 0 for y_1, and -2 for m.
$$y - y_1 = m(x - x_1)$$
$$y - 0 = -2(x - 8)$$
$$y = -2x + 16$$

Using the slope-intercept equation:

Substitute 8 for x, 0 for y, and -2 for m in $y = mx + b$ and solve for b.
$$y = mx + b$$
$$0 = -2 \cdot 8 + b$$
$$0 = -16 + b$$
$$16 = b$$

Then we use the equation $y = mx + b$ and substitute -2 for m and 16 for b.
$$y = -2x + 16$$

17. Using the point-slope equation:

Substitute 0 for x_1, -7 for y_1, and 0 for m.

$$y - y_1 = m(x - x_1)$$
$$y - (-7) = 0(x - 0)$$
$$y + 7 = 0$$
$$y = -7$$

Using the slope-intercept equation:

Substitute 0 for x, -7 for y, and 0 for m in $y = mx + b$ and solve for b.

$$y = mx + b$$
$$-7 = 0 \cdot 0 + b$$
$$-7 = b$$

Then we use the equation $y = mx + b$ and substitute 0 for m and -7 for b.

$$y = 0x - 7, \text{ or } y = -7$$

19. Using the point-slope equation:

Substitute 1 for x_1, -2 for y_1, and $\dfrac{2}{3}$ for m.

$$y - y_1 = m(x - x_1)$$
$$y - (-2) = \frac{2}{3}(x - 1)$$
$$y + 2 = \frac{2}{3}x - \frac{2}{3}$$
$$y = \frac{2}{3}x - \frac{8}{3}$$

Using the slope-intercept equation:

Substitute 1 for x, -2 for y and $\dfrac{2}{3}$ for m in $y = mx + b$ and solve for b.

$$y = mx + b$$
$$-2 = \frac{2}{3} \cdot 1 + b$$
$$-2 = \frac{2}{3} + b$$
$$-\frac{8}{3} = b$$

Then we use the equation $y = mx + b$ and substitute $\dfrac{2}{3}$ for m and $-\dfrac{8}{3}$ for b.

$$y = \frac{2}{3}x - \frac{8}{3}$$

21. First find the slope of the line:

$$m = \frac{6 - 4}{5 - 1} = \frac{2}{4} = \frac{1}{2}$$

Using the point-slope equation:

We choose to use the point $(1, 4)$ and substitute 1 for x_1, 4 for y_1, and $\dfrac{1}{2}$ for m.

$$y - y_1 = m(x - x_1)$$
$$y - 4 = \frac{1}{2}(x - 1)$$
$$y - 4 = \frac{1}{2}x - \frac{1}{2}$$
$$y = \frac{1}{2}x + \frac{7}{2}$$

Using the slope-intercept equation:

We choose $(1, 4)$ and substitute 1 for x, 4 for y, and $\dfrac{1}{2}$ for m in $y = mx + b$. Then we solve for b.

$$y = mx + b$$
$$4 = \frac{1}{2} \cdot 1 + b$$
$$4 = \frac{1}{2} + b$$
$$\frac{7}{2} = b$$

Finally, we use the equation $y = mx + b$ and substitute $\dfrac{1}{2}$ for m and $\dfrac{7}{2}$ for b.

$$y = \frac{1}{2}x + \frac{7}{2}$$

23. First find the slope of the line:

$$m = \frac{-3 - 2}{-3 - 2} = \frac{-5}{-5} = 1$$

Using the point-slope equation:

We choose to use the point $(2, 2)$ and substitute 2 for x_1, 2 for y_1, and 1 for m.

$$y - y_1 = m(x - x_1)$$
$$y - 2 = 1(x - 2)$$
$$y - 2 = x - 2$$
$$y = x$$

Using the slope-intercept equation:

We choose $(2, 2)$ and substitute 2 for x, 2 for y, and 1 for m in $y = mx + b$. Then we solve for b.

$$y = mx + b$$
$$2 = 1 \cdot 2 + b$$
$$2 = 2 + b$$
$$0 = b$$

Finally, we use the equation $y = mx + b$ and substitute 1 for m and 0 for b.

$$y = 1x + 0, \text{ or } y = x$$

25. First find the slope of the line:

$$m = \frac{0 - 7}{-4 - 0} = \frac{-7}{-4} = \frac{7}{4}$$

Using the point-slope equation:

We choose $(0, 7)$ and substitute 0 for x_1, 7 for y_1, and $\dfrac{7}{4}$ for m.

$$y - y_1 = m(x - x_1)$$
$$y - 7 = \frac{7}{4}(x - 0)$$
$$y - 7 = \frac{7}{4}x$$
$$y = \frac{7}{4}x + 7$$

Using the slope-intercept equation:

We choose $(0,7)$ and substitute 0 for x, 7 for y, and $\frac{7}{4}$ for m in $y = mx + b$. Then we solve for b.

$$y = mx + b$$
$$7 = \frac{7}{4} \cdot 0 + b$$
$$7 = b$$

Finally, we use the equation $y = mx + b$ and substitute $\frac{7}{4}$ for m and 7 for b.

$$y = \frac{7}{4}x + 7$$

27. First find the slope of the line:
$$m = \frac{-6 - (-3)}{-4 - (-2)} = \frac{-6 + 3}{-4 + 2} = \frac{-3}{-2} = \frac{3}{2}$$

Using the point-slope equation:

We choose $(-2, -3)$ and substitute -2 for x_1, -3 for y_1, and $\frac{3}{2}$ for m.

$$y - y_1 = m(x - x_1)$$
$$y - (-3) = \frac{3}{2}(x - (-2))$$
$$y + 3 = \frac{3}{2}(x + 2)$$
$$y + 3 = \frac{3}{2}x + 3$$
$$y = \frac{3}{2}x$$

Using the slope-intercept equation:

We choose $(-2, -3)$ and substitute -2 for x, -3 for y, and $\frac{3}{2}$ for m in $y = mx + b$. Then we solve for b.

$$y = mx + b$$
$$-3 = \frac{3}{2}(-2) + b$$
$$-3 = -3 + b$$
$$0 = b$$

Finally, we use the equation $y = mx + b$ and substitute $\frac{3}{2}$ for m and 0 for b.

$$y = \frac{3}{2}x + 0, \text{ or } y = \frac{3}{2}x$$

29. First find the slope of the line:
$$m = \frac{1 - 0}{6 - 0} = \frac{1}{6}$$

Using the point-slope equation:

We choose $(0, 0)$ and substitute 0 for x_1, 0 for y_1, and $\frac{1}{6}$ for m.

$$y - y_1 = m(x - x_1)$$
$$y - 0 = \frac{1}{6}(x - 0)$$
$$y = \frac{1}{6}x$$

Using the slope-intercept equation:

We choose $(0, 0)$ and substitute 0 for x, 0 for y, and $\frac{1}{6}$ for m in $y = mx + b$. Then we solve for b.

$$y = mx + b$$
$$0 = \frac{1}{6} \cdot 0 + b$$
$$0 = b$$

Finally, we use the equation $y = mx + b$ and substitute $\frac{1}{6}$ for m and 0 for b.

$$y = \frac{1}{6}x + 0, \text{ or } y = \frac{1}{6}x$$

31. First find the slope of the line:
$$m = \frac{-\frac{1}{2} - 6}{\frac{1}{4} - \frac{3}{4}} = \frac{-\frac{13}{2}}{-\frac{1}{2}} = 13$$

Using the point-slope equation:

We choose $\left(\frac{3}{4}, 6\right)$ and substitute $\frac{3}{4}$ for x_1, 6 for y_1, and 13 for m.

$$y - y_1 = m(x - x_1)$$
$$y - 6 = 13\left(x - \frac{3}{4}\right)$$
$$y - 6 = 13x - \frac{39}{4}$$
$$y = 13x - \frac{15}{4}$$

Using the slope-intercept equation:

We choose $\left(\frac{3}{4}, 6\right)$ and substitute $\frac{3}{4}$ for x, 6 for y, and 13 for m in $y = mx + b$. Then we solve for b.

$$y = mx + b$$
$$6 = 13 \cdot \frac{3}{4} + b$$
$$6 = \frac{39}{4} + b$$
$$-\frac{15}{4} = b$$

Finally, we use the equation $y = mx + b$ and substitute 13 for m and $-\frac{15}{4}$ for b.

$$y = 13x - \frac{15}{4}$$

33. First solve the equation for y and determine the slope of the given line.

$$x + 2y = 6 \qquad \text{Given line}$$
$$2y = -x + 6$$
$$y = -\frac{1}{2}x + 3$$

The slope of the given line is $-\frac{1}{2}$. The line through $(3, 7)$ must have slope $-\frac{1}{2}$.

Using the point-slope equation:

Substitute 3 for x_1, 7 for y_1, and $-\frac{1}{2}$ for m.

$$y - y_1 = m(x - x_1)$$

$$y - 7 = -\frac{1}{2}(x - 3)$$

$$y - 7 = -\frac{1}{2}x + \frac{3}{2}$$

$$y = -\frac{1}{2}x + \frac{17}{2}$$

Using the slope-intercept equation:

Substitute 3 for x, 7 for y, and $-\frac{1}{2}$ for m and solve for b.

$$y = mx + b$$

$$7 = -\frac{1}{2} \cdot 3 + b$$

$$7 = -\frac{3}{2} + b$$

$$\frac{17}{2} = b$$

Then we use the equation $y = mx + b$ and substitute $-\frac{1}{2}$ for m and $\frac{17}{2}$ for b.

$$y = -\frac{1}{2}x + \frac{17}{2}$$

35. First solve the equation for y and determine the slope of the given line.

$$5x - 7y = 8 \qquad \text{Given line}$$

$$5x - 8 = 7y$$

$$\frac{5}{7}x - \frac{8}{7} = y$$

$$y = \frac{5}{7}x - \frac{8}{7}$$

The slope of the given line is $\frac{5}{7}$. The line through $(2, -1)$ must have slope $\frac{5}{7}$.

Using the point-slope equation:

Substitute 2 for x_1, -1 for y_1, and $\frac{5}{7}$ for m.

$$y - y_1 = m(x - x_1)$$

$$y - (-1) = \frac{5}{7}(x - 2)$$

$$y + 1 = \frac{5}{7}x - \frac{10}{7}$$

$$y = \frac{5}{7}x - \frac{17}{7}$$

Using the slope-intercept equation:

Substitute 2 for x, -1 for y, and $\frac{5}{7}$ for m and solve for b.

$$y = mx + b$$

$$-1 = \frac{5}{7} \cdot 2 + b$$

$$-1 = \frac{10}{7} + b$$

$$-\frac{17}{7} = b$$

Then we use the equation $y = mx + b$ and substitute $\frac{5}{7}$ for m and $-\frac{17}{7}$ for b.

$$y = \frac{5}{7}x - \frac{17}{7}$$

37. First solve the equation for y and determine the slope of the given line.

$$3x - 9y = 2 \qquad \text{Given line}$$

$$3x - 2 = 9y$$

$$\frac{1}{3}x - \frac{2}{9} = y$$

The slope of the given line is $\frac{1}{3}$. The line through $(-6, 2)$ must have slope $\frac{1}{3}$.

Using the point-slope equation:

Substitute -6 for x_1, 2 for y_1, and $\frac{1}{3}$ for m.

$$y - y_1 = m(x - x_1)$$

$$y - 2 = \frac{1}{3}(x - (-6))$$

$$y - 2 = \frac{1}{3}(x + 6)$$

$$y - 2 = \frac{1}{3}x + 2$$

$$y = \frac{1}{3}x + 4$$

Using the slope-intercept equation:

Substitute -6 for x, 2 for y, and $\frac{1}{3}$ for m and solve for b.

$$y = mx + b$$

$$2 = \frac{1}{3}(-6) + b$$

$$2 = -2 + b$$

$$4 = b$$

Then we use the equation $y = mx + b$ and substitute $\frac{1}{3}$ for m and 4 for b.

$$y = \frac{1}{3}x + 4$$

39. First solve the equation for y and determine the slope of the given line.

$$2x + y = -3 \qquad \text{Given line}$$

$$y = -2x - 3$$

The slope of the given line is -2. The slope of the perpendicular line is the opposite of the reciprocal of -2. Thus, the line through $(2, 5)$ must have slope $\frac{1}{2}$.

Using the point-slope equation:

Substitute 2 for x_1, 5 for y_1, and $\frac{1}{2}$ for m.

$$y - y_1 = m(x - x_1)$$

$$y - 5 = \frac{1}{2}(x - 2)$$

$$y - 5 = \frac{1}{2}x - 1$$

$$y = \frac{1}{2}x + 4$$

Using the slope-intercept equation:

Substitute 2 for x, 5 for y, and $\frac{1}{2}$ for m and solve for b.

$$y = mx + b$$

$$5 = \frac{1}{2} \cdot 2 + b$$

$$5 = 1 + b$$

$$4 = b$$

Then we use the equation $y = mx + b$ and substitute $\frac{1}{2}$ for m and 4 for b.

$$y = \frac{1}{2}x + 4$$

41. First solve the equation for y and determine the slope of the given line.

$$3x + 4y = 5 \qquad \text{Given line}$$

$$4y = -3x + 5$$

$$y = -\frac{3}{4}x + \frac{5}{4}$$

The slope of the given line is $-\frac{3}{4}$. The slope of the perpendicular line is the opposite of the reciprocal of $-\frac{3}{4}$. Thus, the line through $(3, -2)$ must have slope $\frac{4}{3}$.

Using the point-slope equation:

Substitute 3 for x_1, -2 for y_1, and $\frac{4}{3}$ for m.

$$y - y_1 = m(x - x_1)$$

$$y - (-2) = \frac{4}{3}(x - 3)$$

$$y + 2 = \frac{4}{3}x - 4$$

$$y = \frac{4}{3}x - 6$$

Using the slope-intercept equation:

Substitute 3 for x, -2 for y, and $\frac{4}{3}$ for m.

$$y = mx + b$$

$$-2 = \frac{4}{3} \cdot 3 + b$$

$$-2 = 4 + b$$

$$-6 = b$$

Then we use the equation $y = mx + b$ and substitute $\frac{4}{3}$ for m and -6 for b.

$$y = \frac{4}{3}x - 6$$

43. First solve the equation for y and determine the slope of the given line.

$$2x + 5y = 7 \qquad \text{Given line}$$

$$5y = -2x + 7$$

$$y = -\frac{2}{5}x + \frac{7}{5}$$

The slope of the given line is $-\frac{2}{5}$. The slope of the perpendicular line is the opposite of the reciprocal of $-\frac{2}{5}$. Thus, the line through $(0, 9)$ must have slope $\frac{5}{2}$.

Using the point-slope equation:

Substitute 0 for x_1, 9 for y_1, and $\frac{5}{2}$ for m.

$$y - y_1 = m(x - x_1)$$

$$y - 9 = \frac{5}{2}(x - 0)$$

$$y - 9 = \frac{5}{2}x$$

$$y = \frac{5}{2}x + 9$$

Using the slope-intercept equation:

Substitute 0 for x, 9 for y, and $\frac{5}{2}$ for m.

$$y = mx + b$$

$$9 = \frac{5}{2} \cdot 0 + b$$

$$9 = b$$

Then we use the equation $y = mx + b$ and substitute $\frac{5}{2}$ for m and 9 for b.

$$y = \frac{5}{2}x + 9$$

45. a) The problem describes a situation in which an hourly fee is charged after an initial assessment of $85. After 1 hour, the total cost is $85 + $40 \cdot 1$. After 2 hours, the total cost is $85 + $40 \cdot 2$. Then after t hours, the total cost is $C(t) = 85 + 40t$, or $C(t) = 40t + 85$, where $t > 0$.

b) For $C(t) = 40t + 85$, the y-intercept is $(0, 85)$ and the slope, or rate of change, is $40 per hour. We plot $(0, 85)$ and from there we count up $40 and to the right 1 hour. This takes us to $(1, 125)$. Then we draw a line through the points, calculating a third value as a check:

$$C(5) = 40 \cdot 5 + 85 = 285$$

c) To find the cost for $6\frac{1}{2}$ hours of moving service, we determine $C(6.5)$:

$$C(6.5) = 40(6.5) + 85 = 345$$

Thus, it would cost \$345 for $6\frac{1}{2}$ hours of moving service.

47. a) The problem describes a situation in which the value of the fax machine decreases at the rate of \$25 per month from an initial value of \$750. After 1 month, the value is $\$750 - \$25 \cdot 1$. After 2 months, the value is $\$750 - \$25 \cdot 2$. Then after t months, the value is $V(t) = 750 - 25t$, where $t \geq 0$.

b) For $V(t) = 750 - 25t$, or $V(t) = -25t + 750$, the y-intercept is $(0, 750)$ and the slope, or rate of change, is $-\$25$ per month. We think of the slope as $\dfrac{-25}{1}$. Plot $(0, 750)$ and from there count down \$25 and to the right 1 month. This takes us to $(1, 725)$. We draw the line through the points, calculating a third value as a check:

$$V(6) = 750 - 25 \cdot 6 = 600$$

c) To find the value of the machine after 13 months, we determine $V(13)$:

$$V(13) = 750 - 25 \cdot 13 = 425$$

Thus, after 13 months the value of the machine is \$425.

49. a) In 1991, $x = 1991 - 1990 = 1$, so one data point is $(1, \, 271,000)$. In 2001, $x = 2001 - 1990 = 11$, so the other data point is $(11, \, 1,430,000)$.

First we find the slope of the line:

$$m = \frac{1,430,000 - 271,000}{11 - 1} = \frac{1,159,000}{10} = 115,900.$$

Using the point-slope equation:

We choose $(1, \, 271,000)$ and substitute 1 for x_1, 271,000 for y_1, and 115,900 for m.

$$y - y_1 = m(x - x_1)$$
$$y - 271,000 = 115,900(x - 1)$$
$$y - 271,000 = 115,900x - 115,900$$
$$y = 115,900x + 155,100, \text{ or}$$
$$S = 115,900x + 155,100$$

Using the slope-intercept equation:

We choose $(1, \, 271,000)$ and substitute 1 for x, 271,000 for y, and 115,900 for m in $y = mx + b$.

$$y = mx + b$$
$$271,000 = 115,900 \cdot 1 + b$$
$$271,000 = 115,900 + b$$
$$155,100 = b$$

Finally, we use the equation $y = mx + b$ and substitute 115,900 for m and 155,100 for b.

$$y = 115,900x + 155,100, \text{ or}$$
$$S = 115,900x + 155,100$$

b) In 2005, $x = 2005 - 1990 = 15$. Substitute 15 for x and compute S.

$$S = 115,900(15) + 155,100$$
$$S = 1,738,500 + 155,100$$
$$S = 1,893,600$$

We estimate the average salary in 2005 to be \$1,893,600.

In 2010, $x = 2010 - 1990 = 20$. Substitute 20 for x and compute S.

$$S = 115,900(20) + 155,100$$
$$S = 2,318,000 + 155,100$$
$$S = 2,473,100$$

We estimate the average salary in 2010 to be \$2,473,100.

51. a) We form pairs of the type (t, R) where t is the number of years since 1930 and R is the record. We have two pairs, $(0, 46.8)$ and $(40, 43.8)$. These are two points on the graph of the linear function we are seeking. First we find the slope:

$$m = \frac{43.8 - 46.8}{40 - 0} = \frac{-3}{40} = -0.075$$

Using the slope and the y-intercept, $(0, 46.8)$ we write the equation of the line.

$$R = -0.075t + 46.8$$
$$R(t) = -0.075t + 46.8 \quad \text{Using function notation}$$

b) 2003 is 73 years since 1930, so to predict the record in 2003, we find $R(73)$:

$$R(73) = -0.075(73) + 46.8$$
$$= 41.325$$

The estimated record is 41.325 seconds in 2003.

2006 is 76 years since 1930, so to predict the record in 2006, we find $R(76)$:

$$R(76) = -0.075(76) + 46.8$$
$$= 41.1$$

The estimated record is 41.1 seconds in 2006.

c) Substitute 40 for $R(t)$ and solve for t:

$$40 = -0.075t + 46.8$$
$$-6.8 = -0.075t$$
$$91 \approx t$$

The record will be 40 seconds about 91 years after 1930, or in 2021.

53. a) We form pairs of the type (t, E) where t is the number of years since 1990 and E is the life expectancy. We have two pairs, $(0, 71.8)$ and $(7, 73.6)$. These are two points on the graph of the linear function we are seeking. First we find the slope.

$$m = \frac{73.6 - 71.8}{7 - 0} = \frac{1.8}{7} = \frac{18}{70} = \frac{9}{35}$$

Using the slope and the y-intercept $(0, 71.8)$, we write the equation of the line.

$$E = \frac{9}{35}t + 71.8$$
$$E(t) = \frac{9}{35}t + 71.8 \quad \text{Using function notation}$$

b) 2007 is 17 years since 1990, so we find $E(17)$:

$$E(17) = \frac{9}{35}(17) + 71.8 \approx 72.6$$

We predict that the life expectancy of males will be about 76.2 years in 2007.

55. Discussion and Writing Exercise

57. $2x + 3 > 51$

$$2x > 48 \quad \text{Subtracting 3}$$
$$x > 24 \quad \text{Dividing by 2}$$

The solution set is $\{x | x > 24\}$, or $(24, \infty)$.

59. $2x + 3 \le 51$

$$2x \le 48 \quad \text{Subtracting 3}$$
$$x \le 24 \quad \text{Dividing by 2}$$

The solution set is $\{x | x \le 24\}$, or $(-\infty, 24]$.

61. $|2x + 3| \le 13$

$$-13 \le 2x + 3 \le 13$$
$$-16 \le 2x \le 10 \quad \text{Subtracting 3}$$
$$-8 \le x \le 5 \quad \text{Dividing by 2}$$

The solution set is $\{x | -8 \le x \le 5\}$, or $[-8, 5]$.

63. $|5x - 4| = -8$

Since the absolute value of a number must be nonnegative, the equation has no solution. The solution set is $\emptyset$.

65. The value C of the computer, in dollars, after t months can be modeled by a line that contains the points $(6, 900)$ and $(8, 750)$. We find an equation relating C and t.

$$m = \frac{750 - 900}{8 - 6} = \frac{-150}{2} = -75$$
$$C - 900 = -75(t - 6)$$
$$C - 900 = -75t + 450$$
$$C = -75t + 1350$$

Using function notation we have $C(t) = -75t + 1350$. To find how much the computer cost we find $C(0)$:

$$C(0) = -75 \cdot 0 + 1350 = 1350$$

The computer cost $1350.

Chapter 3
Systems of Equations

1. Graph both lines on the same set of axes.

The solution (point of intersection) seems to be the point $(3, 1)$.

Check:

$x + y = 4$		$x - y = 2$	
$3 + 1$? 4		$3 - 1$? 2	
4	TRUE	2	TRUE

The solution is $(3, 1)$.

Since the system of equations has a solution it is consistent. Since there is exactly one solution, the equations are independent.

3. Graph both lines on the same set of axes.

The solution (point of intersection) seems to be the point $(1, -2)$.

Check:

$2x - y = 4$		$2x + 3y = -4$	
$2 \cdot 1 - (-2)$? 4		$2 \cdot 1 + 3(-2)$? -4	
$2 + 2$		$2 - 6$	
4	TRUE	-4	TRUE

The solution is $(1, -2)$.

Since the system of equations has a solution, it is consistent. Since there is exactly one solution, the equations are independent.

5. Graph both lines on the same set of axes.

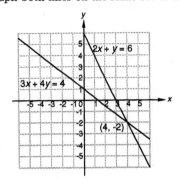

The solution (point of intersection) seems to be the point $(4, -2)$.

Check:

$2x + y = 6$		$3x + 4y = 4$	
$2 \cdot 4 + (-2)$? 6		$3 \cdot 4 + 4(-2)$? 4	
$8 - 2$		$12 - 8$	
6	TRUE	4	TRUE

The solution is $(4, -2)$.

Since the system of equations has a solution, it is consistent. Since there is exactly one solution, the equations are independent.

7. Graph both lines on the same set of axes.

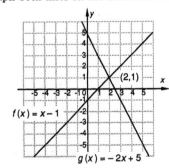

The solution seems to be the point $(2, 1)$.

Check:

$f(x) = x - 1$		$g(x) = -2x + 5$	
1 ? $2 - 1$		1 ? $-2 \cdot 2 + 5$	
1	TRUE	$-4 + 5$	
		1	TRUE

The solution is $(2, 1)$.

Since the system of equations has a solution, it is consistent. Since there is exactly one solution, the equations are independent.

9. Graph both lines on the same set of axes.

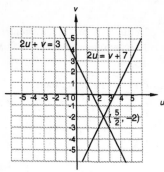

The solution seems to be $\left(\dfrac{5}{2}, -2\right)$.

Check:

$2u + v = 3$	$2u = v + 7$
$2 \cdot \dfrac{5}{2} + (-2) \ ? \ 3$	$2 \cdot \dfrac{5}{2} \ ? \ -2 + 7$
$5 - 2$	$5 \ \big| \ 5 \qquad$ TRUE
$3 \ \big|$ TRUE	

The solution is $\left(\dfrac{5}{2}, -2\right)$.

Since the system of equations has a solution, it is consistent. Since there is exactly one solution, the equations are independent.

11. Graph both lines on the same set of axes.

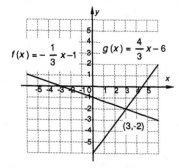

The ordered pair $(3, -2)$ checks in both equations. It is the solution.

Since the system of equations has a solution, it is consistent. Since there is exactly one solution, the equations are independent.

13. Graph both lines on the same set of axes.

The lines are parallel. There is no solution.

Since the system of equations has no solution, it is inconsistent. Since there is no solution, the equations are independent.

15. Graph both lines on the same set of axes.

The graphs are the same. Any solution of one of the equations is also a solution of the other. Each equation has an infinite number of solutions. Thus the system of equations has an infinite number of solutions. Since the system of equations has a solution, it is consistent. Since there are infinitely many solutions, the equations are dependent.

17. Graph both lines on the same set of axes.

The ordered pair $(4, -5)$ checks in both equations. It is the solution.

Since the system of equations has a solution, it is consistent. Since there is exactly one solution, the equations are independent.

19. Graph both lines on the same set of axes.

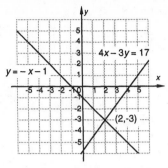

The ordered pair $(2, -3)$ checks in both equations. It is the solution.

Since the system of equations has a solution, it is consistent. Since there is exactly one solution, the equations are independent.

21. Since the system of equations has a solution, it is consistent. Since there is exactly one solution, the equations are independent. The graph of the system consists of a vertical line and a horizontal line, each passing through $(3, 3)$. Thus, system **F** corresponds to this graph.

23. Since the system of equations has a solution, it is consistent. Since there are infinitely many solutions, the equations are dependent. The equations in system B are equivalent, so their graphs are the same. In addition the graph corresponds to the one shown, so system **B** corresponds to this graph.

25. Since the system of equations has no solution, it is inconsistent. Since there is no solution, the equations are independent. The equations in system **D** have the same slope and different y-intercepts and have the graphs shown, so this system corresponds to the given graph.

27. Discussion and Writing Exercise

29. $3x + 4 = x - 2$

$2x + 4 = -2$ Adding $-x$ on both sides

$2x = -6$ Adding -4 on both sides

$x = -3$ Multiplying by $\frac{1}{2}$ on both sides

The solution is -3.

31. $4x - 5x = 8x - 9 + 11x$

$-x = 19x - 9$ Collecting like terms

$-20x = -9$ Adding $-19x$ on both sides

$x = \frac{9}{20}$ Multiplying by $-\frac{1}{20}$ on both sides

The solution is $\frac{9}{20}$.

33. Graph these equations, solving each equation for y first, if necessary. We get $y = \dfrac{13.78 - 2.18x}{7.81}$ and $y = \dfrac{5.79x - 8.94}{3.45}$. Using the INTERSECT feature, we find that the point of intersection is $(2.23, 1.14)$.

35. Graph both lines on the same set of axes.

The solutions appear to be $(-5, 5)$ and $(3, 3)$.

Check:

For $(-5, 5)$:

$y = \lvert x \rvert$			$x + 4y = 15$	
5 ? $\lvert -5 \rvert$			$-5 + 4 \cdot 5$? 15	
	5	TRUE	$-5 + 20$	
			15	TRUE

For $(3, 3)$:

$y = \lvert x \rvert$			$x + 4y = 15$	
3 ? $\lvert 3 \rvert$			$3 + 4 \cdot 3$? 15	
	3	TRUE	$3 + 12$	
			15	TRUE

Both pairs check. The solutions are $(-5, 5)$ and $(3, 3)$.

Exercise Set 3.2

1. $y = 5 - 4x$,   (1)

$2x - 3y = 13$ (2)

We substitute $5 - 4x$ for y in the second equation and solve for x.

$2x - 3y = 13$ (2)

$2x - 3(5 - 4x) = 13$ Substituting

$2x - 15 + 12x = 13$

$14x - 15 = 13$

$14x = 28$

$x = 2$

Next we substitute 2 for x in either equation of the original system and solve for y.

$y = 5 - 4x$ (1)

$y = 5 - 4 \cdot 2$ Substituting

$y = 5 - 8$

$y = -3$

We check the ordered pair $(2, -3)$.

$y = 5 - 4x$		
-3 ? $5 - 4 \cdot 2$		
	$5 - 8$	
-3	-3	TRUE

$$2x - 3y = 13$$

$$\begin{array}{c|c} 2 \cdot 2 - 3(-3) \ ? \ 13 & \\ 4 + 9 & \\ 13 & 13 \quad \text{TRUE} \end{array}$$

Since $(2, -3)$ checks, it is the solution.

3. $2y + x = 9$,   (1)

  $x = 3y - 3$ (2)

We substitute $3y - 3$ for x in the first equation and solve for y.

$$2y + x = 9 \qquad (1)$$

$$2y + (3y - 3) = 9 \qquad \text{Substituting}$$

$$5y - 3 = 9$$

$$5y = 12$$

$$y = \frac{12}{5}$$

Next we substitute $\frac{12}{5}$ for y in either equation of the original system and solve for x.

$$x = 3y - 3 \qquad\qquad\qquad (2)$$

$$x = 3 \cdot \frac{12}{5} - 3 = \frac{36}{5} - \frac{15}{5} = \frac{21}{5}$$

We check the ordered pair $\left(\frac{21}{5}, \frac{12}{5}\right)$.

$$2y + x = 9$$

$$\begin{array}{c|c} 2 \cdot \dfrac{12}{5} + \dfrac{21}{15} \ ? \ 9 & \\[2mm] \dfrac{24}{5} + \dfrac{21}{5} & \\[2mm] \dfrac{45}{5} & \\[2mm] 9 & 9 \quad \text{TRUE} \end{array}$$

$$x = 3y - 3$$

$$\begin{array}{c|c} \dfrac{21}{5} \ ? \ 3 \cdot \dfrac{12}{5} - 3 & \\[2mm] & \dfrac{36}{5} - \dfrac{15}{5} \\[2mm] \dfrac{21}{5} & \dfrac{21}{5} \qquad \text{TRUE} \end{array}$$

Since $\left(\dfrac{21}{5}, \dfrac{12}{5}\right)$ checks, it is the solution.

5. $3s - 4t = 14$,   (1)

  $5s + t = 8$ (2)

We solve the second equation for t.

$$5s + t = 8 \qquad (2)$$

$$t = 8 - 5s \qquad (3)$$

We substitute $8 - 5s$ for t in the first equation and solve for s.

$$3s - 4t = 14 \qquad (1)$$

$$3s - 4(8 - 5s) = 14 \qquad \text{Substituting}$$

$$3s - 32 + 20s = 14$$

$$23s - 32 = 14$$

$$23s = 46$$

$$s = 2$$

Next we substitute 2 for s in Equation (1), (2), or (3). It is easiest to use Equation (3) since it is already solved for t.

$$t = 8 - 5 \cdot 2 = 8 - 10 = -2$$

We check the ordered pair $(2, -2)$.

$$3s - 4t = 14$$

$$\begin{array}{c|c} 3 \cdot 2 - 4(-2) \ ? \ 14 & \\ 6 + 8 & \\ 14 & 14 \quad \text{TRUE} \end{array}$$

$$5s + t = 8$$

$$\begin{array}{c|c} 5 \cdot 2 + (-2) \ ? \ 8 & \\ 10 - 2 & \\ 8 & 8 \quad \text{TRUE} \end{array}$$

Since $(2, -2)$ checks, it is the solution.

7. $9x - 2y = -6$,   (1)

  $7x + 8 = y$ (2)

We substitute $7x + 8$ for y in the first equation and solve for x.

$$9x - 2y = -6 \qquad (1)$$

$$9x - 2(7x + 8) = -6 \qquad \text{Substituting}$$

$$9x - 14x - 16 = -6$$

$$-5x - 16 = -6$$

$$-5x = 10$$

$$x = -2$$

Next we substitute -2 for x in either equation of the original system and solve for y.

$$7x + 8 = y \qquad (2)$$

$$7(-2) + 8 = y$$

$$-14 + 8 = y$$

$$-6 = y$$

We check the ordered pair $(-2, -6)$.

$$9x - 2y = -6$$

$$\begin{array}{c|c} 9(-2) - 2(-6) \ ? \ -6 & \\ -18 + 12 & \\ -6 & \qquad \text{TRUE} \end{array}$$

$$7x + 8 = y$$

$$\begin{array}{c|c} 7(-2) + 8 \ ? \ -6 & \\ -14 + 8 & \\ -6 & \qquad \text{TRUE} \end{array}$$

Since $(-2, -6)$ checks, it is the solution.

9. $-5s + t = 11,$ (1)

$4s + 12t = 4$ (2)

We solve the first equation for t.

$-5s + t = 11$ (1)

$t = 5s + 11$ (3)

We substitute $5s + 11$ for t in the second equation and solve for s.

$4s + 12t = 4$ (2)

$4s + 12(5s + 11) = 4$

$4s + 60s + 132 = 4$

$64s + 132 = 4$

$64s = -128$

$s = -2$

Next we substitute -2 for s in Equation (3).

$t = 5s + 11 = 5(-2) + 11 = -10 + 11 = 1$

We check the ordered pair $(-2, 1)$.

$$\begin{array}{c|c} -5s + t = 11 & \\ \hline -5(-2) + 1 \ ? \ 11 & \\ 10 + 1 & \\ 11 & 11 \quad \text{TRUE} \end{array}$$

$$\begin{array}{c|c} 4s + 12t = 4 & \\ \hline 4(-2) + 12 \cdot 1 \ ? \ 4 & \\ -8 + 12 & \\ 4 & 4 \quad \text{TRUE} \end{array}$$

Since $(-2, 1)$ checks, it is the solution.

11. $2x + 2y = 2,$ (1)

$3x - y = 1$ (2)

We solve the second equation for y.

$3x - y = 1$ (2)

$-y = -3x + 1$

$y = 3x - 1$ (3)

We substitute $3x - 1$ for y in the first equation and solve for x.

$2x + 2y = 2$ (1)

$2x + 2(3x - 1) = 2$

$2x + 6x - 2 = 2$

$8x - 2 = 2$

$8x = 4$

$x = \dfrac{1}{2}$

Next we substitute $\dfrac{1}{2}$ for x in Equation (3).

$y = 3x - 1 = 3 \cdot \dfrac{1}{2} - 1 = \dfrac{3}{2} - 1 = \dfrac{1}{2}$

The ordered pair $\left(\dfrac{1}{2}, \dfrac{1}{2}\right)$ checks in both equations. It is the solution.

13. $3a - b = 7,$ (1)

$2a + 2b = 5$ (2)

We solve the first equation for b.

$3a - b = 7$ (1)

$-b = -3a + 7$

$b = 3a - 7$ (3)

We substitute $3a - 7$ for b in the second equation and solve for a.

$2a + 2b = 5$ (2)

$2a + 2(3a - 7) = 5$

$2a + 6a - 14 = 5$

$8a - 14 = 5$

$8a = 19$

$a = \dfrac{19}{8}$

We substitute $\dfrac{19}{8}$ for a in Equation (3).

$b = 3a - 7 = 3 \cdot \dfrac{19}{8} - 7 = \dfrac{57}{8} - \dfrac{56}{8} = \dfrac{1}{8}$

The ordered pair $\left(\dfrac{19}{8}, \dfrac{1}{8}\right)$ checks in both equations. It is the solution.

15. $2x - 3 = y$ (1)

$y - 2x = 1,$ (2)

We substitute $2x - 3$ for y in the second equation and solve for x.

$y - 2x = 1$ (2)

$2x - 3 - 2x = 1$ Substituting

$-3 = 1$ Collecting like terms

We have a false equation. Therefore, there is no solution.

17. _Familiarize._ Refer to the drawing in the text. Let $l =$ the length of the court and $w =$ the width. Recall that the perimeter P of a rectangle with length l and width w is given by $P = 2l + 2w$.

Translate.

$$\underbrace{\text{The perimeter}}_{2l + 2w} \ \text{is} \ \underbrace{120 \text{ ft.}}_{}$$

$$2l + 2w \quad = \quad 120$$

$$\underbrace{\text{The length}}_{l} \ \text{is twice} \ \underbrace{\text{the width.}}_{w}$$

$$l \quad = \quad 2 \cdot \quad w$$

We have system of equations.

$2l + 2w = 120,$ (1)

$l = 2w$ (2)

Solve. We substitute $2w$ for l in Equation (1) and solve for w.

$2l + 2w = 120$

$2 \cdot 2w + 2w = 120$

$4w + 2w = 120$

$6w = 120$

$w = 20$

Now substitute 20 for w in Equation (2) and find l.

$$l = 2w = 2 \cdot 20 = 40$$

Check. If the length is 40 ft and the width is 20 ft, then the perimeter is $2 \cdot 40 + 2 \cdot 20$, or 120 ft. Also, the length is twice the width. The answer checks.

State. The length of the court is 40 ft, and the width is 20 ft.

19. **Familiarize**. Using the drawing in the text, we let x and y represent the measures of the angles.

Translate.

We have a system of equations.

$$x + y = 180, \quad (1)$$
$$x = 3y - 12 \quad (2)$$

Solve. Substitute $3y - 12$ for x in Equation (1) and solve for y.

$$x + y = 180$$
$$(3y - 12) + y = 180$$
$$4y - 12 = 180$$
$$4y = 192$$
$$y = 48$$

Now substitute 48 for y in Equation (2) and find x.

$$x = 3y - 12 = 3 \cdot 48 - 12 = 132$$

Check. The sum of the measures is $48° + 132°$, or $180°$. Also, $132°$ is $12°$ less than three times $48°$. The answer checks.

State. The measures of the angles are $48°$ and $132°$.

21. **Familiarize**. Let x = number of games won and y = number of games tied. The total points earned in x wins is $2x$; the total points earned in y ties is $1 \cdot y$, or y.

Translate.

We have a system of equations:

$$2x + y = 60,$$
$$x = 9 + y$$

Solve. We solve the system of equations. We use substitution.

$$2(9 + y) + y = 60 \quad \text{Substituting } 9+y \text{ for } x \text{ in (1)}$$
$$18 + 2y + y = 60$$
$$18 + 3y = 60$$
$$3y = 42$$
$$y = 14$$

$$x = 9 + 14 \quad \text{Substituting 14 for } y \text{ in (2)}$$
$$x = 23$$

Check. The number of wins, 23, is 9 more than the number of ties, 14.

Points from wins: $23 \times 2 = 46$

Points from ties: $14 \times 1 = \underline{14}$

                Total   60

The numbers check.

State. The team had 23 wins and 14 ties.

23. Discussion and Writing Exercise

25. $y = 1.3x - 7$

The equation is in slope-intercept form, $y = mx + b$. The slope is 1.3.

27. $A = \dfrac{pq}{7}$

$7A = pq \quad$ Multiplying by 7

$\dfrac{7A}{q} = p \quad$ Dividing by q

29. $-4x + 5(x - 7) = 8x - 6(x + 2)$

$-4x + 5x - 35 = 8x - 6x - 12 \quad$ Removing parentheses

$\quad\quad x - 35 = 2x - 12 \quad\quad$ Collecting like terms

$\quad\quad\quad -35 = x - 12 \quad\quad$ Subtracting x

$\quad\quad\quad -23 = x \quad\quad\quad$ Adding 12

The solution is -23.

31. $2 = m + b, \quad (1) \quad$ Substituting $(1, 2)$

$\quad 4 = -3m + b \quad (2) \quad$ Substituting $(-3, 4)$

$\quad\quad 2 = m + b \quad (1)$

$\quad\underline{-4 = 3m - b} \quad$ Multiplying (2) by -1

$\quad -2 = 4m$

$\quad -\dfrac{1}{2} = m$

Substitute $-\dfrac{1}{2}$ for m in (1).

$2 = -\dfrac{1}{2} + b$

$\dfrac{5}{2} = b$

Thus, $m = -\dfrac{1}{2}$ and $b = \dfrac{5}{2}$.

33. *Familiarize*. Let l = the original length, in inches, and w = the original width, in inches. Then $w - 6$ = the width after 6 in. is cut off.

Translate.

$\underbrace{\text{The original perimeter}}_{2l + 2w}$ $\underset{\downarrow}{\text{is}}$ $\underbrace{156 \text{ in}}_{156}$.

$2l + 2w = 156$

$\underbrace{\text{The length}}_{l}$ $\underset{=}{\text{becomes}}$ $\underset{4}{\text{4}}$ $\underset{\cdot}{\text{times}}$ $\underbrace{\text{the new width}}_{(w - 6)}$.

$l = 4 \cdot (w - 6)$

We have a system of equations:

$2l + 2w = 156$, (1)
$l = 4 \cdot (w - 6)$ (2)

Solve. Substitute $4(w - 6)$ for l in Equation (1) and solve for w.

$$2l + 2w = 156$$
$$2 \cdot 4(w - 6) + 2w = 156$$
$$8w - 48 + 2w = 156$$
$$10w - 48 = 156$$
$$10w = 204$$
$$w = 20.4$$

Now substitute 20.4 for w in Equation (2) and find l.

$$l = 4 \cdot (w - 6) = 4(20.4 - 6) = 4(14.4) = 57.6$$

Check. The original perimeter is $2(57.6) + 2(20.4)$, or $115.2 + 40.8$, or 156 in. If 6 in. is cut off the width, then the width becomes $20.4 - 6$, or 14.4 in., and the length is 4 times the width, or 57.6 in. The answer checks.

State. The length is 57.6 in., and the width is 20.4 in.

Exercise Set 3.3

1. $x + 3y = 7$ (1)
  $\underline{-x + 4y = 7}$ (2)
  $0 + 7y = 14$ Adding
  $7y = 14$
  $y = 2$

Substitute 2 for y in one of the original equations and solve for x.

$x + 3y = 7$ Equation (1)
$x + 3 \cdot 2 = 7$ Substituting
$x + 6 = 7$
$x = 1$

Check:

$$\begin{array}{c|c}
x + 3y = 7 & -x + 4y = 7 \\ \hline
1 + 3 \cdot 2 \; ? \; 7 & -1 + 4 \cdot 2 \; ? \; 7 \\
1 + 6 & -1 + 8 \\
7 \mid \text{TRUE} & 7 \mid \text{TRUE}
\end{array}$$

Since $(1, 2)$ checks, it is the solution.

3. $9x + 5y = 6$ (1)
  $\underline{2x - 5y = -17}$ (2)
  $11x + 0 = -11$ Adding
  $11x = -11$
  $x = -1$

Substitute -1 for x in one of the original equations and solve for y.

$9x + 5y = 6$ Equation (1)
$9(-1) + 5y = 6$ Substituting
$-9 + 5y = 6$
$5y = 15$
$y = 3$

We obtain $(-1, 3)$. This checks, so it is the solution.

5. $5x + 3y = 19$, (1)
  $2x - 5y = 11$ (2)

We multiply twice to make two terms become additive inverses.

From (1): $25x + 15y = 95$ Multiplying by 5
From (2): $\underline{6x - 15y = 33}$ Multiplying by 3
  $31x + 0 = 128$ Adding
  $31x = 128$
  $x = \dfrac{128}{31}$

Substitute $\dfrac{128}{31}$ for x in one of the original equations and solve for y.

$5x + 3y = 19$ Equation (1)
$5 \cdot \dfrac{128}{31} + 3y = 19$ Substituting
$\dfrac{640}{31} + 3y = \dfrac{589}{31}$
$3y = -\dfrac{51}{31}$
$\dfrac{1}{3} \cdot 3y = \dfrac{1}{3} \cdot \left(-\dfrac{51}{31} \right)$
$y = -\dfrac{17}{31}$

We obtain $\left(\dfrac{128}{31}, -\dfrac{17}{31} \right)$. This checks, so it is the solution.

7. $5r - 3s = 24$, (1)
  $3r + 5s = 28$ (2)

We multiply twice to make two terms become additive inverses.

From (1): $25r - 15s = 120$ Multiplying by 5
From (2): $\underline{9r + 15s = 84}$ Multiplying by 3
  $34r + 0 = 204$ Adding
  $34r = 204$
  $r = 6$

Substitute 6 for r in one of the original equations and solve for s.

$$3r + 5s = 28 \quad \text{Equation (2)}$$
$$3 \cdot 6 + 5s = 28 \quad \text{Substituting}$$
$$18 + 5s = 28$$
$$5s = 10$$
$$s = 2$$

We obtain $(6, 2)$. This checks, so it is the solution.

9. $0.3x - 0.2y = 4,$

$\quad 0.2x + 0.3y = 1$

We first multiply each equation by 10 to clear decimals.

$$3x - 2y = 40 \quad (1)$$
$$2x + 3y = 10 \quad (2)$$

We use the multiplication principle with both equations of the resulting system.

From (1): $9x - 6y = 120$ Multiplying by 3

From (2): $\underline{4x + 6y = 20}$ Multiplying by 2

$\qquad\qquad 13x + \quad 0 = 140$ Adding

$\qquad\qquad\qquad 13x = 140$

$$x = \frac{140}{13}$$

Substitute $\dfrac{140}{13}$ for x in one of the equations in which the decimals were cleared and solve for y.

$$2x + 3y = 10 \qquad \text{Equation (2)}$$
$$2 \cdot \frac{140}{13} + 3y = 10 \qquad \text{Substituting}$$
$$\frac{280}{13} + 3y = \frac{130}{13}$$
$$3y = -\frac{150}{13}$$
$$y = -\frac{50}{13}$$

We obtain $\left(\dfrac{140}{13}, -\dfrac{50}{13}\right)$. This checks, so it is the solution.

11. $\dfrac{1}{2}x + \dfrac{1}{3}y = 4,$

$\quad \dfrac{1}{4}x + \dfrac{1}{3}y = 3$

We first multiply each equation by the LCM of the denominators to clear fractions.

$$3x + 2y = 24 \quad \text{Multiplying by 6}$$
$$3x + 4y = 36 \quad \text{Multiplying by 12}$$

We multiply by -1 on both sides of the first equation and then add.

$-3x - 2y = -24$ Multiplying by -1

$\underline{3x + 4y = \quad 36}$

$\quad 0 + 2y = \quad 12$ Adding

$\qquad\quad 2y = 12$

$\qquad\qquad y = 6$

Substitute 6 for y in one of the equations in which the fractions were cleared and solve for x.

$$3x + 2y = 24$$
$$3x + 2 \cdot 6 = 24 \quad \text{Substituting}$$
$$3x + 12 = 24$$
$$3x = 12$$
$$x = 4$$

We obtain $(4, 6)$. This checks, so it is the solution.

13. $\dfrac{2}{5}x + \dfrac{1}{2}y = 2,$

$\quad \dfrac{1}{2}x - \dfrac{1}{6}y = 3$

We first multiply each equation by the LCM of the denominators to clear fractions.

$$4x + 5y = 20 \quad \text{Multiplying by 10}$$
$$3x - \quad y = 18 \quad \text{Multiplying by 6}$$

We multiply by 5 on both sides of the second equation and then add.

$\quad 4x + \quad 5y = \quad 20$

$\underline{15x - \quad 5y = \quad 90}$ Multiplying by 5

$19x + \quad 0 = 110$ Adding

$\qquad\quad 19x = 110$

$$x = \frac{110}{19}$$

Substitute $\dfrac{110}{19}$ for x in one of the equations in which the fractions were cleared and solve for y.

$$3x - y = 18$$
$$3\left(\frac{110}{19}\right) - y = 18 \qquad \text{Substituting}$$
$$\frac{330}{19} - y = \frac{342}{19}$$
$$-y = \frac{12}{19}$$
$$y = -\frac{12}{19}$$

We obtain $\left(\dfrac{110}{19}, -\dfrac{12}{19}\right)$. This checks, so it is the solution.

15. $2x + 3y = 1,$

$\quad 4x + 6y = 2$

Multiply the first equation by -2 and then add.

$-4x - 6y = -2$

$\underline{4x + 6y = \quad 2}$

$\qquad\quad 0 = \quad 0$ Adding

We have an equation that is true for all numbers x and y. The system is dependent and has an infinite number of solutions.

17. $2x - 4y = 5,$

$2x - 4y = 6$

Multiply the first equation by -1 and then add.

$-2x + 4y = -5$

$\underline{2x - 4y = 6}$

$ 0 = 1$

We have a false equation. The system has no solution.

19. $5x - 9y = 7,$

$7y - 3x = -5$

We first write the second equation in the form $Ax + By = C$.

$5x - 9y = 7 \quad (1)$

$-3x + 7y = -5 \quad (2)$

We use the multiplication principle with both equations and then add.

$15x - 27y = 21 \quad$ Multiplying by 3

$\underline{-15x + 35y = -25} \quad$ Multiplying by 5

$ 0 + 8y = -4 \quad$ Adding

$ 8y = -4$

$ y = -\frac{1}{2}$

Substitute $-\frac{1}{2}$ for y in one of the original equations and solve for x.

$5x - 9y = 7 \quad$ Equation (1)

$5x - 9\left(-\frac{1}{2}\right) = 7 \quad$ Substituting

$5x + \frac{9}{2} = \frac{14}{2}$

$5x = \frac{5}{2}$

$x = \frac{1}{2}$

We obtain $\left(\frac{1}{2}, -\frac{1}{2}\right)$. This checks, so it is the solution.

21. $3(a - b) = 15,$

$4a = b + 1$

We first write each equation in the form $Ax + By = C$.

$3a - 3b = 15 \quad (1)$

$4a - b = 1 \quad (2)$

We multiply by -3 on both sides of the second equation and then add.

$3a - 3b = 15$

$\underline{-12a + 3b = -3} \quad$ Multiplying by -3

$-9a + 0 = 12$

$-9a = 12$

$a = -\frac{12}{9}$

$a = -\frac{4}{3}$

Substitute $-\frac{4}{3}$ for a in either Equation (1) or Equation (2) and solve for b.

$4a - b = 1 \quad$ Equation (2)

$4\left(-\frac{4}{3}\right) - b = 1 \quad$ Substituting

$-\frac{16}{3} - b = \frac{3}{3}$

$-b = \frac{19}{3}$

$b = -\frac{19}{3}$

We obtain $\left(-\frac{4}{3}, -\frac{19}{3}\right)$. This checks, so it is the solution.

23. $x - \frac{1}{10}y = 100,$

$y - \frac{1}{10}x = -100$

We first write the second equation in the form $Ax + By = C$.

$x - \frac{1}{10}y = 100$

$-\frac{1}{10}x + y = -100$

Next we multiply each equation by 10 to clear fractions.

$10x - y = 1000 \quad (1)$

$-x + 10y = -1000 \quad (2) \quad$ Equation (1)

We multiply by 10 on both sides of Equation (1) and then add.

$100x - 10y = 10,000 \quad$ Multiplying by 10

$\underline{-x + 10y = -1000}$

$99x + 0 = 9000$

$99x = 9000$

$x = \frac{9000}{99}$

$x = \frac{1000}{11}$

Substitute $\frac{1000}{11}$ for x in one of the equations in which the fractions were cleared and solve for y.

$10x - y = 1000 \quad$ Equation (1)

$10\left(\frac{1000}{11}\right) - y = 1000 \quad$ Substituting

$\frac{10,000}{11} - y = \frac{11,000}{11}$

$-y = \frac{1000}{11}$

$y = -\frac{1000}{11}$

We obtain $\left(\frac{1000}{11}, -\frac{1000}{11}\right)$. This checks, so it is the solution.

25. $0.05x + 0.25y = 22,$

$0.15x + 0.05y = 24$

We first multiply each equation by 100 to clear decimals.

$5x + 25y = 2200$ (1)

$15x + 5y = 2400$ (2)

We multiply by -5 on both sides of the second equation and add.

$$
\begin{array}{ll}
5x + 25y = 2200 & \\
\underline{-75x - 25y = -12,000} & \text{Multiplying by } -5 \\
-70x + 0 = -9800 & \text{Adding}
\end{array}
$$

$$-70x = -9800$$

$$x = \frac{-9800}{-70}$$

$$x = 140$$

Substitute 140 for x in one of the equations in which the decimals were cleared and solve for y.

$5x + 25y = 2200$ Equation (1)

$5 \cdot 140 + 25y = 2200$ Substituting

$700 + 25y = 2200$

$25y = 1500$

$y = 60$

We obtain $(140, 60)$. This checks, so it is the solution.

27. *Familiarize.* Let l = the length of the field and w = the width, in meters. Recall that the perimeter P of a rectangle with length l and width w is given by $P = 2l + 2w$.

Translate.

We have system of equations.

$2l + 2w = 340,$ (1)

$l = 50 + w$ (2)

Solve. First we subtract w on both sides of Equation (2).

$l = 50 + w$

$l - w = 50$

Now we have

$2l + 2w = 340,$ (1)

$l - w = 50.$ (3)

Multiply Equation (3) by 2 and then add.

$$
\begin{array}{l}
2l + 2w = 340 \\
\underline{2l - 2w = 100} \\
4l \quad\quad = 440
\end{array}
$$

$l = 110$

Now substitute 110 for l in one of the original equations and solve for w.

$l = 50 + w$ (2)

$110 = 50 + w$

$60 = w$

Check. The perimeter is $2 \cdot 110 + 2 \cdot 60$, or $220 + 120$, or 340 m. Also, the length, 110 m, exceeds the width, 60 m, by 50 m. The answer checks.

State. The length is 110 m and the width is 60 m.

29. *Familiarize.* Using the drawing in the text, we let x and y represent the measures of the angles.

Translate.

We have system of equations.

$x + y = 90,$ (1)

$y = 6 + 5x$ (2)

Solve. First we subtract $5x$ on both sides of Equation (2).

$y = 6 + 5x$

$-5x + y = 6$ (3)

Now we have

$x + y = 90,$ (1)

$-5x + y = 6.$ (3)

Multiply Equation (1) by 5 and then add.

$$
\begin{array}{l}
5x + 5y = 450 \\
\underline{-5x + y = 6} \\
6y = 456
\end{array}
$$

$y = 76$

Substitute 76 for y in one of the original equations and solve for x.

$x + y = 90$ (1)

$x + 76 = 90$

$x = 14$

Check. The sum of the measures is $14° + 76°$, or $90°$. Also, $6°$ more than 5 times the measure of the $14°$ angle is $5 \cdot 14° + 6° = 70° + 6° = 76°$, the measure of the other angle. The answer checks.

State. The angles measure $14°$ and $76°$.

31. *Familiarize.* Let c = the number of coach seats and f = the number of first-class seats.

Translate.

The total number of seats is 152.

$$c + f = 152$$

We have system of equations.

$$c + f = 152, \quad (1)$$
$$c = 5 + 6f \quad (2)$$

Solve. First we subtract $6f$ on both sides of Equation (2).

$$c = 5 + 6f$$
$$c - 6f = 5 \quad (3)$$

Now we have

$$c + f = 152, \quad (1)$$
$$c - 6f = 5. \quad (3)$$

Multiply Equation (1) by 6 and then add.

$$6c + 6f = 912$$
$$\underline{c - 6f = 5}$$
$$7c = 917$$
$$c = 131$$

Substitute 131 for c in one of the original equations and solve for f.

$$c + f = 152 \quad (1)$$
$$131 + f = 152$$
$$f = 21$$

Check. The total number of seats is $131 + 21$, or 152. Five more than six times the number of first-class seats is $5 + 6 \cdot 21$, or $5 + 126$, or 131, the number of coach seats. The answer checks.

State. There are 131 coach-class seats and 21 first-class seats.

33. Discussion and Writing Exercise

35. $f(x) = 3x^2 - x + 1$
$f(0) = 3 \cdot 0^2 - 0 + 1 = 0 - 0 + 1 = 1$

37. $f(x) = 3x^2 - x + 1$
$f(1) = 3 \cdot 1^2 - 1 + 1 = 3 - 1 + 1 = 3$

39. $f(x) = 3x^2 - x + 1$
$f(-2) = 3(-2)^2 - (-2) + 1 = 12 + 2 + 1 = 15$

41. $f(x) = 3x^2 - x + 1$
$f(-4) = 3(-4)^2 - (-4) + 1 = 48 + 4 + 1 = 53$

43. Graph these equations, solving each equation for y first, if necessary. We get $y = \dfrac{3.5x - 106.2}{2.1}$ and $y = \dfrac{-4.1x - 106.28}{16.7}$. Using the INTERSECT feature, we find that the point of intersection is $(23.12, -12.04)$.

45. Substitute -5 for x and -1 for y in the first equation.

$$A(-5) - 7(-1) = -3$$
$$-5A + 7 = -3$$
$$-5A = -10$$
$$A = 2$$

Then substitute -5 for x and -1 for y in the second equation.

$$-5 - B(-1) = -1$$
$$-5 + B = -1$$
$$B = 4$$

We have $A = 2$, $B = 4$.

47. $(0, -3)$ and $\left(-\dfrac{3}{2}, 6\right)$ are two solutions of $px - qy = -1$.
Substitute 0 for x and -3 for y.

$$p \cdot 0 - q \cdot (-3) = -1$$
$$3q = -1$$
$$q = -\frac{1}{3}$$

Substitute $-\dfrac{3}{2}$ for x and 6 for y.

$$p \cdot \left(-\frac{3}{2}\right) - q \cdot 6 = -1$$
$$-\frac{3}{2}p - 6q = -1$$

Substitute $-\dfrac{1}{3}$ for q and solve for p.

$$-\frac{3}{2}p - 6 \cdot \left(-\frac{1}{3}\right) = -1$$
$$-\frac{3}{2}p + 2 = -1$$
$$-\frac{3}{2}p = -3$$
$$-\frac{2}{3} \cdot \left(-\frac{3}{2}p\right) = -\frac{2}{3} \cdot (-3)$$
$$p = 2$$

Thus, $p = 2$ and $q = -\dfrac{1}{3}$.

Exercise Set 3.4

1. Familiarize. Let x = the number of less expensive brushes sold and y = the number of more expensive brushes sold.

Translate. We organize the information in a table.

Kind of brush	Less expensive	More expensive	Total
Number sold	x	y	45
Price	$8.50	$9.75	
Amount taken in	$8.50x$	$9.75y$	398.75

The "Number sold" row of the table gives us one equation:

$$x + y = 45$$

The "Amount taken in" row gives us a second equation:

$$8.50x + 9.75y = 398.75$$

We have a system of equations:

$$x + y = 45,$$
$$8.50x + 9.75y = 398.75$$

We can multiply the second equation on both sides by 100 to clear the decimals:

$$x + y = 45, \qquad (1)$$
$$850x + 975y = 39,875 \quad (2)$$

Solve. We solve the system of equations using the elimination method. Begin by multiplying Equation (1) by -850.

$$-850x - 850y = -38,250 \quad \text{Multiplying (1)}$$
$$\underline{850x + 975y = 39,875}$$
$$125y = 1625$$
$$y = 13$$

Substitute 13 for y in (1) and solve for x.

$$x + 13 = 45$$
$$x = 32$$

Check. The number of brushes sold is $32 + 13$, or 45. The amount taken in was $\$8.50(32) + \$9.75(13) = \$272 + \$126.75 = \$398.75$. The answer checks.

State. 32 of the less expensive brushes were sold, and 13 of the more expensive brushes were sold.

3. **Familiarize**. Let $h =$ the number of vials of Humulin Insulin sold and $n =$ the number of vials of Novolin Insulin sold.

Translate. We organize the information in a table.

Brand	Humulin	Novolin	Total
Number sold	h	n	65
Price	$15.75	$12.95	
Amount taken in	$15.75h$	$12.95n$	959.35

The "Number sold" row of the table gives us one equation:

$$h + n = 65$$

The "Amount taken in" row gives us a second equation:

$$15.75h + 12.95n = 959.35$$

We have a system of equations:

$$h + n = 65,$$
$$15.75h + 12.95n = 959.35$$

We can multiply the second equation on both sides by 100 to clear the decimals:

$$h + n = 65, \qquad (1)$$
$$1575h + 1295n = 95,935 \quad (2)$$

Solve. We solve the system of equations using the elimination method.

$$-1295h - 1295n = -84,175 \quad \text{Multiplying (1)}$$
$$\underline{1575h + 1295n = 95,935} \qquad \text{by} -1295$$
$$280h = 11,760$$
$$h = 42$$

Substitute 42 for h in (1) and solve for n.

$$42 + n = 65$$
$$n = 23$$

Check. A total of $42 + 23$, or 65 vials, was sold. The amount collected was $\$15.75(42) + \$12.95(23) = \$661.50 + \$297.85 = \$959.35$. The answer checks.

State. 42 vials of Humulin Insulin and 23 vials of Novolin Insulin were sold.

5. **Familiarize**. Let x and y represent the number of 30-sec and 60-sec commercials played, respectively. We will convert 10 min to seconds:

$$10 \text{ min} = 10 \times 1 \text{ min} = 10 \times 60 \text{ sec} = 600 \text{ sec}.$$

Translate. We organize the information in a table.

Type	30-sec	60-sec	Total
Number	x	y	12
Time	$30x$	$60y$	600

The "Number" row of the table gives us one equation:

$$x + y = 12$$

The "Time" row gives us a second equation:

$$30x + 60y = 600$$

We have a system of equations:

$$x + y = 12, \qquad (1)$$
$$30x + 60y = 600 \quad (2)$$

Solve. We solve the system of equations using the elimination method.

$$-30x - 30y = -360 \quad \text{Multiplying (1) by} -30$$
$$\underline{30x + 60y = 600}$$
$$30y = 240$$
$$y = 8$$

Substitute 8 for y in Equation (1) and solve for x.

$$x + 8 = 12$$
$$x = 4$$

Check. If Rudy plays 4 30-sec and 8 60-sec commercials, then the total number of commercials played is $4 + 8$, or 12. Also, the time for 4 30-sec commercials is $4 \cdot 30$, or 120 sec, and the time for 8 60-sec commercials is $8 \cdot 60$, or 480 sec. Then the total commercial time is $120 + 480$, or 600 sec, or 10 min. The answer checks.

State. Rudy plays 4 30-sec commercials and 8 60-sec commercials.

7. **Familiarize**. Let x and y represent the number of pounds of the 40% and the 10% mixture to be used. The final mixture contains 25% (10 lb), or 0.25(10 lb), or 2.5 lb of peanuts.

Translate. We organize the information in a table.

	40% mixture	10% mixture	Wedding mixture
Number of pounds	x	y	10
Percent of peanuts	40%	10%	25%
Pounds of peanuts	$0.4x$	$0.1y$	2.5

The first row of the table gives us one equation:

$$x + y = 10$$

The last row gives us a second equation:

$$0.4x + 0.1y = 2.5$$

After clearing decimals, we have the problem translated to a system of equations:

$$x + y = 10, \quad (1)$$
$$4x + y = 25 \quad (2)$$

Solve. We solve the system of equations using the elimination method.

$$
\begin{aligned}
-x - y &= -10 \quad \text{Multiplying (1) by } -1 \\
4x + y &= 25 \\
\hline
3x &= 15 \\
x &= 5
\end{aligned}
$$

Now substitute 5 for x in Equation (1) and solve for y.

$$5 + y = 10$$
$$y = 5$$

Check. If 5 lb of each mixture is used, the total wedding mixture is $5 + 5$, or 10 lb. The amount of peanuts in the wedding mixture is $0.4(5) + 0.1(5)$, or $2 + 0.5$, or 2.5 lb. The answer checks.

State. 5 lb of each type of mixture should be used.

9. *Familiarize*. Let $x =$ the number of liters of 25% solution and $y =$ the number of liters of 50% solution to be used. The mixture contains $40\%(10 \text{ L})$, or $0.4(10 \text{ L}) = 4 \text{ L}$ of acid.

Translate. We organize the information in a table.

	25% solution	50% solution	Mixture
Number of liters	x	y	10
Percent of acid	25%	50%	40%
Amount of acid	$0.25x$	$0.5y$	4 L

We get one equation from the "Number of liters" row of the table.

$$x + y = 10$$

The last row of the table yields a second equation.

$$0.25x + 0.5y = 4$$

After clearing decimals, we have the problem translated to a system of equations:

$$x + y = 10, \quad (1)$$
$$25x + 50y = 400 \quad (2)$$

Solve. We use the elimination method to solve the system of equations.

$$
\begin{aligned}
-25x - 25y &= -250 \quad \text{Multiplying (1) by } -25 \\
25x + 50y &= 400 \\
\hline
25y &= 150 \\
y &= 6
\end{aligned}
$$

Substitute 6 for y in (1) and solve for x.

$$x + 6 = 10$$
$$x = 4$$

Check. The total amount of the mixture is $4 \text{ lb} + 6 \text{ lb}$, or 10 lb. The amount of acid in the mixture is $0.25(4 \text{ L}) + 0.5(6 \text{ L}) = 1 \text{ L} + 3 \text{ L} = 4 \text{ L}$. The answer checks.

State. 4 L of the 25% solution and 6 L of the 50% solution should be mixed.

11. *Familiarize*. Let $x =$ the amount of the 6% loan and $y =$ the amount of the 9% loan. Recall that the formula for simple interest is

$$\text{Interest} = \text{Principal} \cdot \text{Rate} \cdot \text{Time}.$$

Translate. We organize the information in a table.

	6% loan	9% loan	Total
Principal	x	y	$12,000
Interest Rate	6%	9%	
Time	1 yr	1 yr	
Interest	$0.06x$	$0.09y$	$855

The "Principal" row of the table gives us one equation:

$$x + y = 12,000$$

The last row of the table yields another equation:

$$0.06x + 0.09y = 855$$

After clearing decimals, we have the problem translated to a system of equations:

$$x + y = 12,000 \quad (1)$$
$$6x + 9y = 85,500 \quad (2)$$

Solve. We use the elimination method to solve the system of equations.

$$
\begin{aligned}
-6x - 6y &= -72,000 \quad \text{Multiplying (1) by } -6 \\
6x + 9y &= 85,500 \\
\hline
3y &= 13,500 \\
y &= 4500
\end{aligned}
$$

Substitute 4500 for y in (1) and solve for x.

$$x + 4500 = 12,000$$
$$x = 7500$$

Check. The loans total $7500 + $4500, or $12,000. The total interest is $0.06(\$7500) + 0.09(\$4500) = \$450 + \$405 = \$855$. The answer checks.

State. The 6% loan was for $7500, and the 9% loan was for $4500.

13. *Familiarize*. From the bar graph we see that whole milk is 4% milk fat, milk for cream cheese is 8% milk fat, and cream is 30% milk fat. Let x = the number of pounds of whole milk and y = the number of pounds of cream to be used. The mixture contains 8%(200 lb), or 0.08(200 lb) = 16 lb of milk fat.

Translate. We organize the information in a table.

	Whole milk	Cream	Mixture
Number of pounds	x	y	200
Percent of milk fat	4%	30%	8%
Amount of milk fat	$0.04x$	$0.3y$	16 lb

We get one equation from the " Number of pounds" row of the table:

$$x + y = 200$$

The last row of the table yields a second equation:

$$0.04x + 0.3y = 16$$

After clearing decimals, we have the problem translated to a system of equations:

$$x + y = 200, \quad (1)$$
$$4x + 30y = 1600 \quad (2)$$

Solve. We use the elimination method to solve the system of equations.

$$\begin{aligned} -4x - 4y &= -800 \qquad \text{Multiplying (1) by } -4 \\ 4x + 30y &= 1600 \\ \hline 26y &= 800 \\ y &= \frac{400}{13}, \text{ or } 30\frac{10}{13} \end{aligned}$$

Substitute $\frac{400}{13}$ for y in (1) and solve for x.

$$x + \frac{400}{13} = 200$$
$$x = \frac{2200}{13}, \text{ or } 169\frac{3}{13}$$

Check. The total amount of the mixture is

$\frac{2200}{13}$ lb + $\frac{400}{13}$ lb = $\frac{2600}{13}$ lb = 200 lb. The amount

of milk fat in the mixture is $0.04\left(\frac{2200}{13} \text{ lb}\right) +$

$0.3\left(\frac{400}{13} \text{ lb}\right) = \frac{88}{13}$ lb + $\frac{120}{13}$ lb = $\frac{208}{13}$ lb = 16 lb.

The answer checks.

State. $169\frac{3}{13}$ lb of whole milk and $30\frac{10}{13}$ lb of cream should be mixed.

15. *Familiarize*. Let x = the number of $5 bills and y = the number of $1 bills. The total value of the $5 bills is $5x$, and the total value of the $1 bills is $1 \cdot y$, or y.

Translate.
The total number of bills is 22.

$$\underbrace{x + y} \qquad \underset{=}{\downarrow} \quad \underset{22}{\downarrow}$$

The total value of the bills is $50.

$$\underbrace{5x + y} \qquad \underset{=}{\downarrow} \quad \underset{50}{\downarrow}$$

We have a system of equations:

$$x + y = 22, \quad (1)$$
$$5x + y = 50 \quad (2)$$

Solve. We use the elimination method.

$$\begin{aligned} -x - y &= -22 \qquad \text{Multiplying (1) by } -1 \\ 5x + y &= 50 \\ \hline 4x &= 28 \\ x &= 7 \end{aligned}$$

$$7 + y = 22 \qquad \text{Substituting 7 for } x \text{ in (1)}$$
$$y = 15$$

Check. Total number of bills: $7 + 15 = 22$

Total value of bills: $\$5 \cdot 7 + \$1 \cdot 15 = \$35 + \$15 = \$50$.

The numbers check.

State. There are 7 $5 bills and 15 $1 bills.

17. *Familiarize*. We first make a drawing.

Slow train			
d miles	75 mph	$(t+2)$ hr	

Fast train			
d miles	125 mph	t hr	

From the drawing we see that the distances are the same. Now complete the chart.

$$d = r \cdot t$$

	Distance	Rate	Time	
Slow train	d	75	$t+2$	$\rightarrow d = 75(t+2)$
Fast train	d	125	t	$\rightarrow d = 125t$

Translate. Using $d = rt$ in each row of the table, we get a system of equations:

$$d = 75(t + 2),$$
$$d = 125t$$

Solve. We solve the system of equations.

$$\begin{aligned} 125t &= 75(t + 2) \qquad \text{Using substitution} \\ 125t &= 75t + 150 \\ 50t &= 150 \\ t &= 3 \end{aligned}$$

Then $d = 125t = 125 \cdot 3 = 375$

Check. At 125 mph, in 3 hr the fast train will travel $125 \cdot 3 = 375$ mi. At 75 mph, in $3 + 2$, or 5 hr the slow train will travel $75 \cdot 5 = 375$ mi. The numbers check.

State. The trains will meet 375 mi from the station.

19. *Familiarize*. We first make a drawing. Let $d =$ the distance and $r =$ the speed of the canoe in still water. Then when the canoe travels downstream its speed is $r + 6$, and its speed upstream is $r - 6$. From the drawing we see that the distances are the same.

Downstream, 6 km/h current

d km, $r + 6$, 4 hr

Upstream, 6 km/h current

d km, $r - 6$, 10 hr

Organize the information in a table.

	Distance	Rate	Time
With current	d	$r+6$	4
Against current	d	$r-6$	10

Translate. Using $d = rt$ in each row of the table, we get a system of equations:

$$d = 4(r+6), \qquad d = 4r + 24,$$
$$\text{or}$$
$$d = 10(r-6) \qquad d = 10r - 60$$

Solve. Solve the system of equations.

$$4r + 24 = 10r - 60 \quad \text{Using substitution}$$
$$24 = 6r - 60$$
$$84 = 6r$$
$$14 = r$$

Check. When $r = 14$, then $r + 6 = 14 + 6 = 20$, and the distance traveled in 4 hr is $4 \cdot 20 = 80$ km. Also, $r - 6 = 14 - 6 = 8$, and the distance traveled in 10 hr is $8 \cdot 10 = 80$ km. The answer checks.

State. The speed of the canoe in still water is 14 km/h.

21. *Familiarize*. We first make a drawing. Let $d =$ the distance and $t =$ the time at 32 mph. At 4 mph faster, the speed is 36 mph.

32 mph t hr d mi

36 mph $\left(t - \dfrac{1}{2}\right)$ hr d mi

From the drawing, we see that the distances are the same. List the information in a table.

| d | $=$ | r | $\cdot$ | t |

	Distance	Rate	Time	
Slower trip	d	32	t	$\rightarrow d = 32t$
Faster trip	d	36	$t - \dfrac{1}{2}$	$\rightarrow d = 36\left(t - \dfrac{1}{2}\right)$

Translate. Using $d = rt$ in each row of the table, we get a system of equations:

$$d = 32t, \qquad (1)$$
$$d = 36\left(t - \frac{1}{2}\right) \quad (2)$$

Solve. We solve the system of equations.

$$32t = 36\left(t - \frac{1}{2}\right) \quad \text{Substituting } 32t \text{ for } d \text{ in (2)}$$
$$32t = 36t - 18$$
$$-4t = -18$$
$$t = \frac{18}{4}, \text{ or } \frac{9}{2}$$

The time at 32 mph is $\dfrac{9}{2}$ hr, and the time at 36 mph is $\dfrac{9}{2} - \dfrac{1}{2}$, or 4 hr.

Check. At 32 mph, in $\dfrac{9}{2}$ hr the salesperson will travel $32 \cdot \dfrac{9}{2}$, or 144 mi. At 36 mph, in 4 hr she will travel $36 \cdot 4$, or 144 mi. Since the distances are the same, the numbers check.

State. The towns are 144 mi apart.

23. *Familiarize*. We first make a drawing. Let $t =$ the time, $d =$ the distance traveled at 190 km/h, and $780 - d =$ the distance traveled at 200 km/h.

190 km/h t hr t hr   200 km/h

$\vdash$————— 780 km —————$\dashv$

We list the information in a table.

| d | $=$ | r | $\cdot$ | t |

	Distance	Rate	Time	
Slower plane	d	190	t	$\rightarrow d = 190t$
Faster plane	$780 - d$	200	t	$\rightarrow 780 - d = 200t$

Translate. Using $d = rt$ in each row of the table, we get a system of equations:

$$d = 190t, \quad (1)$$
$$780 - d = 200t \quad (2)$$

Solve. We solve the system of equations.

$$780 - 190t = 200t \quad \text{Substituting } 190t \text{ for } d \text{ in (2)}$$
$$780 = 390t$$
$$2 = t$$

Check. In 2 hr the slower plane will travel $190 \cdot 2$, or 380 km, and the faster plane will travel $200 \cdot 2$, or 400 km. The sum of the distances is $380 + 400$, or 780 km. The value checks.

State. The planes will meet in 2 hr.

25. *Familiarize*. We first make a drawing. Let $d =$ the distance traveled at 420 km/h and $t =$ the time traveled. Then $1000 - d =$ the distance traveled at 330 km/h.

d km, 420 km/h, t hr $1000 - d$ km, 330 km/h, t hr

|——————— 1000 km ———————|

We list the information in a table.

$$d \; = \; r \; \cdot \; t$$

	Distance	Rate	Time	
Faster airplane	d	420	t	$\rightarrow d = 420t$
Slower airplane	$1000 - d$	330	t	$\rightarrow 1000 - d = 330t$

Translate. Using $d = rt$ in each row of the table, we get a system of equations:

$$d = 420t, \quad (1)$$
$$1000 - d = 330t \quad (2)$$

Solve. We use substitution.

$$1000 - 420t = 330t \quad \text{Substituting } 420t \text{ for } d \text{ in (2)}$$
$$1000 = 750t$$
$$\frac{4}{3} = t$$

Check. If $t = \frac{4}{3}$, then $420 \cdot \frac{4}{3} = 560$, the distance traveled by the faster airplane. Also, $330 \cdot \frac{4}{3} = 440$, the distance traveled by the slower plane. The sum of the distances is $560 + 440$, or 1000 km. The values check.

State. The airplanes will meet after $\frac{4}{3}$ hr, or $1\frac{1}{3}$ hr.

27. **Familiarize.** We make a drawing. Note that the plane's speed traveling toward London is $360 + 50$, or 410 mph, and the speed traveling toward New York City is $360 - 50$, or 310 mph. Also, when the plane is d mi from New York City, it is $3458 - d$ mi from London.

New York City   London
310 mph t hours t hours   410 mph

|——————————— 3458 mi ———————————|

|——— d ———|——— 3458 mi $-d$ ———|

Organize the information in a table.

	Distance	Rate	Time
Toward NYC	d	310	t
Toward London	$3458 - d$	410	t

Translate. Using $d = rt$ in each row of the table, we get a system of equations:

$$d = 310t, \quad (1)$$
$$3458 - d = 410t \quad (2)$$

Solve. We solve the system of equations.

$$3458 - 310t = 410t \quad \text{Using substitution}$$
$$3458 = 720t$$
$$4.8028 \approx t$$

Substitute 4.8028 for t in (1).

$$d \approx 310(4.8028) \approx 1489$$

Check. If the plane is 1489 mi from New York City, it can return to New York City, flying at 310 mph, in $1489/310 \approx 4.8$ hr. If the plane is $3458 - 1489$, or 1969 mi from London, it can fly to London, traveling at 410 mph, in $1969/410 \approx 4.8$ hr. Since the times are the same, the answer checks.

State. The point of no return is about 1489 mi from New York City.

29. Discussion and Writing Exercise

31. $f(x) = 4x - 7$
    $f(0) = 4 \cdot 0 - 7 = 0 - 7 = -7$

33. $f(x) = 4x - 7$
    $f(1) = 4 \cdot 1 - 7 = 4 - 7 = -3$

35. $f(x) = 4x - 7$
    $f(-2) = 4(-2) - 7 = -8 - 7 = -15$

37. $f(x) = 4x - 7$
    $f(-4) = 4(-4) - 7 = -16 - 7 = -23$

39. $f(x) = 4x - 7$
    $f\left(\dfrac{3}{4}\right) = 4 \cdot \dfrac{3}{4} - 7 = 3 - 7 = -4$

41. $f(x) = 4x - 7$
    $f(-3h) = 4(-3h) - 7 = -12h - 7$

43. **Familiarize.** Let $x =$ the amount of the original solution that remains after some of the original solution is drained and replaced with pure antifreeze. Let $y =$ the amount of the original solution that is drained and replaced with pure antifreeze.

Translate. We organize the information in a table. Keep in mind that the table contains information regarding the solution *after* some of the original solution is drained and replaced with pure antifreeze.

	Original Solution	Pure Anti-freeze	New Mixture
Amount of solution	x	y	16 L
Percent of antifreeze	30%	100%	50%
Amount of antifreeze in solution	$0.3x$	$1 \cdot y$, or y	$0.5(16)$, or 8

The "Amount of solution" row gives us one equation:
$x + y = 16$

The last row gives us a second equation:
$0.3x + y = 8$

After clearing the decimal we have the following system of equations:

$$x + y = 16, \quad (1)$$
$$3x + 10y = 80 \quad (2)$$

Solve. We use the elimination method.

$$
\begin{array}{rl}
-3x - 3y = -48 & \text{Multiplying (1) by } -3 \\
\underline{3x + 10y = 80} & \\
7y = 32 & \\
y = \dfrac{32}{7}, \text{ or } 4\dfrac{4}{7} &
\end{array}
$$

Although the problem only asks for the amount of pure antifreeze added, we will also find x in order to check.

$$x + 4\frac{4}{7} = 16 \quad \text{Substituting } 4\frac{4}{7} \text{ for } y \text{ in (1)}$$

$$x = 11\frac{3}{7}$$

Check. Total amount of new mixture: $11\dfrac{3}{7} + 4\dfrac{4}{7} =$

16 L

Amount of antifreeze in new mixture:

$$0.3\left(11\frac{3}{7}\right) + 4\frac{4}{7} = \frac{3}{10} \cdot \frac{80}{7} + \frac{32}{7} = \frac{56}{7} = 8 \text{ L}$$

The numbers check.

State. Michelle should drain $4\dfrac{4}{7}$ L of the original solution and replace it with pure antifreeze.

45. Familiarize. Let x and y represent the number of city miles and highway miles that were driven, respectively. Then in city driving, $\dfrac{x}{18}$ gallons of gasoline are used; in highway driving, $\dfrac{y}{24}$ gallons are used.

Translate. We organize the information in a table.

Type of driving	City	Highway	Total
Number of miles	x	y	465
Gallons of gasoline used	$\dfrac{x}{18}$	$\dfrac{y}{24}$	23

The first row of the table gives us one equation:

$$x + y = 465$$

The second row gives us another equation:

$$\frac{x}{18} + \frac{y}{24} = 23$$

After clearing fractions, we have the following system of equations:

$$x + y = 465, \quad (1)$$
$$24x + 18y = 9936 \quad (2)$$

Solve. We solve the system of equations using the elimination method.

$$
\begin{array}{rl}
-18x - 18y = -8370 & \text{Multiplying (1) by } -18 \\
\underline{24x + 18y = 9936} & \\
6x \phantom{{}+ 18y} = 1566 & \\
x = 261 &
\end{array}
$$

Now substitute 261 for x in Equation (1) and solve for y.

$$261 + y = 465$$
$$y = 204$$

Check. The total mileage is $261 + 204$, or 465. In 216 city miles, $261/18$, or 14.5 gal of gasoline are used; in 204 highway miles, $204/24$, or 8.5 gal are used. Then a total of $14.5 + 8.5$ or 23 gal of gasoline are used. The answer checks.

State. 261 miles were driven in the city, and 204 miles were driven on the highway.

47. Familiarize. Let $x =$ the number of gallons of pure brown and $y =$ the number of gallons of neutral stain that should be added to the original 0.5 gal. Note that a total of 1 gal of stain needs to be added to bring the amount of stain up to 1.5 gal. The original 0.5 gal of stain contains 20%(0.5 gal), or 0.2(0.5 gal) = 0.1 gal of brown stain. The final solution contains 60%(1.5 gal), or 0.6(1.5 gal) = 0.9 gal of brown stain. This is composed of the original 0.1 gal and the x gal that are added.

Translate.

The amount of stain added was 1 gal.

$$x + y = 1$$

The amount of brown stain in the final solution is 0.9 gal.

$$0.1 + x = 0.9$$

We have a system of equations.

$$x + y = 1, \quad (1)$$
$$0.1 + x = 0.9 \quad (2)$$

Carry out. First we solve (2) for x.

$$0.1 + x = 0.9$$
$$x = 0.8$$

Then substitute 0.8 for x in (1) and solve for y.

$$0.8 + y = 1$$
$$y = 0.2$$

Check. Total amount of stain: $0.5 + 0.8 + 0.2 = 1.5$ gal

Total amount of brown stain: $0.1 + 0.8 = 0.9$ gal

Total amount of neutral stain: $0.8(0.5) + 0.2 = 0.4 + 0.2 = 0.6$ gal $= 0.4(1.5$ gal$)$

The answer checks.

State. 0.8 gal of pure brown and 0.2 gal of neutral stain should be added.

Exercise Set 3.5

1. $x + y + z = 2$, (1)
$2x - y + 5z = -5$, (2)
$-x + 2y + 2z = 1$ (3)

Add Equations (1) and (2) to eliminate y:

$\quad x + y + z = 2$ (1)
$\quad \underline{2x - y + 5z = -5}$ (2)
$\quad 3x + 6z = -3$ (4) Adding

Use a different pair of equations and eliminate y:

$\quad 4x - 2y + 10z = -10$ Multiplying (2) by 2
$\quad \underline{-x + 2y + 2z = 1}$ (3)
$\quad 3x + 12z = -9$ (5) Adding

Now solve the system of Equations (4) and (5).

$\quad 3x + 6z = -3$ (4)
$\quad 3x + 12z = -9$ (5)

$\quad -3x - 6z = 3$ Multiplying (4) by -1
$\quad \underline{3x + 12z = -9}$ (5)
$\quad 6z = -6$ Adding
$\quad z = -1$

$\quad 3x + 6(-1) = -3$ Substituting -1 for z in (4)
$\quad 3x - 6 = -3$
$\quad 3x = 3$
$\quad x = 1$

$\quad 1 + y + (-1) = 2$ Substituting 1 for x and -1 for z in (1)
$\quad y = 2$ Simplifying

We obtain $(1, 2, -1)$. This checks, so it is the solution.

3. $2x - y + z = 5$, (1)
$6x + 3y - 2z = 10$, (2)
$x - 2y + 3z = 5$ (3)

We start by eliminating z from two different pairs of equations.

$\quad 4x - 2y + 2z = 10$ Multiplying (1) by 2
$\quad \underline{6x + 3y - 2z = 10}$ (2)
$\quad 10x + y = 20$ (4) Adding

$\quad -6x + 3y - 3z = -15$ Multiplying (1) by -3
$\quad \underline{x - 2y + 3z = 5}$ (3)
$\quad -5x + y = -10$ (5) Adding

Now solve the system of Equations (4) and (5).

$\quad 10x + y = 20$ (4)
$\quad \underline{5x - y = 10}$ Multiplying (5) by -1
$\quad 15x = 30$ Adding
$\quad x = 2$

$\quad 10 \cdot 2 + y = 20$ Substituting 2 for x in (4)
$\quad 20 + y = 20$
$\quad y = 0$

$\quad 2 \cdot 2 - 0 + z = 5$ Substituting 2 for x and 0 for y in (1)
$\quad 4 + z = 5$
$\quad z = 1$

We obtain $(2, 0, 1)$. This checks, so it is the solution.

5. $2x - 3y + z = 5$, (1)
$x + 3y + 8z = 22$, (2)
$3x - y + 2z = 12$ (3)

We start by eliminating y from two different pairs of equations.

$\quad 2x - 3y + z = 5$ (1)
$\quad \underline{x + 3y + 8z = 22}$ (2)
$\quad 3x + 9z = 27$ (4) Adding

$\quad x + 3y + 8z = 22$ (2)
$\quad \underline{9x - 3y + 6z = 36}$ Multiplying (3) by 3
$\quad 10x + 14z = 58$ (5) Adding

Solve the system of Equations (4) and (5).

$\quad 3x + 9z = 27$ (4)
$\quad 10x + 14z = 58$ (5)

$\quad 30x + 90z = 270$ Multiplying (4) by 10
$\quad \underline{-30x - 42z = -174}$ Multiplying (5) by -3
$\quad 48z = 96$ Adding
$\quad z = 2$

$\quad 3x + 9 \cdot 2 = 27$ Substituting 2 for z in (4)
$\quad 3x + 18 = 27$
$\quad 3x = 9$
$\quad x = 3$

$\quad 2 \cdot 3 - 3y + 2 = 5$ Substituting 3 for x and 2 for z in (1)
$\quad -3y + 8 = 5$
$\quad -3y = -3$
$\quad y = 1$

We obtain $(3, 1, 2)$. This checks, so it is the solution.

7. $3a - 2b + 7c = 13$, (1)
$a + 8b - 6c = -47$, (2)
$7a - 9b - 9c = -3$ (3)

We start by eliminating a from two different pairs of equations.

$$3a - 2b + 7c = 13 \quad (1)$$
$$\underline{-3a - 24b + 18c = 141} \quad \text{Multiplying (2) by } -3$$
$$-26b + 25c = 154 \quad (4) \quad \text{Adding}$$

$$-7a - 56b + 42c = 329 \quad \text{Multiplying (2) by } -7$$
$$\underline{7a - 9b - 9c = -3} \quad (3)$$
$$-65b + 33c = 326 \quad (5) \quad \text{Adding}$$

Now solve the system of Equations (4) and (5).

$$-26b + 25c = 154 \quad (4)$$
$$-65b + 33c = 326 \quad (5)$$

$$-130b + 125c = 770 \quad \text{Multiplying (4) by 5}$$
$$\underline{130b - 66c = -652} \quad \text{Multiplying (5) by } -2$$
$$59c = 118$$
$$c = 2$$

$$-26b + 25 \cdot 2 = 154 \quad \text{Substituting 2 for } c \text{ in (4)}$$
$$-26b + 50 = 154$$
$$-26b = 104$$
$$b = -4$$

$$a + 8(-4) - 6(2) = -47 \quad \text{Substituting } -4 \text{ for } b \text{ and}$$
$$ 2 \text{ for } c \text{ in (2)}$$
$$a - 32 - 12 = -47$$
$$a - 44 = -47$$
$$a = -3$$

We obtain $(-3, -4, 2)$. This checks, so it is the solution.

9.
$$2x + 3y + z = 17, \quad (1)$$
$$x - 3y + 2z = -8, \quad (2)$$
$$5x - 2y + 3z = 5 \quad (3)$$

We start by eliminating y from two different pairs of equations.

$$2x + 3y + z = 17 \quad (1)$$
$$\underline{x - 3y + 2z = -8} \quad (2)$$
$$3x + 3z = 9 \quad (4) \quad \text{Adding}$$

$$4x + 6y + 2z = 34 \quad \text{Multiplying (1) by 2}$$
$$\underline{15x - 6y + 9z = 15} \quad \text{Multiplying (3) by 3}$$
$$19x + 11z = 49 \quad (5) \quad \text{Adding}$$

Now solve the system of Equations (4) and (5).

$$3x + 3z = 9 \quad (4)$$
$$19x + 11z = 49 \quad (5)$$

$$33x + 33z = 99 \quad \text{Multiplying (4) by 11}$$
$$\underline{-57x - 33z = -147} \quad \text{Multiplying (5) by } -3$$
$$-24x = -48$$
$$x = 2$$

$$3 \cdot 2 + 3z = 9 \quad \text{Substituting 2 for } x \text{ in (4)}$$
$$6 + 3z = 9$$
$$3z = 3$$
$$z = 1$$

$$2 \cdot 2 + 3y + 1 = 17 \quad \text{Substituting 2 for } x \text{ and 1 for}$$
$$ z \text{ in (1)}$$
$$3y + 5 = 17$$
$$3y = 12$$
$$y = 4$$

We obtain $(2, 4, 1)$. This checks, so it is the solution.

11.
$$2x + y + z = -2, \quad (1)$$
$$2x - y + 3z = 6, \quad (2)$$
$$3x - 5y + 4z = 7 \quad (3)$$

We start by eliminating y from two different pairs of equations.

$$2x + y + z = -2 \quad (1)$$
$$\underline{2x - y + 3z = 6} \quad (2)$$
$$4x + 4z = 4 \quad (4) \quad \text{Adding}$$

$$10x + 5y + 5z = -10 \quad \text{Multiplying (1) by 5}$$
$$\underline{3x - 5y + 4z = 7} \quad (3)$$
$$13x + 9z = -3 \quad (5) \quad \text{Adding}$$

Now solve the system of Equations (4) and (5).

$$4x + 4z = 4 \quad (4)$$
$$13x + 9z = -3 \quad (5)$$

$$36x + 36z = 36 \quad \text{Multiplying (4) by 9}$$
$$\underline{-52x - 36z = 12} \quad \text{Multiplying (5) by } -4$$
$$-16x = 48 \quad \text{Adding}$$
$$x = -3$$

$$4(-3) + 4z = 4 \quad \text{Substituting } -3 \text{ for } x \text{ in (4)}$$
$$-12 + 4z = 4$$
$$4z = 16$$
$$z = 4$$

$$2(-3) + y + 4 = -2 \quad \text{Substituting } -3 \text{ for } x \text{ and 4}$$
$$ \text{for } z \text{ in (1)}$$
$$y - 2 = -2$$
$$y = 0$$

We obtain $(-3, 0, 4)$. This checks, so it is the solution.

13.
$$x - y + z = 4, \quad (1)$$
$$5x + 2y - 3z = 2, \quad (2)$$
$$3x - 7y + 4z = 8 \quad (3)$$

We start by eliminating z from two different pairs of equations.

$$3x - 3y + 3z = 12 \quad \text{Multiplying (1) by 3}$$
$$\underline{5x + 2y - 3z = 2} \quad (2)$$
$$8x - y = 14 \quad (4) \quad \text{Adding}$$

$$-4x + 4y - 4z = -16 \quad \text{Multiplying (1) by } -4$$
$$\underline{3x - 7y + 4z = 8} \quad (3)$$
$$-x - 3y = -8 \quad (5) \quad \text{Adding}$$

Now solve the system of Equations (4) and (5).

$$8x - y = 14 \quad (4)$$
$$-x - 3y = -8 \quad (5)$$

$$
\begin{array}{l}
8x - y = 14 \quad (4) \\
\underline{-8x - 24y = -64} \quad \text{Multiplying (5) by 8} \\
- 25y = -50 \\
y = 2
\end{array}
$$

$$8x - 2 = 14 \quad \text{Substituting 2 for } y \text{ in (4)}$$
$$8x = 16$$
$$x = 2$$

$$2 - 2 + z = 4 \quad \text{Substituting 2 for } x \text{ and 2 for}$$
$$ y \text{ in (1)}$$
$$z = 4$$

We obtain $(2, 2, 4)$. This checks, so it is the solution.

15.
$$4x - y - z = 4, \quad (1)$$
$$2x + y + z = -1, \quad (2)$$
$$6x - 3y - 2z = 3 \quad (3)$$

We start by eliminating y from two different pairs of equations.

$$
\begin{array}{l}
4x - y - z = 4 \quad (1) \\
\underline{2x + y + z = -1} \quad (2) \\
6x = 3 \quad (4) \quad \text{Adding}
\end{array}
$$

At this point we can either continue by eliminating y from a second pair of equations or we can solve (4) for x and substitute that value in a different pair of the original equations to obtain a system of two equations in two variables. We take the second option.

$$6x = 3 \quad (4)$$
$$x = \frac{1}{2}$$

Substitute $\frac{1}{2}$ for x in (1):

$$4\left(\frac{1}{2}\right) - y - z = 4$$
$$2 - y - z = 4$$
$$-y - z = 2 \quad (5)$$

Substitute $\frac{1}{2}$ for x in (3):

$$6\left(\frac{1}{2}\right) - 3y - 2z = 3$$
$$3 - 3y - 2z = 3$$
$$-3y - 2z = 0 \quad (6)$$

Solve the system of Equations (5) and (6).

$$
\begin{array}{l}
2y + 2z = -4 \quad \text{Multiplying (5) by } -2 \\
\underline{-3y - 2z = 0} \quad (6) \\
-y = -4 \\
y = 4
\end{array}
$$

$$-4 - z = 2 \quad \text{Substituting 4 for } y \text{ in (5)}$$
$$-z = 6$$
$$z = -6$$

We obtain $\left(\frac{1}{2}, 4, -6\right)$. This checks, so it is the solution.

17.
$$2r + 3s + 12t = 4, \quad (1)$$
$$4r - 6s + 6t = 1, \quad (2)$$
$$r + s + t = 1 \quad (3)$$

We start by eliminating s from two different pairs of equations.

$$
\begin{array}{l}
4r + 6s + 24t = 8 \quad \text{Multiplying (1) by 2} \\
\underline{4r - 6s + 6t = 1} \quad (2) \\
8r + 30t = 9 \quad (4) \quad \text{Adding}
\end{array}
$$

$$
\begin{array}{l}
4r - 6s + 6t = 1 \quad (2) \\
\underline{6r + 6s + 6t = 6} \quad \text{Multiplying (3) by 6} \\
10r + 12t = 7 \quad (5) \quad \text{Adding}
\end{array}
$$

Solve the system of Equations (4) and (5).

$$
\begin{array}{l}
40r + 150t = 45 \quad \text{Multiplying (4) by 5} \\
\underline{-40r - 48t = -28} \quad \text{Multiplying (5) by } -4 \\
102t = 17 \\
t = \frac{17}{102} \\
t = \frac{1}{6}
\end{array}
$$

$$8r + 30\left(\frac{1}{6}\right) = 9 \quad \text{Substituting } \frac{1}{6} \text{ for } t \text{ in (4)}$$
$$8r + 5 = 9$$
$$8r = 4$$
$$r = \frac{1}{2}$$

$$\frac{1}{2} + s + \frac{1}{6} = 1 \quad \text{Substituting } \frac{1}{2} \text{ for } r \text{ and}$$
$$\phantom{\frac{1}{2} + s + \frac{1}{6} = 1 \quad} \frac{1}{6} \text{ for } t \text{ in (3)}$$
$$s + \frac{2}{3} = 1$$
$$s = \frac{1}{3}$$

We obtain $\left(\frac{1}{2}, \frac{1}{3}, \frac{1}{6}\right)$. This checks, so it is the solution.

19.
$$4a + 9b = 8, \quad (1)$$
$$8a + 6c = -1, \quad (2)$$
$$ 6b + 6c = -1 \quad (3)$$

We will use the elimination method. Note that there is no c in Equation (1). We will use equations (2) and (3) to obtain another equation with no c terms.

$$
\begin{array}{l}
8a + 6c = -1 \quad (2) \\
\underline{ - 6b - 6c = 1} \quad \text{Multiplying (3) by } -1 \\
8a - 6b = 0 \quad (4) \quad \text{Adding}
\end{array}
$$

Now solve the system of Equations (1) and (4).

$$-8a - 18b = -16 \quad \text{Multiplying (1) by } -2$$
$$\underline{8a - 6b = 0}$$
$$-24b = -16$$
$$b = \frac{2}{3}$$

$$8a - 6\left(\frac{2}{3}\right) = 0 \quad \text{Substituting } \frac{2}{3} \text{ for } b \text{ in (4)}$$
$$8a - 4 = 0$$
$$8a = 4$$
$$a = \frac{1}{2}$$

$$8\left(\frac{1}{2}\right) + 6c = -1 \quad \text{Substituting } \frac{1}{2} \text{ for } a \text{ in (2)}$$
$$4 + 6c = -1$$
$$6c = -5$$
$$c = -\frac{5}{6}$$

We obtain $\left(\frac{1}{2}, \frac{2}{3}, -\frac{5}{6}\right)$. This checks, so it is the solution.

21.
$$x + y + z = 57, \quad (1)$$
$$-2x + y = 3, \quad (2)$$
$$x - z = 6 \quad (3)$$

We will use the substitution method. Solve Equations (2) and (3) for y and z, respectively. Then substitute in Equation (1) to solve for x.

$$-2x + y = 3 \qquad \text{Solving (2) for } y$$
$$y = 2x + 3$$
$$x - z = 6 \qquad \text{Solving (3) for } z$$
$$-z = -x + 6$$
$$z = x - 6$$

$$x + (2x + 3) + (x - 6) = 57 \quad \text{Substituting in (1)}$$
$$4x - 3 = 57$$
$$4x = 60$$
$$x = 15$$

To find y, substitute 15 for x in $y = 2x + 3$:
$$y = 2 \cdot 15 + 3 = 33$$

To find z, substitute 15 for x in $z = x - 6$:
$$z = 15 - 6 = 9$$

We obtain $(15, 33, 9)$. This checks, so it is the solution.

23.
$$r + s = 5, \quad (1)$$
$$3s + 2t = -1, \quad (2)$$
$$4r + t = 14 \quad (3)$$

We will use the elimination method. Note that there is no t in Equation (1). We will use Equations (2) and (3) to obtain another equation with no t terms.

$$3s + 2t = -1 \quad (2)$$
$$\underline{-8r - 2t = -28 \quad \text{Multiplying (3) by } -2}$$
$$-8r + 3s = -29 \quad (4) \quad \text{Adding}$$

Now solve the system of Equations (1) and (4).

$$r + s = 5 \quad (1)$$
$$-8r + 3s = -29 \quad (4)$$

$$8r + 8s = 40 \quad \text{Multiplying (1) by 8}$$
$$\underline{-8r + 3s = -29 \quad (4)}$$
$$11s = 11 \quad \text{Adding}$$
$$s = 1$$

$$r + 1 = 5 \quad \text{Substituting 1 for } s \text{ in (1)}$$
$$r = 4$$

$$4 \cdot 4 + t = 14 \quad \text{Substituting 4 for } r \text{ in (3)}$$
$$16 + t = 14$$
$$t = -2$$

We obtain $(4, 1, -2)$. This checks, so it is the solution.

25. Discussion and Writing Exercise

27.
$$F = 3ab$$
$$\frac{F}{3b} = a \quad \text{Dividing by } 3b$$

29.
$$F = \frac{1}{2}t(c - d)$$
$$2F = t(c - d) \quad \text{Multiplying by 2}$$
$$2F = tc - td \quad \text{Removing parentheses}$$
$$2F + td = tc \quad \text{Adding } td$$
$$\frac{2F + td}{t} = c, \text{ or} \quad \text{Dividing by } t$$
$$\frac{2F}{t} + d = c$$

31.
$$Ax - By = c$$
$$Ax = By + c \quad \text{Adding } By$$
$$Ax - c = By \quad \text{Subtracting } c$$
$$\frac{Ax - c}{B} = y \quad \text{Dividing by } B$$

33. $y = -\frac{2}{3}x - \frac{5}{4}$

The equation is in slope-intercept form, $y = mx + b$. The slope is $-\frac{2}{3}$, and the y-intercept is $\left(0, -\frac{5}{4}\right)$.

35.
$$2x - 5y = 10$$
$$-5y = -2x + 10$$
$$-\frac{1}{5}(-5y) = -\frac{1}{5}(-2x + 10)$$
$$y = \frac{2}{5}x - 2$$

The equation is now in slope-intercept form, $y = mx + b$. The slope is $\frac{2}{5}$, and the y-intercept is $(0, -2)$.

37.
$$w + x + y + z = 2, \quad (1)$$
$$w + 2x + 2y + 4z = 1, \quad (3)$$
$$w - x + y + z = 6, \quad (3)$$
$$w - 3x - y + z = 2 \quad (4)$$

Start by eliminating w from three different pairs of equations.

$$\begin{array}{l} w + x + y + z = 2 \quad (1) \\ \underline{-w - 2x - 2y - 4z = -1} \text{ Multiplying (2) by } -1 \\ -x - y - 3z = 1 \quad (5) \quad \text{Adding} \end{array}$$

$$\begin{array}{l} w + x + y + z = 2 \quad (1) \\ \underline{-w + x - y - z = -6} \text{ Multiplying (3) by } -1 \\ 2x = -4 \quad (6) \quad \text{Adding} \end{array}$$

$$\begin{array}{l} w + x + y + z = 2 \quad (1) \\ \underline{-w + 3x + y - z = -2} \text{ Multiplying (4) by } -1 \\ 4x + 2y = 0 \quad (7) \quad \text{Adding} \end{array}$$

We can solve (6) for x:
$$2x = -4$$
$$x = -2$$

Substitute -2 for x in (7):
$$4(-2) + 2y = 0$$
$$-8 + 2y = 0$$
$$2y = 8$$
$$y = 4$$

Substitute -2 for x and 4 for y in (5):
$$-(-2) - 4 - 3z = 1$$
$$-2 - 3z = 1$$
$$-3z = 3$$
$$z = -1$$

Substitute -2 for x, 4 for y, and -1 for z in (1):
$$w - 2 + 4 - 1 = 2$$
$$w + 1 = 2$$
$$w = 1$$

We obtain $(1, -2, 4, -1)$. This checks, so it is the solution.

Exercise Set 3.6

1. Familiarize. Let $x =$ the number of 10-oz cups, $y =$ the number of 14-oz cups, and $z =$ the number of 20-oz cups that Reggie filled. Note that five 96-oz pots contain $5 \cdot 96$ oz, or 480 oz of coffee. Also, x 10-oz cups contain a total of $10x$ oz of coffee and bring in $\$1.09x$, y 14-oz cups contain $14y$ oz and bring in $\$1.29y$, and z 20-oz cups contain $20z$ oz and bring in $\$1.49z$.

Translate.

The total number of coffees served was 34.

$$x + y + z = 34$$

The total amount of coffee served was 480 oz.

$$10x + 14y + 20z = 480$$

The total amount collected was $44.06.

$$1.09x + 1.29y + 1.49z = 44.06$$

Now we have a system of equations.
$$x + y + z = 34,$$
$$10x + 14y + 20z = 480,$$
$$1.09x + 1.29y + 1.49z = 43.46$$

Solve. Solving the system we get $(8, 20, 6)$.

Check. The total number of coffees served was $8 + 20 + 6$, or 34, The total amount of coffee served was $10 \cdot 8 + 14 \cdot 20 + 20 \cdot 6 = 80 + 280 + 120 = 480$ oz. The total amount collected was $\$1.09(8) + \$1.29(20) + \$1.49(6) = \$8.72 + \$25.80 + \$8.94 = \$43.46$. The numbers check.

State. Reggie filled 8 10-oz cups, 20 14-oz cups, and 6 20-oz cups.

3. Familiarize. We first make a drawing.

We let x, y, and z represent the measures of angles A, B, and C, respectively. The measures of the angles of a triangle add up to $180°$.

Translate.

The sum of the measures is $180°$.

$$x + y + z = 180$$

The measure of angle B is three times the measure of angle A.

$$y = 3x$$

The measure of angle C is $20°$ more than the measure of angle A.

$$z = x + 20$$

We now have a system of equations.
$$x + y + z = 180,$$
$$y = 3x,$$
$$z = x + 20$$

Solve. Solving the system we get $(32, 96, 52)$.

Check. The sum of the measures is $32° + 96° + 52°$, or $180°$. Three times the measure of angle A is $3 \cdot 32°$, or $96°$, the measure of angle B. $20°$ more than the measure of angle A is $32° + 20°$, or $52°$, the measure of angle C. The numbers check.

State. The measures of angles A, B, and C are $32°$, $96°$, and $52°$, respectively.

5. *Familiarize*. Let x = the cost of automatic transmission, y = the cost of power door locks, and z = the cost of air conditioning. The prices of the options are added to the basic price of $12,685.

***Translate*.**

We now have a system of equations.

$$12,685 + x + y = 14,070,$$
$$12,685 + z + y = 13,580,$$
$$12,685 + z + x = 13,925$$

***Solve*.** Solving the system we get $(865, 520, 375)$.

***Check*.** The basic model with automatic transmission and power door locks costs $12,685 + $865 + $520, or $14,070. The basic model with AC and power door locks costs $12,685 + $375 + $520, or $13,580. The basic model with AC and automatic transmission costs $12,685 + $375 + $865, or $13,925. The numbers check.

***State*.** Automatic transmission costs $865, power door locks cost $520, and AC costs $375.

7. *Familiarize*. It helps to organize the information in a table. We let x, y, and z represent the weekly productions of the individual machines.

Machines Working	A	B	C
Weekly Production	x	y	z

Machines Working	A & B	B & C	A, B, & C
Weekly Production	3400	4200	5700

***Translate*.** From the table, we obtain three equations.

$x + y + z = 5700$ (All three machines working)

$x + y \quad\;\; = 3400$ (A and B working)

$\quad\; y + z = 4200$ (B and C working)

***Solve*.** Solving the system we get $(1500, 1900, 2300)$.

***Check*.** The sum of the weekly productions of machines A, B & C is $1500 + 1900 + 2300$, or 5700. The sum of the weekly productions of machines A and B is $1500 + 1900$, or 3400. The sum of the weekly productions of machines B and C is $1900 + 2300$, or 4200. The numbers check.

***State*.** In a week Machine A can polish 1500 lenses, Machine B can polish 1900 lenses, and Machine C can polish 2300 lenses.

9. *Familiarize*. Let x = the amount invested in the first fund, y = the amount invested in the second fund, and z = the amount invested in the third fund. Then the earnings from the investments were $0.1x$, $0.06y$, and $0.15z$.

***Translate*.**

Now we have a system of equations.

$$x + y + z = 80,000$$
$$0.1x + 0.06y + 0.15z = 8850,$$
$$0.1x = 750 + 0.15z$$

***Solve*.** Solving the system we get $(45,000,\ 10,000,\ 25,000)$.

***Check*.** The total investment was $45,000 + $10,000 + $25,000, or $80,000. The total earnings were $0.1($45,000) + 0.06(10,000) + 0.15(25,000) = $4500 + $600 + $3750 = 8850. The earnings from the first fund, $4500, were $750 more than the earnings from the second fund, $3750.

***State*.** $45,000 was invested in the first fund, $10,000 in the second fund, and $25,000 in the third fund.

11. *Familiarize*. Let x, y, and z represent the number of fraternal twin births for Asian-Americans, African-Americans, and Caucasians in the U.S., respectively, out of every 15,400 births.

Translate. Out of every 15,400 births, we have the following statistics:

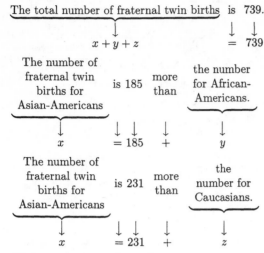

The total number of fraternal twin births is 739.

$$x + y + z = 739$$

The number of fraternal twin births for Asian-Americans is 185 more than the number for African-Americans.

$$x = 185 + y$$

The number of fraternal twin births for Asian-Americans is 231 more than the number for Caucasians.

$$x = 231 + z$$

We have a system of equations.

$$x + y + z = 739,$$
$$x = 185 + y,$$
$$x = 231 + y$$

Solve. Solving the system we get $(385, 200, 154)$.

Check. The total of the numbers is 739. Also 385 is 185 more than 200, and it is 231 more than 154.

State. Out of every 15,400 births, there are 385 births of fraternal twins for Asian-Americans, 200 for African-Americans, and 154 for Caucasians.

13. *Familiarize.* Let r = the number of servings of roast beef, p = the number of baked potatoes, and b = the number of servings of broccoli. Then r servings of roast beef contain $300r$ Calories, $20r$ g of protein, and no vitamin C. In p baked potatoes there are $100p$ Calories, $5p$ g of protein, and $20p$ mg of vitamin C. And b servings of broccoli contain $50b$ Calories, $5b$ g of protein, and $100b$ mg of vitamin C. The patient requires 800 Calories, 55 g of protein, and 220 mg of vitamin C.

Translate. Write equations for the total number of calories, the total amount of protein, and the total amount of vitamin C.

$$300r + 100p + 50b = 800 \quad \text{(Calories)}$$
$$20r + 5p + 5b = 55 \quad \text{(protein)}$$
$$20p + 100b = 220 \quad \text{(vitamin C)}$$

We now have a system of equations.

Solve. Solving the system we get $(2, 1, 2)$.

Check. Two servings of roast beef provide 600 Calories, 40 g of protein, and no vitamin C. One baked potato provides 100 Calories, 5 g of protein, and 20 mg of vitamin C. And 2 servings of broccoli provide 100 Calories, 10 g of protein, and 200 mg of vitamin C. Together, then, they provide 800 Calories, 55 g of protein, and 220 mg of vitamin C. The values check.

State. The dietician should prepare 2 servings of roast beef, 1 baked potato, and 2 servings of broccoli.

15. *Familiarize.* Let x, y, and z represent the number of par-3, par-4, and par-5 holes, respectively. Then a par golfer shoots $3x$ on the par-3 holes, $4x$ on the par-4 holes, and $5x$ on the par-5 holes.

Translate.

The total number of holes is 18.

$$x + y + z = 18$$

A par golfer's score is 70.

$$3x + 4y + 5z = 70$$

The number of par-4 holes is 2 times the number of par-5 holes.

$$y = 2 \cdot z$$

We have a system of equations.

$$x + y + z = 18,$$
$$3x + 4y + 5z = 70,$$
$$y = 2z$$

Solve. Solving the system we get $(6, 8, 4)$.

Check. The numbers add up to 18. A par golfer would shoot $3 \cdot 6 + 4 \cdot 8 + 5 \cdot 4$, or 70. The number of par-4 holes, 8, is twice the number of par-5 holes, 4. The numbers check.

State. There are 6 par-3 holes, 8 par-4 holes, and 4 par-5 holes.

17. *Familiarize.* Let x, y, and z represent the number of 2-point field goals, 3-point field goals, and 1-point foul shots made, respectively. The total number of points scored from each of these types of goals is $2x$, $3y$, and z.

Translate.

The total number of points was 92.

$$2x + 3y + z = 92$$

The total number of baskets was 50.

$$x + y + z = 50$$

The number of 2-pointers was 19 more than the number of foul shots.

$$x = 19 + z$$

Now we have a system of equations.

$$2x + 3y + z = 92,$$
$$x + y + z = 50,$$
$$x = 19 + z$$

Solve. Solving the system we get $(32, 5, 13)$.

Check. The total number of points was $2 \cdot 32 + 3 \cdot 5 + 13 = 64 + 15 + 13 = 92$. The number of baskets was $32 + 5 + 13$, or 50. The number of 2-pointers, 32, was 19 more than the number of foul shots, 13. The numbers check.

State. The Knicks made 32 two-point field goals, 5 three-point field goals, and 13 foul shots.

19. Discussion and Writing Exercise

21. Discussion and Writing Exercise

23. The correspondence is not a function, because an input (in fact, both inputs) corresponds to more than one output.

25. We cannot calculate $f(x)$ when the denominator is 0. We set the denominator equal to 0 and solve for x.

$$x + 7 = 0$$
$$x = -7$$

The domain is $\{x | x \text{ is a real number } and\ x \neq -7\}$, or $(-\infty, -7) \cup (-7, \infty)$.

27. Substitute $-\dfrac{3}{5}$ for m and -7 for b in the slope-intercept equation.

$$y = mx + b$$
$$y = -\frac{3}{5}x - 7$$

29. *Familiarize.* We first make a drawing with additional labels.

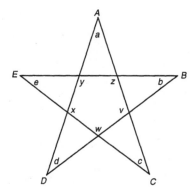

We let a, b, c, d, and e represent the angle measures at the tips of the star. We also label the interior angles of the pentagon v, w, x, y, and z. We recall the following geometric fact:

The sum of the measures of the interior angles of a polygon of n sides is given by $(n-2)180°$.

Using this fact we know:

1. The sum of the angle measures of a triangle is $(3-2)180°$, or $180°$.

2. The sum of the angle measures of a pentagon is $(5-2)180°$, or $3(180°)$.

Translate. Using fact (1) listed above we obtain a system of 5 equations.

$$a + v + d = 180$$
$$b + w + e = 180$$
$$c + x + a = 180$$
$$d + y + b = 180$$
$$e + z + c = 180$$

Solve. Adding we obtain

$$2a + 2b + 2c + 2d + 2e + v + w + x + y + z = 5(180)$$
$$2(a + b + c + d + e) + (v + w + x + y + z) = 5(180)$$

Using fact (2) listed above we substitute $3(180)$ for $(v + w + x + y + z)$ and solve for $(a + b + c + d + e)$.

$$2(a + b + c + d + e) + 3(180) = 5(180)$$
$$2(a + b + c + d + e) = 2(180)$$
$$a + b + c + d + e = 180$$

Check. We should repeat the above calculations.

State. The sum of the angle measures at the tips of the star is $180°$.

31. *Familiarize.* Let $x =$ the one's digit, $y =$ the ten's digit, and $z =$ the hundred's digit. Then the number is represented by $100z + 10y + x$. When the digits are reversed, the resulting number is represented by $100x + 10y + z$.

Translate.

$$\underbrace{\text{The sum of the digits}}_{x + y + z} \quad \underbrace{\text{is}}_{=} \quad \underbrace{14.}_{14}$$

$$\underbrace{\text{The ten's digit}}_{y} \quad \underbrace{\text{is}}_{=} \quad \underbrace{2}_{2} \quad \underbrace{\substack{\text{more} \\ \text{than}}}_{+} \quad \underbrace{\substack{\text{the one's} \\ \text{digit.}}}_{x}$$

$$\underbrace{\text{The number}}_{100z + 10y + x} \quad \underbrace{\substack{\text{is the} \\ \text{same as}}}_{=} \quad \underbrace{\substack{\text{the number with the} \\ \text{digits reversed.}}}_{100x + 10y + z}$$

Now we have a system of equations.

$$x + y + z = 14,$$
$$y = 2 + x,$$
$$100z + 10y + x = 100x + 10y + z$$

Solve. Solving the system we get $(4, 6, 4)$.

Check. If the number is 464, then the sum of the digits is $4+6+4$, or 14. The ten's digit, 6, is 2 more than the one's digit, 4. If the digits are reversed the number is unchanged. The result checks.

State. The number is 464.

Exercise Set 3.7

1. We use alphabetical order to replace x by -3 and y by 3.

Since $-6 < -5$ is true, $(-3, 3)$ is a solution.

3. We use alphabetical order to replace x by 5 and y by 9.

$$\frac{2x - y > -1}{2 \cdot 5 - 9 \ ? \ -1}$$
$$10 - 9$$
$$1 \qquad \text{TRUE}$$

Since $1 > -1$ is true, $(5, 9)$ is a solution.

5. Graph: $y > 2x$

We first graph the line $y = 2x$. We draw the line dashed since the inequality symbol is $>$. To determine which half-plane to shade, test a point not on the line. We try $(1, 1)$ and substitute:

$$\frac{y > 2x}{1 \ ? \ 2 \cdot 1}$$
$$2 \qquad \text{FALSE}$$

Since $1 > 2$ is false, $(1, 1)$ is not a solution, nor are any points in the half-plane containing $(1, 1)$. The points in the opposite half-plane are solutions, so we shade that half-plane and obtain the graph.

7. Graph: $y < x + 1$

First graph the line $y = x + 1$. Draw it dashed since the inequality symbol is $<$. Test the point $(0, 0)$ to determine if it is a solution.

$$\frac{y < x + 1}{0 \ ? \ 0 + 1}$$
$$1 \qquad \text{TRUE}$$

Since $0 < 1$ is true, we shade the half-plane containing $(0, 0)$ and obtain the graph.

9. Graph: $y > x - 2$

First graph the line $y = x - 2$. Draw a dashed line since the inequality symbol is $>$. Test the point $(0, 0)$ to determine if it is a solution.

$$\frac{y > x - 2}{0 \ ? \ 0 - 2}$$
$$-2 \qquad \text{TRUE}$$

Since $0 > -2$ is true, we shade the half-plane containing $(0, 0)$ and obtain the graph.

11. Graph: $x + y < 4$

First graph $x + y = 4$. Draw the line dashed since the inequality symbol is $<$. Test the point $(0, 0)$ to determine if it is a solution.

$$\frac{x + y < 4}{0 + 0 \ ? \ 4}$$
$$0 \qquad \text{TRUE}$$

Since $0 < 4$ is true, we shade the half-plane containing $(0, 0)$ and obtain the graph.

13. Graph: $3x + 4y \le 12$

We first graph $3x + 4y = 12$. Draw the line solid since the inequality symbol is $\le$. Test the point $(0, 0)$ to determine if it is a solution.

$$\frac{3x + 4y \le 12}{3 \cdot 0 + 4 \cdot 0 \ ? \ 12}$$
$$0 \qquad \text{TRUE}$$

Since $0 \le 12$ is true, we shade the half-plane containing $(0, 0)$ and obtain the graph.

15. Graph: $2y - 3x > 6$

We first graph $2y - 3x = 6$. Draw the line dashed since the inequality symbol is $>$. Test the point $(0,0)$ to determine if it is a solution.

$$\frac{2y - 3x > 6}{2 \cdot 0 - 3 \cdot 0 \; ? \; 6}$$
$$0 \quad \Big| \quad \text{FALSE}$$

Since $0 > 6$ is false, we shade the half-plane that does not contain $(0,0)$ and obtain the graph.

17. Graph: $3x - 2 \leq 5x + y$

$$-2 \leq 2x + y$$

We first graph $-2 = 2x + y$. Draw the line solid since the inequality symbol is $\leq$. Test the point $(0,0)$ to determine if it is a solution.

$$\frac{-2 \leq 2x + y}{-2 \; ? \; 2 \cdot 0 + 0}$$
$$\Big| \quad 0 \qquad \text{TRUE}$$

Since $-2 \leq 0$ is true, we shade the half-plane containing $(0,0)$ and obtain the graph.

19. Graph: $x < 5$

We first graph $x = 5$. Draw the line dashed since the inequality symbol is $<$. Test the point $(0,0)$ to determine if it is a solution.

$$\frac{x < 5}{0 \; ? \; 5 \quad \text{TRUE}}$$

Since $0 < 5$ is true, we shade the half-plane containing $(0,0)$ and obtain the graph.

21. Graph: $y > 2$

We first graph $y = 2$. We draw the line dashed since the inequality symbol is $>$. Test the point $(0,0)$ to determine if it is a solution.

$$\frac{y > 2}{0 \; ? \; 2 \quad \text{FALSE}}$$

Since $0 > 2$ is false, we shade the half-plane that does not contain $(0,0)$ and obtain the graph.

23. Graph: $2x + 3y \leq 6$

We first graph $2x + 3y = 6$. We draw the line solid since the inequality symbol is $\leq$. Test the point $(0,0)$ to determine if it is a solution.

$$\frac{2x + 3y \leq 6}{2 \cdot 0 + 3 \cdot 0 \; ? \; 6}$$
$$0 \quad \Big| \quad \text{TRUE}$$

Since $0 \leq 6$ is true, we shade the half-plane containing $(0,0)$ and obtain the graph.

25. The intercepts of the graph of the related equation are $(0, -2)$ and $(3, 0)$, so inequality **F** could be the correct one. Since $(0, 0)$ is in the solution set of this inequality and the half-plane containing $(0, 0)$ is shaded, we know that inequality **F** corresponds to this graph.

27. The intercepts of the graph of the related equation are $(-5, 0)$ and $(0, 3)$, so inequality **B** could be the correct one. Since $(0, 0)$ is in the solution set of this inequality and the half-plane containing $(0, 0)$ is shaded, we know that inequality **B** corresponds to this graph.

29. The intercepts of the graph of the related equation are $(-3, 0)$ and $(0, -3)$, so inequality **C** could be the correct one. Since $(0, 0)$ is not in the solution set of the inequality and the half-plane that does not contain $(0, 0)$ is shaded, we know that inequality **C** corresponds to this graph.

31. Graph: $y \geq x$,

$\qquad\qquad y \leq -x + 2$

We graph the lines $y = x$ and $y = -x + 2$, using solid lines. We indicate the region for each inequality by the arrows at the ends of the lines. Note where the regions overlap, and shade the region of solutions.

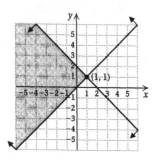

To find the vertex we solve the system of related equations:

$\qquad y = x$,

$\qquad y = -x + 2$

Solving, we obtain the vertex $(1, 1)$.

33. Graph: $y > x$,

$\qquad\qquad y < -x + 1$

We graph the lines $y = x$ and $y = -x + 1$, using dashed lines. We indicate the region for each inequality by arrows at the ends of the lines. Note where the regions overlap, and shade the region of solutions.

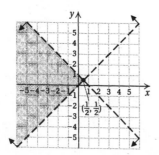

To find the vertex we solve the system of related equations:

$\qquad y = x$,

$\qquad y = -x + 1$

Solving, we obtain the vertex $\left(\dfrac{1}{2}, \dfrac{1}{2}\right)$.

35. Graph: $y \geq -2$,

$\qquad\qquad x \geq 1$

We graph the lines $y = -2$ and $x = 1$, using solid lines. We indicate the region for each inequality by arrows. Shade the region where they overlap.

To find the vertex, we solve the system of related equations:

$\qquad y = -2$,

$\qquad x = 1$

Solving, we obtain the vertex $(1, -2)$.

37. Graph: $x \leq 3$,

$\qquad\qquad y \geq -3x + 2$

Graph the lines $x = 3$ and $y = -3x + 2$, using solid lines. Indicate the region for each inequality by arrows, and shade the region where they overlap.

To find the vertex we solve the system of related equations:

$\qquad x = 3$,

$\qquad y = -3x + 2$

Solving, we obtain the vertex $(3, -7)$.

39. Graph: $y \leq 2x + 1$, $\quad$ (1)

$\qquad\qquad y \geq -2x + 1$, $\quad$ (2)

$\qquad\qquad x \leq 2$ $\qquad\qquad$ (3)

Shade the intersection of the graphs of $y \leq 2x + 1$, $y \geq -2x + 1$, and $x \leq 2$.

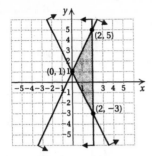

To find the vertices we solve three different systems of equations. From (1) and (2) we obtain the vertex $(0,1)$. From (1) and (3) we obtain the vertex $(2,5)$. From (2) and (3) we obtain the vertex $(2,-3)$.

41. Graph: $x + y \leq 1$,

$x - y \leq 2$

Graph the lines $x + y = 1$ and $x - y = 2$, using solid lines. Indicate the region for each inequality by arrows, and shade the region where they overlap.

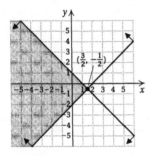

To find the vertex we solve the system of related equations:

$x + y = 1$,

$x - y = 2$

The vertex is $\left(\dfrac{3}{2}, -\dfrac{1}{2}\right)$.

43. Graph: $x + 2y \leq 12$, (1)

$2x + y \leq 12$, (2)

$x \geq 0$, (3)

$y \geq 0$ (4)

Shade the intersection of the graphs of the four inequalities above.

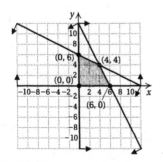

To find the vertices we solve four different systems of equations, as follows:

System of equations	Vertex
From (1) and (2)	$(4,4)$
From (1) and (3)	$(0,6)$
From (2) and (4)	$(6,0)$
From (3) and (4)	$(0,0)$

45. Graph: $8x + 5y \leq 40$, (1)

$x + 2y \leq 8$, (2)

$x \geq 0$, (3)

$y \geq 0$ (4)

Shade the intersection of the graphs of the four inequalities above.

To find the vertices we solve four different systems of equations, as follows:

System of equations	Vertex
From (1) and (2)	$\left(\dfrac{40}{11}, \dfrac{24}{11}\right)$
From (1) and (4)	$(5,0)$
From (2) and (3)	$(0,4)$
From (3) and (4)	$(0,0)$

47. Discussion and Writing Exercise

49. $5(3x - 4) = -2(x + 5)$

$15x - 20 = -2x - 10$

$17x - 20 = -10$

$17x = 10$

$x = \dfrac{10}{17}$

The solution is $\dfrac{10}{17}$.

51. $2(x - 1) + 3(x - 2) - 4(x - 5) = 10$

$2x - 2 + 3x - 6 - 4x + 20 = 10$

$x + 12 = 10$

$x = -2$

The solution is -2.

53. $5x + 7x = -144$

$12x = -144$

$x = -12$

The solution is -12.

55. $f(x) = |2 - x|$

$f(0) = |2 - 0| = |2| = 2$

57. $f(x) = |2 - x|$

$f(1) = |2 - 1| = |1| = 1$

59. $f(x) = |2 - x|$

$f(-2) = |2 - (-2)| = |4| = 4$

61. $f(x) = |2 - x|$

$f(-4) = |2 - (-4)| = |6| = 6$

63. Both the width and the height must be positive, but they must be less than 62 in. in order to be checked as luggage, so we have:

$0 < w \leq 62,$

$0 < h \leq 62$

The girth is represented by $2w + 2h$ and the length is 62 in. In order to meet postal regulations the sum of the girth and the length cannot exceed 108 in., so we have:

$62 + 2w + 2h \leq 108,$ or

$2w + 2h \leq 46,$ or

$w + h \leq 23$

Thus, have a system of inequalities:

$0 < w \leq 62,$

$0 < h \leq 62,$

$w + h \leq 23$

65.

67.

69. Left to the student

Exercise Set 3.8

1. $C(x) = 25x + 270{,}000$ $R(x) = 70x$

a) $P(x) = R(x) - C(x)$

$\qquad = 70x - (25x + 270{,}000)$

$\qquad = 70x - 25x - 270{,}000$

$\qquad = 45x - 270{,}000$

b) To find the break-even point we solve the system

$\qquad R(x) = 70x,$

$\qquad C(x) = 25x + 270{,}000.$

Since both $R(x)$ and $C(x)$ are in dollars and they are equal at the break-even point, we can rewrite the system:

$\qquad d = 70x, \qquad\qquad (1)$

$\qquad d = 25x + 270{,}000 \quad (2)$

We solve using substitution.

$\quad 70x = 25x + 270{,}000$ Substituting $65x$

$\qquad\qquad\qquad\qquad\qquad$ for d in (2)

$\quad 45x = 270{,}000$

$\qquad x = 6000$

Thus, 6000 units must be produced and sold in order to break even.

The amount taken in is $R(6000) = 70 \cdot 6000 = \$420{,}000$. Thus, the break-even point is $(6000, \$420{,}000)$.

3. $C(x) = 10x + 120{,}000$ $R(x) = 60x$

a) $P(x) = R(x) - C(x)$

$\qquad = 60x - (10x + 120{,}000)$

$\qquad = 60x - 10x - 120{,}000$

$\qquad = 50x - 120{,}000$

b) Solve the system

$\qquad R(x) = 60x,$

$\qquad C(x) = 10x + 120{,}000.$

Since both $R(x)$ and $C(x)$ are in dollars and they are equal at the break-even point, we can rewrite the system:

$\qquad d = 60x, \qquad\qquad (1)$

$\qquad d = 10x + 120{,}000 \quad (2)$

We solve using substitution.

$\quad 60x = 10x + 120{,}000$ Substituting $60x$

$\qquad\qquad\qquad\qquad\qquad$ for d in (2)

$\quad 50x = 120{,}000$

$\qquad x = 2400$

Thus, 2400 units must be produced and sold in order to break even.

The amount taken in is $R(2400) = 60 \cdot 2400 = \$144{,}000$. Thus, the break-even point is $(2400, \$144{,}000)$.

5. $C(x) = 20x + 10,000 \qquad R(x) = 100x$

a) $P(x) = R(x) - C(x)$

$\qquad = 100x - (20x + 10,000)$

$\qquad = 100x - 20x - 10,000$

$\qquad = 80x - 10,000$

b) Solve the system

$\qquad R(x) = 100x,$

$\qquad C(x) = 20x + 10,000.$

Since both $R(x)$ and $C(x)$ are in dollars and they are equal at the break-even point, we can rewrite the system:

$\qquad d = 100x, \qquad\qquad (1)$

$\qquad d = 20x + 10,000 \quad (2)$

We solve using substitution.

$\quad 100x = 20x + 10,000$ Substituting $100x$

$\qquad\qquad\qquad\qquad\qquad$ for d in (2)

$\quad 80x = 10,000$

$\qquad x = 125$

Thus, 125 units must be produced and sold in order to break even.

The amount taken in is $R(125) = 100 \cdot 125 = \$12,500$. Thus, the break-even point is $(125, \$12,500)$.

7. $C(x) = 22x + 16,000 \qquad R(x) = 40x$

a) $P(x) = R(x) - C(x)$

$\qquad = 40x - (22x + 16,000)$

$\qquad = 40x - 22x - 16,000$

$\qquad = 18x - 16,000$

b) Solve the system

$\qquad R(x) = 40x,$

$\qquad C(x) = 22x + 16,000.$

Since both $R(x)$ and $C(x)$ are in dollars and they are equal at the break-even point, we can rewrite the system:

$\qquad d = 40x, \qquad\qquad (1)$

$\qquad d = 22x + 16,000 \quad (2)$

We solve using substitution.

$\quad 40x = 22x + 16,000$ Substituting $40x$ for

$\qquad\qquad\qquad\qquad\qquad$ d in (2)

$\quad 18x = 16,000$

$\qquad x \approx 889$ units

Thus, 889 units must be produced and sold in order to break even.

The amount taken in is $R(889) = 40 \cdot 889 = \$35,560$. Thus, the break-even point is $(889, \$35,560)$.

9. $C(x) = 50x + 195,000 \qquad R(x) = 125x$

a) $P(x) = R(x) - C(x)$

$\qquad = 125x - (50x + 195,000)$

$\qquad = 125x - 50x - 195,000$

$\qquad = 75x - 195,000$

b) Solve the system

$\qquad R(x) = 125x,$

$\qquad C(x) = 50x + 195,000.$

Since $R(x) = C(x)$ at the break-even point, we can rewrite the system:

$\qquad R(x) = 125x, \qquad\qquad (1)$

$\qquad R(x) = 50x + 195,000 \quad (2)$

We solve using substitution.

$\quad 125x = 50x + 195,000$ Substituting $125x$

$\qquad\qquad\qquad\qquad\qquad$ for $R(x)$ in (2)

$\quad 75x = 195,000$

$\qquad x = 2600$

To break even 2600 units must be produced and sold.

The amount taken in is $R(2600) = 125 \cdot 2600 = \$325,000$. Thus, the break-even point is $(2600, \$325,000)$.

11. a) $C(x) = $ Fixed costs + Variable costs

$\qquad C(x) = 22,500 + 40x,$

where x is the number of lamps produced.

b) Each lamp sells for \$85. The total revenue is 85 times the number of lamps sold. We assume that all lamps produced are sold.

$\qquad R(x) = 85x$

c) $P(x) = R(x) - C(x)$

$\qquad P(x) = 85x - (22,500 + 40x)$

$\qquad\qquad = 85x - 22,500 - 40x$

$\qquad\qquad = 45x - 22,500$

d) $P(3000) = 45(3000) - 22,500$

$\qquad\qquad = 135,000 - 22,500$

$\qquad\qquad = 112,500$

The company will realize a profit of \$112,500 when 3000 lamps are produced and sold.

$\qquad P(400) = 45(400) - 22,500$

$\qquad\qquad = 18,000 - 22,500$

$\qquad\qquad = -4500$

The company will realize a \$4500 loss when 400 lamps are produced and sold.

e) Solve the system

$\qquad R(x) = 85x,$

$\qquad C(x) = 22,500 + 40x.$

Since both $R(x)$ and $C(x)$ are in dollars and they are equal at the break-even point, we can rewrite the system:

$\qquad d = 85x, \qquad\qquad (1)$

$\qquad d = 22,500 + 40x \quad (2)$

We solve using substitution.

$85x = 22,500 + 40x$ Substituting $85x$ for d
                                                    in (2)

$45x = 22,500$

$x = 500$

The firm will break even if it produces and sells 500 lamps and takes in a total of $R(500) = 85 \cdot 500 = \$42,500$ in revenue. Thus, the break-even point is (500, $42,500).

13. a) $C(x) =$ Fixed costs + Variable costs

$C(x) = 16,404 + 6x$,

where x is the number of caps produced, in dozens.

b) Each dozen caps sell for \$18. The total revenue is 18 times the number of caps sold, in dozens. We assume that all caps produced are sold.

$R(x) = 18x$

c) $P(x) = R(x) - C(x)$

$P(x) = 18x - (16,404 + 6x)$

$\quad\;\; = 18x - 16,404 - 6x$

$\quad\;\; = 12x - 16,404$

d) $P(3000) = 12(3000) - 16,404$

$\qquad\qquad = 36,000 - 16,404$

$\qquad\qquad = 19,596$

The company will realize a profit of \$19,596 when 3000 dozen caps are produced and sold.

$P(1000) = 12(1000) - 16,404$

$\qquad\qquad = 12,000 - 16,404$

$\qquad\qquad = -4404$

The company will realize a \$4404 loss when 1000 dozen caps are produced and sold.

e) Solve the system

$R(x) = 18x$,

$C(x) = 16,404 + 6x$.

Since both $R(x)$ and $C(x)$ are in dollars and they are equal at the break-even point, we can rewrite the system:

$d = 18x$,   (1)

$d = 16,404 + 6x$ (2)

We solve using substitution.

$18x = 16,404 + 6x$ Substituting $18x$ for d
                                                    in (2)

$12x = 16,404$

$x = 1367$

The firm will break even if it produces and sells 1367 dozen caps and takes in a total of $R(1367) = 18 \cdot 1367 = \$24,606$ in revenue. Thus, the break-even point is (1367,\$24,606).

15. $D(p) = 1000 - 10p$,

$S(p) = 230 + p$

Since both demand and supply are quantities, the system can be rewritten:

$q = 1000 - 10p$,   (1)

$q = 230 + p$ (2)

Substitute $1000 - 10p$ for q in (2) and solve.

$1000 - 10p = 230 + p$

$770 = 11p$

$70 = p$

The equilibrium price is \$70 per unit. To find the equilibrium quantity we substitute \$70 into either $D(p)$ or $S(p)$.

$D(70) = 1000 - 10 \cdot 70 = 1000 - 700 = 300$

The equilibrium quantity is 300 units.

The equilibrium point is ($70, 300).

17. $D(p) = 760 - 13p$,

$S(p) = 430 + 2p$

Rewrite the system:

$q = 760 - 13p$,   (1)

$q = 430 + 2p$ (2)

Substitute $760 - 13p$ for q in (2) and solve.

$760 - 13p = 430 + 2p$

$330 = 15p$

$22 = p$

The equilibrium price is \$22 per unit.

To find the equilibrium quantity we substitute \$22 into either $D(p)$ or $S(p)$.

$S(22) = 430 + 2(22) = 430 + 44 = 474$

The equilibrium quantity is 474 units.

The equilibrium point is ($22, 474).

19. $D(p) = 7500 - 25p$,

$S(p) = 6000 + 5p$

Rewrite the system:

$q = 7500 - 25p$,   (1)

$q = 6000 + 5p$ (2)

Substitute $7500 - 25p$ for q in (2) and solve.

$7500 - 25p = 6000 + 5p$

$1500 = 30p$

$50 = p$

The equilibrium price is \$50 per unit.

To find the equilibrium quantity we substitute \$50 into either $D(p)$ or $S(p)$.

$D(50) = 7500 - 25(50) = 7500 - 1250 = 6250$

The equilibrium quantity is 6250 units.

The equilibrium point is ($50, 6250).

21. $D(p) = 1600 - 53p,$

$\quad S(p) = 320 + 75p$

Rewrite the system:

$\quad q = 1600 - 53p, \quad (1)$

$\quad q = 320 + 75p \quad\;\; (2)$

Substitute $1600 - 53p$ for q in (2) and solve.

$1600 - 53p = 320 + 75p$

$\qquad 1280 = 128p$

$\qquad\; 10 = p$

The equilibrium price is \$10 per unit.

To find the equilibrium quantity we substitute \$10 into either $D(p)$ or $S(p)$.

$S(10) = 320 + 75(10) = 320 + 750 = 1070$

The equilibrium quantity is 1070 units.

The equilibrium point is $(\$10, 1070)$.

23. Discussion and Writing Exercise

25. $5y - 3x = 8$

$\qquad 5y = 3x + 8$

$\qquad \dfrac{1}{5} \cdot 5y = \dfrac{1}{5}(3x + 8)$

$\qquad\qquad y = \dfrac{3}{5}x + \dfrac{8}{5}$

The equation is now in slope-intercept form, $y = mx + b$

The slope is $\dfrac{3}{5}$, and the y-intercept is $\left(0, \dfrac{8}{5}\right)$.

27. $\qquad 2y = 3.4x + 98$

$\qquad \dfrac{1}{2} \cdot 2y = \dfrac{1}{2}(3.4x + 98)$

$\qquad\qquad y = 1.7x + 49$

The equation is now in slope-intercept form, $y = mx + b$.

The slope is 1.7, and the y-intercept is $(0, 49)$.

Chapter 4

Polynomials and Polynomial Functions

Exercise Set 4.1

---

1. $-9x^4 - x^3 + 7x^2 + 6x - 8$

Term	$-9x^4$	$-x^3$	$7x^2$	$6x$	-8
Degree	4	3	2	1	0
Degree of polynomial	4				
Leading term	$-9x^4$				
Leading coefficient	-9				

3. $t^3 + 4t^7 + s^2t^4 - 2$

Term	t^3	$4t^7$	s^2t^4	-2
Degree	3	7	6	0
Degree of polynomial	7			
Leading term	$4t^7$			
Leading coefficient	4			

5. $u^7 + 8u^2v^6 + 3uv + 4u - 1$

Term	u^7	$8u^2v^6$	$3uv$	$4u$	-1
Degree	7	8	2	1	0
Degree of polynomial	8				
Leading term	$8u^2v^6$				
Leading coefficient	8				

7. $-4y^3 - 6y^2 + 7y + 23$

9. $-xy^3 + x^2y^2 + x^3y + 1$

11. $-9b^5y^5 - 8b^2y^3 + 2by$

13. $5 + 12x - 4x^3 + 8x^5$

15. $3xy^3 + x^2y^2 - 9x^3y + 2x^4$

17. $-7ab + 4ax - 7ax^2 + 4x^6$

19. $P(x) = 3x^2 - 2x + 5$
$P(4) = 3 \cdot 4^2 - 2 \cdot 4 + 5$
$\quad = 48 - 8 + 5$
$\quad = 45$

$P(-2) = 3(-2)^2 - 2(-2) + 5$
$\quad = 12 + 4 + 5$
$\quad = 21$
$P(0) = 3 \cdot 0^2 - 2 \cdot 0 + 5$
$\quad = 0 - 0 + 5$
$\quad = 5$

21. $p(x) = 9x^3 + 8x^2 - 4x - 9$
$p(-3) = 9(-3)^3 + 8(-3)^2 - 4(-3) - 9$
$\quad = -243 + 72 + 12 - 9$
$\quad = -168$
$p(0) = 9 \cdot 0^3 + 8 \cdot 0^2 - 4 \cdot 0 - 9$
$\quad = 0 + 0 - 0 - 9$
$\quad = -9$
$p(1) = 9 \cdot 1^3 + 8 \cdot 1^2 - 4 \cdot 1 - 9$
$\quad = 9 + 8 - 4 - 9$
$\quad = 4$
$p\left(\dfrac{1}{2}\right) = 9\left(\dfrac{1}{2}\right)^3 + 8\left(\dfrac{1}{2}\right)^2 - 4 \cdot \dfrac{1}{2} - 9$
$\quad = \dfrac{9}{8} + 2 - 2 - 9$
$\quad = -\dfrac{63}{8},\ \text{or}\ -7\dfrac{7}{8}$

23. $s(t) = 16t^2$

a) $s(3) = 16 \cdot 3^2 = 16 \cdot 9 = 144$
The scaffold is 144 ft high.

b) $s(8) = 16 \cdot 8^2 = 16 \cdot 64 = 1024$
The cliff is 1024 ft high.

25. a) Locate 2 on the horizontal axis. From there move vertically to the graph and then horizontally to the $M(t)$-axis. This locates a value of about 340. Thus, about 340 mg of ibuprofen is in the the bloodstream 2 hr after 400 mg have been swallowed.

b) Locate 4 on the horizontal axis. From there move vertically to the graph and then horizontally to the $M(t)$-axis. This locates a value of about 185. Thus, about 185 mg of ibuprofen is in the the bloodstream 4 hr after 400 mg have been swallowed.

c) Locate 5 on the horizontal axis. From there move vertically to the graph and then horizontally to the $M(t)$-axis. This locates a value of about 65. Thus, $M(5) \approx 65$.

d) Locate 3 on the horizontal axis. From there move vertically to the graph and then horizontally to the $M(t)$-axis. This locates a value of about 300. Thus, $M(3) \approx 300$.

27. $R(x) = 280x - 0.4x^2$

 a) $R(75) = 280 \cdot 75 - 0.4(75)^2$

        $= 21,000 - 0.4(5625)$

        $= 21,000 - 2250 = 18,750$

   The total revenue is $18,750.

 b) $R(100) = 280(100) - 0.4(100)^2$

        $= 28,000 - 4000$

        $= 24,000$

   The total revenue is $24,000.

29. We subtract:

$P(x) = R(x) - C(x)$

     $= 280x - 0.4x^2 - (7000 + 0.6x^2)$

     $= 280x - 0.4x^2 + (-7000 - 0.6x^2)$ Adding the opposite

     $= -x^2 + 280x - 7000$

The total profit is given by $P(x) = -x^2 + 280x - 7000$.

31. Substitute 162 for G, 78 for W_1, and 68 for L_2.

$M = G - W_1 - L_2 + 1$

   $= 162 - 78 - 68 + 1$

   $= 17$

The magic number is 17.

33. Substitute 162 for G, 86 for W_1, and 69 for L_2.

$M = G - W_1 - L_2 + 1$

   $= 162 - 86 - 69 + 1$

   $= 8$

The magic number is 8.

35. $6x^2 - 7x^2 + 3x^2 = (6 - 7 + 3)x^2 = 2x^2$

37. $7x - 2y - 4x + 6y$

$= (7 - 4)x + (-2 + 6)y$

$= 3x + 4y$

39. $3a + 9 - 2 + 8a - 4a + 7$

$= (3 + 8 - 4)a + (9 - 2 + 7)$

$= 7a + 14$

41. $3a^2b + 4b^2 - 9a^2b - 6b^2$

$= (3 - 9)a^2b + (4 - 6)b^2$

$= -6a^2b - 2b^2$

43. $8x^2 - 3xy + 12y^2 + x^2 - y^2 + 5xy + 4y^2$

$= (8 + 1)x^2 + (-3 + 5)xy + (12 - 1 + 4)y^2$

$= 9x^2 + 2xy + 15y^2$

45. $4x^2y - 3y + 2xy^2 - 5x^2y + 7y + 7xy^2$

$= (4 - 5)x^2y + (-3 + 7)y + (2 + 7)xy^2$

$= -x^2y + 4y + 9xy^2$

47. $(3x^2 + 5y^2 + 6) + (2x^2 - 3y^2 - 1)$

$= (3 + 2)x^2 + (5 - 3)y^2 + (6 - 1)$

$= 5x^2 + 2y^2 + 5$

49. $(2a + 3b - c) + (4a - 2b + 2c)$

$= (2 + 4)a + (3 - 2)b + (-1 + 2)c$

$= 6a + b + c$

51. $(a^2 - 3b^2 + 4c^2) + (-5a^2 + 2b^2 - c^2)$

$= (1 - 5)a^2 + (-3 + 2)b^2 + (4 - 1)c^2$

$= -4a^2 - b^2 + 3c^2$

53. $(x^2 + 3x - 2xy - 3) + (-4x^2 - x + 3xy + 2)$

$= (1 - 4)x^2 + (3 - 1)x + (-2 + 3)xy + (-3 + 2)$

$= -3x^2 + 2x + xy - 1$

55. $(7x^2y - 3xy^2 + 4xy) + (-2x^2y - xy^2 + xy)$

$= (7 - 2)x^2y + (-3 - 1)xy^2 + (4 + 1)xy$

$= 5x^2y - 4xy^2 + 5xy$

57. $(2r^2 + 12r - 11) + (6r^2 - 2r + 4) + (r^2 - r - 2)$

$= (2 + 6 + 1)r^2 + (12 - 2 - 1)r + (-11 + 4 - 2)$

$= 9r^2 + 9r - 9$

59. $\left(\frac{2}{3}xy + \frac{5}{6}xy^2 + 5.1x^2y\right) + \left(-\frac{4}{5}xy + \frac{3}{4}xy^2 - 3.4x^2y\right)$

$= \left(\frac{2}{3} - \frac{4}{5}\right)xy + \left(\frac{5}{6} + \frac{3}{4}\right)xy^2 + (5.1 - 3.4)x^2y$

$= \left(\frac{10}{15} - \frac{12}{15}\right)xy + \left(\frac{10}{12} + \frac{9}{12}\right)xy^2 + 1.7x^2y$

$= -\frac{2}{15}xy + \frac{19}{12}xy^2 + 1.7x^2y$

61. $5x^3 - 7x^2 + 3x - 6$

 a) $-(5x^3 - 7x^2 + 3x - 6)$ Writing an inverse sign in front

 b) $-5x^3 + 7x^2 - 3x + 6$ Writing the opposite of each term

63. $-13y^2 + 6ay^4 - 5by^2$

 a) $-(-13y^2 + 6ay^4 - 5by^2)$

 b) $13y^2 - 6ay^4 + 5by^2$

65. $(7x - 2) - (-4x + 5)$

$= (7x - 2) + (4x - 5)$ Adding the opposite

$= 11x - 7$

67. $(-3x^2 + 2x + 9) - (x^2 + 5x - 4)$

$= (-3x^2 + 2x + 9) + (-x^2 - 5x + 4)$ Adding the opposite

$= -4x^2 - 3x + 13$

69. $(5a - 2b + c) - (3a + 2b - 2c)$

$= (5a - 2b + c) + (-3a - 2b + 2c)$

$= 2a - 4b + 3c$

71. $(3x^2 - 2x - x^3) - (5x^2 - 8x - x^3)$

$= (3x^2 - 2x - x^3) + (-5x^2 + 8x + x^3)$

$= -2x^2 + 6x$

73. $(5a^2 + 4ab - 3b^2) - (9a^2 - 4ab + 2b^2)$

  $= (5a^2 + 4ab - 3b^2) + (-9a^2 + 4ab - 2b^2)$

  $= -4a^2 + 8ab - 5b^2$

75. $(6ab - 4a^2b + 6ab^2) - (3ab^2 - 10ab - 12a^2b)$

  $= (6ab - 4a^2b + 6ab^2) + (-3ab^2 + 10ab + 12a^2b)$

  $= 16ab + 8a^2b + 3ab^2$

77. $(0.09y^4 - 0.052y^3 + 0.93) -$
  $\qquad (0.03y^4 - 0.084y^3 + 0.94y^2)$

  $= (0.09y^4 - 0.052y^3 + 0.93) +$
  $\qquad (-0.03y^4 + 0.084y^3 - 0.94y^2)$

  $= 0.06y^4 + 0.032y^3 - 0.94y^2 + 0.93$

79. $\left(\dfrac{5}{8}x^4 - \dfrac{1}{4}x^2 - \dfrac{1}{2}\right) - \left(-\dfrac{3}{8}x^4 + \dfrac{3}{4}x^2 + \dfrac{1}{2}\right)$

  $= \left(\dfrac{5}{8}x^4 - \dfrac{1}{4}x^2 - \dfrac{1}{2}\right) + \left(\dfrac{3}{8}x^4 - \dfrac{3}{4}x^2 - \dfrac{1}{2}\right)$

  $= x^4 - x^2 - 1$

81. Discussion and Writing Exercise

83. Graph: $f(x) = \dfrac{2}{3}x - 1$.

   We find some ordered pairs that are solutions. By choosing multiples of 3 for x we can avoid fractional values when calculating $f(x)$.

   For $x = -3$, $f(-3) = \dfrac{2}{3}(-3) - 1 = -2 - 1 = -3$.

   For $x = 0$, $f(0) = \dfrac{2}{3} \cdot 0 - 1 = 0 - 1 = -1$.

   For $x = 3$, $f(3) = \dfrac{2}{3} \cdot 3 - 1 = 2 - 1 = 1$.

x	$f(x)$	$(x, f(x))$
-3	-3	$(-3, -3)$
0	-1	$(0, -1)$
3	1	$(3, 1)$

   We plot these points and draw the graph.

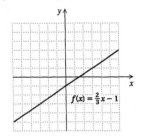

85. Graph: $g(x) = \dfrac{4}{x - 3}$.

   We choose x-values and find the corresponding values of $g(x)$. We list the results in a table.

x	$f(x)$	$(x, f(x))$
-5	$-\dfrac{1}{2}$	$\left(-5, -\dfrac{1}{2}\right)$
-3	$-\dfrac{2}{3}$	$\left(-3, -\dfrac{2}{3}\right)$
-1	-1	$(-1, -1)$
0	$-\dfrac{4}{3}$	$\left(0, -\dfrac{4}{3}\right)$
1	-2	$(1, -2)$
2	-4	$(2, -4)$
4	4	$(4, 4)$
5	2	$(5, 2)$
6	$\dfrac{4}{3}$	$\left(6, \dfrac{4}{3}\right)$
7	1	$(7, 1)$
9	$\dfrac{2}{3}$	$\left(9, \dfrac{2}{3}\right)$

   Since $4/0$ is undefined, we cannot use 3 as a first coordinate. The graph has two branches, one on each side of the line $x = 3$.

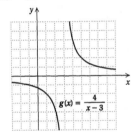

87. $3(y - 2) = 3 \cdot y - 3 \cdot 2 = 3y - 6$

89. $-14(3p - 2q - 10) = -14 \cdot 3p - (-14)(2q) - (-14)(10)$
  $= -42p + 28q + 140$

91. Graph: $y = \dfrac{4}{3}x + 2$.

   First we plot the y-intercept $(0, 2)$. Starting at $(0, 2)$ and using the slope, $\dfrac{4}{3}$, we find another point by moving 4 units up and 3 units to the right. We get to the point $(3, 6)$. We can also think of the slope as $\dfrac{-4}{-3}$. Starting again at $(0, 2)$, move 4 units down and 3 units to the left to the point $(-3, -2)$. Plot the points and draw the line.

93. Graph: $y = 0.4x - 3$

We write the equation as $y = \frac{4}{10}x - 3$, or $y = \frac{2}{5}x - 3$. First we plot the y-intercept $(0, -3)$. Starting at $(0, -3)$ and using the slope, $\frac{2}{5}$, we find another point by moving 2 units up and 5 units to the right. We get to the point $(5, -1)$. We can also think of the slope as $\frac{-2}{-5}$. Starting again at $(0, -3)$, move 2 units down and 5 units to the left to the point $(-5, -5)$. Plot the points and draw the line.

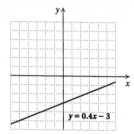

95. First we find the number of truffles in the display.

$$N(x) = \frac{1}{6}x^3 + \frac{1}{2}x^2 + \frac{1}{3}x$$

$$N(5) = \frac{1}{6} \cdot 5^3 + \frac{1}{2} \cdot 5^2 + \frac{1}{3} \cdot 5$$

$$= \frac{1}{6} \cdot 125 + \frac{1}{2} \cdot 25 + \frac{5}{3}$$

$$= \frac{125}{6} + \frac{25}{2} + \frac{5}{3}$$

$$= \frac{125}{6} + \frac{75}{6} + \frac{10}{6}$$

$$= \frac{210}{6} = 35$$

There are 35 truffles in the display. Now find the volume of one truffle. Each truffle's diameter is 3 cm, so the radius is $\frac{3}{2}$, or 1.5 cm.

$$V(r) = \frac{4}{3}\pi r^3$$

$$V(1.5) \approx \frac{4}{3}(3.14)(1.5)^3 \approx 14.13 \text{ cm}^3$$

Finally, multiply the number of truffles and the volume of a truffle to find the total volume of chocolate.

$$35(14.13 \text{ cm}^3) = 494.55 \text{ cm}^3$$

The display contains about 494.55 cm^3 of chocolate.

97. $(47x^{4a} + 3x^{3a} + 22x^{2a} + x^a + 1) +$
$\qquad (37x^{3a} + 8x^{2a} + 3)$
$= 47x^{4a} + (3 + 37)x^{3a} + (22 + 8)x^{2a} + x^a + (1 + 3)$
$= 47x^{4a} + 40x^{3a} + 30x^{2a} + x^a + 4$

99. Left to the student

Exercise Set 4.2

1. $8y^2 \cdot 3y = (8 \cdot 3)(y^2 \cdot y) = 24y^3$

3. $2x(-10x^2y) = [2(-10)](x \cdot x^2)(y) = -20x^3y$

5. $(5x^5y^4)(-2xy^3) = [5(-2)](x^5 \cdot x)(y^4 \cdot y^3) = -10x^6y^7$

7. $\quad 2z(7 - x)$
$= 2z \cdot 7 - 2z \cdot x \quad$ Using a distributive law
$= 14z - 2zx \qquad$ Multiplying monomials

9. $\quad 6ab(a + b)$
$= 6ab \cdot a + 6ab \cdot b \quad$ Using a distributive law
$= 6a^2b + 6ab^2 \qquad$ Multiplying monomials

11. $\quad 5cd(3c^2d - 5cd^2)$
$= 5cd \cdot 3c^2d - 5cd \cdot 5cd^2$
$= 15c^3d^2 - 25c^2d^3$

13. $\quad (5x + 2)(3x - 1)$
$= 15x^2 - 5x + 6x - 2 \qquad$ FOIL
$= 15x^2 + x - 2$

15. $\quad (s + 3t)(s - 3t)$
$= s^2 - (3t)^2 \qquad (A + B)(A - B) = A^2 - B^2$
$= s^2 - 9t^2$

17. $\quad (x - y)(x - y)$
$= x^2 - 2xy + y^2 \quad (A - B)^2 = A^2 - 2AB + B^2$

19. $\quad (x^3 + 8)(x^3 - 5)$
$= x^6 - 5x^3 + 8x^3 - 40 \qquad$ FOIL
$= x^6 + 3x^3 - 40$

21. $\quad (a^2 - 2b^2)(a^2 - 3b^2)$
$= a^4 - 3a^2b^2 - 2a^2b^2 + 6b^4 \qquad$ FOIL
$= a^4 - 5a^2b^2 + 6b^4$

23. $\quad (x - 4)(x^2 + 4x + 16)$
$= (x - 4)(x^2) + (x - 4)(4x) + (x - 4)(16)$
$\qquad\qquad\qquad\qquad$ Using a distributive law
$= x(x^2) - 4(x^2) + x(4x) - 4(4x) + x(16) - 4(16)$
$\qquad\qquad\qquad\qquad$ Using a distributive law
$= x^3 - 4x^2 + 4x^2 - 16x + 16x - 64$
$\qquad\qquad\qquad\qquad$ Multiplying monomials
$= x^3 - 64 \qquad$ Collecting like terms

25. $\quad (x + y)(x^2 - xy + y^2)$
$= (x + y)x^2 + (x + y)(-xy) + (x + y)(y^2)$
$= x(x^2) + y(x^2) + x(-xy) + y(-xy) + x(y^2) + y(y^2)$
$= x^3 + x^2y - x^2y - xy^2 + xy^2 + y^3$
$= x^3 + y^3$

27.
$$a^2 + a - 1$$
$$\underline{a^2 + 4a - 5}$$
$$-5a^2 - 5a + 5 \quad \text{Multiplying by } -5$$
$$4a^3 + 4a^2 - 4a \quad \text{Multiplying by } 4a$$
$$\underline{a^4 + a^3 - a^2 \quad \text{Multiplying by } a^2}$$
$$a^4 + 5a^3 - 2a^2 - 9a + 5 \quad \text{Adding}$$

29.
$$4a^2b - 2ab + 3b^2$$
$$\underline{ab - 2b + a}$$
$$4a^3b - 2a^2b + 3ab^2 \qquad (1)$$
$$-6b^3 \qquad +4ab^2 - 8a^2b^2 \qquad (2)$$
$$3ab^3 \qquad\qquad - 2a^2b^2 + 4a^3b^2 \quad (3)$$
$$\overline{3ab^3 - 6b^3 + 4a^3b - 2a^2b + 7ab^2 - 10a^2b^2 + 4a^3b^2} \quad (4)$$

(1) Multiplying by a

(2) Multiplying by $-2b$

(3) Multiplying by ab

(4) Adding

31. $\left(x + \dfrac{1}{4}\right)\left(x + \dfrac{1}{4}\right)$

$$= x^2 + \frac{1}{4}x + \frac{1}{4}x + \frac{1}{16} \qquad \text{FOIL}$$

$$= x^2 + \frac{1}{2}x + \frac{1}{16}$$

33. $\left(\dfrac{1}{2}x - \dfrac{2}{3}\right)\left(\dfrac{1}{4}x + \dfrac{1}{3}\right)$

$$= \frac{1}{8}x^2 + \frac{1}{6}x - \frac{1}{6}x - \frac{2}{9} \qquad \text{FOIL}$$

$$= \frac{1}{8}x^2 - \frac{2}{9}$$

35. $(1.3x - 4y)(2.5x + 7y)$

$$= 3.25x^2 + 9.1xy - 10xy - 28y^2 \qquad \text{FOIL}$$

$$= 3.25x^2 - 0.9xy - 28y^2$$

37. $(a + 8)(a + 5)$

$$= a^2 + 5a + 8a + 40 \qquad \text{FOIL}$$

$$= a^2 + 13a + 40$$

39. $(y + 7)(y - 4)$

$$= y^2 - 4y + 7y - 28 \qquad \text{FOIL}$$

$$= y^2 + 3y - 28$$

41. $\left(3a + \dfrac{1}{2}\right)^2$

$$= (3a)^2 + 2(3a)\left(\frac{1}{2}\right) + \left(\frac{1}{2}\right)^2$$
$$(A + B)^2 = A^2 + 2AB + B^2$$

$$= 9a^2 + 3a + \frac{1}{4}$$

43. $(x - 2y)^2$

$$= x^2 - 2(x)(2y) + (2y)^2$$
$$(A - B)^2 = A^2 - 2AB + B^2$$

$$= x^2 - 4xy + 4y^2$$

45. $\left(b - \dfrac{1}{3}\right)\left(b - \dfrac{1}{2}\right)$

$$= b^2 - \frac{1}{2}b - \frac{1}{3}b + \frac{1}{6} \qquad \text{FOIL}$$

$$= b^2 - \frac{3}{6}b - \frac{2}{6}b + \frac{1}{6}$$

$$= b^2 - \frac{5}{6}b + \frac{1}{6}$$

47. $(2x + 9)(x + 2)$

$$= 2x^2 + 4x + 9x + 18 \qquad \text{FOIL}$$

$$= 2x^2 + 13x + 18$$

49. $(20a - 0.16b)^2$

$$= (20a)^2 - 2(20a)(0.16b) + (0.16b)^2$$
$$(A - B)^2 = A^2 - 2AB + B^2$$

$$= 400a^2 - 6.4ab + 0.0256b^2$$

51. $(2x - 3y)(2x + y)$

$$= 4x^2 + 2xy - 6xy - 3y^2 \qquad \text{FOIL}$$

$$= 4x^2 - 4xy - 3y^2$$

53. $(x^3 + 2)^2$

$$= (x^3)^2 + 2 \cdot x^3 \cdot 2 + 2^2 \quad (A + B)^2 = A^2 + 2AB + B^2$$

$$= x^6 + 4x^3 + 4$$

55. $(2x^2 - 3y^2)^2$

$$= (2x^2)^2 - 2(2x^2)(3y^2) + (3y^2)^2$$
$$(A - B)^2 = A^2 - 2AB + B^2$$

$$= 4x^4 - 12x^2y^2 + 9y^4$$

57. $(a^3b^2 + 1)^2$

$$= (a^3b^2)^2 + 2 \cdot a^3b^2 \cdot 1 + 1^2$$
$$(A + B)^2 = A^2 + 2AB + B^2$$

$$= a^6b^4 + 2a^3b^2 + 1$$

59. $(0.1a^2 - 5b)^2$

$$= (0.1a^2)^2 - 2(0.1a^2)(5b) + (5b)^2$$
$$(A - B)^2 = A^2 - 2AB + B^2$$

$$= 0.01a^4 - a^2b + 25b^2$$

61. $A = P(1 + i)^2$

$$A = P(1 + 2i + i^2) \qquad \text{FOIL}$$

$$A = P + 2Pi + Pi^2 \qquad \text{Multiplying by } P$$

63. $(d + 8)(d - 8)$

$$= d^2 - 8^2 \qquad (A + B)(A - B) = A^2 - B^2$$

$$= d^2 - 64$$

65. $(2c + 3)(2c - 3)$

$$= (2c)^2 - 3^2 \qquad (A + B)(A - B) = A^2 - B^2$$

$$= 4c^2 - 9$$

67. $(6m - 5n)(6m + 5n)$

$$= (6m)^2 - (5n)^2 \qquad (A + B)(A - B) = A^2 - B^2$$

$$= 36m^2 - 25n^2$$

69. $(x^2 + yz)(x^2 - yz)$

$= (x^2)^2 - (yz)^2$ $(A+B)(A-B) = A^2 - B^2$

$= x^4 - y^2z^2$

71. $(-mn + m^2)(mn + m^2)$

$= (m^2 - mn)(m^2 + mn)$

$= (m^2)^2 - (mn)^2$ $(A+B)(A-B) = A^2 - B^2$

$= m^4 - m^2n^2$

73. $(-3pq + 4p^2)(4p^2 - 3pq)$

$= (4p^2 - 3pq)(4p^2 + 3pq)$

$= (4p^2)^2 - (3pq)^2$

$= 16p^4 - 9p^2q^2$

75. $\left(\dfrac{1}{2}p - \dfrac{2}{3}q\right)\left(\dfrac{1}{2}p + \dfrac{2}{3}q\right)$

$= \left(\dfrac{1}{2}p\right)^2 - \left(\dfrac{2}{3}q\right)^2$

$= \dfrac{1}{4}p^2 - \dfrac{4}{9}q^2$

77. $(x+1)(x-1)(x^2+1)$

$= (x^2 - 1^2)(x^2 + 1)$

$= (x^2 - 1)(x^2 + 1)$

$= (x^2)^2 - 1^2$

$= x^4 - 1$

79. $(a-b)(a+b)(a^2 - b^2)$

$= (a^2 - b^2)(a^2 - b^2)$

$= (a^2 - b^2)^2$

$= (a^2)^2 - 2(a^2)(b^2) + (b^2)^2$

$= a^4 - 2a^2b^2 + b^4$

81. $(a+b+1)(a+b-1)$

$= [(a+b)+1][(a+b)-1]$

$= (a+b)^2 - 1^2$

$= a^2 + 2ab + b^2 - 1$

83. $(2x + 3y + 4)(2x + 3y - 4)$

$= [(2x + 3y) + 4][(2x + 3y) - 4]$

$= (2x + 3y)^2 - 4^2$

$= 4x^2 + 12xy + 9y^2 - 16$

85. a) Replace each occurrence of x by $t - 1$.

$f(t-1) = 5(t-1) + (t-1)^2$

$= 5t - 5 + t^2 - 2t + 1$

$= t^2 + 3t - 4$

b) $f(a+h) - f(a)$

$= [5(a+h) + (a+h)^2] - [5a + a^2]$

$= 5a + 5h + a^2 + 2ah + h^2 - 5a - a^2$

$= 5h + 2ah + h^2$

87. a) $f(a+2) = 2 - 4(a+2) - 3(a+2)^2$

$= 2 - 4(a+2) - 3(a^2 + 4a + 4)$

$= 2 - 4a - 8 - 3a^2 - 12a - 12$

$= -3a^2 - 16a - 18$

b) $f(a+h) - f(a)$

$= [2 - 4a(a+h) - 3(a+h)^2] - (2 - 4a - 3a^2)$

$= [2 - 4(a+h) - 3(a^2 + 2ah + h^2)] - (2 - 4a - 3a^2)$

$= 2 - 4a - 4h - 3a^2 - 6ah - 3h^2 - 2 + 4a + 3a^2$

$= -4h - 6ah - 3h^2$

89. Discussion and Writing Exercise

91. *Familiarize*. When Rachel's sister catches up with her, their distances traveled are the same. Let $d =$ this distance. Also let $t =$ the time for Rachel's sister to catch up with her. Then $t + 2 =$ the time Rachel travels before her sister catches up with her. Organize the information in a table.

$$d = r \cdot t$$

	Distance	Rate	Time
Rachel	d	55	$t+2$
Sister	d	75	t

***Translate*.** Using $d = r \cdot t$ in each row of the table, we get a system of equations.

$d = 55(t+2)$,   (1)

$d = 75t$ (2)

***Solve*.** We use the substitution method. First, substitute $75t$ for d in Equation (1) and solve for t.

$75t = 55(t+2)$

$75t = 55t + 110$

$20t = 110$

$t = 5.5$

If the sister's time is 5.5 hr, then Rachel's time is $5.5 + 2$, or 7.5 hr.

***Check*.** At 55 mph, in 7.5 hr Rachel travels $55(7.5)$, or 412.5 mi. At 75 mph, in 5.5 hr her sister travels $75(5.5)$, or 412.5 mi. Since the distances are the same, the answer checks.

***State*.** Rachel's sister will catch up with her 5.5 hr after the sister leaves (or 7.5 hr after Rachel leaves).

93. $5x + 9y = 2$ (1)

$\underline{4x - 9y = 10}$ (2)

$9x = 12$ Adding

$x = \dfrac{4}{3}$

Substitute $\dfrac{4}{3}$ for x in one of the equations and solve for y.

$$5x + 9y = 2 \qquad (1)$$

$$5 \cdot \frac{4}{3} + 9y = 2$$

$$\frac{20}{3} + 9y = 2$$

$$9y = -\frac{14}{3}$$

$$y = -\frac{14}{27}$$

The ordered pair $\left(\frac{4}{3}, -\frac{14}{27}\right)$ checks. It is the solution.

95. $2x - 3y = 1$, $\quad (1)$

$\quad\;\; 4x - 6y = 2 \quad (2)$

We multiply Equation (1) by -2 and add.

$$-4x + 6y = -2$$
$$\underline{4x - 6y = 2}$$
$$0 = 0$$

We get an equation that is true for all values of x and y. There are infinitely many solutions.

97. Left to the student

99. $(z^{n^2})^{n^3}(z^{4n^3})^{n^2} = z^{n^5} \cdot z^{4n^5} = z^{n^5 + 4n^5} = z^{5n^5}$

101. $(r^2 + s^2)^2(r^2 + 2rs + s^2)(r^2 - 2rs + s^2)$

$= (r^2 + s^2)^2(r + s)^2(r - s)^2$

$= (r^2 + s^2)^2[(r + s)(r - s)]^2$

$= (r^2 + s^2)^2(r^2 - s^2)^2$

$= [(r^2 + s^2)(r^2 - s^2)]^2$

$= (r^4 - s^4)^2$

$= r^8 - 2r^4s^4 + s^8$

103. $\left(3x^5 - \frac{5}{11}\right)^2$

$= (3x^5)^2 - 2(3x^5)\left(\frac{5}{11}\right) + \left(\frac{5}{11}\right)^2$

$= 9x^{10} - \frac{30}{11}x^5 + \frac{25}{121}$

105. $(x^a + y^b)(x^a - y^b)(x^{2a} + y^{2b})$

$= (x^{2a} - y^{2b})(x^{2a} + y^{2b})$

$= x^{4a} - y^{4b}$

107. $(x - 1)(x^2 + x + 1)(x^3 + 1)$

$= (x^3 + x^2 + x - x^2 - x - 1)(x^3 + 1)$

$= (x^3 - 1)(x^3 + 1)$

$= x^6 - 1$

1. $6a^2 + 3a$

$= 3a \cdot 2a + 3a \cdot 1$

$= 3a(2a + 1)$

3. $x^3 + 9x^2$

$= x^2 \cdot x + x^2 \cdot 9$

$= x^2(x + 9)$

5. $8x^2 - 4x^4$

$= 4x^2 \cdot 2 - 4x^2 \cdot x^2$

$= 4x^2(2 - x^2)$

7. $4x^2y - 12xy^2$

$= 4xy \cdot x - 4xy \cdot 3y$

$= 4xy(x - 3y)$

9. $3y^2 - 3y - 9$

$= 3 \cdot y^2 - 3 \cdot y - 3 \cdot 3$

$= 3(y^2 - y - 3)$

11. $4ab - 6ac + 12ad$

$= 2a \cdot 2b - 2a \cdot 3c + 2a \cdot 6d$

$= 2a(2b - 3c + 6d)$

13. $10a^4 + 15a^2 - 25a - 30$

$= 5 \cdot 2a^4 + 5 \cdot 3a^2 - 5 \cdot 5a - 5 \cdot 6$

$= 5(2a^4 + 3a^2 - 5a - 6)$

15. $-5x - 45 = -5(x + 9)$

17. $-6a - 84 = -6(a + 14)$

19. $-2x^2 + 2x - 24 = -2(x^2 - x + 12)$

21. $-3y^2 + 24y = -3y(y - 8)$

23. $-3y^3 + 12y^2 - 15y + 24 = -3(y^3 - 4y^2 + 5y - 8)$

25. $N(x) = \frac{1}{3}x^3 + \frac{1}{2}x^2 + \frac{1}{6}x$

$N(x) = x\left(\frac{1}{3}x^2 + \frac{1}{2}x + \frac{1}{6}\right) \quad$ Factoring out x

27. a) $\; h(t) = -16t^2 + 72t$

$\quad\;\; h(t) = -8t(2t - 9)$

b) $\; h(2) = -16 \cdot 2^2 + 72 \cdot 2 = 80$

$\quad\; h(2) = -8(2)(2 \cdot 2 - 9) = -8(2)(-5) = 80$

The expressions have the same value for $t = 2$, so the factorization is probably correct.

29. $R(x) = 280x - 0.4x^2$

$\quad\;\; R(x) = 0.4x(700 - x)$

31. $a(b - 2) + c(b - 2) = (a + c)(b - 2)$

33.
$$(x-2)(x+5) + (x-2)(x+8)$$
$$= (x-2)[(x+5) + (x+8)]$$
$$= (x-2)(2x+13)$$

35. $a^2(x-y) + a^2(x-y) = 2a^2(x-y)$

37.
$$ac + ad + bc + bd$$
$$= a(c+d) + b(c+d)$$
$$= (a+b)(c+d)$$

39.
$$b^3 - b^2 + 2b - 2$$
$$= b^2(b-1) + 2(b-1)$$
$$= (b^2+2)(b-1)$$

41.
$$y^3 - 8y^2 + y - 8$$
$$= y^2(y-8) + 1(y-8)$$
$$= (y^2+1)(y-8)$$

43.
$$24x^3 - 36x^2 + 72x - 108$$
$$= 12(2x^3 - 3x^2 + 6x - 9)$$
$$= 12[x^2(2x-3) + 3(2x-3)]$$
$$= 12(x^2+3)(2x-3)$$

45. $a^4 - a^3 + a^2 + a = a(a^3 - a^2 + a + 1)$

47.
$$2y^4 + 6y^2 + 5y^2 + 15$$
$$= 2y^2(y^2+3) + 5(y^2+3)$$
$$= (2y^2+5)(y^2+3)$$

49. Discussion and Writing Exercise

51. $c + 10 \leq -10$

$\qquad c \leq -20$ Subtracting 10

The solution set is $\{c | c \leq -20\}$, or $(-\infty, -20]$.

53. $\dfrac{1}{2}(5x-8) > 2$

$\qquad 5x - 8 > 4$ Multiplying by 2

$\qquad\quad 5x > 12$ Adding 8

$\qquad\quad\quad x > \dfrac{12}{5}$ Dividing by 5

The solution set is $\left\{ x \Big| x > \dfrac{12}{5} \right\}$, or $\left(\dfrac{12}{5}, \infty \right)$.

55. $|x-6| = -4$

The absolute value of a number is always nonnegative. Thus, there is no solution. The solution set is $\emptyset$.

57. $|2x-1| = |x+5|$

$2x - 1 = x + 5 \quad or \quad 2x - 1 = -(x+5)$

$\quad x - 1 = 5 \qquad or \quad 2x - 1 = -x - 5$

$\qquad\quad x = 6 \qquad or \qquad 3x - 1 = -5$

$\qquad\quad x = 6 \qquad or \qquad\quad 3x = -4$

$\qquad\quad x = 6 \qquad or \qquad\qquad x = -\dfrac{4}{3}$

The solution set is $\left\{ 6, -\dfrac{4}{3} \right\}$.

59. $f(x) = 2x^2 - 7$

We can substitute any number for x, so the domain is the set of all real numbers.

61. $7x - 3 = 0$ when $x = \dfrac{3}{7}$, so the domain is

$\left\{ x \Big| x \text{ is a real number } and \ x \neq \dfrac{3}{7} \right\}$, or

$\left(-\infty, \dfrac{3}{7} \right) \cup \left(\dfrac{3}{7}, \infty \right)$.

63. $x^5 y^4 + \underline{\quad} = x^3 y (\underline{\quad} + xy^5)$

The term that goes in the first blank is the product of $x^3 y$ and xy^5, or $x^4 y^6$.

The term that goes in the second blank is the expression that is multiplied with $x^3 y$ to obtain $x^5 y^4$, or $x^2 y^3$. Thus, we have

$$x^5 y^4 + x^4 y^6 = x^3 y(x^2 y^3 + xy^5).$$

65.
$$rx^2 - rx + 5r + sx^2 - sx + 5s$$
$$= r(x^2 - x + 5) + s(x^2 - x + 5)$$
$$= (x^2 - x + 5)(r + s)$$

67.
$$a^4 x^4 + a^4 x^2 + 5a^4 + a^2 x^4 + a^2 x^2 + 5a^2 +$$
$$\qquad\qquad\qquad\qquad\qquad 5x^4 + 5x^2 + 25$$
$$= a^4(x^4 + x^2 + 5) + a^2(x^4 + x^2 + 5) + 5(x^4 + x^2 + 5)$$
$$= (x^4 + x^2 + 5)(a^4 + a^2 + 5)$$

69. $x^{1/3} - 7x^{4/3} = x^{1/3} \cdot 1 - 7x \cdot x^{1/3} = x^{1/3}(1 - 7x)$

71.
$$x^{1/3} - 5x^{1/2} + 3x^{3/4}$$
$$= x^{4/12} - 5x^{6/12} + 3x^{9/12}$$
$$= x^{4/12}(1 - 5x^{2/12} + 3x^{5/12})$$
$$= x^{1/3}(1 - 5x^{1/6} + 3x^{5/12})$$

73.
$$3a^{n+1} + 6a^n - 15a^{n+2}$$
$$= 3a^n \cdot a + 3a^n \cdot 2 - 3a^n(5a^2)$$
$$= 3a^n(a + 2 - 5a^2)$$

75.
$$7y^{2a+b} - 5y^{a+b} + 3y^{a+2b}$$
$$= y^{a+b} \cdot 7y^a - y^{a+b}(5) + y^{a+b} \cdot 3y^b$$
$$= y^{a+b}(7y^a - 5 + 3y^b)$$

Exercise Set 4.4

1. $x^2 + 13x + 36$

We look for two numbers whose product is 36 and whose sum is 13. Since both 36 and 13 are positive, we need consider only positive factors.

Pairs of Factors	Sums of Factors
1, 36	37
2, 18	20
3, 12	15
4, 9	13
6, 6	12

The numbers we need are 4 and 9. The factorization is $(x+4)(x+9)$.

3. $t^2 - 8t + 15$

Since the constant term, 15, is positive and the coefficient of the middle term, -8, is negative, we look for a factorization of 15 in which both factors are negative. Their sum must be -8.

Pairs of Factors	Sums of Factors
$-1, -15$	-16
$-3, -5$	-8

The numbers we need are -3 and -5. The factorization is $(t-3)(t-5)$.

5. $x^2 - 8x - 33$

Since the constant term, -33, is negative, we look for a factorization of -33 in which one factor is positive and one factor is negative. The sum of the factors must be -8, so the negative factor must have the larger absolute value. Thus we consider only pairs of factors in which the negative factor has the larger absolute value.

Pairs of Factors	Sums of Factors
$1, -33$	-32
$3, -11$	-8

The numbers we want are 3 and -11. The factorization is $(x+3)(x-11)$.

7. $2y^2 - 16y + 32$
    $= 2(y^2 - 8y + 16)$ Removing the common factor

We now factor $y^2 - 8y + 16$. We look for two numbers whose product is 16 and whose sum is -8. Since the constant term is positive and the coefficient of the middle term is negative, we look for a factorization of 16 in which both factors are negative.

Pairs of Factors	Sums of Factors
$-1, -16$	-17
$-2, -8$	-10
$-4, -4$	-8

The numbers we need are -4 and -4.
    $y^2 - 8y + 16 = (y-4)(y-4)$

We must not forget to include the common factor 2.
    $2y^2 - 16y + 32 = 2(y-4)(y-4)$.

9. $p^2 + 3p - 54$

Since the constant term is negative, we look for a factorization of -54 in which one factor is positive and one factor is negative. We consider only pairs of factors in which the positive factor has the larger absolute value, since the sum of the factors, 3, is positive.

Pairs of Factors	Sums of Factors
$54, -1$	53
$27, -2$	25
$18, -3$	15
$9, -6$	3

The numbers we need are 9 and -6. The factorization is $(p+9)(p-6)$.

11. $12x + x^2 + 27 = x^2 + 12x + 27$

We look for two numbers whose product is 27 and whose sum is 12. Since both 27 and 12 are positive, we need consider only positive factors.

Pairs of Factors	Sums of Factors
$1, 27$	28
$3, 9$	12

The numbers we want are 3 and 9. The factorization is $(x+3)(x+9)$.

13. $y^2 - \frac{2}{3}y + \frac{1}{9}$

Since the constant term, $\frac{1}{9}$, is positive and the coefficient of the middle term, $-\frac{2}{3}$, is negative, we look for a factorization of $\frac{1}{9}$ in which both factors are negative. Their sum must be $-\frac{2}{3}$.

Pairs of Factors	Sums of Factors
$-1, -\frac{1}{9}$	$-\frac{10}{9}$
$-\frac{1}{3}, -\frac{1}{3}$	$-\frac{2}{3}$

The numbers we need are $-\frac{1}{3}$ and $-\frac{1}{3}$. The factorization is $\left(y - \frac{1}{3}\right)\left(y - \frac{1}{3}\right)$.

15. $t^2 - 4t + 3$

Since the constant term, 3, is positive and the coefficient of the middle term, -4, is negative, we look for a factorization of 3 in which both factors are negative. Their sum must be -4. The only possibility is $-1, -3$. These are the numbers we need. The factorization is $(t-1)(t-3)$.

17. $5x + x^2 - 14 = x^2 + 5x - 14$

Since the constant term, -14, is negative, we look for a factorization of -14 in which one factor is positive and one factor is negative. Their sum must be 5, so the positive factor must have the larger absolute value. We consider only pairs of factors in which the positive factor has the larger absolute value.

Pairs of Factors	Sums of Factors
$-1, 14$	13
$-2, 7$	5

The numbers we need are -2 and 7. The factorization is $(x-2)(x+7)$.

19. $x^2 + 5x + 6$

We look for two numbers whose product is 6 and whose sum is 5. Since 6 and 5 are both positive, we need consider only positive factors.

Pairs of Factors	Sums of Factors
$1, 6$	7
$2, 3$	5

The numbers we need are 2 and 3. The factorization is $(x+2)(x+3)$.

21. $56 + x - x^2 = -x^2 + x + 56 = -1(x^2 - x - 56)$

We now factor $x^2 - x - 56$. Since the constant term, -56, is negative, we look for a factorization of -56 in which one factor is positive and one factor is negative. We consider only pairs of factors in which the negative factor has the larger absolute value, since the sum of the factors, -1, is negative.

Pairs of Factors	Sums of Factors
$-56,\ \ 1$	-55
$-28,\ \ 2$	-26
$-14,\ \ 4$	-10
$-8,\ \ 7$	-1

The numbers we need are -8 and 7. Thus, $x^2 - x - 56 = (x - 8)(x + 7)$. We must not forget to include the factor that was factored out earlier:

$$-x^2 + x + 56$$
$$= -1(x^2 - x - 56)$$
$$= -1(x - 8)(x + 7)$$
$$= (-x + 8)(x + 7) \qquad \text{Multiplying } x - 8 \text{ by } -1$$
$$= (x - 8)(-x - 7) \qquad \text{Multiplying } x + 7 \text{ by } -1$$

23. $32y + 4y^2 - y^3$

There is a common factor, y. We also factor out -1 in order to make the leading coefficient positive.

$$32y + 4y^2 - y^3 = -y(-32 - 4y + y^2)$$
$$= -y(y^2 - 4y - 32)$$

Now we factor $y^2 - 4y - 32$. Since the constant term, -32, is negative, we look for a factorization of -32 in which one factor is positive and one factor is negative. We consider only pairs of factors in which the negative factor has the larger absolute value, since the sum of the factors, -4, is negative.

Pairs of Factors	Sums of Factors
$-32,\ \ 1$	-31
$-16,\ \ 2$	-14
$-8,\ \ 4$	-4

The numbers we need are -8 and 4. Thus, $y^2 - 4y - 32 = (y - 8)(y + 4)$. We must not forget to include the common factor:

$$32y + 4y^2 - y^3$$
$$= -y(y^2 - 4y - 32)$$
$$= -y(y - 8)(y + 4)$$
$$= -1 \cdot y(y - 8)(y + 4)$$
$$= y(-y + 8)(y + 4) \qquad \text{Multiplying } y - 8 \text{ by } -1$$
$$= y(y - 8)(-y - 4) \qquad \text{Multiplying } y + 4 \text{ by } -1$$

25. $x^4 + 11x^2 - 80$

First make a substitution. We let $u = x^2$, so $u^2 = x^4$. Then we consider $u^2 + 11u - 80$. We look for pairs of factors of -80, one positive and one negative, such that the positive factor has the larger absolute value and the sum of the factors is 11.

Pairs of Factors	Sums of Factors
$80, -1$	79
$40, -2$	38
$20, -4$	16
$16, -5$	11
$10, -8$	2

The numbers we need are 16 and -5. Then $u^2 + 11u - 80 = (u + 16)(u - 5)$. Replacing u by x^2 we obtain the factorization of the original trinomial: $(x^2 + 16)(x^2 - 5)$.

27. $x^2 - 3x + 7$

There are no factors of 7 whose sum is -3. This trinomial is not factorable into binomials with integer coefficients.

29. $x^2 + 12xy + 27y^2$

We look for numbers p and q such that $x^2 + 12xy + 27y^2 = (x + py)(x + qy)$. Our thinking is much the same as if we were factoring $x^2 + 12x + 27$. We look for factors of 27 whose sum is 12. Those factors are 9 and 3. Then

$$x^2 + 12xy + 27y^2 = (x + 9y)(x + 3y).$$

31. $45 + 4x - x^2 = -x^2 + 4x + 45 = -1(x^2 - 4x - 45)$

Now we factor $x^2 - 4x - 45$. We look for two numbers whose product is -45 and whose sum is -4. The numbers we need are -9 and 5. We have:

$$-x^2 + 4x + 45$$
$$= -1(x^2 - 4x - 45)$$
$$= -1(x - 9)(x + 5)$$
$$= (-x + 9)(x + 5) \qquad \text{Multiplying } x - 9 \text{ by } -1$$
$$= (x - 9)(-x - 5) \qquad \text{Multiplying } x + 5 \text{ by } -1$$

33. $-z^2 + 36 - 9z = -z^2 - 9z + 36 = -1(z^2 + 9z - 36)$

Now we factor $z^2 + 9z - 36$. We look for two numbers whose product is -36 and whose sum is 9. The numbers we need are 12 and -3. We have:

$$-z^2 - 9z + 36$$
$$= -1(z^2 + 9z - 36)$$
$$= -1(z + 12)(z - 3)$$
$$= (-z - 12)(z - 3) \qquad \text{Multiplying } z + 12 \text{ by } -1$$
$$= (z + 12)(-z + 3) \qquad \text{Multiplying } z - 3 \text{ by } -1$$

35. $x^4 + 50x^2 + 49$

Substitute u for x^2 (and hence u^2 for x^4). Consider $u^2 + 50u + 49$. We look for a pair of positive factors of 49 whose sum is 50.

Pairs of Factors	Sums of Factors
$7,\ \ 7$	14
$1,\ \ 49$	50

The numbers we need are 1 and 49. Then $u^2 + 50u + 49 = (u + 1)(u + 49)$. Replacing u by x^2 we have

$$x^4 + 50x^2 + 49 = (x^2 + 1)(x^2 + 49).$$

37. $x^6 + 11x^3 + 18$

Substitute u for x^3 (and hence u^2 for x^6). Consider $u^2 + 11u + 18$. We look for two numbers whose product is 18 and whose sum is 11. Since both 18 and 11 are positive, we need consider only positive factors.

Pairs of Factors	Sums of Factors
1, 18	19
2, 9	11
3, 6	9

The numbers we need are 2 and 9. Then $u^2 + 11u + 18 = (u+2)(u+9)$. Replacing u by x^3 we obtain the factorization of the original trinomial: $(x^3 + 2)(x^3 + 9)$.

39. $x^8 - 11x^4 + 24$

Substitute u for x^4 (and hence u^2 for x^8). Consider $u^2 - 11u + 24$. Since the constant term, 24, is positive and the coefficient of the middle term, -11, is negative, we look for a factorization of 24 in which both factors are negative. Their sum must be -11.

Pairs of Factors	Sums of Factors
$-1, -24$	-25
$-2, -12$	-14
$-3, -8$	-11
$-4, -6$	-10

The numbers we need are -3 and -8. Then $u^2 - 11u + 24 = (u-3)(u-8)$. Replacing u by x^4 we obtain the factorization of the original trinomial: $(x^4 - 3)(x^4 - 8)$.

41. Discussion and Writing Exercise

43. *Familiarize.* Let x = the number of pounds of Countryside rice and y = the number of pounds of Mystic rice to be used in the mixture.

Translate. We organize the information in a table.

	Countryside	Mystic	Mixture
Number of pounds	x	y	25
Percent of wild rice	10%	50%	35%
Pounds of wild rice	$0.1x$	$0.5x$	$0.35(25)$

From the "Number of pounds" row of the table we get one equation.

$$x + y = 25$$

We get a second equation from the last row of the table.

$$0.1x + 0.5x = 0.35(25), \text{ or}$$
$$0.1x + 0.5x = 8.75$$

Clearing decimals, we have the following system of equations:

$$x + y = 25, \quad (1)$$
$$10x + 50y = 875 \quad (2)$$

Solve. We use the elimination method to solve the system of equations. We multiply Equation (1) by -10 and add.

$$
\begin{array}{rcr}
-10x - 10y &=& -250 \\
10x + 50y &=& 875 \\
\hline
40y &=& 625 \\
y &=& 15.625
\end{array}
$$

Now substitute 15.625 for y in Equation (1) and solve for x.

$$x + 15.625 = 25$$
$$x = 9.375$$

Check. The total weight of the mixture is $9.375 + 15.625$, or 25 lb. The amount of wild rice in the mixture is $0.1(9.375) + 0.5(15.625) = 0.9375 + 7.8125 = 8.75$ lb. This is 35% of 25 lb. The numbers check.

State. 9.375 lb, or $9\frac{3}{8}$ lb, of Countryside Rice and 15.625 lb, or $15\frac{5}{8}$ lb of Mystic Rice should be used.

45. The graph is that of a function, because no vertical line can cross the graph at more than one point.

47. The graph is not that of a function, because a vertical line can cross the graph at more than one point.

49. $f(x) = x^2 - 2$

$f(x)$ can be calculated for any number x, so the domain is the set of all real numbers.

51. $f(x) = \dfrac{3}{4x - 7}$

We cannot calculate $\dfrac{3}{4x - 7}$ when the denominator is 0.

$$4x - 7 = 0$$
$$4x = 7$$
$$x = \frac{7}{4}$$

The domain is $\left\{ x \middle| x \text{ is a real number and } x \neq \frac{7}{4} \right\}$, or

$$\left(-\infty, \frac{7}{4} \right) \cup \left(\frac{7}{4}, \infty \right).$$

53. All such m are the sums of the factors of 75.

Pair of Factors	Sum of Factors
75, 1	76
$-75, -1$	-76
25, 3	28
$-25, -3$	-28
15, 5	20
$-15, -5$	-20

m can be 76, -76, 28, -28, 20, or -20.

55. $20(-365) = -7300$ and $20 + (-365) = -345$ so the other factor is $(x - 365)$.

Exercise Set 4.5

1. $3x^2 - 14x - 5$

We will use the FOIL method.

1) There is no common factor (other than 1 or -1).

2) We factor the first term, $3x^2$. The factors are $3x$ and x. We have this possibility:

$$(3x+\ \ )(x+\ \ )$$

3) Next we factor the last term, -5. The possibilities are $-1, 5$ and $1, -5$.

4) We look for combinations of factors from steps (2) and (3) such that the sum of their products is the middle term, $-14x$. We try the possibilities:

$$(3x - 1)(x + 5) = 3x^2 + 14x - 5$$
$$(3x + 1)(x - 5) = 3x^2 - 14x - 5$$

The factorization is $(3x + 1)(x - 5)$.

3. $10y^3 + y^2 - 21y$

We will use the ac-method.

1) Look for a common factor. We factor out y:

$$y(10y^2 + y - 21)$$

2) Factor the trinomial $10y^2 + y - 21$. Multiply the leading coefficient, 10, and the constant, -21.

$$10(-21) = -210$$

3) Look for a factorization of -210 in which the sum of the factors is the coefficient of the middle term, 1.

Pairs of Factors	Sums of Factors
$-1,\quad 210$	209
$1,\ -210$	-209
$-2,\quad 105$	103
$2,\ -105$	-103
$-3,\quad 70$	67
$3,\ -70$	-67
$-5,\quad 42$	37
$5,\ -42$	-37
$-6,\quad 35$	29
$6,\ -35$	-29
$-7,\quad 30$	23
$7,\ -30$	-23
$-10,\quad 21$	11
$10,\ -21$	-11
$-14,\quad 15$	$1 \quad \leftarrow -14+15=1$
$14,\ -15$	-1

4) Next, split the middle term, y, as follows:

$$y = -14y + 15y$$

5) Factor by grouping:

$$10y^2 + y - 21 = 10y^2 - 14y + 15y - 21$$
$$= 2y(5y - 7) + 3(5y - 7)$$
$$= (2y + 3)(5y - 7)$$

We must include the common factor to get a factorization of the original trinomial:

$$10y^3 + y^2 - 21y = y(2y + 3)(5y - 7)$$

5. $3c^2 - 20c + 32$

We will use the FOIL method.

1) There is no common factor(other than 1 or -1).

2) Factor the first term, $3c^2$. The factors are $3c$ and c. We have this possibility:

$$(3c+\ \ )(c+\ \ )$$

3) Next we factor the last term, 32. The possibilities are $1, 32$ and $-1, -32$ and $2, 16$ and $-2, -16$ and $4, 8$ and $-4, -8$.

4) We look for a combination of factors from steps (2) and (3) such that the sum of their products is the middle term, $-20c$. Trial and error leads us to the correct factorization, $(3c - 8)(c - 4)$.

7. $35y^2 + 34y + 8$

We will use the ac-method.

1) There is no common factor (other than 1 or -1).

2) Multiply the leading coefficient, 35, and the constant, 8: $35(8) = 280$

3) Try to factor 280 so the sum of the factors is 34. We need only consider pairs of positive factors since 280 and 34 are both positive.

Pairs of Factors	Sums of Factors
$280,\quad 1$	281
$140,\quad 2$	142
$70,\quad 4$	74
$56,\quad 5$	61
$40,\quad 7$	47
$28, 10$	38
$20, 14$	34

4) Split $34y$ as follows:

$$34y = 20y + 14y$$

5) Factor by grouping:

$$35y^2 + 34y + 8 = 35y^2 + 20y + 14y + 8$$
$$= 5y(7y + 4) + 2(7y + 4)$$
$$= (7y + 4)(5y + 2)$$

9. $4t + 10t^2 - 6 = 10t^2 + 4t - 6$

We will use the FOIL method.

1) Factor out the common factor, 2:

$$2(5t^2 + 2t - 3)$$

2) Now we factor out the trinomial $5t^2 + 2t - 3$.

Factor the first term, $5t^2$. The factors are $5t$ and t. We have this possibility:

$$(5t+ \quad)(t+ \quad)$$

3) Factor the last term, -3. The factors are $1, -3$ and $-1, 3$.

4) Look for factors in steps (2) and (3) such that the sum of the products is the middle term, $2t$. Trial and error leads us to the correct factorization:
$$5t^2 + 2t - 3 = (5t - 3)(t + 1)$$

We must include the common factor to get a factorization of the original trinomial:
$$4t + 10t^2 - 6 = 2(5t - 3)(t + 1)$$

11. $8x^2 - 16 - 28x = 8x^2 - 28x - 16$

We will use the ac-method.

1) Factor out the common factor, 4:
$$4(2x^2 - 7x - 4)$$

2) Now we factor the trinomial $2x^2 - 7x - 4$. Multiply the leading coefficient, 2, and the constant, -4: $2(-4) = -8$

3) Factor -8 so the sum of the factors is -7. We need only consider parts of factors in which the negative factor has the larger absolute value, since their sum is negative.

Pairs of Factors	Sums of Factors
$-4, \quad 2$	-2
$-8, \quad 1$	-7

4) Split $-7x$ as follows:
$$-7x = -8x + x$$

5) Factor by grouping:
$$2x^2 - 7x - 4 = 2x^2 - 8x + x - 4$$
$$= 2x(x - 4) + (x - 4)$$
$$= (x - 4)(2x + 1)$$

We must include the common factor to get a factorization of the original trinomial:
$$8x^2 - 16 - 28x = 4(x - 4)(2x + 1)$$

13. $12x^3 - 31x^2 + 20x$

We will use the FOIL method.

1) Factor out the common factor, x:
$$x(12x^2 - 31x + 20)$$

2) We now factor the trinomial $12x^2 - 31x + 20$. Factor the first term, $12x^2$. The factors are $12x, x$ and $6x, 2x$ and $4x, 3x$. We have these possibilities:
$(12x+ \quad)(x+ \quad)$, $(6x+ \quad)(2x+ \quad)$, $(4x+ \quad)(3x+ \quad)$

3) Factor the last term, 20. The factors are 20, 1 and $-20, -1$ and 10, 2 and $-10, -2$ and 5, 4 and $-5, -4$.

4) Look for factors in steps (2) and (3) such that the sum of the products is the middle term, $-31x$. Trial and error leads us to the correct factorization:
$$12x^2 - 31x + 20 = (4x - 5)(3x - 4)$$

We must include the common factor to get a factorization of the original trinomial:
$$12x^3 - 31x^2 + 20x = x(4x - 5)(3x - 4)$$

15. $14x^4 - 19x^3 - 3x^2$

We will use the ac-method.

1) Factor out the common factor, x^2:
$$x^2(14x^2 - 19x - 3)$$

2) Now we factor the trinomial $14x^2 - 19x - 3$. Multiply the leading coefficient, 14, and the constant, -3: $14(-3) = -42$

3) Factor -42 so the sum of the factors is -19. We need only consider pairs of factors in which the negative factor has the larger absolute value, since the sum is negative.

Pairs of Factors	Sums of Factors
$-42, \quad 1$	-41
$-21, \quad 2$	-19
$-14, \quad 3$	-11
$-7, \quad 6$	-1

4) Split $-19x$ as follows:
$$-19x = -21x + 2x$$

5) Factor by grouping:
$$14x^2 - 19x - 3 = 14x^2 - 21x + 2x - 3$$
$$= 7x(2x - 3) + 2x - 3$$
$$= (2x - 3)(7x + 1)$$

We must include the common factor to get a factorization of the original trinomial:
$$14x^4 - 19x^3 - 3x^2 = x^2(2x - 3)(7x + 1)$$

17. $3a^2 - a - 4$

We will use the FOIL method.

1) There is no common factor (other than 1 or -1).

2) Factor the first term, $3a^2$. The factors are $3a$ and a. We have this possibility: $(3a+ \quad)(a+ \quad)$

3) Factor the last term, -4. The factors are $4, -1$ and $-4, 1$ and $2, -2$.

4) Look for factors in steps (2) and (3) such that the sum of the products is the middle term, $-a$. Trial and error leads us to the correct factorization:
$$(3a - 4)(a + 1)$$

19. $9x^2 + 15x + 4$

We will use the ac-method.

1) There is no common factor (other than 1 or -1).

2) Multiply the leading coefficient and the constant: $9(4) = 36$

3) Factor 36 so the sum of the factors is 15. We need only consider pairs of positive factors since 36 and 15 are both positive.

Pairs of Factors	Sums of Factors
36, 1	37
18, 2	20
12, 3	15
9, 4	13
6, 6	12

4) Split $15x$ as follows:
$$15x = 12x + 3x$$

5) Factor by grouping:
$$9x^2 + 15x + 4 = 9x^2 + 12x + 3x + 4$$
$$= 3x(3x + 4) + 3x + 4$$
$$= (3x + 4)(3x + 1)$$

21. $3 + 35z - 12z^2 = -12z^2 + 35z + 3$

We will use the FOIL method.

1) Factor out -1 so the leading coefficient is positive:
$-1(12z^2 - 35z - 3)$

2) Now we factor the trinomial $12z^2 - 35z - 3$. Factor the first term, $12z^2$. The factors are $12z$, z and $6z$, $2z$ and $4z$, $3z$. We have these possibilities: $(12z+ \ )(z+ \ )$, $(6z+ \ )(2z+ \ )$, $(4z+ \ )(3z+ \ )$

3) Factor the last term, -3. The factors are 3, -1 and -3, 1.

4) Look for factors in steps (2) and (3) such that the sum of the products is the middle term, $-35z$. Trial and error leads us to the correct factorization: $(12z + 1)(z - 3)$

We must include the common factor to get a factorization of the original trinomial:
$$3 + 35z - 12z^2 = -1(12z + 1)(z - 3), \text{ or}$$
$$(-12z - 1)(z - 3), \text{ or } (12z + 1)(-z + 3)$$

23. $-4t^2 - 4t + 15$

We will use the ac-method.

1) Factor out -1 so the leading coefficient is positive:
$-1(4t^2 + 4t - 15)$

2) Now we factor the trinomial $4t^2 + 4t - 15$. Multiply the leading coefficient and the constant: $4(-15) = -60$

3) Factor -60 so the sum of the factors is 4. The desired factorization is $10(-6)$.

4) Split $4t$ as follows:
$$4t = 10t - 6t$$

5) Factor by grouping:
$$4t^2 + 4t - 15 = 4t^2 + 10t - 6t - 15$$
$$= 2t(2t + 5) - 3(2t + 5)$$
$$= (2t + 5)(2t - 3)$$

We must include the common factor to get a factorization of the original trinomial:
$$-4t^2 - 4t + 15 = -1(2t + 5)(2t - 3), \text{ or}$$
$$(-2t - 5)(2t - 3), \text{ or } (2t + 5)(-2t + 3)$$

25. $3x^3 - 5x^2 - 2x$

We will use the FOIL method.

1) Factor out the common factor, x:
$x(3x^2 - 5x - 2)$

2) Now we factor the trinomial $3x^2 - 5x - 2$. Factor the first term, $3x^2$. The factors are $3x$ and x. We have this possibility: $(3x+ \ )(x+ \ )$

3) Factor the last term, -2. The factors are 2, -1 and -2, 1.

4) Look for factors in steps (2) and (3) such that the sum of the products is the middle term, $-5x$. Trial and error leads us to the correct factorization: $(3x + 1)(x - 2)$

We must include the common factor to get a factorization of the original trinomial:
$$3x^3 - 5x^2 - 2x = x(3x + 1)(x - 2)$$

27. $24x^2 - 2 - 47x = 24x^2 - 47x - 2$

We will use the ac-method.

1) There is no common factor (other than 1 or -1).

2) Multiply the leading coefficient and the constant: $24(-2) = -48$

3) Factor -48 so the sum of the factors is -47. The desired factorization is $-48 \cdot 1$.

4) Split $-47x$ as follows:
$$-47x = -48x + x$$

5) Factor by grouping:
$$24x^2 - 47x - 2 = 24x^2 - 48x + x - 2$$
$$= 24x(x - 2) + (x - 2)$$
$$= (x - 2)(24x + 1)$$

29. $21x^2 + 37x + 12$

We will use the FOIL method.

1) There is no common factor (other than 1 or -1).

2) Factor the first term $21x^2$. The factors are $21x$, x and $7x$, $3x$. We have these possibilities: $(21x+ \ )(x+ \ )$ and $(7x+ \ )(3x+ \ )$.

3) Factor the last term, 12. The factors are 12, 1 and -12, -1 and 6, 2 and -6, -2 and 4, 3 and -4, -3.

4) Look for factors in steps (2) and (3) such that the sum of the products is the middle term, $37x$. Trial and error leads us to the correct factorization: $(7x + 3)(3x + 4)$

31. $40x^4 + 16x^2 - 12$

We will use the ac-method.

1) Factor out the common factor, 4.
$$4(10x^4 + 4x^2 - 3)$$

Now we will factor the trinomial $10x^4 + 4x^2 - 3$. Substitute u for x^2 (and u^2 for x^4), and factor $10u^2 + 4u - 3$.

2) Multiply the leading coefficient and the constant: $10(-3) = -30$

3) Factor -30 so the sum of the factors is 4. This cannot be done. The trinomial $10u^2 + 4u - 3$ cannot be factored into binomials with integer coefficients. We have

$$40x^4 + 16x^2 - 12 = 4(10x^4 + 4x^2 - 3)$$

33. $12a^2 - 17ab + 6b^2$

We will use the FOIL method. (Our thinking is much the same as if we were factoring $12a^2 - 17a + 6$.)

1) There is no common factor (other than 1 or -1).

2) Factor the first term, $12a^2$. The factors are $12a$, a and $6a$, $2a$ and $4a$, $3a$. We have these possibilities: $(12a+ \quad)(a+ \quad)$ and $(6a+ \quad)(2a+ \quad)$ and $(4a+ \quad)(3a+ \quad)$.

3) Factor the last term, $6b^2$. The factors are $6b$, b and $-6b$, $-b$ and $3b$, $2b$ and $-3b$, $-2b$.

4) Look for factors in steps (2) and (3) such that the sum of the products is the middle term, $-17ab$. Trial and error leads us to the correct factorization: $(4a - 3b)(3a - 2b)$

35. $2x^2 + xy - 6y^2$

We will use the ac-method.

1) There is no common factor (other than 1 or -1).

2) Multiply the coefficients of the first and last terms: $2(-6) = -12$

3) Factor -12 so the sum of the factors is 1. The desired factorization is $4(-3)$.

4) Split xy as follows:

$$xy = 4xy - 3xy$$

5) Factor by grouping:

$$2x^2 + xy - 6y^2 = 2x^2 + 4xy - 3xy - 6y^2$$
$$= 2x(x + 2y) - 3y(x + 2y)$$
$$= (x + 2y)(2x - 3y)$$

37. $12x^2 - 58xy + 56y^2$

We will use the FOIL method.

1) Factor out the common factor, 2:

$$2(6x^2 - 29xy + 28y^2)$$

2) Now we factor the trinomial $6x^2 - 29xy + 28y^2$. Factor the first term, $6x^2$. The factors are $6x$, x and $3x$, $2x$. We have these possibilities: $(6x+ \quad)(x+ \quad)$ and $(3x+ \quad)(2x+ \quad)$.

3) Factor the last term, $28y^2$. The factors are $28y$, y and $-28y$, $-y$ and $14y$, $2y$ and $-14y$, $-2y$ and $7y$, $4y$ and $-7y$, $-4y$.

4) Look for factors in steps (2) and (3) such that the sum of the products is the middle term, $-29xy$. Trial and error leads us to the correct factorization: $(3x - 4y)(2x - 7y)$

We must include the common factor to get a factorization of the original trinomial:

$$12x^2 - 58xy + 56y^2 = 2(3x - 4y)(2x - 7y)$$

39. $9x^2 - 30xy + 25y^2$

We will use the ac-method.

1) There is no common factor (other than 1 or -1).

2) Multiply the coefficients of the first and last terms: $9(25) = 225$

3) Factor 225 so the sum of the factors is -30. The desired factorization is $-15(-15)$.

4) Split $-30xy$ as follows:

$$-30xy = -15xy - 15xy$$

5) Factor by grouping:

$$9x^2 - 30xy + 25y^2 = 9x^2 - 15xy - 15xy + 25y^2$$
$$= 3x(3x - 5y) - 5y(3x - 5y)$$
$$= (3x - 5y)(3x - 5y)$$

41. $3x^6 + 4x^3 - 4$

We will use the FOIL method.

1) There is no common factor (other than 1 or -1). Substitute u for x^3 (and hence u^2 for x^6). We factor $3u^2 + 4u - 4$.

2) Factor the first term, $3u^2$. The factors are $3u$ and u. We have this possibility: $(3u+ \quad)(u+ \quad)$

3) Factor the last term, -4. The factors are -1, 4 and 1, -4 and -2, 2.

4) Look for factors in steps (2) and (3) such that the sum of the products is the middle term, $4u$. Trial and error leads us to the correct factorization of $3u^2 + 4u - 4$: $(3u - 2)(u + 2)$. Replacing u with x^3 we have the factorization of the original trinomial: $(3x^3 - 2)(x^3 + 2)$.

43. a) $h(10) = -16(0)^2 + 80(0) + 224 = 224$ ft

$h(1) = -16(1)^2 + 80(1) + 224 = 288$ ft

$h(3) = -16(3)^2 + 80(3) + 224 = 320$ ft

$h(4) = -16(4)^2 + 80(4) + 224 = 288$ ft

$h(6) = -16(6)^2 + 80(6) + 224 = 128$ ft

b) $h(t) = -16t^2 + 80t + 224$

We will use the grouping method.

1) Factor out -16 so the leading coefficient is positive: $-16(t^2 - 5t - 14)$

2) Factor the trinomial $t^2 - 5t - 14$. Multiply the leading coefficient and the constant: $1(-14) = -14$

3) Factor -14 so the sum of the factors is -5. The desired factorization is $-7 \cdot 2$.

4) Split $-5t$ as follows:

$$-5t = -7t + 2t$$

5) Factor by grouping:
$$t^2 - 5t - 14 = t^2 - 7t + 2t - 14$$
$$= t(t-7) + 2(t-7)$$
$$= (t-7)(t+2)$$

We must include the common factor to get a factorization of the original trinomial.
$$h(t) = -16(t-7)(t+2)$$

45. Discussion and Writing Exercise

47. $x + 2y - z = 0,$ (1)
$$4x + 2y + 5z = 6,$$ (2)
$$2x - y + z = 5$$ (3)

First we will eliminate z from Equations (1) and (2).
$$5x + 10y - 5z = 0 \quad \text{Multiplying (1) by 5}$$
$$\underline{4x + 2y + 5z = 6 \quad (2)}$$
$$9x + 12y \quad\quad = 6 \quad (4)$$

Now add Equations (1) and (3) to eliminate z.
$$x + 2y - z = 0$$
$$\underline{2x - y + z = 5}$$
$$3x + y \quad\quad = 5 \quad (5)$$

Now solve the system composed of Equations (4) and (5). We multiply Equation (5) by -3 and add.
$$9x + 12y = 6$$
$$\underline{-9x - 3y = -15}$$
$$9y = -9$$
$$y = -1$$

Substitute -1 for y in Equation (4) or (5) and solve for x. We use Equation (5) here.
$$3x - 1 = 5$$
$$3x = 6$$
$$x = 2$$

Now substitute 2 for x and -1 for y in one of the original equations and solve for z. We use Equation (3).
$$2 \cdot 2 - (-1) + z = 5$$
$$4 + 1 + z = 5$$
$$5 + z = 5$$
$$z = 0$$

The triple $(2, -1, 0)$ checks, so it is the solution.

49. $2x + 9y + 6z = 5,$ (1)
$$x - y + z = 4,$$ (2)
$$3x + 2y + 3z = 7$$ (3)

First we will eliminate x from Equations (1) and (2).
$$2x + 9y + 6z = 5 \quad (1)$$
$$\underline{-2x + 2y - 2z = -8 \quad \text{Multiplying (2) by } -2}$$
$$11y + 4z = -3 \quad (4)$$

Now eliminate x from Equations (2) and (3).

$$-3x + 3y - 3z = -12 \quad \text{Multiplying (2) by } -3$$
$$\underline{3x + 2y + 3z = 7 \quad (3)}$$
$$5y \quad\quad = -5$$
$$y = -1$$

Note that the last step eliminated z as well as x, allowing us to solve for y. Now substitute -1 for y in Equation (4) and solve for z.
$$11(-1) + 4z = -3$$
$$-11 + 4z = -3$$
$$4z = 8$$
$$z = 2$$

Substitute -1 for y and 2 for z in one of the original equations and solve for x. We use Equation (2).
$$x - (-1) + 2 = 4$$
$$x + 1 + 2 = 4$$
$$x + 3 = 4$$
$$x = 1$$

The triple $(1, -1, 2)$ checks, so it is the solution.

51. Write the first equation in slope-intercept form.
$$y - 2x = 18$$
$$y = 2x + 18$$

The second equation, $2x - 7 = y$, or $y = 2x - 7$, is in slope-intercept form.

Since the equations have the same slope, 2, and different y-intercepts, $(0, 8)$ and $(0, -7)$, the graphs of the equations are parallel lines.

53. Write each equation in slope-intercept form.
$$2x + 5y = 4 \quad\quad\quad\quad 2x - 5y = -3$$
$$5y = -2x + 4 \quad\quad\quad -5y = -2x - 3$$
$$y = -\frac{2}{5}x + \frac{4}{5} \quad\quad\quad y = \frac{2}{5}x + \frac{3}{5}$$

The slope of the first line is $-\dfrac{2}{5}$, and the slope of the second is $\dfrac{2}{5}$. The slopes are not the same nor is their product -1, so the graphs of the equations are neither parallel nor perpendicular.

55. First we find the slope.
$$m = \frac{-4 - (-3)}{5 - (-2)} = \frac{-1}{7} = -\frac{1}{7}$$

Now substitute $-\dfrac{1}{7}$ for m and the coordinates of either point in the slope-intercept equation $y = mx + b$ and solve for b. We will use the point $(5, -4)$.
$$y = mx + b$$
$$-4 = -\frac{1}{7} \cdot 5 + b$$
$$-4 = -\frac{5}{7} + b$$
$$-\frac{23}{7} = b$$

Now use the equation $y = mx + b$ again, substituting $-\dfrac{1}{7}$ for m and $-\dfrac{23}{7}$ for b.

$$y = -\frac{1}{7}x - \frac{23}{7}$$

57. First we find the slope.

$$m = \frac{-4 - 3}{7 - (-10)} = \frac{-7}{17} = -\frac{7}{17}$$

Now substitute $-\dfrac{7}{17}$ for m and the coordinates of either point in the slope-intercept equation $y = mx + b$ and solve for b. We will use the point $(-10, 3)$.

$$y = mx + b$$
$$3 = -\frac{7}{17}(-10) + b$$
$$3 = \frac{70}{17} + b$$
$$-\frac{19}{17} = b$$

Now use the equation $y = mx + b$ again, substituting $-\dfrac{7}{17}$ for m and $-\dfrac{19}{17}$ for b.

$$y = -\frac{7}{17}x - \frac{19}{17}$$

59. Left to the student

61. $p^2q^2 + 7pq + 12$

The factorization will be of the form $(pq + \quad)(pq + \quad)$. We look for factors of 12 whose sum is 7. The factors we need are 4 and 3. The factorization is $(pq + 4)(pq + 3)$.

63. $x^2 - \dfrac{4}{25} + \dfrac{3}{5}x = x^2 + \dfrac{3}{5}x - \dfrac{4}{25}$

We look for factors of $-\dfrac{4}{25}$ whose sum is $\dfrac{3}{5}$. The factors are $\dfrac{4}{5}$ and $-\dfrac{1}{5}$. The factorization is $\left(x + \dfrac{4}{5}\right)\left(x - \dfrac{1}{5}\right)$.

65. $y^2 + 0.4y - 0.05$

We look for factors of -0.05 whose sum is 0.4. The factors are -0.1 and 0.5. The factorization is $(y - 0.1)(y + 0.5)$.

67. $7a^2b^2 + 6 + 13ab = 7a^2b^2 + 13ab + 6$

We will use the grouping method. There is no common factor (other than 1 or -1). Multiply the leading coefficient and the constant: $7(6) = 42$. Factor 42 so the sum of the factors is 13. The desired factorization is $6 \cdot 7$. Split the middle term and factor by grouping.

$$7a^2b^2 + 13ab + 6 = 7a^2b^2 + 6ab + 7ab + 6$$
$$= ab(7ab + 6) + 7ab + 6$$
$$= (7ab + 6)(ab + 1)$$

69. $3x^2 + 12x - 495$

Factor out the common factor, 3.

$$3(x^2 + 4x - 165)$$

Now factor $x^2 + 4x - 165$. Find factors of -165 whose sum is 4. The factors are -11 and 15. Then $x^2 + 4x - 165 = (x - 11)(x + 15)$, and $3x^2 + 12x - 495 = 3(x - 11)(x + 15)$.

71. $216x + 78x^2 + 6x^3 = 6x^3 + 78x^2 + 216x$

Factor out the common factor, $6x$.

$$6x(x^2 + 13x + 36)$$

Now factor $x^2 + 13x + 36$. Look for factors of 36 whose sum is 13. The factors are 9 and 4. Then $x^2 + 13x + 36 = (x + 9)(x + 4)$, and $6x^3 + 78x^2 + 216x = 6x(x + 9)(x + 4)$.

73. $x^{2a} + 5x^a - 24$

$x^{2a} = (x^a)^2$, so the factorization is of the form $(x^a + \quad)(x^a + \quad)$.

Look for factors of -24 whose sum is 5. The factors are 8 and -3. Then the factorization is $(x^a + 8)(x^a - 3)$.

Exercise Set 4.6

1. $x^2 - 4x + 4 = (x - 2)^2$ — Find the square terms and write their square roots with a minus sign between them.

3. $y^2 + 18y + 81 = (y + 9)^2$ — Find the square terms and write their square roots with a minus sign between them.

5. $x^2 + 1 + 2x = x^2 + 2x + 1$ — Writing in descending order
$\quad\quad = (x + 1)^2$ — Factoring the trinomial square

7. $9y^2 + 12y + 4 = (3y + 2)^2$ — Find the square terms and write their square roots with a minus sign between them.

9. $-18y^2 + y^3 + 81y = y^3 - 18y^2 + 81y$ — Writing in descending order
$\quad\quad = y(y^2 - 18y + 81)$ — Removing the common factor
$\quad\quad = y(y - 9)^2$ — Factoring the trinomial square

11. $12a^2 + 36a + 27 = 3(4a^2 + 12a + 9)$ — Removing the common factor
$\quad\quad = 3(2a + 3)^2$ — Factoring the trinomial square

13. $2x^2 - 40x + 200 = 2(x^2 - 20x + 100)$
$\quad\quad = 2(x - 10)^2$

15. $1 - 8d + 16d^2 = (1 - 4d)^2$, or $(4d - 1)^2$ — Find the square terms and write their square roots with a minus sign between them.

17. $y^4 - 8y^2 + 16 = (y^2 - 4)^2$ — Find the square terms and write their square roots with a minus sign between them.
$\quad\quad = [(y + 2)(y - 2)]^2$ — Factoring the difference of squares
$\quad\quad = (y + 2)^2(y - 2)^2$

19. $0.25x^2 + 0.30x + 0.09 = (0.5x + 0.3)^2$ Find the square terms and write their square roots with a plus sign between them.

21. $p^2 - 2pq + q^2 = (p - q)^2$

23. $a^2 + 4ab + 4b^2 = (a + 2b)^2$

25. $25a^2 - 30ab + 9b^2 = (5a - 3b)^2$

27. $y^6 + 26y^3 + 169 = (y^3 + 13)^2$ Find the square terms and write their square roots with a plus sign between them

29. $16x^{10} - 8x^5 + 1 = (4x^5 - 1)^2$ $[16x^{10} = (4x^5)^2]$

31. $x^4 + 2y^2y^2 + y^4 = (x^2 + y^2)^2$

33. $x^2 - 16 = x^2 - 4^2 = (x + 4)(x - 4)$

35. $p^2 - 49 = p^2 - 7^2 = (p + 7)(p - 7)$

37. $p^2q^2 - 25 = (pq)^2 - 5^2 = (pq + 5)(pq - 5)$

39. $6x^2 - 6y^2$
$= 6(x^2 - y^2)$ Removing the common factor
$= 6(x + y)(x - y)$ Factoring the difference of squares

41. $4xy^4 - 4xz^4$
$= 4x(y^4 - z^4)$ Removing the common factor
$= 4x[(y^2)^2 - (z^2)^2]$
$= 4x(y^2 + z^2)(y^2 - z^2)$ Factoring the difference of squares
$= 4x(y^2 + z^2)(y + z)(y - z)$ Factoring $y^2 - z^2$

43. $4a^3 - 49a = a(4a^2 - 49)$
$= a[(2a)^2 - 7^2]$
$= a(2a + 7)(2a - 7)$

45. $3x^8 - 3y^8 = 3(x^8 - y^8)$
$= 3[(x^4)^2 - (y^4)^2)]$
$= 3(x^4 + y^4)(x^4 - y^4)$
$= 3(x^4 + y^4)[(x^2)^2 - (y^2)^2]$
$= 3(x^4 + y^4)(x^2 + y^2)(x^2 - y^2)$
$= 3(x^4 + y^4)(x^2 + y^2)(x + y)(x - y)$ •

47. $9a^4 - 25a^2b^4 = a^2(9a^2 - 25b^4)$
$= a^2[(3a)^2 - (5b^2)^2]$
$= a^2(3a + 5b^2)(3a - 5b^2)$

49. $\dfrac{1}{36} - z^2 = \left(\dfrac{1}{6}\right)^2 - z^2 = \left(\dfrac{1}{6} + z\right)\left(\dfrac{1}{6} - z\right)$

51. $0.04x^2 - 0.09y^2 = (0.2x)^2 - (0.3y)^2$
$= (0.2x + 0.3y)(0.2x - 0.3y)$

53. $m^3 - 7m^2 - 4m + 28$
$= m^2(m - 7) - 4(m - 7)$ Factoring by grouping
$= (m^2 - 4)(m - 7)$
$= (m + 2)(m - 2)(m - 7)$ Factoring the difference of squares

55. $a^3 - ab^2 - 2a^2 + 2b^2$
$= a(a^2 - b^2) - 2(a^2 - b^2)$ Factoring by grouping
$= (a - 2)(a^2 - b^2)$
$= (a - 2)(a + b)(a - b)$ Factoring the difference of squares

57. $(a + b)^2 - 100 = (a + b)^2 - 10^2$
$= (a + b + 10)(a + b - 10)$

59. $a^2 + 2ab + b^2 - 9$
$= (a^2 + 2ab + b^2) - 9$ Grouping as a difference of squares
$= (a + b)^2 - 3^2$
$= (a + b + 3)(a + b - 3)$

61. $r^2 - 2r + 1 - 4s^2$
$= (r^2 - 2r + 1) - 4s^2$ Grouping as a difference of squares
$= (r - 1)^2 - (2s)^2$
$= (r - 1 + 2s)(r - 1 - 2s)$

63. $2m^2 + 4mn + 2n^2 - 50b^2$
$= 2(m^2 + 2mn + n^2 - 25b^2)$ Removing the common factor
$= 2[(m^2 + 2mn + n^2) - 25b^2]$ Grouping as a difference of squares
$= 2[(m + n)^2 - (5b)^2]$
$= 2(m + n + 5b)(m + n - 5b)$

65. $9 - (a^2 + 2ab + b^2) = 9 - (a + b)^2$
$= [3 + (a + b)][3 - (a + b)]$, or
$(3 + a + b)(3 - a - b)$

67. $z^3 + 27 = z^3 + 3^3$
$= (z + 3)(z^2 - 3z + 9)$
$A^3 + B^3 = (A + B)(A^2 - AB + B^2)$

69. $x^3 - 1 = x^3 - 1^3$
$= (x - 1)(x^2 + x + 1)$
$A^3 - B^3 = (A - B)(A^2 + AB + B^2)$

71. $y^3 + 125 = y^3 + 5^3$
$= (y + 5)(y^2 - 5y + 25)$
$A^3 + B^3 = (A + B)(A^2 - AB + B^2)$

73. $8a^3 + 1 = (2a)^3 + 1^3$
$= (2a + 1)(4a^2 - 2a + 1)$
$A^3 + B^3 = (A + B)(A^2 - AB + B^2)$

75. $y^3 - 8 = y^3 - 2^3$
$$= (y - 2)(y^2 + 2y + 4)$$
$$A^3 - B^3 = (A - B)(A^2 + AB + B^2)$$

77. $8 - 27b^3 = 2^3 - (3b)^3$
$$= (2 - 3b)(4 + 6b + 9b^2)$$

79. $64y^3 + 1 = (4y)^3 + 1^3$
$$= (4y + 1)(16y^2 - 4y + 1)$$

81. $8x^3 + 27 = (2x)^3 + 3^3$
$$= (2x + 3)(4x^2 - 6x + 9)$$

83. $a^3 - b^3 = (a - b)(a^2 + ab + b^2)$

85. $a^3 + \dfrac{1}{8} = a^3 + \left(\dfrac{1}{2}\right)^3$
$$= \left(a + \dfrac{1}{2}\right)\left(a^2 - \dfrac{1}{2}a + \dfrac{1}{4}\right)$$

87. $2y^3 - 128 = 2(y^3 - 64)$
$$= 2(y^3 - 4^3)$$
$$= 2(y - 4)(y^2 + 4y + 16)$$

89. $24a^3 + 3 = 3(8a^3 + 1)$
$$= 3[(2a)^3 + 1^3]$$
$$= 3(2a + 1)(4a^2 - 2a + 1)$$

91. $rs^3 + 64r = r(s^3 + 64)$
$$= r(s^3 + 4^3)$$
$$= r(s + 4)(s^2 - 4s + 16)$$

93. $5x^3 - 40z^3 = 5(x^3 - 8z^3)$
$$= 5[x^3 - (2z)^3]$$
$$= 5(x - 2z)(x^2 + 2xz + 4z^2)$$

95. $x^3 + 0.001 = x^3 + (0.1)^3$
$$= (x + 0.1)(x^2 - 0.1x + 0.01)$$

97. $64x^6 - 8t^6 = 8(8x^6 - t^6)$
$$= 8[(2x^2)^3 - (t^2)^3]$$
$$= 8(2x^2 - t^2)(4x^4 + 2x^2t^2 + t^4)$$

99. $2y^4 - 128y = 2y(y^3 - 64)$
$$= 2y(y^3 - 4^3)$$
$$= 2y(y - 4)(y^2 + 4y + 16)$$

101. $z^6 - 1$
$$= (z^3)^2 - 1^2 \qquad \text{Writing as a difference of squares}$$
$$= (z^3 + 1)(z^3 - 1) \qquad \text{Factoring a difference of squares}$$
$$= (z + 1)(z^2 - z + 1)(z - 1)(z^2 + z + 1)$$
$$\qquad\qquad\qquad \text{Factoring a sum and a}$$
$$\qquad\qquad\qquad \text{difference of cubes}$$

103. $t^6 + 64y^6 = (t^2)^3 + (4y^2)^3$
$$= (t^2 + 4y^2)(t^4 - 4t^2y^2 + 16y^4)$$

105. Discussion and Writing Exercise

107. $7x - 2y = -11, \quad (1)$
$\qquad 2x + 7y = 18 \qquad (2)$

To eliminate y, multiply Equation (1) by 7 and Equation (2) by 2 and add.

$$49x - 14y = -77$$
$$\underline{4x + 14y = \quad 36}$$
$$53x \qquad\quad = -41$$
$$x = -\dfrac{41}{53}$$

Now substitute $-\dfrac{41}{53}$ for x in one of the original equations and solve for y.

$$2x + 7y = 18 \qquad (2)$$
$$2\left(-\dfrac{41}{53}\right) + 7y = 18$$
$$-\dfrac{82}{53} + 7y = 18$$
$$7y = \dfrac{1036}{53}$$
$$y = \dfrac{148}{53}$$

The pair $\left(-\dfrac{41}{53}, \dfrac{148}{53}\right)$ checks, so it is the solution.

109. $x - y = -12, \quad (1)$
$$\underline{x + y = \quad 14 \quad (2)}$$
$$2x \qquad = \quad 2 \quad \text{Adding}$$
$$x = \quad 1$$

Now substitute 1 for x in one of the original equations and solve for y.

$$x + y = 14 \quad (2)$$
$$1 + y = 14$$
$$y = 13$$

The pair $(1, 13)$ checks, so it is the solution.

111. $x - y \leq 5,$
$\qquad x + y \geq 3$

Graph the lines $x - y = 5$ and $x + y = 3$ using solid lines. We indicate the region for each inequality by arrows. Shade the region where they overlap.

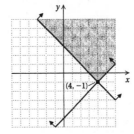

To find the vertex, solve the system of related equations:
$$x - y = 5$$
$$x + y = 3$$

Solving, we obtain the vertex $(4, -1)$.

113. $x - y \geq 5,$ (1)

$x + y \leq 3,$ (2)

$x \geq 1$ (3)

Shade the intersection of the graphs of $x - y \geq 5$, $x + y \leq 3$, and $x \geq 1$.

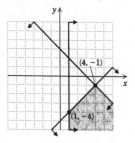

To find the vertices we solve two different systems of equations. From (1) and (2) we obtain the vertex $(4, -1)$. From (1) and (3) we obtain the vertex $(1, -4)$.

115. To find an equation of the line through $(-2, -4)$ parallel to $x - y = 5$, we first write $x - y = 5$ in slope-intercept form.

$$x - y = 5$$
$$-y = -x + 5$$
$$y = x - 5$$

The slope of $y = x - 5$ is 1, so we want to find an equation with slope 1 containing the point $(-2, -4)$. First substitute 1 for m, -2 for x, and -4 for y in $y = mx + b$.

$$y = mx + b$$
$$-4 = 1(-2) + b$$
$$-4 = -2 + b$$
$$-2 = b$$

Now use $y = mx + b$ again, substituting 1 for m and -2 for b.

$$y = 1 \cdot x - 2, \text{ or } y = x - 2$$

We have seen above that the slope of $x - y = 5$ is 1. Then the slope of a line perpendicular to this line is the opposite of the reciprocal of 1, or -1. Thus, we want to find an equation of the line with slope -1 containing $(-2, -4)$. First substitute -1 for m, -2 for x, and -4 for y in $y = mx + b$.

$$y = mx + b$$
$$-4 = -1(-2) + b$$
$$-4 = 2 + b$$
$$-6 = b$$

Now use $y = mx + b$ again, substituting -1 for m and -6 for b.

$$y = -1 \cdot x - 6, \text{ or } y = -x - 6$$

117. To find an equation of the line through $(4, 5)$ parallel to $y = -\frac{1}{2}x + 3$, we first observe that the slope of $y = -\frac{1}{2}x + 3$ is $-\frac{1}{2}$. Thus, we want to find an equation of

the line with slope $-\frac{1}{2}$ containing $(4, 5)$. Begin by substituting $-\frac{1}{2}$ for m, 4 for x, and 5 for y in $y = mx + b$.

$$y = mx + b$$
$$5 = -\frac{1}{2} \cdot 4 + b$$
$$5 = -2 + b$$
$$7 = b$$

Now use $y = mx + b$ again, substituting $-\frac{1}{2}$ for m and 7 for b.

$$y = -\frac{1}{2}x + 7$$

The slope of a line perpendicular to $y = -\frac{1}{2}x + 3$ is the opposite of the reciprocal of $-\frac{1}{2}$, or 2. Thus, we want to find an equation of the line with slope 2 containing $(4, 5)$. First substitute 2 for m, 4 for x, and 5 for y in $y = mx + b$.

$$y = mx + b$$
$$5 = 2 \cdot 4 + b$$
$$5 = 8 + b$$
$$-3 = b$$

Now use $y = mx + b$ again, substituting 2 for m and -3 for b.

$$y = 2x - 3$$

119. If $P(x) = x^2$, then

$$P(a + h) - P(a)$$
$$= (a + h)^2 - a^2$$
$$= [(a + h) + a][(a + h) - a]$$
$$= (2a + h)h, \text{ or } h(2a + h)$$

121. If $P(x) = x^3$, then

$$P(a + h) - P(a)$$
$$= (a + h)^3 - a^3$$
$$= (a + h - a)[(a + h)^2 + (a + h)(a) + a^2]$$
$$= h(a^2 + 2ah + h^2 + a^2 + ah + a^2)$$
$$= h(3a^2 + 3ah + h^2)$$

123. The model shows a cube with volume a^3 from which a portion whose volume is b^3 has been removed. This leaves a remaining volume which can be expressed as $a^2(a - b) + ab(a - b) + b^2(a - b)$, or $(a - b)(a^2 + ab + b^2)$. Thus, $a^3 - b^3 = (a - b)(a^2 + ab + b^2)$.

125. $x^4y^4 - 8x^2y^2 + 16 = (x^2y^2 - 4)^2$
$$= [(xy + 2)(xy - 2)]^2$$
$$= (xy + 2)^2(xy - 2)^2$$

127. $5c^{100} - 80d^{100}$
$$= 5(c^{100} - 16d^{100})$$
$$= 5(c^{50} + 4d^{50})(c^{50} - 4d^{50})$$
$$= 5(c^{50} + 4d^{50})(c^{25} + 2d^{25})(c^{25} - 2d^{25})$$

129. $x^{4a} - y^{2b} = (x^{2a})^2 - (y^b)^2 = (x^{2a} + y^b)(x^{2a} - y^b)$

131. $x^{6a} + y^{3b} = (x^{2a})^3 + (y^b)^3$
$$= (x^{2a} + y^b)(x^{4a} - x^{2a}y^b + y^{2b})$$

133. $3x^{3a} + 24y^{3b} = 3(x^{3a} + 8y^{3b})$
$$= 3[(x^a)^3 + (2y^b)^3]$$
$$= 3(x^a + 2y^b)(x^{2a} - 2x^a y^b + 4y^{2b})$$

135. $\frac{1}{24}x^3y^3 + \frac{1}{3}z^3 = \frac{1}{3}\left(\frac{1}{8}x^3y^3 + z^3\right)$
$$= \frac{1}{3}\left[\left(\frac{1}{2}xy\right)^3 + z^3\right]$$
$$= \frac{1}{3}\left(\frac{1}{2}xy + z\right)\left(\frac{1}{4}x^2y^2 - \frac{1}{2}xyz + z^2\right)$$

137. $(x+y)^3 - x^3$
$$= [(x+y) - x][(x+y)^2 + x(x+y) + x^2]$$
$$= (x + y - x)(x^2 + 2xy + y^2 + x^2 + xy + x^2)$$
$$= y(3x^2 + 3xy + y^2)$$

139. $(a+2)^3 - (a-2)^3$
$$= [(a+2) - (a-2)][(a+2)^2 + (a+2)(a-2) + (a-2)^2]$$
$$= (a+2-a+2)(a^2+4a+4+a^2-4+a^2-4a+4)$$
$$= 4(3a^2 + 4)$$

Exercise Set 4.7

1. $y^2 - 225$
$$= y^2 - 15^2 \quad \text{Difference of squares}$$
$$= (y + 15)(y - 15)$$

3. $2x^2 + 11x + 12$
$$= (2x + 3)(x + 4) \qquad \text{FOIL or } ac\text{-method}$$

5. $5x^4 - 20$
$$= 5(x^4 - 4) \quad \text{Removing the common factor}$$
$$= 5[(x^2)^2 - 2^2] \quad \text{Difference of squares}$$
$$= 5(x^2 + 2)(x^2 - 2)$$

7. $p^2 + 36 + 12p$
$$= p^2 + 12p + 36 \quad \text{Trinomial square}$$
$$= (p + 6)^2$$

9. $2x^2 - 10x - 132$
$$= 2(x^2 - 5x - 66)$$
$$= 2(x - 11)(x + 6) \quad \text{Trial and error}$$

11. $9x^2 - 25y^2$
$$= (3x)^2 - (5y)^2 \quad \text{Difference of squares}$$
$$= (3x + 5y)(3x - 5y)$$

13. $m^6 - 1$
$$= (m^3)^2 - 1^2 \quad \text{Difference of squares}$$
$$= (m^3 + 1)(m^3 - 1) \quad \text{Sum and difference of cubes}$$
$$= (m + 1)(m^2 - m + 1)(m - 1)(m^2 + m + 1)$$

15. $x^2 + 6x - y^2 + 9$
$$= x^2 + 6x + 9 - y^2$$
$$= (x + 3)^2 - y^2 \quad \text{Difference of squares}$$
$$= [(x + 3) + y][(x + 3) - y]$$
$$= (x + 3 + y)(x + 3 - y)$$

17. $250x^3 - 128y^3$
$$= 2(125x^3 - 64y^3)$$
$$= 2[(5x)^3 - (4y)^3] \quad \text{Difference of cubes}$$
$$= 2(5x - 4y)(25x^2 + 20xy + 16y^2)$$

19. $8m^3 + m^6 - 20$
$$= m^6 + 8m^3 - 20$$
$$= (m^3)^2 + 8m^3 - 20$$
$$= (m^3 - 2)(m^3 + 10) \quad \text{Trial and error}$$

21. $ac + cd - ab - bd$
$$= c(a + d) - b(a + d) \quad \text{Factoring by grouping}$$
$$= (c - b)(a + d)$$

23. $50b^2 - 5ab - a^2$
$$= (5b - a)(10b + a) \quad \text{FOIL or } ac\text{-method}$$

25. $-7x^2 + 2x^3 + 4x - 14$
$$= 2x^3 - 7x^2 + 4x - 14$$
$$= x^2(2x - 7) + 2(2x - 7) \quad \text{Factoring by grouping}$$
$$= (x^2 + 2)(2x - 7)$$

27. $2x^3 + 6x^2 - 8x - 24$
$$= 2(x^3 + 3x^2 - 4x - 12)$$
$$= 2[x^2(x + 3) - 4(x + 3)] \quad \text{Factoring by grouping}$$
$$= 2(x^2 - 4)(x + 3) \qquad \text{Difference of squares}$$
$$= 2(x + 2)(x - 2)(x + 3)$$

29. $16x^3 + 54y^3$
$$= 2(8x^3 + 27y^3)$$
$$= 2[(2x)^3 + (3y)^3] \quad \text{Sum of cubes}$$
$$= 2(2x + 3y)(4x^2 - 6xy + 9y^2)$$

31. $36y^2 - 35 + 12y$
$$= 36y^2 + 12y - 35$$
$$= (6y - 5)(6y + 7) \quad \text{FOIL or } ac\text{-method}$$

33. $a^8 - b^8 \qquad \text{Difference of squares}$
$$= (a^4 + b^4)(a^4 - b^4) \qquad \text{Difference of squares}$$
$$= (a^4 + b^4)(a^2 + b^2)(a^2 - b^2) \quad \text{Difference of squares}$$
$$= (a^4 + b^4)(a^2 + b^2)(a + b)(a - b)$$

35. $a^3b - 16ab^3$
$$= ab(a^2 - 16b^2) \quad \text{Difference of squares}$$
$$= ab(a + 4b)(a - 4b)$$

37. $\dfrac{1}{16}x^2 - \dfrac{1}{6}xy^2 + \dfrac{1}{9}y^4$

$= \dfrac{1}{16}x^2 - \dfrac{1}{6}xy^2 + \dfrac{1}{9}(y^2)^2$ Trinomial square

$= \left(\dfrac{1}{4}x - \dfrac{1}{3}y^2\right)^2$

39. $5x^3 - 5x^2y - 5xy^2 + 5y^3$

$= 5(x^3 - x^2y - xy^2 + y^3)$

$= 5[x^2(x - y) - y^2(x - y)]$ Factoring by grouping

$= 5(x^2 - y^2)(x - y)$

$= 5(x + y)(x - y)(x - y)$ Factoring the difference
                                        of squares

$= 5(x + y)(x - y)^2$

41. $42ab + 27a^2b^2 + 8$

$= 27a^2b^2 + 42ab + 8$

$= (9ab + 2)(3ab + 4)$ FOIL or ac-method

43. $8y^4 - 125y$

$= y(8y^3 - 125)$

$= y[(2y)^3 - 5^3]$ Difference of cubes

$= y(2y - 5)(4y^2 + 10y + 25)$

45. $a^2 - b^2 - 6b - 9$

$= a^2 - (b^2 + 6b + 9)$ Factoring out -1

$= a^2 - (b + 3)^2$ Difference of squares

$= [a + (b + 3)][a - (b + 3)]$

$= (a + b + 3)(a - b - 3)$

47. Discussion and Writing Exercise

49. Familiarize. Let $x =$ the number of correct answers and $y =$ the number of incorrect answers. Then the total number of points awarded for the correct answers is $2x$, the total number of points deducted for the incorrect answers is $\dfrac{1}{2}y$, and the total score is $2x - \dfrac{1}{2}y$. Assume that all the questions were answered.

Translate.

The number of questions is 75.

$$x + y = 75$$

The total score is 100.

$$2x - \dfrac{1}{2}y = 100$$

After clearing the fraction in the second equation, we have a system of equations.

$$x + y = 75,$$
$$4x - y = 200$$

Solve. We use the elimination method. Begin by adding the equations.

$$x + y = 75$$
$$\underline{4x - y = 200}$$
$$5x = 275$$
$$x = 55$$

Now substitute 55 for x in the first equation and solve for y.

$$55 + y = 75$$
$$y = 20$$

Check. If there are 55 correct answers and 20 incorrect answers, the total number of questions is $55+20$, or 75. For the 55 correct answers, $2 \cdot 55$ or 110 points are awarded; for the 20 incorrect answers, $\dfrac{1}{2} \cdot 20$ or 10, points are deducted. Then the total score is $110 - 10$ or 100. The answer checks.

State. There were 55 correct answers and 20 incorrect answers.

51. $30y^4 - 97xy^2 + 60x^2$

$= (5y^2 - 12x)(6y^2 - 5x)$ FOIL or ac-method

53. $5x^3 - \dfrac{5}{27}$

$= 5\left(x^3 - \dfrac{1}{27}\right)$

$= 5\left[x^3 - \left(\dfrac{1}{3}\right)^3\right]$ Difference of cubes

$= 5\left(x - \dfrac{1}{3}\right)\left(x^2 + \dfrac{1}{3}x + \dfrac{1}{9}\right)$

55. $(x - p)^2 - p^2$ Difference of squares

$= (x - p + p)(x - p - p)$

$= x(x - 2p)$

57. $(y - 1)^4 - (y - 1)^2$

$= (y - 1)^2[(y - 1)^2 - 1]$
                    Removing the common factor

$= (y - 1)^2[(y - 1) + 1][(y - 1) - 1]$
                    Factoring the difference of squares

$= (y - 1)^2(y)(y - 2)$, or $y(y - 1)^2(y - 2)$

59. $4x^2 + 4xy + y^2 - r^2 + 6rs - 9s^2$

$= (4x^2 + 4xy + y^2) - 1(r^2 - 6rs + 9s^2)$ Grouping

$= (2x + y)^2 - (r - 3s)^2$ Difference of squares

$= [(2x + y) + (r - 3s)][(2x + y) - (r - 3s)]$

$= (2x + y + r - 3s)(2x + y - r + 3s)$

61. $c^{2w+1} + 2c^{w+1} + c$

$= c^{2w} \cdot c + 2c^w \cdot c + c$

$= c(c^{2w} + 2c^w + 1)$

$= c[(c^w)^2 + 2(c^w) + 1]$ Trinomial square

$= c(c^w + 1)^2$

63. $3(x + 1)^2 + 9(x + 1) - 12$

$= 3[(x + 1)^2 + 3(x + 1) - 4]$

$= 3[(x + 1) + 4][(x + 1) - 1]$ Factor $u^2 + 3u - 4$
                                      where $u = x + 1$

$= 3(x + 5)(x)$, or

$3x(x + 5)$

65. $\quad x^6 - 2x^5 + x^4 - x^2 + 2x - 1$

$\quad = x^4(x^2 - 2x + 1) - (x^2 - 2x + 1)$

$\quad = (x^2 - 2x + 1)(x^4 - 1)$

$\quad = (x - 1)^2(x^2 + 1)(x + 1)(x - 1)$

$\quad = (x - 1)^3(x^2 + 1)(x + 1)$

67. $\quad y^9 - y$

$\quad = y(y^8 - 1)$

$\quad = y(y^4 + 1)(y^4 - 1)$

$\quad = y(y^4 + 1)(y^2 + 1)(y^2 - 1)$

$\quad = y(y^4 + 1)(y^2 + 1)(y + 1)(y - 1)$

Exercise Set 4.8

1. $\quad x^2 + 3x = 28$

$x^2 + 3x - 28 = 0 \quad$ Getting 0 on one side

$(x + 7)(x - 4) = 0 \quad$ Factoring

$x + 7 = 0 \quad or \quad x - 4 = 0 \quad$ Principle of zero products

$\quad x = -7 \quad or \quad\quad x = 4$

The solutions are -7 and 4.

3. $\quad y^2 + 9 = 6y$

$y^2 - 6y + 9 = 0 \quad$ Getting 0 on one side

$(y - 3)(y - 3) = 0 \quad$ Factoring

$y - 3 = 0 \quad or \quad y - 3 = 0 \quad$ Principle of zero products

$\quad y = 3 \quad or \quad\quad y = 3$

There is only one solution, 3.

5. $\quad x^2 + 20x + 100 = 0$

$(x + 10)(x + 10) = 0 \quad$ Factoring

$x + 10 = 0 \quad or \quad x + 10 = 0 \quad$ Principle of zero products

$\quad x = -10 \quad or \quad\quad x = -10$

There is only one solution, -10.

7. $\quad 9x + x^2 + 20 = 0$

$x^2 + 9x + 20 = 0 \quad$ Changing order

$(x + 5)(x + 4) = 0 \quad$ Factoring

$x + 5 = 0 \quad or \quad x + 4 = 0 \quad$ Principle of zero products

$\quad x = -5 \quad or \quad\quad x = -4$

The solutions are -5 and -4.

9. $\quad x^2 + 8x = 0$

$x(x + 8) = 0 \quad$ Factoring

$x = 0 \quad or \quad x + 8 = 0 \quad$ Principle of zero products

$\quad x = 0 \quad or \quad\quad x = -8$

The solutions are 0 and -8.

11. $\quad x^2 - 25 = 0$

$(x + 5)(x - 5) = 0 \quad$ Factoring

$x + 5 = 0 \quad or \quad x - 5 = 0 \quad$ Principle of zero products

$\quad x = -5 \quad or \quad\quad x = 5$

The solutions are -5 and 5.

13. $\quad z^2 = 144$

$z^2 - 144 = 0 \quad$ Getting 0 on one side

$(z + 12)(z - 12) = 0 \quad$ Factoring

$z + 12 = 0 \quad or \quad z - 12 = 0 \quad$ Principle of zero products

$\quad z = -12 \quad or \quad\quad z = 12$

The solutions are -12 and 12.

15. $\quad y^2 + 2y = 63$

$y^2 + 2y - 63 = 0$

$(y + 9)(y - 7) = 0$

$y + 9 = 0 \quad or \quad y - 7 = 0$

$\quad y = -9 \quad or \quad\quad y = 7$

The solutions are -9 and 7.

17. $\quad 32 + 4x - x^2 = 0$

$\quad 0 = x^2 - 4x - 32$

$\quad 0 = (x - 8)(x + 4)$

$x - 8 = 0 \quad or \quad x + 4 = 0$

$\quad x = 8 \quad or \quad\quad x = -4$

The solutions are 8 and -4.

19. $\quad 3b^2 + 8b + 4 = 0$

$(3b + 2)(b + 2) = 0$

$3b + 2 = 0 \quad or \quad b + 2 = 0$

$\quad 3b = -2 \quad or \quad\quad b = -2$

$\quad b = -\dfrac{2}{3} \quad or \quad\quad b = -2$

The solutions are $-\dfrac{2}{3}$ and -2.

21. $\quad 8y^2 - 10y + 3 = 0$

$(4y - 3)(2y - 1) = 0$

$4y - 3 = 0 \quad or \quad 2y - 1 = 0$

$\quad 4y = 3 \quad or \quad\quad 2y = 1$

$\quad y = \dfrac{3}{4} \quad or \quad\quad y = \dfrac{1}{2}$

The solutions are $\dfrac{3}{4}$ and $\dfrac{1}{2}$.

23. $\quad 6z - z^2 = 0$

$\quad 0 = z^2 - 6z$

$\quad 0 = z(z - 6)$

$z = 0 \quad or \quad z - 6 = 0$

$z = 0 \quad or \quad\quad z = 6$

The solutions are 0 and 6.

25.
$$12z^2 + z = 6$$
$$12z^2 + z - 6 = 0$$
$$(4z + 3)(3z - 2) = 0$$
$$4z + 3 = 0 \quad or \quad 3z - 2 = 0$$
$$4z = -3 \quad or \quad 3z = 2$$
$$z = -\frac{3}{4} \quad or \quad z = \frac{2}{3}$$
The solutions are $-\frac{3}{4}$ and $\frac{2}{3}$.

27.
$$7x^2 - 7 = 0$$
$$7(x^2 - 1) = 0$$
$$7(x + 1)(x - 1) = 0$$
$$x + 1 = 0 \quad or \quad x - 1 = 0$$
$$x = -1 \quad or \quad x = 1$$
The solutions are -1 and 1.

29.
$$21r^2 + r - 10 = 0$$
$$(3r - 2)(7r + 5) = 0$$
$$3r - 2 = 0 \quad or \quad 7r + 5 = 0$$
$$3r = 2 \quad or \quad 7r = -5$$
$$r = \frac{2}{3} \quad or \quad r = -\frac{5}{7}$$
The solutions are $\frac{2}{3}$ and $-\frac{5}{7}$.

31.
$$15y^2 = 3y$$
$$15y^2 - 3y = 0$$
$$3y(5y - 1) = 0$$
$$3y = 0 \quad or \quad 5y - 1 = 0$$
$$y = 0 \quad or \quad 5y = 1$$
$$y = 0 \quad or \quad y = \frac{1}{5}$$
The solutions are 0 and $\frac{1}{5}$.

33.
$$14 = x(x - 5)$$
$$14 = x^2 - 5x$$
$$0 = x^2 - 5x - 14 \quad \text{Getting 0 on one side}$$
$$0 = (x - 7)(x + 2)$$
$$x - 7 = 0 \quad or \quad x + 2 = 0$$
$$x = 7 \quad or \quad x = -2$$
The solutions are 7 and -2.

35.
$$2x^3 - 2x^2 = 12x$$
$$2x^3 - 2x^2 - 12x = 0$$
$$2x(x^2 - x - 6) = 0$$
$$2x(x - 3)(x + 2) = 0$$
$$2x = 0 \quad or \quad x - 3 = 0 \quad or \quad x + 2 = 0$$
$$x = 0 \quad or \quad x = 3 \quad or \quad x = -2$$
The solutions are 0, 3, and -2.

37.
$$2x^3 = 128x$$
$$2x^3 - 128x = 0$$
$$2x(x^2 - 64) = 0$$
$$2x(x + 8)(x - 8) = 0$$
$$x = 0 \quad or \quad x + 8 = 0 \quad or \quad x - 8 = 0$$
$$x = 0 \quad or \quad x = -8 \quad or \quad x = 8$$
The solutions are 0, -8, and 8.

39.
$$t^4 - 26t^2 + 25 = 0$$
$$(t^2 - 1)(t^2 - 25) = 0$$
$$(t + 1)(t - 1)(t + 5)(t - 5) = 0$$
$$t + 1 = 0 \quad or \quad t - 1 = 0 \quad or \quad t + 5 = 0 \quad or \quad t - 5 = 0$$
$$t = -1 \quad or \quad t = 1 \quad or \quad t = -5 \quad or \quad t = 5$$
The solutions are -1, 1, -5, and 5.

41. We set $f(x)$ equal to 8.
$$x^2 + 12x + 40 = 8$$
$$x^2 + 12x + 32 = 0$$
$$(x + 8)(x + 4) = 0$$
$$x + 8 = 0 \quad or \quad x + 4 = 0$$
$$x = -8 \quad or \quad x = -4$$
The values of x for which $f(x) = 8$ are -8 and -4.

43. We set $g(x)$ equal to 12.
$$2x^2 + 5x = 12$$
$$2x^2 + 5x - 12 = 0$$
$$(2x - 3)(x + 4) = 0$$
$$2x - 3 = 0 \quad or \quad x + 4 = 0$$
$$2x = 3 \quad or \quad x = -4$$
$$x = \frac{3}{2} \quad or \quad x = -4$$

The values of x for which $g(x) = 12$ are $\frac{3}{2}$ and -4.

45. We set $h(x)$ equal to -27.
$$12x + x^2 = -27$$
$$12x + x^2 + 27 = 0$$
$$x^2 + 12x + 27 = 0 \quad \text{Rearranging}$$
$$(x + 3)(x + 9) = 0$$
$$x + 3 = 0 \quad or \quad x + 9 = 0$$
$$x = -3 \quad or \quad x = -9$$
The values of x for which $h(x) = -27$ are -3 and -9.

47. $f(x) = \dfrac{3}{x^2 - 4x - 5}$

$f(x)$ cannot be calculated for any x-value for which the denominator, $x^2 - 4x - 5$, is 0. To find the excluded values, we solve:
$$x^2 - 4x - 5 = 0$$
$$(x - 5)(x + 1) = 0$$
$$x - 5 = 0 \quad or \quad x + 1 = 0$$
$$x = 5 \quad or \quad x = -1$$

The domain of f is $\{x | x$ is a real number *and* $x \neq 5$ *and* $x \neq -1\}$.

49. $f(x) = \dfrac{x}{6x^2 - 54}$

$f(x)$ cannot be calculated for any x-value for which the denominator, $6x^2 - 54$, is 0. To find the excluded values, we solve:

$$6x^2 - 54 = 0$$
$$6(x^2 - 9) = 0$$
$$6(x + 3)(x - 3) = 0$$
$$x + 3 = 0 \quad or \quad x - 3 = 0$$
$$x = -3 \quad or \qquad x = 3$$

The domain of f is $\{x | x$ is a real number *and* $x \neq -3$ *and* $x \neq 3\}$.

51. $f(x) = \dfrac{x - 5}{9x - 18x^2}$

$f(x)$ cannot be calculated for any x-value for which the denominator, $9x - 18x^2$, is 0. To find the excluded values, we solve:

$$9x - 18x^2 = 0$$
$$9x(1 - 2x) = 0$$
$$9x = 0 \quad or \quad 1 - 2x = 0$$
$$x = 0 \quad or \qquad -2x = -1$$
$$x = 0 \quad or \qquad x = \frac{1}{2}$$

The domain of f is $\left\{ x | x \text{ is a real number } and \right.$ $\left. x \neq 0 \text{ and } x \neq \frac{1}{2} \right\}$.

53. $f(x) = \dfrac{7}{5x^3 - 35x^2 + 50x}$

$f(x)$ cannot be calculated for any x-value for which the denominator, $5x^3 - 35x^2 + 50x$, is 0. To find the excluded values, we solve:

$$5x^3 - 35x^2 + 50x = 0$$
$$5x(x^2 - 7x + 10) = 0$$
$$5x(x - 2)(x - 5) = 0$$
$$5x = 0 \quad or \quad x - 2 = 0 \quad or \quad x - 5 = 0$$
$$x = 0 \quad or \qquad x = 2 \quad or \qquad x = 5$$

The domain of f is $\{x | x$ is a real number *and* $x \neq 0$ *and* $x \neq 2$ *and* $x \neq 5\}$.

55. From the graph we see that the x-intercepts are $(-5, 0)$ and $(9, 0)$. The solutions of the equation are the first coordinates of the x-intercepts, -5 and 9.

57. From the graph we see that the x-intercepts are $(-4, 0)$ and $(8, 0)$. The solutions of the equation are the first coordinates of the x-intercepts, -4 and 8.

59. *Familiarize.* Let $w =$ the width of the envelope. Then $w + 4 =$ the length. Recall that the area of a rectangle is given by length $\times$ width.

Translate.

$$\underbrace{\text{The area}}_{w(w + 4)} \quad \underbrace{\text{is}}_{=} \quad \underbrace{96 \text{ cm}^2}_{96}.$$

Solve. We solve the equation.

$$w(w + 4) = 96$$
$$w^2 + 4w = 96$$
$$w^2 + 4w - 96 = 0$$
$$(w + 12)(w - 8) = 0$$
$$w + 12 = 0 \quad or \quad w - 8 = 0$$
$$w = -12 \quad or \qquad w = 8$$

Check. The width cannot be negative so we check only 8. If the width is 8 cm, then the length is $8 + 4$, or 12 cm, and the area is $8 \cdot 12$, or 96 cm^2. The answer checks.

State. The length is 12 cm, and the width is 8 cm.

61. *Familiarize.* Using the labels on the drawing in the text, we let x represent the base of the triangle and $x + 2$ represent the height. Recall that the formula for the area of the triangle with base b and height h is $\frac{1}{2}bh$.

Translate.

$$\underbrace{\text{The area}}_{\frac{1}{2}x(x + 2)} \quad \underbrace{\text{is}}_{=} \quad \underbrace{12 \text{ ft}^2}_{12}.$$

Solve. We solve the equation:

$$\frac{1}{2}x(x + 2) = 12$$
$$x(x + 2) = 24 \quad \text{Multiplying by 2}$$
$$x^2 + 2x = 24$$
$$x^2 + 2x - 24 = 0$$
$$(x + 6)(x - 4) = 0$$
$$x + 6 = 0 \quad or \quad x - 4 = 0$$
$$x = -6 \quad or \qquad x = 4$$

Check. We check only 4 since the length of the base cannot be negative. If the base is 4 ft, then the height is $4 + 2$, or 6 ft, and the area is $\frac{1}{2} \cdot 4 \cdot 6$, or 12 ft^2. The answer checks.

State. The height is 6 ft, and the base is 4 ft.

63. *Familiarize.* We make a drawing. We let $l =$ the length of the flower bed and $w =$ the width.

Recall the formula for the area of a rectangle: $A = lw$.

Translate. We translate to a system of equations.

$$108 = lw, \quad \text{Substituting 108 for } A$$
$$l = w + 3$$

Solve. We will use the system of equations to find an equation in one variable. We substitute $w + 3$ for l in the first equation.

$$108 = (w + 3)w$$
$$108 = w^2 + 3w$$
$$0 = w^2 + 3w - 108$$
$$0 = (w + 12)(w - 9)$$

$$w + 12 = 0 \quad or \quad w - 9 = 0$$
$$w = -12 \quad or \quad w = 9$$

Check. Width cannot be negative, so -12 cannot be a solution. If the width is 9 and the length is 3 m longer, or 12, then the area will be $12 \cdot 9$, or 108 m². We have a solution.

State. The length is 12 m, and the width is 9 m.

65. *Familiarize*. If $d =$ the distance from the base of the tower to the end of the wire, then $d + 4 =$ the height of the tower.

Translate. We use the Pythagorean theorem.

$$d^2 + (d + 4)^2 = 20^2$$

Solve. We solve the equation.

$$d^2 + (d^2 + 8d + 16) = 400$$
$$2d^2 + 8d + 16 = 400$$
$$2d^2 + 8d - 384 = 0$$
$$2(d + 16)(d - 12) = 0$$

$$d + 16 = 0 \quad or \quad d - 12 = 0$$
$$d = -16 \quad or \quad d = 12$$

Check. The distance cannot be negative, so we check only 12. If $d = 12$, then $d + 4 = 16$ and $12^2 + 16^2 = 400 = 20^2$. The answer checks.

State. The distance d is 12 ft, and the height of the tower is 16 ft.

67. *Familiarize*. Let x represent the first integer, $x + 2$ the second, and $x + 4$ the third.

Translate.

Square of the third	is 76	more than	square of the second.
$(x + 4)^2$	$= 76$	$+$	$(x + 2)^2$

Solve. We solve the equation:

$$(x + 4)^2 = 76 + (x + 2)^2$$
$$x^2 + 8x + 16 = 76 + x^2 + 4x + 4$$
$$x^2 + 8x + 16 = x^2 + 4x + 80$$
$$4x = 64$$
$$x = 16$$

Check. We check the integers 16, 18, and 20. The square of 20, or 400, is 76 more than 324, the square of 18. The answer checks.

State. The integers are 16, 18, and 20.

69. *Familiarize*. We make a drawing and label it. We let x represent the length of a side of the original square.

Translate.

Area of new square	is	144 cm^2.
$(x + 6)^2$	$=$	144

Solve. We solve the equation:

$$(x + 6)^2 = 144$$
$$x^2 + 12x + 36 = 144$$
$$x^2 + 12x - 108 = 0$$
$$(x - 6)(x + 18) = 0$$

$$x - 6 = 0 \quad or \quad x + 18 = 0$$
$$x = 6 \quad or \quad x = -18$$

Check. We only check 6 since the length of a side cannot be negative. If we increase the length by 6, the new length is $6 + 6$, or 12 cm. Then the new area is $12 \cdot 12$, or 144 cm². We have a solution.

State. The length of a side of the original square is 6 cm.

71. *Familiarize*. Using the labels in the text, we let $x =$ the width of the frame, in centimeters. Then we see that $20 - 2x =$ the length of the picture and $12 - 2x =$ the width of the picture. Recall that the area A of a rectangle with length l and width w is given by $A = lw$.

Translate.

The area of the picture	is	84 cm^2.
$(20 - 2x)(12 - 2x)$	$=$	84

Solve. We solve the equation.

$$(20 - 2x)(12 - 2x) = 84$$
$$240 - 64x + 4x^2 = 84$$
$$4x^2 - 64x + 156 = 0$$
$$4(x^2 - 16x + 39) = 0$$
$$x^2 - 16x + 39 = 0$$
$$(x - 13)(x - 3) = 0$$

$$x - 13 = 0 \quad or \quad x - 3 = 0$$
$$x = 13 \quad or \quad x = 3$$

Check. If the width of the frame were 13 cm, then the width of the picture would be $12 - 2 \cdot 13$, or -14 cm. This is not possible, so 13 cannot be a solution. If the width of the frame is 3 cm, then the length and width of the picture are $20 - 2 \cdot 3$, or 14 cm, and $12 - 2 \cdot 3$, or 6 cm, respectively. The area of the picture is 14 cm $\cdot$ 6 cm, or 84 cm². The number 3 checks.

State. The frame is 3 cm wide.

73. Familiarize. Let $w =$ the width of the parking lot. Then $w + 50 =$ the length.

Translate. We use the Pythagorean theorem.

$$a^2 + b^2 = c^2$$

$$w^2 + (w + 50)^2 = 250^2$$

Solve. We solve the equation:

$$w^2 + (w + 50)^2 = 250^2$$

$$w^2 + w^2 + 100w + 2500 = 62{,}500$$

$$2w^2 + 100w + 2500 = 62{,}500$$

$$2w^2 + 100w - 60{,}000 = 0$$

$$w^2 + 50w - 30{,}000 = 0 \qquad \text{Dividing by 2}$$

$$(w - 150)(w + 200) = 0$$

$$w - 150 = 0 \quad or \quad w + 200 = 0$$

$$w = 150 \quad or \qquad w = -200$$

Check. Since the width cannot be negative, -200 cannot be a solution. We check 150. When $w = 150$, then $w + 150 = 200$, and $150^2 + 200^2 = 250^2$. The answer checks.

State. The parking lot is 150 ft by 200 ft.

75. Familiarize. Let $x =$ the other leg of the triangle. Then $x + 1 =$ the hypotenuse.

Translate. We use the Pythagorean theorem.

$$a^2 + b^2 = c^2$$

$$9^2 + x^2 = (x + 1)^2$$

Solve. We solve the equation:

$$9^2 + x^2 = (x + 1)^2$$

$$81 + x^2 = x^2 + 2x + 1$$

$$80 = 2x$$

$$40 = x$$

Check. When $x = 40$, then $x + 1 = 41$, and $9^2 + 40^2 = 1681 = 41^2$. The numbers check.

State. The other sides have lengths of 40 m and 41 m.

77. Familiarize. We will use the equation $h(t) = -16t^2 + 80t + 224$.

Translate.

$$\underbrace{\text{Height}}_{\downarrow} \quad \text{is} \quad \underbrace{0 \text{ ft.}}_{\downarrow \quad \downarrow}$$

$$-16t^2 + 80t + 224 \;=\; 0$$

Solve. We solve the equation:

$$-16(t^2 - 5t - 14) = 0$$

$$-16(t - 7)(t + 2) = 0$$

$$t - 7 = 0 \quad or \quad t + 2 = 0$$

$$t = 7 \quad or \qquad t = -2$$

Check. The number -2 is not a solution, since time cannot be negative in this application. When $t = 7$, $h(t) = -16 \cdot 7^2 + 80 \cdot 7 + 224 = 0$. We have a solution.

State. The object reaches the ground after 7 sec.

79. Discussion and Writing Exercise

81. $|4 - (-3)| = |7| = 7$, or $|-3 - 4| = |-7| = 7$

83. $|3 - (-4)| = |7| = 7$, or $|-4 - 3| = |-7| = 7$

85. $|3.6 - 4.9| = |-1.3| = 1.3$, or $|4.9 - 3.6| = |1.3| = 1.3$

87. $|-123 - 568| = |-691| = 691$, or $|568 - (-123)| = |691| = 691$

89. First find the slope.

$$m = \frac{-4 - 7}{-8 - (-2)} = \frac{-11}{-6} = \frac{11}{6}$$

Now substitute $\dfrac{11}{6}$ for m and the coordinates of one of the given points for x and y in the equation $y = mx + b$ and solve for b. We will use the point $(-2, 7)$.

$$y = mx + b$$

$$7 = \frac{11}{6}(-2) + b$$

$$7 = -\frac{11}{3} + b$$

$$\frac{32}{3} = b$$

Now use $y = mx + b$ again, substituting $\dfrac{11}{6}$ for m and $\dfrac{32}{3}$ for b.

$$y = \frac{11}{6}x + \frac{32}{3}$$

91. First find the slope.

$$m = \frac{4 - 7}{8 - (-2)} = \frac{-3}{10} = -\frac{3}{10}$$

Now substitute $-\dfrac{3}{10}$ for m and the coordinates of one of the given points for x and y in the equation $y = mx + b$ and solve for b. We will use the point $(-2, 7)$.

$$y = mx + b$$

$$7 = -\frac{3}{10}(-2) + b$$

$$7 = \frac{3}{5} + b$$

$$\frac{32}{5} = b$$

Now we use $y = mx + b$ again, substituting $-\dfrac{3}{10}$ for m and $\dfrac{32}{5}$ for b.

$$y = -\frac{3}{10}x + \frac{32}{5}$$

93.

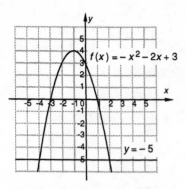

The solutions of $-x^2 - 2x + 3 = 0$ are the first coordinates of the x-intercepts. From the graph we see that these are -3 and 1. The solution set is $\{-3, 1\}$.

To solve $-x^2 - 2x + 3 \geq -5$ we find the x-values for which $f(x) \geq -5$. From the graph we see that these are the values in the interval $[-4, 2]$. The solution set can also be expressed as $\{x| -4 \leq x \leq 2\}$.

95. Left to the student

97. a) One method is to graph $y = x^4 - 3x^3 - x^2 + 5$ and then use the ZERO feature. The solutions are 1.2522305 and 3.1578935.

b) One method is to graph $y_1 = x^4 - 3x^3 - x^2 + 5$ and $y_2 = 5$. Then use the INTERSECT feature to find the first coordinates of the points of intersection of the graphs. The solutions are -0.3027756, 0, and 3.3027756.

c) One method is to graph $y_1 = x^4 - 3x^3 - x^2 + 5$ and $y_2 = -8$. Then use the INTERSECT feature to find the first coordinates of the points of intersection of the graphs. The solutions are 2.1387475 and 2.7238657.

d) One method is to graph $y_1 = x^4$ and $y_2 = 1 + 3x^3 + x^2$. Then use the INTERSECT feature to find the first coordinates of the points of intersection of the graphs. The solutions are -0.7462555 and 3.3276509.

Chapter 5

Rational Expressions, Equations, and Functions

Exercise Set 5.1

1. $\dfrac{5t^2 - 64}{3t + 17}$

We set the denominator equal to 0 and solve.

$$3t + 17 = 0$$
$$3t = -17$$
$$t = -\frac{17}{3}$$

The expression is not defined for the number $-\dfrac{17}{3}$.

3. $\dfrac{x^3 - x^2 + x + 2}{x^2 + 12x + 35}$

We set the denominator equal to 0 and solve.

$$x^2 + 12x + 35 = 0$$
$$(x + 5)(x + 7) = 0$$
$$x + 5 = 0 \quad or \quad x + 7 = 0$$
$$x = -5 \quad or \qquad x = -7$$

The expression is not defined for the numbers -5 and -7.

5. In Exercise 1 we found that the only replacement for which the rational expression $\dfrac{5t^2 - 64}{3t + 17}$ is not defined is $-\dfrac{17}{3}$. Then the domain of $f(t) = \dfrac{5t^2 - 64}{3t + 17}$ is $\left(-\infty, -\dfrac{17}{3}\right) \cup \left(-\dfrac{17}{3}, \infty\right)$.

7. In Exercise 3 we found that the replacements for which the rational expression $\dfrac{x^3 - x^2 + x + 2}{x^2 + 12x + 35}$ is not defined are -7 and -5. Then the domain of $f(x) = \dfrac{x^3 - x^2 + x + 2}{x^2 + 12x + 35}$ is $(-\infty, -7) \cup (-7, -5) \cup (-5, \infty)$.

9. $\dfrac{7x}{7x} \cdot \dfrac{x+2}{x+8} = \dfrac{7x(x+2)}{7x(x+8)}$ Multiplying numerators and multiplying denominators

11. $\dfrac{q-5}{q+3} \cdot \dfrac{q+5}{q+5} = \dfrac{(q-5)(q+5)}{(q+3)(q+5)}$ Multiplying numerators and multiplying denominators

13. $\dfrac{15y^5}{5y^4} = \dfrac{3 \cdot 5 \cdot y^4 \cdot y}{5 \cdot y^4 \cdot 1}$ Factoring the numerator and the denominator

$= \dfrac{5y^4}{5y^4} \cdot \dfrac{3y}{1}$ Factoring the rational expression

$= 1 \cdot 3y$ $\dfrac{5y^4}{5y^4} = 1$

$= 3y$ Removing a factor of 1

15. $\dfrac{16p^3}{24p^7} = \dfrac{8p^3 \cdot 2}{8p^3 \cdot 3p^4}$ Factoring the numerator and the denominator

$= \dfrac{8p^3}{8p^3} \cdot \dfrac{2}{3p^4}$ Factoring the rational expression

$= 1 \cdot \dfrac{2}{3p^4}$ $\dfrac{8p^3}{8p^3} = 1$

$= \dfrac{2}{3p^4}$ Removing a factor of 1

17. $\dfrac{9a - 27}{9} = \dfrac{9(a-3)}{9 \cdot 1}$ Factoring the numerator and the denominator

$= \dfrac{9}{9} \cdot \dfrac{a-3}{1}$

$= \dfrac{a-3}{1}$ Removing a factor of 1

$= a - 3$

19. $\dfrac{12x - 15}{21} = \dfrac{3(4x-5)}{3 \cdot 7}$ Factoring the numerator and the denominator

$= \dfrac{3}{3} \cdot \dfrac{4x-5}{7}$

$= \dfrac{4x-5}{7}$ Removing a factor of 1

21. $\dfrac{4y - 12}{4y + 12} = \dfrac{4(y-3)}{4(y+3)} = \dfrac{4}{4} \cdot \dfrac{y-3}{y+3} = \dfrac{y-3}{y+3}$

23. $\dfrac{t^2 - 16}{t^2 - 8t + 16} = \dfrac{(t+4)(t-4)}{(t-4)(t-4)} = \dfrac{t+4}{t-4} \cdot \dfrac{t-4}{t-4} = \dfrac{t+4}{t-4}$

25. $\dfrac{x^2 - 9x + 8}{x^2 + 3x - 4} = \dfrac{(x-8)(x-1)}{(x+4)(x-1)} = \dfrac{x-8}{x+4} \cdot \dfrac{x-1}{x-1} = \dfrac{x-8}{x+4}$

27. $\dfrac{w^3 - z^3}{w^2 - z^2} = \dfrac{(w-z)(w^2 + wz + z^2)}{(w+z)(w-z)} =$

$\dfrac{w-z}{w-z} \cdot \dfrac{w^2 + wz + z^2}{w+z} = \dfrac{w^2 + wz + z^2}{w+z}$

29. $\dfrac{x^4}{3x+6} \cdot \dfrac{5x+10}{5x^7}$

$= \dfrac{x^4(5x+10)}{(3x+6)(5x^7)}$ Multiplying the numerators and the denominators

$= \dfrac{x^4(5)(x+2)}{3(x+2)(5)(x^4)(x^3)}$ Factoring the numerator and the denominator

$= \dfrac{x^4(5)(x+2)(1)}{3(x+2)(5)(x^4)(x^3)}$ Removing a factor of 1: $\dfrac{(x^4)(5)(x+2)}{(x+2)(5)(x^4)} = 1$

$= \dfrac{1}{3x^3}$ Simplifying

31. $\dfrac{x^2 - 16}{x^2} \cdot \dfrac{x^2 - 4x}{x^2 - x - 12}$

$= \dfrac{(x^2 - 16)(x^2 - 4x)}{x^2(x^2 - x - 12)}$ Multiplying the numerators and the denominators

$= \dfrac{(x + 4)(x - 4)(x)(x - 4)}{x \cdot x(x - 4)(x + 3)}$ Factoring the numerator and the denominator

$= \dfrac{(x + 4)(x\!\!\!\!\diagup4)(\diagup x)(x - 4)}{\diagup x \cdot x(x\!\!\!\!\diagup4)(x + 3)}$ Removing a factor of 1

$= \dfrac{(x + 4)(x - 4)}{x(x + 3)}$

33. $\dfrac{y^2 - 16}{2y + 6} \cdot \dfrac{y + 3}{y - 4} = \dfrac{(y^2 - 16)(y + 3)}{(2y + 6)(y - 4)}$

$= \dfrac{(y + 4)(y - 4)(y + 3)}{2(y + 3)(y - 4)}$

$= \dfrac{(y + 4)(y\!\!\!\!\diagup4)(y\!\!\!\!\diagup3)}{2(y\!\!\!\!\diagup3)(y\!\!\!\!\diagup4)}$

$= \dfrac{y + 4}{2}$

35. $\dfrac{x^2 - 2x - 35}{2x^3 - 3x^2} \cdot \dfrac{4x^3 - 9x}{7x - 49}$

$= \dfrac{(x^2 - 2x - 35)(4x^3 - 9x)}{(2x^3 - 3x^2)(7x - 49)}$

$= \dfrac{(x - 7)(x + 5)(x)(2x + 3)(2x - 3)}{x \cdot x(2x - 3)(7)(x - 7)}$

$= \dfrac{(x\!\!\!\!\diagup7)(x + 5)(\diagup x)(2x + 3)(2x\!\!\!\!\diagup3)}{\diagup x \cdot x(2x\!\!\!\!\diagup3)(7)(x\!\!\!\!\diagup7)}$

$= \dfrac{(x + 5)(2x + 3)}{7x}$

37. $\dfrac{c^3 + 8}{c^2 - 4} \cdot \dfrac{c^2 - 4c + 4}{c^2 - 2c + 4}$

$= \dfrac{(c^3 + 8)(c^2 - 4c + 4)}{(c^2 - 4)(c^2 - 2c + 4)}$

$= \dfrac{(c + 2)(c^2 - 2c + 4)(c - 2)(c - 2)}{(c + 2)(c - 2)(c^2 - 2c + 4) \cdot 1}$

$= \dfrac{(c + 2)(c^2 - 2c + 4)(c - 2)}{(c + 2)(c^2 - 2c + 4)(c - 2)} \cdot \dfrac{c - 2}{1}$

$= \dfrac{c - 2}{1}$

$= c - 2$

39. $\dfrac{x^2 - y^2}{x^3 - y^3} \cdot \dfrac{x^2 + xy + y^2}{x^2 + 2xy + y^2}$

$= \dfrac{(x^2 - y^2)(x^2 + xy + y^2)}{(x^3 - y^3)(x^2 + 2xy + y^2)}$

$= \dfrac{(x + y)(x - y)(x^2 + xy + y^2) \cdot 1}{(x - y)(x^2 + xy + y^2)(x + y)(x + y)}$

$= \dfrac{(x + y)(x - y)(x^2 + xy + y^2)}{(x + y)(x - y)(x^2 + xy + y^2)} \cdot \dfrac{1}{x + y}$

$= \dfrac{1}{x + y}$

41. $\dfrac{12x^8}{3y^4} \div \dfrac{16x^3}{6y}$

$= \dfrac{12x^8}{3y^4} \cdot \dfrac{6y}{16x^3}$ Multiplying by the reciprocal of the divisor

$= \dfrac{12x^8(6y)}{3y^4(16x^3)}$ Multiplying the numerators and the denominators

$= \dfrac{3 \cdot 4 \cdot x^3 \cdot x^5 \cdot 2 \cdot 3 \cdot y}{3 \cdot y \cdot y^3 \cdot 4 \cdot 2 \cdot 2 \cdot x^3}$ Factoring the numerator and the denominator

$= \dfrac{\diagup 3 \cdot \diagup 4 \cdot \diagup{x^3} \cdot x^5 \cdot \diagup 2 \cdot 3 \cdot \diagup y}{\diagup 3 \cdot \diagup y \cdot y^3 \cdot \diagup 4 \cdot \diagup 2 \cdot 2 \cdot \diagup{x^3}}$ Removing a factor of 1

$= \dfrac{3x^5}{2y^3}$

43. $\dfrac{3y + 15}{y} \div \dfrac{y + 5}{y} = \dfrac{3y + 15}{y} \cdot \dfrac{y}{y + 5}$

$= \dfrac{(3y + 15)(y)}{y(y + 5)}$

$= \dfrac{3(y + 5)(y)}{y(y + 5) \cdot 1}$

$= \dfrac{3(y\!\!\!\!\diagup5)(\diagup y)}{\diagup y(y\!\!\!\!\diagup5) \cdot 1}$

$= \dfrac{3}{1}$

$= 3$

45. $\dfrac{y^2 - 9}{y} \div \dfrac{y + 3}{y + 2} = \dfrac{y^2 - 9}{y} \cdot \dfrac{y + 2}{y + 3}$

$= \dfrac{(y^2 - 9)(y + 2)}{y(y + 3)}$

$= \dfrac{(y + 3)(y - 3)(y + 2)}{y(y + 3)}$

$= \dfrac{(y\!\!\!\!\diagup3)(y - 3)(y + 2)}{y(y\!\!\!\!\diagup3)}$

$= \dfrac{(y - 3)(y + 2)}{y}$

47. $\dfrac{4a^2 - 1}{a^2 - 4} \div \dfrac{2a - 1}{a - 2} = \dfrac{4a^2 - 1}{a^2 - 4} \cdot \dfrac{a - 2}{2a - 1}$

$= \dfrac{(4a^2 - 1)(a - 2)}{(a^2 - 4)(2a - 1)}$

$= \dfrac{(2a + 1)(2a - 1)(a - 2)}{(a + 2)(a - 2)(2a - 1)}$

$= \dfrac{(2a + 1)(2a\!\!\!\!\diagup1)(a\!\!\!\!\diagup2)}{(a + 2)(a\!\!\!\!\diagup2)(2a\!\!\!\!\diagup1)}$

$= \dfrac{2a + 1}{a + 2}$

49. $\dfrac{x^2 - 16}{x^2 - 10x + 25} \div \dfrac{3x - 12}{x^2 - 3x - 10}$

$= \dfrac{x^2 - 16}{x^2 - 10x + 25} \cdot \dfrac{x^2 - 3x - 10}{3x - 12}$

$= \dfrac{(x^2 - 16)(x^2 - 3x - 10)}{(x^2 - 10x + 25)(3x - 12)}$

$= \dfrac{(x + 4)(x - 4)(x - 5)(x + 2)}{(x - 5)(x - 5)(3)(x - 4)}$

$= \dfrac{(x + 4)(\cancel{x - 4})(\cancel{x - 5})(x + 2)}{(\cancel{x - 5})(x - 5)(3)(\cancel{x - 4})}$

$= \dfrac{(x + 4)(x + 2)}{3(x - 5)}$

51. $\dfrac{y^3 + 3y}{y^2 - 9} \div \dfrac{y^2 + 5y - 14}{y^2 + 4y - 21}$

$= \dfrac{y^3 + 3y}{y^2 - 9} \cdot \dfrac{y^2 + 4y - 21}{y^2 + 5y - 14}$

$= \dfrac{(y^3 + 3y)(y^2 + 4y - 21)}{(y^2 - 9)(y^2 + 5y - 14)}$

$= \dfrac{y(y^2 + 3)(y + 7)(y - 3)}{(y + 3)(y - 3)(y + 7)(y - 2)}$

$= \dfrac{y(y^2 + 3)(\cancel{y + 7})(\cancel{y - 3})}{(y + 3)(\cancel{y - 3})(\cancel{y + 7})(y - 2)}$

$= \dfrac{y(y^2 + 3)}{(y + 3)(y - 2)}$

53. $\dfrac{x^3 - 64}{x^3 + 64} \div \dfrac{x^2 - 16}{x^2 - 4x + 16}$

$= \dfrac{x^3 - 64}{x^3 + 64} \cdot \dfrac{x^2 - 4x + 16}{x^2 - 16}$

$= \dfrac{(x^3 - 64)(x^2 - 4x + 16)}{(x^3 + 64)(x^2 - 16)}$

$= \dfrac{(x - 4)(x^2 + 4x + 16)(x^2 - 4x + 16)}{(x + 4)(x^2 - 4x + 16)(x + 4)(x - 4)}$

$= \dfrac{(x - 4)(x^2 - 4x + 16)}{(x - 4)(x^2 - 4x + 16)} \cdot \dfrac{x^2 + 4x + 16}{(x + 4)(x + 4)}$

$= \dfrac{x^2 + 4x + 16}{(x + 4)(x + 4)}, \text{ or } \dfrac{x^2 + 4x + 16}{(x + 4)^2}$

55. $\left[\dfrac{r^2 - 4s^2}{r + 2s} \div (r + 2s)\right] \cdot \dfrac{2s}{r - 2s}$

$= \left[\dfrac{r^2 - 4s^2}{r + 2s} \cdot \dfrac{1}{r + 2s}\right] \cdot \dfrac{2s}{r - 2s}$

$= \dfrac{(r^2 - 4s^2)(1)(2s)}{(r + 2s)(r + 2s)(r - 2s)}$

$= \dfrac{(r + 2s)(r - 2s)(2s)}{(r + 2s)(r + 2s)(r - 2s)}$

$= \dfrac{(\cancel{r + 2s})(\cancel{r - 2s})(2s)}{(\cancel{r + 2s})(r + 2s)(\cancel{r - 2s})}$

$= \dfrac{2s}{r + 2s}$

57. Discussion and Writing Exercise

59. The function can be written as a set of six ordered pairs, $\{(-4, 3), (-2, 1), (0, -3), (2, -2), (4, 0), (6, 4)\}$.

The domain is the set of all first coordinates, $\{-4, -2, 0, 2, 4, 6\}$.

The range is the set of all second coordinates, $\{-3, -2, 0, 1, 3, 4\}$.

61. The domain is the set of all x-values on the graph, $[-5, 5]$.

The range is the set of all y-values on the graph, $[-4, 4]$.

63. $6a^2 + 5ab - 25b^2$

We can factor this using the FOIL method or the grouping method. The factorization is $(3a - 5b)(2a + 5b)$.

65. $10x^2 - 80x + 70 = 10(x^2 - 8x + 7)$

To factor $x^2 - 8x + 7$ we find factors of 7 whose sum is -8. The numbers we need are -1 and -7, so $x^2 - 8x + 7 = (x - 1)(x - 7)$. Then $10x^2 - 80x + 70 = 10(x - 1)(x - 7)$.

67. $21p^2 + p - 10$

We can factor this using the FOIL method or the grouping method. The factorization is $(7p + 5)(3p - 2)$.

69. $2x^3 - 16x^2 - 66x = 2x(x^2 - 8x - 33)$

To factor $x^2 - 8x - 33$ we find factors of -33 whose sum is -8. The numbers we need are -11 and 3, so $x^2 - 8x - 33 = (x - 11)(x + 3)$. Then $2x^3 - 16x^2 - 66x = 2x(x - 11)(x + 3)$.

71. $\dfrac{x(x + 1) - 2(x + 3)}{(x + 1)(x + 2)(x + 3)} = \dfrac{x^2 + x - 2x - 6}{(x + 1)(x + 2)(x + 3)}$

$= \dfrac{x^2 - x - 6}{(x + 1)(x + 2)(x + 3)}$

$= \dfrac{(x - 3)(x + 2)}{(x + 1)(x + 2)(x + 3)}$

$= \dfrac{(x - 3)(\cancel{x + 2})}{(x + 1)(\cancel{x + 2})(x + 3)}$

$= \dfrac{x - 3}{(x + 1)(x + 3)}$

73. $\dfrac{m^2 - t^2}{m^2 + t^2 + m + t + 2mt} = \dfrac{m^2 - t^2}{(m^2 + 2mt + t^2) + (m + t)}$

$= \dfrac{(m + t)(m - t)}{(m + t)^2 + (m + t)}$

$= \dfrac{(m + t)(m - t)}{(m + t)[(m + t) + 1]}$

$= \dfrac{(\cancel{m + t})(m - t)}{(\cancel{m + t})(m + t + 1)}$

$= \dfrac{m - t}{m + t + 1}$

75. $g(x) = \dfrac{2x + 3}{4x - 1}$

$g(5) = \dfrac{2 \cdot 5 + 3}{4 \cdot 5 - 1} = \dfrac{10 + 3}{20 - 1} = \dfrac{13}{19}$

$g(0) = \dfrac{2 \cdot 0 + 3}{4 \cdot 0 - 1} = \dfrac{3}{-1} = -3$

$g\left(\dfrac{1}{4}\right) = \dfrac{2 \cdot \dfrac{1}{4} + 3}{4 \cdot \dfrac{1}{4} - 1} = \dfrac{\dfrac{1}{2} + 3}{1 - 1} = \dfrac{\dfrac{7}{2}}{0}$; since division by 0 is not

defined, $g(0)$ is not defined.

$g(a+h) = \dfrac{2(a+h) + 3}{4(a+h) - 1} = \dfrac{2a + 2h + 3}{4a + 4h - 1}$

Exercise Set 5.2

1. $15 = 3 \cdot 5$

$40 = 2 \cdot 2 \cdot 2 \cdot 5$

LCM $= 2 \cdot 2 \cdot 2 \cdot 3 \cdot 5$, or 120

(We used each factor the greatest number of times that it occurs in any one prime factorization.)

3. $18 = 2 \cdot 3 \cdot 3$

$48 = 2 \cdot 2 \cdot 2 \cdot 2 \cdot 3$

LCM $= 2 \cdot 2 \cdot 2 \cdot 2 \cdot 3 \cdot 3$, or 144

5. $30 = 2 \cdot 3 \cdot 5$

$105 = 3 \cdot 5 \cdot 7$

LCM $= 2 \cdot 3 \cdot 5 \cdot 7$, or 210

7. $9 = 3 \cdot 3$

$15 = 3 \cdot 5$

$5 = 5$

LCM $= 3 \cdot 3 \cdot 5$, or 45

9. $\dfrac{5}{6} + \dfrac{4}{15} = \dfrac{5}{2 \cdot 3} + \dfrac{4}{3 \cdot 5}$,   LCD $= 2 \cdot 3 \cdot 5$, or 30

$= \dfrac{5}{2 \cdot 3} \cdot \dfrac{5}{5} + \dfrac{4}{3 \cdot 5} \cdot \dfrac{2}{2}$

$= \dfrac{25}{2 \cdot 3 \cdot 5} + \dfrac{8}{2 \cdot 3 \cdot 5}$

$= \dfrac{33}{2 \cdot 3 \cdot 5} = \dfrac{\cancel{3} \cdot 11}{2 \cdot \cancel{3} \cdot 5}$

$= \dfrac{11}{10}$

11. $\dfrac{7}{36} + \dfrac{1}{24}$

$= \dfrac{7}{2 \cdot 2 \cdot 3 \cdot 3} + \dfrac{1}{2 \cdot 2 \cdot 2 \cdot 3}$,   LCD $= 2 \cdot 2 \cdot 2 \cdot 3 \cdot 3$, or 72

$= \dfrac{7}{2 \cdot 2 \cdot 3 \cdot 3} \cdot \dfrac{2}{2} + \dfrac{1}{2 \cdot 2 \cdot 2 \cdot 3} \cdot \dfrac{3}{3}$

$= \dfrac{14}{2 \cdot 2 \cdot 2 \cdot 3 \cdot 3} + \dfrac{3}{2 \cdot 2 \cdot 2 \cdot 3 \cdot 3}$

$= \dfrac{17}{2 \cdot 2 \cdot 2 \cdot 3 \cdot 3}$

$= \dfrac{17}{72}$

13. $\dfrac{3}{4} + \dfrac{7}{30} + \dfrac{1}{16}$

$= \dfrac{3}{2 \cdot 2} + \dfrac{7}{2 \cdot 3 \cdot 5} + \dfrac{1}{2 \cdot 2 \cdot 2 \cdot 2}$,   LCD $= 2 \cdot 2 \cdot 2 \cdot 2 \cdot 3 \cdot 5$

$= \dfrac{3}{2 \cdot 2} \cdot \dfrac{2 \cdot 2 \cdot 3 \cdot 5}{2 \cdot 2 \cdot 3 \cdot 5} + \dfrac{7}{2 \cdot 3 \cdot 5} \cdot \dfrac{2 \cdot 2 \cdot 2}{2 \cdot 2 \cdot 2} +$

$ \dfrac{1}{2 \cdot 2 \cdot 2 \cdot 2} \cdot \dfrac{3 \cdot 5}{3 \cdot 5}$

$= \dfrac{180}{2 \cdot 2 \cdot 2 \cdot 2 \cdot 3 \cdot 5} + \dfrac{56}{2 \cdot 2 \cdot 2 \cdot 2 \cdot 3 \cdot 5} + \dfrac{15}{2 \cdot 2 \cdot 2 \cdot 2 \cdot 3 \cdot 5}$

$= \dfrac{251}{2 \cdot 2 \cdot 2 \cdot 2 \cdot 3 \cdot 5}$

$= \dfrac{251}{240}$

15. $21x^2y = 3 \cdot 7 \cdot x \cdot x \cdot y$

$7xy = 7 \cdot x \cdot y$

LCM $= 3 \cdot 7 \cdot x \cdot x \cdot y$, or $21x^2y$

17. $y^2 - 100 = (y+10)(y-10)$

$10y + 100 = 10(y+10)$

LCM $= 10(y+10)(y-10)$

19. $15ab^2 = 3 \cdot 5 \cdot a \cdot b \cdot b$

$3ab = 3 \cdot a \cdot b$

$10a^3b = 2 \cdot 5 \cdot a \cdot a \cdot a \cdot b$

LCM $= 2 \cdot 3 \cdot 5 \cdot a \cdot a \cdot a \cdot b \cdot b$, or $30a^3b^2$

21. $5y - 15 = 5(y-3)$

$y^2 - 6y + 9 = (y-3)(y-3)$

LCM $= 5(y-3)(y-3)$, or $5(y-3)^2$

23. $y^2 - 25 = (y+5)(y-5)$

$5 - y$

We can use $y - 5$ from the prime factorization of $y^2 - 25$ or $5 - y$ from the second expression, but not both.

LCM $= (y+5)(y-5)$, or $(y+5)(5-y)$

25. $2r^2 - 5r - 12 = (2r+3)(r-4)$

$3r^2 - 13r + 4 = (3r-1)(r-4)$

$r^2 - 16 = (r+4)(r-4)$

LCM $= (2r+3)(3r-1)(r+4)(r-4)$

27. $x^5 + 4x^3 = x^3(x^2+4) = x \cdot x \cdot x(x^2+4)$

$x^3 - 4x^2 + 4x = x(x^2 - 4x + 4) = x(x-2)(x-2)$

LCM $= x \cdot x \cdot x(x-2)(x-2)(x^2+4)$, or $x^3(x-2)^2(x^2+4)$

29. $x^5 - 2x^4 + x^3 = x^3(x^2 - 2x + 1) = x \cdot x \cdot x(x-1)(x-1)$

$2x^3 + 2x = 2x(x^2+1)$

$5x + 5 = 5(x+1)$

LCM $= 2 \cdot 5 \cdot x \cdot x \cdot x(x-1)(x-1)(x+1)(x^2+1)$, or $10x^3(x-1)^2(x+1)(x^2+1)$

31. $\dfrac{x-2y}{x+y}+\dfrac{x+9y}{x+y}$

$=\dfrac{x-2y+x+9y}{x+y}$ Adding the numerators

$=\dfrac{2x+7y}{x+y}$

33. $\dfrac{4y+2}{y-2}-\dfrac{y-3}{y-2}$

$=\dfrac{4y+2-(y-3)}{y-2}$ Subtracting numerators

$=\dfrac{4y+2-y+3}{y-2}$

$=\dfrac{3y+5}{y-2}$

35. $\dfrac{a^2}{a-b}+\dfrac{b^2}{b-a}$

$=\dfrac{a^2}{a-b}+\dfrac{b^2}{b-a}\cdot\dfrac{-1}{-1}$ Multiplying by 1, using $\dfrac{-1}{-1}$

$=\dfrac{a^2}{a-b}+\dfrac{-b^2}{a-b}$

$=\dfrac{a^2-b^2}{a-b}$ Adding numerators

$=\dfrac{(a+b)(a-b)}{a-b}$ Factoring the numerator

$=\dfrac{(a+b)(a-b)}{1(a-b)}$ Removing a factor of 1

$=\dfrac{a+b}{1}$

$=a+b$

37. $\dfrac{6}{y}-\dfrac{7}{-y}$

$=\dfrac{6}{y}-\dfrac{7}{-y}\cdot\dfrac{-1}{-1}$ Multiplying by 1, using $\dfrac{-1}{-1}$

$=\dfrac{6}{y}-\dfrac{-7}{y}$

$=\dfrac{6-(-7)}{y}$ Subtracting numerators

$=\dfrac{13}{y}$

39. $\dfrac{4a-2}{a^2-49}+\dfrac{5+3a}{49-a^2}$

$=\dfrac{4a-2}{a^2-49}+\dfrac{5+3a}{49-a^2}\cdot\dfrac{-1}{-1}$ Multiplying by 1, using $\dfrac{-1}{-1}$

$=\dfrac{4a-2}{a^2-49}+\dfrac{-5-3a}{a^2-49}$

$=\dfrac{4a-2-5-3a}{a^2-49}$ Adding numerators

$=\dfrac{a-7}{a^2-49}$

$=\dfrac{a-7}{(a+7)(a-7)}$ Factoring

$=\dfrac{(a-7)\cdot1}{(a+7)(a-7)}$ Removing a factor of 1

$=\dfrac{1}{a+7}$

41. $\dfrac{a^3}{a-b}+\dfrac{b^3}{b-a}$

$=\dfrac{a^3}{a-b}+\dfrac{b^3}{b-a}\cdot\dfrac{-1}{-1}$

$=\dfrac{a^3}{a-b}+\dfrac{-b^3}{a-b}$

$=\dfrac{a^3-b^3}{a-b}$

$=\dfrac{(a-b)(a^2+ab+b^2)}{a-b}$

$=\dfrac{(a-b)(a^2+ab+b^2)}{(a-b)\cdot1}$

$=a^2+ab+b^2$

43. $\dfrac{y-2}{y+4}+\dfrac{y+3}{y-5}$ LCD $=(y+4)(y-5)$

$=\dfrac{y-2}{y+4}\cdot\dfrac{y-5}{y-5}+\dfrac{y+3}{y-5}\cdot\dfrac{y+4}{y+4}$

$=\dfrac{(y^2-7y+10)+(y^2+7y+12)}{(y+4)(y-5)}$

$=\dfrac{2y^2+22}{(y+4)(y-5)}$, or $\dfrac{2y^2+22}{y^2-y-20}$

45. $\dfrac{4xy}{x^2-y^2}+\dfrac{x-y}{x+y}$

$=\dfrac{4xy}{(x+y)(x-y)}+\dfrac{x-y}{x+y}$ LCD $=(x+y)(x-y)$

$=\dfrac{4xy}{(x+y)(x-y)}+\dfrac{x-y}{x+y}\cdot\dfrac{x-y}{x-y}$

$=\dfrac{4xy+x^2-2xy+y^2}{(x+y)(x-y)}$

$=\dfrac{x^2+2xy+y^2}{(x+y)(x-y)}=\dfrac{(x+y)(x+y)}{(x+y)(x-y)}$

$=\dfrac{(x+y)(x+y)}{(x+y)(x-y)}=\dfrac{x+y}{x-y}$

47. $\dfrac{9x+2}{3x^2-2x-8}+\dfrac{7}{3x^2+x-4}$

$=\dfrac{9x+2}{(3x+4)(x-2)}+\dfrac{7}{(3x+4)(x-1)}$

$\qquad\qquad\text{LCD}=(3x+4)(x-2)(x-1)$

$=\dfrac{9x+2}{(3x+4)(x-2)}\cdot\dfrac{x-1}{x-1}+\dfrac{7}{(3x+4)(x-1)}\cdot\dfrac{x-2}{x-2}$

$=\dfrac{9x^2-7x-2+7x-14}{(3x+4)(x-2)(x-1)}$

$=\dfrac{9x^2-16}{(3x+4)(x-2)(x-1)}=\dfrac{(3x+4)(3x-4)}{(3x+4)(x-2)(x-1)}$

$=\dfrac{\cancel{(3x+4)}(3x-4)}{\cancel{(3x+4)}(x-2)(x-1)}$

$=\dfrac{3x-4}{(x-2)(x-1)},\text{ or }\dfrac{3x-4}{x^2-3x+2}$

49. $\dfrac{4}{x+1}+\dfrac{x+2}{x^2-1}+\dfrac{3}{x-1}$

$=\dfrac{4}{x+1}+\dfrac{x+2}{(x+1)(x-1)}+\dfrac{3}{x-1}$

$\qquad\qquad\text{LCD}=(x+1)(x-1)$

$=\dfrac{4}{x+1}\cdot\dfrac{x-1}{x-1}+\dfrac{x+2}{(x+1)(x-1)}+\dfrac{3}{x-1}\cdot\dfrac{x+1}{x+1}$

$=\dfrac{4x-4+x+2+3x+3}{(x+1)(x-1)}$

$=\dfrac{8x+1}{(x+1)(x-1)},\text{ or }\dfrac{8x+1}{x^2-1}$

51. $\dfrac{x-1}{3x+15}-\dfrac{x+3}{5x+25}$

$=\dfrac{x-1}{3(x+5)}-\dfrac{x+3}{5(x+5)}$

$\qquad\qquad\text{LCD}=3\cdot5(x+5),\text{ or }15(x+5)$

$=\dfrac{x-1}{3(x+5)}\cdot\dfrac{5}{5}-\dfrac{x+3}{5(x+5)}\cdot\dfrac{3}{3}$

$=\dfrac{5x-5-(3x+9)}{15(x+5)}$

$=\dfrac{5x-5-3x-9}{15(x+5)}$

$=\dfrac{2x-14}{15(x+5)},\text{ or }\dfrac{2x-14}{15x+75}$

53. $\dfrac{5ab}{a^2-b^2}-\dfrac{a-b}{a+b}$

$=\dfrac{5ab}{(a+b)(a-b)}-\dfrac{a-b}{a+b}\qquad\text{LCD}=(a+b)(a-b)$

$=\dfrac{5ab}{(a+b)(a-b)}-\dfrac{a-b}{a+b}\cdot\dfrac{a-b}{a-b}$

$=\dfrac{5ab-(a^2-2ab+b^2)}{(a+b)(a-b)}$

$=\dfrac{5ab-a^2+2ab-b^2}{(a+b)(a-b)}$

$=\dfrac{-a^2+7ab-b^2}{(a+b)(a-b)},\text{ or }\dfrac{-a^2+7ab-b^2}{a^2-b^2}$

55. $\dfrac{3y}{y^2-7y+10}-\dfrac{2y}{y^2-8y+15}$

$=\dfrac{3y}{(y-5)(y-2)}-\dfrac{2y}{(y-5)(y-3)}$

$\qquad\qquad\text{LCD}=(y-5)(y-2)(y-3)$

$=\dfrac{3y}{(y-5)(y-2)}\cdot\dfrac{y-3}{y-3}-\dfrac{2y}{(y-5)(y-3)}\cdot\dfrac{y-2}{y-2}$

$=\dfrac{3y^2-9y-(2y^2-4y)}{(y-5)(y-2)(y-3)}$

$=\dfrac{3y^2-9y-2y^2+4y}{(y-5)(y-2)(y-3)}$

$=\dfrac{y^2-5y}{(y-5)(y-2)(y-3)}=\dfrac{y(y-5)}{(y-5)(y-2)(y-3)}$

$=\dfrac{y\cancel{(y-5)}}{\cancel{(y-5)}(y-2)(y-3)}$

$=\dfrac{y}{(y-2)(y-3)},\text{ or }\dfrac{y}{y^2-5y+6}$

57. $\dfrac{y}{y^2-y-20}+\dfrac{2}{y+4}$

$=\dfrac{y}{(y-5)(y+4)}+\dfrac{2}{y+4}\qquad\text{LCD}=(y-5)(y+4)$

$=\dfrac{y}{(y-5)(y+4)}+\dfrac{2}{y+4}\cdot\dfrac{y-5}{y-5}$

$=\dfrac{y+2y-10}{(y-5)(y+4)}$

$=\dfrac{3y-10}{(y-5)(y+4)},\text{ or }\dfrac{3y-10}{y^2-y-20}$

59. $\dfrac{3y+2}{y^2+5y-24}+\dfrac{7}{y^2+4y-32}$

$=\dfrac{3y+2}{(y+8)(y-3)}+\dfrac{7}{(y+8)(y-4)}$

$\qquad\qquad\text{LCD}=(y+8)(y-3)(y-4)$

$=\dfrac{3y+2}{(y+8)(y-3)}\cdot\dfrac{y-4}{y-4}+\dfrac{7}{(y+8)(y-4)}\cdot\dfrac{y-3}{y-3}$

$=\dfrac{3y^2-10y-8+7y-21}{(y+8)(y-3)(y-4)}$

$=\dfrac{3y^2-3y-29}{(y+8)(y-3)(y-4)}$

61. $\dfrac{3x-1}{x^2+2x-3}-\dfrac{x+4}{x^2-9}$

$=\dfrac{3x-1}{(x+3)(x-1)}-\dfrac{x+4}{(x+3)(x-3)}$

$\qquad\qquad\text{LCD}=(x+3)(x-1)(x-3)$

$=\dfrac{3x-1}{(x+3)(x-1)}\cdot\dfrac{x-3}{x-3}-\dfrac{x+4}{(x+3)(x-3)}\cdot\dfrac{x-1}{x-1}$

$=\dfrac{3x^2-10x+3-(x^2+3x-4)}{(x+3)(x-1)(x-3)}$

$=\dfrac{3x^2-10x+3-x^2-3x+4}{(x+3)(x-1)(x-3)}$

$=\dfrac{2x^2-13x+7}{(x+3)(x-1)(x-3)}$

63.
$$\frac{1}{x+1} - \frac{x}{x-2} + \frac{x^2+2}{x^2-x-2}$$

$$= \frac{1}{x+1} - \frac{x}{x-2} + \frac{x^2+2}{(x-2)(x+1)}$$

$$\text{LCD} = (x+1)(x-2)$$

$$= \frac{1}{x+1} \cdot \frac{x-2}{x-2} - \frac{x}{x-2} \cdot \frac{x+1}{x+1} + \frac{x^2+2}{(x-2)(x+1)}$$

$$= \frac{x-2-(x^2+x)+x^2+2}{(x+1)(x-2)}$$

$$= \frac{x-2-x^2-x+x^2+2}{(x+1)(x-2)}$$

$$= \frac{0}{(x+1)(x-2)}$$

$$= 0$$

65.
$$\frac{x-1}{x-2} - \frac{x+1}{x+2} + \frac{x-6}{x^2-4}$$

$$= \frac{x-1}{x-2} - \frac{x+1}{x+2} + \frac{x-6}{(x+2)(x-2)}$$

$$\text{LCD} = (x-2)(x+2)$$

$$= \frac{x-1}{x-2} \cdot \frac{x+2}{x+2} - \frac{x+1}{x+2} \cdot \frac{x-2}{x-2} + \frac{x-6}{(x+2)(x-2)}$$

$$= \frac{(x^2+x-2)-(x^2-x-2)+(x-6)}{(x-2)(x+2)}$$

$$= \frac{x^2+x-2-x^2+x+2+x-6}{(x-2)(x+2)}$$

$$= \frac{3x-6}{(x-2)(x+2)}$$

$$= \frac{3(x-2)}{(x-2)(x+2)}$$

$$= \frac{3\cancel{(x-2)}}{\cancel{(x-2)}(x+2)}$$

$$= \frac{3}{x+2}$$

67.
$$\frac{4x}{x^2-1} + \frac{3x}{1-x} - \frac{4}{x-1}$$

$$= \frac{4x}{x^2-1} + \frac{3x}{1-x} \cdot \frac{-1}{-1} - \frac{4}{x-1}$$

$$= \frac{4x}{(x+1)(x-1)} + \frac{-3x}{x-1} - \frac{4}{x-1}$$

$$\text{LCD} = (x+1)(x-1)$$

$$= \frac{4x}{(x+1)(x-1)} + \frac{-3x}{x-1} \cdot \frac{x+1}{x+1} - \frac{4}{x-1} \cdot \frac{x+1}{x+1}$$

$$= \frac{4x-3x^2-3x-4x-4}{(x+1)(x-1)}$$

$$= \frac{-3x^2-3x-4}{x^2-1}$$

69.
$$\frac{1}{x+y} + \frac{1}{y-x} - \frac{2x}{x^2-y^2}$$

$$= \frac{1}{x+y} + \frac{1}{y-x} \cdot \frac{-1}{-1} - \frac{2x}{x^2-y^2}$$

$$= \frac{1}{x+y} + \frac{-1}{x-y} - \frac{2x}{(x+y)(x-y)}$$

$$\text{LCD} = (x+y)(x-y)$$

$$= \frac{1}{x+y} \cdot \frac{x-y}{x-y} + \frac{-1}{x-y} \cdot \frac{x+y}{x+y} - \frac{2x}{(x+y)(x-y)}$$

$$= \frac{x-y-x-y-2x}{(x+y)(x-y)}$$

$$= \frac{-2x-2y}{(x+y)(x-y)} = \frac{-2(x+y)}{(x+y)(x-y)}$$

$$= \frac{-2\cancel{(x+y)}}{\cancel{(x+y)}(x-y)}$$

$$= \frac{-2}{x-y}, \text{ or } \frac{2}{y-x}$$

71. Discussion and Writing Exercise

73. Graph: $2x - 3y > 6$

We first graph the line $2x - 3y = 6$. The intercepts are $(0, -2)$ and $(3, 0)$. We draw the line dashed since the inequality symbol is $>$. To determine which half-plane to shade, we consider a test point not on the line. We try $(0, 0)$:

$$\begin{array}{c|c} \multicolumn{2}{c}{2x - 3y > 6} \\ \hline 2 \cdot 0 - 3 \cdot 0 \ ? \ 6 & \\ 0 \ | & \text{FALSE} \end{array}$$

Since $0 > 6$ is false, we shade the half-plane that does not contain $(0, 0)$.

75. Graph: $5x + 3y \leq 15$

We first graph the line $5x + 3y = 15$. The intercepts are $(3, 0)$ and $(0, 5)$. We draw the line solid since the inequality symbol is $\leq$. To determine which half-plane to shade, we consider a test point not on the line. We try $(0, 0)$:

$$\begin{array}{c|c} \multicolumn{2}{c}{5x + 3y \leq 15} \\ \hline 5 \cdot 0 + 3 \cdot 0 \ ? \ 15 & \\ 0 \ | & \text{TRUE} \end{array}$$

Since $0 \leq 15$ is true, we shade the half-plane that contains $(0, 0)$.

$5x + 3y \leq 15$

77. $t^3 - 8 = t^3 - 2^3$
$$= (t - 2)(t^2 + 2t + 4)$$

79. $23x^4 + 23x$
$$= 23x(x^3 + 1)$$
$$= 23x(x + 1)(x^2 - x + 1)$$

81. $\dfrac{15x^{-7}y^{12}z^4}{35x^{-2}y^6z^{-3}} = \dfrac{15}{35}x^{-7-(-2)}y^{12-6}z^{4-(-3)}$
$$= \frac{3}{7}x^{-5}y^6z^7, \text{ or}$$
$$= \frac{3y^6z^7}{7x^5}$$

83. From the graph or from the equation of the function we see that the domain is $(-\infty, 2) \cup (2, \infty)$. From the graph we see that the range is $(-\infty, 0) \cup (0, \infty)$.

85. $x^8 - x^4 = x^4(x^2 + 1)(x + 1)(x - 1)$
$x^5 - x^2 = x^2(x - 1)(x^2 + x + 1)$
$x^5 - x^3 = x^3(x + 1)(x - 1)$
$x^5 + x^2 = x^2(x + 1)(x^2 - x + 1)$
LCM =
$x^4(x^2 + 1)(x + 1)(x - 1)(x^2 + x + 1)(x^2 - x + 1)$

87. $\dfrac{x + y + 1}{y - (x + 1)} + \dfrac{x + y - 1}{x - (y - 1)} - \dfrac{x - y - 1}{1 - (y - x)}$
$$= \frac{x + y + 1}{-x + y - 1} + \frac{x + y - 1}{x - y + 1} - \frac{x - y - 1}{x - y + 1}$$
$$= \frac{x + y + 1}{-x + y - 1} \cdot \frac{-1}{-1} + \frac{x + y - 1}{x - y + 1} - \frac{x - y - 1}{x - y + 1}$$
$$= \frac{-x - y - 1}{x - y + 1} + \frac{x + y - 1}{x - y + 1} - \frac{x - y - 1}{x - y + 1}$$
$$= \frac{-x - y - 1 + x + y - 1 - (x - y - 1)}{x - y + 1}$$
$$= \frac{-x - y - 1 + x + y - 1 - x + y + 1}{x - y + 1}$$
$$= \frac{-x + y - 1}{x - y + 1}$$
$$= \frac{-(x - y + 1)}{x - y + 1}$$
$$= \frac{-1 \cdot (x - y + 1)}{1 \cdot (x - y + 1)}$$
$$= \frac{-1}{1} \cdot \frac{x - y + 1}{x - y + 1}$$
$$= -1$$

89. $\dfrac{x}{x^4 - y^4} - \dfrac{1}{x^2 + 2xy + y^2}$
$$= \frac{x}{(x^2 + y^2)(x + y)(x - y)} - \frac{1}{(x + y)(x + y)}$$
$$= \frac{x}{(x^2 + y^2)(x + y)(x - y)} \cdot \frac{x + y}{x + y} -$$
$$\frac{1}{(x + y)(x + y)} \cdot \frac{(x^2 + y^2)(x - y)}{(x^2 + y^2)(x - y)}$$
$$= \frac{x^2 + xy}{(x^2 + y^2)(x + y)(x - y)(x + y)} -$$
$$\frac{x^3 - x^2y + xy^2 - y^3}{(x^2 + y^2)(x + y)(x - y)(x + y)}$$
$$= \frac{x^2 + xy - (x^3 - x^2y + xy^2 - y^3)}{(x^2 + y^2)(x + y)(x - y)(x + y)}$$
$$= \frac{x^2 + xy - x^3 + x^2y - xy^2 + y^3}{(x^2 + y^2)(x + y)(x - y)(x + y)}$$

Exercise Set 5.3

1. $\dfrac{24x^6 + 18x^5 - 36x^2}{6x^2}$
$$= \frac{24x^6}{6x^2} + \frac{18x^5}{6x^2} - \frac{36x^2}{6x^2}$$
$$= 4x^4 + 3x^3 - 6$$

3. $\dfrac{45y^7 - 20y^4 + 15y^2}{5y^2}$
$$= \frac{45y^7}{5y^2} - \frac{20y^4}{5y^2} + \frac{15y^2}{5y^2}$$
$$= 9y^5 - 4y^2 + 3$$

5. $(32a^4b^3 + 14a^3b^2 - 22a^2b) \div 2a^2b$
$$= \frac{32a^4b^3 + 14a^3b^2 - 22a^2b}{2a^2b}$$
$$= \frac{32a^4b^3}{2a^2b} + \frac{14a^3b^2}{2a^2b} - \frac{22a^2b}{2a^2b}$$
$$= 16a^2b^2 + 7ab - 11$$

7.
$$\begin{array}{r} x + 7 \\ x + 3 \overline{\smash{\big)}\ x^2 + 10x + 21} \\ \underline{x^2 + 3x} \\ 7x + 21 \\ \underline{7x + 21} \\ 0 \end{array}$$
$(x^2 + 10x) - (x^2 + 3x) = 7x$

The answer is $x + 7$.

9.
$$\begin{array}{r} a - 12 \\ a + 4 \overline{\smash{\big)}\ a^2 - 8a - 16} \\ \underline{a^2 + 4a} \\ -12a - 16 \\ \underline{-12a - 48} \\ 32 \end{array}$$
$(a^2 - 8a) - (a^2 + 4a) = -12a$
$(-12a - 16) - (-12a - 48) = 32$

The answer is $a - 12$, R 32, or $a - 12 + \dfrac{32}{a + 4}$.

11.

$$\begin{array}{r} x + 2 \\ x + 5 \overline{\smash{\big)}\ x^2 + 7x + 14} \\ \underline{x^2 + 5x} \\ 2x + 14 \\ \underline{2x + 10} \\ 4 \end{array}$$

$(x^2+7x)-(x^2+5x)=2x$

$(2x+14)-(2x+10)=4$

The answer is $x + 2$, R 4, or $x + 2 + \dfrac{4}{x+5}$.

13.

$$\begin{array}{r} 2y^2 - y + 2 \\ 2y + 4 \overline{\smash{\big)}\ 4y^3 + 6y^2 + 0y + 14} \\ \underline{4y^3 + 8y^2} \\ -2y^2 + 0y \\ \underline{-2y^2 - 4y} \\ 4y + 14 \\ \underline{4y + 8} \\ 6 \end{array}$$

The answer is $2y^2 - y + 2$, R 6, or $2y^2 - y + 2 + \dfrac{6}{2y+4}$.

15.

$$\begin{array}{r} 2y^2 + 2y - 1 \\ 5y - 2 \overline{\smash{\big)}\ 10y^3 + 6y^2 - 9y + 10} \\ \underline{10y^3 - 4y^2} \\ 10y^2 - 9y \\ \underline{10y^2 - 4y} \\ -5y + 10 \\ \underline{-5y + 2} \\ 8 \end{array}$$

The answer is $2y^2 + 2y - 1$, R 8, or $2y^2 + 2y - 1 + \dfrac{8}{5y-2}$.

17.

$$\begin{array}{r} 2x^2 - x - 9 \\ x^2 + 2 \overline{\smash{\big)}\ 2x^4 - x^3 - 5x^2 + x - 6} \\ \underline{2x^4 \qquad + 4x^2} \\ -x^3 - 9x^2 + x \\ \underline{-x^3 \qquad - 2x} \\ -9x^2 + 3x - 6 \\ \underline{-9x^2 \qquad - 18} \\ 3x + 12 \end{array}$$

The answer is $2x^2 - x - 9$, R $(3x + 12)$, or

$2x^2 - x - 9 + \dfrac{3x+12}{x^2+2}$.

19.

$$\begin{array}{r} 2x^3 + 5x^2 + 17x + 51 \\ x^2 - 3x \overline{\smash{\big)}\ 2x^5 - x^4 + 2x^3 + 0x^2 - x} \\ \underline{2x^5 - 6x^4} \\ 5x^4 + 2x^3 \\ \underline{5x^4 - 15x^3} \\ 17x^3 + 0x^2 \\ \underline{17x^3 - 51x^2} \\ 51x^2 - x \\ \underline{51x^2 - 153x} \\ 152x \end{array}$$

The answer is $2x^3 + 5x^2 + 17x + 51$, R $152x$, or

$2x^3 + 5x^2 + 17x + 51 + \dfrac{152x}{x^2-3x}$.

21. $(x^3 - 2x^2 + 2x - 5) \div (x - 1)$

$$\begin{array}{r} 1 \,\big|\ \begin{array}{rrrr} 1 & -2 & 2 & -5 \\ & 1 & -1 & 1 \\ \hline 1 & -1 & 1 & | -4 \end{array} \end{array}$$

The answer is $x^2 - x + 1$, R -4, or $x^2 - x + 1 + \dfrac{-4}{x-1}$.

23. $(a^2 + 11a - 19) \div (a + 4) =$

$(a^2 + 11a - 19) \div [a - (-4)]$

$$\begin{array}{r} -4 \,\big|\ \begin{array}{rrr} 1 & 11 & -19 \\ & -4 & -28 \\ \hline 1 & 7 & | -47 \end{array} \end{array}$$

The answer is $a + 7$, R -47, or $a + 7 + \dfrac{-47}{a+4}$.

25. $(x^3 - 7x^2 - 13x + 3) \div (x - 2)$

$$\begin{array}{r} 2 \,\big|\ \begin{array}{rrrr} 1 & -7 & -13 & 3 \\ & 2 & -10 & -46 \\ \hline 1 & -5 & -23 & | -43 \end{array} \end{array}$$

The answer is $x^2 - 5x - 23$, R -43, or $x^2 - 5x - 23 + \dfrac{-43}{x-2}$.

27. $(3x^3 + 7x^2 - 4x + 3) \div (x + 3) =$

$(3x^3 + 7x^2 - 4x + 3) \div [x - (-3)]$

$$\begin{array}{r} -3 \,\big|\ \begin{array}{rrrr} 3 & 7 & -4 & 3 \\ & -9 & 6 & -6 \\ \hline 3 & -2 & 2 & | -3 \end{array} \end{array}$$

The answer is $3x^2 - 2x + 2$, R -3, or $3x^2 - 2x + 2 + \dfrac{-3}{x+3}$.

29. $(y^3 - 3y + 10) \div (y - 2) =$

$(y^3 + 0y^2 - 3y + 10) \div (y - 2)$

$$\begin{array}{r} 2 \,\big|\ \begin{array}{rrrr} 1 & 0 & -3 & 10 \\ & 2 & 4 & 2 \\ \hline 1 & 2 & 1 & | 12 \end{array} \end{array}$$

The answer is $y^2 + 2y + 1$, R 12, or $y^2 + 2y + 1 + \dfrac{12}{y-2}$.

31. $(3x^4 - 25x^2 - 18) \div (x - 3) =$

$(3x^4 + 0x^3 - 25x^2 + 0x - 18) \div (x - 3)$

$$\begin{array}{r} 3 \,\big|\ \begin{array}{rrrrr} 3 & 0 & -25 & 0 & -18 \\ & 9 & 27 & 6 & 18 \\ \hline 3 & 9 & 2 & 6 & | 0 \end{array} \end{array}$$

The answer is $3x^3 + 9x^2 + 2x + 6$.

33. $(x^3 - 8) \div (x - 2) = (x^3 + 0x^2 + 0x - 8) \div (x - 2)$

$$\begin{array}{r} 2 \,\big|\ \begin{array}{rrrr} 1 & 0 & 0 & -8 \\ & 2 & 4 & 8 \\ \hline 1 & 2 & 4 & | 0 \end{array} \end{array}$$

The answer is $x^2 + 2x + 4$.

35. $(y^4 - 16) \div (y - 2) =$

$(y^4 + 0y^3 + 0y^2 + 0y - 16) \div (y - 2)$

$$\begin{array}{r} 2 \,\big|\ \begin{array}{rrrrr} 1 & 0 & 0 & 0 & -16 \\ & 2 & 4 & 8 & 16 \\ \hline 1 & 2 & 4 & 8 & | 0 \end{array} \end{array}$$

The answer is $y^3 + 2y^2 + 4y + 8$.

37. Discussion and Writing Exercise

39. Graph: $2x - 3y < 6$

We first graph the line $2x - 3y = 6$. The intercepts are $(0, -2)$ and $(3, 0)$. We draw the line dashed since the inequality symbol is $<$. To determine which half-plane to shade, we consider a test point not on the line. We try $(0, 0)$:

$$\frac{2x - 3y < 6}{2 \cdot 0 - 3 \cdot 0 \; ? \; 6}$$
$$0 \; | \quad \text{TRUE}$$

Since $0 < 6$ is true, we shade the half-plane that contains $(0, 0)$.

41. Graph $y > 4$.

We first graph the line $y = 4$. This is a horizontal line 4 units above the x-axis. We draw the line dashed since the inequality symbol is $>$. To determine which half-plane to shade, we write $y > 4$ as $0x + y > 4$ and consider a test point not on the line. We try $(0, 0)$:

$$\frac{0x + y > 4}{0 \cdot 0 + 0 \; ? \; 4}$$
$$0 \; | \quad \text{FALSE}$$

Since $0 > 4$ is false, we shade the half-plane that does not contain $(0, 0)$.

43. Graph: $f(x) = x^2$.

We select x-values and find the corresponding y-values. We plot these ordered pairs and draw the graph.

x	y
-2	4
-1	1
0	0
1	1
2	4

45. Graph: $f(x) = 3 - x^2$.

We select x-values and find the corresponding y-values. We plot these ordered pairs and draw the graph.

x	y
-3	-6
-2	-1
-1	2
0	3
1	2
2	-1
3	-6

47.
$$x^2 - 5x = 0$$
$$x(x - 5) = 0$$
$$x = 0 \quad or \quad x - 5 = 0$$
$$x = 0 \quad or \quad \quad\quad x = 5$$
The solutions are 0 and 5.

49.
$$12x^2 = 17x + 5$$
$$12x^2 - 17x - 5 = 0$$
$$(4x + 1)(3x - 5) = 0$$
$$4x + 1 = 0 \quad or \quad 3x - 5 = 0$$
$$4x = -1 \quad or \quad\quad 3x = 5$$
$$x = -\frac{1}{4} \quad or \quad\quad x = \frac{5}{3}$$
The solutions are $-\frac{1}{4}$ and $\frac{5}{3}$.

51. $f(x) = 4x^3 + 16x^2 - 3x - 45$
$$f(-3) = 4(-3)^3 + 16(-3)^2 - 3(-3) - 45$$
$$= -108 + 144 + 9 - 45$$
$$= 0$$

Since $f(-3) = 0$, we know that -3 is a solution of $f(x) = 0$. That is, $f(x) = 0$ when $x = -3$, or when $x + 3 = 0$. We find $f(x) \div (x + 3)$.

$$
\begin{array}{r}
4x^2 + 4x - 15 \\
x + 3 \overline{\smash{\big)}\, 4x^3 + 16x^2 - 3x - 45} \\
\underline{4x^3 + 12x^2} \\
4x^2 - 3x \\
\underline{4x^2 + 12x } \\
-15x - 45 \\
\underline{-15x - 45} \\
0
\end{array}
$$

Now we know that $(x + 3)(4x^2 + 4x - 15) = 0$. To find the other solutions of $f(x) = 0$ we solve $4x^2 + 4x - 15 = 0$.

$$4x^2 + 4x - 15 = 0$$
$$(2x - 3)(2x + 5) = 0$$
$$2x - 3 = 0 \quad or \quad 2x + 5 = 0$$
$$2x = 3 \quad or \quad\quad 2x = -5$$
$$x = \frac{3}{2} \quad or \quad\quad x = -\frac{5}{2}$$

Then the solutions of $f(x) = 0$ are -3, $\frac{3}{2}$, and $-\frac{5}{2}$.

53.

$$
\begin{array}{r}
x - 5 \\
x + 2 \overline{\smash{)}\, x^2 - 3x + 2k} \\
\underline{x^2 + 2x} \\
-5x + 2k \\
\underline{-5x - 10} \\
2k + 10
\end{array}
$$

The remainder is 7. Thus, we solve the following equation for k.

$$2k + 10 = 7$$
$$2k = -3$$
$$k = -\frac{3}{2}$$

55.

$$
\begin{array}{r}
a^2 + ab \\
a^2 + 3ab + 2b^2 \overline{\smash{)}\, a^4 + 4a^3b + 5a^2b^2 + 2ab^3} \\
\underline{a^4 + 3a^3b + 2a^2b^2} \\
a^3b + 3a^2b^2 + 2ab^3 \\
\underline{a^3b + 3a^2b^2 + 2ab^3} \\
0
\end{array}
$$

The answer is $a^2 + ab$.

Exercise Set 5.4

1. $\dfrac{2 + \dfrac{3}{5}}{4 - \dfrac{1}{2}}$

The LCM of the denominators is $5 \cdot 2$, or 10. We multiply by 1 using 10/10.

$$
\frac{2 + \dfrac{3}{5}}{4 - \dfrac{1}{2}} = \frac{2 + \dfrac{3}{5}}{4 - \dfrac{1}{2}} \cdot \frac{10}{10}
$$

$$
= \frac{\left(2 + \dfrac{3}{5}\right) \cdot 10}{\left(4 - \dfrac{1}{2}\right) \cdot 10}
$$

$$
= \frac{2 \cdot 10 + \dfrac{3}{5} \cdot 10}{4 \cdot 10 - \dfrac{1}{2} \cdot 10}
$$

$$
= \frac{20 + 6}{40 - 5}
$$

$$
= \frac{26}{35}
$$

3. $\dfrac{\dfrac{2}{3} + \dfrac{4}{5}}{\dfrac{3}{4} - \dfrac{1}{2}}$

The LCM of the denominators is $3 \cdot 5 \cdot 2 \cdot 2$, or 60. We multiply by 1 using 60/60.

$$
\frac{\dfrac{2}{3} + \dfrac{4}{5}}{\dfrac{3}{4} - \dfrac{1}{2}} = \frac{\dfrac{2}{3} + \dfrac{4}{5}}{\dfrac{3}{4} - \dfrac{1}{2}} \cdot \frac{60}{60}
$$

$$
= \frac{\left(\dfrac{2}{3} + \dfrac{4}{5}\right) \cdot 60}{\left(\dfrac{3}{4} - \dfrac{1}{2}\right) \cdot 60}
$$

$$
= \frac{\dfrac{2}{3} \cdot 60 + \dfrac{4}{5} \cdot 60}{\dfrac{3}{4} \cdot 60 - \dfrac{1}{2} \cdot 60}
$$

$$
= \frac{40 + 48}{45 - 30}
$$

$$
= \frac{88}{15}
$$

5. $\dfrac{\dfrac{x}{y^2}}{\dfrac{y^3}{x^2}} = \dfrac{x}{y^2} \cdot \dfrac{x^2}{y^3}$ Multiplying by the reciprocal of the divisor

$$
= \frac{x^3}{y^5}
$$

7. $= \dfrac{\dfrac{9x^2 - y^2}{xy}}{\dfrac{3x - y}{y}}$

$$
= \frac{9x^2 - y^2}{xy} \cdot \frac{y}{3x - y} \quad \text{Multiplying by the reciprocal of the divisor}
$$

$$
= \frac{(9x^2 - y^2)(y)}{xy(3x - y)}
$$

$$
= \frac{(3x + y)(3x - y)(y)}{xy(3x - y)}
$$

$$
= \frac{3x + y}{x}
$$

9. $\dfrac{\dfrac{1}{a} + 2}{\dfrac{1}{a} - 1}$

The LCM of all the denominators is a. We multiply by 1 using a/a.

$$
\frac{\dfrac{1}{a} + 2}{\dfrac{1}{a} - 1} = \frac{\dfrac{1}{a} + 2}{\dfrac{1}{a} - 1} \cdot \frac{a}{a}
$$

$$
= \frac{\left(\dfrac{1}{a} + 2\right) \cdot a}{\left(\dfrac{1}{a} - 1\right) \cdot a}
$$

$$
= \frac{\dfrac{1}{a} \cdot a + 2a}{\dfrac{1}{a} \cdot a - a}
$$

$$
= \frac{1 + 2a}{1 - a}
$$

11. $\dfrac{x - \dfrac{1}{x}}{x + \dfrac{1}{x}}$

The LCM of all the denominators is x. We multiply by 1 using x/x.

$$\frac{x - \dfrac{1}{x}}{x + \dfrac{1}{x}} = \frac{x - \dfrac{1}{x}}{x + \dfrac{1}{x}} \cdot \frac{x}{x}$$

$$= \frac{\left(x - \dfrac{1}{x}\right) \cdot x}{\left(x + \dfrac{1}{x}\right) \cdot x}$$

$$= \frac{x \cdot x - \dfrac{1}{x} \cdot x}{x \cdot x + \dfrac{1}{x} \cdot x}$$

$$= \frac{x^2 - 1}{x^2 + 1}$$

13. $\dfrac{\dfrac{3}{x} + \dfrac{4}{y}}{\dfrac{4}{x} - \dfrac{3}{y}}$

The LCM of all the denominators is xy. We multiply by 1 using $\dfrac{xy}{xy}$.

$$\frac{\dfrac{3}{x} + \dfrac{4}{y}}{\dfrac{4}{x} - \dfrac{3}{y}} = \frac{\dfrac{3}{x} + \dfrac{4}{y}}{\dfrac{4}{x} - \dfrac{3}{y}} \cdot \frac{xy}{xy}$$

$$= \frac{\left(\dfrac{3}{x} + \dfrac{4}{y}\right) \cdot xy}{\left(\dfrac{4}{x} - \dfrac{3}{y}\right) \cdot xy}$$

$$= \frac{\dfrac{3}{x} \cdot xy + \dfrac{4}{y} \cdot xy}{\dfrac{4}{x} \cdot xy - \dfrac{3}{y} \cdot xy}$$

$$= \frac{3y + 4x}{4y - 3x}$$

15. $\dfrac{a - \dfrac{3a}{b}}{b - \dfrac{b}{a}}$

$$= \frac{a - \dfrac{3a}{b}}{b - \dfrac{b}{a}} \cdot \frac{ab}{ab} \quad \text{Using the LCM of the denominators}$$

$$= \frac{\left(a - \dfrac{3a}{b}\right) \cdot ab}{\left(b - \dfrac{b}{a}\right) \cdot ab}$$

$$= \frac{a(ab) - \dfrac{3a}{b} \cdot ab}{b(ab) - \dfrac{b}{a} \cdot ab}$$

$$= \frac{a^2 b - 3a^2}{ab^2 - b^2}$$

$$= \frac{a^2(b - 3)}{b^2(a - 1)}$$

17. $\dfrac{\dfrac{1}{a} + \dfrac{1}{b}}{\dfrac{a^2 - b^2}{ab}}$

$$= \frac{\dfrac{1}{a} + \dfrac{1}{b}}{\dfrac{a^2 - b^2}{ab}} \cdot \frac{ab}{ab} \quad \text{Using the LCM of the denominators}$$

$$= \frac{\left(\dfrac{1}{a} + \dfrac{1}{b}\right) \cdot ab}{\left(\dfrac{a^2 - b^2}{ab}\right) \cdot ab}$$

$$= \frac{\dfrac{1}{a} \cdot ab + \dfrac{1}{b} \cdot ab}{\dfrac{a^2 - b^2}{ab} \cdot ab}$$

$$= \frac{b + a}{a^2 - b^2} = \frac{b + a}{(a + b)(a - b)}$$

$$= \frac{a + b}{a + b} \cdot \frac{1}{a - b} \qquad (b + a = a + b)$$

$$= \frac{1}{a - b}$$

19. $\dfrac{\dfrac{1}{x+h} - \dfrac{1}{x}}{h}$

$= \dfrac{\dfrac{1}{x+h} \cdot \dfrac{x}{x} - \dfrac{1}{x} \cdot \dfrac{x+h}{x+h}}{h}$ Adding in the numerator

$= \dfrac{\dfrac{x-x-h}{x(x+h)}}{h} = \dfrac{\dfrac{-h}{x(x+h)}}{h}$

$= \dfrac{-h}{x(x+h)} \cdot \dfrac{1}{h}$ Multiplying by the reciprocal of the divisor

$= \dfrac{-h}{hx(x+h)}$

$= \dfrac{h}{h} \cdot \dfrac{-1}{x(x+h)}$ Removing a factor of 1

$= \dfrac{-1}{x(x+h)}$, or $-\dfrac{1}{x(x+h)}$

21. $\dfrac{\dfrac{x^2 - x - 12}{x^2 - 2x - 15}}{\dfrac{x^2 + 8x + 12}{x^2 - 5x - 14}}$

$= \dfrac{x^2 - x - 12}{x^2 - 2x - 15} \cdot \dfrac{x^2 - 5x - 14}{x^2 + 8x + 12}$ Multiplying by the reciprocal of the divisor

$= \dfrac{(x^2 - x - 12)(x^2 - 5x - 14)}{(x^2 - 2x - 15)(x^2 + 8x + 12)}$

$= \dfrac{(x+3)(x-4)(x-7)(x+2)}{(x-5)(x+3)(x+6)(x+2)}$ Removing a factor of 1

$= \dfrac{(x-4)(x-7)}{(x-5)(x+6)}$

23. $\dfrac{\dfrac{1}{x+2} + \dfrac{4}{x-3}}{\dfrac{2}{x-3} - \dfrac{7}{x+2}}$

$= \dfrac{\dfrac{1}{x+2} + \dfrac{4}{x-3}}{\dfrac{2}{x-3} - \dfrac{7}{x+2}} \cdot \dfrac{(x+2)(x-3)}{(x+2)(x-3)}$ Using the LCM of the denominators

$= \dfrac{\dfrac{1}{x+2} \cdot (x+2)(x-3) + \dfrac{4}{x-3} \cdot (x+2)(x-3)}{\dfrac{2}{x-3} \cdot (x+2)(x-3) - \dfrac{7}{x+2} \cdot (x+2)(x-3)}$

$= \dfrac{x-3+4(x+2)}{2(x+2)-7(x-3)}$

$= \dfrac{x-3+4x+8}{2x+4-7x+21}$

$= \dfrac{5x+5}{-5x+25}$

$= \dfrac{5(x+1)}{5(-x+5)}$ Removing a factor of 1

$= \dfrac{x+1}{-x+5}$, or $\dfrac{x+1}{5-x}$

25. $\dfrac{\dfrac{6}{x^2-4} - \dfrac{5}{x+2}}{\dfrac{7}{x^2-4} - \dfrac{4}{x-2}}$

$= \dfrac{\dfrac{6}{(x+2)(x-2)} - \dfrac{5}{x+2} \cdot \dfrac{x-2}{x-2}}{\dfrac{7}{(x+2)(x-2)} - \dfrac{4}{x-2} \cdot \dfrac{(x+2)}{(x+2)}}$

Finding the LCM of the denominators and multiplying by 1

$= \dfrac{\dfrac{6}{(x+2)(x-2)} - \dfrac{5x-10}{(x+2)(x-2)}}{\dfrac{7}{(x+2)(x-2)} - \dfrac{4x+8}{(x+2)(x-2)}}$

$= \dfrac{\dfrac{6-5x+10}{(x+2)(x-2)}}{\dfrac{7-4x-8}{(x+2)(x-2)}}$ Subtracting in the numerator and in the denominator

$= \dfrac{\dfrac{16-5x}{(x+2)(x-2)}}{\dfrac{-1-4x}{(x+2)(x-2)}}$

$= \dfrac{16-5x}{(x+2)(x-2)} \cdot \dfrac{(x+2)(x-2)}{-1-4x}$

Multiplying by the reciprocal of the denominator

$= \dfrac{(16-5x)(x+2)(x-2)}{(x+2)(x-2)(-1-4x)}$ Removing a factor of 1

$= \dfrac{(16-5x)(x+2)(x-2)}{(x+2)(x-2)(-1-4x)}$ Removing a factor of 1

$= \dfrac{16-5x}{-1-4x}$

$= \dfrac{-1 \cdot (5x-16)}{-1(4x+1)}$ Removing a factor of 1

$= \dfrac{5x-16}{4x+1}$

27.

$$\dfrac{\dfrac{1}{z^2} - \dfrac{1}{w^2}}{\dfrac{1}{z^3} + \dfrac{1}{w^3}}$$

$$= \dfrac{\dfrac{1}{z^2} - \dfrac{1}{w^2}}{\dfrac{1}{z^3} + \dfrac{1}{w^3}} \cdot \dfrac{z^3 w^3}{z^3 w^3} \qquad \begin{array}{l}\text{Multiplying by the LCM of} \\ \text{the denominators}\end{array}$$

$$= \dfrac{\left(\dfrac{1}{z^2} - \dfrac{1}{w^2}\right) \cdot z^3 w^3}{\left(\dfrac{1}{z^3} + \dfrac{1}{w^3}\right) \cdot z^3 w^3}$$

$$= \dfrac{zw^3 - z^3 w}{w^3 + z^3}$$

$$= \dfrac{zw(w^2 - z^2)}{(w + z)(w^2 - wz + z^2)}$$

$$= \dfrac{zw(w + z)(w - z)}{(w + z)(w^2 - wz + z^2)}$$

$$= \dfrac{zw(w - z)}{w^2 - wz + z^2}$$

29.

$$\dfrac{\dfrac{3}{x^2 + 2x - 3} - \dfrac{1}{x^2 - 3x - 10}}{\dfrac{3}{x^2 - 6x + 5} - \dfrac{1}{x^2 + 5x + 6}}$$

$$= \dfrac{\dfrac{3}{(x + 3)(x - 1)} - \dfrac{1}{(x - 5)(x + 2)}}{\dfrac{3}{(x - 5)(x - 1)} - \dfrac{1}{(x + 3)(x + 2)}}$$

$$= \dfrac{\dfrac{3}{(x+3)(x-1)} - \dfrac{1}{(x-5)(x+2)}}{\dfrac{3}{(x-5)(x-1)} - \dfrac{1}{(x+3)(x+2)}} \cdot$$

$$\dfrac{(x+3)(x-1)(x-5)(x+2)}{(x+3)(x-1)(x-5)(x+2)}$$

Multiplying by 1, using the LCD

$$= \dfrac{3(x - 5)(x + 2) - (x + 3)(x - 1)}{3(x + 3)(x + 2) - (x - 1)(x - 5)}$$

$$= \dfrac{3(x^2 - 3x - 10) - (x^2 + 2x - 3)}{3(x^2 + 5x + 6) - (x^2 - 6x + 5)}$$

$$= \dfrac{3x^2 - 9x - 30 - x^2 - 2x + 3}{3x^2 + 15x + 18 - x^2 + 6x - 5}$$

$$= \dfrac{2x^2 - 11x - 27}{2x^2 + 21x + 13}$$

31. Discussion and Writing Exercise

33.

$$4x^3 + 20x^2 + 6x$$

$$= 2x(2x^2 + 10x + 3) \qquad \begin{array}{l}\text{Factoring out the largest} \\ \text{common factor}\end{array}$$

The trinomial $2x^2 + 10x + 3$ cannot be factored as a product of binomials so we have the complete factorization.

35. $y^3 - 8 = y^3 - 2^3 = (y - 2)(y^2 + 2y + 4)$

37. $1000x^3 + 1 = (10x)^3 + 1^3 = (10x + 1)(100x^2 - 10x + 1)$

39. $y^3 - 64x^3 = y^3 - (4x)^3 = (y - 4x)(y^2 + 4xy + 16x^2)$

41.

$$T = \dfrac{r + s}{3}$$

$$3T = r + s \qquad \text{Multiplying by 3}$$

$$3T - r = s \qquad \text{Subtracting } r$$

43.

$$f(x) = x^2 - 3$$

$$f(-5) = (-5)^2 - 3 = 25 - 3 = 22$$

45. $f(a) = \dfrac{3}{a^2}$, $f(a + h) = \dfrac{3}{(a + h)^2}$

$$\dfrac{f(a + h) - f(a)}{h} = \dfrac{\dfrac{3}{(a + h)^2} - \dfrac{3}{a^2}}{h}$$

$$= \dfrac{3a^2 - 3(a + h)^2}{a^2(a + h)^2} \cdot \dfrac{1}{h}$$

$$= \dfrac{3a^2 - 3a^2 - 6ah - 3h^2}{a^2(a + h)^2} \cdot \dfrac{1}{h}$$

$$= \dfrac{-6ah - 3h^2}{a^2(a + h)^2 h}$$

$$= \dfrac{-3h(2a + h)}{a^2(a + h)^2 h}$$

$$= \dfrac{-3h(2a + h)}{a^2(a + h)^2 h}$$

$$= \dfrac{-3(2a + h)}{x^2(a + h)^2}, \text{ or}$$

$$= \dfrac{-6a - 3h}{a^2(a + h)^2}$$

47. $f(a) = \dfrac{1}{1 - a}$, $f(a + h) = \dfrac{1}{1 - (a + h)} = \dfrac{1}{1 - a - h}$

$$\dfrac{f(a + h) - f(a)}{h}$$

$$= \dfrac{\dfrac{1}{1 - a - h} - \dfrac{1}{1 - a}}{h}$$

$$= \dfrac{1 - a - (1 - a - h)}{(1 - a - h)(1 - a)} \cdot \dfrac{1}{h}$$

$$= \dfrac{1 - a - 1 + a + h}{(1 - a - h)(1 - a)} \cdot \dfrac{1}{h}$$

$$= \dfrac{h}{(1 - a - h)(1 - a)h}$$

$$= \dfrac{h \cdot 1}{(1 - a - h)(1 - a)h}$$

$$= \dfrac{1}{(1 - a - h)(1 - a)}$$

49. $\dfrac{5x^{-1} - 5y^{-1} + 10x^{-1}y^{-1}}{6x^{-1} - 6y^{-1} + 12x^{-1}y^{-1}}$

$= \dfrac{\dfrac{5}{x} - \dfrac{5}{y} + \dfrac{10}{xy}}{\dfrac{6}{x} - \dfrac{6}{y} + \dfrac{12}{xy}}$

$= \dfrac{\dfrac{5}{x} - \dfrac{5}{y} + \dfrac{10}{xy}}{\dfrac{6}{x} - \dfrac{6}{y} + \dfrac{12}{xy}} \cdot \dfrac{xy}{xy}$

$= \dfrac{5y - 5x + 10}{6y - 6x + 12}$

$= \dfrac{5(y - x + 2)}{6(y - x + 2)}$

$= \dfrac{5}{6} \cdot \dfrac{y - x + 2}{y - x + 2}$

$= \dfrac{5}{6}$

51. $\dfrac{1}{x^2 - \dfrac{1}{x}} = \dfrac{1}{x^2 \cdot \dfrac{x}{x} - \dfrac{1}{x}} = \dfrac{1}{\dfrac{x^3}{x} - \dfrac{1}{x}} =$

$\dfrac{1}{\dfrac{x^3 - 1}{x}} = 1 \cdot \dfrac{x}{x^3 - 1} = \dfrac{x}{x^3 - 1}$

53. $\dfrac{1}{\dfrac{a^3 + b^3}{a + b}} = 1 \cdot \dfrac{a + b}{a^3 + b^3}$

$= \dfrac{1 \cdot (a + b)}{(a + b)(a^2 - ab + b^2)}$

$= \dfrac{1}{a^2 - ab + b^2}$

Exercise Set 5.5

1. $\dfrac{y}{10} = \dfrac{2}{5} + \dfrac{3}{8}$, LCM is 40

$40 \cdot \dfrac{y}{10} = 40 \cdot \left(\dfrac{2}{5} + \dfrac{3}{8}\right)$ Multiplying by the LCM

$4y = 40 \cdot \dfrac{2}{5} + 40 \cdot \dfrac{3}{8}$ Removing parentheses

$4y = 16 + 15$

$4y = 31$

$y = \dfrac{31}{4}$

Check: $\dfrac{y}{10} = \dfrac{2}{5} + \dfrac{3}{8}$

$\dfrac{\dfrac{31}{4}}{10} \ ? \ \dfrac{2}{5} + \dfrac{3}{8}$

$\dfrac{31}{4} \cdot \dfrac{1}{10} \ \bigg| \ \dfrac{16}{40} + \dfrac{15}{40}$

$\dfrac{31}{40} \ \bigg| \ \dfrac{31}{40}$ TRUE

The solution is $\dfrac{31}{4}$.

3. $\dfrac{1}{4} - \dfrac{5}{6} = \dfrac{1}{a}$, LCM is $12a$

$12a \cdot \left(\dfrac{1}{4} - \dfrac{5}{6}\right) = 12a \cdot \dfrac{1}{a}$ Multiplying by the LCM

$12a \cdot \dfrac{1}{4} - 12a \cdot \dfrac{5}{6} = 12$

$3a - 10a = 12$

$-7a = 12$

$a = -\dfrac{12}{7}$

Check: $\dfrac{1}{4} - \dfrac{5}{6} = \dfrac{1}{a}$

$\dfrac{1}{4} - \dfrac{5}{6} \ ? \ \dfrac{1}{-\dfrac{12}{7}}$

$\dfrac{3}{12} - \dfrac{10}{12} \ \bigg| \ 1 \cdot \left(-\dfrac{7}{12}\right)$

$-\dfrac{7}{12} \ \bigg| \ -\dfrac{7}{12}$ TRUE

The solution is $-\dfrac{12}{7}$.

5. $\dfrac{x}{3} - \dfrac{x}{4} = 12$, LCM is 12

$12 \cdot \left(\dfrac{x}{3} - \dfrac{x}{4}\right) = 12 \cdot 12$

$12 \cdot \dfrac{x}{3} - 12 \cdot \dfrac{x}{4} = 144$

$4x - 3x = 144$

$x = 144$

Check: $\dfrac{x}{3} - \dfrac{x}{4} = 12$

$\dfrac{144}{3} - \dfrac{144}{4} \ ? \ 12$

$48 - 36 \ \bigg|$

$12 \ \bigg|$ TRUE

The solution is 144.

7. $x + \dfrac{8}{x} = -9$, LCM is x

$x\left(x + \dfrac{8}{x}\right) = x(-9)$

$x \cdot x + x \cdot \dfrac{8}{x} = -9x$

$x^2 + 8 = -9x$

$x^2 + 9x + 8 = 0$

$(x + 1)(x + 8) = 0$

$x + 1 = 0$ *or* $x + 8 = 0$ Principle of zero products

$x = -1$ *or* $x = -8$

Check:

For -1:

$$x + \frac{8}{x} = -9$$

$$\begin{array}{c|c} -1 + \dfrac{8}{-1} & ? -9 \\ \hline -1 - 8 & \\ -9 & \text{TRUE} \end{array}$$

For -8:

$$x + \frac{8}{x} = -9$$

$$\begin{array}{c|c} -8 + \dfrac{8}{-8} & ? -9 \\ \hline -8 - 1 & \\ -9 & \text{TRUE} \end{array}$$

The solutions are -1 and -8.

9. $\dfrac{3}{y} + \dfrac{7}{y} = 5$, LCM is y

$$y\left(\frac{3}{y} + \frac{7}{y}\right) = y \cdot 5$$

$$y \cdot \frac{3}{y} + y \cdot \frac{7}{y} = 5y$$

$$3 + 7 = 5y$$

$$10 = 5y$$

$$2 = y$$

Check: $\dfrac{3}{y} + \dfrac{7}{y} = 5$

$$\begin{array}{c|c} \dfrac{3}{2} + \dfrac{7}{2} & ? 5 \\ \dfrac{10}{2} & \\ 5 & \text{TRUE} \end{array}$$

The solution is 2.

11. $\dfrac{1}{2} = \dfrac{z-5}{z+1}$, LCM is $2(z+1)$

$$2(z+1) \cdot \frac{1}{2} = 2(z+1) \cdot \frac{z-5}{z+1}$$

$$z + 1 = 2(z - 5)$$

$$z + 1 = 2z - 10$$

$$11 = z$$

Check: $\dfrac{1}{2} = \dfrac{z-5}{z+1}$

$$\begin{array}{c|c} \dfrac{1}{2} & ? \dfrac{11-5}{11+1} \\ & \dfrac{6}{12} \\ & \dfrac{1}{2} \quad \text{TRUE} \end{array}$$

The solution is 11.

13. $\dfrac{3}{y+1} = \dfrac{2}{y-3}$, LCM is $(y+1)(y-3)$

$$(y+1)(y-3) \cdot \frac{3}{y+1} = (y+1)(y-3) \cdot \frac{2}{y-3}$$

$$3(y-3) = 2(y+1)$$

$$3y - 9 = 2y + 2$$

$$y = 11$$

Check: $\dfrac{3}{y+1} = \dfrac{2}{y-3}$

$$\begin{array}{c|c} \dfrac{3}{11+1} & ? \dfrac{2}{11-3} \\ \dfrac{3}{12} & \dfrac{2}{8} \\ \dfrac{1}{4} & \dfrac{1}{4} \quad \text{TRUE} \end{array}$$

The solution is 11.

15. $\dfrac{y-1}{y-3} = \dfrac{2}{y-3}$, LCM is $y-3$

$$(y-3) \cdot \frac{y-1}{y-3} = (y-3) \cdot \frac{2}{y-3}$$

$$y - 1 = 2$$

$$y = 3$$

Check: $\dfrac{y-1}{y-3} = \dfrac{2}{y-3}$

$$\begin{array}{c|c} \dfrac{3-1}{3-3} & ? \dfrac{2}{3-3} \\ \dfrac{2}{0} & \dfrac{2}{0} \quad \text{UNDEFINED} \end{array}$$

We know that 3 is not a solution of the original equation, because it results in division by 0. The equation has no solution.

17. $\dfrac{x+1}{x} = \dfrac{3}{2}$, LCM is $2x$

$$2x \cdot \frac{x+1}{x} = 2x \cdot \frac{3}{2}$$

$$2(x+1) = x \cdot 3$$

$$2x + 2 = 3x$$

$$2 = x$$

Check: $\dfrac{x+1}{x} = \dfrac{3}{2}$

$$\begin{array}{c|c} \dfrac{2+1}{2} & ? \dfrac{3}{2} \\ \dfrac{3}{2} & \quad \text{TRUE} \end{array}$$

The solution is 2.

19.
$$\frac{1}{2} - \frac{4}{9x} = \frac{4}{9} - \frac{1}{6x}, \text{ LCM is } 18x$$

$$18x\left(\frac{1}{2} - \frac{4}{9x}\right) = 18x\left(\frac{4}{9} - \frac{1}{6x}\right)$$

$$18x \cdot \frac{1}{2} - 18x \cdot \frac{4}{9x} = 18x \cdot \frac{4}{9} - 18x \cdot \frac{1}{6x}$$

$$9x - 8 = 8x - 3$$

$$x = 5$$

Since 5 checks, it is the solution.

21.
$$\frac{60}{x} - \frac{60}{x-5} = \frac{2}{x}, \text{ LCM is } x(x-5)$$

$$x(x-5)\left(\frac{60}{x} - \frac{60}{x-5}\right) = x(x-5) \cdot \frac{2}{x}$$

$$60(x-5) - 60x = 2(x-5)$$

$$60x - 300 - 60x = 2x - 10$$

$$-300 = 2x - 10$$

$$-290 = 2x$$

$$-145 = x$$

Since -145 checks, it is the solution.

23.
$$\frac{7}{5x-2} = \frac{5}{4x}, \text{ LCM is } 4x(5x-2)$$

$$4x(5x-2) \cdot \frac{7}{5x-2} = 4x(5x-2) \cdot \frac{5}{4x}$$

$$4x \cdot 7 = 5(5x-2)$$

$$28x = 25x - 10$$

$$3x = -10$$

$$x = -\frac{10}{3}$$

Since $-\dfrac{10}{3}$ checks, it is the solution.

25.
$$\frac{x}{x-2} + \frac{x}{x^2-4} = \frac{x+3}{x+2}$$

$$\frac{x}{x-2} + \frac{x}{(x+2)(x-2)} = \frac{x+3}{x+2}$$

$$\text{LCM is } (x+2)(x-2)$$

$$(x+2)(x-2)\left(\frac{x}{x-2} + \frac{x}{(x+2)(x-2)}\right) =$$

$$(x+2)(x-2) \cdot \frac{x+3}{x+2}$$

$$x(x+2) + x =$$

$$(x-2)(x+3)$$

$$x^2 + 2x + x = x^2 + x - 6$$

$$3x = x - 6$$

$$2x = -6$$

$$x = -3$$

Since -3 checks, it is the solution.

27.
$$\frac{6}{x^2-4x+3} - \frac{1}{x-3} = \frac{1}{4x-4}$$

$$\frac{6}{(x-3)(x-1)} - \frac{1}{x-3} = \frac{1}{4(x-1)}$$

$$\text{LCM is } 4(x-3)(x-1)$$

$$4(x-3)(x-1)\left(\frac{6}{(x-3)(x-1)} - \frac{1}{x-3}\right) =$$

$$4(x-3)(x-1) \cdot \frac{1}{4(x-1)}$$

$$4 \cdot 6 - 4(x-1) = x-3$$

$$24 - 4x + 4 \quad x-3$$

$$-5x = -31$$

$$x = \frac{31}{5}$$

Since $\dfrac{31}{5}$ checks, it is the solution.

29.
$$\frac{5}{y+3} = \frac{1}{4y^2-36} + \frac{2}{y-3}$$

$$\frac{5}{y+3} = \frac{1}{4(y+3)(y-3)} + \frac{2}{y-3}$$

$$\text{LCM is } 4(y+3)(y-3)$$

$$4(y+3)(y-3) \cdot \frac{5}{y+3} =$$

$$4(y+3)(y-3)\left(\frac{1}{4(y+3)(y-3)} + \frac{2}{y-3}\right)$$

$$4 \cdot 5(y-3) = 1 + 4 \cdot 2(y+3)$$

$$20y - 60 = 1 + 8y + 24$$

$$12y = 85$$

$$y = \frac{85}{12}$$

Since $\dfrac{85}{12}$ checks, it is the solution.

31.
$$\frac{a}{2a-6} - \frac{3}{a^2-6a+9} = \frac{a-2}{3a-9}$$

$$\frac{a}{2(a-3)} - \frac{3}{(a-3)(a-3)} = \frac{a-2}{3(a-3)}$$

$$\text{LCM is } 2 \cdot 3(a-3)(a-3)$$

$$6(a-3)(a-3)\left(\frac{a}{2(a-3)} - \frac{3}{(a-3)(a-3)}\right) =$$

$$6(a-3)(a-3) \cdot \frac{a-2}{3(a-3)}$$

$$3a(a-3) - 6 \cdot 3 = 2(a-3)(a-2)$$

$$3a^2 - 9a - 18 = 2(a^2 - 5a + 6)$$

$$3a^2 - 9a - 18 = 2a^2 - 10a + 12$$

$$a^2 + a - 30 = 0$$

$$(a+6)(a-5) = 0$$

$$a + 6 = 0 \quad or \quad a - 5 = 0$$

$$a = -6 \quad or \quad a = 5$$

Both -6 and 5 check. The solutions are -6 and 5.

33.
$$\frac{2x+3}{x-1} = \frac{10}{x^2-1} + \frac{2x-3}{x+1}$$
$$\frac{2x+3}{x-1} = \frac{10}{(x+1)(x-1)} + \frac{2x-3}{x+1}$$
$$\text{LCM is } (x+1)(x-1)$$
$$(x+1)(x-1)\cdot\frac{2x+3}{x-1} =$$
$$(x+1)(x-1)\Big(\frac{10}{(x+1)(x-1)} + \frac{2x-3}{x+1}\Big)$$
$$(x+1)(2x+3) = 10 + (x-1)(2x-3)$$
$$2x^2 + 5x + 3 = 10 + 2x^2 - 5x + 3$$
$$5x + 3 = 13 - 5x$$
$$10x = 10$$
$$x = 1$$

We know that 1 is not a solution of the original equation, because it results in division by 0. The equation has no solution.

35. $\dfrac{4}{x+3} + \dfrac{7}{x^2-3x+9} = \dfrac{108}{x^3+27}$

Note: $x^3 + 27 = (x+3)(x^2 - 3x + 9)$

Thus the LCM is $(x+3)(x^2 - 3x + 9)$.
$$(x+3)(x^2-3x+9)\Big(\frac{4}{x+3} + \frac{7}{x^2-3x+9}\Big) =$$
$$(x+3)(x^2-3x+9)\Big(\frac{108}{(x+3)(x^2-3x+9)}\Big)$$
$$4(x^2 - 3x + 9) + 7(x+3) = 108$$
$$4x^2 - 12x + 36 + 7x + 21 = 108$$
$$4x^2 - 5x - 51 = 0$$
$$(4x - 17)(x+3) = 0$$

$$4x - 17 = 0 \quad or \quad x + 3 = 0$$
$$4x = 17 \quad or \quad x = -3$$
$$x = \frac{17}{4} \quad or \quad x = -3$$

We know that -3 is not a solution of the original equation, because it results in division by 0. Since $\dfrac{17}{4}$ checks, it is the solution.

37.
$$\frac{5x}{x-7} - \frac{35}{x+7} = \frac{490}{x^2-49}$$
$$\frac{5x}{x-7} - \frac{35}{x+7} = \frac{490}{(x+7)(x-7)}$$
$$\text{LCM is } (x+7)(x-7)$$
$$(x+7)(x-7)\Big(\frac{5x}{x-7} - \frac{35}{x+7}\Big) =$$
$$(x+7)(x-7)\cdot\frac{490}{(x+7)(x-7)}$$
$$5x(x+7) - 35(x-7) = 490$$
$$5x^2 + 35x - 35x + 245 = 490$$
$$5x^2 + 245 = 490$$
$$5x^2 - 245 = 0$$
$$5(x^2 - 49) = 0$$
$$5(x+7)(x-7) = 0$$

$$x + 7 = 0 \quad or \quad x - 7 = 0$$
$$x = -7 \quad or \quad x = 7$$

The numbers -7 and 7 are possible solutions. Each makes a denominator 0, so the equation has no solution.

39.
$$\frac{x-1}{3} + \frac{6x+1}{15} + \frac{2(x-2)}{13-7x} = \frac{2(x+2)}{5},$$
$$\text{LCM is } 15(13-7x)$$
$$15(13-7x)\Big(\frac{x-1}{3} + \frac{6x+1}{15} + \frac{2(x-2)}{13-7x}\Big) =$$
$$15(13-7x)\cdot\frac{2(x+2)}{5}$$
$$5(13-7x)(x-1) + (13-7x)(6x+1) + 15\cdot 2(x-2) =$$
$$3(13-7x)(2)(x+2)$$
$$5(-7x^2 + 20x - 13) + (-42x^2 + 71x + 13) + 30x - 60 =$$
$$6(-7x^2 - x + 26)$$
$$-35x^2 + 100x - 65 - 42x^2 + 71x + 13 + 30x - 60 =$$
$$-42x^2 - 6x + 156$$
$$-77x^2 + 201x - 112 = -42x^2 - 6x + 156$$
$$0 = 35x^2 - 207x + 268$$
$$0 = (35x - 67)(x-4)$$

$$35x - 67 = 0 \quad or \quad x - 4 = 0$$
$$35x = 67 \quad or \quad x = 4$$
$$x = \frac{67}{35} \quad or \quad x = 4$$

Both numbers check. The solutions are $\dfrac{67}{35}$ and 4.

41. We find all values of x for which $2x - \dfrac{6}{x} = 1$. First note that $x \neq 0$. Then multiply on both sides by the LCD, x.

$$x\left(2x - \frac{6}{x}\right) = x \cdot 1$$

$$x \cdot 2x - x \cdot \frac{6}{x} = x$$

$$2x^2 - 6 = x$$

$$2x^2 - x - 6 = 0$$

$$(2x + 3)(x - 2) = 0$$

$$x = -\frac{3}{2} \ or \ x = 2$$

Both values check. The solutions are $-\frac{3}{2}$ and 2.

43. We find all values of x for which $\frac{x-3}{x+2} = \frac{1}{5}$. First note that $x \neq -2$. Then multiply on both sides by the LCD, $5(x+2)$.

$$5(x+2) \cdot \frac{x-3}{x+2} = 5(x+2) \cdot \frac{1}{5}$$

$$5(x-3) = x+2$$

$$5x - 15 = x + 2$$

$$4x = 17$$

$$x = \frac{17}{4}$$

This value checks. The solution is $\frac{17}{4}$.

45. We find all values of x for which $\frac{6}{x} - \frac{6}{2x} = 5$. First note that $x \neq 0$. Then multiply on both sides by the LCD, $2x$.

$$2x\left(\frac{6}{x} - \frac{6}{2x}\right) = 2x \cdot 5$$

$$2x \cdot \frac{6}{x} - 2x \cdot \frac{6}{2x} = 10x$$

$$12 - 6 = 10x$$

$$6 = 10x$$

$$\frac{3}{5} = x$$

This value checks. The solution is $\frac{3}{5}$.

47. Discussion and Writing Exercise

49.
$$1 - t^6$$
$$= 1^2 - (t^3)^2$$
$$= (1 + t^3)(1 - t^3)$$
$$= (1 + t)(1 - t + t^2)(1 - t)(1 + t + t^2)$$

51.
$$a^3 - 8b^3$$
$$= a^3 - (2b)^3$$
$$= (a - 2b)(a^2 + 2ab + 4b^2)$$

53. a) Graph $y_1 = \frac{x+3}{x+2} - \frac{x+4}{x+3}$ and $y_2 = \frac{x+5}{x+4} - \frac{x+6}{x+5}$ and use the INTERSECT feature to find the point of intersection of the graphs. It is $(-3.5, 1.\overline{3})$.

b) Set $f(x)$ equal to $g(x)$ and solve for x.
$$\frac{x+3}{x+2} - \frac{x+4}{x+3} = \frac{x+5}{x+4} - \frac{x+6}{x+5}$$
Note that $x \neq -2$ and $x \neq -3$ and $x \neq -4$ and $x \neq -5$.

$$(x+2)(x+3)(x+4)(x+5)\left(\frac{x+3}{x+2} - \frac{x+4}{x+3}\right) =$$
$$(x+2)(x+3)(x+4)(x+5)\left(\frac{x+5}{x+4} - \frac{x+6}{x+5}\right)$$
$$(x+3)(x+4)(x+5)(x+3) - (x+2)(x+4)(x+5)(x+4) =$$
$$(x+2)(x+3)(x+5)(x+5) - (x+2)(x+3)(x+4)(x+6)$$
$$x^4 + 15x^3 + 83x^2 + 201x + 180 -$$
$$(x^4 + 15x^3 + 82x^2 + 192x + 160) =$$
$$x^4 + 15x^3 + 81x^2 + 185x + 150 -$$
$$(x^4 + 15x^3 + 80x^2 + 180x + 144)$$
$$x^2 + 9x + 20 = x^2 + 5x + 6$$
$$4x = -14$$
$$x = -\frac{7}{2}$$

This value checks. When $x = -\frac{7}{2}$, $f(x) = g(x)$. This confirms that the graphs of $f(x)$ and $g(x)$ intersect when $x = -\frac{7}{2}$, or -3.5.

c) Answers will vary.

Exercise Set 5.6

1. *Familiarize*. Let t = the time it takes them, working together, to fill the order.

Translate. Using the work principle, we get the following equation:
$$\frac{t}{5} + \frac{t}{9} = 1$$

Solve. We solve the equation.
$$\frac{t}{5} + \frac{t}{9} = 1, \ \text{LCM is } 45$$
$$45\left(\frac{t}{5} + \frac{t}{9}\right) = 45 \cdot 1$$
$$45 \cdot \frac{t}{5} + 45 \cdot \frac{t}{9} = 45$$
$$9t + 5t = 45$$
$$14t = 45$$
$$t = \frac{45}{14}, \ \text{or } 3\frac{3}{14}$$

Check. We verify the work principle.
$$\frac{\frac{45}{14}}{5} + \frac{\frac{45}{14}}{9} = \frac{45}{14} \cdot \frac{1}{5} + \frac{45}{14} \cdot \frac{1}{9} = \frac{9}{14} + \frac{5}{14} = \frac{14}{14} = 1$$

State. It will take them $3\frac{3}{14}$ hr, working together.

3. **Familiarize.** Let $t =$ the time it will take to fill the pool using both the pipe and the hose.

Translate. Using the work principle, we get the following equation:

$$\frac{t}{12} + \frac{t}{30} = 1$$

Solve. We solve the equation.

$$\frac{t}{12} + \frac{t}{30} = 1, \text{ LCM is } 60$$

$$60\left(\frac{t}{12} + \frac{t}{30}\right) = 60 \cdot 1$$

$$\frac{60t}{12} + \frac{60t}{30} = 60$$

$$5t + 2t = 60$$

$$7t = 60$$

$$t = \frac{60}{7}, \text{ or } 8\frac{4}{7}$$

Check. We verify the work principle.

$$\frac{\frac{60}{7}}{12} + \frac{\frac{60}{7}}{30} = \frac{60}{7} \cdot \frac{1}{12} + \frac{60}{7} \cdot \frac{1}{30} = \frac{5}{7} + \frac{2}{7} = 1$$

State. It will take them $8\frac{4}{7}$ hr to fill the pool using both the pipe and the hose.

5. **Familiarize.** Let $t =$ the time it will take to print the order if both presses are used.

Translate. Using the work principle, we get the following equation:

$$\frac{t}{4.5} + \frac{t}{5.5} = 1$$

Solve. We solve the equation.

$$\frac{t}{4.5} + \frac{t}{5.5} = 1, \text{ LCM is } (4.5)(5.5)$$

$$(4.5)(5.5)\left(\frac{t}{4.5} + \frac{t}{5.5}\right) = (4.5)(5.5)(1)$$

$$(4.5)(5.5) \cdot \frac{t}{4.5} + (4.5)(5.5) \cdot \frac{t}{5.5} = 24.75$$

$$5.5t + 4.5t = 24.75$$

$$10t = 24.75$$

$$t = 2.475, \text{ or } 2\frac{19}{40}$$

Check. We verify the work principle.

$$\frac{2.475}{4.5} + \frac{2.475}{5.5} = 0.55 + 0.45 = 1$$

State. It will take 2.475 hr, or $2\frac{19}{40}$ hr, to print the order if both presses are used.

7. **Familiarize.** Let $a =$ the number of days it takes Juan to paint the house. Then $4a =$ the number of days it takes Ariel to paint the house.

Translate. Using the work principle, we get the following equation:

$$\frac{8}{a} + \frac{8}{4a} = 1, \text{ or } \frac{8}{a} + \frac{2}{a} = 1$$

Solve. We solve the equation.

$$\frac{8}{a} + \frac{2}{a} = 1$$

$$\frac{10}{a} = 1 \quad \text{Adding}$$

$$10 = a \quad \text{Multiplying by } a$$

Check. If it takes Juan 10 days to paint the house, then it takes Ariel $4 \cdot 10$, or 40 days. We verify the work principle.

$$\frac{8}{10} + \frac{8}{40} = \frac{4}{5} + \frac{1}{5} = \frac{5}{5} = 1$$

State. It would take Juan 10 days to paint the house alone, and it would take Ariel 40 days.

9. **Familiarize.** Let $t =$ the number of hours it would take Skyler to split the firewood working alone. Then $t - 6 =$ the time it would take Jake to split the firewood working alone.

Translate. Using the work principle, we get the following equation:

$$\frac{4}{t} + \frac{4}{t-6} = 1$$

Solve. We solve the equation.

$$\frac{4}{t} + \frac{4}{t-6} = 1, \text{ LCM is } t(t-6)$$

$$t(t-6)\left(\frac{4}{t} + \frac{4}{t-6}\right) = t(t-6) \cdot 1$$

$$t(t-6) \cdot \frac{4}{t} + t(t-6) \cdot \frac{4}{t-6} = t(t-6)$$

$$4(t-6) + 4t = t^2 - 6t$$

$$4t - 24t + 4t = t^2 - 6t$$

$$8t - 24 = t^2 - 6t$$

$$0 = t^2 - 14t + 24$$

$$0 = (t-2)(t-12)$$

$$t - 2 = 0 \quad or \quad t - 12 = 0$$

$$t = 2 \quad or \quad\quad t = 12$$

Check. If it takes Skyler 2 hr to split the firewood, then it would take Jack $2 - 6$, or -4 hr. Since negative values of time have no meaning in this application, 2 is not a solution.

If it takes Skyler 12 hr to split the firewood, then it would take Jake $12 - 6$, or 6 hr. We verify the work principle.

$$\frac{4}{12} + \frac{4}{6} = \frac{1}{3} + \frac{2}{3} = 1$$

State. It would take Skyler 12 hr to split the firewood working alone, and it would take Jake 6 hr.

11. **Familiarize.** Let $w =$ the waist measurement that allows Marta to meet the recommendation.

Translate. We translate to a proportion. We write 0.85 as $\frac{85}{100}$.

$$\begin{array}{c} \text{Waist} \rightarrow \\ \text{Hip} \rightarrow \end{array} \frac{85}{100} = \frac{w}{40} \begin{array}{c} \leftarrow \text{Waist} \\ \leftarrow \text{Hip} \end{array}$$

Solve. We solve the proportion.

$$\frac{85}{100} = \frac{w}{40}$$

$85 \cdot 40 = 100w$ Equating cross products

$$\frac{85 \cdot 40}{100} = w$$

$$34 = w$$

Check. We substitute into the proportion and check cross products.

$$\frac{85}{100} = \frac{34}{40}; \ 85 \cdot 40 = 3400; \ 100 \cdot 34 = 3400$$

Since the cross products are the same, the answer checks.

State. Marta's waist measurement should be 34 in. or less to meet the recommendation.

13. a) **Familiarize.** Let $h =$ the number of home runs Barry Bonds would hit in the 162-game season.

Translate. We translate to a proportion.

Home runs $\rightarrow$ $\dfrac{50}{118} = \dfrac{h}{162}$ $\leftarrow$ Home runs
Games $\rightarrow$ $\leftarrow$ Games

Solve. We solve the proportion.

$$\frac{50}{118} = \frac{h}{162}$$

$50 \cdot 162 = 118h$ Equating cross products

$$\frac{50 \cdot 162}{118} = h$$

$$69 \approx h$$

Check. We substitute into the proportion and check cross products.

$$\frac{50}{118} = \frac{69}{162}; \ 50 \cdot 162 = 8100; \ 118 \cdot 69 = 8142$$

The cross products are approximately the same. Remember that we rounded the value of h. The answer checks.

State. If he continued to bat at the same rate, Bonds would hit about 69 home runs in the 162-game season.

b) Bonds would not break McGwire's record.

15. Familiarize. Let $t =$ the number of trees required to produce beans for 638 kg of coffee.

Translate. We translate to a proportion.

Trees $\rightarrow$ $\dfrac{14}{7.7} = \dfrac{t}{638}$ $\leftarrow$ Trees
Coffee $\rightarrow$ $\leftarrow$ Coffee

Solve. We solve the proportion.

$$\frac{14}{7.7} = \frac{t}{638}$$

$14 \cdot 638 = 7.7t$ Equating cross products

$$\frac{14 \cdot 638}{7.7} = t$$

$$1160 = t$$

Check. We substitute into the proportion and check cross products.

$$\frac{14}{7.7} = \frac{1160}{638}; \ 14 \cdot 638 = 8932; \ 7.7(1160) = 8932$$

Since the cross products are the same, the answer checks.

State. The beans from 1160 trees are required to produce 638 kg of coffee.

17. Familiarize. Let $T =$ the number of trout in the lake.

Translate. We translate to a proportion.

Trout tagged originally $\rightarrow$ $\dfrac{112}{T} = \dfrac{32}{82}$ $\leftarrow$ Tagged trout caught later
Trout in lake $\rightarrow$ $\leftarrow$ Trout caught later

Solve. We solve the proportion.

$$\frac{112}{T} = \frac{32}{82}$$

$112 \cdot 82 = T \cdot 32$ Equating cross products

$$\frac{112 \cdot 82}{32} = T$$

$$287 = T$$

Check. We substitute into the proportion and check cross products.

$$\frac{112}{287} = \frac{32}{82}; \ 112 \cdot 82 = 9184; \ 287 \cdot 32 = 9184$$

Since the cross products are the same, the answer checks.

State. There are 287 trout in the lake.

19. a) **Familiarize.** Let $w =$ the number of tons the rocket will weigh on Mars.

Translate. We translate to a proportion.

Weight on Mars $\rightarrow$ $\dfrac{0.4}{1} = \dfrac{w}{12}$ $\leftarrow$ Weight on Mars
Weight on earth $\rightarrow$ $\leftarrow$ Weight on earth

Solve. We solve the proportion.

$$\frac{0.4}{1} = \frac{w}{12}$$

$0.4 \cdot 12 = 1 \cdot w$ Equating cross products

$$4.8 = w$$

Check. We substitute into the proportion and check cross products.

$$\frac{0.4}{1} = \frac{4.8}{12}; \ 0.4(12) = 4.8; \ 1 \cdot (4.8) = 4.8$$

Since the cross products are the same, the answer checks.

State. A 12-T rocket will weigh 4.8 T on Mars.

b) **Familiarize.** Let $w =$ the number of pounds the astronaut will weigh on Mars.

Translate. We translate to a proportion.

Weight on Mars $\rightarrow$ $\dfrac{0.4}{1} = \dfrac{w}{120}$ $\leftarrow$ Weight on Mars
Weight on earth $\rightarrow$ $\leftarrow$ Weight on earth

Solve. We solve the proportion.

$$\frac{0.4}{1} = \frac{w}{120}$$

$0.4 \cdot 120 = 1 \cdot w$ Equating cross products

$$48 = w$$

Check. We substitute into the proportion and check cross products.

$$\frac{0.4}{1} = \frac{48}{120}; \ 0.4(120) = 48; \ 1 \cdot 48 = 48$$

Since the cross products are the same, the answer checks.

State. A 120-lb astronaut will weigh 48 lb on Mars.

21. Familiarize. Let x = the number that is added to each of the given numbers.

Translate. We translate to a proportion.
$$\frac{1+x}{2+x} = \frac{3+x}{5+x}$$

Solve. We solve the proportion.
$$\frac{1+x}{2+x} = \frac{3+x}{5+x}$$
$$(1+x)(5+x) = (2+x)(3+x) \quad \text{Equating cross products}$$
$$5 + 6x + x^2 = 6 + 5x + x^2$$
$$x = 1$$

Check. We substitute into the proportion and check cross products.
$$\frac{1+1}{2+1} = \frac{3+1}{5+1}, \text{ or } \frac{2}{3} = \frac{4}{6}; \ 2 \cdot 6 = 12; \ 3 \cdot 4 = 12$$
Since the cross products are the same, the answer checks.

State. The number is 1.

23. Familiarize. We first make a drawing. Let r = the boat's speed in still water in mph. Then $r - 4$ = the speed upstream and $r + 4$ = the speed downstream.

$$\text{Upstream} \quad 6 \text{ miles} \quad r - 4 \text{ mph}$$
$$12 \text{ miles} \quad r + 4 \text{ mph} \quad \text{Downstream}$$

We organize the information in a table. The time is the same both upstream and downstream so we use t for each time.

	Distance	Speed	Time
Upstream	6	$r-4$	t
Downstream	12	$r+4$	t

Translate. Using the formula Time = Distance/Rate in each row of the table and the fact that the times are the same, we can write an equation.
$$\frac{6}{r-4} = \frac{12}{r+4}$$

Solve. We solve the equation.
$$\frac{6}{r-4} = \frac{12}{r+4},$$
$$\text{LCD is } (r-4)(r+4)$$
$$(r-4)(r+4) \cdot \frac{6}{r-4} = (r-4)(r+4) \cdot \frac{12}{r+4}$$
$$6(r+4) = 12(r-4)$$
$$6r + 24 = 12r - 48$$
$$72 = 6r$$
$$12 = r$$

Check. If the boat's speed in still water is 12 mph, then its speed upstream is $12-4$, or 8 mph, and its speed downstream is $12+4$, or 16 mph. Traveling 6 mi at 8 mph takes the boat $\frac{6}{8} = \frac{3}{4}$ hr. Traveling 12 mi at 16 mph takes the boat $\frac{12}{16} = \frac{3}{4}$ hr. Since the times are the same, the answer checks.

State. The boat's speed in still water is 12 mph.

25. Familiarize. Using the labels on the drawing in the text, we let c = the speed of the current. Then $10 - c$ = the speed of the tugboat upstream and $10 + c$ = the speed downstream. We organize the information in a table.

	Distance	Speed	Time
Upstream	24	$10 - c$	$\frac{24}{10-c}$
Downstream	24	$10 + c$	$\frac{24}{10+c}$

Translate. Since the total time is 5 hr, we use the last column of the table to write an equation.
$$\frac{24}{10-c} + \frac{24}{10+c} = 5$$

Solve. We solve the equation.
$$\frac{24}{10-c} + \frac{24}{10+c} = 5,$$
$$\text{LCD is } (10-c)(10+c)$$
$$(10-c)(10+c)\left(\frac{24}{10-c} + \frac{24}{10+c}\right) = (10-c)(10+c) \cdot 5$$
$$24(10+c) + 24(10-c) = 5(100 - c^2)$$
$$240 + 24c + 240 - 24c = 500 - 5c^2$$
$$480 = 500 - 5c^2$$
$$5c^2 - 20 = 0$$
$$5(c^2 - 4) = 0$$
$$5(c+2)(c-2) = 0$$
$$c + 2 = 0 \quad or \quad c - 2 = 0$$
$$c = -2 \quad or \quad\quad c = 2$$

Check. Since negative time has no meaning in this application, we check only 2. If the current is 2 mph, then the boat's speed upstream is $10 - 2$, or 8 mph, and the speed downstream is $10 + 2$, or 12 mph. Traveling 24 mi at 8 mph takes 24/8, or 3 hr; traveling 24 mi at 12 mph takes 24/12, or 2 hr. The total time is $3 + 2$, or 5 hr, so the answer checks.

State. The speed of the current is 2 mph.

27. Familiarize. We first make a drawing. Let r = Camille's speed on a nonmoving sidewalk in ft/sec. Then her speed moving forward on the moving sidewalk is $r + 1.8$, and her speed in the opposite direction is $r - 1.8$.

$$\text{Forward} \quad\quad r + 1.8 \quad\quad 105 \text{ ft}$$
$$\text{Opposite}$$
$$51 \text{ ft} \quad r - 1.8 \quad \text{direction}$$

We organize the information in a table. The time is the same both forward and in the opposite direction so we use t for each time.

	Distance	Speed	Time
Forward	105	$r+1.8$	t
Opposite direction	51	$r-1.8$	t

Translate. Using the formula Time = Distance/Rate in each row of the table and the fact that the times are the same, we can write an equation.

$$\frac{105}{r+1.8} = \frac{51}{r-1.8}$$

Solve. We solve the equation.

$$\frac{105}{r+1.8} = \frac{51}{r-1.8},$$

LCD is $(r+1.8)(r-1.8)$

$$(r+1.8)(r-1.8) \cdot \frac{105}{r+1.8} = (r+1.8)(r-1.8) \cdot \frac{51}{r-1.8}$$

$$105(r-1.8) = 51(r+1.8)$$

$$105r - 189 = 51r + 91.8$$

$$54r = 280.8$$

$$r = 5.2$$

Check. If Camille's speed on a nonmoving sidewalk is 5.2 ft/sec, then her speed moving forward on the moving sidewalk is $5.2 + 1.8$, or 7 ft/sec, and her speed moving in the opposite direction on the sidewalk is $5.2 - 1.8$, or 3.4 ft/sec. Moving 105 ft at 7 ft/sec takes $\frac{105}{7} = 15$ sec. Moving 51 ft at 3.4 ft/sec takes 15 sec. Since the times are the same, the answer checks.

State. Camille would be walking 5.2 ft/sec on a nonmoving sidewalk.

29. *Familiarize*. Let r = Simone's walking speed, in mph. Then $r - 2$ = Rosanna's speed. The times are the same, so we let t = the time. We organize the information in a table.

	Distance	Speed	Time
Simone	8	r	t
Rosanna	5	$r-2$	t

Translate. Using the formula Time = Distance/Rate in each row of the table and the fact that the times are the same, we can write an equation.

$$\frac{8}{r} = \frac{5}{r-2}$$

Solve. We solve the equation.

$$\frac{8}{r} = \frac{5}{r-2}, \text{ LCD is } r(r-2)$$

$$r(r-2) \cdot \frac{8}{r} = r(r-2) \cdot \frac{5}{r-2}$$

$$8(r-2) = 5r$$

$$8r - 16 = 5r$$

$$3r = 16$$

$$r = \frac{16}{3}$$

Check. If Simone's speed is $\frac{16}{3}$ mph, then Rosanna's speed is $\frac{16}{3} - 2$, or $\frac{10}{3}$ mph. Walking 8 mi at $\frac{16}{3}$ mph takes Simone $8/(16/3)$, or $\frac{3}{2}$ hr. Walking 5 mi at $\frac{10}{3}$ mph takes Rosanna $5/(10/3)$, or $\frac{3}{2}$ hr. Since the times are the same, the answer checks.

State. Simone's speed is $\frac{16}{3}$, or $5\frac{1}{3}$ mph, and Rosanna's speed is $\frac{10}{3}$, or $3\frac{1}{3}$ mph.

31. Discussion and Writing Exercise

33. The domain is the set of all x-values on the graph, $[-5, 5]$. The range is the set of all y-values on the graph, $[-4, 3]$.

35. The domain is the set of all x-values on the graph, $[-5, 5]$. The range is the set of all y-values on the graph, $[-5, 3]$.

37. Graph: $x - 4y \geq 4$

We first graph the line $x - 4y = 4$. The intercepts are $(0, -1)$ and $(4, 0)$. We draw the line solid since the inequality symbol is $\geq$. To determine which half-plane to shade, we consider a test point not on the line. We try $(0, 0)$:

$$\begin{array}{c|c} x - 4y \geq 4 \\ \hline 0 - 4 \cdot 0 \; ? \; 4 \\ 0 & \text{FALSE} \end{array}$$

Since $0 \geq 4$ is false, we shade the half-plane that does not contain $(0, 0)$.

39. Graph: $f(x) = |x + 3|$

We select x-values and find the corresponding y-values. We plot these ordered pairs and draw the graph.

x	y
-5	2
-3	0
-1	2
0	3
2	5

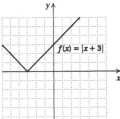

41. *Familiarize*. Let d = the distance, in miles, Melissa lives from work. Also let t = the travel time in hours, when Melissa arrives on time. Note that 1 min = $\frac{1}{60}$ hr and 5 min = $\frac{5}{60}$, or $\frac{1}{12}$ hr.

Translate. Melissa's travel time at 50 mph is $\frac{d}{50}$. This is $\frac{1}{60}$ hr more than t, so we write an equation using this information:

$$\frac{d}{50} = t + \frac{1}{60}$$

Her travel time at 60 mph, $\frac{d}{60}$, is $\frac{1}{12}$ hr less than t, so we write a second equation:

$$\frac{d}{60} = t - \frac{1}{12}$$

We have a system of equations:

$$\frac{d}{50} = t + \frac{1}{60},$$

$$\frac{d}{60} = t - \frac{1}{12}$$

Solve. Solving the system of equations, we get $\left(30, \frac{7}{12}\right)$.

Check. Traveling 30 mi at 50 mph takes $\frac{30}{50}$, or $\frac{3}{5}$ hr. Since $\frac{7}{12} + \frac{1}{60} = \frac{36}{60} = \frac{3}{5}$, this time makes Melissa $\frac{1}{60}$ hr, or 1 min late. Traveling 30 mi at 60 mph takes $\frac{30}{60}$, or $\frac{1}{2}$ hr. Since $\frac{7}{12} - \frac{1}{12} = \frac{6}{12} = \frac{1}{2}$, this time makes Melissa $\frac{1}{12}$ hr, or 5 min early. The answer checks.

State. Melissa lives 30 mi from work.

43. Familiarize. Let x = the number of miles driven in the city and y = the number of miles driven on the highway. Then $\frac{x}{22.5}$ = the number of gallons of gasoline used in city driving and $\frac{y}{30}$ = the number of gallons used in highway driving.

Translate. The total number of miles is 465, so we have one equation:

$$x + y = 465$$

The total amount of gasoline used is 18.4 gal, so we have a second equation.

$$\frac{x}{22.5} + \frac{y}{30} = 18.4$$

After clearing fractions, we have the following system of equations:

$$x + y = 465,$$

$$30x + 22.5y = 12,420$$

Solve. The solution of the system of equations is $(261, 204)$.

Check. If 261 city miles and 204 highway miles are driven, the total number of miles is $261 + 204$, or 465. In 261 city miles $261/22.5$ or 11.6 gal, of gasoline are used; in 204 highway miles $204/30$, or 6.8 gal, are used. Then the total amount of gasoline used is $11.6 + 6.8$, or 18.4 gal. The answer checks.

State. 261 mi were driven in the city, and 204 mi were driven on the highway.

45. Familiarize. It helps to first make a drawing.

The minute hand moves 60 units per hour while the hour hand moves 5 units per hour, where one unit represents one minute on the face of the clock. When the hands are in the same position the first time, the hour hand will have moved x units and the minute hand will have moved $x + 20$ units. The times are the same.

We organize the information in a table.

	Distance	Speed	Time
Minute	$x + 20$	60	t
Hour	x	5	t

Translate. Since Time = Distance/Speed and since the times are the same, we can write an equation:

$$\frac{x + 20}{60} = \frac{x}{5}$$

Solve. We solve the equation.

$$\frac{x + 20}{60} = \frac{x}{5}, \quad \text{LCD is 60}$$

$$60 \cdot \frac{x + 20}{60} = 60 \cdot \frac{x}{5}$$

$$x + 20 = 12x$$

$$20 = 11x$$

$$\frac{20}{11} = x, \text{ or}$$

$$1\frac{9}{11} = x$$

When the hour hand has moved $1\frac{9}{11}$ units, the minute hand has moved $20 + 1\frac{9}{11}$, or $21\frac{9}{11}$ units, so the time will be $21\frac{9}{11}$ minutes after 4:00.

Check. At 60 units per hour the minute hand moves $21\frac{9}{11}$ units in $60/(240/11)$, or $11/4$ min. At 5 units per hour the hour hand moves $1\frac{9}{11}$ units in $5/(20/11)$, or $11/4$ min. Since the times are the same, the answer checks.

State. The hands will first be in the same position $21\frac{9}{11}$ min after 4:00.

Exercise Set 5.7

1.
$$\frac{W_1}{W_2} = \frac{d_1}{d_2}$$

$$W_2 d_2 \cdot \frac{W_1}{W_2} = W_2 d_2 \cdot \frac{d_1}{d_2} \quad \text{Multiplying by the LCM}$$

$$d_2 W_1 = W_2 d_1$$

$$\frac{d_2 W_1}{d_1} = W_2 \quad \text{Dividing by } d_1$$

3.
$$\frac{1}{R} = \frac{1}{r_1} + \frac{1}{r_2}$$

$$Rr_1r_2 \cdot \frac{1}{R} = Rr_1r_2\left(\frac{1}{r_1} + \frac{1}{r_2}\right) \quad \text{Multiplying by}$$
the LCM

$$r_1r_2 = Rr_2 + Rr_1$$

$$r_1r_2 - Rr_2 = Rr_1 \qquad \text{Subtracting } Rr_2$$

$$r_2(r_1 - R) = Rr_1 \qquad \text{Factoring}$$

$$r_2 = \frac{Rr_1}{r_1 - R} \qquad \text{Dividing by } r_1 - R$$

5.
$$s = \frac{(v_1 + v_2)t}{2}$$

$$2 \cdot s = 2 \cdot \frac{(v_1 + v_2)t}{2} \quad \text{Multiplying by } 2$$

$$2s = (v_1 + v_2)t$$

$$\frac{2s}{v_1 + v_2} = t \qquad \text{Dividing by } v_1 + v_2$$

7.
$$R = \frac{gs}{g + s}$$

$$(g + s) \cdot R = (g + s) \cdot \frac{gs}{g + s} \quad \text{Multiplying by } g + s$$

$$R(g + s) = gs$$

$$Rg + Rs = gs \qquad \text{Removing parentheses}$$

$$Rg = gs - Rs \qquad \text{Subtracting } Rs$$

$$Rg = s(g - R) \qquad \text{Factoring}$$

$$\frac{Rg}{g - R} = s \qquad \text{Dividing by } g - R$$

9.
$$\frac{1}{p} + \frac{1}{q} = \frac{1}{f}$$

$$pqf\left(\frac{1}{p} + \frac{1}{q}\right) = pqf \cdot \frac{1}{f} \quad \text{Multiplying by } pqf$$

$$pqf \cdot \frac{1}{p} + pqf \cdot \frac{1}{q} = pq$$

$$qf + pf = pq$$

$$qf = pq - pf \qquad \text{Subtracting } pf$$

$$qf = p(q - f) \qquad \text{Factoring}$$

$$\frac{qf}{q - f} = p \qquad \text{Dividing by } q - f$$

11.
$$\frac{t}{a} + \frac{t}{b} = 1$$

$$ab\left(\frac{t}{a} + \frac{t}{b}\right) = ab \cdot 1 \qquad \text{Multiplying by } ab$$

$$ab \cdot \frac{t}{a} + ab \cdot \frac{t}{b} = ab \qquad \text{Removing parentheses}$$

$$bt + at = ab$$

$$bt = ab - at \qquad \text{Subtracting } at$$

$$bt = a(b - t) \qquad \text{Factoring}$$

$$\frac{bt}{b - t} = a \qquad \text{Dividing by } b - t$$

13.
$$I = \frac{nE}{E + nr}$$

$$(E + nr)I = (E + nr) \cdot \frac{nE}{E + nr} \quad \text{Multiplying by}$$
$E + nr$

$$EI + nrI = nE$$

$$nrI = nE - EI \qquad \text{Subtracting } EI$$

$$nrI = E(n - I) \qquad \text{Factoring}$$

$$\frac{nrI}{n - I} = E \qquad \text{Dividing by } n - I$$

15.
$$I = \frac{704.5W}{H^2}$$

$$H^2I = 704.5W \quad \text{Multiplying by } H^2$$

$$H^2 = \frac{704.5W}{I} \quad \text{Dividing by } I$$

17.
$$\frac{E}{e} = \frac{R + r}{r}$$

$$er \cdot \frac{E}{e} = er \cdot \frac{R + r}{r} \quad \text{Multiplying by } er$$
$$Er = eR + er$$

$$Er - er = eR \qquad \text{Subtracting } er$$

$$r(E - e) = eR \qquad \text{Factoring}$$

$$r = \frac{eR}{E - e} \qquad \text{Dividing by } E - e$$

19.
$$V = \frac{1}{3}\pi h^2(3R - h)$$

$$\frac{3}{\pi h^2} \cdot V = \frac{3}{\pi h^2} \cdot \frac{1}{3}\pi h^2(3R - h) \quad \text{Multiplying}$$
by $\dfrac{3}{\pi h^2}$

$$\frac{3V}{\pi h^2} = 3R - h$$

$$\frac{3V}{\pi h^2} + h = 3R \qquad \text{Adding } h$$

$$\frac{1}{3}\left(\frac{3V}{\pi h^2} + h\right) = \frac{1}{3} \cdot 3R \qquad \text{Multiplying by } \frac{1}{3}$$

$$\frac{V}{\pi h^2} + \frac{h}{3} = R, \text{ or}$$

$$\frac{3V + \pi h^3}{3\pi h^2} = R$$

21.
$$P = \frac{A}{1 + r}$$

$$P(1 + r) = \frac{A}{1 + r} \cdot (1 + r) \quad \text{Multiplying by}$$
the LCD

$$P(1 + r) = A$$

$$1 + r = \frac{A}{P} \qquad \text{Dividing by } P$$

$$r = \frac{A}{P} - 1, \text{ or } \frac{A - P}{P}$$

23.
$$\frac{V^2}{R^2} = \frac{2g}{R+h}$$

$$(R+h) \cdot \frac{V^2}{R^2} = (R+h) \cdot \frac{2g}{R+h} \quad \begin{array}{l}\text{Multiplying} \\ \text{by } (R+h)\end{array}$$

$$\frac{(R+h)V^2}{R^2} = 2g$$

$$R + h = \frac{2gR^2}{V^2} \qquad \text{Multiplying by } \frac{R^2}{V^2}$$

$$h = \frac{2gR^2}{V^2} - R \quad \text{Adding } -R$$

The result can also be expressed as

$$h = \frac{2gR^2 - RV^2}{V^2}.$$

25.
$$A = \frac{2Tt + Qq}{2T + Q}$$

$$(2T + Q) \cdot A = (2T + Q) \cdot \frac{2Tt + Qq}{2T + Q}$$

$$2AT + AQ = 2Tt + Qq$$

$$AQ - Qq = 2Tt - 2AT \quad \begin{array}{l}\text{Adding } -2AT \\ \text{and } -Qq\end{array}$$

$$Q(A - q) = 2Tt - 2AT$$

$$Q = \frac{2Tt - 2AT}{A - q}$$

27. Discussion and Writing Exercise

29. Familiarize. Let x = the number of 30-min tapes bought and y = the number of 60-min tapes. We will express all times in minutes so we convert 10 hr to minutes: 10 hr = 10×60 min = 600 min. The recording time for the 30-min tapes is $30x$, and the recording time for the 60-min tapes is $60y$.

Translate. Esther buys 12 tapes, so we have one equation:

$$x + y = 12$$

The total recording time is 600 min, so we have a second equation:

$$30x + 60y = 600$$

We have a system of equations:

$$x + y = 12,$$
$$30x + 60y = 600$$

Solve. The solution of the system of equations is $(4, 8)$, so 4 30-min tapes and 8 60-min tapes were bought.

Check. The total number of tapes is $4 + 8$, or 12. The total recording time is $30 \cdot 4 + 8 \cdot 60$, or 600 min. The answer checks.

State. Esther bought 4 30-min tapes and 8 60-min tapes.

31. $f(x) = x^3 - x$
$$f(2) = 2^3 - 2 = 8 - 2 = 6$$

33. $f(x) = x^3 - x$
$$f(2a) = (2a)^3 - 2a = 8a^3 - 2a$$

35. First we find the slope.
$$m = \frac{5 - (-3)}{-2 - 8} = \frac{8}{-10} = -\frac{4}{5}$$
Now we use the slope and one of the given points to find b. We will use $(-2, 5)$. Substitute -2 for x, 5 for y, and $-\frac{4}{5}$ for m in $y = mx + b$ and solve for b.

$$y = mx + b$$
$$5 = -\frac{4}{5}(-2) + b$$
$$5 = \frac{8}{5} + b$$
$$\frac{17}{5} = b$$

Use $y = mx + b$ again, substituting $-\frac{4}{5}$ for m and $\frac{17}{5}$ for b. The equation is
$$y = -\frac{4}{5}x + \frac{17}{5}.$$

Exercise Set 5.8

1. $y = kx$
$$40 = k \cdot 8 \quad \text{Substituting}$$
$$5 = k \qquad \text{Solving for } k$$
The variation constant is 5.
The equation of variation is $y = 5x$.

3. $y = kx$
$$4 = k \cdot 30 \quad \text{Substituting}$$
$$\frac{4}{30} = k, \text{ or} \quad \text{Solving for } k$$
$$\frac{2}{15} = k \qquad \text{Simplifying}$$
The variation constant is $\frac{2}{15}$.
The equation of variation is $y = \frac{2}{15}x$.

5. $y = kx$
$$0.9 = k \cdot 0.4 \quad \text{Substituting}$$
$$\frac{0.9}{0.4} = k, \text{ or}$$
$$\frac{9}{4} = k$$
The variation constant is $\frac{9}{4}$.
The equation of variation is $y = \frac{9}{4}x$.

7. Let p = the number of people using the cans.
$$N = kp \qquad N \text{ varies directly as } p.$$
$$60,000 = k \cdot 250 \quad \text{Substituting}$$
$$\frac{60,000}{250} = k \qquad \text{Solving for } k$$
$$240 = k \qquad \text{Variation constant}$$

$N = 240p$ Equation of variation

$N = 240(1,008,000)$ Substituting

$N = 241,920,000$

In Dallas 241,920,000 cans are used each year.

9. $d = kw$ d varies directly as w.

$40 = k \cdot 3$ Substituting

$\dfrac{40}{3} = k$ Variation constant

$d = \dfrac{40}{3}w$ Equation of variation

$d = \dfrac{40}{3} \cdot 5$ Substituting

$d = \dfrac{200}{3}$, or $66\dfrac{2}{3}$

The spring is stretched $66\dfrac{2}{3}$ cm by a 5-kg barbell.

11. Let $F =$ the number of grams of fat and $w =$ the weight.

$F = kw$ F varies directly as w.

$60 = k \cdot 120$ Substituting

$\dfrac{60}{120} = k$, or   Solving for k

$\dfrac{1}{2} = k$ Variation constant

$F = \dfrac{1}{2}w$ Equation of variation

$F = \dfrac{1}{2} \cdot 180$ Substituting

$F = 90$

The maximum daily fat intake for a person weighing 180 lb is 90 g.

13. Let $m =$ the mass of the body.

$W = km$ W varies directly as m.

$64 = k \cdot 96$ Substituting

$\dfrac{64}{96} = k$ Solving for k

$\dfrac{2}{3} = k$ Variation constant

$W = \dfrac{2}{3}m$ Equation of variation

$W = \dfrac{2}{3} \cdot 60$ Substituting

$W = 40$

There are 40 kg of water in a 60-kg person.

15. $y = \dfrac{k}{x}$

$14 = \dfrac{k}{7}$ Substituting

$7 \cdot 14 = k$ Solving for k

$98 = k$

The variation constant is 98.

The equation of variation is $y = \dfrac{98}{x}$.

17. $y = \dfrac{k}{x}$

$3 = \dfrac{k}{12}$ Substituting

$12 \cdot 3 = k$ Solving for k

$36 = k$

The variation constant is 36.

The equation of variation is $y = \dfrac{36}{x}$.

19. $y = \dfrac{k}{x}$

$0.1 = \dfrac{k}{0.5}$ Substituting

$0.5(0.1) = k$ Solving for k

$0.05 = k$

The variation constant is 0.05.

The equation of variation is $y = \dfrac{0.05}{x}$.

21. $T = \dfrac{k}{P}$ T varies inversely as P.

$5 = \dfrac{k}{7}$ Substituting

$35 = k$ Variation constant

$T = \dfrac{35}{P}$ Equation of variation

$T = \dfrac{35}{10}$ Substituting

$T = 3.5$

It will take 10 bricklayers 3.5 hr to complete the job.

23. $I = \dfrac{k}{R}$ I varies inversely as R.

$\dfrac{1}{2} = \dfrac{k}{240}$ Substituting

$240 \cdot \dfrac{1}{2} = k$

$120 = k$ Variation constant

$I = \dfrac{120}{R}$ Equation of variation

$I = \dfrac{120}{540}$ Substituting

$I = \dfrac{2}{9}$

When the resistance is 540 ohms, the current is $\dfrac{2}{9}$ ampere.

25. $P = \dfrac{k}{W}$ P varies inversely as W.

$330 = \dfrac{k}{3.2}$ Substituting

$1056 = k$ Variation constant

$$P = \frac{1056}{W} \quad \text{Equation of variation}$$

$$550 = \frac{1056}{W} \quad \text{Substituting}$$

$$550W = 1056 \quad \text{Multiplying by } W$$

$$W = \frac{1056}{550} \quad \text{Dividing by 550}$$

$$W = 1.92 \quad \text{Simplifying}$$

A tone with a pitch of 550 vibrations per second has a wavelength of 1.92 ft.

27. $\quad V = \dfrac{k}{P} \quad V$ varies inversely as P.

$$200 = \frac{k}{32} \quad \text{Substituting}$$

$$6400 = k \quad \text{Variation constant}$$

$$V = \frac{6400}{P} \quad \text{Equation of variation}$$

$$V = \frac{6400}{40} \quad \text{Substituting}$$

$$V = 160$$

The volume is 160 cm^3 under a pressure of 40 kg/cm^2.

29. $\quad y = kx^2$

$$0.15 = k(0.1)^2 \quad \text{Substituting}$$

$$0.15 = 0.01k$$

$$\frac{0.15}{0.01} = k$$

$$15 = k$$

The equation of variation is $y = 15x^2$.

31. $\qquad y = \dfrac{k}{x^2}$

$$0.15 = \frac{k}{(0.1)^2} \quad \text{Substituting}$$

$$0.15 = \frac{k}{0.01}$$

$$0.15(0.01) = k$$

$$0.0015 = k$$

The equation of variation is $y = \dfrac{0.0015}{x^2}$.

33. $\quad y = kxz$

$$56 = k \cdot 7 \cdot 8 \quad \text{Substituting}$$

$$56 = 56k$$

$$1 = k$$

The equation of variation is $y = xz$.

35. $\qquad y = kxz^2$

$$105 = k \cdot 14 \cdot 5^2 \quad \text{Substituting}$$

$$105 = 350k$$

$$\frac{105}{350} = k$$

$$\frac{3}{10} = k$$

The equation of variation is $y = \dfrac{3}{10}xz^2$.

37. $\qquad y = k\dfrac{xz}{wp}$

$$\frac{3}{28} = k\frac{3 \cdot 10}{7 \cdot 8} \quad \text{Substituting}$$

$$\frac{3}{28} = k \cdot \frac{30}{56}$$

$$\frac{3}{28} \cdot \frac{56}{30} = k$$

$$\frac{1}{5} = k$$

The equation of variation is $y = \dfrac{xz}{5wp}$.

39. $\qquad d = kr^2$

$$200 = k \cdot 60^2 \quad \text{Substituting}$$

$$200 = 3600k$$

$$\frac{200}{3600} = k$$

$$\frac{1}{18} = k$$

The equation of variation is $d = \dfrac{1}{18}r^2$.

Substitute 72 for d and find r.

$$72 = \frac{1}{18}r^2$$

$$1296 = r^2$$

$$36 = r$$

A car can travel 36 mph and still stop in 72 ft.

41. $\qquad I = \dfrac{k}{d^2}$

$$90 = \frac{k}{5^2} \quad \text{Substituting}$$

$$90 = \frac{k}{25}$$

$$2250 = k$$

The equation of variation is $I = \dfrac{2250}{d^2}$.

Substitute 40 for I and find d.

$$40 = \frac{2250}{d^2}$$

$$40d^2 = 2250$$

$$d^2 = 56.25$$

$$d = 7.5$$

The distance from 5 m to 7.5 m is $7.5 - 5$, or 2.5 m, so it is 2.5 m further to a point where the intensity is 40 W/m^2.

43. $E = \dfrac{kR}{I}$

We first find k.

$$3.18 = \frac{k \cdot 71}{201} \quad \text{Substituting}$$

$$3.18\left(\frac{201}{71}\right) = k \quad \text{Multiplying by } \frac{201}{71}$$

$$9 \approx k$$

The equation of variation is $E = \dfrac{9R}{I}$.

Substitute 3.18 for E and 300 for I and solve R.

$$3.18 = \frac{9R}{300}$$

$$3.18\left(\frac{300}{9}\right) = R \qquad \text{Multiplying by } \frac{300}{9}$$

$$106 = R$$

Shawn Estes would have given up 106 earned runs if he had pitched 300 innings.

45. $Q = kd^2$

We first find k.

$$225 = k \cdot 5^2$$

$$225 = 25k$$

$$9 = k$$

The equation of variation is $Q = 9d^2$.

Substitute 9 for d and compute Q.

$$Q = 9 \cdot 9^2$$

$$Q = 9 \cdot 81$$

$$Q = 729$$

729 gallons of water are emptied by a pipe that is 9 in. in diameter.

47. Discussion and Writing Exercise

49. $(x - 3)(x + 4) = 0$

$$x - 3 = 0 \ \ or \ \ x + 4 = 0$$

$$x = 3 \ \ or \ \ \qquad x = -4$$

The solutions are 3 and -4.

51. $\quad 12x^2 - 11x + 2 = 0$

$$(4x - 1)(3x - 2) = 0$$

$$4x - 1 = 0 \ \ or \ \ 3x - 2 = 0$$

$$4x = 1 \ \ or \ \qquad 3x = 2$$

$$x = \frac{1}{4} \ \ or \ \qquad x = \frac{2}{3}$$

The solutions are $\dfrac{1}{4}$ and $\dfrac{2}{3}$.

53. Substitute $-\dfrac{2}{3}$ for m and -5 for b in the slope-intercept equation, $y = mx + b$. The equation is $y = -\dfrac{2}{3}x - 5$.

55. a) First we find the slope. In 2000, $t = 0$ and in 2003, $t = 3$.

$$m = \frac{10.6 - 5.4}{3 - 0} = \frac{5.2}{3} \approx 1.73$$

Now use the slope, 1.73, and the y-intercept, $(5.4, 0)$ to write the function:

$$S(t) = mt + b$$

$$S(t) = 1.73t + 5.4, \text{ where } S(t) \text{ is in billions}$$
$$\text{of dollars}$$

b) In 2005, $t = 5$. We find $S(5)$.

$$S(t) = 1.73t + 5.4$$

$$S(5) = 1.73 \cdot 5 + 5.4$$

$$\approx 8.7 + 5.4$$

$$\approx 14.1$$

Online spending for advertising will be about \$14.1 billion in 2005.

57. We are told $A = kd^2$, and we know $A = \pi r^2$ so we have:

$$kd^2 = \pi r^2$$

$$kd^2 = \pi\left(\frac{d}{2}\right)^2 \qquad r = \frac{d}{2}$$

$$kd^2 = \frac{\pi d^2}{4}$$

$$k = \frac{\pi}{4} \qquad\qquad \text{Variation constant}$$

59. $Q = \dfrac{kp^2}{q^3}$

Q varies directly as the square of p and inversely as the cube of q.

Chapter 6

Radical Expressions, Equations, and Functions

Exercise Set 6.1

1. The square roots of 16 are 4 and -4, because $4^2 = 16$ and $(-4)^2 = 16$.

3. The square roots of 144 are 12 and -12, because $12^2 = 144$ and $(-12)^2 = 144$.

5. The square roots of 400 are 20 and -20, because $20^2 = 400$ and $(-20)^2 = 400$.

7. $-\sqrt{\dfrac{49}{36}} = -\dfrac{7}{6}$ Since $\sqrt{\dfrac{49}{36}} = \dfrac{7}{6}$, $-\sqrt{\dfrac{49}{36}} = -\dfrac{7}{6}$.

9. $\sqrt{196} = 14$ Remember, $\sqrt{}$ indicates the principle square root.

11. $\sqrt{0.0036} = 0.06$

13. $\sqrt{347} \approx 18.628$

15. $\sqrt{\dfrac{285}{74}} \approx 1.962$

17. $9\sqrt{y^2 + 16}$

    The radicand is the expression written under the radical sign, $y^2 + 16$.

19. $x^4 y^5 \sqrt{\dfrac{x}{y-1}}$

    The radicand is the expression written under the radical sign, $\dfrac{x}{y-1}$.

21. $f(x) = \sqrt{5x - 10}$

    $f(6) = \sqrt{5 \cdot 6 - 10} = \sqrt{20} \approx 4.472$

    $f(2) = \sqrt{5 \cdot 2 - 10} = \sqrt{0} = 0$

    $f(1) = \sqrt{5 \cdot 1 - 10} = \sqrt{-5}$

    Since negative numbers do not have real-number square roots, $f(1)$ does not exist as a real number.

$f(-1) = \sqrt{5(-1) - 10} = \sqrt{-15}$

Since negative numbers do not have real-number square roots, $f(-1)$ does not exist as a real number.

23. $g(x) = \sqrt{x^2 - 25}$

$g(-6) = \sqrt{(-6)^2 - 25} = \sqrt{11} \approx 3.317$

$g(3) = \sqrt{3^2 - 25} = \sqrt{-16}$

Since negative numbers do not have real-number square roots, $g(3)$ does not exist as a real number.

$g(6) = \sqrt{6^2 - 25} = \sqrt{11} \approx 3.317$

$g(13) = \sqrt{13^2 - 25} = \sqrt{144} = 12$

25. The domain of $f(x) = \sqrt{5x - 10}$ is the set of all x-values for which $5x - 10 \geq 0$.

$$5x - 10 \geq 0$$
$$5x \geq 10$$
$$x \geq 2$$

The domain is $\{x | x \geq 2\}$, or $[2, \infty)$.

27. $S(x) = 2\sqrt{5x}$

$S(30) = 2\sqrt{5 \cdot 30} = 2\sqrt{150} \approx 24.5$

The speed of a car that left skid marks of length 30 ft was about 24.5 mph.

$S(150) = 2\sqrt{5 \cdot 150} = 2\sqrt{750} \approx 54.8$

The speed of a car that left skid marks of length 150 ft was about 54.8 mph.

29. Graph: $f(x) = 2\sqrt{x}$.

We find some ordered pairs, plot points, and draw the curve.

x	$f(x)$	$(x, f(x))$
0	0	$(0, 0)$
1	2	$(1, 2)$
2	2.8	$(2, 2.8)$
3	3.5	$(3, 3.5)$
4	4	$(4, 4)$
5	4.5	$(5, 4.5)$

31. Graph: $F(x) = -3\sqrt{x}$.

We find some ordered pairs, plot points, and draw the curve.

x	$f(x)$	$(x, f(x))$
0	0	$(0, 0)$
1	-3	$(1, -3)$
2	-4.2	$(2, -4.2)$
3	-5.2	$(3, -5.2)$
4	-6	$(4, -6)$
5	-6.7	$(5, -6.7)$

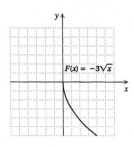

33. Graph: $f(x) = \sqrt{x}$.

We find some ordered pairs, plot points, and draw the curve.

x	$f(x)$	$(x, f(x))$
0	0	$(0, 0)$
1	1	$(1, 1)$
2	1.4	$(2, 1.4)$
3	1.7	$(3, 1.7)$
4	2	$(4, 2)$
5	2.2	$(5, 2.2)$

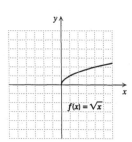

35. Graph: $f(x) = \sqrt{x - 2}$.

We find some ordered pairs, plot points, and draw the curve.

x	$f(x)$	$(x, f(x))$
2	0	$(2, 0)$
3	1	$(3, 1)$
4	1.4	$(4, 1.4)$
5	1.7	$(5, 1.7)$
7	2.2	$(7, 2.2)$
9	2.6	$(9, 2.6)$

37. Graph: $f(x) = \sqrt{12 - 3x}$.

We find some ordered pairs, plot points, and draw the curve.

x	$f(x)$	$(x, f(x))$
-5	5.2	$(-5, 5.2)$
-3	4.6	$(-3, 4.6)$
-1	3.9	$(-1, 3.9)$
0	3.5	$(0, 3.5)$
2	2.4	$(2, 2.4)$
4	0	$(4, 0)$

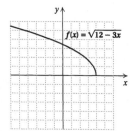

39. Graph: $g(x) = \sqrt{3x + 9}$.

We find some ordered pairs, plot points, and draw the curve.

x	$f(x)$	$(x, f(x))$
-3	0	$(-3, 0)$
-1	2.4	$(-1, 2.4)$
0	3	$(0, 3)$
1	3.5	$(1, 3.5)$
3	4.2	$(3, 4.2)$
5	4.9	$(5, 4.9)$

41. $\sqrt{16x^2} = \sqrt{(4x)^2} = |4x| = 4|x|$

(The absolute value is used to ensure that the principal square root is nonnegative.)

43. $\sqrt{(-12c)^2} = |-12c| = |-12| \cdot |c| = 12|c|$

(The absolute value is used to ensure that the principal square root is nonnegative.)

45. $\sqrt{(p+3)^2} = |p+3|$

(The absolute value is used to ensure that the principal square root is nonnegative.)

47. $\sqrt{x^2 - 4x + 4} = \sqrt{(x-2)^2} = |x - 2|$

(The absolute value is used to ensure that the principal square root is nonnegative.)

49. $\sqrt[3]{27} = 3$ $[3^3 = 27]$

51. $\sqrt[3]{-64x^3} = -4x$ $[(-4x)^3 = -64x^3]$

53. $\sqrt[3]{-216} = -6$ $[(-6)^3 = -216]$

55. $\sqrt[3]{0.343(x+1)^3} = 0.7(x+1)$

$$[(0.7(x+1))^3 = 0.343(x+1)^3]$$

57.
$$f(x) = \sqrt[3]{x+1}$$
$$f(7) = \sqrt[3]{7+1} = \sqrt[3]{8} = 2$$
$$f(26) = \sqrt[3]{26+1} = \sqrt[3]{27} = 3$$
$$f(-9) = \sqrt[3]{-9+1} = \sqrt[3]{-8} = -2$$
$$f(-65) = \sqrt[3]{-65+1} = \sqrt[3]{-64} = -4$$

59.
$$f(x) = -\sqrt[3]{3x+1}$$
$$f(0) = -\sqrt[3]{3 \cdot 0 + 1} = -\sqrt[3]{1} = -1$$
$$f(-7) = -\sqrt[3]{3(-7) + 1} = -\sqrt[3]{-20}, \text{or } \sqrt[3]{20} \approx 2.7144$$
$$f(21) = -\sqrt[3]{3 \cdot 21 + 1} = -\sqrt[3]{64} = -4$$
$$f(333) = -\sqrt[3]{3 \cdot 333 + 1} = -\sqrt[3]{1000} = -10$$

61. $-\sqrt[4]{625} = -5$ Since $5^4 = 625$, then $\sqrt[4]{625} = 5$ and $-\sqrt[4]{625} = -5$.

63. $\sqrt[5]{-1} = -1$ Since $(-1)^5 = -1$

65. $\sqrt[5]{-\dfrac{32}{243}} = -\dfrac{2}{3}$ Since $\left(-\dfrac{2}{3}\right)^5 = -\dfrac{32}{243}$

67. $\sqrt[6]{x^6} = |x|$

The index is even so we use absolute-value notation.

69. $\sqrt[4]{(5a)^4} = |5a| = 5|a|$

The index is even so we use absolute-value notation.

71. $\sqrt[10]{(-6)^{10}} = |-6| = 6$

73. $\sqrt[414]{(a+b)^{414}} = |a+b|$

The index is even so we use absolute-value notation.

75. $\sqrt[7]{y^7} = y$

We do not use absolute-value notation when the index is odd.

77. $\sqrt[5]{(x-2)^5} = x-2$

We do not use absolute-value notation when the index is odd.

79. Discussion and Writing Exercise

81. $x^2 + x - 2 = 0$

$(x+2)(x-1) = 0$ Factoring

$x + 2 = 0$ or $x - 1 = 0$ Principle of zero products

$x = -2$ or $x = 1$

The solutions are -2 and 1.

83. $4x^2 - 49 = 0$

$(2x+7)(2x-7) = 0$ Factoring

$2x + 7 = 0$ or $2x - 7 = 0$ Principle of zero products

$2x = -7$ or $2x = 7$

$x = -\dfrac{7}{2}$ or $x = \dfrac{7}{2}$

The solutions are $-\dfrac{7}{2}$ and $\dfrac{7}{2}$.

85. $3x^2 + x = 10$

$3x^2 + x - 10 = 0$

$(3x-5)(x+2) = 0$

$3x - 5 = 0$ or $x + 2 = 0$

$3x = 5$ or $x = -2$

$x = \dfrac{5}{3}$ or $x = -2$

The solutions are $\dfrac{5}{3}$ and -2.

87. $4x^3 - 20x^2 + 25x = 0$

$x(4x^2 - 20x + 25) = 0$

$x(2x-5)(2x-5) = 0$

$x = 0$ or $2x - 5 = 0$ or $2x - 5 = 0$

$x = 0$ or $2x = 5$ or $2x = 5$

$x = 0$ or $x = \dfrac{5}{2}$ or $x = \dfrac{5}{2}$

The solutions are 0 and $\dfrac{5}{2}$.

89. $(a^3b^2c^5)^3 = a^{3\cdot3}b^{2\cdot3}c^{5\cdot3} = a^9b^6c^{15}$

91. $f(x) = \dfrac{\sqrt{x+3}}{\sqrt{2-x}}$

In the numerator we must have $x + 3 \geq 0$, or $x \geq -3$, and in the denominator we must have $2 - x > 0$, or $x < 2$. Thus, we have $x \geq -3$ *and* $x < 2$, so

Domain of $f = \{x | -3 \leq x < 2\}$, or $[-3, 2)$.

93. From 3 on the x-axis, go up to the graph and across to the y-axis to find $f(3) = \sqrt{3} \approx 1.7$.

From 5 on the x-axis, go up to the graph and across to the y-axis to find $f(5) = \sqrt{5} \approx 2.2$.

From 10 on the x-axis, go up to the graph and across to the y-axis to find $f(10) = \sqrt{10} \approx 3.2$.

95. a) $f(x) = \sqrt[3]{x}$

Domain $= (-\infty, \infty)$; range $= (-\infty, \infty)$

b) $g(x) = \sqrt[3]{4x-5}$

Domain $= (-\infty, \infty)$; range $= (-\infty, \infty)$

c) $q(x) = 2 - \sqrt{x+3}$

Domain $= [-3, \infty)$; range $= (-\infty, 2]$

d) $h(x) = \sqrt[4]{x}$

Domain $= [0, \infty)$; range $= [0, \infty)$

e) $t(x) = \sqrt[4]{x-3}$

Domain $= [3, \infty)$; range $= [0, \infty)$

Exercise Set 6.2

1. $y^{1/7} = \sqrt[7]{y}$

3. $(8)^{1/3} = \sqrt[3]{8} = 2$

5. $(a^3b^3)^{1/5} = \sqrt[5]{a^3b^3}$

7. $16^{3/4} = \sqrt[4]{16^3} = (\sqrt[4]{16})^3 = 2^3 = 8$

9. $49^{3/2} = \sqrt{49^3} = (\sqrt{49})^3 = 7^3 = 343$

11. $\sqrt{17} = 17^{1/2}$

13. $\sqrt[3]{18} = 18^{1/3}$

15. $\sqrt[5]{xy^2z} = (xy^2z)^{1/5}$

17. $(\sqrt{3mn})^3 = (3mn)^{3/2}$

19. $(\sqrt[7]{8x^2y})^5 = (8x^2y)^{5/7}$

21. $27^{-1/3} = \dfrac{1}{27^{1/3}} = \dfrac{1}{\sqrt[3]{27}} = \dfrac{1}{3}$

23. $100^{-3/2} = \dfrac{1}{100^{3/2}} = \dfrac{1}{(\sqrt{100})^3} = \dfrac{1}{10^3} = \dfrac{1}{1000}$

25. $x^{-1/4} = \dfrac{1}{x^{1/4}}$

27. $(2rs)^{-3/4} = \dfrac{1}{(2rs)^{3/4}}$

29. $2a^{3/4}b^{-1/2}c^{2/3} = 2 \cdot a^{3/4} \cdot \dfrac{1}{b^{1/2}} \cdot c^{2/3} = \dfrac{2a^{3/4}c^{2/3}}{b^{1/2}}$

31. $\left(\dfrac{7x}{8yz}\right)^{-3/5} = \left(\dfrac{8yz}{7x}\right)^{3/5}$ $\left(\text{Since } \left(\dfrac{a}{b}\right)^{-n} = \left(\dfrac{b}{a}\right)^n\right)$

33. $\dfrac{1}{x^{-2/3}} = x^{2/3}$

35. $2^{-1/3}x^4y^{-2/7} = \dfrac{1}{2^{1/3}} \cdot x^4 \cdot \dfrac{1}{y^{2/7}} = \dfrac{x^4}{2^{1/3}y^{2/7}}$

37. $\dfrac{7x}{\sqrt[3]{z}} = \dfrac{7x}{z^{1/3}}$

39. $\dfrac{5a}{3c^{-1/2}} = \dfrac{5a}{3} \cdot c^{1/2} = \dfrac{5ac^{1/2}}{3}$

41. $5^{3/4} \cdot 5^{1/8} = 5^{3/4+1/8} = 5^{6/8+1/8} = 5^{7/8}$

43. $\dfrac{7^{5/8}}{7^{3/8}} = 7^{5/8-3/8} = 7^{2/8} = 7^{1/4}$

45. $\dfrac{4.9^{-1/6}}{4.9^{-2/3}} = 4.9^{-1/6-(-2/3)} = 4.9^{-1/6+4/6} = 4.9^{3/6} = 4.9^{1/2}$

47. $(6^{3/8})^{2/7} = 6^{3/8 \cdot 2/7} = 6^{6/56} = 6^{3/28}$

49. $a^{2/3} \cdot a^{5/4} = a^{2/3+5/4} = a^{8/12+15/12} = a^{23/12}$

51. $(a^{2/3} \cdot b^{5/8})^4 = (a^{2/3})^4(b^{5/8})^4 = a^{8/3}b^{20/8} = a^{8/3}b^{5/2}$

53. $(x^{2/3})^{-3/7} = x^{2/3(-3/7)} = x^{-2/7} = \dfrac{1}{x^{2/7}}$

55. $\sqrt[6]{a^2} = a^{2/6}$　Converting to exponential notation

$\phantom{\sqrt[6]{a^2}} = a^{1/3}$　Simplifying the exponent

$\phantom{\sqrt[6]{a^2}} = \sqrt[3]{a}$　Returning to radical notation

57. $\sqrt[3]{x^{15}} = x^{15/3}$　Converting to exponential notation

$\phantom{\sqrt[3]{x^{15}}} = x^5$　Simplifying

59. $\sqrt[6]{x^{-18}} = x^{-18/6}$　Converting to exponential notation

$\phantom{\sqrt[6]{x^{-18}}} = x^{-3}$　Simplifying

$\phantom{\sqrt[6]{x^{-18}}} = \dfrac{1}{x^3}$

61. $(\sqrt[3]{ab})^{15} = (ab)^{15/3}$　Converting to exponential notation

$\phantom{(\sqrt[3]{ab})^{15}} = (ab)^5$　Simplifying the exponent

$\phantom{(\sqrt[3]{ab})^{15}} = a^5b^5$　Using the law of exponents

63. $\sqrt[14]{128} = \sqrt[14]{2^7} = 2^{7/14} = 2^{1/2} = \sqrt{2}$

65. $\sqrt[6]{4x^2} = (2^2x^2)^{1/6} = 2^{2/6}x^{2/6}$

$\phantom{\sqrt[6]{4x^2}} = 2^{1/3}x^{1/3} = (2x)^{1/3} = \sqrt[3]{2x}$

67. $\sqrt{x^4y^6} = (x^4y^6)^{1/2} = x^{4/2}y^{6/2} = x^2y^3$

69. $\sqrt[5]{32c^{10}d^{15}} = (2^5c^{10}d^{15})^{1/5} = 2^{5/5}c^{10/5}d^{15/5}$

$\phantom{\sqrt[5]{32c^{10}d^{15}}} = 2c^2d^3$

71. $\sqrt[3]{7} \cdot \sqrt[4]{5} = 7^{1/3} \cdot 5^{1/4} = 7^{4/12} \cdot 5^{3/12} = $

$(7^4 \cdot 5^3)^{1/12} = \sqrt[12]{7^4 \cdot 5^3}$

73. $\sqrt[4]{5} \cdot \sqrt[5]{7} = 5^{1/4} \cdot 7^{1/5} = 5^{5/20} \cdot 7^{4/20} = (5^5 \cdot 7^4)^{1/20} = $

$\sqrt[20]{5^5 \cdot 7^4}$

75. $\sqrt{x}\sqrt[3]{2x} = x^{1/2} \cdot (2x)^{1/3} = x^{3/6} \cdot (2x)^{2/6} = $

$[x^3(2x)^2]^{1/6} = (x^3 \cdot 4x^2)^{1/6} = (4x^5)^{1/6} = \sqrt[6]{4x^5}$

77. $(\sqrt[5]{a^2b^4})^{15} = (a^2b^4)^{15/5} = (a^2b^4)^3 = a^6b^{12}$

79. $\sqrt[3]{\sqrt[6]{m}} = \sqrt[3]{m^{1/6}} = (m^{1/6})^{1/3} = m^{1/18} = \sqrt[18]{m}$

81. $x^{1/3} \cdot y^{1/4} \cdot z^{1/6} = x^{4/12} \cdot y^{3/12} \cdot z^{2/12} = $

$(x^4y^3z^2)^{1/12} = \sqrt[12]{x^4y^3z^2}$

83. $\left(\dfrac{c^{-4/5}d^{5/9}}{c^{3/10}d^{1/6}}\right)^3 = (c^{-4/5-3/10}d^{5/9-1/6})^3 = $

$(c^{-8/10-3/10}d^{10/18-3/18})^3 = (c^{-11/10}d^{7/18})^3 = $

$c^{-33/10}d^{7/6} = c^{-99/30}d^{35/30} = (c^{-99}d^{35})^{1/30} = $

$\left(\dfrac{d^{35}}{c^{99}}\right)^{1/30} = \sqrt[30]{\dfrac{d^{35}}{c^{99}}}$

85. Discussion and Writing Exercise

87. $A = \dfrac{ab}{a+b}$

$A(a+b) = ab$　　Multiplying by $a+b$

$Aa + Ab = ab$

$Ab = ab - Aa$　　Subtracting Aa

$Ab = a(b - A)$　　Factoring

$\dfrac{Ab}{b-A} = a$　　Dividing by $b - A$

89. $Q = \dfrac{st}{s-t}$

$Q(s-t) = st$　　Multiplying by $s - t$

$Qs - Qt = st$

$Qs = st + Qt$　　Adding Qt

$Qs = t(s + Q)$　　Factoring

$\dfrac{Qs}{s+Q} = t$　　Dividing by $s + Q$

91.

$y_1 = x^{1/2},\ y_2 = 3x^{2/5},$
$y_3 = x^{4/7},\ y_4 = \frac{1}{5}x^{3/4}$

Exercise Set 6.3

1. $\sqrt{24} = \sqrt{4 \cdot 6} = \sqrt{4}\,\sqrt{6} = 2\sqrt{6}$

3. $\sqrt{90} = \sqrt{9 \cdot 10} = \sqrt{9}\,\sqrt{10} = 3\sqrt{10}$

5. $\sqrt[3]{250} = \sqrt[3]{125 \cdot 2} = \sqrt[3]{125}\,\sqrt[3]{2} = 5\sqrt[3]{2}$

7. $\sqrt{180x^4} = \sqrt{36 \cdot 5 \cdot x^4} = \sqrt{36x^4}\,\sqrt{5} = 6x^2\sqrt{5}$

9. $\sqrt[3]{54x^8} = \sqrt[3]{27 \cdot 2 \cdot x^6 \cdot x^2} = \sqrt[3]{27x^6}\,\sqrt[3]{2x^2} = 3x^2\sqrt[3]{2x^2}$

11. $\sqrt[3]{80t^8} = \sqrt[3]{8 \cdot 10 \cdot t^6 \cdot t^2} = \sqrt[3]{8t^6}\,\sqrt[3]{10t^2} = 2t^2\sqrt[3]{10t^2}$

13. $\sqrt[4]{80} = \sqrt[4]{16 \cdot 5} = \sqrt[4]{16}\,\sqrt[4]{5} = 2\sqrt[4]{5}$

15. $\sqrt{32a^2b} = \sqrt{16a^2 \cdot 2b} = \sqrt{16a^2} \cdot \sqrt{2b} = 4a\sqrt{2b}$

17. $\sqrt[4]{243x^8y^{10}} = \sqrt[4]{81x^8y^8 \cdot 3y^2} = \sqrt[4]{81x^8y^8}\sqrt[4]{3y^2} = 3x^2y^2\sqrt[4]{3y^2}$

19. $\sqrt[5]{96x^7y^{15}} = \sqrt[5]{32x^5y^{15} \cdot 3x^2} = \sqrt[5]{32x^5y^{15}}\sqrt[5]{3x^2} = 2xy^3\sqrt[5]{3x^2}$

21. $\sqrt{10}\sqrt{5} = \sqrt{10 \cdot 5} = \sqrt{50} = \sqrt{25 \cdot 2} = 5\sqrt{2}$

23. $\sqrt{15}\sqrt{6} = \sqrt{15 \cdot 6} = \sqrt{90}$
$= \sqrt{9 \cdot 10} = \sqrt{9}\sqrt{10} = 3\sqrt{10}$

25. $\sqrt[3]{2}\sqrt[3]{4} = \sqrt[3]{2 \cdot 4} = \sqrt[3]{8} = 2$

27. $\sqrt{45}\sqrt{60} = \sqrt{45 \cdot 60} = \sqrt{2700}$
$= \sqrt{900 \cdot 3} = \sqrt{900}\sqrt{3} = 30\sqrt{3}$

29. $\sqrt{3x^3}\sqrt{6x^5} = \sqrt{18x^8} = \sqrt{9x^8 \cdot 2} = 3x^4\sqrt{2}$

31. $\sqrt{5b^3}\sqrt{10c^4} = \sqrt{5b^3 \cdot 10c^4}$
$= \sqrt{50b^3c^4}$
$= \sqrt{25 \cdot 2 \cdot b^2 \cdot b \cdot c^4}$
$= \sqrt{25b^2c^4}\sqrt{2b}$
$= 5bc^2\sqrt{2b}$

33. $\sqrt[3]{5a^2}\sqrt[3]{2a} = \sqrt[3]{5a^2 \cdot 2a} = \sqrt[3]{10a^3} = \sqrt[3]{a^3 \cdot 10} = a\sqrt[3]{10}$

35. $\sqrt[3]{y^4}\sqrt[3]{16y^5} = \sqrt[3]{y^4 \cdot 16y^5}$
$= \sqrt[3]{16y^9}$
$= \sqrt[3]{8 \cdot 2 \cdot y^9}$
$= \sqrt[3]{8y^9}\sqrt[3]{2}$
$= 2y^3\sqrt[3]{2}$

37. $\sqrt[4]{16}\sqrt[4]{64} = \sqrt[4]{16 \cdot 64} = \sqrt[4]{1024} = \sqrt[4]{256 \cdot 4} = \sqrt[4]{256}\sqrt[4]{4} = 4\sqrt[4]{4}$

39. $\sqrt{12a^3b}\sqrt{8a^4b^2} = \sqrt{12a^3b \cdot 8a^4b^2} = \sqrt{96a^7b^3} = \sqrt{16a^6b^2 \cdot 6ab} = \sqrt{16a^6b^2}\sqrt{6ab} = 4a^3b\sqrt{6ab}$

41. $\sqrt{2}\sqrt[3]{5}$
$= 2^{1/2} \cdot 5^{1/3}$ Converting to exponential notation
$= 2^{3/6} \cdot 5^{2/6}$ Rewriting so that exponents have a common denominator
$= (2^3 \cdot 5^2)^{1/6}$ Using $a^n b^n = (ab)^n$
$= \sqrt[6]{2^3 \cdot 5^2}$ Converting to radical notation
$= \sqrt[6]{8 \cdot 25}$ Simplifying
$= \sqrt[6]{200}$ Multiplying

43. $\sqrt[4]{3}\sqrt{2}$
$= 3^{1/4} \cdot 2^{1/2}$ Converting to exponential notation
$= 3^{1/4} \cdot 2^{2/4}$ Rewriting so that exponents have a common denominator
$= (3 \cdot 2^2)^{1/4}$ Using $a^n b^n = (ab)^n$
$= \sqrt[4]{3 \cdot 2^2}$ Converting to radical notation
$= \sqrt[4]{3 \cdot 4}$ Squaring 2
$= \sqrt[4]{12}$ Multiplying

45. $\sqrt{a}\sqrt[4]{a^3}$
$= a^{1/2} \cdot a^{3/4}$ Converting to exponential notation
$= a^{5/4}$ Adding exponents
$= a^{1+1/4}$ Writing 5/4 as a mixed number
$= a \cdot a^{1/4}$ Factoring
$= a\sqrt[4]{a}$ Returning to radical notation

47. $\sqrt[5]{b^2}\sqrt{b^3}$
$= b^{2/5} \cdot b^{3/2}$ Converting to exponential notation
$= b^{19/10}$ Adding exponents
$= b^{1+9/10}$ Writing 19/10 as a mixed number
$= b \cdot b^{9/10}$ Factoring
$= b\sqrt[10]{b^9}$ Returning to radical notation

49. $\sqrt{xy^3}\sqrt[3]{x^2y} = (xy^3)^{1/2}(x^2y)^{1/3}$
$= (xy^3)^{3/6}(x^2y)^{2/6}$
$= [(xy^3)^3(x^2y)^2]^{1/6}$
$= \sqrt[6]{x^3y^9 \cdot x^4y^2}$
$= \sqrt[6]{x^7y^{11}}$
$= \sqrt[6]{x^6y^6 \cdot xy^5}$
$= xy\sqrt[6]{xy^5}$

51. $\dfrac{\sqrt{90}}{\sqrt{5}} = \sqrt{\dfrac{90}{5}} = \sqrt{18} = \sqrt{9 \cdot 2} = \sqrt{9}\sqrt{2} = 3\sqrt{2}$

53. $\dfrac{\sqrt{35q}}{\sqrt{7q}} = \sqrt{\dfrac{35q}{7q}} = \sqrt{5}$

55. $\dfrac{\sqrt[3]{54}}{\sqrt[3]{2}} = \sqrt[3]{\dfrac{54}{2}} = \sqrt[3]{27} = 3$

57. $\dfrac{\sqrt{56xy^3}}{\sqrt{8x}} = \sqrt{\dfrac{56xy^3}{8x}} = \sqrt{7y^3} = \sqrt{y^2 \cdot 7y} = \sqrt{y^2}\sqrt{7y} = y\sqrt{7y}$

59. $\dfrac{\sqrt[3]{96a^4b^2}}{\sqrt[3]{12a^2b}} = \sqrt[3]{\dfrac{96a^4b^2}{12a^2b}} = \sqrt[3]{8a^2b} = \sqrt[3]{8}\sqrt[3]{a^2b} = 2\sqrt[3]{a^2b}$

61. $\dfrac{\sqrt{128xy}}{2\sqrt{2}} = \dfrac{1}{2}\dfrac{\sqrt{128xy}}{\sqrt{2}} = \dfrac{1}{2}\sqrt{\dfrac{128xy}{2}} = \dfrac{1}{2}\sqrt{64xy} = \dfrac{1}{2}\sqrt{64}\sqrt{xy} = \dfrac{1}{2} \cdot 8\sqrt{xy} = 4\sqrt{xy}$

63. $\dfrac{\sqrt[4]{48x^9y^{13}}}{\sqrt[4]{3xy^5}} = \sqrt[4]{\dfrac{48x^9y^{13}}{3xy^5}} = \sqrt[4]{16x^8y^8} = 2x^2y^2$

65. $\dfrac{\sqrt[3]{a}}{\sqrt{a}}$

$= \dfrac{a^{1/3}}{a^{1/2}}$ Converting to exponential notation

$= a^{1/3-1/2}$ Subtracting exponents

$= a^{2/6-3/6}$

$= a^{-1/6}$

$= \dfrac{1}{a^{1/6}}$

$= \dfrac{1}{\sqrt[6]{a}}$ Converting to radical notation

67. $\dfrac{\sqrt[3]{a^2}}{\sqrt[4]{a}}$

$= \dfrac{a^{2/3}}{a^{1/4}}$ Converting to exponential notation

$= a^{2/3-1/4}$ Subtracting exponents

$= a^{5/12}$ Converting back

$= \sqrt[12]{a^5}$ to radical notation

69. $\dfrac{\sqrt[4]{x^2y^3}}{\sqrt[3]{xy}}$

$= \dfrac{(x^2y^3)^{1/4}}{(xy)^{1/3}}$ Converting to exponential notation

$= \dfrac{x^{2/4}y^{3/4}}{x^{1/3}y^{1/3}}$ Using the power and product rules

$= x^{2/4-1/3}y^{3/4-1/3}$ Subtracting exponents

$= x^{2/12}y^{5/12}$

$= (x^2y^5)^{1/2}$ Converting back to

$= \sqrt[12]{x^2y^5}$ radical notation

71. $\sqrt{\dfrac{25}{36}} = \dfrac{\sqrt{25}}{\sqrt{36}} = \dfrac{5}{6}$

73. $\sqrt{\dfrac{16}{49}} = \dfrac{\sqrt{16}}{\sqrt{49}} = \dfrac{4}{7}$

75. $\sqrt[3]{\dfrac{125}{27}} = \dfrac{\sqrt[3]{125}}{\sqrt[3]{27}} = \dfrac{5}{3}$

77. $\sqrt{\dfrac{49}{y^2}} = \dfrac{\sqrt{49}}{\sqrt{y^2}} = \dfrac{7}{y}$

79. $\sqrt{\dfrac{25y^3}{x^4}} = \dfrac{\sqrt{25y^3}}{\sqrt{x^4}} = \dfrac{\sqrt{25y^2 \cdot y}}{\sqrt{x^4}} = \dfrac{\sqrt{25y^2}\sqrt{y}}{\sqrt{x^4}} =$

$\dfrac{5y\sqrt{y}}{x^2}$

81. $\sqrt[3]{\dfrac{27a^4}{8b^3}} = \dfrac{\sqrt[3]{27a^4}}{\sqrt[3]{8b^3}} = \dfrac{\sqrt[3]{27a^3 \cdot a}}{\sqrt[3]{8b^3}} = \dfrac{\sqrt[3]{27a^3}\sqrt[3]{a}}{\sqrt[3]{8b^3}} =$

$\dfrac{3a\sqrt[3]{a}}{2b}$

83. $\sqrt[4]{\dfrac{81x^4}{16}} = \dfrac{\sqrt[4]{81x^4}}{\sqrt[4]{16}} = \dfrac{3x}{2}$

85. $\sqrt[5]{\dfrac{32x^8}{y^{10}}} = \dfrac{\sqrt[5]{32x^8}}{\sqrt[5]{y^{10}}} = \dfrac{\sqrt[5]{32 \cdot x^5 \cdot x^3}}{\sqrt[5]{y^{10}}} = \dfrac{\sqrt[5]{32x^5}\sqrt[5]{x^3}}{\sqrt[5]{y^{10}}} =$

$\dfrac{2x\sqrt[5]{x^3}}{y^2}$

87. $\sqrt[6]{\dfrac{x^{13}}{y^6z^{12}}} = \dfrac{\sqrt[6]{x^{13}}}{\sqrt[6]{y^6z^{12}}} = \dfrac{\sqrt[6]{x^{12} \cdot x}}{\sqrt[6]{y^6z^{12}}} = \dfrac{\sqrt[6]{x^{12}}\sqrt[6]{x}}{\sqrt[6]{y^6z^{12}}} = \dfrac{x^2\sqrt[6]{x}}{yz^2}$

89. Discussion and Writing Exercise

91. *Familiarize.* We will use the formula $d = rt$. When the boat travels downstream, its rate is $14 + 7$, or 21 mph. Its rate traveling upstream is $14 - 7$ or 7 mph.

Translate. We substitute in the formula.

Downstream: $56 = 21t$

Upstream: $56 = 7t$

Solve. We solve the equation.

Downstream: $56 = 21t$

$\dfrac{56}{21} = t$

$\dfrac{8}{3} = t$, or

$2\dfrac{2}{3} = t$

Upstream: $56 = 7t$

$8 = t$

Check. At a rate of 21 mph, in $\dfrac{8}{3}$ hr the boat would travel $21 \cdot \dfrac{8}{3}$, or 56 mi. At a rate of 7 mph, in 8 hr the boat would travel $7 \cdot 8$, or 56 mi. The answer checks.

State. It will take the boat $2\dfrac{2}{3}$ hr to travel 56 mi downstream and 8 hr to travel 56 mi upstream.

93. $\dfrac{12x}{x-4} - \dfrac{3x^2}{x+4} = \dfrac{384}{x^2-16}$

$\dfrac{12x}{x-4} - \dfrac{3x^2}{x+4} = \dfrac{384}{(x+4)(x-4)}$,

LCM is $(x+4)(x-4)$.

$(x+4)(x-4)\left[\dfrac{12x}{x-4} - \dfrac{3x^2}{x+4}\right] = (x+4)(x-4) \cdot \dfrac{384}{(x+4)(x-4)}$

$12x(x+4) - 3x^2(x-4) = 384$

$12x^2 + 48x - 3x^3 + 12x^2 = 384$

$-3x^3 + 24x^2 + 48x - 384 = 0$

$-3(x^3 - 8x^2 - 16x + 128) = 0$

$-3[x^2(x-8) - 16(x-8)] = 0$

$-3(x-8)(x^2-16) = 0$

$-3(x-8)(x+4)(x-4) = 0$

$x - 8 = 0$ *or* $x + 4 = 0$ *or* $x - 4 = 0$

$x = 8$ *or* $x = -4$ *or* $x = 4$

Check: For 8:

$$\frac{12x}{x-4} - \frac{3x^2}{x+4} = \frac{384}{x^2-16}$$

$$\frac{12 \cdot 8}{8-4} - \frac{3 \cdot 8^2}{8+4} \ ? \ \frac{384}{8^2-16}$$

$$\frac{96}{4} - \frac{192}{12} \ \Big| \ \frac{384}{48}$$

$$24 - 16 \ \Big| \ 8$$

$$8 \ \Big| \qquad \text{TRUE}$$

8 is a solution.

For -4:

$$\frac{12x}{x-4} - \frac{3x^2}{x+4} = \frac{384}{x^2-16}$$

$$\frac{12(-4)}{-4-4} - \frac{3(-4)^2}{-4+4} \ ? \ \frac{384}{(-4)^2-16}$$

$$\frac{-48}{-8} - \frac{48}{0} \ \Big| \ \frac{384}{16-16} \qquad \text{UNDEFINED}$$

-4 is not a solution.

For 4:

$$\frac{12x}{x-4} - \frac{3x^2}{x+4} = \frac{384}{x^2-16}$$

$$\frac{12 \cdot 4}{4-4} - \frac{3 \cdot 4^2}{4+4} \ ? \ \frac{384}{4^2-16}$$

$$\frac{48}{0} - \frac{48}{8} \ \Big| \ \frac{384}{16-16} \qquad \text{UNDEFINED}$$

4 is not a solution.

The solution is 8.

95.

$$\frac{18}{x^2-3x} = \frac{2x}{x-3} - \frac{6}{x}$$

$$\frac{18}{x(x-3)} = \frac{2x}{x-3} - \frac{6}{x},$$

$$\text{LCM is } x(x-3)$$

$$x(x-3) \cdot \frac{18}{x(x-3)} = x(x-3)\left(\frac{2x}{x-3} - \frac{6}{x}\right)$$

$$18 = x(x-3) \cdot \frac{2x}{x-3} - x(x-3) \cdot \frac{6}{x}$$

$$18 = 2x^2 - 6x + 18$$

$$0 = 2x^2 - 6x$$

$$0 = 2x(x-3)$$

$$2x = 0 \ \text{ or } \ x-3 = 0$$

$$x = 0 \ \text{ or } \qquad x = 3$$

Each value makes a denominator 0. There is no solution.

97. a) $T = 2\pi\sqrt{\dfrac{65}{980}} \approx 1.62 \text{ sec}$

b) $T = 2\pi\sqrt{\dfrac{98}{980}} \approx 1.99 \text{ sec}$

c) $T = 2\pi\sqrt{\dfrac{120}{980}} \approx 2.20 \text{ sec}$

99. $\dfrac{\sqrt{44x^2y^9z}\sqrt{22y^9z^6}}{(\sqrt{11xy^8z^2})^2} = \dfrac{\sqrt{44 \cdot 22x^2y^{18}z^7}}{\sqrt{11 \cdot 11x^2y^{16}z^4}} =$

$$\sqrt{\frac{44 \cdot 22x^2y^{18}z^7}{11 \cdot 11x^2y^{16}z^4}} = \sqrt{4 \cdot 2y^2z^3} = \sqrt{4y^2z^2 \cdot 2z} = 2yz\sqrt{2z}$$

Exercise Set 6.4

1. $7\sqrt{5} + 4\sqrt{5} = (7+4)\sqrt{5}$ Factoring out $\sqrt{5}$

$$= 11\sqrt{5}$$

3. $6\sqrt[3]{7} - 5\sqrt[3]{7} = (6-5)\sqrt[3]{7}$ Factoring out $\sqrt[3]{7}$

$$= \sqrt[3]{7}$$

5. $4\sqrt[3]{y} + 9\sqrt[3]{y} = (4+9)\sqrt[3]{y} = 13\sqrt[3]{y}$

7. $5\sqrt{6} - 9\sqrt{6} - 4\sqrt{6} = (5-9-4)\sqrt{6} = -8\sqrt{6}$

9. $4\sqrt[3]{3} - \sqrt{5} + 2\sqrt[3]{3} + \sqrt{5} =$

$$(4+2)\sqrt[3]{3} + (-1+1)\sqrt{5} = 6\sqrt[3]{3}$$

11. $8\sqrt{27} - 3\sqrt{3} = 8\sqrt{9 \cdot 3} - 3\sqrt{3}$ } Factoring the first radical

$$= 8\sqrt{9} \cdot \sqrt{3} - 3\sqrt{3}$$

$$= 8 \cdot 3\sqrt{3} - 3\sqrt{3} \quad \text{Taking the square root}$$

$$= 24\sqrt{3} - 3\sqrt{3}$$

$$= (24-3)\sqrt{3} \quad \text{Factoring out } \sqrt{3}$$

$$= 21\sqrt{3}$$

13. $8\sqrt{45} + 7\sqrt{20} = 8\sqrt{9 \cdot 5} + 7\sqrt{4 \cdot 5}$ } Factoring the radicals

$$= 8\sqrt{9} \cdot \sqrt{5} + 7\sqrt{4} \cdot \sqrt{5}$$

$$= 8 \cdot 3\sqrt{5} + 7 \cdot 2\sqrt{5} \quad \text{Taking the square roots}$$

$$= 24\sqrt{5} + 14\sqrt{5}$$

$$= (24+14)\sqrt{5} \quad \text{Factoring out } \sqrt{5}$$

$$= 38\sqrt{5}$$

15. $18\sqrt{72} + 2\sqrt{98} = 18\sqrt{36 \cdot 2} + 2\sqrt{49 \cdot 2} =$

$$18\sqrt{36} \cdot \sqrt{2} + 2\sqrt{49} \cdot \sqrt{2} = 18 \cdot 6\sqrt{2} + 2 \cdot 7\sqrt{2} =$$

$$108\sqrt{2} + 14\sqrt{2} = (108+14)\sqrt{2} = 122\sqrt{2}$$

17. $3\sqrt[3]{16} + \sqrt[3]{54} = 3\sqrt[3]{8 \cdot 2} + \sqrt[3]{27 \cdot 2} =$

$$3\sqrt[3]{8} \cdot \sqrt[3]{2} + \sqrt[3]{27} \cdot \sqrt[3]{2} = 3 \cdot 2\sqrt[3]{2} + 3\sqrt[3]{2} =$$

$$6\sqrt[3]{2} + 3\sqrt[3]{2} = (6+3)\sqrt[3]{2} = 9\sqrt[3]{2}$$

19. $2\sqrt{128} - \sqrt{18} + 4\sqrt{32} =$

$$2\sqrt{64 \cdot 2} - \sqrt{9 \cdot 2} + 4\sqrt{16 \cdot 2} =$$

$$2\sqrt{64} \cdot \sqrt{2} - \sqrt{9} \cdot \sqrt{2} + 4\sqrt{16} \cdot \sqrt{2} =$$

$$2 \cdot 8\sqrt{2} - 3\sqrt{2} + 4 \cdot 4\sqrt{2} = 16\sqrt{2} - 3\sqrt{2} + 16\sqrt{2} =$$

$$(16 - 3 + 16)\sqrt{2} = 29\sqrt{2}$$

21. $\sqrt{5a} + 2\sqrt{45a^3} = \sqrt{5a} + 2\sqrt{9a^2 \cdot 5a} =$

$$\sqrt{5a} + 2\sqrt{9a^2} \cdot \sqrt{5a} = \sqrt{5a} + 2 \cdot 3a\sqrt{5a} =$$

$$\sqrt{5a} + 6a\sqrt{5a} = (1 + 6a)\sqrt{5a}$$

23. $\sqrt[3]{24x} - \sqrt[3]{3x^4} = \sqrt[3]{8 \cdot 3x} - \sqrt[3]{x^3 \cdot 3x} =$

$\sqrt[3]{8} \cdot \sqrt[3]{3x} - \sqrt[3]{x^3} \cdot \sqrt[3]{3x} = 2\sqrt[3]{3x} - x\sqrt[3]{3x} =$

$(2 - x)\sqrt[3]{3x}$

25. $5\sqrt[3]{32} - \sqrt[3]{108} + 2\sqrt[3]{256} =$

$5\sqrt[3]{8 \cdot 4} - \sqrt[3]{27 \cdot 4} + 2\sqrt[3]{64 \cdot 4} =$

$5\sqrt[3]{8} \cdot \sqrt[3]{4} - \sqrt[3]{27} \cdot \sqrt[3]{4} + 2\sqrt[3]{64} \cdot \sqrt[3]{4} =$

$5 \cdot 2\sqrt[3]{4} - 3\sqrt[3]{4} + 2 \cdot 4\sqrt[3]{4} = 10\sqrt[3]{4} - 3\sqrt[3]{4} + 8\sqrt[3]{4} =$

$(10 - 3 + 8)\sqrt[3]{4} = 15\sqrt[3]{4}$

27. $\sqrt[3]{6x^4} + \sqrt[3]{48x} - \sqrt[3]{6x}$

$= \sqrt[3]{x^3 \cdot 6x} + \sqrt[3]{8 \cdot 6x} - \sqrt[3]{6x}$

$= \sqrt[3]{x^3} \cdot \sqrt[3]{6x} + \sqrt[3]{8} \cdot \sqrt[3]{6x} - \sqrt[3]{6x}$

$= x\sqrt[3]{6x} + 2\sqrt[3]{6x} - \sqrt[3]{6x}$

$= (x + 2 - 1)\sqrt[3]{6x}$

$= (x + 1)\sqrt[3]{6x}$

29. $\sqrt{4a - 4} + \sqrt{a - 1} = \sqrt{4(a - 1)} + \sqrt{a - 1}$

$= \sqrt{4} \cdot \sqrt{a - 1} + \sqrt{a - 1}$

$= 2\sqrt{a - 1} + \sqrt{a - 1}$

$= (2 + 1)\sqrt{a - 1}$

$= 3\sqrt{a - 1}$

31. $\sqrt{x^3 - x^2} + \sqrt{9x - 9} = \sqrt{x^2(x - 1)} + \sqrt{9(x - 1)}$

$= \sqrt{x^2}\sqrt{x - 1} + \sqrt{9}\sqrt{x - 1}$

$= x\sqrt{x - 1} + 3\sqrt{x - 1}$

$= (x + 3)\sqrt{x - 1}$

33. $\sqrt{5}(4 - 2\sqrt{5}) = \sqrt{5} \cdot 4 - 2(\sqrt{5})^2$ Distributive law

$= 4\sqrt{5} - 2 \cdot 5$

$= 4\sqrt{5} - 10$

35. $\sqrt{3}(\sqrt{2} - \sqrt{7}) = \sqrt{3}\ \sqrt{2} - \sqrt{3}\ \sqrt{7}$ Distributive law

$= \sqrt{6} - \sqrt{21}$

37. $\sqrt{3}(2\sqrt{5} - 3\sqrt{4}) = \sqrt{3}(2\sqrt{5} - 3 \cdot 2) =$

$\sqrt{3} \cdot 2\sqrt{5} - \sqrt{3} \cdot 6 = 2\sqrt{15} - 6\sqrt{3}$

39. $\sqrt[3]{2}(\sqrt[3]{4} - 2\sqrt[3]{32}) = \sqrt[3]{2} \cdot \sqrt[3]{4} - \sqrt[3]{2} \cdot 2\sqrt[3]{32} =$

$\sqrt[3]{8} - 2\sqrt[3]{64} = 2 - 2 \cdot 4 = 2 - 8 = -6$

41. $\sqrt[3]{a}(\sqrt[3]{2a^2} + \sqrt[3]{16a^2}) = \sqrt[3]{a} \cdot \sqrt[3]{2a^2} + \sqrt[3]{a} \cdot \sqrt[3]{16a^2} =$

$\sqrt[3]{2a^3} + \sqrt[3]{16a^3} = \sqrt[3]{a^3 \cdot 2} + \sqrt[3]{8a^3 \cdot 2} = a\sqrt[3]{2} + 2a\sqrt[3]{2} =$

$3a\sqrt[3]{2}$

43. $(\sqrt{3} - \sqrt{2})(\sqrt{3} + \sqrt{2}) = (\sqrt{3})^2 - (\sqrt{2})^2 = 3 - 2 = 1$

45. $(\sqrt{8} + 2\sqrt{5})(\sqrt{8} - 2\sqrt{5}) = (\sqrt{8})^2 - (2\sqrt{5})^2 =$

$8 - 4 \cdot 5 = 8 - 20 = -12$

47. $(7 + \sqrt{5})(7 - \sqrt{5}) = 7^2 - (\sqrt{5})^2 = 49 - 5 = 44$

49. $(2 - \sqrt{3})(2 + \sqrt{3}) = 2^2 - (\sqrt{3})^2 = 4 - 3 = 1$

51. $(\sqrt{8} + \sqrt{5})(\sqrt{8} - \sqrt{5}) = (\sqrt{8})^2 - (\sqrt{5})^2 = 8 - 5 = 3$

53. $(3 + 2\sqrt{7})(3 - 2\sqrt{7}) = 3^2 - (2\sqrt{7})^2 =$

$9 - 4 \cdot 7 = 9 - 28 = -19$

55. $(\sqrt{a} + \sqrt{b})(\sqrt{a} - \sqrt{b}) = (\sqrt{a})^2 - (\sqrt{b})^2 = a - b$

57. $(3 - \sqrt{5})(2 + \sqrt{5})$

$= 3 \cdot 2 + 3\sqrt{5} - 2\sqrt{5} - (\sqrt{5})^2$ Using FOIL

$= 6 + 3\sqrt{5} - 2\sqrt{5} - 5$

$= 1 + \sqrt{5}$ Simplifying

59. $(\sqrt{3} + 1)(2\sqrt{3} + 1)$

$= \sqrt{3} \cdot 2\sqrt{3} + \sqrt{3} \cdot 1 + 1 \cdot 2\sqrt{3} + 1^2$ Using FOIL

$= 2 \cdot 3 + \sqrt{3} + 2\sqrt{3} + 1$

$= 7 + 3\sqrt{3}$ Simplifying

61. $(2\sqrt{7} - 4\sqrt{2})(3\sqrt{7} + 6\sqrt{2}) =$

$2\sqrt{7} \cdot 3\sqrt{7} + 2\sqrt{7} \cdot 6\sqrt{2} - 4\sqrt{2} \cdot 3\sqrt{7} - 4\sqrt{2} \cdot 6\sqrt{2} =$

$6 \cdot 7 + 12\sqrt{14} - 12\sqrt{14} - 24 \cdot 2 =$

$42 + 12\sqrt{14} - 12\sqrt{14} - 48 = -6$

63. $(\sqrt{a} + \sqrt{2})(\sqrt{a} + \sqrt{3}) =$

$(\sqrt{a})^2 + \sqrt{a} \cdot \sqrt{3} + \sqrt{2} \cdot \sqrt{a} + \sqrt{2} \cdot \sqrt{3} =$

$a + \sqrt{3a} + \sqrt{2a} + \sqrt{6}$

65. $(2\sqrt[3]{3} + \sqrt[3]{2})(\sqrt[3]{3} - 2\sqrt[3]{2}) =$

$2\sqrt[3]{3} \cdot \sqrt[3]{3} - 2\sqrt[3]{3} \cdot 2\sqrt[3]{2} + \sqrt[3]{2} \cdot \sqrt[3]{3} - \sqrt[3]{2} \cdot 2\sqrt[3]{2} =$

$2\sqrt[3]{9} - 4\sqrt[3]{6} + \sqrt[3]{6} - 2\sqrt[3]{4} = 2\sqrt[3]{9} - 3\sqrt[3]{6} - 2\sqrt[3]{4}$

67. $(2 + \sqrt{3})^2 = 2^2 + 4\sqrt{3} + (\sqrt{3})^2$ Squaring a binomial

$= 4 + 4\sqrt{3} + 3$

$= 7 + 4\sqrt{3}$

69. $(\sqrt[5]{9} - \sqrt[5]{3})(\sqrt[5]{8} + \sqrt[5]{27})$

$= \sqrt[5]{9} \cdot \sqrt[5]{8} + \sqrt[5]{9} \cdot \sqrt[5]{27} - \sqrt[5]{3} \cdot \sqrt[5]{8} - \sqrt[5]{3} \cdot \sqrt[5]{27}$

Using FOIL

$= \sqrt[5]{72} + \sqrt[5]{243} - \sqrt[5]{24} - \sqrt[5]{81}$

$= \sqrt[5]{72} + 3 - \sqrt[5]{24} - \sqrt[5]{81}$

71. Discussion and Writing Exercise

73. $\dfrac{x^3 + 4x}{x^2 - 16} \div \dfrac{x^2 + 8x + 15}{x^2 + x - 20}$

$= \dfrac{x^3 + 4x}{x^2 - 16} \cdot \dfrac{x^2 + x - 20}{x^2 + 8x + 15}$

$= \dfrac{(x^3 + 4x)(x^2 + x - 20)}{(x^2 - 16)(x^2 + 8x + 15)}$

$= \dfrac{x(x^2 + 4)(x + 5)(x - 4)}{(x + 4)(x - 4)(x + 3)(x + 5)}$

$= \dfrac{x(x^2 + 4)(x + 5)(x - 4)}{(x + 4)(x - 4)(x + 3)(x + 5)}$

$= \dfrac{x(x^2 + 4)}{(x + 4)(x + 3)}$

75. $\dfrac{a^3+8}{a^2-4}\cdot\dfrac{a^2-4a+4}{a^2-2a+4}$

$=\dfrac{(a^3+8)(a^2-4a+4)}{(a^2-4)(a^2-2a+4)}$

$=\dfrac{(a+2)(a^2-2a+4)(a-2)(a-2)}{(a+2)(a-2)(a^2-2a+4)(1)}$

$=\dfrac{(a+2)(a^2-2a+4)(a-2)}{(a+2)(a^2-2a+4)(a-2)}\cdot\dfrac{a-2}{1}$

$=a-2$

77. $\dfrac{x-\dfrac{1}{3}}{x+\dfrac{1}{4}}=\dfrac{x-\dfrac{1}{3}}{x+\dfrac{1}{4}}\cdot\dfrac{12}{12}$

$=\dfrac{\left(x-\dfrac{1}{3}\right)(12)}{\left(x+\dfrac{1}{4}\right)(12)}$

$=\dfrac{12x-4}{12x+3},\ \text{or}\ \dfrac{4(3x-1)}{3(4x+1)}$

79. $\dfrac{\dfrac{1}{p}-\dfrac{1}{q}}{\dfrac{1}{p^2}-\dfrac{1}{q^2}}=\dfrac{\dfrac{1}{p}-\dfrac{1}{q}}{\dfrac{1}{p^2}-\dfrac{1}{q^2}}\cdot\dfrac{p^2q^2}{p^2q^2}$

$=\dfrac{\left(\dfrac{1}{p}-\dfrac{1}{q}\right)(p^2q^2)}{\left(\dfrac{1}{p^2}-\dfrac{1}{q^2}\right)(p^2q^2)}$

$=\dfrac{p^2q^2\cdot\dfrac{1}{p}-p^2q^2\cdot\dfrac{1}{q}}{p^2q^2\cdot\dfrac{1}{p^2}-p^2q^2\cdot\dfrac{1}{q^2}}$

$=\dfrac{pq^2-p^2q}{q^2-p^2}$

$=\dfrac{pq(q-p)}{(q+p)(q-p)}$

$=\dfrac{pq(q-p)}{(q+p)(q-p)}$

$=\dfrac{pq}{q+p}$

81.

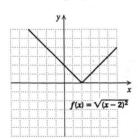

$f(x)=\sqrt{(x-2)^2}$

Since $(x-2)^2$ is nonnegative for all values of x, the domain of f is $\{x|x$ is a real number$\}$, or $(-\infty,\infty)$.

83. $\sqrt{9+3\sqrt5}\sqrt{9-3\sqrt5}=\sqrt{(9+3\sqrt5)(9-3\sqrt5)}=$

$\sqrt{9^2-(3\sqrt5)^2}=\sqrt{81-9\cdot5}=\sqrt{81-45}=\sqrt{36}=6$

85. $(\sqrt3+\sqrt5-\sqrt6)^2=[(\sqrt3+\sqrt5)-\sqrt6]^2=$

$(\sqrt3+\sqrt5)^2-2(\sqrt3+\sqrt5)(\sqrt6)+(\sqrt6)^2=$

$3+2\sqrt{15}+5-2\sqrt{18}-2\sqrt{30}+6=$

$14+2\sqrt{15}-2\sqrt{9\cdot2}-2\sqrt{30}=$

$14+2\sqrt{15}-6\sqrt2-2\sqrt{30}$

87. $(\sqrt[3]{9}-2)(\sqrt[3]{9}+4)$

$=\sqrt[3]{9}\sqrt[3]{9}+4\sqrt[3]{9}-2\sqrt[3]{9}-2\cdot4$

$=\sqrt[3]{81}+2\sqrt[3]{9}-8$

$=\sqrt[3]{27\cdot3}+2\sqrt[3]{9}-8$

$=3\sqrt[3]{3}+2\sqrt[3]{9}-8$

Exercise Set 6.5

1. $\sqrt{\dfrac{5}{3}}=\sqrt{\dfrac{5}{3}\cdot\dfrac{3}{3}}=\sqrt{\dfrac{15}{9}}=\dfrac{\sqrt{15}}{\sqrt9}=\dfrac{\sqrt{15}}{3}$

3. $\sqrt{\dfrac{11}{2}}=\sqrt{\dfrac{11}{2}\cdot\dfrac{2}{2}}=\sqrt{\dfrac{22}{4}}=\dfrac{\sqrt{22}}{\sqrt4}=\dfrac{\sqrt{22}}{2}$

5. $\dfrac{2\sqrt3}{7\sqrt5}=\dfrac{2\sqrt3}{7\sqrt5}\cdot\dfrac{\sqrt5}{\sqrt5}=\dfrac{2\sqrt{15}}{7\sqrt{5^2}}=\dfrac{2\sqrt{15}}{7\cdot5}=\dfrac{2\sqrt{15}}{35}$

7. $\sqrt[3]{\dfrac{16}{9}}=\sqrt[3]{\dfrac{16}{9}\cdot\dfrac{3}{3}}=\sqrt[3]{\dfrac{48}{27}}=\dfrac{\sqrt[3]{8\cdot6}}{\sqrt[3]{27}}=\dfrac{2\sqrt[3]{6}}{3}$

9. $\dfrac{\sqrt[3]{3a}}{\sqrt[3]{5c}}=\dfrac{\sqrt[3]{3a}}{\sqrt[3]{5c}}\cdot\dfrac{\sqrt[3]{5^2c^2}}{\sqrt[3]{5^2c^2}}=\dfrac{\sqrt[3]{75ac^2}}{\sqrt[3]{5^3c^3}}=\dfrac{\sqrt[3]{75ac^2}}{5c}$

11. $\dfrac{\sqrt[3]{2y^4}}{\sqrt[3]{6x^4}}=\dfrac{\sqrt[3]{2y^4}}{\sqrt[3]{6x^4}}\cdot\dfrac{\sqrt[3]{6^2x^2}}{\sqrt[3]{6^2x^2}}=\dfrac{\sqrt[3]{72x^2y^4}}{\sqrt[3]{6^3x^6}}=\dfrac{\sqrt[3]{8y^3\cdot9x^2y}}{6x^2}=$

$\dfrac{2y\sqrt[3]{9x^2y}}{6x^2}=\dfrac{y\sqrt[3]{9x^2y}}{3x^2}$

13. $\dfrac{1}{\sqrt[4]{st}}=\dfrac{1}{\sqrt[4]{st}}\cdot\dfrac{\sqrt[4]{s^3t^3}}{\sqrt[4]{s^3t^3}}=\dfrac{\sqrt[4]{s^3t^3}}{\sqrt[4]{s^4t^4}}=\dfrac{\sqrt[4]{s^3t^3}}{st}$

15. $\sqrt{\dfrac{3x}{20}}=\sqrt{\dfrac{3x}{20}\cdot\dfrac{5}{5}}=\sqrt{\dfrac{15x}{100}}=\dfrac{\sqrt{15x}}{\sqrt{100}}=\dfrac{\sqrt{15x}}{10}$

17. $\sqrt[3]{\dfrac{4}{5x^5y^2}}=\sqrt[3]{\dfrac{4}{5x^5y^2}\cdot\dfrac{25xy}{5^2xy}}=\sqrt[3]{\dfrac{100xy}{5^3x^6y^3}}=$

$\dfrac{\sqrt[3]{100xy}}{\sqrt[3]{5^3x^6y^3}}=\dfrac{\sqrt[3]{100xy}}{5x^2y}$

19. $\sqrt[4]{\dfrac{1}{8x^7y^3}}=\sqrt[4]{\dfrac{1}{2^3x^7y^3}\cdot\dfrac{2xy}{2xy}}=\sqrt[4]{\dfrac{2xy}{2^4x^8y^4}}=\dfrac{\sqrt[4]{2xy}}{\sqrt[4]{2^4x^8y^4}}=$

$\dfrac{\sqrt[4]{2xy}}{2x^2y}$

21. $\dfrac{9}{6-\sqrt{10}}=\dfrac{9}{6-\sqrt{10}}\cdot\dfrac{6+\sqrt{10}}{6+\sqrt{10}}=\dfrac{9(6+\sqrt{10})}{6^2-(\sqrt{10})^2}=$

$\dfrac{9(6+\sqrt{10})}{36-10}=\dfrac{54+9\sqrt{10}}{26}$

23. $\dfrac{-4\sqrt{7}}{\sqrt{5}-\sqrt{3}} = \dfrac{-4\sqrt{7}}{\sqrt{5}-\sqrt{3}} \cdot \dfrac{\sqrt{5}+\sqrt{3}}{\sqrt{5}+\sqrt{3}} =$

$\dfrac{-4\sqrt{7}(\sqrt{5}+\sqrt{3})}{(\sqrt{5})^2-(\sqrt{3})^2} = \dfrac{-4\sqrt{7}(\sqrt{5}+\sqrt{3})}{5-3} =$

$\dfrac{-4\sqrt{7}(\sqrt{5}+\sqrt{3})}{2} = -2\sqrt{7}(\sqrt{5}+\sqrt{3}) = -2\sqrt{35}-2\sqrt{21}$

25. $\dfrac{\sqrt{5}-2\sqrt{6}}{\sqrt{3}-4\sqrt{5}} = \dfrac{\sqrt{5}-2\sqrt{6}}{\sqrt{3}-4\sqrt{5}} \cdot \dfrac{\sqrt{3}+4\sqrt{5}}{\sqrt{3}+4\sqrt{5}} =$

$\dfrac{\sqrt{15}+4\cdot 5-2\sqrt{18}-8\sqrt{30}}{(\sqrt{3})^2-(4\sqrt{5})^2} =$

$\dfrac{\sqrt{15}+20-2\sqrt{9\cdot 2}-8\sqrt{30}}{3-16\cdot 5} =$

$\dfrac{\sqrt{15}+20-6\sqrt{2}-8\sqrt{30}}{-77}$, or $-\dfrac{\sqrt{15}+20-6\sqrt{2}-8\sqrt{30}}{77}$

27. $\dfrac{2-\sqrt{a}}{3+\sqrt{a}} = \dfrac{2-\sqrt{a}}{3+\sqrt{a}} \cdot \dfrac{3-\sqrt{a}}{3-\sqrt{a}} = \dfrac{6-2\sqrt{a}-3\sqrt{a}+a}{9-a} =$

$\dfrac{6-5\sqrt{a}+a}{9-a}$

29. $\dfrac{5\sqrt{3}-3\sqrt{2}}{3\sqrt{2}-2\sqrt{3}} = \dfrac{5\sqrt{3}-3\sqrt{2}}{3\sqrt{2}-2\sqrt{3}} \cdot \dfrac{3\sqrt{2}+2\sqrt{3}}{3\sqrt{2}+2\sqrt{3}} =$

$\dfrac{15\sqrt{6}+10\cdot 3-9\cdot 2-6\sqrt{6}}{9\cdot 2-4\cdot 3} = \dfrac{12+9\sqrt{6}}{6} =$

$\dfrac{3(4+3\sqrt{6})}{3\cdot 2} = \dfrac{4+3\sqrt{6}}{2}$

31. $\dfrac{\sqrt{x}-\sqrt{y}}{\sqrt{x}+\sqrt{y}} = \dfrac{\sqrt{x}-\sqrt{y}}{\sqrt{x}+\sqrt{y}} \cdot \dfrac{\sqrt{x}-\sqrt{y}}{\sqrt{x}-\sqrt{y}} =$

$\dfrac{x-\sqrt{xy}-\sqrt{xy}+y}{x-y} = \dfrac{x-2\sqrt{xy}+y}{x-y}$

33. Discussion and Writing Exercise

35. $\dfrac{1}{2} - \dfrac{1}{3} = \dfrac{5}{t}$, LCM is $6t$

$6t\left(\dfrac{1}{2}-\dfrac{1}{3}\right) = 6t\left(\dfrac{5}{t}\right)$

$3t - 2t = 30$

$t = 30$

Check:

$\dfrac{1}{2} - \dfrac{1}{3} = \dfrac{1}{t}$

$\begin{array}{c|c} \dfrac{1}{2} - \dfrac{1}{3} & \dfrac{5}{30} \\ \hline \dfrac{3}{6} - \dfrac{2}{6} & \dfrac{1}{6} \\ \dfrac{1}{6} & \text{TRUE} \end{array}$

The solution is 30.

37. $\dfrac{1}{x^3-y^2} \div \dfrac{1}{(x-y)(x^2+xy+y^2)}$

$= \dfrac{1}{(x-y)(x^2+xy+y^2)} \cdot \dfrac{(x-y)(x^2+xy+y^2)}{1}$

$= \dfrac{(x-y)(x^2+xy+y^2)}{(x-y)(x^2+xy+y^2)}$

$= 1$

39. Left to the student

41. $\sqrt{a^2-3} - \dfrac{a^2}{\sqrt{a^2-3}}$

$= \sqrt{a^2-3} - \dfrac{a^2}{\sqrt{a^2-3}} \cdot \dfrac{\sqrt{a^2-3}}{\sqrt{a^2-3}}$

$= \sqrt{a^2-3} - \dfrac{a^2\sqrt{a^2-3}}{a^2-3}$

$= \sqrt{a^2-3} \cdot \dfrac{a^2-3}{a^2-3} - \dfrac{a^2\sqrt{a^2-3}}{a^2-3}$

$= \dfrac{a^2\sqrt{a^2-3}-3\sqrt{a^2-3}-a^2\sqrt{a^2-3}}{a^2-3}$

$= \dfrac{-3\sqrt{a^2-3}}{a^2-3}$, or $-\dfrac{3\sqrt{a^2-3}}{a^2-3}$

Exercise Set 6.6

1. $\sqrt{2x-3} = 4$

$(\sqrt{2x-3})^2 = 4^2$ Principle of powers

$2x - 3 = 16$

$2x = 19$

$x = \dfrac{19}{2}$

Check: $\dfrac{\sqrt{2x-3} = 4}{}$

$\begin{array}{c|c} \sqrt{2\cdot\dfrac{19}{2}-3} \;?\; 4 & \\ \sqrt{19-3} & \\ \sqrt{16} & \\ 4 & \text{TRUE} \end{array}$

The solution is $\dfrac{19}{2}$.

3. $\sqrt{6x} + 1 = 8$

$\sqrt{6x} = 7$ Subtracting to isolate the radical

$(\sqrt{6x})^2 = 7^2$ Principle of powers

$6x = 49$

$x = \dfrac{49}{6}$

Check: $\dfrac{\sqrt{6x} + 1 = 8}{}$

$\begin{array}{c|c} \sqrt{6\cdot\dfrac{49}{6}}+1 \;?\; 8 & \\ \sqrt{49}+1 & \\ 7+1 & \\ 8 & \text{TRUE} \end{array}$

The solution is $\dfrac{49}{6}$.

5. $\sqrt{y+7} - 4 = 4$

$\sqrt{y+7} = 8$ Adding to isolate the radical

$(\sqrt{y+7})^2 = 8^2$ Principle of powers

$y + 7 = 64$

$y = 57$

Check: $\dfrac{\sqrt{y+7} - 4 = 4}{}$

$\sqrt{57+7} - 4 \ ? \ 4$

$\sqrt{64} - 4$

$8 - 4$

$4 \ \Big| \ $ TRUE

The solution is 57.

7. $\sqrt{5y+8} = 10$

$(\sqrt{5y+8})^2 = 10^2$ Principle of powers

$5y + 8 = 100$

$5y = 92$

$y = \dfrac{92}{5}$

Check: $\dfrac{\sqrt{5y+8} = 10}{}$

$\sqrt{5 \cdot \dfrac{92}{5} + 8} \ ? \ 10$

$\sqrt{92+8}$

$\sqrt{100}$

$10 \ \Big| \ $ TRUE

The solution is $\dfrac{92}{5}$.

9. $\sqrt[3]{x} = -1$

$(\sqrt[3]{x})^3 = (-1)^3$ Principle of powers

$x = -1$

Check: $\dfrac{\sqrt[3]{x} = -1}{}$

$\sqrt[3]{-1} \ ? \ -1$

$-1 \ \Big| \ $ TRUE

The solution is -1.

11. $\sqrt{x+2} = -4$

$(\sqrt{x+2})^2 = (-4)^2$

$x + 2 = 16$

$x = 14$

Check: $\dfrac{\sqrt{x+2} = -4}{}$

$\sqrt{14+2} \ ? \ -4$

$\sqrt{16}$

$4 \ \Big| \ $ FALSE

The number 14 does not check. The equation has no solution. We might have observed at the outset that this equation has no solution because the principle square root of a number is never negative.

13. $\sqrt[3]{x+5} = 2$

$(\sqrt[3]{x+5})^3 = 2^3$

$x + 5 = 8$

$x = 3$

Check: $\dfrac{\sqrt[3]{x+5} = 2}{}$

$\sqrt[3]{3+5} \ ? \ 2$

$\sqrt[3]{8}$

$2 \ \Big| \ $ TRUE

The solution is 3.

15. $\sqrt[4]{y-3} = 2$

$(\sqrt[4]{y-3})^4 = 2^4$

$y - 3 = 16$

$y = 19$

Check: $\dfrac{\sqrt[4]{y-3} = 2}{}$

$\sqrt[4]{19-3} \ ? \ 2$

$\sqrt[4]{16}$

$2 \ \Big| \ $ TRUE

The solution is 19.

17. $\sqrt[3]{6x+9} + 8 = 5$

$\sqrt[3]{6x+9} = -3$

$(\sqrt[3]{6x+9})^3 = (-3)^3$

$6x + 9 = -27$

$6x = -36$

$x = -6$

Check: $\dfrac{\sqrt[3]{6x+9} + 8 = 5}{}$

$\sqrt[3]{6(-6)+9} + 8 \ ? \ 5$

$\sqrt[3]{-27} + 8$

$-3 + 8$

$5 \ \Big| \ $ TRUE

The solution is -6.

19. $8 = \dfrac{1}{\sqrt{x}}$

$8 \cdot \sqrt{x} = \dfrac{1}{\sqrt{x}} \cdot \sqrt{x}$

$8\sqrt{x} = 1$

$(8\sqrt{x})^2 = 1^2$

$64x = 1$

$x = \dfrac{1}{64}$

Check: $8 = \dfrac{1}{\sqrt{x}}$

$$8 \ ? \ \dfrac{1}{\sqrt{\dfrac{1}{64}}}$$

$$\dfrac{1}{\dfrac{1}{8}}$$

$$8 \qquad \text{TRUE}$$

The solution is $\dfrac{1}{64}$.

21.
$$x - 7 = \sqrt{x - 5}$$
$$(x - 7)^2 = (\sqrt{x - 5})^2$$
$$x^2 - 14x + 49 = x - 5$$
$$x^2 - 15x + 54 = 0$$
$$(x - 6)(x - 9) = 0$$
$$x - 6 = 0 \quad or \quad x - 9 = 0$$
$$x = 6 \quad or \qquad x = 9$$

Check: For 6: $x - 7 = \sqrt{x - 5}$

$$6 - 7 \ ? \ \sqrt{6 - 5}$$
$$-1 \ \Big| \ \sqrt{1}$$
$$-1 \ \Big| \ 1 \quad \text{FALSE}$$

Check: For 9: $x - 7 = \sqrt{x - 5}$

$$9 - 7 \ ? \ \sqrt{9 - 5}$$
$$2 \ \Big| \ \sqrt{4}$$
$$2 \ \Big| \ 2 \quad \text{TRUE}$$

The number 6 does not check, but 9 does. The solution is 9.

23. $2\sqrt{x + 1} + 7 = x$
$$2\sqrt{x + 1} = x - 7$$
$$(2\sqrt{x + 1})^2 = (x - 7)^2$$
$$4(x + 1) = x^2 - 14x + 49$$
$$4x + 4 = x^2 - 14x + 49$$
$$0 = x^2 - 18x + 45$$
$$0 = (x - 3)(x - 15)$$
$$x - 3 = 0 \quad or \quad x - 15 = 0$$
$$x = 3 \quad or \qquad x = 15$$

Check: For 3: $2\sqrt{x + 1} + 7 = x$

$$2\sqrt{3 + 1} + 7 \ ? \ 3$$
$$2\sqrt{4} + 7$$
$$2 \cdot 2 + 7$$
$$4 + 7$$
$$11 \ \Big| \ 3 \quad \text{FALSE}$$

Check: For 15: $2\sqrt{x + 1} + 7 = x$

$$2\sqrt{15 + 1} + 7 \ ? \ 15$$
$$2\sqrt{16} + 7$$
$$2 \cdot 4 + 7$$
$$8 + 7$$
$$15 \ \Big| \ 15 \quad \text{TRUE}$$

The number 3 does not check, but 15 does. The solution is 15.

25. $3\sqrt{x - 1} - 1 = x$
$$3\sqrt{x - 1} = x + 1$$
$$(3\sqrt{x - 1})^2 = (x + 1)^2$$
$$9(x - 1) = x^2 + 2x + 1$$
$$9x - 9 = x^2 + 2x + 1$$
$$0 = x^2 - 7x + 10$$
$$0 = (x - 2)(x - 5)$$
$$x - 2 = 0 \quad or \quad x - 5 = 0$$
$$x = 2 \quad or \qquad x = 5$$

Check: For 2: $3\sqrt{x - 1} - 1 = x$

$$3\sqrt{2 - 1} - 1 \ ? \ 2$$
$$3\sqrt{1} - 1$$
$$3 \cdot 1 - 1$$
$$3 - 1$$
$$2 \ \Big| \ 2 \quad \text{TRUE}$$

Check: For 5: $3\sqrt{x - 1} - 1 = x$

$$3\sqrt{5 - 1} - 1 \ ? \ 5$$
$$3\sqrt{4} - 1$$
$$3 \cdot 2 - 1$$
$$6 - 1$$
$$5 \ \Big| \ 5 \quad \text{TRUE}$$

Both numbers check. The solutions are 2 and 5.

27.
$$x - 3 = \sqrt{27 - 3x}$$
$$(x - 3)^2 = (\sqrt{27 - 3x})^2$$
$$x^2 - 6x + 9 = 27 - 3x$$
$$x^2 - 3x - 18 = 0$$
$$(x - 6)(x + 3) = 0$$
$$x - 6 = 0 \quad or \quad x + 3 = 0$$
$$x = 6 \quad or \qquad x = -3$$

Check: For 6: $x - 3 = \sqrt{27 - 3x}$

$$6 - 3 \ ? \ \sqrt{27 - 3 \cdot 6}$$
$$3 \ \Big| \ \sqrt{27 - 18}$$
$$\Big| \ \sqrt{9}$$
$$3 \ \Big| \ 3 \quad \text{TRUE}$$

Check: For -3:

$$x - 3 = \sqrt{27 - 3x}$$

$$\overline{-3 - 3 \ ? \ \sqrt{27 - 3(-3)}}$$

$$-6 \ \Big| \ \sqrt{27 + 9}$$

$$\sqrt{36}$$

$$-6 \ \Big| \ 6 \quad \text{FALSE}$$

The number 6 checks but -3 does not. The solution is 6.

29.
$$\sqrt{3y + 1} = \sqrt{2y + 6}$$
$$(\sqrt{3y + 1})^2 = (\sqrt{2y + 6})^2$$
$$3y + 1 = 2y + 6$$
$$y = 5$$

Check:

$$\sqrt{3y + 1} = \sqrt{2y + 6}$$

$$\overline{\sqrt{3 \cdot 5 + 1} \ ? \ \sqrt{2 \cdot 5 + 6}}$$

$$\sqrt{16} \ \Big| \ \sqrt{16} \quad \text{TRUE}$$

The solution is 5.

31.
$$\sqrt{y - 5} + \sqrt{y} = 5$$
$$\sqrt{y - 5} = 5 - \sqrt{y} \qquad \text{Isolating one radical}$$
$$(\sqrt{y - 5})^2 = (5 - \sqrt{y})^2$$
$$y - 5 = 25 - 10\sqrt{y} + y$$
$$10\sqrt{y} = 30 \qquad \text{Isolating the remaining radical}$$
$$\sqrt{y} = 3 \qquad \text{Dividing by 10}$$
$$(\sqrt{y})^2 = 3^2$$
$$y = 9$$

The number 9 checks, so it is the solution.

33.
$$3 + \sqrt{z - 6} = \sqrt{z + 9}$$
$$(3 + \sqrt{z - 6})^2 = (\sqrt{z + 9})^2$$
$$9 + 6\sqrt{z - 6} + z - 6 = z + 9$$
$$6\sqrt{z - 6} = 6$$
$$\sqrt{z - 6} = 1 \qquad \text{Dividing by 6}$$
$$(\sqrt{z - 6})^2 = 1^2$$
$$z - 6 = 1$$
$$z = 7$$

The number 7 checks, so it is the solution.

35.
$$\sqrt{20 - x} + 8 = \sqrt{9 - x} + 11$$
$$\sqrt{20 - x} = \sqrt{9 - x} + 3 \qquad \text{Isolating one radical}$$
$$(\sqrt{20 - x})^2 = (\sqrt{9 - x} + 3)^2$$
$$20 - x = 9 - x + 6\sqrt{9 - x} + 9$$
$$2 = 6\sqrt{9 - x} \qquad \text{Isolating the remaining radical}$$
$$1 = 3\sqrt{9 - x} \qquad \text{Dividing by 2}$$
$$1^2 = (3\sqrt{9 - x})^2$$
$$1 = 9(9 - x)$$
$$1 = 81 - 9x$$
$$9x = 80$$
$$x = \frac{80}{9}$$

The number $\frac{80}{9}$ checks, so it is the solution.

37.
$$\sqrt{4y + 1} - \sqrt{y - 2} = 3$$
$$\sqrt{4y + 1} = 3 + \sqrt{y - 2} \qquad \text{Isolating one radical}$$

$$(\sqrt{4y + 1})^2 = (3 + \sqrt{y - 2})^2$$
$$4y + 1 = 9 + 6\sqrt{y - 2} + y - 2$$
$$3y - 6 = 6\sqrt{y - 2} \qquad \text{Isolating the remaining radical}$$
$$y - 2 = 2\sqrt{y - 2} \qquad \text{Multiplying by } \frac{1}{3}$$
$$(y - 2)^2 = (2\sqrt{y - 2})^2$$
$$y^2 - 4y + 4 = 4(y - 2)$$
$$y^2 - 4y + 4 = 4y - 8$$
$$y^2 - 8y + 12 = 0$$
$$(y - 6)(y - 2) = 0$$
$$y - 6 = 0 \ \ or \ \ y - 2 = 0$$
$$y = 6 \ \ or \qquad y = 2$$

The numbers 6 and 2 check, so they are the solutions.

39.
$$\sqrt{x + 2} + \sqrt{3x + 4} = 2$$
$$\sqrt{x + 2} = 2 - \sqrt{3x + 4} \qquad \text{Isolating one radical}$$
$$(\sqrt{x + 2})^2 = (2 - \sqrt{3x - 4})^2$$
$$x + 2 = 4 - 4\sqrt{3x + 4} + 3x + 4$$
$$-2x - 6 = -4\sqrt{3x + 4} \qquad \text{Isolating the remaining radical}$$
$$x + 3 = 2\sqrt{3x + 4} \qquad \text{Dividing by 2}$$
$$(x + 3)^2 = (2\sqrt{3x + 4})^2$$
$$x^2 + 6x + 9 = 4(3x + 4)$$
$$x^2 + 6x + 9 = 12x + 16$$
$$x^2 - 6x - 7 = 0$$
$$(x - 7)(x + 1) = 0$$
$$x - 7 = 0 \ \ or \ \ x + 1 = 0$$
$$x = 7 \ \ or \qquad x = -1$$

Check: For 7:

$$\frac{\sqrt{x+2}+\sqrt{3x+4}=2}{\sqrt{7+2}+\sqrt{3\cdot 7+4}\ ?\ 2}$$

$$\sqrt{9}+\sqrt{25}$$

$$8 \quad\bigg|\quad \text{FALSE}$$

Check: For -1:

$$\frac{\sqrt{x+2}+\sqrt{3x+4}=2}{\sqrt{-1+2}+\sqrt{3(-1)+4}\ ?\ 2}$$

$$\sqrt{1}+\sqrt{1}$$

$$2 \quad\bigg|\quad \text{TRUE}$$

Since -1 checks but 7 does not, the solution is -1.

41. $\sqrt{3x-5}+\sqrt{2x+3}+1=0$

$$\sqrt{3x-5}+1=-\sqrt{2x+3}$$

$$(\sqrt{3x-5}+1)^2=(-\sqrt{2x+3})^2$$

$$3x-5+2\sqrt{3x-5}+1=2x+3$$

$$2\sqrt{3x-5}=-x+7$$

$$(2\sqrt{3x-5})^2=(-x+7)^2$$

$$4(3x-5)=x^2-14x+49$$

$$12x-20=x^2-14x+49$$

$$0=x^2-26x+69$$

$$0=(x-23)(x-3)$$

$$x-23=0 \quad or \quad x-3=0$$

$$x=23 \quad or \quad x=3$$

Neither number checks. There is no solution. (At the outset we might have observed that there is no solution since the sum on the left side of the equation must be at least 1.)

43. $2\sqrt{t-1}-\sqrt{3t-1}=0$

$$2\sqrt{t-1}=\sqrt{3t-1}$$

$$(2\sqrt{t-1})^2=(\sqrt{3t-1})^2$$

$$4(t-1)=3t-1$$

$$4t-4=3t-1$$

$$t=3$$

Since 3 checks, it is the solution.

45. $V=3.5\sqrt{h}$

$$V=3.5\sqrt{9000}$$

$$V\approx 332$$

You can see about 332 km to the horizon at an altitude of 9000 m.

47.

$$V=3.5\sqrt{h}$$

$$50.4=3.5\sqrt{h}$$

$$(50.4)^2=(3.5\sqrt{h})^2$$

$$2540.16=12.25h$$

$$207.36=h$$

The altitude is 207.36 m.

49.

$$V=3.5\sqrt{h}$$

$$21=3.5\sqrt{h}$$

$$21^2=(3.5\sqrt{h})^2$$

$$441=12.25h$$

$$36=h$$

The height of the steeplejack's eyes is 36 m.

51. $V=3.5\sqrt{h}$

$$V=3.5\sqrt{37}$$

$$V\approx 21$$

The sailor can see about 21 km to the horizon.

53. At 55 mph: $\qquad r=2\sqrt{5L}$

$$55=2\sqrt{5L}$$

$$27.5=\sqrt{5L}$$

$$(27.5)^2=(\sqrt{5L})^2$$

$$756.25=5L$$

$$151.25=L$$

At 55 mph, a car will skid 151.25 ft.

At 75 mph: $\qquad r=2\sqrt{5L}$

$$75=2\sqrt{5L}$$

$$37.5=\sqrt{5L}$$

$$(37.5)^2=(\sqrt{5L})^2$$

$$1406.25=5L$$

$$281.25=L$$

At 75 mph, a car will skid 281.25 ft.

55.

$$S=21.9\sqrt{5t+2457}$$

$$1113=21.9\sqrt{5t+2457}$$

$$\frac{1113}{21.9}=\sqrt{5t+2457}$$

$$\left(\frac{1113}{21.9}\right)^2=(\sqrt{5t+2457})^2$$

$$2583\approx 5t+2457$$

$$126\approx 5t$$

$$25.2\approx t$$

The temperature was approximately $25°F$.

57.
$$T = 2\pi\sqrt{\frac{L}{32}}$$

$$1 = 2(3.14)\sqrt{\frac{L}{32}}$$

$$1 = 6.28\sqrt{\frac{L}{32}}$$

$$1^2 = \left(6.28\sqrt{\frac{L}{32}}\right)^2$$

$$1 = 39.4384 \cdot \frac{L}{32}$$

$$\frac{32}{39.4384} = L$$

$$0.81 \approx L$$

The pendulum is about 0.81 ft long.

59. Discussion and Writing Exercise

61. *Familiarize.* Let $t = $ the time it will take Julia and George to paint the room working together.

Translate. We use the work principle.
$$\frac{t}{a} + \frac{t}{b} = 1$$
$$\frac{t}{8} + \frac{t}{10} = 1$$

Solve. We first multiply by 40 to clear fractions.
$$40\left(\frac{t}{8} + \frac{t}{10}\right) = 40 \cdot 1$$
$$40 \cdot \frac{t}{8} + 40 \cdot \frac{t}{10} = 40$$
$$5t + 4t = 40$$
$$9t = 40$$
$$t = \frac{40}{9}, \text{ or } 4\frac{4}{9}$$

Check. In $\frac{40}{9}$ hr, Julia does $\frac{40}{9}\left(\frac{1}{8}\right)$, or $\frac{5}{9}$, of the job and George does $\frac{40}{9}\left(\frac{1}{10}\right)$, or $\frac{4}{9}$, of the job. Together they do $\frac{5}{9} + \frac{4}{9}$, or 1 entire job. The answer checks.

State. It will take them $4\frac{4}{9}$ hr to paint the room, working together.

63. *Familiarize.* Let $d = $ the distance the cyclist would travel in 56 days at the same rate.

Translate. We translate to a proportion.
$$\begin{array}{l} \text{Distance} \rightarrow \\ \text{Days} \rightarrow \end{array} \frac{702}{14} = \frac{d}{56} \begin{array}{l} \leftarrow \text{Distance} \\ \leftarrow \text{Days} \end{array}$$

Solve. We equate cross products.
$$\frac{702}{14} = \frac{d}{56}$$
$$702 \cdot 56 = 14 \cdot d$$
$$\frac{702 \cdot 56}{14} = d$$
$$2808 = d$$

Check. We substitute in the proportion and check cross products.
$$\frac{702}{14} = \frac{2808}{56}; \ 702 \cdot 56 = 39,312; \ 14 \cdot 2808 = 39,312$$
The cross products are the same, so the answer checks.

State. The cyclist would have traveled 2808 mi in 56 days.

65.
$$x^2 + 2.8x = 0$$
$$x(x + 2.8) = 0$$
$$x = 0 \ \text{ or } \ x + 2.8 = 0$$
$$x = 0 \ \text{ or } \qquad x = -2.8$$
The solutions are 0 and -2.8.

67.
$$x^2 - 64 = 0$$
$$(x + 8)(x - 8) = 0$$
$$x + 8 = 0 \ \text{ or } \ x - 8 = 0$$
$$x = -8 \ \text{ or } \qquad x = 8$$
The solutions are -8 and 8.

69. $f(x) = x^2$
$$\begin{aligned} f(a + h) - f(a) &= (a + h)^2 - a^2 \\ &= a^2 + 2ah + h^2 - a^2 \\ &= 2ah + h^2 \end{aligned}$$

71. $f(x) = 2x^2 - 3x$
$$\begin{aligned} &f(a + h) - f(a) \\ &= 2(a + h)^2 - 3(a + h) - (2a^2 - 3a) \\ &= 2(a^2 + 2ah + h^2) - 3a - 3h - 2a^2 + 3a \\ &= 2a^2 + 4ah + 2h^2 - 3a - 3h - 2a^2 + 3a \\ &= 4ah + 2h^2 - 3h \end{aligned}$$

73. Left to the student

75.
$$\sqrt[3]{\frac{z}{4}} - 10 = 2$$
$$\sqrt[3]{\frac{z}{4}} = 12$$
$$\left(\sqrt[3]{\frac{z}{4}}\right)^3 = 12^3$$
$$\frac{z}{4} = 1728$$
$$z = 6912$$

The number 6912 checks, so it is the solution.

77.
$$\sqrt{\sqrt{y+49}-\sqrt{y}} = \sqrt{7}$$
$$\left(\sqrt{\sqrt{y+49}-\sqrt{y}}\right)^2 = (\sqrt{7})^2$$
$$\sqrt{y+49}-\sqrt{y} = 7$$
$$\sqrt{y+49} = 7+\sqrt{y}$$
$$(\sqrt{y+49})^2 = (7+\sqrt{y})^2$$
$$y+49 = 49+14\sqrt{y}+y$$
$$0 = 14\sqrt{y}$$
$$0 = \sqrt{y}$$
$$0^2 = (\sqrt{y})^2$$
$$0 = y$$

The number 0 checks and is the solution.

79.
$$\sqrt{\sqrt{x^2+9x+34}} = 2$$
$$\left(\sqrt{\sqrt{x^2+9x+34}}\right)^2 = 2^2$$
$$\sqrt{x^2+9x+34} = 4$$
$$(\sqrt{x^2+9x+34})^2 = 4^2$$
$$x^2+9x+34 = 16$$
$$x^2+9x+18 = 0$$
$$(x+6)(x+3) = 0$$
$$x+6 = 0 \quad\text{or}\quad x+3 = 0$$
$$x = -6 \quad\text{or}\quad x = -3$$

Both values check. The solutions are -6 and -3.

81.
$$\sqrt{x-2}-\sqrt{x+2}+2 = 0$$
$$\sqrt{x-2}+2 = \sqrt{x+2}$$
$$(\sqrt{x-2}+2)^2 = (\sqrt{x+2})^2$$
$$(x-2)+4\sqrt{x-2}+4 = x+2$$
$$4\sqrt{x-2} = 0$$
$$\sqrt{x-2} = 0$$
$$(\sqrt{x-2})^2 = 0^2$$
$$x-2 = 0$$
$$x = 2$$

The number 2 checks, so it is the solution.

83.
$$\sqrt{a^2+30a} = a+\sqrt{5a}$$
$$(\sqrt{a^2+30a})^2 = (a+\sqrt{5a})^2$$
$$a^2+30a = a^2+2a\sqrt{5a}+5a$$
$$25a = 2a\sqrt{5a}$$
$$(25a)^2 = (2a\sqrt{5a})^2$$
$$625a^2 = 4a^2\cdot 5a$$
$$625a^2 = 20a^3$$
$$0 = 20a^3-625a^2$$
$$0 = 5a^2(4a-125)$$
$$5a^2 = 0 \quad\text{or}\quad 4a-125 = 0$$
$$a^2 = 0 \quad\text{or}\qquad 4a = 125$$
$$a = 0 \quad\text{or}\qquad a = \frac{125}{4}$$

Both values check. The solutions are 0 and $\frac{125}{4}$.

85.
$$\frac{x-1}{\sqrt{x^2+3x+6}} = \frac{1}{4},$$
$$\text{LCM} = 4\sqrt{x^2+3x+6}$$
$$4\sqrt{x^2+3x+6}\cdot\frac{x-1}{\sqrt{x^2+3x+6}} = 4\sqrt{x^2+3x+6}\cdot\frac{1}{4}$$
$$4x-4 = \sqrt{x^2+3x+6}$$
$$16x^2-32x+16 = x^2+3x+6$$
$$\text{Squaring both sides}$$
$$15x^2-35x+10 = 0$$
$$3x^2-7x+2 = 0 \qquad\text{Dividing by 5}$$
$$(3x-1)(x-2) = 0$$
$$3x-1 = 0 \quad\text{or}\quad x-2 = 0$$
$$3x = 1 \quad\text{or}\qquad x = 2$$
$$x = \frac{1}{3} \quad\text{or}\qquad x = 2$$

The number 2 checks but $\frac{1}{3}$ does not. The solution is 2.

87.
$$\sqrt{y^2+6}+y-3 = 0$$
$$\sqrt{y^2+6} = 3-y$$
$$(\sqrt{y^2+6})^2 = (3-y)^2$$
$$y^2+6 = 9-6y+y^2$$
$$-3 = -6y$$
$$\frac{1}{2} = y$$

The number $\frac{1}{2}$ checks and is the solution.

89.

$$\sqrt{y+1} - \sqrt{2y-5} = \sqrt{y-2}$$
$$(\sqrt{y+1} - \sqrt{2y-5})^2 = (\sqrt{y-2})^2$$
$$y+1 - 2\sqrt{(y+1)(2y-5)} + 2y - 5 = y - 2$$
$$-2\sqrt{2y^2 - 3y - 5} = -2y + 2$$
$$\sqrt{2y^2 - 3y - 5} = y - 1$$

Dividing by -2

$$(\sqrt{2y^2 - 3y - 5})^2 = (y-1)^2$$
$$2y^2 - 3y - 5 = y^2 - 2y + 1$$
$$y^2 - y - 6 = 0$$
$$(y-3)(y+2) = 0$$

$y - 3 = 0 \ \ or \ \ y + 2 = 0$

$y = 3 \ \ or \ \ \ \ \ \ y = -2$

The number 3 checks but -2 does not. The solution is 3.

Exercise Set 6.7

1. $a = 3, \quad b = 5$

Find c.

$c^2 = a^2 + b^2$ Pythagorean equation

$c^2 = 3^2 + 5^2$ Substituting

$c^2 = 9 + 25$

$c^2 = 34$

$c = \sqrt{34}$ Exact answer

$c \approx 5.831$ Approximation

3. $a = 15, \quad b = 15$

Find c.

$c^2 = a^2 + b^2$ Pythagorean equation

$c^2 = 15^2 + 15^2$ Substituting

$c^2 = 225 + 225$

$c^2 = 450$

$c = \sqrt{450}$ Exact answer

$c \approx 21.213$ Approximation

5. $b = 12, \quad c = 13$

Find a.

$a^2 + b^2 = c^2$ Pythagorean equation

$a^2 + 12^2 = 13^2$ Substituting

$a^2 + 144 = 169$

$a^2 = 25$

$a = 5$

7. $c = 7, \quad a = \sqrt{6}$

Find b.

$c^2 = a^2 + b^2$ Pythagorean equation

$7^2 = (\sqrt{6})^2 + b^2$ Substituting

$49 = 6 + b^2$

$43 = b^2$

$\sqrt{43} = b$ Exact answer

$6.557 \approx b$ Approximation

9. $b = 1, \quad c = \sqrt{13}$

Find a.

$a^2 + b^2 = c^2$ Pythagorean equation

$a^2 + 1^2 = (\sqrt{13})^2$ Substituting

$a^2 + 1 = 13$

$a^2 = 12$

$a = \sqrt{12}$ Exact answer

$a \approx 3.464$ Approximation

11. $a = 1, \quad c = \sqrt{n}$

Find b.

$a^2 + b^2 = c^2$

$1^2 + b^2 = (\sqrt{n})^2$

$1 + b^2 = n$

$b^2 = n - 1$

$b = \sqrt{n-1}$

13. We add labels to the drawing in the text. We let $h =$ the height of the bulge.

Note that 1 mi = 5280 ft, so 1 mi + 1 ft = 5280 + 1, or 5281 ft.

We use the Pythagorean equation to find h.

$$5281^2 = 5280^2 + h^2$$
$$27,888,961 = 27,878,400 + h^2$$
$$10,561 = h^2$$
$$\sqrt{10,561} = h$$
$$102.767 \approx h$$

The bulge is $\sqrt{10,561}$ ft, or about 102.767 ft high.

15. We add some labels to the drawing in the text.

Note that $d = s + 2x$. We use the Pythagorean equation to find x.

$$x^2 + x^2 = s^2$$
$$2x^2 = s^2$$
$$x^2 = \frac{s^2}{2}$$
$$x = \sqrt{\frac{s^2}{2}}$$
$$x = \frac{s}{\sqrt{2}}$$
$$x = \frac{s\sqrt{2}}{2} \quad \text{Rationalizing the denominator}$$

Then $d = s + 2x = s + 2\left(\dfrac{s\sqrt{2}}{2}\right) = s + s\sqrt{2}.$

17. We make a drawing and let d = the length of the guy wire.

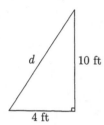

We use the Pythagorean equation to find d.
$$d^2 = 4^2 + 10^2$$
$$d^2 = 16 + 100$$
$$d^2 = 116$$
$$d = \sqrt{116}$$
$$d \approx 10.770$$

The wire is $\sqrt{116}$ ft, or about 10.770 ft long.

19.
$$L = \frac{0.000169d^{2.27}}{h}$$
$$L = \frac{0.000169(200)^{2.27}}{4}$$
$$\approx 7.1$$

The length of the letters should be about 7.1 ft.

21. We make a drawing. Let x = the width of the rectangle. Then $x + 1$ = the length.

We first find the length and width of the rectangle. Recall the formula for the area of a rectangle, $A = lw$. We substitute 90 for A, $x + 1$ for l, and x for w in this formula and solve for x.

$$90 = (x + 1)x$$
$$90 = x^2 + x$$
$$0 = x^2 + x - 90$$
$$0 = (x + 10)(x - 9)$$
$$x + 10 = 0 \quad \text{or} \quad x - 9 = 0$$
$$x = -10 \quad \text{or} \quad x = 9$$

Since the width cannot be negative, we know that the width is 9 cm. Thus the length is 10 cm. (These numbers check since 9 and 10 are consecutive integers and the area of a rectangle with width 9 cm and length 10 cm is $10 \cdot 9$, or 90 cm^2.)

Now we find the length of the diagonal of the rectangle. We make another drawing, letting d = the length of the diagonal.

We use the Pythagorean equation to find d.
$$d^2 = 9^2 + 10^2$$
$$d^2 = 81 + 100$$
$$d^2 = 181$$
$$d = \sqrt{181}$$
$$d \approx 13.454$$

The length of the diagonal is $\sqrt{181}$ cm, or about 13.454 cm.

23. We use the drawing in the text, replacing w with 16 in.

We use the Pythagorean equation to find h.
$$h^2 + 16^2 = 20^2$$
$$h^2 + 256 = 400$$
$$h^2 = 144$$
$$h = 12$$

The height is 12 in.

25. We first make a drawing. A point on the x-axis has coordinates $(x, 0)$ and is $|x|$ units from the origin.

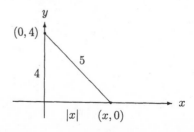

We use the Pythagorean equation to find x.

$$4^2 + |x|^2 = 5^2$$
$$16 + x^2 = 25 \quad |x|^2 = x^2$$
$$x^2 - 9 = 0 \quad \text{Subtracting 25}$$
$$(x + 3)(x - 3) = 0$$
$$x - 3 = 0 \quad \text{or} \quad x + 3 = 0$$
$$x = 3 \quad \text{or} \qquad x = -3$$

The points are $(3, 0)$ and $(-3, 0)$.

27. We make a drawing, letting $d =$ the distance the wire will run diagonally, disregarding the slack.

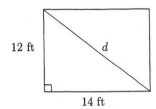

We use the Pythagorean equation to find d.

$$d^2 = 12^2 + 14^2$$
$$d^2 = 144 + 196$$
$$d^2 = 340$$
$$d = \sqrt{340}$$

Adding 4 ft of slack on each end, we find that a wire of length $\sqrt{340} + 4 + 4$, or $\sqrt{340} + 8$ ft should be purchased. This is approximately 26.439 ft of wire.

29. Referring to the drawing in the text, we let $t =$ the travel. Then we use the Pythagorean equation.

$$t^2 = (17.75)^2 + (10.25)^2$$
$$t^2 = 315.0625 + 105.0625$$
$$t^2 = 420.125$$
$$t = \sqrt{420.125}$$
$$t \approx 20.497$$

The travel is $\sqrt{420.125}$ in., or about 20.497 in.

31. Discussion and Writing Exercise

33. *Familiarize*. Let $r =$ the speed of the Carmel Crawler. Then $r + 14 =$ the speed of the Zionsville Flash. We organize the information in a table.

	Distance	Speed	Time
Crawler	230	r	t
Flash	290	$r + 14$	t

***Translate*.** Using the formula $t = d/r$ and noting that the times are the same, we have

$$\frac{230}{r} = \frac{290}{r + 14}.$$

***Solve*.** We first clear fractions by multiplying by the LCM of the denominators, $r(r + 14)$.

$$r(r + 14) \cdot \frac{230}{r} = r(r + 14) \cdot \frac{290}{r + 14}$$
$$230(r + 14) = 290r$$
$$230r + 3220 = 290r$$
$$3220 = 60r$$
$$\frac{161}{3} = r, \text{ or}$$
$$53\frac{2}{3} = r$$

If $r = 53\frac{2}{3}$, then $r + 14 = 67\frac{2}{3}$.

***Check*.** At $53\frac{2}{3}$, or $\frac{161}{3}$ mph, the Crawler travels 230 mi in $\frac{230}{161/3}$, or about 4.3 hr. At $67\frac{2}{3}$, or $\frac{203}{3}$ mph, the Flash travels 290 mi in $\frac{290}{203/3}$, or about 4.3 hr. Since the times are the same, the answer checks.

***State*.** The Carmel Crawler's speed is $53\frac{2}{3}$ mph, and the Zionsville Flash's speed is $67\frac{2}{3}$ mph.

35.
$$2x^2 + 11x - 21 = 0$$
$$(2x - 3)(x + 7) = 0$$
$$2x - 3 = 0 \quad \text{or} \quad x + 7 = 0$$
$$x = \frac{3}{2} \quad \text{or} \qquad x = -7$$

The solutions are $\frac{3}{2}$ and -7.

37.
$$\frac{x + 2}{x + 3} = \frac{x - 4}{x - 5},$$

LCM is $(x + 3)(x - 5)$

$$(x + 3)(x - 5) \cdot \frac{x + 2}{x + 3} = (x + 3)(x - 5) \cdot \frac{x - 4}{x - 5}$$
$$(x - 5)(x + 2) = (x + 3)(x - 4)$$
$$x^2 - 3x - 10 = x^2 - x - 12$$
$$-2x = -2$$
$$x = 1$$

The number 1 checks, so it is the solution.

39.
$$\frac{x - 5}{x - 7} = \frac{4}{3}, \text{ LCM is } 3(x - 7)$$
$$3(x - 7) \cdot \frac{x - 5}{x - 7} = 3(x - 7) \cdot \frac{4}{3}$$
$$3(x - 5) = 4(x - 7)$$
$$3x - 15 = 4x - 28$$
$$13 = x$$

The number 13 checks and is the solution.

41.

$c^2 = 6^2 + 12^2 = 36 + 144 = 180$

$c = \sqrt{180}$ ft

Area of the roof $= 2 \cdot \sqrt{180} \cdot 32 = 64\sqrt{180}$ ft^2

Number of packets $= \dfrac{64\sqrt{180}}{33\frac{1}{3}} \approx 26$

Kit should buy 26 packets of shingles.

43.

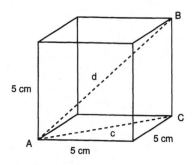

First find the length of a diagonal of the base of the cube. It is the hypotenuse of an isosceles right triangle with $a = 5$ cm. Then $c = a\sqrt{2} = 5\sqrt{2}$ cm.

Triangle ABC is a right triangle with legs of $5\sqrt{2}$ cm and 5 cm and hypotenuse d. Use the Pythagorean equation to find d, the length of the diagonal that connects two opposite corners of the cube.

$d^2 = (5\sqrt{2})^2 + 5^2$

$d^2 = 25 \cdot 2 + 25$

$d^2 = 50 + 25$

$d^2 = 75$

$d = \sqrt{75}$

Exact answer: $d = \sqrt{75}$ cm

Exercise Set 6.8

1. $\sqrt{-35} = \sqrt{-1 \cdot 35} = \sqrt{-1} \cdot \sqrt{35} = i\sqrt{35}$, or $\sqrt{35}i$

3. $\sqrt{-16} = \sqrt{-1 \cdot 16} = \sqrt{-1} \cdot \sqrt{16} = i \cdot 4 = 4i$

5. $-\sqrt{-12} = -\sqrt{-1 \cdot 12} = -\sqrt{-1} \cdot \sqrt{12} = -i \cdot 2\sqrt{3} = -2\sqrt{3}i$, or $-2i\sqrt{3}$

7. $\sqrt{-3} = \sqrt{-1 \cdot 3} = \sqrt{-1} \cdot \sqrt{3} = i\sqrt{3}$, or $\sqrt{3}i$

9. $\sqrt{-81} = \sqrt{-1 \cdot 81} = \sqrt{-1} \cdot \sqrt{81} = i \cdot 9 = 9i$

11. $\sqrt{-98} = \sqrt{-1 \cdot 98} = \sqrt{-1} \cdot \sqrt{98} = i \cdot 7\sqrt{2} = 7\sqrt{2}i$, or $7i\sqrt{2}$

13. $-\sqrt{-49} = -\sqrt{-1 \cdot 49} = -\sqrt{-1} \cdot \sqrt{49} = -i \cdot 7 = -7i$

15. $4 - \sqrt{-60} = 4 - \sqrt{-1 \cdot 60} = 4 - \sqrt{-1} \cdot \sqrt{60} = 4 - i \cdot 2\sqrt{15} = 4 - 2\sqrt{15}i$, or $4 - 2i\sqrt{15}$

17. $\sqrt{-4} + \sqrt{-12} = \sqrt{-1 \cdot 4} + \sqrt{-1 \cdot 12} = \sqrt{-1} \cdot \sqrt{4} + \sqrt{-1} \cdot \sqrt{12} = i \cdot 2 + i \cdot 2\sqrt{3} = (2 + 2\sqrt{3})i$

19. $\quad (7 + 2i) + (5 - 6i)$

$= (7 + 5) + (2 - 6)i \quad$ Collecting like terms

$= 12 - 4i$

21. $\quad (4 - 3i) + (5 - 2i)$

$= (4 + 5) + (-3 - 2)i \quad$ Collecting like terms

$= 9 - 5i$

23. $(9 - i) + (-2 + 5i) = (9 - 2) + (-1 + 5)i$

$= 7 + 4i$

25. $(6 - i) - (10 + 3i) = (6 - 10) + (-1 - 3)i$

$= -4 - 4i$

27. $(4 - 2i) - (5 - 3i) = (4 - 5) + [-2 - (-3)]i$

$= -1 + i$

29. $(9 + 5i) - (-2 - i) = [9 - (-2)] + [5 - (-1)]i$

$= 11 + 6i$

31. $\sqrt{-36} \cdot \sqrt{-9} = \sqrt{-1} \cdot \sqrt{36} \cdot \sqrt{-1} \cdot \sqrt{9}$

$= i \cdot 6 \cdot i \cdot 3$

$= i^2 \cdot 18$

$= -1 \cdot 18 \qquad i^2 = -1$

$= -18$

33. $\sqrt{-7} \cdot \sqrt{-2} = \sqrt{-1} \cdot \sqrt{7} \cdot \sqrt{-1} \cdot \sqrt{2}$

$= i \cdot \sqrt{7} \cdot i \cdot \sqrt{2}$

$= i^2(\sqrt{14})$

$= -1(\sqrt{14}) \qquad i^2 = -1$

$= -\sqrt{14}$

35. $-3i \cdot 7i = -21 \cdot i^2$

$= -21(-1) \qquad i^2 = -1$

$= 21$

37. $-3i(-8 - 2i) = -3i(-8) - 3i(-2i)$

$= 24i + 6i^2$

$= 24i + 6(-1) \qquad i^2 = -1$

$= 24i - 6$

$= -6 + 24i$

39. $(3 + 2i)(1 + i)$

$= 3 + 3i + 2i + 2i^2$ Using FOIL

$= 3 + 3i + 2i - 2$ $i^2 = -1$

$= 1 + 5i$

41. $(2 + 3i)(6 - 2i)$

$= 12 - 4i + 18i - 6i^2$ Using FOIL

$= 12 - 4i + 18i + 6$ $i^2 = -1$

$= 18 + 14i$

43. $(6 - 5i)(3 + 4i) = 18 + 24i - 15i - 20i^2$

$= 18 + 24i - 15i + 20$

$= 38 + 9i$

45. $(7 - 2i)(2 - 6i) = 14 - 42i - 4i + 12i^2$

$= 14 - 42i - 4i - 12$

$= 2 - 46i$

47. $(3 - 2i)^2 = 3^2 - 2 \cdot 3 \cdot 2i + (2i)^2$ Squaring a binomial

$= 9 - 12i + 4i^2$

$= 9 - 12i - 4$ $i^2 = -1$

$= 5 - 12i$

49. $(1 + 5i)^2$

$= 1^2 + 2 \cdot 1 \cdot 5i + (5i)^2$ Squaring a binomial

$= 1 + 10i + 25i^2$

$= 1 + 10i - 25$ $i^2 = -1$

$= -24 + 10i$

51. $(-2 + 3i)^2 = 4 - 12i + 9i^2 = 4 - 12i - 9 =$

$-5 - 12i$

53. $i^7 = i^6 \cdot i = (i^2)^3 \cdot i = (-1)^3 \cdot i = -1 \cdot i = -i$

55. $i^{24} = (i^2)^{12} = (-1)^{12} = 1$

57. $i^{42} = (i^2)^{21} = (-1)^{21} = -1$

59. $i^9 = (i^2)^4 \cdot i = (-1)^4 \cdot i = 1 \cdot i = i$

61. $i^6 = (i^2)^3 = (-1)^3 = -1$

63. $(5i)^3 = 5^3 \cdot i^3 = 125 \cdot i^2 \cdot i = 125(-1)(i) = -125i$

65. $7 + i^4 = 7 + (i^2)^2 = 7 + (-1)^2 = 7 + 1 = 8$

67. $i^{28} - 23i = (i^2)^{14} - 23i = (-1)^{14} - 23i = 1 - 23i$

69. $i^2 + i^4 = -1 + (i^2)^2 = -1 + (-1)^2 = -1 + 1 = 0$

71. $i^5 + i^7 = i^4 \cdot i + i^6 \cdot i = (i^2)^2 \cdot i + (i^2)^3 \cdot i =$

$(-1)^2 \cdot i + (-1)^3 \cdot i = 1 \cdot i + (-1)i = i - i = 0$

73. $1 + i + i^2 + i^3 + i^4 = 1 + i + i^2 + i^2 \cdot i + (i^2)^2$

$= 1 + i + (-1) + (-1) \cdot i + (-1)^2$

$= 1 + i - 1 - i + 1$

$= 1$

75. $5 - \sqrt{-64} = 5 - \sqrt{-1} \cdot \sqrt{64} = 5 - i \cdot 8 = 5 - 8i$

77. $\dfrac{8 - \sqrt{-24}}{4} = \dfrac{8 - \sqrt{-1} \cdot \sqrt{24}}{4} = \dfrac{8 - i \cdot 2\sqrt{6}}{4} =$

$\dfrac{2(4 - i\sqrt{6})}{2 \cdot 2} = \dfrac{\cancel{2}(4 - i\sqrt{6})}{\cancel{2} \cdot 2} = \dfrac{4 - i\sqrt{6}}{2} = 2 - \dfrac{\sqrt{6}}{2}i$

79. $\dfrac{4 + 3i}{3 - i} = \dfrac{4 + 3i}{3 - i} \cdot \dfrac{3 + i}{3 + i}$

$= \dfrac{(4 + 3i)(3 + i)}{(3 - i)(3 + i)}$

$= \dfrac{12 + 4i + 9i + 3i^2}{9 - i^2}$

$= \dfrac{12 + 13i - 3}{9 - (-1)}$

$= \dfrac{9 + 13i}{10}$

$= \dfrac{9}{10} + \dfrac{13}{10}i$

81. $\dfrac{3 - 2i}{2 + 3i} = \dfrac{3 - 2i}{2 + 3i} \cdot \dfrac{2 - 3i}{2 - 3i}$

$= \dfrac{(3 - 2i)(2 - 3i)}{(2 + 3i)(2 - 3i)}$

$= \dfrac{6 - 9i - 4i + 6i^2}{4 - 9i^2}$

$= \dfrac{6 - 13i - 6}{4 - 9(-1)}$

$= \dfrac{-13i}{13}$

$= -i$

83. $\dfrac{8 - 3i}{7i} = \dfrac{8 - 3i}{7i} \cdot \dfrac{-7i}{-7i}$

$= \dfrac{-56i + 21i^2}{-49i^2}$

$= \dfrac{-21 - 56i}{49}$

$= -\dfrac{21}{49} - \dfrac{56}{49}i$

$= -\dfrac{3}{7} - \dfrac{8}{7}i$

85. $\dfrac{4}{3 + i} = \dfrac{4}{3 + i} \cdot \dfrac{3 - i}{3 - i}$

$= \dfrac{12 - 4i}{9 - i^2}$

$= \dfrac{12 - 4i}{9 - (-1)}$

$= \dfrac{12 - 4i}{10}$

$= \dfrac{12}{10} - \dfrac{4}{10}i$

$= \dfrac{6}{5} - \dfrac{2}{5}i$

87.

$$\frac{2i}{5-4i} = \frac{2i}{5-4i} \cdot \frac{5+4i}{5+4i}$$

$$= \frac{10i+8i^2}{25-16i^2}$$

$$= \frac{10i+8(-1)}{25-16(-1)}$$

$$= \frac{-8+10i}{41}$$

$$= -\frac{8}{41} + \frac{10}{41}i$$

89.

$$\frac{4}{3i} = \frac{4}{3i} \cdot \frac{-3i}{-3i}$$

$$= \frac{-12i}{-9i^2}$$

$$= \frac{-12i}{-9(-1)}$$

$$= \frac{-12i}{9}$$

$$= -\frac{4}{3}i$$

91.

$$\frac{9-4i}{8i} = \frac{2-4i}{8i} \cdot \frac{-8i}{-8i}$$

$$= \frac{-16i+32i^2}{-64i^2}$$

$$= \frac{-16i+32(-1)}{-64(-1)}$$

$$= \frac{-32-16i}{64}$$

$$= -\frac{32}{64} - \frac{16}{64}i$$

$$= -\frac{1}{2} - \frac{1}{4}i$$

93.

$$\frac{6+3i}{6-3i} = \frac{6+3i}{6-3i} \cdot \frac{6+3i}{6+3i}$$

$$= \frac{36+18i+18i+9i^2}{36-9i^2}$$

$$= \frac{36+36i-9}{36-9(-1)}$$

$$= \frac{27+36i}{45}$$

$$= \frac{27}{45} + \frac{36}{45}i$$

$$= \frac{3}{5} + \frac{4}{5}i$$

95. Substitute $1-2i$ for x in the equation.

$$\frac{x^2 - 2x + 5 = 0}{(1-2i)^2 - 2(1-2i) + 5 \ ? \ 0}$$

$$1 - 4i + 4i^2 - 2 + 4i + 5 \ \Big|$$

$$1 - 4i - 4 - 2 + 4i + 5 \ \Big|$$

$$0 \ \Big| \quad \text{TRUE}$$

$1-2i$ is a solution.

97. Substitute $2+i$ for x in the equation.

$$\frac{x^2 - 4x - 5 = 0}{(2+i)^2 - 4(2+i) - 5 \ ? \ 0}$$

$$4 + 4i + i^2 - 8 - 4i - 5 \ \Big|$$

$$4 + 4i - 1 - 8 - 4i - 5 \ \Big|$$

$$-10 \ \Big| \quad \text{FALSE}$$

$2+i$ is not a solution.

99. Discussion and Writing Exercise

101.

$$\frac{196}{x^2 - 7x + 49} - \frac{2x}{x+7} = \frac{2058}{x^3 + 343}$$

Note: $x^3 + 343 = (x+7)(x^2 - 7x + 49)$.

The LCM $= (x+7)(x^2 - 7x + 49)$.

$$(x+7)(x^2 - 7x + 49)\left(\frac{196}{x^2 - 7x + 49} - \frac{2x}{x+7}\right) =$$

$$(x+7)(x^2 - 7x + 49) \cdot \frac{2058}{x^3 + 343}$$

$$196(x+7) - 2x(x^2 - 7x + 49) = 2058$$

$$196x + 1372 - 2x^3 + 14x^2 - 98x = 2058$$

$$98x - 686 - 2x^3 + 14x^2 = 0$$

$$49x - 343 - x^3 + 7x^2 = 0 \quad \text{Dividing by 2}$$

$$49(x-7) - x^2(x-7) = 0$$

$$(49 - x^2)(x-7) = 0$$

$$(7-x)(7+x)(x-7) = 0$$

$$7 - x = 0 \quad or \quad 7 + x = 0 \quad or \quad x - 7 = 0$$

$$7 = x \quad or \quad x = -7 \quad or \quad x = 7$$

Only 7 checks. It is the solution.

103. $|3x + 7| = 22$

$$3x + 7 = -22 \quad or \quad 3x + 7 = 22$$

$$3x = -29 \quad or \quad 3x = 15$$

$$x = -\frac{29}{3} \quad or \quad x = 5$$

The solutions are $-\frac{29}{3}$ and 5.

105. $|3x + 7| \geq 22$

$$3x + 7 \leq -22 \quad or \quad 3x + 7 \geq 22$$

$$3x \leq -29 \quad or \quad 3x \geq 15$$

$$x \leq -\frac{29}{3} \quad or \quad x \geq 5$$

The solution set is $\left\{x \Big| x \leq -\frac{29}{3} \ or \ x \geq 5\right\}$, or $\left(-\infty, -\frac{29}{3}\right] \cup [5, \infty)$.

107. $g(2i) = \dfrac{(2i)^4 - (2i)^2}{2i - 1} = \dfrac{16i^4 - 4i^2}{-1 + 2i} = \dfrac{20}{-1 + 2i} =$

$\dfrac{20}{-1 + 2i} \cdot \dfrac{-1 - 2i}{-1 - 2i} = \dfrac{-20 - 40i}{5} = -4 - 8i;$

$g(i + 1) = \dfrac{(i + 1)^4 - (i + 1)^2}{(i + 1) - 1} =$

$\dfrac{(i + 1)^2[(i + 1)^2 - 1]}{i} = \dfrac{2i(2i - 1)}{i} = 2(2i - 1) =$

$-2 + 4i;$

$g(2i - 1) = \dfrac{(2i - 1)^4 - (2i - 1)^2}{(2i - 1) - 1} =$

$\dfrac{(2i - 1)^2[(2i - 1)^2 - 1]}{2i - 2} = \dfrac{(-3 - 4i)(-4 - 4i)}{-2 + 2i} =$

$\dfrac{(-3 - 4i)(-2 - 2i)}{-1 + i} = \dfrac{-2 + 14i}{-1 + i} =$

$\dfrac{-2 + 14i}{-1 + i} \cdot \dfrac{-1 - i}{-1 - i} = \dfrac{16 - 12i}{2} = 8 - 6i$

109. $\dfrac{1}{8}\left(-24 - \sqrt{-1024}\right) = \dfrac{1}{8}(-24 - 32i) = -3 - 4i$

111. $7\sqrt{-64} - 9\sqrt{-256} = 7 \cdot 8i - 9 \cdot 16i = 56i - 144i = -88i$

113. $(1 - i)^3(1 + i)^3 =$

$(1 - i)(1 + i) \cdot (1 - i)(1 + i) \cdot (1 - i)(1 + i) =$

$(1 - i^2)(1 - i^2)(1 - i^2) = (1 + 1)(1 + 1)(1 + 1) =$

$2 \cdot 2 \cdot 2 = 8$

115. $\dfrac{6}{1 + \dfrac{3}{i}} = \dfrac{6}{\dfrac{i + 3}{i}} = \dfrac{6i}{i + 3} = \dfrac{6i}{i + 3} \cdot \dfrac{-i + 3}{-i + 3} =$

$\dfrac{-6i^2 + 18i}{-i^2 + 9} = \dfrac{6 + 18i}{10} = \dfrac{6}{10} + \dfrac{18}{10}i = \dfrac{3}{5} + \dfrac{9}{5}i$

117. $\dfrac{i - i^{38}}{1 + i} = \dfrac{i - (i^2)^{19}}{1 + i} = \dfrac{i - (-1)^{19}}{1 + i} = \dfrac{i - (-1)}{1 + i} =$

$\dfrac{i + 1}{1 + i} = 1$

Chapter 7

Quadratic Equations and Functions

Exercise Set 7.1

1. a) $6x^2 = 30$

$\quad\quad x^2 = 5$ Dividing by 6

$\quad x = \sqrt{5}$ or $x = -\sqrt{5}$ Principle of square roots

Check: $\quad\quad\dfrac{6x^2 = 30}{6(\pm\sqrt{5})\;?\;30}$
$\quad\quad\quad\quad\quad\; 6\cdot 5$
$\quad\quad\quad\quad\quad\;\; 30 \quad\quad\mid\quad$ TRUE

The solutions are $\sqrt{5}$ and $-\sqrt{5}$, or $\pm\sqrt{5}$.

b) The real-number solutions of the equation $6x^2 = 30$ are the first coordinates of the x-intercepts of the graph of $f(x) = 6x^2 - 30$. Thus, the x-intercepts are $(-\sqrt{5}, 0)$ and $(\sqrt{5}, 0)$.

3. a) $9x^2 + 25 = 0$

$\quad\quad 9x^2 = -25$ Subtracting 25

$\quad\quad x^2 = -\dfrac{25}{9}$ Dividing by 9

$\quad x = \sqrt{-\dfrac{25}{9}}$ or $x = -\sqrt{-\dfrac{25}{9}}$ Principle of square roots

$\quad x = \dfrac{5}{3}i$ or $\quad x = -\dfrac{5}{3}i$ Simplifying

Check: $\quad\quad\dfrac{9x^2 + 25 = 0}{9\left(\pm\dfrac{5}{3}i\right) + 25\;?\;0}$

$\quad\quad\quad 9\left(-\dfrac{25}{9}\right) + 25$

$\quad\quad\quad\quad -25 + 25$

$\quad\quad\quad\quad\quad\quad 0 \quad\mid\quad$ TRUE

The solutions are $\dfrac{5}{3}i$ and $-\dfrac{5}{3}i$, or $\pm\dfrac{5}{3}i$.

b) Since the equation $9x^2 + 25 = 0$ has no real-number solutions, the graph of $f(x) = 9x^2 + 25$ has no x-intercepts.

5. $\quad 2x^2 - 3 = 0$

$\quad\quad 2x^2 = 3$

$\quad\quad x^2 = \dfrac{3}{2}$

$\quad x = \sqrt{\dfrac{3}{2}}$ or $\;x = -\sqrt{\dfrac{3}{2}}$ Principle of square roots

$\quad x = \sqrt{\dfrac{3}{2}\cdot\dfrac{2}{2}}$ or $\;x = -\sqrt{\dfrac{3}{2}\cdot\dfrac{2}{2}}$ Rationalizing denominators

$\quad x = \dfrac{\sqrt{6}}{2}$ or $\;x = -\dfrac{\sqrt{6}}{2}$

Check: $\quad\quad\dfrac{2x^2 - 3 = 0}{2\left(\pm\dfrac{\sqrt{6}}{2}\right)^2 - 3\;?\;0}$

$\quad\quad\quad 2\cdot\dfrac{6}{4} - 3$

$\quad\quad\quad\quad 3 - 3$

$\quad\quad\quad\quad\quad 0 \quad\mid\quad$ TRUE

The solutions are $\dfrac{\sqrt{6}}{2}$ and $-\dfrac{\sqrt{6}}{2}$, or $\pm\dfrac{\sqrt{6}}{2}$. Using a calculator, we find that the solutions are approximately ± 1.225.

7. $(x + 2)^2 = 49$

$\quad x + 2 = 7$ or $\;x + 2 = -7$ Principle of square roots

$\quad\quad x = 5$ or $\quad\quad x = -9$

The solutions are 5 and -9.

9. $(x - 4)^2 = 16$

$\quad x - 4 = 4$ or $\;x - 4 = -4$ Principle of square roots

$\quad\quad x = 8$ or $\quad\quad x = 0$

The solutions are 8 and 0.

11. $(x - 11)^2 = 7$

$\quad x - 11 = \sqrt{7}$ or $\;x - 11 = -\sqrt{7}$

$\quad\quad x = 11 + \sqrt{7}$ or $\quad\quad x = 11 - \sqrt{7}$

The solutions are $11 + \sqrt{7}$ and $11 - \sqrt{7}$, or $11 \pm \sqrt{7}$. Using a calculator, we find that the solutions are approximately 8.354 and 13.646.

13. $(x - 7)^2 = -4$

$\quad x - 7 = \sqrt{-4}$ or $\;x - 7 = -\sqrt{-4}$

$\quad x - 7 = 2i$ or $\;x - 7 = -2i$

$\quad\quad x = 7 + 2i$ or $\quad\quad x = 7 - 2i$

The solutions are $7 + 2i$ and $7 - 2i$, or $7 \pm 2i$.

15. $(x - 9)^2 = 81$

$\quad x - 9 = 9$ or $\;x - 9 = -9$

$\quad\quad x = 18$ or $\quad\quad x = 0$

The solutions are 18 and 0.

17. $\left(x - \dfrac{3}{2}\right)^2 = \dfrac{7}{2}$

$\quad x - \dfrac{3}{2} = \sqrt{\dfrac{7}{2}} \qquad or \quad x - \dfrac{3}{2} = -\sqrt{\dfrac{7}{2}}$

$\quad x - \dfrac{3}{2} = \sqrt{\dfrac{7}{2} \cdot \dfrac{2}{2}} \quad or \quad x - \dfrac{3}{2} = -\sqrt{\dfrac{7}{2} \cdot \dfrac{2}{2}}$

$\quad x - \dfrac{3}{2} = \dfrac{\sqrt{14}}{2} \qquad or \quad x - \dfrac{3}{2} = -\dfrac{\sqrt{14}}{2}$

$\qquad x = \dfrac{3}{2} + \dfrac{\sqrt{14}}{2} \quad or \qquad x = \dfrac{3}{2} - \dfrac{\sqrt{14}}{2}$

$\qquad x = \dfrac{3 + \sqrt{14}}{2} \quad or \qquad x = \dfrac{3 - \sqrt{14}}{2}$

The solutions are $\dfrac{3 + \sqrt{14}}{2}$ and $\dfrac{3 - \sqrt{14}}{2}$, or $\dfrac{3 \pm \sqrt{14}}{2}$. Using a calculator, we find that the solutions are approximately -0.371 and 3.371.

19. $x^2 + 6x + 9 = 64$

$\quad (x + 3)^2 = 64$

$\quad x + 3 = 8 \ \ or \ \ x + 3 = -8$

$\qquad x = 5 \ \ or \qquad x = -11$

The solutions are 5 and -11.

21. $y^2 - 14y + 49 = 4$

$\quad (y - 7)^2 = 4$

$\quad y - 7 = 2 \ \ or \ \ y - 7 = -2$

$\qquad y = 9 \ \ or \qquad y = 5$

The solutions are 9 and 5.

23. $x^2 + 4x \quad = 2 \qquad$ Original equation

$\quad x^2 + 4x + 4 = 2 + 4 \quad$ Adding 4: $\left(\dfrac{4}{2}\right)^2 = 2^2 = 4$

$\qquad (x + 2)^2 = 6$

$\quad x + 2 = \sqrt{6} \qquad or \ \ x + 2 = -\sqrt{6} \qquad$ Principle of square roots

$\qquad x = -2 + \sqrt{6} \ \ or \qquad x = -2 - \sqrt{6}$

The solutions are $-2 \pm \sqrt{6}$.

25. $x^2 - 22x \qquad = 11 \qquad$ Original equation

$\quad x^2 - 22x + 121 = 11 + 121 \quad$ Adding 121: $\left(\dfrac{-22}{2}\right)^2 =$

$\qquad (x - 11)^2 = 132 \qquad\qquad (-11)^2 = 121$

$\quad x - 11 = \sqrt{132} \qquad or \ \ x - 11 = -\sqrt{132}$

$\quad x - 11 = 2\sqrt{33} \qquad or \ \ x - 11 = -2\sqrt{33}$

$\qquad x = 11 + 2\sqrt{33} \ \ or \qquad x = 11 - 2\sqrt{33}$

The solutions are $11 \pm 2\sqrt{33}$.

27. $x^2 + x \qquad = 1$

$\quad x^2 + x + \dfrac{1}{4} = 1 + \dfrac{1}{4} \quad$ Adding $\dfrac{1}{4}$: $\left(\dfrac{1}{2}\right)^2 = \dfrac{1}{4}$

$\qquad \left(x + \dfrac{1}{2}\right)^2 = \dfrac{5}{4}$

$\quad x + \dfrac{1}{2} = \dfrac{\sqrt{5}}{2} \qquad or \ \ x + \dfrac{1}{2} = -\dfrac{\sqrt{5}}{2}$

$\qquad x = \dfrac{-1 + \sqrt{5}}{2} \quad or \qquad x = \dfrac{-1 - \sqrt{5}}{2}$

The solutions are $\dfrac{-1 \pm \sqrt{5}}{2}$.

29. $t^2 - 5t \qquad = 7$

$\quad t^2 - 5t + \dfrac{25}{4} = 7 + \dfrac{25}{4} \quad$ Adding $\dfrac{25}{4}$: $\left(\dfrac{-5}{2}\right)^2 = \dfrac{25}{4}$

$\qquad \left(t - \dfrac{5}{2}\right)^2 = \dfrac{53}{4}$

$\quad t - \dfrac{5}{2} = \dfrac{\sqrt{53}}{2} \qquad or \ \ t - \dfrac{5}{2} = -\dfrac{\sqrt{53}}{2}$

$\qquad t = \dfrac{5 + \sqrt{53}}{2} \quad or \qquad t = \dfrac{5 - \sqrt{53}}{2}$

The solutions are $\dfrac{5 \pm \sqrt{53}}{2}$.

31. $x^2 + \dfrac{3}{2}x \qquad = 3$

$\quad x^2 + \dfrac{3}{2}x + \dfrac{9}{16} = 3 + \dfrac{9}{16} \quad \left(\dfrac{1}{2} \cdot \dfrac{3}{2}\right)^2 = \left(\dfrac{3}{4}\right)^2 = \dfrac{9}{16}$

$\qquad \left(x + \dfrac{3}{4}\right)^2 = \dfrac{57}{16}$

$\quad x + \dfrac{3}{4} = \dfrac{\sqrt{57}}{4} \qquad or \ \ x + \dfrac{3}{4} = -\dfrac{\sqrt{57}}{4}$

$\qquad x = \dfrac{-3 + \sqrt{57}}{4} \quad or \qquad x = \dfrac{-3 - \sqrt{57}}{4}$

The solutions are $\dfrac{-3 \pm \sqrt{57}}{4}$.

33. $m^2 - \dfrac{9}{2}m \qquad = \dfrac{3}{2} \qquad$ Original equation

$\quad m^2 - \dfrac{9}{2}m + \dfrac{81}{16} = \dfrac{3}{2} + \dfrac{81}{16} \quad \left[\dfrac{1}{2}\left(-\dfrac{9}{2}\right)\right]^2 = \left(-\dfrac{9}{4}\right)^2 = \dfrac{81}{16}$

$\qquad \left(m - \dfrac{9}{4}\right)^2 = \dfrac{105}{16}$

$\quad m - \dfrac{9}{4} = \dfrac{\sqrt{105}}{4} \qquad or \ \ m - \dfrac{9}{4} = -\dfrac{\sqrt{105}}{4}$

$\qquad m = \dfrac{9 + \sqrt{105}}{4} \quad or \qquad m = \dfrac{9 - \sqrt{105}}{4}$

The solutions are $\dfrac{9 \pm \sqrt{105}}{4}$.

35. $x^2 + 6x - 16 = 0$

$\quad x^2 + 6x \qquad = 16 \qquad$ Adding 16

$\quad x^2 + 6x + 9 = 16 + 9 \qquad \left(\dfrac{6}{2}\right)^2 = 3^2 = 9$

$\qquad (x + 3)^2 = 25$

$\quad x + 3 = 5 \ \ or \ \ x + 3 = -5$

$\qquad x = 2 \ \ or \qquad x = -8$

The solutions are 2 and -8.

37. $x^2 + 22x + 102 = 0$

$x^2 + 22x \qquad = -102 \qquad$ Subtracting 102

$x^2 + 22x + 121 = -102 + 121 \qquad \left(\dfrac{22}{2}\right)^2 = 11^2 = 121$

$(x + 11)^2 = 19$

$x + 11 = \sqrt{19} \qquad or \quad x + 11 = -\sqrt{19}$

$\qquad x = -11 + \sqrt{19} \quad or \qquad x = -11 - \sqrt{19}$

The solutions are $-11 \pm \sqrt{19}$.

39. $x^2 - 10x - 4 = 0$

$x^2 - 10x \qquad = 4 \qquad\qquad$ Adding 4

$x^2 - 10x + 25 = 4 + 25 \qquad \left(\dfrac{-10}{2}\right)^2 = (-5)^2 = 25$

$(x - 5)^2 = 29$

$x - 5 = \sqrt{29} \qquad or \quad x - 5 = -\sqrt{29}$

$\qquad x = 5 + \sqrt{29} \quad or \qquad x = 5 - \sqrt{29}$

The solutions are $5 \pm \sqrt{29}$.

41. a) $x^2 + 7x - 2 = 0$

$x^2 + 7x \qquad = 2 \qquad\qquad$ Adding 2

$x^2 + 7x + \dfrac{49}{4} = 2 + \dfrac{49}{4} \qquad \left(\dfrac{7}{2}\right)^2 = \dfrac{49}{4}$

$\left(x + \dfrac{7}{2}\right)^2 = \dfrac{57}{4}$

$x + \dfrac{7}{2} = \dfrac{\sqrt{57}}{2} \qquad or \quad x + \dfrac{7}{2} = -\dfrac{\sqrt{57}}{2}$

$\qquad x = \dfrac{-7 + \sqrt{57}}{2} \quad or \qquad x = \dfrac{-7 - \sqrt{57}}{2}$

The solutions are $\dfrac{-7 \pm \sqrt{57}}{2}$.

b) The real-number solutions of the equation $x^2 + 7x - 2 = 0$ are the first coordinates of the x-intercepts of the graph of $f(x) = x^2 + 7x - 2$. Thus, the x-intercepts are $\left(\dfrac{-7 - \sqrt{57}}{2}, 0\right)$ and $\left(\dfrac{-7 + \sqrt{57}}{2}, 0\right)$.

43. a) $\qquad 2x^2 - 5x + 8 = 0$

$\dfrac{1}{2}(2x^2 - 5x + 8) = \dfrac{1}{2} \cdot 0 \qquad$ Multiplying by $\dfrac{1}{2}$ to make the x^2-coefficient 1

$x^2 - \dfrac{5}{2}x + 4 = 0$

$x^2 - \dfrac{5}{2}x \qquad = -4 \qquad$ Subtracting 4

$x^2 - \dfrac{5}{2}x + \dfrac{25}{16} = -4 + \dfrac{25}{16}$

$\left[\dfrac{1}{2}\left(-\dfrac{5}{2}\right)\right]^2 = \left(-\dfrac{5}{4}\right)^2 = \dfrac{25}{16}$

$\left(x - \dfrac{5}{4}\right)^2 = -\dfrac{64}{16} + \dfrac{25}{16}$

$\left(x - \dfrac{5}{4}\right)^2 = -\dfrac{39}{16}$

$x - \dfrac{5}{4} = \sqrt{-\dfrac{39}{16}} \qquad or \quad x - \dfrac{5}{4} = -\sqrt{-\dfrac{39}{16}}$

$x - \dfrac{5}{4} = i\sqrt{\dfrac{39}{16}} \qquad or \quad x - \dfrac{5}{4} = -i\sqrt{\dfrac{39}{16}}$

$x = \dfrac{5}{4} + i\dfrac{\sqrt{39}}{4} \qquad or \qquad x = \dfrac{5}{4} - i\dfrac{\sqrt{39}}{4}$

The solutions are $\dfrac{5}{4} \pm i\dfrac{\sqrt{39}}{4}$.

b) Since the equation $2x^2 - 5x + 8 = 0$ has no real-number solutions, the graph of $f(x) = 2x^2 - 5x + 8$ has no x-intercepts.

45. $x^2 - \dfrac{3}{2}x - \dfrac{1}{2} = 0$

$x^2 - \dfrac{3}{2}x \qquad = \dfrac{1}{2}$

$x^2 - \dfrac{3}{2}x + \dfrac{9}{16} = \dfrac{1}{2} + \dfrac{9}{16} \qquad \left[\dfrac{1}{2}\left(-\dfrac{3}{2}\right)\right]^2 = \left(-\dfrac{3}{4}\right)^2 = \dfrac{9}{16}$

$\left(x - \dfrac{3}{4}\right)^2 = \dfrac{17}{16}$

$x - \dfrac{3}{4} = \dfrac{\sqrt{17}}{4} \qquad or \quad x - \dfrac{3}{4} = -\dfrac{\sqrt{17}}{4}$

$x = \dfrac{3 + \sqrt{17}}{4} \qquad or \qquad x = \dfrac{3 - \sqrt{17}}{4}$

The solutions are $\dfrac{3 \pm \sqrt{17}}{4}$.

47. $2x^2 - 3x - 17 = 0$

$\frac{1}{2}(2x^2 - 3x - 17) = \frac{1}{2} \cdot 0$ Multiplying by $\frac{1}{2}$ to make the x^2-coefficient 1

$x^2 - \frac{3}{2}x - \frac{17}{2} = 0$

$x^2 - \frac{3}{2}x \qquad = \frac{17}{2}$ Adding $\frac{17}{2}$

$x^2 - \frac{3}{2}x + \frac{9}{16} = \frac{17}{2} + \frac{9}{16}$ $\left[\frac{1}{2}\left(-\frac{3}{2}\right)\right]^2 =$

$\left(-\frac{3}{4}\right)^2 = \frac{9}{16}$

$\left(x - \frac{3}{4}\right)^2 = \frac{145}{16}$

$x - \frac{3}{4} = \frac{\sqrt{145}}{4}$ or $x - \frac{3}{4} = -\frac{\sqrt{145}}{4}$

$x = \frac{3 + \sqrt{145}}{4}$ or $x = \frac{3 - \sqrt{145}}{4}$

The solutions are $\frac{3 \pm \sqrt{145}}{4}$.

49. $3x^2 - 4x - 1 = 0$

$\frac{1}{3}(3x^2 - 4x - 1) = \frac{1}{3} \cdot 0$ Multiplying to make the x^2-coefficient 1

$x^2 - \frac{4}{3}x - \frac{1}{3} = 0$

$x^2 - \frac{4}{3}x \qquad = \frac{1}{3}$ Adding $\frac{1}{3}$

$x^2 - \frac{4}{3}x + \frac{4}{9} = \frac{1}{3} + \frac{4}{9}$ $\left[\frac{1}{2}\left(-\frac{4}{3}\right)\right]^2 =$

$\left(-\frac{2}{3}\right)^2 = \frac{4}{9}$

$\left(x - \frac{2}{3}\right)^2 = \frac{7}{9}$

$x - \frac{2}{3} = \frac{\sqrt{7}}{3}$ or $x - \frac{2}{3} = -\frac{\sqrt{7}}{3}$

$x = \frac{2 + \sqrt{7}}{3}$ or $x = \frac{2 - \sqrt{7}}{3}$

The solutions are $\frac{2 \pm \sqrt{7}}{3}$.

51. $x^2 + x + 2 = 0$

$x^2 + x \qquad = -2$ Subtracting 2

$x^2 + x + \frac{1}{4} = -2 + \frac{1}{4}$ $\left(\frac{1}{2}\right)^2 = \frac{1}{4}$

$\left(x + \frac{1}{2}\right)^2 = -\frac{7}{4}$

$x + \frac{1}{2} = \sqrt{-\frac{7}{4}}$ or $x + \frac{1}{2} = -\sqrt{-\frac{7}{4}}$

$x + \frac{1}{2} = i\sqrt{\frac{7}{4}}$ or $x + \frac{1}{2} = -i\sqrt{\frac{7}{4}}$

$x = -\frac{1}{2} + i\frac{\sqrt{7}}{2}$ or $x = -\frac{1}{2} - i\frac{\sqrt{7}}{2}$

The solutions are $-\frac{1}{2} \pm i\frac{\sqrt{7}}{2}$.

53. $x^2 - 4x + 13 = 0$

$x^2 - 4x \qquad = -13$ Subtracting 13

$x^2 - 4x + 4 = -13 + 4$ $\left(\frac{-4}{2}\right)^2 = (-2)^2 = 4$

$(x - 2)^2 = -9$

$x - 2 = \sqrt{-9}$ or $x - 2 = -\sqrt{-9}$

$x - 2 = 3i$ or $x - 2 = -3i$

$x = 2 + 3i$ or $x = 2 - 3i$

The solutions are $2 \pm 3i$.

55. $V = 48T^2$

$36 = 48T^2$ Substituting 36 for V

$\frac{36}{48} = T^2$ Solving for T^2

$0.75 = T^2$

$\sqrt{0.75} = T$

$0.866 \approx T$

The hang time is 0.866 sec.

57. $s(t) = 16t^2$

$850 = 16t^2$ Substituting 850 for $s(t)$

$\frac{850}{16} = t^2$ Solving for t^2

$53.125 = t^2$

$\sqrt{53.125} = t$

$7.3 \approx t$

It will take about 7.3 sec for an object to fall from the top.

59. $s(t) = 16t^2$

$745 = 16t^2$ Substituting 745 for $s(t)$

$\frac{745}{16} = t^2$ Solving for t^2

$46.5625 = t^2$

$\sqrt{46.5625} = t$

$6.8 \approx t$

It will take about 6.8 sec for an object to fall from the top.

61. Discussion and Writing Exercise

63. a) First find the slope.

$m = \frac{410 - 275}{5 - 1} = \frac{135}{4} = 33.75$

Now find the function. We substitute in the point-slope equation, using the point $(1, 275)$.

$T - T_1 = m(t - t_1)$

$T - 275 = 33.75(t - 1)$

$T - 275 = 33.75t - 33.75$

$T = 33.75t + 241.25$

Using the function notation we have $T(t) = 33.75t + 241.25$.

b) Since $2005 - 1995 = 10$, the year 2005 is 10 years since 1995. We find $T(10)$.

$$T(t) = 33.75t + 241.25$$
$$T(10) = 33.75(10) + 241.25$$
$$= 337.5 + 241.25$$
$$= 578.75$$

In 2005 about 578.75 thousand, or 578,750 people, will visit a doctor for tattoo removal.

c) Since $1,085,000 = 1085$ thousand, we substitute 1085 for $T(t)$ and solve for t.

$$T(t) = 33.75t + 241.25$$
$$1085 = 33.75t + 241.25$$
$$843.75 = 33.75t$$
$$25 = t$$

1,085,000 people will visit a doctor for tattoo removal 25 yr after 1995, or in 2020.

65. Graph $f(x) = 5 - 2x$

We find some ordered pairs $(x, f(x))$, plot them, and draw the graph.

x	$f(x)$	$(x, f(x))$
0	5	$(0, 5)$
1	3	$(1, 3)$
3	-1	$(3, -1)$
5	-5	$(5, -5)$

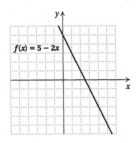

67. Graph $f(x) = |5 - 2x|$

We find some ordered pairs $(x, f(x))$, plot them, and draw the graph.

x	$f(x)$	$(x, f(x))$
0	5	$(0, 5)$
1	3	$(1, 3)$
$\frac{5}{2}$	0	$\left(\frac{5}{2}, 0\right)$
3	1	$(3, 1)$
5	5	$(5, 5)$

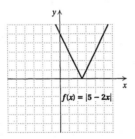

69. $\sqrt{\dfrac{2}{5}} = \sqrt{\dfrac{2}{5} \cdot \dfrac{5}{5}} = \sqrt{\dfrac{10}{25}} = \dfrac{\sqrt{10}}{\sqrt{25}} = \dfrac{\sqrt{10}}{5}$

71. Left to the student

73. In order for $x^2 + bx + 64$ to be a trinomial square, the following must be true:

$$\left(\frac{b}{2}\right)^2 = 64$$
$$\frac{b^2}{4} = 64$$
$$b^2 = 256$$
$$b = 16 \ \ or \ \ b = -16$$

75. $x(2x^2 + 9x - 56)(3x + 10) = 0$

$$x(2x - 7)(x + 8)(3x + 10) = 0$$

$x=0$ or $2x - 7=0$ or $x + 8=0$ or $3x + 10=0$

$x=0$ or $\quad x=\dfrac{7}{2}$ or $\quad x=-8$ or $\quad x=-\dfrac{10}{3}$

The solutions are -8, $-\dfrac{10}{3}$, 0, and $\dfrac{7}{2}$.

Exercise Set 7.2

1. $x^2 + 6x + 4 = 0$

$a = 1, \ b = 6, \ c = 4$

$$x = \frac{-b \pm \sqrt{b^2 - 4ac}}{2a}$$

$$x = \frac{-6 \pm \sqrt{6^2 - 4 \cdot 1 \cdot 4}}{2 \cdot 1} = \frac{-6 \pm \sqrt{36 - 16}}{2}$$

$$x = \frac{-6 \pm \sqrt{20}}{2} = \frac{-6 \pm 2\sqrt{5}}{2}$$

$$x = \frac{2(-3 \pm \sqrt{5})}{2} = -3 \pm \sqrt{5}$$

The solutions are $-3 + \sqrt{5}$ and $-3 - \sqrt{5}$.

3. $\qquad 3p^2 = -8p - 1$

$3p^2 + 8p + 1 = 0 \qquad$ Finding standard form

$a = 3, \ b = 8, \ c = 1$

$$p = \frac{-b \pm \sqrt{b^2 - 4ac}}{2a}$$

$$p = \frac{-8 \pm \sqrt{8^2 - 4 \cdot 3 \cdot 1}}{2 \cdot 3} = \frac{-8 \pm \sqrt{64 - 12}}{6}$$

$$x = \frac{-8 \pm \sqrt{52}}{6} = \frac{-8 \pm 2\sqrt{13}}{6}$$

$$x = \frac{2(-4 \pm \sqrt{13})}{2 \cdot 3} = \frac{-4 \pm \sqrt{13}}{3}$$

The solutions are $\dfrac{-4 + \sqrt{13}}{3}$ and $\dfrac{-4 - \sqrt{13}}{3}$.

5. $x^2 - x + 1 = 0$

$a = 1, \ b = -1, \ c = 1$

$$x = \frac{-(-1) \pm \sqrt{(-1)^2 - 4 \cdot 1 \cdot 1}}{2 \cdot 1} = \frac{1 \pm \sqrt{1 - 4}}{2}$$

$$x = \frac{1 \pm \sqrt{-3}}{2} = \frac{1 \pm i\sqrt{3}}{2} = \frac{1}{2} \pm i\frac{\sqrt{3}}{2}$$

The solutions are $\dfrac{1}{2} + i\dfrac{\sqrt{3}}{2}$ and $\dfrac{1}{2} - i\dfrac{\sqrt{3}}{2}$.

7. $\qquad x^2 + 13 = 4x$

$x^2 - 4x + 13 = 0 \qquad$ Finding standard form

$a = 1, \ b = -4, \ c = 13$

$$x = \frac{-(-4) \pm \sqrt{(-4)^2 - 4 \cdot 1 \cdot 13}}{2 \cdot 1} = \frac{4 \pm \sqrt{16 - 52}}{2}$$

$$x = \frac{4 \pm \sqrt{-36}}{2} = \frac{4 \pm 6i}{2} = 2 \pm 3i$$

The solutions are $2 + 3i$ and $2 - 3i$.

9. $r^2 + 3r = 8$

     $r^2 + 3r - 8 = 0$ Finding standard form

     $a = 1,\ b = 3,\ c = -8$

$$r = \frac{-3 \pm \sqrt{3^2 - 4 \cdot 1 \cdot (-8)}}{2 \cdot 1} = \frac{-3 \pm \sqrt{9 + 32}}{2}$$

$$r = \frac{-3 \pm \sqrt{41}}{2}$$

The solutions are $\dfrac{-3 + \sqrt{41}}{2}$ and $\dfrac{-3 - \sqrt{41}}{2}$.

11. $1 + \dfrac{2}{x} + \dfrac{5}{x^2} = 0$

     $x^2 + 2x + 5 = 0$ Multiplying by x^2, the LCM of the denominators

     $a = 1,\ b = 2,\ c = 5$

$$x = \frac{-2 \pm \sqrt{2^2 - 4 \cdot 1 \cdot 5}}{2 \cdot 1} = \frac{-2 \pm \sqrt{4 - 20}}{2}$$

$$x = \frac{-2 \pm \sqrt{-16}}{2} = \frac{-2 \pm 4i}{2} = -1 \pm 2i$$

The solutions are $-1 + 2i$ and $-1 - 2i$.

13. a) $3x + x(x - 2) = 0$

     $3x + x^2 - 2x = 0$

         $x^2 + x = 0$

         $x(x + 1) = 0$

   $x = 0$ or $x + 1 = 0$

   $x = 0$ or $x = -1$

The solutions are 0 and -1.

b) The solutions of the equation $3x + x(x - 2) = 0$ are the first coordinates of the x-intercepts of the graph of $f(x) = 3x + x(x - 2)$. Thus, the x-intercepts are $(-1, 0)$ and $(0, 0)$.

15. a) $11x^2 - 3x - 5 = 0$

     $a = 11,\ b = -3,\ c = -5$

$$x = \frac{-(-3) \pm \sqrt{(-3)^2 - 4 \cdot 11 \cdot (-5)}}{2 \cdot 11}$$

$$x = \frac{3 \pm \sqrt{9 + 220}}{22} = \frac{3 \pm \sqrt{229}}{22}$$

The solutions are $\dfrac{3 + \sqrt{229}}{22}$ and $\dfrac{3 - \sqrt{229}}{22}$.

b) The solutions of the equation $11x^2 - 3x - 5 = 0$ are the first coordinates of the x-intercepts of the graph of $f(x) = 11x^2 - 3x - 5$. Thus, the x-intercepts are $\left(\dfrac{3 - \sqrt{229}}{22}, 0\right)$ and $\left(\dfrac{3 + \sqrt{229}}{22}, 0\right)$.

17. a) $25x^2 - 20x + 4 = 0$

     $(5x - 2)(5x - 2) = 0$

   $5x - 2 = 0$ or $5x - 2 = 0$

     $5x = 2$ or $5x = 2$

      $x = \dfrac{2}{5}$ or $x = \dfrac{2}{5}$

The solution is $\dfrac{2}{5}$.

b) The solution of the equation $25x^2 - 20x + 4 = 0$ is the first coordinate of the x-intercept of $f(x) = 25x^2 - 20x + 4$. Thus, the x-intercept is $\left(\dfrac{2}{5}, 0\right)$.

19. $4x(x - 2) - 5x(x - 1) = 2$

     $4x^2 - 8x - 5x^2 + 5x = 2$ Removing parentheses

         $-x^2 - 3x = 2$

      $-x^2 - 3x - 2 = 0$

       $x^2 + 3x + 2 = 0$ Multiplying by -1

     $(x + 2)(x + 1) = 0$

   $x + 2 = 0$ or $x + 1 = 0$

     $x = -2$ or $x = -1$

The solutions are -2 and -1.

21. $14(x - 4) - (x + 2) = (x + 2)(x - 4)$

     $14x - 56 - x - 2 = x^2 - 2x - 8$

        $13x - 58 = x^2 - 2x - 8$

           $0 = x^2 - 15x + 50$

           $0 = (x - 10)(x - 5)$

   $x - 10 = 0$ or $x - 5 = 0$

     $x = 10$ or $x = 5$

The solutions are 10 and 5.

23. $5x^2 = 17x - 2$

     $5x^2 - 17x + 2 = 0$

     $a = 5,\ b = -17,\ c = 2$

$$x = \frac{-(-17) \pm \sqrt{(-17)^2 - 4 \cdot 5 \cdot 2}}{2 \cdot 5}$$

$$x = \frac{17 \pm \sqrt{289 - 40}}{10} = \frac{17 \pm \sqrt{249}}{10}$$

The solutions are $\dfrac{17 + \sqrt{249}}{10}$ and $\dfrac{17 - \sqrt{249}}{10}$.

25. $x^2 + 5 = 4x$

     $x^2 - 4x + 5 = 0$

     $a = 1,\ b = -4,\ c = 5$

$$x = \frac{-(-4) \pm \sqrt{(-4)^2 - 4 \cdot 1 \cdot 5}}{2 \cdot 1} = \frac{4 \pm \sqrt{16 - 20}}{2}$$

$$x = \frac{4 \pm \sqrt{-4}}{2} = \frac{4 \pm 2i}{2} = 2 \pm i$$

The solutions are $2 + i$ and $2 - i$.

27.
$$x + \frac{1}{x} = \frac{13}{6}, \text{ LCM is } 6x$$

$$6x\left(x + \frac{1}{x}\right) = 6x \cdot \frac{13}{6}$$

$$6x^2 + 6 = 13x$$

$$6x^2 - 13x + 6 = 0$$

$$(2x - 3)(3x - 2) = 0$$

$$2x - 3 = 0 \text{ or } 3x - 2 = 0$$

$$2x = 3 \text{ or } 3x = 2$$

$$x = \frac{3}{2} \text{ or } x = \frac{2}{3}$$

The solutions are $\frac{3}{2}$ and $\frac{2}{3}$.

29.
$$\frac{1}{y} + \frac{1}{y+2} = \frac{1}{3}, \text{ LCM is } 3y(y+2)$$

$$3y(y+2)\left(\frac{1}{y} + \frac{1}{y+2}\right) = 3y(y+2) \cdot \frac{1}{3}$$

$$3(y+2) + 3y = y(y+2)$$

$$3y + 6 + 3y = y^2 + 2y$$

$$6y + 6 = y^2 + 2y$$

$$0 = y^2 - 4y - 6$$

$$a = 1, \ b = -4, \ c = -6$$

$$y = \frac{-(-4) \pm \sqrt{(-4)^2 - 4 \cdot 1 \cdot (-6)}}{2 \cdot 1} = \frac{4 \pm \sqrt{16 + 24}}{2}$$

$$y = \frac{4 \pm \sqrt{40}}{2} = \frac{4 \pm 2\sqrt{10}}{2}$$

$$y = \frac{2(2 \pm \sqrt{10})}{2 \cdot 1} = 2 \pm \sqrt{10}$$

The solutions are $2 + \sqrt{10}$ and $2 - \sqrt{10}$.

31.
$$(2t - 3)^2 + 17t = 15$$

$$4t^2 - 12t + 9 + 17t = 15$$

$$4t^2 + 5t - 6 = 0$$

$$(4t - 3)(t + 2) = 0$$

$$4t - 3 = 0 \text{ or } t + 2 = 0$$

$$t = \frac{3}{4} \text{ or } t = -2$$

The solutions are $\frac{3}{4}$ and -2.

33.
$$(x - 2)^2 + (x + 1)^2 = 0$$

$$x^2 - 4x + 4 + x^2 + 2x + 1 = 0$$

$$2x^2 - 2x + 5 = 0$$

$$a = 2, \ b = -2, \ c = 5$$

$$x = \frac{-(-2) \pm \sqrt{(-2)^2 - 4 \cdot 2 \cdot 5}}{2 \cdot 2} = \frac{2 \pm \sqrt{4 - 40}}{4}$$

$$x = \frac{2 \pm \sqrt{-36}}{4} = \frac{2 \pm 6i}{4}$$

$$x = \frac{2(1 \pm 3i)}{2 \cdot 2} = \frac{1 \pm 3i}{2} = \frac{1}{2} \pm \frac{3}{2}i$$

The solutions are $\frac{1}{2} + \frac{3}{2}i$ and $\frac{1}{2} - \frac{3}{2}i$.

35.
$$x^3 - 1 = 0$$

$$(x - 1)(x^2 + x + 1) = 0$$

$$x - 1 = 0 \text{ or } x^2 + x + 1 = 0$$

$$x = 1 \text{ or } \qquad x = \frac{-1 \pm \sqrt{1^2 - 4 \cdot 1 \cdot 1}}{2 \cdot 1}$$

$$x = 1 \text{ or } \qquad x = \frac{-1 \pm \sqrt{-3}}{2}$$

$$x = 1 \text{ or } \qquad x = \frac{-1 \pm i\sqrt{3}}{2} = -\frac{1}{2} \pm i\frac{\sqrt{3}}{2}$$

The solutions are 1, $-\frac{1}{2} + i\frac{\sqrt{3}}{2}$, and $-\frac{1}{2} - i\frac{\sqrt{3}}{2}$.

37. $x^2 + 6x + 4 = 0$

$$a = 1, \ b = 6, \ c = 4$$

$$x = \frac{-6 \pm \sqrt{6^2 - 4 \cdot 1 \cdot 4}}{2 \cdot 1} = \frac{-6 \pm \sqrt{36 - 16}}{2}$$

$$x = \frac{-6 \pm \sqrt{20}}{2} = \frac{-6 \pm \sqrt{4 \cdot 5}}{2}$$

$$x = \frac{-6 \pm 2\sqrt{5}}{2} = \frac{2(-3 \pm \sqrt{5})}{2}$$

$$x = -3 \pm \sqrt{5}$$

We can use a calculator to approximate the solutions:

$-3 + \sqrt{5} \approx -0.764$; $-3 - \sqrt{5} \approx -5.236$

The solutions are $-3 + \sqrt{5}$ and $-3 - \sqrt{5}$, or approximately -0.764 and -5.236.

39. $x^2 - 6x + 4 = 0$

$$a = 1, \ b = -6, \ c = 4$$

$$x = \frac{-(-6) \pm \sqrt{(-6)^2 - 4 \cdot 1 \cdot 4}}{2 \cdot 1} = \frac{6 \pm \sqrt{36 - 16}}{2}$$

$$x = \frac{6 \pm \sqrt{20}}{2} = \frac{6 \pm \sqrt{4 \cdot 5}}{2}$$

$$x = \frac{6 \pm 2\sqrt{5}}{2} = \frac{2(3 \pm \sqrt{5})}{2}$$

$$x = 3 \pm \sqrt{5}$$

We can use a calculator to approximate the solutions:

$3 + \sqrt{5} \approx 5.236$; $3 - \sqrt{5} \approx 0.764$

The solutions are $3 + \sqrt{5}$ and $3 - \sqrt{5}$, or approximately 5.236 and 0.764.

41. $2x^2 - 3x - 7 = 0$

$$a = 2, \ b = -3, \ c = -7$$

$$x = \frac{-(-3) \pm \sqrt{(-3)^2 - 4 \cdot 2 \cdot (-7)}}{2 \cdot 2} = \frac{3 \pm \sqrt{9 + 56}}{4}$$

$$x = \frac{3 \pm \sqrt{65}}{4}$$

We can use a calculator to approximate the solutions:

$$\frac{3 + \sqrt{65}}{4} \approx 2.766; \ \frac{3 - \sqrt{65}}{4} \approx -1.266$$

The solutions are $\frac{3 + \sqrt{65}}{4}$ and $\frac{3 - \sqrt{65}}{4}$, or approximately 2.766 and -1.266.

43.
$$5x^2 = 3 + 8x$$
$$5x^2 - 8x - 3 = 0$$
$$a = 5, \ b = -8, \ c = -3$$
$$x = \frac{-(-8) \pm \sqrt{(-8)^2 - 4 \cdot 5 \cdot (-3)}}{2 \cdot 5} = \frac{8 \pm \sqrt{64 + 60}}{10}$$
$$x = \frac{8 \pm \sqrt{124}}{10} = \frac{8 \pm \sqrt{4 \cdot 31}}{10}$$
$$x = \frac{8 \pm 2\sqrt{31}}{10} = \frac{2(4 \pm \sqrt{31})}{2 \cdot 5}$$
$$x = \frac{4 \pm \sqrt{31}}{5}$$

We can use a calculator to approximate the solutions:

$$\frac{4 + \sqrt{31}}{5} \approx 1.914; \quad \frac{4 - \sqrt{31}}{5} \approx -0.314$$

The solutions are $\dfrac{4 + \sqrt{31}}{5}$ and $\dfrac{4 - \sqrt{31}}{5}$, or approximately 1.914 and -0.314.

45. Discussion and Writing Exercise

47.
$$x = \sqrt{x + 2}$$
$$x^2 = (\sqrt{x + 2})^2 \quad \text{Principle of powers}$$
$$x^2 = x + 2$$
$$x^2 - x - 2 = 0$$
$$(x - 2)(x + 1) = 0$$
$$x - 2 = 0 \quad or \quad x + 1 = 0$$
$$x = 2 \quad or \qquad x = -1$$

The number 2 checks but -1 does not, so the solution is 2.

49.
$$\sqrt{x + 2} = \sqrt{2x - 8}$$
$$(\sqrt{x + 2})^2 = (\sqrt{2x + 8})^2 \quad \text{Principle of powers}$$
$$x + 2 = 2x - 8$$
$$2 = x - 8$$
$$10 = x$$

The number 10 checks, so it is the solution.

51. $\sqrt{x + 5} = -7$

Since the square root of a number must be nonnegative, this equation has no solution.

53.
$$\sqrt[3]{4x - 7} = 2$$
$$(\sqrt[3]{4x - 7})^3 = 2^3 \quad \text{Principle of powers}$$
$$4x - 7 = 8$$
$$4x = 15$$
$$x = \frac{15}{4}$$

The number $\dfrac{15}{4}$ checks, so it is the solution.

55. The solutions of $2.2x^2 + 0.5x - 1 = 0$ are approximately -0.797 and 0.570.

57. $2x^2 - x - \sqrt{5} = 0$
$$a = 2, \ b = -1, \ c = -\sqrt{5}$$
$$x = \frac{-(-1) \pm \sqrt{(-1)^2 - 4 \cdot 2 \cdot (-\sqrt{5})}}{2 \cdot 2} = \frac{1 \pm \sqrt{1 + 8\sqrt{5}}}{4}$$
The solutions are $\dfrac{1 + \sqrt{1 + 8\sqrt{5}}}{4}$ and $\dfrac{1 - \sqrt{1 + 8\sqrt{5}}}{4}$.

59. $ix^2 - x - 1 = 0$
$$a = i, \ b = -1, \ c = -1$$
$$x = \frac{-(-1) \pm \sqrt{(-1)^2 - 4 \cdot i \cdot (-1)}}{2 \cdot i} = \frac{1 \pm \sqrt{1 + 4i}}{2i}$$
$$x = \frac{1 \pm \sqrt{1 + 4i}}{2i} \cdot \frac{i}{i} = \frac{i \pm i\sqrt{1 + 4i}}{2i^2} = \frac{i \pm i\sqrt{1 + 4i}}{-2}$$
$$x = \frac{-i \pm i\sqrt{1 + 4i}}{2}$$
The solutions are $\dfrac{-i + i\sqrt{1 + 4i}}{2}$ and $\dfrac{-i - i\sqrt{1 + 4i}}{2}$.

61.
$$\frac{x}{x + 1} = 4 + \frac{1}{3x^2 - 3}$$
$$\frac{x}{x + 1} = 4 + \frac{1}{3(x + 1)(x - 1)},$$
$$\text{LCM is } 3x(x + 1)(x - 1)$$
$$3(x + 1)(x - 1) \cdot \frac{x}{x + 1} =$$
$$3(x + 1)(x - 1)\left(4 + \frac{1}{3(x + 1)(x - 1)}\right)$$
$$3x(x - 1) = 12(x + 1)(x - 1) + 1$$
$$3x^2 - 3x = 12x^2 - 12 + 1$$
$$0 = 9x^2 + 3x - 11$$
$$a = 9, \ b = 3, \ c = -11$$
$$x = \frac{-3 \pm \sqrt{3^2 - 4 \cdot 9 \cdot (-11)}}{2 \cdot 9} = \frac{-3 \pm \sqrt{9 + 396}}{18}$$
$$x = \frac{-3 \pm \sqrt{405}}{18} = \frac{-3 \pm 9\sqrt{5}}{18}$$
$$x = \frac{3(-1 \pm 3\sqrt{5})}{3 \cdot 6} = \frac{-1 \pm 3\sqrt{5}}{6}$$
The solutions are $\dfrac{-1 + 3\sqrt{5}}{6}$ and $\dfrac{-1 - 3\sqrt{5}}{6}$.

63. Replace $f(x)$ with 13.
$$13 = (x - 3)^2$$
$$\pm\sqrt{13} = x - 3$$
$$3 \pm \sqrt{13} = x$$
The solutions are $3 + \sqrt{13}$ and $3 - \sqrt{13}$.

Exercise Set 7.3

1. Familiarize. We make a drawing and label it. We let $x =$ the length of the rectangle. Then $x - 7 =$ the width.

Translate. We use the formula for the area of a rectangle.

$$A = lw$$

$$18 = x(x - 7) \quad \text{Substituting}$$

Solve. We solve the equation.

$$18 = x^2 - 7x$$

$$0 = x^2 - 7x - 18$$

$$0 = (x - 9)(x + 2)$$

$$x - 9 = 0 \quad or \quad x + 2 = 0$$

$$x = 9 \quad or \qquad x = -2$$

Check. We only check 9 since the length cannot be negative. If $x = 9$, then $x - 7 = 9 - 7$, or 2, and the area is $9 \cdot 2$, or 18 ft^2. The value checks.

State. The length of 9 ft, and the width is 2 ft.

3. Familiarize. We make a drawing and label it. We let $x =$ the width of the rectangle. Then $2x =$ the length.

Translate.

$$A = lw$$

$$162 = 2x \cdot x \quad \text{Substituting}$$

Solve. We solve the equation.

$$162 = 2x^2$$

$$81 = x^2$$

$$\pm 9 = x$$

Check. We only check 9 since the width cannot be negative. If $x = 9$, then $2x = 2 \cdot 9$, or 18, and the area is $18 \cdot 9$, or 162 yd^2. The value checks.

State. The length is 18 yd, and the width is 9 yd.

5. Familiarize. Let h represent the height of the sail. Then $h - 9$ represents the base. Recall that the formula for the area of a triangle is $A = \dfrac{1}{2} \times$ base $\times$ height.

Translate. The area is 56 m^2. We substitute in the formula.

$$\frac{1}{2}(h - 9)h = 56$$

Solve. We solve the equation:

$$\frac{1}{2}(h - 9)h = 56$$

$$(h - 9)h = 112 \quad \text{Multiplying by 2}$$

$$h^2 - 9h = 112$$

$$h^2 - 9h - 112 = 0$$

$$(h - 16)(h + 7) = 0$$

$$h - 16 = 0 \quad or \quad h + 7 = 0$$

$$h = 16 \quad or \qquad h = -7$$

Check. We check only 16, since height cannot be negative. If the height is 16 m, the base is $16 - 9$, or 7 m, and the area is $\dfrac{1}{2} \cdot 7 \cdot 16$, or 56 m^2. We have a solution.

State. The height is 16 m, and the base is 7 m.

7. Familiarize. Let h represent the height of the sail. Then $h - 8$ represents the base. Recall that the formula for the area of a triangle is $A = \dfrac{1}{2} \times$ base $\times$ height.

Translate. The area 56 ft^2. We substitute n the formula.

$$\frac{1}{2}(h - 8)h = 56$$

Solve. We solve the equation.

$$\frac{1}{2}(h - 8)h = 56$$

$$(h - 8)h = 112 \quad \text{Multiplying by 2}$$

$$h^2 - 8h = 112$$

$$h^2 - 8h - 112 = 0$$

We use the quadratic formula.

$$h = \frac{-b \pm \sqrt{b^2 - 4ac}}{2a}$$

$$= \frac{-(-8) \pm \sqrt{(-8)^2 - 4 \cdot 1 \cdot (-112)}}{2 \cdot 1}$$

$$= \frac{8 \pm \sqrt{64 + 448}}{2} = \frac{8 \pm \sqrt{512}}{2}$$

$$= \frac{8 \pm \sqrt{256 \cdot 2}}{2} = \frac{8 \pm 16\sqrt{2}}{2}$$

$$= \frac{8(1 \pm 2\sqrt{2})}{2} = 4(1 \pm 2\sqrt{2})$$

$$= 4 \pm 8\sqrt{2}$$

Check. The number $4 - 8\sqrt{2}$ is negative. We do not check it since the height cannot be negative. If the height is $4 + 8\sqrt{2}$ ft, then the base is $4 + 8\sqrt{2} - 8$, or $-4 + 8\sqrt{2}$ ft, and the area is $\dfrac{1}{2}(-4 + 8\sqrt{2})(4 + 8\sqrt{2})$, or $\dfrac{1}{2}(-16 + 128)$, or $\dfrac{1}{2}(112)$, or 56 ft^2. The answer checks.

State. The base of the sail is $-4 + 8\sqrt{2}$ ft, and the height is $4 + 8\sqrt{2}$ ft.

9. Familiarize. We make a drawing and label it. We let $x =$ the width of the frame.

The length and width of the picture that shows are represented by $20 - 2x$ and $12 - 2x$. The area of the picture that shows is 84 cm^2.

Translate. Using the formula for the area of a rectangle, $A = l \cdot w$, we have

$$84 = (20 - 2x)(12 - 2x).$$

Solve. We solve the equation.

$$84 = (20 - 2x)(12 - 2x)$$

$$84 = 240 - 64x + 4x^2$$

$$0 = 156 - 64x + 4x^2$$

$$0 = 4x^2 - 64x + 156$$

$$0 = x^2 - 16x + 39 \qquad \text{Dividing by 4}$$

$$0 = (x - 13)(x - 3)$$

$$x - 13 = 0 \quad or \quad x - 3 = 0$$

$$x = 13 \quad or \qquad x = 3$$

Check. We see that 13 is not a solution, because when $x = 13$, then $20 - 2x = -6$ and $12 - 2x = -14$ and the dimensions of the frame cannot be negative. We check 3. When $x = 3$, then $20 - 2x = 14$ and $12 - 2x = 6$ and $14 \cdot 6 = 84$, the area of the picture that shows. The number 3 checks.

State. The width of the frame is 3 cm.

11. *Familiarize*. Using the labels on the drawing in the text, we let x and $x + 2$ represent the lengths of the legs of the right triangle.

Translate. We use the Pythagorean equation.

$$a^2 + b^2 = c^2$$

$$x^2 + (x + 2)^2 = 10^2 \qquad \text{Substituting}$$

Solve. We solve the equation.

$$x^2 + x^2 + 4x + 4 = 100$$

$$2x^2 + 4x + 4 = 100$$

$$2x^2 + 4x - 96 = 0$$

$$x^2 + 2x - 48 = 0 \qquad \text{Dividing by 2}$$

$$(x + 8)(x - 6) = 0$$

$$x + 8 = 0 \quad or \quad x - 6 = 0$$

$$x = -8 \quad or \qquad x = 6$$

Check. We only check 6 since the length of a leg cannot be negative. When $x = 6$, then $x + 2 = 8$, and $6^2 + 8^2 = 100 = 10^2$. The number 6 checks.

State. The lengths of the legs are 6 ft and 8 ft.

13. *Familiarize*. The page numbers on facing pages are consecutive integers. Let $x =$ the number on the left-hand page. Then $x + 1 =$ the number on the right-hand page.

Translate.

$$\underbrace{\text{The product of the page numbers}}_{x(x+1)} \quad \text{is 812.} \atop = 812$$

Solve. We solve the equation.

$$x^2 + x = 812$$

$$x^2 + x - 812 = 0$$

$$(x + 29)(x - 28) = 0$$

$$x + 29 = 0 \quad or \quad x - 28 = 0$$

$$x = -29 \quad or \qquad x = 28$$

Check. We only check 28 since a page number cannot be negative. If $x = 28$, then $x + 1 = 29$ and $28 \cdot 29 = 812$. The number 28 checks.

State. The page numbers are 28 and 29.

15. *Familiarize*. We make a drawing and label it. We let $x =$ the length and $x - 4 =$ the width.

Translate. We use the formula for the area of a rectangle.

$$A = lw$$

$$10 = x(x - 4) \qquad \text{Substituting}$$

Solve. We solve the equation.

$$10 = x^2 - 4x$$

$$0 = x^2 - 4x - 10$$

$$x = \frac{-b \pm \sqrt{b^2 - 4ac}}{2a} = \frac{-(-4) \pm \sqrt{(-4)^2 - 4 \cdot 1 \cdot (-10)}}{2 \cdot 1}$$

$$x = \frac{4 \pm \sqrt{16 + 40}}{2} = \frac{4 \pm \sqrt{56}}{2} = \frac{4 \pm \sqrt{4 \cdot 14}}{2}$$

$$x = \frac{4 \pm 2\sqrt{14}}{2} = 2 \pm \sqrt{14}$$

Check. We only need to check $2 + \sqrt{14}$ since $2 - \sqrt{14}$ is negative and the length cannot be negative. If $x = 2 + \sqrt{14}$, then $x - 4 = (2 + \sqrt{14}) - 4$, or $\sqrt{14} - 2$. Using a calculator we find that the length is $2 + \sqrt{14} \approx 5.742$ ft and the width is $\sqrt{14} - 2 \approx 1.742$ ft, and $(5.742)(1.742) = 10.003 \approx 10$. Our result checks.

State. The length is $2 + \sqrt{14}$ ft ≈ 5.742 ft; the width is $\sqrt{14} - 2$ ft ≈ 1.742 ft.

17. *Familiarize*. We make a drawing and label it. We let $x =$ the width of the margin.

The length and width of the printed text are represented by $20 - 2x$ and $14 - 2x$. The area of the printed text is 100 in^2.

Translate. We use the formula for the area of a rectangle.

$$A = lw$$

$$100 = (20 - 2x)(14 - 2x)$$

Solve. We solve the equation.

$$100 = 280 - 68x + 4x^2$$

$$0 = 4x^2 - 68x + 180$$

$$0 = x^2 - 17x + 45 \qquad \text{Dividing by 4}$$

$$x = \frac{-b \pm \sqrt{b^2 - 4ac}}{2a} = \frac{-(-17) \pm \sqrt{(-17)^2 - 4 \cdot 1 \cdot 45}}{2 \cdot 1}$$

$$x = \frac{17 \pm \sqrt{289 - 180}}{2} = \frac{17 \pm \sqrt{109}}{2}$$

$$x \approx 13.720 \quad or \quad x \approx 3.280$$

Check. If $x \approx 13.720$, then $20 - 2x \approx -7.440$ and $14 - 2x \approx -13.440$. Since the width of the margin cannot be negative, 13.720 is not a solution. If $x \approx 3.280$, then $20 - 2x \approx 13.440$ and $14 - 2x \approx 7.440$ and $(13.440)(7.440) = 99.99 \approx 100$. The number $\frac{17 - \sqrt{109}}{2} \approx 3.280$ checks.

State. The width of the margin is $\frac{17 - \sqrt{109}}{2}$ in. ≈ 3.280 in.

19. **Familiarize**. We make a drawing. We let $x =$ the length of the shorter leg and $x + 14 =$ the length of the longer leg.

Translate. We use the Pythagorean equation.

$$a^2 + b^2 = c^2$$

$$x^2 + (x + 14)^2 = 24^2 \qquad \text{Substituting}$$

Solve. We solve the equation.

$$x^2 + x^2 + 28x + 196 = 576$$

$$2x^2 + 28x - 380 = 0$$

$$x^2 + 14x - 190 = 0 \qquad \text{Dividing by 2}$$

$$x = \frac{-b \pm \sqrt{b^2 - 4ac}}{2a} = \frac{-14 \pm \sqrt{14^2 - 4 \cdot 1 \cdot (-190)}}{2 \cdot 1}$$

$$x = \frac{-14 \pm \sqrt{196 + 760}}{2} = \frac{-14 \pm \sqrt{956}}{2} = \frac{-14 \pm \sqrt{4 \cdot 239}}{2}$$

$$x = \frac{-14 \pm 2\sqrt{239}}{2} = -7 \pm \sqrt{239}$$

$$x \approx 8.460 \text{ or } x \approx -22.460$$

Check. Since the length of a leg cannot be negative, we only need to check 8.460. If $x = -7 + \sqrt{239} \approx 8.460$, then $x + 14 = -7 + \sqrt{239} + 14 = 7 + \sqrt{239} \approx 22.460$ and $(8.460)^2 + (22.460)^2 = 576.0232 \approx 576 = 24^2$. The number $-7 + \sqrt{239} \approx 8.460$ checks.

State. The lengths of the legs are $-7 + \sqrt{239}$ ft ≈ 8.460 ft and $7 + \sqrt{239}$ ft ≈ 22.460 ft.

21. **Familiarize**. We first make a drawing, labeling it with the known and unknown information. We can also organize the information in a table. We let r represent the speed and t the time for the first part of the trip.

r mph t hr $r - 10$ mph $4 - t$ hr

      120 mi   100 mi

Trip	Distance	Speed	Time
1st part	120	r	t
2nd part	100	$r - 10$	$4 - t$

Translate. Using $r = \frac{d}{t}$, we get two equations from the table, $r = \frac{120}{t}$ and $r - 10 = \frac{100}{4 - t}$.

Solve. We substitute $\frac{120}{t}$ for r in the second equation and solve for t.

$$\frac{120}{t} - 10 = \frac{100}{4 - t}, \quad \text{LCD is } t(4 - t)$$

$$t(4 - t)\left(\frac{120}{t} - 10\right) = t(4 - t) \cdot \frac{100}{4 - t}$$

$$120(4 - t) - 10t(4 - t) = 100t$$

$$480 - 120t - 40t + 10t^2 = 100t$$

$$10t^2 - 260t + 480 = 0 \qquad \text{Standard form}$$

$$t^2 - 26t + 48 = 0 \qquad \text{Multiplying by } \frac{1}{10}$$

$$(t - 2)(t - 24) = 0$$

$$t = 2 \quad or \quad t = 24$$

Check. Since the time cannot be negative (If $t = 24$, $4 - t = -20$.), we check only 2 hr. If $t = 2$, then $4 - t = 2$. The speed of the first part is $\frac{120}{2}$, or 60 mph. The speed of the second part is $\frac{100}{2}$, or 50 mph. The speed of the second part is 10 mph slower than the first part. The value checks.

State. The speed of the first part was 60 mph, and the speed of the second part was 50 mph.

23. **Familiarize**. We first make a drawing. We also organize the information in a table. We let $r =$ the speed and $t =$ the time of the slower trip.

200 mi r mph t hr

200 mi $r + 10$ mph $t - 1$ hr

Trip	Distance	Speed	Time
Slower	200	r	t
Faster	200	$r + 10$	$t - 1$

Translate. Using $t = d/r$, we get two equations from the table:

$$t = \frac{200}{r} \text{ and } t - 1 = \frac{200}{r + 10}$$

Solve. We substitute $\frac{200}{r}$ for t in the second equation and solve for r.

$$\frac{200}{r} - 1 = \frac{200}{r + 10}, \text{ LCD is } r(r+10)$$

$$r(r+10)\left(\frac{200}{r} - 1\right) = r(r+10) \cdot \frac{200}{r+10}$$

$$200(r+10) - r(r+10) = 200r$$

$$200r + 2000 - r^2 - 10r = 200r$$

$$0 = r^2 + 10r - 2000$$

$$0 = (r+50)(r-40)$$

$$r = -50 \ \ or \ \ r = 40$$

Check. Since negative speed has no meaning in this problem, we check only 40. If $r = 40$, then the time for the slower trip is $\frac{200}{40}$, or 5 hours. If $r = 40$, then $r + 10 = 50$ and the time for the faster trip is $\frac{200}{50}$, or 4 hours. This is 1 hour less time than the slower trip took, so we have an answer to the problem.

State. The speed is 40 mph.

25. **Familiarize**. We make a drawing and then organize the information in a table. We let r = the speed and t = the time of the Cessna.

| 600 mi | r mph | t hr |
| 1000 mi | $r + 50$ mph | $t + 1$ hr |

Plane	Distance	Speed	Time
Cessna	600	r	t
Beechcraft	1000	$r + 50$	$t + 1$

Translate. Using $t = d/r$, we get two equations from the table:

$$t = \frac{600}{r} \ \text{ and } \ t + 1 = \frac{1000}{r+50}$$

Solve. We substitute $\frac{600}{r}$ for t in the second equation and solve for r.

$$\frac{600}{r} + 1 = \frac{1000}{r+50},$$

$$\text{LCD is } r(r+50)$$

$$r(r+50)\left(\frac{600}{r} + 1\right) = r(r+50) \cdot \frac{1000}{r+50}$$

$$600(r+50) + r(r+50) = 1000r$$

$$600r + 30,000 + r^2 + 50r = 1000r$$

$$r^2 - 350r + 30,000 = 0$$

$$(r-150)(r-200) = 0$$

$$r = 150 \ \ or \ \ r = 200$$

Check. If $r = 150$, then the Cessna's time is $\frac{600}{150}$, or 4 hr and the Beechcraft's time is $\frac{1000}{150+50}$, or $\frac{1000}{200}$, or 5 hr. If $r = 200$, then the Cessna's time is $\frac{600}{200}$, or 3 hr and the Beechcraft's time is $\frac{1000}{200+50}$, or $\frac{1000}{250}$, or 4 hr. Since the Beechcraft's time is 1 hr longer in each case, both values check. There are two solutions.

State. The speed of the Cessna is 150 mph and the speed of the Beechcraft is 200 mph; or the speed of the Cessna is 200 mph and the speed of the Beechcraft is 250 mph.

27. **Familiarize**. We make a drawing and then organize the information in a table. We let r represent the speed and t the time of the trip to Hillsboro.

		Hillsboro
40 mi	r mph	t hr
40 mi	$r - 6$ mph	$14 - t$ hr

Trip	Distance	Speed	Time
To Hillsboro	40	r	t
Return	40	$r - 6$	$14 - t$

Translate. Using $t = \frac{d}{r}$, we get two equations from the table,

$$t = \frac{40}{r} \ \text{ and } \ 14 - t = \frac{40}{r-6}.$$

Solve. We substitute $\frac{40}{r}$ for t in the second equation and solve for r.

$$14 - \frac{40}{r} = \frac{40}{r-6},$$

$$\text{LCD is } r(r-6)$$

$$r(r-6)\left(14 - \frac{40}{r}\right) = r(r-6) \cdot \frac{40}{r-6}$$

$$14r(r-6) - 40(r-6) = 40r$$

$$14r^2 - 84r - 40r + 240 = 40r$$

$$14r^2 - 164r + 240 = 0$$

$$7r^2 - 82r + 120 = 0$$

$$(7r - 12)(r - 10) = 0$$

$$r = \frac{12}{7} \ \ or \ \ r = 10$$

Check. Since negative speed has no meaning in this problem (If $r = \frac{12}{7}$, then $r - 6 = -\frac{30}{7}$.), we check only 10 mph. If $r = 10$, then the time of the trip to Hillsboro is $\frac{40}{10}$, or 4 hr. The speed of the return trip is $10 - 6$, or 4 mph, and the time is $\frac{40}{4}$, or 10 hr. The total time for the round trip is 4 hr + 10 hr, or 14 hr. The value checks.

State. Naoki's speed on the trip to Hillsboro was 10 mph and it was 4 mph on the return trip.

29. **Familiarize**. We make a drawing and organize the information in a table. Let r represent the speed of the barge in still water, and let t represent the time of the trip upriver.

24 mi	$r - 4$ mph	t hr	
			Upriver
Downriver	24 mi	$r + 4$ mph	$5 - t$ hr

Trip	Distance	Speed	Time
Upriver	24	$r-4$	t
Downriver	24	$r+4$	$5-t$

Translate. Using $t = \dfrac{d}{r}$, we get two equations from the table,

$$t = \frac{24}{r-4} \text{ and } 5 - t = \frac{24}{r+4}.$$

Solve. We substitute $\dfrac{24}{r-4}$ for t in the second equation and solve for r.

$$5 - \frac{24}{r-4} = \frac{24}{r+4},$$
$$\text{LCD is } (r{-}4)(r{+}4)$$
$$(r-4)(r+4)\left(5 - \frac{24}{r-4}\right) = (r-4)(r+4) \cdot \frac{24}{r+4}$$
$$5(r-4)(r+4) - 24(r+4) = 24(r-4)$$
$$5r^2 - 80 - 24r - 96 = 24r - 96$$
$$5r^2 - 48r - 80 = 0$$

We use the quadratic formula.

$$r = \frac{-(-48) \pm \sqrt{(-48)^2 - 4 \cdot 5 \cdot (-80)}}{2 \cdot 5}$$
$$r = \frac{48 \pm \sqrt{3904}}{10}$$
$$r \approx 11 \ \ or \ \ r \approx -1.5$$

Check. Since negative speed has no meaning in this problem, we check only 11 mph. If $r \approx 11$, then the speed upriver is about $11 - 4$, or 7 mph, and the time is about $\dfrac{24}{7}$, or 3.4 hr. The speed downriver is about $11 + 4$, or 15 mph, and the time is about $\dfrac{24}{15}$, or 1.6 hr. The total time of the round trip is $3.4 + 1.6$, or 5 hr. The value checks.

State. The barge must be able to travel about 11 mph in still water.

31. $A = 6s^2$

$\quad \dfrac{A}{6} = s^2 \quad$ Dividing by 6

$\quad \sqrt{\dfrac{A}{6}} = s \quad$ Taking the positive square root

33. $F = \dfrac{Gm_1m_2}{r^2}$

$\quad Fr^2 = Gm_1m_2 \quad$ Multiplying by r^2

$\quad r^2 = \dfrac{Gm_1m_2}{F} \quad$ Dividing by F

$\quad r = \sqrt{\dfrac{Gm_1m_2}{F}} \quad$ Taking the positive square root

35. $E = mc^2$

$\quad \dfrac{E}{m} = c^2 \quad$ Dividing by m

$\quad \sqrt{\dfrac{E}{m}} = c \quad$ Taking the square root

37. $a^2 + b^2 = c^2$

$\quad b^2 = c^2 - a^2 \quad$ Subtracting a^2

$\quad b = \sqrt{c^2 - a^2} \quad$ Taking the square root

39. $N = \dfrac{k^2 - 3k}{2}$

$\quad 2N = k^2 - 3k$

$\quad 0 = k^2 - 3k - 2N \quad$ Standard form

$\quad a = 1, \ b = -3, \ c = -2N$

$\quad k = \dfrac{-(-3) \pm \sqrt{(-3)^3 - 4 \cdot 1 \cdot (-2N)}}{2 \cdot 1} \quad$ Using the quadratic formula

$\quad k = \dfrac{3 \pm \sqrt{9 + 8N}}{2}$

Since taking the negative square root would result in a negative answer, we take the positive one.

$\quad k = \dfrac{3 + \sqrt{9 + 8N}}{2}$

41. $A = 2\pi r^2 + 2\pi rh$

$\quad 0 = 2\pi r^2 + 2\pi rh - A \quad$ Standard form

$\quad a = 2\pi, \ b = 2\pi h, \ c = -A$

$\quad r = \dfrac{-2\pi h \pm \sqrt{(2\pi h)^2 - 4 \cdot 2\pi \cdot (-A)}}{2 \cdot 2\pi} \quad$ Using the quadratic formula

$\quad r = \dfrac{-2\pi h \pm \sqrt{4\pi^2 h^2 + 8\pi A}}{4\pi}$

$\quad r = \dfrac{-2\pi h \pm 2\sqrt{\pi^2 h^2 + 2\pi A}}{4\pi}$

$\quad r = \dfrac{-\pi h \pm \sqrt{\pi^2 h^2 + 2\pi A}}{2\pi}$

Since taking the negative square root would result in a negative answer, we take the positive one.

$\quad r = \dfrac{-\pi h + \sqrt{\pi^2 h^2 + 2\pi A}}{2\pi}$

43. $T = 2\pi \sqrt{\dfrac{L}{g}}$

$\quad \dfrac{T}{2\pi} = \sqrt{\dfrac{L}{g}} \quad$ Dividing by 2π

$\quad \dfrac{T^2}{4\pi^2} = \dfrac{L}{g} \quad$ Squaring

$\quad gT^2 = 4\pi^2 L \quad$ Multiplying by $4\pi^2 g$

$\quad g = \dfrac{4\pi^2 L}{T^2} \quad$ Dividing by T^2

45. $I = \dfrac{704.5W}{H^2}$

$\quad H^2 I = 704.5W \quad$ Multiplying by H^2

$\quad H^2 = \dfrac{704.5W}{I} \quad$ Dividing by I

$\quad H = \sqrt{\dfrac{704.5W}{I}}$

47.
$$m = \frac{m_0}{\sqrt{1 - \frac{v^2}{c^2}}}$$

$$m^2 = \frac{m_0^2}{1 - \frac{v^2}{c^2}} \qquad \text{Principle of powers}$$

$$m^2\left(1 - \frac{v^2}{c^2}\right) = m_0^2$$

$$m^2 - \frac{m^2 v^2}{c^2} = m_0^2$$

$$m^2 - m_0^2 = \frac{m^2 v^2}{c^2}$$

$$c^2(m^2 - m_0^2) = m^2 v^2$$

$$\frac{c^2(m^2 - m_0^2)}{m^2} = v^2$$

$$\sqrt{\frac{c^2(m^2 - m_0^2)}{m^2}} = v$$

$$\frac{c\sqrt{m^2 - m_0^2}}{m} = v$$

49. Discussion and Writing Exercise

51.
$$\frac{1}{x-1} + \frac{1}{x^2 - 3x + 2}$$
$$= \frac{1}{x-1} + \frac{1}{(x-1)(x-2)}, \text{ LCD is } (x-1)(x-2)$$
$$= \frac{1}{x-1} \cdot \frac{x-2}{x-2} + \frac{1}{(x-1)(x-2)}$$
$$= \frac{x-2}{(x-1)(x-2)} + \frac{1}{(x-1)(x-2)}$$
$$= \frac{x-2+1}{(x-1)(x-2)}$$
$$= \frac{x-1}{(x-1)(x-2)}$$
$$= \frac{(x-1)\cdot 1}{(x-1)(x-2)}$$
$$= \frac{1}{x-2}$$

53.
$$\frac{2}{x+3} - \frac{x}{x-1} + \frac{x^2+2}{x^2+2x-3}$$
$$= \frac{2}{x+3} - \frac{x}{x-1} + \frac{x^2+2}{(x+3)(x-1)},$$
$$\qquad \text{LCD is } (x+3)(x-1)$$
$$= \frac{2}{x+3} \cdot \frac{x-1}{x-1} - \frac{x}{x-1} \cdot \frac{x+3}{x+3} + \frac{x^2+2}{(x+3)(x-1)}$$
$$= \frac{2(x-1)}{(x+3)(x-1)} - \frac{x(x+3)}{(x-1)(x+3)} + \frac{x^2+2}{(x+3)(x-1)}$$
$$= \frac{2(x-1) - x(x+3) + x^2 + 2}{(x+3)(x-1)}$$
$$= \frac{2x - 2 - x^2 - 3x + x^2 + 2}{(x+3)(x-1)}$$
$$= \frac{-x}{(x+3)(x-1)}$$

55. $\sqrt{-20} = \sqrt{-1 \cdot 4 \cdot 5} = i \cdot 2 \cdot \sqrt{5} = 2\sqrt{5}i$, or $2i\sqrt{5}$

57.
$$\frac{\frac{4}{a^2 b}}{\frac{3}{a} - \frac{4}{b^2}} = \frac{\frac{4}{a^2 b}}{\frac{3}{a} - \frac{4}{b^2}} \cdot \frac{a^2 b^2}{a^2 b^2}$$
$$= \frac{\frac{4}{a^2 b} \cdot a^2 b^2}{\frac{3}{a} \cdot a^2 b^2 - \frac{4}{b^2} \cdot a^2 b^2}$$
$$= \frac{4b}{3ab^2 - 4a^2}, \text{ or } \frac{4b}{a(3b^2 - 4a)}$$

59.
$$\frac{1}{a-1} = a + 1$$
$$\frac{1}{a-1} \cdot a - 1 = (a+1)(a-1)$$
$$1 = a^2 - 1$$
$$2 = a^2$$
$$\pm\sqrt{2} = a$$

61. Let s represent a length of a side of the cube, let S represent the surface area of the cube, and let A represent the surface area of the sphere. Then the diameter of the sphere is s, so the radius r is $s/2$. From Exercise 32, we know, $A = 4\pi r^2$, so when $r = s/2$ we have $A = 4\pi\left(\frac{s}{2}\right)^2 = 4\pi \cdot \frac{s^2}{4} = \pi s^2$. From the formula for the surface area of a cube (See Exercise 31.) we know that $S = 6s^2$, so $\frac{S}{6} = s^2$ and then $A = \pi \cdot \frac{S}{6}$, or $A(S) = \frac{\pi S}{6}$.

63.
$$\frac{w}{l} = \frac{l}{w+l}$$
$$l(w+l) \cdot \frac{w}{l} = l(w+l) \cdot \frac{l}{w+l}$$
$$w(w+l) = l^2$$
$$w^2 + lw = l^2$$
$$0 = l^2 - lw - w^2$$

Use the quadratic formula with $a = 1$, $b = -w$, and $c = -w^2$.
$$l = \frac{-(-w) \pm \sqrt{(-w)^2 - 4 \cdot 1 \cdot (-w^2)}}{2 \cdot 1}$$
$$l = \frac{w \pm \sqrt{w^2 + 4w^2}}{2} = \frac{w \pm \sqrt{5w^2}}{2}$$
$$l = \frac{w \pm w\sqrt{5}}{2}$$

Since $\frac{w - w\sqrt{5}}{2}$ is negative we use the positive square root:
$$l = \frac{w + w\sqrt{5}}{2}$$

Exercise Set 7.4

---

1. $x^2 - 8x + 16 = 0$

$a = 1$, $b = -8$, $c = 16$

We compute the discriminant.

$$b^2 - 4ac = (-8)^2 - 4 \cdot 1 \cdot 16$$
$$= 64 - 64$$
$$= 0$$

Since $b^2 - 4ac = 0$, there is just one solution, and it is a real number.

3. $x^2 + 1 = 0$

$a = 1$, $b = 0$, $c = 1$

We compute the discriminant.
$$b^2 - 4ac = 0^2 - 4 \cdot 1 \cdot 1$$
$$= -4$$

Since $b^2 - 4ac < 0$, there are two nonreal solutions.

5. $x^2 - 6 = 0$

$a = 1$, $b = 0$, $c = -6$

We compute the discriminant.
$$b^2 - 4ac = 0^2 - 4 \cdot 1 \cdot (-6)$$
$$= 24$$

Since $b^2 - 4ac > 0$, there are two real solutions.

7. $4x^2 - 12x + 9 = 0$

$a = 4$, $b = -12$, $c = 9$

We compute the discriminant.
$$b^2 - 4ac = (-12)^2 - 4 \cdot 4 \cdot 9$$
$$= 144 - 144$$
$$= 0$$

Since $b^2 - 4ac = 0$, there is just one solution, and it is a real number.

9. $x^2 - 2x + 4 = 0$

$a = 1$, $b = -2$, $c = 4$

We compute the discriminant.
$$b^2 - 4ac = (-2)^2 - 4 \cdot 1 \cdot 4$$
$$= 4 - 16$$
$$= -12$$

Since $b^2 - 4ac < 0$, there are two nonreal solutions.

11. $9t^2 - 3t = 0$

$a = 9$, $b = -3$, $c = 0$

We compute the discriminant.
$$b^2 - 4ac = (-3)^2 - 4 \cdot 9 \cdot 0$$
$$= 9 - 0$$
$$= 9$$

Since $b^2 - 4ac > 0$, there are two real solutions.

13. $y^2 = \frac{1}{2}y + \frac{3}{5}$

$y^2 - \frac{1}{2}y - \frac{3}{5} = 0$ Standard form

$a = 1$, $b = -\frac{1}{2}$, $c = -\frac{3}{5}$

We compute the discriminant.

$$b^2 - 4ac = \left(-\frac{1}{2}\right)^2 - 4 \cdot 1 \cdot \left(-\frac{3}{5}\right)$$
$$= \frac{1}{4} + \frac{12}{5}$$
$$= \frac{53}{20}$$

Since $b^2 - 4ac > 0$, there are two real solutions.

15. $4x^2 - 4\sqrt{3}x + 3 = 0$

$a = 4$, $b = -4\sqrt{3}$, $c = 3$

We compute the discriminant.
$$b^2 - 4ac = (-4\sqrt{3})^2 - 4 \cdot 4 \cdot 3$$
$$= 48 - 48$$
$$= 0$$

Since $b^2 - 4ac = 0$, there is just one solution, and it is a real number.

17. The solutions are -4 and 4.
$$x = -4 \quad or \quad x = 4$$
$$x + 4 = 0 \quad or \quad x - 4 = 0$$
$$(x + 4)(x - 4) = 0 \quad \text{Principle of zero products}$$
$$x^2 - 16 = 0 \quad (A + B)(A - B) = A^2 - B^2$$

19. The solutions are -2 and -7.
$$x = -2 \quad or \quad x = -7$$
$$x + 2 = 0 \quad or \quad x + 7 = 0$$
$$(x + 2)(x + 7) = 0 \quad \text{Principle of zero products}$$
$$x^2 + 9x + 14 = 0 \quad \text{FOIL}$$

21. The only solution is 8. It must be a double solution.
$$x = 8 \quad or \quad x = 8$$
$$x - 8 = 0 \quad or \quad x - 8 = 0$$
$$(x - 8)(x - 8) = 0 \quad \text{Principle of zero products}$$
$$x^2 - 16x + 64 = 0 \quad (A - B)^2 = A^2 - 2AB + B^2$$

23. The solutions are $-\frac{2}{5}$ and $\frac{6}{5}$.
$$x = -\frac{2}{5} \quad or \quad x = \frac{6}{5}$$
$$x + \frac{2}{5} = 0 \quad or \quad x - \frac{6}{5} = 0$$
$$5x + 2 = 0 \quad or \quad 5x - 6 = 0 \quad \text{Clearing fractions}$$
$$(5x + 2)(5x - 6) = 0 \quad \text{Principle of zero products}$$
$$25x^2 - 20x - 12 = 0 \quad \text{FOIL}$$

25. The solutions are $\frac{k}{3}$ and $\frac{m}{4}$.
$$x = \frac{k}{3} \quad or \quad x = \frac{m}{4}$$
$$x - \frac{k}{3} = 0 \quad or \quad x - \frac{m}{4} = 0$$
$$3x - k = 0 \quad or \quad 4x - m = 0 \quad \text{Clearing fractions}$$

$$(3x - k)(4x - m) = 0 \qquad \text{Principle of zero}$$
$$\text{products}$$
$$12x^2 - 3mx - 4kx + km = 0 \qquad \text{FOIL}$$
$$12x^2 - (3m + 4k)x + km = 0 \qquad \text{Collecting like terms}$$

27. The solutions are $-\sqrt{3}$ and $2\sqrt{3}$.

$$x = -\sqrt{3} \quad or \qquad x = 2\sqrt{3}$$
$$x + \sqrt{3} = 0 \qquad or \quad x - 2\sqrt{3} = 0$$
$$(x + \sqrt{3})(x - 2\sqrt{3}) = 0 \qquad \text{Principle of zero}$$
$$\text{products}$$
$$x^2 - 2\sqrt{3}x + \sqrt{3}x - 2(\sqrt{3})^2 = 0 \qquad \text{FOIL}$$
$$x^2 - \sqrt{3}x - 6 = 0$$

29. $x^4 - 6x^2 + 9 = 0$

Let $u = x^2$ and think of x^4 as $(x^2)^2$.

$$u^2 - 6u + 9 = 0 \qquad \text{Substituting } u \text{ for } x^2$$
$$(u - 3)(u - 3) = 0$$
$$u - 3 = 0 \quad or \quad u - 3 = 0$$
$$u = 3 \quad or \qquad u = 3$$

Now we substitute x^2 for u and solve the equation:

$$x^2 = 3$$
$$x = \pm\sqrt{3}$$

Both $\sqrt{3}$ and $-\sqrt{3}$ check. They are the solutions.

31. $x - 10\sqrt{x} + 9 = 0$

Let $u = \sqrt{x}$ and think of x as $(\sqrt{x})^2$.

$$u^2 - 10u + 9 = 0 \qquad \text{Substituting } u \text{ for } \sqrt{x}$$
$$(u - 9)(u - 1) = 0$$
$$u - 9 = 0 \quad or \quad u - 1 = 0$$
$$u = 9 \quad or \qquad u = 1$$

Now we substitute $\sqrt{x}$ for u and solve these equations:

$$\sqrt{x} = 9 \quad or \quad \sqrt{x} = 1$$
$$x = 81 \quad or \qquad x = 1$$

The numbers 81 and 1 both check. They are the solutions.

33. $(x^2 - 6x) - 2(x^2 - 6x) - 35 = 0$

Let $u = x^2 - 6x$.

$$u^2 - 2u - 35 = 0 \qquad \text{Substituting } u \text{ for } x^2 - 6x$$
$$(u - 7)(u + 5) = 0$$
$$u - 7 = 0 \quad or \quad u + 5 = 0$$
$$u = 7 \quad or \qquad u = -5$$

Now we substitute $x^2 - 6x$ for u and solve these equations:

$$x^2 - 6x = 7 \quad or \qquad x^2 - 6x = -5$$
$$x^2 - 6x - 7 = 0 \quad or \qquad x^2 - 6x + 5 = 0$$
$$(x - 7)(x + 1) = 0 \quad or \quad (x - 5)(x - 1) = 0$$
$$x = 7 \text{ or } x = -1 \text{ or } x = 5 \text{ or } x = 1$$

The numbers -1, 1, 5, and 7 check. They are the solutions.

35. $x^{-2} - 5^{-1} - 36 = 0$

Let $u = x^{-1}$.

$$u^2 - 5u - 36 = 0 \qquad \text{Substituting } u \text{ for } x^{-1}$$
$$(u - 9)(u + 4) = 0$$
$$u - 9 = 0 \quad or \quad u + 4 = 0$$
$$u = 9 \quad or \qquad u = -4$$

Now we substitute x^{-1} for u and solve these equations:

$$x^{-1} = 9 \quad or \quad x^{-1} = -4$$
$$\frac{1}{x} = 9 \quad or \quad \frac{1}{x} = -4$$
$$\frac{1}{9} = x \quad or \quad -\frac{1}{4} = x$$

Both $\frac{1}{9}$ and $-\frac{1}{4}$ check. They are the solutions.

37. $(1 + \sqrt{x})^2 + (1 + \sqrt{x}) - 6 = 0$

Let $u = 1 + \sqrt{x}$.

$$u^2 + u - 6 = 0 \qquad \text{Substituting } u \text{ for } 1 + \sqrt{x}$$
$$(u + 3)(u - 2) = 0$$
$$u + 3 = 0 \qquad or \qquad u - 2 = 0$$
$$u = -3 \qquad or \qquad u = 2$$
$$1 + \sqrt{x} = -3 \quad or \quad 1 + \sqrt{x} = 2 \qquad \text{Substituting}$$
$$1 + \sqrt{x} \text{ for } u$$
$$\sqrt{x} = -4 \qquad or \qquad \sqrt{x} = 1$$
$$\text{No solution} \qquad \qquad x = 1$$

The number 1 checks. It is the solution.

39. $(y^2 - 5y)^2 - 2(y^2 - 5y) - 24 = 0$

Let $u = y^2 - 5y$.

$$u^2 - 2u - 24 = 0 \qquad \text{Substituting } u \text{ for } y^2 - 5y$$
$$(u - 6)(u + 4) = 0$$
$$u - 6 = 0 \quad or \qquad u + 4 = 0$$
$$u = 6 \quad or \qquad u = -4$$
$$y^2 - 5y = 6 \quad or \qquad y^2 - 5y = -4$$
$$\text{Substituting } y^2 - 5y \text{ for } u$$
$$y^2 - 5y - 6 = 0 \quad or \quad y^2 - 5y + 4 = 0$$
$$(y - 6)(y + 1) = 0 \quad or \quad (y - 4)(y - 1) = 0$$
$$y = 6 \text{ or } y = -1 \text{ or } y = 4 \text{ or } y = 1$$

The numbers -1, 1, 4, and 6 check. They are the solutions.

41. $t^4 - 6t^2 - 4 = 0$

Let $u = t^2$.

$u^2 - 6u - 4 = 0$ Substituting u for t^2

$u = \dfrac{-(-6) \pm \sqrt{(-6)^2 - 4 \cdot 1 \cdot (-4)}}{2 \cdot 1}$

$u = \dfrac{6 \pm \sqrt{52}}{2} = \dfrac{6 \pm 2\sqrt{13}}{2}$

$u = 3 \pm \sqrt{13}$

Now we substitute t^2 for u and solve these equations:

$t^2 = 3 + \sqrt{13}$ or $t^2 = 3 - \sqrt{13}$

$t = \pm\sqrt{3 + \sqrt{13}}$ or $t = \pm\sqrt{3 - \sqrt{13}}$

All four numbers check. They are the solutions.

43. $2x^{-2} + x^{-1} - 1 = 0$

Let $u = x^{-1}$.

$2u^2 + u - 1 = 0$ Substituting u for x^{-1}

$(2u - 1)(u + 1) = 0$

$2u - 1 = 0$ or $u + 1 = 0$

$2u = 1$ or $u = -1$

$u = \dfrac{1}{2}$ or $u = -1$

$x^{-1} = \dfrac{1}{2}$ or $x^{-1} = -1$ Substituting x^{-1}
for u

$\dfrac{1}{x} = \dfrac{1}{2}$ or $\dfrac{1}{x} = -1$

$x = 2$ or $x = -1$

Both 2 and -1 check. They are the solutions.

45. $6x^4 - 19x^2 + 15 = 0$

Let $u = x^2$.

$6u^2 - 19u + 15 = 0$ Substituting u for x^2

$(3u - 5)(2u - 3) = 0$

$3u - 5 = 0$ or $2u - 3 = 0$

$3u = 5$ or $2u = 3$

$u = \dfrac{5}{3}$ or $u = \dfrac{3}{2}$

$x^2 = \dfrac{5}{3}$ or $x^2 = \dfrac{3}{2}$ Substituting x^2
for u

$x = \pm\sqrt{\dfrac{5}{3}}$ or $x = \pm\sqrt{\dfrac{3}{2}}$

$x = \pm\dfrac{\sqrt{15}}{3}$ or $x = \pm\dfrac{\sqrt{6}}{2}$

               Rationalizing denominators

All four numbers check. They are the solutions.

47. $x^{2/3} - 4x^{1/3} - 5 = 0$

Let $u = x^{1/3}$.

$u^2 - 4u - 5 = 0$ Substituting u for $x^{1/3}$

$(u - 5)(u + 1) = 0$

$u - 5 = 0$ or $u + 1 = 0$

$u = 5$ or $u = -1$

$x^{1/3} = 5$ or $x^{1/3} = -1$ Substituting $x^{1/3}$
                     for u

$(x^{1/3})^3 = 5^3$ or $(x^{1/3})^3 = (-1)^3$ Principle
                                 of powers

$x = 125$ or $x = -1$

Both 125 and -1 check. They are the solutions.

49. $\left(\dfrac{x-4}{x+1}\right)^2 - 2\left(\dfrac{x-4}{x+1}\right) - 35 = 0$

Let $u = \dfrac{x-4}{x+1}$.

$u^2 - 2u - 35 = 0$ Substituting u for $\dfrac{x-4}{x+1}$

$(u - 7)(u + 5) = 0$

$u - 7 = 0$ or $u + 5 = 0$

$u = 7$ or $u = -5$

$\dfrac{x-4}{x+1} = 7$ or $\dfrac{x-4}{x+1} = -5$ Substituting

                                      $\dfrac{x-4}{x+1}$ for u

$x - 4 = 7(x + 1)$ or $x - 4 = -5(x + 1)$

$x - 4 = 7x + 7$ or $x - 4 = -5x - 5$

$-6x = 11$ or $6x = -1$

$x = -\dfrac{11}{6}$ or $x = -\dfrac{1}{6}$

Both $-\dfrac{11}{6}$ and $-\dfrac{1}{6}$ check. They are the solutions.

51. $9\left(\dfrac{x+2}{x+3}\right)^2 - 6\left(\dfrac{x+2}{x+3}\right) + 1 = 0$

Let $u = \dfrac{x+2}{x+3}$.

$9u^2 - 6u + 1 = 0$ Substituting u for $\dfrac{x+2}{x+3}$

$(3u - 1)(3u - 1) = 0$

$3u - 1 = 0$ or $3u - 1 = 0$

$3u = 1$ or $3u = 1$

$u = \dfrac{1}{3}$ or $u = \dfrac{1}{3}$

Now we substitute $\dfrac{x+2}{x+3}$ for u and solve the equation:

$\dfrac{x+2}{x+3} = \dfrac{1}{3}$

$3(x + 2) = x + 3$ Multiplying by $3(x+3)$

$3x + 6 = x + 3$

$2x = -3$

$x = -\dfrac{3}{2}$

The number $-\dfrac{3}{2}$ checks. It is the solution.

53. $\left(\dfrac{x^2-2}{x}\right)^2 - 7\left(\dfrac{x^2-2}{x}\right) - 18 = 0$

Let $u = \dfrac{x^2-2}{x}$.

$u^2 - 7u - 18 = 0$ Substituting u for $\dfrac{x^2-2}{x}$

$(u-9)(u+2) = 0$

$u - 9 = 0 \quad or \quad u + 2 = 0$

$u = 9 \quad or \quad u = -2$

$\dfrac{x^2-2}{x} = 9 \quad or \quad \dfrac{x^2-2}{x} = -2$

Substituting $\dfrac{x^2-2}{x}$ for u

$x^2 - 2 = 9x \quad or \quad x^2 - 2 = -2x$

$x^2 - 9x - 2 = 0 \quad or \quad x^2 + 2x - 2 = 0$

$x = \dfrac{-(-9) \pm \sqrt{(-9)^2 - 4\cdot1\cdot(-2)}}{2\cdot1}$

$x = \dfrac{9 \pm \sqrt{89}}{2}$

or

$x = \dfrac{-2 \pm \sqrt{2^2 - 4\cdot1\cdot(-2)}}{2\cdot1} = \dfrac{-2 \pm \sqrt{12}}{2}$

$x = \dfrac{-2 \pm 2\sqrt{3}}{2} = -1 \pm \sqrt{3}$

All four numbers check. They are the solutions.

55. The x-intercepts occur where $f(x) = 0$. Thus, we must have $5x + 13\sqrt{x} - 6 = 0$.

Let $u = \sqrt{x}$.

$5u^2 + 13u - 6 = 0$ Substituting

$(5u - 2)(u + 3) = 0$

$u = \dfrac{2}{5} \ or \ u = -3$

Now replace u with $\sqrt{x}$ and solve these equations:

$\sqrt{x} = \dfrac{2}{5} \quad or \quad \sqrt{x} = -3$

$x = \dfrac{4}{25} \qquad$ No solution

The number $\dfrac{4}{25}$ checks. Thus, the x-intercept is $\left(\dfrac{4}{25}, 0\right)$.

57. The x-intercepts occur where $f(x) = 0$. Thus, we must have $(x^2 - 3x)^2 - 10(x^2 - 3x) + 24 = 0$.

Let $u = x^2 - 3x$.

$u^2 - 10u + 24 = 0$ Substituting

$(u-6)(u-4) = 0$

$u = 6 \ or \ u = 4$

Now replace u with $x^2 - 3x$ and solve these equations:

$x^2 - 3x = 6 \quad or \quad x^2 - 3x = 4$

$x^2 - 3x - 6 = 0 \quad or \quad x^2 - 3x - 4 = 0$

$x = \dfrac{-(-3) \pm \sqrt{(-3)^2 - 4(1)(-6)}}{2\cdot1}$ *or*

$(x-4)(x+1) = 0$

$x = \dfrac{3 \pm \sqrt{33}}{2} \ or \ x = 4 \ or \ x = -1$

All four numbers check. Thus, the x-intercepts are $\left(\dfrac{3+\sqrt{33}}{2}, 0\right)$, $\left(\dfrac{3-\sqrt{33}}{2}, 0\right)$, $(4, 0)$, and $(-1, 0)$.

59. Discussion and Writing Exercise

61. *Familiarize.* Let $x =$ the number of pounds of Kenyan coffee and $y =$ the number of pounds of Peruvian coffee in the mixture. We organize the information in a table.

Type of Coffee	Kenyan	Peruvian	Mixture
Price per pound	$6.75	$11.25	$8.55
Number of pounds	x	y	50
Total cost	$6.75x$	$11.25y$	8.55×50, or $427.50

Translate. From the last two rows of the table we get a system of equations.

$x + y = 50,$

$6.75x + 11.25y = 427.50$

Solve. Solving the system of equations, we get $(30, 20)$.

Check. The total number of pounds in the mixture is $30 + 20$, or 50. The total cost of the mixture is $\$6.75(30) + \$11.25(20) = \$427.50$. The values check.

State. The mixture should consist of 30 lb of Kenyan coffee and 20 lb of Peruvian coffee.

63. $\sqrt{8x} \cdot \sqrt{2x} = \sqrt{8x \cdot 2x} = \sqrt{16x^2} = \sqrt{(4x)^2} = 4x$

65. $\sqrt[4]{9a^2} \cdot \sqrt[4]{18a^3} = \sqrt[4]{9a^2 \cdot 18a^3} =$
$\sqrt[4]{3\cdot3\cdot a^2\cdot 3\cdot3\cdot2\cdot a^2\cdot a} = \sqrt[4]{3^4 a^4 \cdot 2a} = \sqrt[4]{3^4}\sqrt[4]{a^4}\sqrt[4]{2a} =$
$3a\sqrt[4]{2a}$

67. Graph $f(x) = -\dfrac{3}{5}x + 4$.

Choose some values for x, find the corresponding values of $f(x)$, plot the points $(x, f(x))$, and draw the graph.

x	$f(x)$	$(x, f(x))$
-5	7	$(-5, 7)$
0	4	$(0, 4)$
5	1	$(5, 1)$

$f(x) = -\frac{3}{5}x + 4$

69. Graph $y = 4$.

The graph of $y = 4$ is a horizontal line with y-intercept $(0, 4)$.

71. Left to the student

73. a) $kx^2 - 2x + k = 0$; one solution is -3

We first find k by substituting -3 for x.

$$k(-3)^2 - 2(-3) + k = 0$$
$$9k + 6 + k = 0$$
$$10k = -6$$
$$k = -\frac{6}{10}$$
$$k = -\frac{3}{5}$$

b) $-\frac{3}{5}x^2 - 2x + \left(-\frac{3}{5}\right) = 0$ Substituting $-\frac{3}{5}$ for k

$$3x^2 + 10x + 3 = 0 \quad \text{Multiplying by } -5$$
$$(3x + 1)(x + 3) = 0$$

$3x + 1 = 0 \quad or \quad x + 3 = 0$

$3x = -1 \quad or \quad\quad x = -3$

$x = -\frac{1}{3} \quad or \quad\quad x = -3$

The other solution is $-\frac{1}{3}$.

75. For $ax^2 + bx + c = 0$, $-\frac{b}{a}$ is the sum of the solutions and $\frac{c}{a}$ is the product of the solutions. Thus $-\frac{b}{a} = \sqrt{3}$ and $\frac{c}{a} = 8$.

$$ax^2 + bx + c = 0$$
$$x^2 + \frac{b}{a}x + \frac{c}{a} = 0 \quad \text{Multiplying by } \frac{1}{a}$$
$$x^2 - \left(-\frac{b}{a}\right)x + \frac{c}{a} = 0$$
$$x^2 - \sqrt{3}x + 8 = 0 \quad \begin{array}{l}\text{Substituting } \sqrt{3} \text{ for} \\ -\frac{b}{a} \text{ and } 8 \text{ for } \frac{c}{a}\end{array}$$

77. The graph includes the points $(-3, 0)$, $(0, -3)$, and $(1, 0)$. Substituting in $y = ax^2 + bx + c$, we have three equations.

$$0 = 9a - 3b + c,$$
$$-3 = \qquad\quad c,$$
$$0 = a + b + c$$

The solution of this system of equations is $a = 1$, $b = 2$, $c = -3$.

79. $\dfrac{x}{x-1} - 6\sqrt{\dfrac{x}{x-1}} - 40 = 0$

Let $u = \sqrt{\dfrac{x}{x-1}}$.

$$u^2 - 6u - 40 = 0 \quad \text{Substituting for } \sqrt{\dfrac{x}{x-1}}$$
$$(u - 10)(u + 4) = 0$$

$u = 10 \qquad or \qquad u = -4$

$\sqrt{\dfrac{x}{x-1}} = 10 \quad or \quad \sqrt{\dfrac{x}{x-1}} = -4$

Substituting for u

$\dfrac{x}{x-1} = 100 \qquad or \qquad$ No solution

$x = 100x - 100 \quad \text{Multiplying by } (x - 1)$

$100 = 99x$

$\dfrac{100}{99} = x$

This number checks. It is the solution.

81. $\sqrt{x-3} - \sqrt[4]{x-3} = 12$

$$(x - 3)^{1/2} - (x - 3)^{1/4} - 12 = 0$$

Let $u = (x - 3)^{1/4}$.

$$u^2 - u - 12 = 0 \quad \text{Substituting for } (x - 3)^{1/4}$$
$$(u - 4)(u + 3) = 0$$

$u = 4 \qquad or \qquad u = -3$

$(x - 3)^{1/4} = 4 \quad or \quad (x - 3)^{1/4} = -3$

Substituting for u

$x - 3 = 4^4 \qquad or \qquad$ No solution

$x - 3 = 256$

$x = 259$

This number checks. It is the solution.

83. $x^6 - 28x^3 + 27 = 0$

Let $u = x^3$.

$$u^2 - 28u + 27 = 0 \quad \text{Substituting for } x^3$$
$$(u - 27)(u - 1) = 0$$

$u = 27 \quad or \quad u = 1$

$x^3 = 27 \quad or \quad x^3 = 1 \quad \text{Substituting for } u$

$x = 3 \quad or \quad x = 1$

Both 3 and 1 check. They are the solutions.

Exercise Set 7.5

1. $f(x) = 4x^2$

$f(x) = 4x^2$ is of the form $f(x) = ax^2$. Thus we know that the vertex is $(0,0)$ and $x = 0$ is the line of symmetry.

We know that $f(x) = 0$ when $x = 0$ since the vertex is $(0,0)$.

For $x = 1$, $f(x) = 4x^2 = 4 \cdot 1^2 = 4$.

For $x = -1$, $f(x) = 4x^2 = 4 \cdot (-1)^2 = 4$.

For $x = 2$, $f(x) = 4x^2 = 4 \cdot 2^2 = 16$.

For $x = -2$, $f(x) = 4x^2 = 4 \cdot (-2)^2 = 16$.

We complete the table.

x	$f(x)$	
0	0	← Vertex
1	4	
2	16	
-1	4	
-2	16	

We plot the ordered pairs $(x, f(x))$ from the table and connect them with a smooth curve.

3. $f(x) = \frac{1}{3}x^2$ is of the form $f(x) = ax^2$. Thus we know that the vertex is $(0,0)$ and $x = 0$ is the line of symmetry. We choose some numbers for x and find the corresponding values for $f(x)$. Then we plot the ordered pairs $(x, f(x))$ and connect them with a smooth curve.

For $x = 3$, $f(x) = \frac{1}{3}x^2 = \frac{1}{3} \cdot 3^2 = 3$.

For $x = -3$, $f(x) = \frac{1}{3}x^2 = \frac{1}{3} \cdot (-3)^2 = 3$.

For $x = 6$, $f(x) = \frac{1}{3}x^2 = \frac{1}{3} \cdot 6^2 = 12$.

For $x = -6$, $f(x) = \frac{1}{3}x^2 = \frac{1}{3} \cdot (-6)^2 = 12$.

x	$f(x)$	
0	0	← Vertex
1	$\frac{1}{3}$	
2	$\frac{4}{3}$	
-1	$\frac{1}{3}$	
-2	$\frac{4}{3}$	

5. $f(x) = -\frac{1}{2}x^2$ is of the form $f(x) = ax^2$. Thus we know that the vertex is $(0,0)$ and $x = 0$ is the line of symmetry. We choose some numbers for x and find the corresponding values for $f(x)$. Then we plot the ordered pairs $(x, f(x))$ and connect them with a smooth curve.

For $x = 2$, $f(x) = -\frac{1}{2}x^2 = -\frac{1}{2} \cdot 2^2 = -2$.

For $x = -2$, $f(x) = -\frac{1}{2}x^2 = -\frac{1}{2} \cdot (-2)^2 = -2$.

For $x = 4$, $f(x) = -\frac{1}{2}x^2 = -\frac{1}{2} \cdot 4^2 = -8$.

For $x = -4$, $f(x) = -\frac{1}{2}x^2 = -\frac{1}{2} \cdot (-4)^2 = -8$.

x	$f(x)$	
0	0	← Vertex
2	-2	
-2	-2	
4	-8	
-4	-8	

7. $f(x) = -4x^2$ is of the form $f(x) = ax^2$. Thus we know that the vertex is $(0,0)$ and $x = 0$ is the line of symmetry. We choose some numbers for x and find the corresponding values for $f(x)$. Then we plot the ordered pairs $(x, f(x))$ and connect them with a smooth curve.

For $x = 1$, $f(x) = -4x^2 = -4 \cdot 1^2 = -4$.

For $x = -1$, $f(x) = -4x^2 = -4 \cdot (-1)^2 = -4$.

For $x = 2$, $f(x) = -4x^2 = -4 \cdot 2^2 = -16$.

For $x = -2$, $f(x) = -4x^2 = -4 \cdot (-2)^2 = -16$.

x	$f(x)$	
0	0	← Vertex
1	-4	
-1	-4	
2	-16	
-2	-16	

9. $f(x) = (x+3)^2 = [x-(-3)]^2$ is of the form $f(x) = a(x-h)^2$.

Thus we know that the vertex is $(-3, 0)$ and $x = -3$ is the line of symmetry. We choose some numbers for x and find the corresponding values for $f(x)$. Then we plot the ordered pairs $(x, f(x))$ and connect them with a smooth curve.

x	$f(x)$	
-3	0	← Vertex
-2	1	
-1	4	
-4	1	
-5	4	

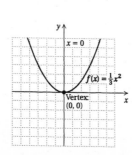

11. Graph: $f(x) = 2(x-4)^2$

We choose some values of x and compute $f(x)$. Then we plot these ordered pairs and connect them with a smooth curve.

x	$f(x)$
4	0
5	2
3	2
6	8
2	8

The graph of $f(x) = 2(x-4)^2$ looks like the graph of $f(x) = 2x^2$ except that it is translated 4 units to the right. The vertex is $(4,0)$, and the line of symmetry is $x = 4$.

13. Graph: $f(x) = -2(x+2)^2$

We choose some values of x and compute $f(x)$. Then we plot these ordered pairs and connect them with a smooth curve.

x	$f(x)$
1	-18
0	-8
-1	-2
-2	0
-3	-2
-4	-8

We can express the equation in the equivalent form $f(x) = -2[x - (-2)]^2$. Then we know that the graph looks like the graph of $f(x) = -2x^2$ translated 2 units to the left. The vertex is $(-2, 0)$, and the line of symmetry is $x = -2$.

15. Graph: $f(x) = 3(x-1)^2$

We choose some values of x and compute $f(x)$. Then we plot these ordered pairs and connect them with a smooth curve.

x	$f(x)$
1	0
2	3
0	3
3	12
-1	12

The graph of $f(x) = 3(x-1)^2$ looks like the graph of $f(x) = 3x^2$ except that it is translated 1 unit to the right. The vertex is $(1, 0)$, and the line of symmetry is $x = 1$.

17. Graph: $f(x) = -\frac{3}{2}(x+2)^2$

We choose some values of x and compute $f(x)$. Then we plot these ordered pairs and connect them with a smooth curve.

x	$f(x)$
-4	-6
-2	0
0	-6
2	-24

We can express the equation in the equivalent form $f(x) = -\frac{3}{2}[x - (-2)]^2$. Then we know that the graph looks like the graph of $f(x) = -\frac{3}{2}x^2$ translated 2 units to the left. The vertex is $(-2, 0)$, and the line of symmetry is $x = -2$.

19. Graph: $f(x) = (x-3)^2 + 1$

We choose some values of x and compute $f(x)$. Then we plot these ordered pairs and connect them with a smooth curve.

x	$f(x)$
3	1
4	2
2	2
5	5
1	5

The graph of $f(x) = (x-3)^2 + 1$ looks like the graph of $f(x) = x^2$ except that it is translated 3 units right and 1 unit up. The vertex is $(3, 1)$, and the line of symmetry is $x = 3$. The equation is of the form $f(x) = a(x-h)^2 + k$ with $a = 1$. Since $1 > 0$, we know that 1 is the minimum value.

21. Graph: $f(x) = -3(x+4)^2 + 1$

$$f(x) = -3[x - (-4)]^2 + 1$$

We choose some values of x and compute $f(x)$. Then we plot these ordered pairs and connect them with a smooth curve.

x	$f(x)$
-4	1
$-3\frac{1}{2}$	$\frac{1}{4}$
$-4\frac{1}{2}$	$\frac{1}{4}$
-3	-2
-5	-2
-2	-11
-6	-11

The graph of $f(x) = -3(x+4)^2 + 1$ looks like the graph of $f(x) = 3x^2$ except that it is translated 4 units left and 1 unit up and opens downward. The vertex is $(-4, 1)$, and the line of symmetry is $x = -4$. Since $-3 < 0$, we know that 1 is the maximum value.

23. Graph: $f(x) = \frac{1}{2}(x+1)^2 + 4$

$$f(x) = \frac{1}{2}[x - (-1)]^2 + 4$$

We choose some values of x and compute $f(x)$. Then we plot these ordered pairs and connect them with a smooth curve.

x	$f(x)$
1	6
2	$8\frac{1}{2}$
0	$4\frac{1}{2}$
−1	4
−2	$4\frac{1}{2}$
−3	6

The graph of $f(x) = \frac{1}{2}(x+1)^2 + 4$ looks like the graph of $f(x) = \frac{1}{2}x^2$ except that it is translated 1 unit left and 4 units up. The vertex is $(-1, 4)$, and the line of symmetry is $x = -1$. Since $\frac{1}{2} > 0$, we know that 4 is the minimum value.

25. Graph: $f(x) = -(x+1)^2 - 2$
$$f(x) = -[x - (-1)]^2 + (-2)$$

We choose some values of x and compute $f(x)$. Then we plot these ordered pairs and connect them with a smooth curve.

x	$f(x)$
−1	−2
0	−3
−2	−3
1	−6
−3	−6

The graph of $f(x) = -(x+1)^2 - 2$ looks like the graph of $f(x) = x^2$ except that it is translated 1 unit left and 2 units down and opens downward. The vertex is $(-1, -2)$, and the line of symmetry is $x = -1$. Since $-1 < 0$, we know that -2 is the maximum value.

27. Discussion and Writing Exercise

29.
$$x - 5 = \sqrt{x+7}$$
$$(x-5)^2 = (\sqrt{x+7})^2 \quad \text{Principle of powers}$$
$$x^2 - 10x + 25 = x + 7$$
$$x^2 - 11x + 18 = 0$$
$$(x-9)(x-2) = 0$$
$$x - 9 = 0 \quad or \quad x - 2 = 0$$
$$x = 9 \quad or \quad x = 2$$

Check: For 9:

$$
\begin{array}{c|c}
x - 5 = \sqrt{x+7} \\
\hline
9 - 5 \ ? \ \sqrt{9+7} \\
4 & \sqrt{16} \\
 & 4 \\
\end{array}
$$
                                        TRUE

For 2:

$$
\begin{array}{c|c}
x - 5 = \sqrt{x+7} \\
\hline
2 - 5 \ ? \ \sqrt{2+7} \\
-3 & \sqrt{9} \\
 & 3 \\
\end{array}
$$
                                        FALSE

Only 9 checks. It is the solution.

31. $\sqrt{x+4} = -11$

The equation has no solution, because the principal square root of a number is always nonnegative.

33. Left to the student

Exercise Set 7.6

1. $f(x) = x^2 - 2x - 3 = (x^2 - 2x) - 3$

We complete the square inside the parentheses. We take half the x-coefficient and square it.

$$\frac{1}{2} \cdot (-2) = -1 \text{ and } (-1)^2 = 1$$

Then we add $1 - 1$ inside the parentheses.
$$
\begin{aligned}
f(x) &= (x^2 - 2x + 1 - 1) - 3 \\
&= (x^2 - 2x + 1) - 1 - 3 \\
&= (x-1)^2 - 4 \\
&= (x-1)^2 + (-4)
\end{aligned}
$$

Vertex: $(1, -4)$

Line of symmetry: $x = 1$

The coefficient of x^2 is 1, which is positive, so the graph opens up. This tells us that -4 is a minimum.

We plot a few points and draw the curve.

x	$f(x)$
1	−4
2	−3
0	−3
3	0
−1	0
4	5
−2	5

3. $f(x) = -x^2 - 4x - 2 = -(x^2 + 4x) - 2$

We complete the square inside the parentheses. We take half the x-coefficient and square it.

$$\frac{1}{2} \cdot 4 = 2 \text{ and } 2^2 = 4$$

Then we add $4 - 4$ inside the parentheses.

$$f(x) = -(x^2 + 4x + 4 - 4) - 2$$
$$= -(x^2 + 4x + 4) + (-1)(-4) - 2$$
$$= -(x + 2)^2 + 4 - 2$$
$$= -(x + 2)^2 + 2$$
$$= -[x - (-2)]^2 + 2$$

Vertex: $(-2, 2)$

Line of symmetry: $x = -2$

The coefficient of x^2 is -1, which is negative, so the graph opens down. This tells us that 2 is a maximum.

We plot a few points and draw the curve.

x	$f(x)$
-2	2
-4	-2
-3	1
-1	1
0	-2

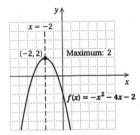

5. $f(x) = 3x^2 - 24x + 50 = 3(x^2 - 8x) + 50$

We complete the square inside the parentheses. We take half the x-coefficient and square it.

$$\frac{1}{2} \cdot (-8) = -4 \text{ and } (-4)^2 = 16$$

Then we add $16 - 16$ inside the parentheses.

$$f(x) = 3(x^2 - 8x + 16 - 16) + 50$$
$$= 3(x^2 - 8x + 16) - 48 + 50$$
$$= 3(x - 4)^2 + 2$$

Vertex: $(4, 2)$

Line of symmetry: $x = 4$

The coefficient of x^2 is 3, which is positive, so the graph opens up. This tells us that 2 is a minimum.

We plot a few points and draw the curve.

x	$f(x)$
4	2
5	5
3	5
6	14
2	14

7. $f(x) = -2x^2 - 2x + 3 = -2(x^2 + x) + 3$

We complete the square inside the parentheses. We take half the x-coefficient and square it.

$$\frac{1}{2} \cdot 1 = \frac{1}{2} \text{ and } \left(\frac{1}{2}\right)^2 = \frac{1}{4}$$

Then we add $\frac{1}{4} - \frac{1}{4}$ inside the parentheses.

$$f(x) = -2\left(x^2 + x + \frac{1}{4} - \frac{1}{4}\right) + 3$$
$$= -2\left(x^2 + x + \frac{1}{4}\right) + (-2)\left(-\frac{1}{4}\right) + 3$$
$$= -2\left(x + \frac{1}{2}\right)^2 + \frac{1}{2} + 3$$
$$= -2\left(x + \frac{1}{2}\right)^2 + \frac{7}{2}$$
$$= -2\left[x - \left(-\frac{1}{2}\right)\right]^2 + \frac{7}{2}$$

Vertex: $\left(-\frac{1}{2}, \frac{7}{2}\right)$

Line of symmetry: $x = -\frac{1}{2}$

The coefficient of x^2 is -2, which is negative, so the graph opens down. This tells us that $\frac{7}{2}$ is a maximum.

We plot a few points and draw the curve.

x	$f(x)$
1	7
$-\frac{1}{2}$	$\frac{7}{2}$
-2	-1
-1	3
0	3
1	-1

9. $f(x) = 5 - x^2 = -x^2 + 5 = -(x - 0)^2 + 5$

Vertex: $(0, 5)$

Line of symmetry: $x = 0$

The coefficient of x^2 is -1, which is negative, so the graph opens down. This tells us that 5 is a maximum.

We plot a few points and draw the curve.

x	$f(x)$
0	5
1	4
-1	4
2	1
-2	1
3	-4
-3	-4

11. $f(x) = 2x^2 + 5x - 2 = 2\left(x^2 + \frac{5}{2}x\right) - 2$

We complete the square inside the parentheses. We take half the x-coefficient and square it.

$$\frac{1}{2} \cdot \frac{5}{2} = \frac{5}{4} \text{ and } \left(\frac{5}{4}\right)^2 = \frac{25}{16}$$

Then we add $\frac{25}{16} - \frac{25}{16}$ inside the parentheses.

$$f(x) = 2\left(x^2 + \frac{5}{2}x + \frac{25}{16} - \frac{25}{16}\right) - 2$$

$$= 2\left(x^2 + \frac{5}{2}x + \frac{25}{16}\right) + 2\left(-\frac{25}{16}\right) - 2$$

$$= 2\left(x + \frac{5}{4}\right)^2 - \frac{25}{8} - 2$$

$$= 2\left(x + \frac{5}{4}\right)^2 - \frac{41}{8}$$

$$= 2\left[x - \left(-\frac{5}{4}\right)\right]^2 + \left(-\frac{41}{8}\right)$$

Vertex: $\left(-\frac{5}{4}, -\frac{41}{8}\right)$

Line of symmetry: $x = -\frac{5}{4}$

The coefficient of x^2 is 2, which is positive, so the graph opens up. This tells us that $-\frac{41}{8}$ is a minimum.

We plot a few points and draw the curve.

x	$f(x)$
$-\frac{5}{4}$	$-\frac{41}{8}$
-3	1
-2	-4
-1	-5
0	-2
1	5

13. $f(x) = x^2 - 6x + 1$

The y-intercept is $(0, f(0))$. Since $f(0) = 0^2 - 6 \cdot 0 + 1 = 1$, the y-intercept is $(0, 1)$.

To find the x-intercepts, we solve $x^2 - 6x + 1 = 0$. Using the quadratic formula gives us $x = 3 \pm 2\sqrt{2}$.

Thus, the x-intercepts are $(3 - 2\sqrt{2}, 0)$ and $(3 + 2\sqrt{2}, 0)$, or approximately $(0.172, 0)$ and $(5.828, 0)$.

15. $f(x) = -x^2 + x + 20$

The y-intercept is $(0, f(0))$. Since $f(0) = -0^2 + 0 + 20 = 20$, the y-intercept is $(0, 20)$.

To find the x-intercepts, we solve $-x^2 + x + 20 = 0$. Factoring and using the principle of zero products gives us $x = -4$ or $x = 5$. Thus, the x-intercepts are $(-4, 0)$ and $(5, 0)$.

17. $f(x) = 4x^2 + 12x + 9$

The y-intercept is $(0, f(0))$. Since $f(0) = 4 \cdot 0^2 + 12 \cdot 0 + 9 = 9$, the y-intercept is $(0, 9)$.

To find the x-intercepts, we solve $4x^2 + 12x + 9 = 0$. Factoring and using the principle of zero products gives us $x = -\frac{3}{2}$. Thus, the x-intercept is $\left(-\frac{3}{2}, 0\right)$.

19. $f(x) = 4x^2 - x + 8$

The y-intercept is $(0, f(0))$. Since $f(0) = 4 \cdot 0^2 - 0 + 8 = 8$, the y-intercept is $(0, 8)$.

To find the x-intercepts, we solve $4x^2 - x + 8 = 0$. Using the quadratic formula gives us $x = \frac{1 \pm i\sqrt{127}}{8}$. Since there are no real-number solutions, there are no x-intercepts.

21. Discussion and Writing Exercise

23. a)
$$D = kw$$
$$420 = k \cdot 28$$
$$\frac{420}{28} = k$$
$$15 = k$$

The equation of variation is $D = 15w$.

b) We substitute 42 for w and compute D.
$$D = 15w$$
$$D = 15 \cdot 42$$
$$D = 630$$

630 mg would be recommended for a child who weighs 42 kg.

25.
$$y = \frac{k}{x}$$
$$125 = \frac{k}{2}$$
$$250 = k \quad \text{Variation constant}$$
$$y = \frac{250}{x} \quad \text{Equation of variation}$$

27.
$$y = kx$$
$$125 = k \cdot 2$$
$$\frac{125}{2} = k \quad \text{Variation constant}$$
$$y = \frac{125}{2}x \quad \text{Equation of variation}$$

29. a) Minimum: -6.954

b) Maximum: 7.014

31. $f(x) = |x^2 - 1|$

We plot some points and draw the curve. Note that it will lie entirely on or above the x-axis since absolute value is never negative.

x	$f(x)$
-3	8
-2	3
-1	0
0	1
1	0
2	3
3	8

33. $f(x) = |x^2 - 3x - 4|$

We plot some points and draw the curve. Note that it will lie entirely on or above the x-axis since absolute value is never negative.

x	$f(x)$
-4	24
-3	14
-2	6
-1	0
0	4
1	6
2	6
3	4
4	0
5	6
6	14

$f(x) = |x^2 - 3x - 4|$

x	$f(x)$
-5	$\frac{3}{2}$
-3	0
-1	$-\frac{1}{2}$
0	$-\frac{3}{8}$
1	0
3	$\frac{3}{2}$
5	4

$x = -1$

$(-1, -\frac{1}{2})$ Minimum: $-\frac{1}{2}$

$f(x) = \frac{x^2}{8} + \frac{x}{4} - \frac{3}{8}$

35. The horizontal distance from $(-1, 0)$ to $(3, -5)$ is $|3 - (-1)|$, or 4, so by symmetry the other x-intercept is $(3 + 4, 0)$, or $(7, 0)$. Substituting the three ordered pairs $(-1, 0)$, $(3, -5)$, and $(7, 0)$ in the equation $f(x) = ax^2 + bx + c$ yields a system of equations:

$$0 = a(-1)^2 + b(-1) + c,$$
$$-5 = a \cdot 3^2 + b \cdot 3 + c,$$
$$0 = a \cdot 7^2 + b \cdot 7 + c$$

or

$$0 = a - b + c,$$
$$-5 = 9a + 3b + c,$$
$$0 = 49a + 7b + c$$

The solution of this system of equations is $\left(\frac{5}{16}, -\frac{15}{8}, -\frac{35}{16}\right)$, so $f(x) = \frac{5}{16}x^2 - \frac{15}{8}x - \frac{35}{16}$.

37. $f(x) = \dfrac{x^2}{8} + \dfrac{x}{4} - \dfrac{3}{8}$

The x-coordinate of the vertex is $-b/2a$:

$$-\frac{b}{2a} = -\frac{\frac{1}{4}}{2 \cdot \frac{1}{8}} = -\frac{\frac{1}{4}}{\frac{1}{4}} = -1$$

The second coordinate is $f(-1)$:

$$f(-1) = \frac{(-1)^2}{8} + \frac{-1}{4} - \frac{3}{8}$$
$$= \frac{1}{8} - \frac{1}{4} - \frac{3}{8}$$
$$= -\frac{1}{2}$$

The vertex is $\left(-1, -\dfrac{1}{2}\right)$.

The line of symmetry is $x = -1$.

The coefficient of x^2 is $\dfrac{1}{8}$, which is positive, so the graph opens up. This tells us that $-\dfrac{1}{2}$ is a minimum.

We plot some points and draw the graph.

39. Graph $y_1 = x^2 - 4x + 2$ and $y_2 = 2 + x$ and use INTERSECT to find the points of intersection. They are $(0, 2)$ and $(5, 7)$.

Exercise Set 7.7

1. *Familiarize*. Referring to the drawing in the text, we let $l =$ the length of the atrium and $w =$ the width. Then the perimeter of each floor is $2l + 2w$, and the area is $l \cdot w$.

Translate. Using the formula for perimeter we have:

$$2l + 2w = 720$$
$$2l = 720 - 2w$$
$$l = \frac{720 - 2w}{2}$$
$$l = 360 - w$$

Substituting $360 - w$ for l in the formula for area, we get a quadratic function.

$$A = lw = (360 - w)w = 360w - w^2 = -w^2 + 360w$$

Carry out. We complete the square in order to find the vertex of the quadratic function.

$$A = -w^2 + 360w$$
$$= -(w^2 - 360w)$$
$$= -(w^2 - 360w + 32,400 - 32,400)$$
$$= -(w^2 - 360w + 32,400) + (-1)(-32,400)$$
$$= -(w - 180)^2 + 32,400$$

The vertex is $(180, 32,400)$. The coefficient of w^2 is negative, so the graph of a function is a parabola that opens down. This tells us that the function has a maximum value and that value occurs when $w = 180$. When $w = 180$, $l = 360 - w = 360 - 180 = 180$.

Check. We could find the value of the function for some values of w less than 180 and for some values greater than 180, determining that the maximum value we found, 32,400, is larger than these function values. We could also use the graph of the function to check the maximum value. Our answer checks.

State. Floors with dimensions 180 ft by 180 ft will allow an atrium with maximum area.

3. *Familiarize*. Let x represent the height of the file and y represent the width. We make a drawing.

***Translate*.** We have two equations.

$2x + y = 14$

$V = 8xy$

Solve the first equation for y.

$y = 14 - 2x$

Substitute for y in the second equation.

$V = 8x(14 - 2x)$

$V = -16x^2 + 112x$

***Carry out*.** Completing the square, we get

$$V = -16\left(x - \frac{7}{2}\right)^2 + 196.$$

The maximum function value of 196 occurs when $x = \frac{7}{2}$. When $x = \frac{7}{2}$, $y = 14 - 2 \cdot \frac{7}{2} = 7$.

***Check*.** Check a function value for x less than $\frac{7}{2}$ and for x greater than $\frac{7}{2}$.

$$V(3) = -16 \cdot 3^2 + 112 \cdot 3 = 192$$
$$V(4) = -16 \cdot 4^2 + 112 \cdot 4 = 192$$

Since 196 is greater than these numbers, it looks as though we have a maximum.

We could also use the graph of the function to check the maximum value.

***State*.** The file should be $\frac{7}{2}$ in., or 3.5 in., tall.

5. *Familiarize and Translate*. We want to find the value of x for which $C(x) = 0.1x^2 - 0.7x + 2.425$ is a minimum.

***Carry out*.** We complete the square.

$C(x) = 0.1(x^2 - 7x + 12.25) + 2.425 - 1.225$

$C(x) = 0.1(x - 3.5)^2 + 1.2$

The minimum function value of 1.2 occurs when $x = 3.5$.

***Check*.** Check a function value for x less than 3.5 and for x greater than 3.5.

$C(3) = 0.1(3)^2 - 0.7(3) + 2.425 = 1.225$

$C(4) = 0.1(4)^2 - 0.7(4) + 2.425 = 1.225$

Since 1.2 is less than these numbers, it looks as though we have a minimum.

We could also use the graph of the function to check the minimum value.

***State*.** The shop should build 3.5 hundred, or 350 bicycles.

7. *Familiarize*. We make a drawing and label it.

***Translate*.** We have two equations.

$l + 2w = 40$

$A = lw$

Solve the first equation for l.

$l = 40 - 2w$

Substitute for l in the second equation.

$A = (40 - 2w)w = 40w - 2w^2$

$ = -2w^2 + 40w$

***Carry out*.** Completing the square, we get

$A = -2(w - 10)^2 + 200$

The maximum function value is 200. It occurs when $w = 10$. When $w = 10$, $l = 40 - 2 \cdot 10 = 20$.

***Check*.** Check a function value for w less than 10 and for w greater than 10.

$$A(9) = -2 \cdot 9^2 + 40 \cdot 9 = 198$$
$$A(11) = -2 \cdot 11^2 + 40 \cdot 11 = 198$$

Since 200 is greater than these numbers, it looks as though we have a maximum. We could also use the graph of the function to check the maximum value.

***State*.** The maximum area of 200 ft^2 will occur when the dimensions are 10 ft by 20 ft.

9. *Familiarize and Translate*. We are given the function $N(x) = -0.4x^2 + 9x + 11$.

***Carry out*.** To find the value of x for which $N(x)$ is a maximum, we first find $-\frac{b}{2a}$:

$$-\frac{b}{2a} = -\frac{9}{2(-0.4)} = 11.25$$

Now we find the maximum value of the function $N(11.25)$:

$N(11.25) = -0.4(11.25)^2 + 9(11.25) + 11 = 61.625$

***Check*.** We can go over the calculations again. We could also solve the problem again by completing the square. The answer checks.

***State*.** Daily ticket sales will peak 11 days after the concert was announced. About 62 tickets will be sold that day.

11. Find the total profit:

$P(x) = R(x) - C(x)$

$P(x) = (1000x - x^2) - (3000 + 20x)$

$P(x) = -x^2 + 980x - 3000$

To find the maximum value of the total profit and the value of x at which it occurs we complete the square:

$$P(x) = -(x^2 - 980x) - 3000$$
$$= -(x^2 - 980x + 240,100 - 240,100) - 3000$$
$$= -(x^2 - 980x + 240,100) - (-240,100) - 3000$$
$$= -(x - 490)^2 + 237,100$$

The maximum profit of $237,100 occurs at $x = 490$.

13. ***Familiarize***. Let x and y represent the numbers.

Translate. The sum of the numbers is 22, so we have $x + y = 22$. Solving for y, we get $y = 22 - x$. The product of the numbers is xy. Substituting $22 - x$ for y in the product, we get a quadratic function:

$$P = xy = x(22 - x) = 22x - x^2 = -x^2 + 22x$$

Carry out. The coefficient of x^2 is negative, so the graph of the function is a parabola that opens down and a maximum exists. We complete the square in order to find the vertex of the quadratic function.

$$P = -x^2 + 22x$$
$$= -(x^2 - 22x)$$
$$= -(x^2 - 22x + 121 - 121)$$
$$= -(x^2 - 22x + 121) + (-1)(-121)$$
$$= -(x - 11)^2 + 121$$

The vertex is $(11, 121)$. This tells us that the maximum product is 121. The maximum occurs when $x = 11$. Note that when $x = 11$, $y = 22 - x = 22 - 11 = 11$, so the numbers that yield the maximum product are 11 and 11.

Check. We could find the value of the function for some values of x less than 11 and for some greater than 11, determining that the maximum value we found is larger than these function values. We could also use the graph of the function to check the maximum value. Our answer checks.

State. The maximum product is 121. The numbers 11 and 11 yield this product.

15. ***Familiarize***. Let x and y represent the numbers.

Translate. The difference of the numbers is 4, so we have $x - y = 4$. Solve for x, we get $x = y + 4$. The product of the numbers is xy. Substituting $y + 4$ for x in the product, we get a quadratic function:

$$P = xy = (y + 4)y = y^2 + 4y$$

Carry out. The coefficient of y^2 is positive, so the graph of the function opens up and a minimum exists. We complete the square in order to find the vertex of the quadratic function.

$$P = y^2 + 4y$$
$$= y^2 + 4y + 4 - 4$$
$$= (y + 2)^2 - 4$$
$$= [y - (-2)]^2 + (-4)$$

The vertex is $(-2, 4)$. This tells us that the minimum product is -4. The minimum occurs when $y = -2$. Note that when $y = -2$, $x = y + 4 = -2 + 4 = 2$, so the numbers that yield the minimum product are 2 and -2.

Check. We could find the value of the function for some values of y less than -2 and for some greater than -2,

determining that the minimum value we found is smaller than these function values. We could also use the graph of the function to check the minimum value. Our answer checks.

State. The minimum product is -4. The numbers 2 and -2 yield this product.

17. ***Familiarize***. We let x and y represent the two numbers, and we let P represent their product.

Translate. We have two equations.
$$x + y = -12,$$
$$P = xy$$

Solve the first equation for y.
$$y = -12 - x$$

Substitute for y in the second equation.
$$P = x(-12 - x) = -12x - x^2$$
$$= -x^2 - 12x$$

Carry out. Completing the square, we get
$$P = -(x + 6)^2 + 36$$

The maximum function value is 36. It occurs when $x = -6$. When $x = -6$, $y = -12 - (-6)$, or -6.

Check. Check a function value for x less than -6 and for x greater than -6.
$$P(-7) = -(-7)^2 - 12(-7) = 35$$
$$P(-5) = -(-5)^2 - 12(-5) = 35$$

Since 36 is greater than these numbers, it looks as though we have a maximum.

We could also use the graph of the function to check the maximum value.

State. The maximum product of 36 occurs for the numbers -6 and -6.

19. The data seem to fit a linear function $f(x) = mx + b$.

21. The data fall and then rise in a curved manner fitting a quadratic function $f(x) = ax^2 + bx + c$, $a > 0$.

23. The data fall, then rise, then fall again so they do not fit a linear or a quadratic function but might fit a polynomial function that is neither quadratic nor linear.

25. The data rise and then fall in a curved manner fitting a quadratic function $f(x) = ax^2 + bx + c$, $a < 0$.

27. We look for a function of the form $f(x) = ax^2 + bx + c$. Substituting the data points, we get
$$4 = a(1)^2 + b(1) + c,$$
$$-2 = a(-1)^2 + b(-1) + c,$$
$$13 = a(2)^2 + b(2) + c,$$
or
$$4 = a + b + c,$$
$$-2 = a - b + c,$$
$$13 = 4a + 2b + c.$$

Solving this system, we get
$$a = 2, \ b = 3, \text{ and } c = -1.$$

Therefore the function we are looking for is

$$f(x) = 2x^2 + 3x - 1.$$

29. We look for a function of the form $f(x) = ax^2 + bx + c$. Substituting the data points, we get

$$0 = a(2)^2 + b(2) + c,$$
$$3 = a(4)^2 + b(4) + c,$$
$$-5 = a(12)^2 + b(12) + c,$$

or

$$0 = 4a + 2b + c,$$
$$3 = 16a + 4b + c,$$
$$-5 = 144a + 12b + c.$$

Solving this system, we get

$$a = -\frac{1}{4},\ b = 3,\ c = -5.$$

Therefore the function we are looking for is

$$f(x) = -\frac{1}{4}x^2 + 3x - 5.$$

31. a) We look for a function of the form $A(s) = as^2 + bs + c$, where $A(s)$ represents the number of nighttime accidents (for every 200 million km) and s represents the travel speed (in km/h). We substitute the given values of s and $A(s)$.

$$400 = a(60)^2 + b(60) + c,$$
$$250 = a(80)^2 + b(80) + c,$$
$$250 = a(100)^2 + b(100) + c,$$

or

$$400 = 3600a + 60b + c,$$
$$250 = 6400a + 80b + c,$$
$$250 = 10,000a + 100b + c.$$

Solving the system of equations, we get

$$a = \frac{3}{16},\ b = -\frac{135}{4},\ c = 1750.$$

Thus, the function $A(s) = \frac{3}{16}s^2 - \frac{135}{4}s + 1750$ fits the data.

b) Find $A(50)$.

$$A(50) = \frac{3}{16}(50)^2 - \frac{135}{4}(50) + 1750 = 531.25$$

About 531 accidents per 200,000,000 km driven occur at 50 km/h.

33. *Familiarize*. Think of a coordinate system placed on the drawing in the text with the origin at the point where the arrow is released. Then three points on the arrow's parabolic path are $(0,0)$, $(63, 27)$, and $(126, 0)$. We look for a function of the form $h(d) = ad^2 + bd + c$, where $h(d)$ represents the arrow's height and d represents the distance the arrow has traveled horizontally.

Translate. We substitute the values given above for d and $h(d)$.

$$0 = a \cdot 0^2 + b \cdot 0 + c,$$
$$27 = a \cdot 63^2 + b \cdot 63 + c,$$
$$0 = a \cdot 126^2 + b \cdot 126 + c$$

or

$$0 = c,$$
$$27 = 3969a + 63b + c,$$
$$0 = 15,876a + 126b + c$$

Solve. Solving the system of equations, we get

$$a = -\frac{1}{147} \approx -0.0068,\ b = \frac{6}{7} \approx 0.8571,\ \text{and } c = 0.$$

Check. Recheck the calculations.

State. The function $h(d) = -\frac{1}{147}d^2 + \frac{6}{7}d \approx -0.0068d^2 + 0.8571d$ expresses the arrow's height as a function of the distance it has traveled horizontally.

35. Discussion and Writing Exercise

37. $\sqrt[4]{5x^3y^5}\ \sqrt[4]{125x^2y^3} = \sqrt[4]{625x^5y^8} = \sqrt[4]{625x^4y^8 \cdot x} = \sqrt[4]{625x^4y^8} \cdot \sqrt[4]{x} = 5xy^2\sqrt[4]{x}$

39.
$$\sqrt{4x - 4} = \sqrt{x + 4} + 1$$
$$(\sqrt{4x - 4})^2 = (\sqrt{x + 4} + 1)^2$$
$$4x - 4 = x + 4 + 2\sqrt{x + 4} + 1$$
$$3x - 9 = 2\sqrt{x + 4}$$
$$(3x - 9)^2 = (2\sqrt{x + 4})^2$$
$$9x^2 - 54x + 81 = 4(x + 4)$$
$$9x^2 - 54x + 81 = 4x + 16$$
$$9x^2 - 58x + 65 = 0$$
$$(9x - 13)(x - 5) = 0$$
$$9x - 13 = 0 \quad or \quad x - 5 = 0$$
$$9x = 13 \quad or \qquad x = 5$$
$$x = \frac{13}{9} \quad or \qquad x = 5$$

Only 5 checks. It is the solution.

41. $-35 = \sqrt{2x + 5}$

The equation has no solution, because the principle square root of a number is always nonnegative.

43. We will let x represent the number of years since 1997 and y represent the gross profit, in billions of dollars. Enter the data points (x, y) in STAT lists and use the quartic regression feature to find the equation $y = -0.290x^4 + 2.699x^3 - 8.306x^2 + 9.190x + 12.235$, where x is the number of years after 1997 and y is in billions of dollars.

Exercise Set 7.8

---

1. $(x - 6)(x + 2) > 0$

The solutions of $(x - 6)(x + 2) = 0$ are 6 and -2. They divide the real-number line into three intervals as shown:

We try test numbers in each interval.

A: Test -3, $y = (-3-6)(-3+2) = 9 > 0$

B: Test 0, $y = (0-6)(0+2) = -12 < 0$

C: Test 7, $y = (7-6)(7+2) = 9 > 0$

The expression is positive for all values of x in intervals A and C. The solution set is $\{x | x < -2 \text{ or } x > 6\}$, or $(-\infty, -2) \cup (6, \infty)$.

From the graph in the text we see that the value of $(x-6)(x+2)$ is positive to the left of -2 and to the right of 6. This verifies the answer we found algebraically.

3. $4 - x^2 \geq 0$

$(2+x)(2-x) \geq 0$

The solutions of $(2+x)(2-x) = 0$ are -2 and 2. They divide the real-number line into three intervals as shown.

We try test numbers in each interval.

A: Test -3, $y = 4 - (-3)^2 = -5 < 0$

B: Test 0, $y = 4 - 0^2 = 4 > 0$

C: Test 3, $y = 4 - 3^2 = -5 < 0$

The expression is positive for values of x in interval B. Since the inequality symbol is $\geq$ we also include the intercepts. The solution set is $\{x | -2 \leq x \leq 2\}$, or $[-2, 2]$.

From the graph we see that $4 - x^2 \geq 0$ at the intercepts and between them. This verifies the answer we found algebraically.

5. $3(x+1)(x-4) \leq 0$

The solutions of $3(x+1)(x-4) = 0$ are -1 and 4. They divide the real-number line into three intervals as shown:

We try test numbers in each interval.

A: Test -2, $y = 3(-2+1)(-2-4) = 18 > 0$

B: Test 0, $y = 3(0+1)(0-4) = -12 < 0$

C: Test 5, $y = 3(5+1)(5-4) = 18 > 0$

The expression is negative for all numbers in interval B. The inequality symbol is $\leq$, so we need to include the intercepts. The solution set is $\{x | -1 \leq x \leq 4\}$, or $[-1, 4]$.

7. $x^2 - x - 2 < 0$

$(x+1)(x-2) < 0$ Factoring

The solutions of $(x+1)(x-2) = 0$ are -1 and 2. They divide the real-number line into three intervals as shown:

We try test numbers in each interval.

A: Test -2, $y = (-2+1)(-2-2) = 4 > 0$

B: Test 0, $y = (0+1)(0-2) = -2 < 0$

C: Test 3, $y = (3+1)(3-2) = 4 > 0$

The expression is negative for all numbers in interval B. The solution set is $\{x | -1 < x < 2\}$, or $(-1, 2)$.

9. $x^2 - 2x + 1 \geq 0$

$(x-1)^2 \geq 0$

The solution of $(x-1)^2 = 0$ is 1. For all real-number values of x except 1, $(x-1)^2$ will be positive. Thus the solution set is $\{x | x \text{ is a real number}\}$, or $(-\infty, \infty)$.

11. $x^2 + 8 < 6x$

$x^2 - 6x + 8 < 0$

$(x-4)(x-2) < 0$

The solutions of $(x-4)(x-2) = 0$ are 4 and 2. They divide the real-number line into three intervals as shown:

We try test numbers in each interval.

A: Test 0, $y = (0-4)(0-2) = 8 > 0$

B: Test 3, $y = (3-4)(3-2) = -1 < 0$

C: Test 5, $y = (5-4)(5-2) = 3 > 0$

The expression is negative for all numbers in interval B. The solution set is $\{x | 2 < x < 4\}$, or $(2, 4)$.

13. $3x(x+2)(x-2) < 0$

The solutions of $3x(x+2)(x-2) = 0$ are 0, -2, and 2. They divide the real-number line into four intervals as shown:

We try test numbers in each interval.

A: Test -3, $y = 3(-3)(-3+2)(-3-2) = -45 < 0$

B: Test -1, $y = 3(-1)(-1+2)(-1-2) = 9 > 0$

C: Test 1, $y = 3(1)(1+2)(1-2) = -9 < 0$

D: Test 3, $y = 3(3)(3+2)(3-2) = 45 > 0$

The expression is negative for all numbers in intervals A and C. The solution set is $\{x | x < -2 \text{ or } 0 < x < 2\}$, or $(-\infty, -2) \cup (0, 2)$.

15. $(x+9)(x-4)(x+1) > 0$

The solutions of $(x+9)(x-4)(x+1) = 0$ are -9, 4, and -1. They divide the real-number line into four intervals as shown:

We try test numbers in each interval.

A: Test -10, $y = (-10+9)(-10-4)(-10+1) = -126 < 0$

B: Test -2, $y = (-2+9)(-2-4)(-2+1) = 42 > 0$

C: Test 0, $y = (0+9)(0-4)(0+1) = -36 < 0$

D: Test 5, $y = (5+9)(5-4)(5+1) = 84 > 0$

The expression is positive for all values of x in intervals B and D. The solution set is $\{x| -9 < x < -1 \ or \ x > 4\}$, or $(-9, -1) \cup (4, \infty)$.

17. $(x+3)(x+2)(x-1) < 0$

The solutions of $(x+3)(x+2)(x-1) = 0$ are -3, -2, and 1. They divide the real-number line into four intervals as shown:

We try test numbers in each interval.

A: Test -4, $y = (-4+3)(-4+2)(-4-1) = -10 < 0$

B: Test $-\dfrac{5}{2}$, $y = \left(-\dfrac{5}{2}+3\right)\left(-\dfrac{5}{2}+2\right)\left(-\dfrac{5}{2}-1\right) = \dfrac{7}{8} > 0$

C: Test 0, $y = (0+3)(0+2)(0-1) = -6 < 0$

D: Test 2, $y = (2+3)(2+2)(2-1) = 20 > 0$

The expression is negative for all numbers in intervals A and C. The solution set is $\{x|x < -3 \ or \ -2 < x < 1\}$, or $(-\infty, -3) \cup (-2, 1)$.

19. $\dfrac{1}{x-6} < 0$

We write the related equation by changing the $<$ symbol to $=$:

$$\frac{1}{x-6} = 0$$

We solve the related equation.

$$(x-6) \cdot \frac{1}{x-6} = (x-6) \cdot 0$$

$$1 = 0$$

We get a false equation, so the related equation has no solution.

Next we find the numbers for which the rational expression is undefined by setting the denominator equal to 0 and solving:

$$x - 6 = 0$$

$$x = 6$$

We use 6 to divide the number line into two intervals as shown:

We try test numbers in each interval.

A: Test 0, $\dfrac{1}{x-6} < 0$

$\dfrac{1}{0-6}$? 0

$-\dfrac{1}{6}$ $\bigg|$ TRUE

The number 0 is a solution of the inequality, so the interval A is part of the solution set.

B: Test 7, $\dfrac{1}{x-6} < 0$

$\dfrac{1}{7-6}$? 0

1 $\bigg|$ FALSE

The number 7 is not a solution of the inequality, so the interval B is not part of the solution set. The solution set is $\{x|x < 6\}$, or $(-\infty, 6)$.

21. $\dfrac{x+1}{x-3} > 0$

Solve the related equation.

$$\frac{x+1}{x-3} = 0$$

$$x + 1 = 0$$

$$x = -1$$

Find the numbers for which the rational expression is undefined.

$$x - 3 = 0$$

$$x = 3$$

Use the numbers -1 and 3 to divide the number line into intervals as shown:

Try test numbers in each interval.

A: Test -2, $\dfrac{x+1}{x-3} > 0$

$\dfrac{-2+1}{-2-3}$? 0

$\dfrac{-1}{-5}$

$\dfrac{1}{5}$ $\bigg|$ TRUE

The number -2 is a solution of the inequality, so the interval A is part of the solution set.

B: Test 0, $\dfrac{x+1}{x-3} > 0$

$\dfrac{0+1}{0-3}$? 0

$-\dfrac{1}{3}$ $\bigg|$ FALSE

The number 0 is not a solution of the inequality, so the interval B is not part of the solution set.

C: Test 4, $\dfrac{x+1}{x-3} > 0$

$\dfrac{4+1}{4-3}$? 0

$\dfrac{5}{1}$

5 $\bigg|$ TRUE

The number 4 is a solution of the inequality, so the interval C is part of the solution set. The solution set is

$\{x | x < -1 \ or \ x > 3\}$, or $(-\infty, -1) \cup (3, \infty)$.

23. $\dfrac{3x + 2}{x - 3} \le 0$

Solve the related equation.

$$\dfrac{3x + 2}{x - 3} = 0$$

$$3x + 2 = 0$$

$$3x = -2$$

$$x = -\dfrac{2}{3}$$

Find the numbers for which the rational expression is undefined.

$$x - 3 = 0$$

$$x = 3$$

Use the numbers $-\dfrac{2}{3}$ and 3 to divide the number line into intervals as shown:

Try test numbers in each interval.

A: Test -1,
$$\dfrac{3x + 2}{x - 3} \le 0$$

$$\dfrac{3(-1) + 2}{-1 - 3} \ ? \ 0$$

$$\dfrac{-1}{-4}$$

$$\dfrac{1}{4} \ \Big| \quad \text{FALSE}$$

The number -1 is not a solution of the inequality, so interval A is not part of the solution set.

B: Test 0,
$$\dfrac{3x + 2}{x - 3} \le 0$$

$$\dfrac{3 \cdot 0 + 2}{0 - 3} \ ? \ 0$$

$$\dfrac{2}{-3}$$

$$-\dfrac{2}{3} \ \Big| \quad \text{TRUE}$$

The number 0 is a solution of the inequality, so the interval B is part of the solution set.

C: Test 4,
$$\dfrac{3x + 2}{x - 3} \le 0$$

$$\dfrac{3 \cdot 4 + 2}{4 - 3} \ ? \ 0$$

$$14 \ \Big| \quad \text{FALSE}$$

The number 4 is not a solution of the inequality, so interval C is not part of the solution set. The solution set includes the interval B. The number $-\dfrac{2}{3}$ is also included

since the inequality symbol is $\le$ and $-\dfrac{2}{3}$ is the solution of the related equation. The number 3 is not included because the rational expression is undefined for 3. The solution set is $\left\{ x \ \Big| -\dfrac{2}{3} \le x < 3 \right\}$, or $\left[-\dfrac{2}{3}, 3 \right)$.

25. $\dfrac{x - 1}{x - 2} > 3$

Solve the related equation.

$$\dfrac{x - 1}{x - 2} = 3$$

$$x - 1 = 3(x - 2)$$

$$x - 1 = 3x - 6$$

$$5 = 2x$$

$$\dfrac{5}{2} = x$$

Find the numbers for which the rational expression is undefined.

$$x - 2 = 0$$

$$x = 2$$

Use the numbers $\dfrac{5}{2}$ and 2 to divide the number line into intervals as shown:

Try test numbers in each interval.

A: Test 0,
$$\dfrac{x - 1}{x - 2} > 3$$

$$\dfrac{0 - 1}{0 - 2} \ ? \ 3$$

$$\dfrac{1}{2} \ \Big| \quad \text{FALSE}$$

The number 0 is not a solution of the inequality, so interval A is not part of the solution set.

B: Test $\dfrac{9}{4}$,
$$\dfrac{x - 1}{x - 2} > 3$$

$$\dfrac{\dfrac{9}{4} - 1}{\dfrac{9}{4} - 2} \ ? \ 3$$

$$\dfrac{\dfrac{5}{4}}{\dfrac{1}{4}}$$

$$5 \ \Big| \quad \text{TRUE}$$

The number $\dfrac{9}{4}$ is a solution of the inequality, so the interval B is part of the solution set.

C: Test 3,
$$\dfrac{x - 1}{x - 2} > 3$$

$$\dfrac{3 - 1}{3 - 2} \ ? \ 3$$

$$2 \ \Big| \quad \text{FALSE}$$

The number 3 is not a solution of the inequality, so the interval C is not part of the solution set. The solution set is $\left\{x \middle| 2 < x < \frac{5}{2}\right\}$, or $\left(2, \frac{5}{2}\right)$.

27. $\dfrac{(x-2)(x+1)}{x-5} < 0$

Solve the related equation.

$$\frac{(x-2)(x+1)}{x-5} = 0$$

$$(x-2)(x+1) = 0$$

$$x = 2 \text{ or } x = -1$$

Find the numbers for which the rational expression is undefined.

$$x - 5 = 0$$

$$x = 5$$

Use the numbers 2, -1, and 5 to divide the number line into intervals as shown:

Try test numbers in each interval.

A: Test -2,
$$\frac{(x-2)(x+1)}{x-5} < 0$$
$$\frac{(-2-2)(-2+1)}{-2-5} \text{ ? } 0$$
$$\frac{-4(-1)}{-7}$$
$$-\frac{4}{7} \quad \text{TRUE}$$

Interval A is part of the solution set.

B: Test 0,
$$\frac{(x-2)(x+1)}{x-5} < 0$$
$$\frac{(0-2)(0+1)}{0-5} \text{ ? } 0$$
$$\frac{-2 \cdot 1}{-5}$$
$$\frac{2}{5} \quad \text{FALSE}$$

Interval B is not part of the solution set.

C: Test 3,
$$\frac{(x-2)(x+1)}{x-5} < 0$$
$$\frac{(3-2)(3+1)}{3-5} \text{ ? } 0$$
$$\frac{1 \cdot 4}{-2}$$
$$-2 \quad \text{TRUE}$$

Interval C is part of the solution set.

D: Test 6,

$$\frac{(x-2)(x+1)}{x-5} < 0$$
$$\frac{(6-2)(6+1)}{6-5} \text{ ? } 0$$
$$\frac{4 \cdot 7}{1}$$
$$28 \quad \text{FALSE}$$

Interval D is not part of the solution set.

The solution set is $\{x | x < -1 \text{ or } 2 < x < 5\}$, or $(-\infty, -1) \cup (2, 5)$.

29. $\dfrac{x+3}{x} \leq 0$

Solve the related equation.

$$\frac{x+3}{x} = 0$$

$$x + 3 = 0$$

$$x = -3$$

Find the numbers for which the rational expression is undefined.

$$x = 0$$

Use the numbers -3 and 0 to divide the number line into intervals as shown:

Try test numbers in each interval.

A: Test -4,
$$\frac{x+3}{x} \leq 0$$
$$\frac{-4+3}{-4} \text{ ? } 0$$
$$\frac{1}{4} \quad \text{FALSE}$$

Interval A is not part of the solution set.

B: Test -1,
$$\frac{x+3}{x} \leq 0$$
$$\frac{-1+3}{-1} \text{ ? } 0$$
$$-2 \quad \text{TRUE}$$

Interval B is part of the solution set.

C: Test 1,
$$\frac{x+3}{x} \leq 0$$
$$\frac{1+3}{1} \text{ ? } 0$$
$$4 \quad \text{FALSE}$$

Interval C is not part of the solution set.

The solution set includes the interval B. The number -3 is also included since the inequality symbol is $\leq$ and -3 is a solution of the related equation. The number 0 is not included because the rational expression is undefined for 0. The solution set is $\{x | -3 \leq x < 0\}$, or $[-3, 0)$.

31. $\dfrac{x}{x-1} > 2$

Solve the related equation.

$$\frac{x}{x-1} = 2$$

$$x = 2x - 2$$

$$2 = x$$

Find the numbers for which the rational expression is undefined.

$$x - 1 = 0$$

$$x = 1$$

Use the numbers 1 and 2 to divide the number line into intervals as shown:

Try test numbers in each interval.

A: Test 0,

$$\frac{x}{x-1} > 2$$

$$\frac{0}{0-1} \;?\; 2$$

$$0 \;|\; \text{FALSE}$$

Interval A is not part of the solution set.

B: Test $\dfrac{3}{2}$,

$$\frac{x}{x-1} > 2$$

$$\frac{\frac{3}{2}}{\frac{3}{2}-1} \;?\; 2$$

$$\frac{\frac{3}{2}}{\frac{1}{2}}$$

$$3 \;|\; \text{TRUE}$$

Interval B is part of the solution set.

C: Test 3,

$$\frac{x}{x-1} > 2$$

$$\frac{3}{3-1} \;?\; 2$$

$$\frac{3}{2} \;|\; \text{FALSE}$$

Interval C is not part of the solution set.

The solution set is $\{x | 1 < x < 2\}$, or $(1, 2)$.

33. $\dfrac{x-1}{(x-3)(x+4)} < 0$

Solve the related equation.

$$\frac{x-1}{(x-3)(x+4)} = 0$$

$$x - 1 = 0$$

$$x = 1$$

Find the numbers for which the rational expression is undefined.

$$(x-3)(x+4) = 0$$

$$x = 3 \text{ or } x = -4$$

Use the numbers 1, 3, and -4 to divide the number line into intervals as shown:

Try test numbers in each interval.

A: Test -5,

$$\frac{x-1}{(x-3)(x+4)} < 0$$

$$\frac{-5-1}{(-5-3)(-5+4)} \;?\; 0$$

$$\frac{-6}{-8(-1)}$$

$$-\frac{3}{4} \;\Big|\; \text{TRUE}$$

Interval A is part of the solution set.

B: Test 0,

$$\frac{x-1}{(x-3)(x+4)} < 0$$

$$\frac{0-1}{(0-3)(0+4)} \;?\; 0$$

$$\frac{-1}{-3 \cdot 4}$$

$$\frac{1}{12} \;\Big|\; \text{FALSE}$$

Interval B is not part of the solution set.

C: Test 2,

$$\frac{x-1}{(x-3)(x+4)} < 0$$

$$\frac{2-1}{(2-3)(2+4)} \;?\; 0$$

$$\frac{1}{-1 \cdot 6}$$

$$-\frac{1}{6} \;\Big|\; \text{TRUE}$$

Interval C is part of the solution set.

D: Test 4,

$$\frac{x-1}{(x-3)(x+4)} < 0$$

$$\frac{4-1}{(4-3)(4+4)} \;?\; 0$$

$$\frac{3}{1 \cdot 8}$$

$$\frac{3}{8} \;\Big|\; \text{FALSE}$$

Interval D is not part of the solution set.

The solution set is $\{x | x < -4 \text{ or } 1 < x < 3\}$, or $(-\infty, -4) \cup (1, 3)$.

35. $3 < \dfrac{1}{x}$

Solve the related equation.

$$3 = \frac{1}{x}$$

$$x = \frac{1}{3}$$

Find the numbers for which the rational expression is undefined.

$$x = 0$$

Use the numbers 0 and $\dfrac{1}{3}$ to divide the number line into intervals as shown:

Try test numbers in each interval.

A: Test -1,

$$3 < \frac{1}{x}$$

$$3 \; ? \; \frac{1}{-1}$$

$$\Big| \; -1 \qquad \text{FALSE}$$

Interval A is not part of the solution set.

B: Test $\dfrac{1}{6}$,

$$3 < \frac{1}{x}$$

$$3 \; ? \; \frac{1}{\frac{1}{6}}$$

$$\Big| \; 6 \qquad \text{TRUE}$$

Interval B is part of the solution set.

C: Test 1,

$$3 < \frac{1}{x}$$

$$3 \; ? \; \frac{1}{1}$$

$$\Big| \; 1 \qquad \text{FALSE}$$

Interval C is not part of the solution set.

The solution set is $\left\{ x \Big| 0 < x < \dfrac{1}{3} \right\}$, or $\left(0, \dfrac{1}{3} \right)$.

37. $\dfrac{(x-1)(x+2)}{(x+3)(x-4)} > 0$

Solve the related equation.

$$\frac{(x-1)(x+2)}{(x+3)(x-4)} = 0$$

$$(x-1)(x+2) = 0$$

$$x = 1 \text{ or } x = -2$$

Find the numbers for which the rational expression is undefined.

$(x+3)(x-4) = 0$

$x = -3 \text{ or } x = 4$

Use the numbers 1, -2, -3, and 4 to divide the number line into intervals as shown:

Try test numbers in each interval.

A: Test -4,

$$\frac{(x-1)(x+2)}{(x+3)(x-4)} > 0$$

$$\frac{(-4-1)(-4+2)}{(-4+3)(-4-4)} \; ? \; 0$$

$$\frac{-5(-2)}{-1(-8)} \Big|$$

$$\frac{5}{4} \; \Big| \qquad \text{TRUE}$$

Interval A is part of the solution set.

B: Test $-\dfrac{5}{2}$,

$$\frac{(x-1)(x+2)}{(x+3)(x-4)} > 0$$

$$\frac{\left(-\frac{5}{2}-1\right)\left(-\frac{5}{2}+2\right)}{\left(-\frac{5}{2}+3\right)\left(-\frac{5}{2}-4\right)} \; ? \; 0$$

$$\frac{-\frac{7}{2}\left(-\frac{1}{2}\right)}{\frac{1}{2}\left(-\frac{13}{2}\right)} \Big|$$

$$-\frac{7}{13} \; \Big| \qquad \text{FALSE}$$

Interval B is not part of the solution set.

C: Test 1,

$$\frac{(x-1)(x+2)}{(x+3)(x-4)} > 0$$

$$\frac{(0-1)(0+2)}{(0+3)(0-4)} \; ? \; 0$$

$$\frac{-1 \cdot 2}{3(-4)} \Big|$$

$$\frac{1}{6} \; \Big| \qquad \text{TRUE}$$

Interval C is part of the solution set.

D: Test 2,

$$\frac{(x-1)(x+2)}{(x+3)(x-4)} > 0$$

$$\frac{(2-1)(2+2)}{(2+3)(2-4)} \; ? \; 0$$

$$\frac{1 \cdot 4}{5(-2)} \Big|$$

$$-\frac{2}{5} \; \Big| \qquad \text{FALSE}$$

Interval D is not part of the solution set.

E: Test 5,

$$\frac{(x-1)(x+2)}{(x+3)(x-4)} > 0$$

$$\frac{(5-1)(5+2)}{(5+3)(5-4)} \ ?\ 0$$

$$\frac{4 \cdot 7}{8 \cdot 1}$$

$$\frac{7}{2} \quad \Big| \quad \text{TRUE}$$

Interval E is part of the solution set.

The solution set is $\{x|x < -3 \ or \ -2 < x < 1 \ or \ x > 4\}$, or $(-\infty, -3) \cup (-2, 1) \cup (4, \infty)$.

39. Discussion and Writing Exercise

41. $\sqrt[3]{\dfrac{125}{27}} = \dfrac{\sqrt[3]{125}}{\sqrt[3]{27}} = \dfrac{5}{3}$

43. $\sqrt{\dfrac{16a^3}{b^4}} = \dfrac{\sqrt{16a^3}}{\sqrt{b^4}} = \dfrac{\sqrt{16a^2 \cdot a}}{\sqrt{b^4}} = \dfrac{\sqrt{16a^2}\sqrt{a}}{\sqrt{b^4}} = \dfrac{4a}{b^2}\sqrt{a}$

45.
$$\begin{aligned}
3\sqrt{8} - 5\sqrt{2} &= 3\sqrt{4 \cdot 2} - 5\sqrt{2}\\
&= 3\sqrt{4}\sqrt{2} - 5\sqrt{2}\\
&= 3 \cdot 2\sqrt{2} - 5\sqrt{2}\\
&= 6\sqrt{2} - 5\sqrt{2}\\
&= \sqrt{2}
\end{aligned}$$

47.
$$\begin{aligned}
5\sqrt[3]{16a^4} + 7\sqrt[3]{2a} &= 5\sqrt[3]{8a^3 \cdot 2a} + 7\sqrt[3]{2a}\\
&= 5\sqrt[3]{8a^3}\sqrt[3]{2a} + 7\sqrt[3]{2a}\\
&= 5 \cdot 2a\sqrt[3]{2a} + 7\sqrt[3]{2a}\\
&= 10a\sqrt[3]{2a} + 7\sqrt[3]{2a}\\
&= (10a + 7)\sqrt[3]{2a}
\end{aligned}$$

49. For Exercise 11, graph $y_1 = x^2 + 8$ and $y_2 = 6x$. Then determine the values of x for which the graph of y_1 lies below the graph of y_2.

For Exercise 22, graph $y_1 = \dfrac{x-2}{x+5}$ and $y_2 = 0$. Then determine the values of x for which the graph of y_1 lies below the graph of y_2. Since the graph of $y_2 = 0$ is the x-axis, this could also be done by graphing $y_1 = \dfrac{x-2}{x+5}$ and determining the values of x for which the graph of y_1 lies below the x-axis.

For Exercise 25, graph $y_1 = \dfrac{x-1}{x-2}$ and $y_2 = 3$. Then determine the values of x for which the graph of y_1 lies above the graph of y_2.

51.
$$x^2 - 2x \le 2$$
$$x^2 - 2x - 2 \le 0$$

The solutions of $x^2 - 2x - 2 = 0$ are found using the quadratic formula. They are $1 \pm \sqrt{3}$, or about 2.7 and -0.7. These numbers divide the number line into three intervals as shown:

```
        A          B          C
   <----+-----+----+----+----+---->
       1 - √3      1 + √3
```

We try test numbers in each interval.

A: Test -1, $y = (-1)^2 - 2(-1) - 2 = 1 > 0$

B: Test 0, $y = 0^2 - 2 \cdot 0 - 2 = -2 < 0$

C: Test 3, $y = 3^2 - 2 \cdot 3 - 2 = 1 > 0$

The expression is negative for all values of x in interval B. The inequality symbol is $\le$, so we must also include the intercepts. The solution set is $\{x|1 - \sqrt{3} \le x \le 1 + \sqrt{3}\}$, or $[1 - \sqrt{3}, 1 + \sqrt{3}]$.

53.
$$x^4 + 2x^2 > 0$$
$$x^2(x^2 + 2) > 0$$

$x^2 > 0$ for all $x \ne 0$, and $x^2 + 2 > 0$ for all values of x. Then $x^2(x^2 + 2) > 0$ for all $x \ne 0$. The solution set is $\{x|x \ne 0\}$, or the set of all real numbers except 0, or $(-\infty, 0) \cup (0, \infty)$.

55. $\left|\dfrac{x+2}{x-1}\right| < 3$

$$-3 < \frac{x+2}{x-1} < 3$$

We rewrite the inequality using "and."

$$-3 < \frac{x+2}{x-1} \quad and \quad \frac{x+2}{x-1} < 3$$

We will solve each inequality and then find the intersection of their solution sets.

Solve: $-3 < \dfrac{x+2}{x-1}$

Solve the related equation.

$$-3 = \frac{x+2}{x-1}$$
$$-3x + 3 = x + 2$$
$$1 = 4x$$
$$\frac{1}{4} = x$$

Find the numbers for which the rational expression is undefined.

$$x - 1 = 0$$
$$x = 1$$

Use the numbers $\dfrac{1}{4}$ and 1 to divide the number line into intervals as shown:

```
        A        B        C
   <----+----+---+---+---+---->
        1/4      1
```

Try test numbers in each interval.

A: Test 0,

$$-3 < \frac{x+2}{x-1}$$

$$-3 \ ?\ \frac{0+2}{0-1}$$

$$\Big| \ -2 \quad \text{TRUE}$$

Interval A is part of the solution set.

B: Test $\dfrac{1}{2}$,

$$-3 < \dfrac{x+2}{x-1}$$

$$-3 \ ? \ \dfrac{\frac{1}{2}+2}{\frac{1}{2}-1}$$

$$\dfrac{\frac{5}{2}}{-\frac{1}{2}}$$

$$-5 \quad \text{FALSE}$$

Interval B is not part of the solution set.

C: Test 2,

$$-3 < \dfrac{x+2}{x-1}$$

$$-3 \ ? \ \dfrac{2+2}{2-1}$$

$$4 \quad \text{TRUE}$$

Interval C is part of the solution set.

The solution set of $-3 < \dfrac{x+2}{x-1}$ is $\left\{x \middle| x < \dfrac{1}{4} \ or \ x > 1\right\}$, or $\left(-\infty, \dfrac{1}{4}\right) \cup (1, \infty)$.

Solve: $\dfrac{x+2}{x-1} > 3$

Solve the related equation.

$$\dfrac{x+2}{x-1} = 3$$

$$x + 2 = 3x - 3$$

$$5 = 2x$$

$$\dfrac{5}{2} = x$$

From our work above we know that the rational expression is undefined for 1.

Use the numbers $\dfrac{5}{2}$ and 1 to divide the number line into intervals as shown:

$$1 \qquad \dfrac{5}{2}$$

Try test numbers in each interval.

A: Test 0,

$$\dfrac{x+2}{x-1} < 3$$

$$\dfrac{0+2}{0-1} \ ? \ 3$$

$$-2 \quad \text{TRUE}$$

Interval A is part of the solution set.

B: Test 2,

$$\dfrac{x+2}{x-1} < 3$$

$$\dfrac{2+2}{2-1} \ ? \ 3$$

$$4 \quad \text{FALSE}$$

Interval B is not part of the solution set.

C: Test 3,

$$\dfrac{x+2}{x-1} < 3$$

$$\dfrac{3+2}{3-1} \ ? \ 3$$

$$\dfrac{5}{2} \quad \text{TRUE}$$

Interval C is part of the solution set.

The solution set of $\dfrac{x+2}{x-1} < 3$ is $\left\{x \middle| x < 1 \ or \ x > \dfrac{5}{2}\right\}$, or $\left(-\infty, 1\right) \cup \left(\dfrac{5}{2}, \infty\right)$.

The solution set of the original inequality is

$$\left\{x \middle| x < \dfrac{1}{4} \ or \ x > 1\right\} \cap \left\{x \middle| x < 1 \ or \ x > \dfrac{5}{2}\right\}, \text{ or}$$

$$\left\{x \middle| x < \dfrac{1}{4} \ or \ x > \dfrac{5}{2}\right\}, \text{ or } \left(-\infty, \dfrac{1}{4}\right) \cup \left(\dfrac{5}{2}, \infty\right).$$

57. a) Solve: $-16t^2 + 32t + 1920 > 1920$

$$-16t^2 + 32t > 0$$

$$t^2 - 2t < 0$$

$$t(t - 2) < 0$$

The solutions of $t(t - 2) = 0$ are 0 and 2. They divide the number line into three intervals as shown:

$$0 \qquad 2$$

Try test numbers in each interval.

A: Test -1, $y = -1(-1 - 2) = 3 > 0$

B: Test 1, $y = 1(1 - 2) = -1 < 0$

C: Test 3, $y = 3(3 - 2) = 3 > 0$

The expression is negative for all values of t in interval B. The solution set is $\{t | 0 < t < 2\}$, or $(0, 2)$.

b) Solve: $-16t^2 + 32t + 1920 < 640$

$$-16t^2 + 32t + 1280 < 0$$

$$t^2 - 2t - 80 > 0$$

$$(t - 10)(t + 8) > 0$$

The solutions of $(t - 10)(t + 8) = 0$ are 10 and -8. They divide the number line into three intervals as shown:

$$-8 \qquad 10$$

Try test numbers in each interval.

A: Test -10, $y = (-10 - 10)(-10 + 8) = 40 > 0$

B: Test 0, $y = (0 - 10)(0 + 8) = -80 < 0$

C: Test 20, $y = (20 - 10)(20 + 8) = 80 = 280 > 0$

The expression is positive for all values of t in intervals A and C. However, since negative values of t have no meaning in this problem, we disregard interval A. Thus, the solution set is $\{t | t > 10\}$, or $(10, \infty)$.

Chapter 8

Exponential and Logarithmic Functions

Exercise Set 8.1

1. Graph: $f(x) = 2^x$

We compute some function values and keep the results in a table.

$f(0) = 2^0 = 1$

$f(1) = 2^1 = 2$

$f(2) = 2^2 = 4$

$f(-1) = 2^{-1} = \dfrac{1}{2^1} = \dfrac{1}{2}$

$f(-2) = 2^{-2} = \dfrac{1}{2^2} = \dfrac{1}{4}$

x	$f(x)$
0	1
1	2
2	4
3	8
-1	$\dfrac{1}{2}$
-2	$\dfrac{1}{4}$
-3	$\dfrac{1}{8}$

Next we plot these points and connect them with a smooth curve.

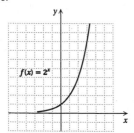

3. Graph: $f(x) = 5^x$

We compute some function values and keep the results in a table.

$f(0) = 5^0 = 1$

$f(1) = 5^1 = 5$

$f(2) = 5^2 = 25$

$f(-1) = 5^{-1} = \dfrac{1}{5^1} = \dfrac{1}{5}$

$f(-2) = 5^{-2} = \dfrac{1}{5^2} = \dfrac{1}{25}$

x	$f(x)$
0	1
1	5
2	25
-1	$\dfrac{1}{5}$
-2	$\dfrac{1}{25}$

Next we plot these points and connect them with a smooth curve.

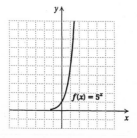

5. Graph: $f(x) = 2^{x+1}$

We compute some function values and keep the results in a table.

$f(0) = 2^{0+1} = 2^1 = 2$

$f(-1) = 2^{-1+1} = 2^0 = 1$

$f(-2) = 2^{-2+1} = 2^{-1} = \dfrac{1}{2^1} = \dfrac{1}{2}$

$f(-3) = 2^{-3+1} = 2^{-2} = \dfrac{1}{2^2} = \dfrac{1}{4}$

$f(1) = 2^{1+1} = 2^2 = 4$

$f(2) = 2^{2+1} = 2^3 = 8$

x	$f(x)$
0	2
-1	1
-2	$\dfrac{1}{2}$
-3	$\dfrac{1}{4}$
1	4
2	8

Next we plot these points and connect them with a smooth curve.

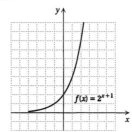

7. Graph: $f(x) = 3^{x-2}$

We compute some function values and keep the results in a table.

$f(0) = 3^{0-2} = 3^{-2} = \dfrac{1}{3^2} = \dfrac{1}{9}$

$f(1) = 3^{1-2} = 3^{-1} = \dfrac{1}{3^1} = \dfrac{1}{3}$

$f(2) = 3^{2-2} = 3^0 = 1$

$f(3) = 3^{3-2} = 3^1 = 3$

$f(4) = 3^{4-2} = 3^2 = 9$

$f(-1) = 3^{-1-2} = 3^{-3} = \dfrac{1}{3^3} = \dfrac{1}{27}$

$f(-2) = 3^{-2-2} = 3^{-4} = \dfrac{1}{3^4} = \dfrac{1}{81}$

x	$f(x)$
0	$\dfrac{1}{9}$
1	$\dfrac{1}{3}$
2	1
3	3
4	9
-1	$\dfrac{1}{27}$
-2	$\dfrac{1}{81}$

Next we plot these points and connect them with a smooth curve.

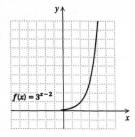

$f(x) = 3^{x-2}$

9. Graph: $f(x) = 2^x - 3$

We construct a table of values. Then we plot the points and connect them with a smooth curve.

$f(0) = 2^0 - 3 = 1 - 3 = -2$

$f(1) = 2^1 - 3 = 2 - 3 = -1$

$f(2) = 2^2 - 3 = 4 - 3 = 1$

$f(3) = 2^3 - 3 = 8 - 3 = 5$

$f(-1) = 2^{-1} - 3 = \dfrac{1}{2} - 3 = -\dfrac{5}{2}$

$f(-2) = 2^{-2} - 3 = \dfrac{1}{4} - 3 = -\dfrac{11}{4}$

x	$f(x)$
0	-2
1	-1
2	1
3	5
-1	$-\dfrac{5}{2}$
-2	$-\dfrac{11}{4}$

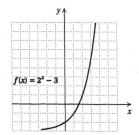

$f(x) = 2^x - 3$

11. Graph: $f(x) = 5^{x+3}$

We construct a table of values. Then we plot the points and connect them with a smooth curve.

$f(0) = 5^{0+3} = 5^3 = 125$

$f(-1) = 5^{-1+3} = 5^2 = 25$

$f(-2) = 5^{-2+3} = 5^1 = 5$

$f(-3) = 5^{-3+3} = 5^0 = 1$

$f(-4) = 5^{-4+3} = 5^{-1} = \dfrac{1}{5}$

$f(-5) = 5^{-5+3} = 5^{-2} = \dfrac{1}{25}$

x	$f(x)$
0	125
-1	25
-2	5
-3	1
-4	$\dfrac{1}{5}$
-5	$\dfrac{1}{25}$

$f(x) = 5^{x+3}$

13. Graph: $f(x) = \left(\dfrac{1}{2}\right)^x$

We construct a table of values. Then we plot the points and connect them with a smooth curve.

$f(0) = \left(\dfrac{1}{2}\right)^0 = 1$

$f(1) = \left(\dfrac{1}{2}\right)^1 = \dfrac{1}{2}$

$f(2) = \left(\dfrac{1}{2}\right)^2 = \dfrac{1}{4}$

$f(3) = \left(\dfrac{1}{2}\right)^3 = \dfrac{1}{8}$

$f(-1) = \left(\dfrac{1}{2}\right)^{-1} = \dfrac{1}{\left(\dfrac{1}{2}\right)^1} = \dfrac{1}{\dfrac{1}{2}} = 2$

$f(-2) = \left(\dfrac{1}{2}\right)^{-2} = \dfrac{1}{\left(\dfrac{1}{2}\right)^2} = \dfrac{1}{\dfrac{1}{4}} = 4$

$f(-3) = \left(\dfrac{1}{2}\right)^{-3} = \dfrac{1}{\left(\dfrac{1}{2}\right)^3} = \dfrac{1}{\dfrac{1}{8}} = 8$

x	$f(x)$
0	1
1	$\dfrac{1}{2}$
2	$\dfrac{1}{4}$
3	$\dfrac{1}{8}$
-1	2
-2	4
-3	8

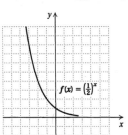

$f(x) = \left(\dfrac{1}{2}\right)^x$

15. Graph: $f(x) = \left(\dfrac{1}{5}\right)^x$

We construct a table of values. Then we plot the points and connect them with a smooth curve.

$f(0) = \left(\dfrac{1}{5}\right)^0 = 1$

$f(1) = \left(\dfrac{1}{5}\right)^1 = \dfrac{1}{5}$

$f(2) = \left(\dfrac{1}{5}\right)^2 = \dfrac{1}{25}$

$f(-1) = \left(\dfrac{1}{5}\right)^{-1} = \dfrac{1}{\dfrac{1}{5}} = 5$

$f(-2) = \left(\dfrac{1}{5}\right)^{-2} = \dfrac{1}{\dfrac{1}{25}} = 25$

x	$f(x)$
0	1
1	$\dfrac{1}{5}$
2	$\dfrac{1}{25}$
-1	5
-2	25

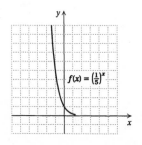

$f(x) = \left(\dfrac{1}{5}\right)^x$

17. Graph: $f(x) = 2^{2x-1}$

We construct a table of values. Then we plot the points and connect them with a smooth curve.

$f(0) = 2^{2 \cdot 0 - 1} = 2^{-1} = \dfrac{1}{2}$

$f(1) = 2^{2 \cdot 1 - 1} = 2^1 = 2$

$f(2) = 2^{2 \cdot 2 - 1} = 2^3 = 8$

$f(-1) = 2^{2(-1)-1} = 2^{-3} = \dfrac{1}{8}$

$f(-2) = 2^{2(-2)-1} = 2^{-5} = \dfrac{1}{32}$

x	$f(x)$
0	$\dfrac{1}{2}$
1	2
2	8
-1	$\dfrac{1}{8}$
-2	$\dfrac{1}{32}$

19. Graph: $x = 2^y$

We can find ordered pairs by choosing values for y and then computing values for x.

For $y = 0$, $x = 2^0 = 1$.

For $y = 1$, $x = 2^1 = 2$.

For $y = 2$, $x = 2^2 = 4$.

For $y = 3$, $x = 2^3 = 8$.

For $y = -1$, $x = 2^{-1} = \dfrac{1}{2^1} = \dfrac{1}{2}$.

For $y = -2$, $x = 2^{-2} = \dfrac{1}{2^2} = \dfrac{1}{4}$.

For $y = -3$, $x = 2^{-3} = \dfrac{1}{2^3} = \dfrac{1}{8}$.

x	y
1	0
2	1
4	2
8	3
$\dfrac{1}{2}$	-1
$\dfrac{1}{4}$	-2
$\dfrac{1}{8}$	-3

⌐ (1) Choose values for y.

└─ (2) Compute values for x.

We plot these points and connect them with a smooth curve.

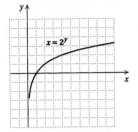

21. Graph: $x = \left(\dfrac{1}{2}\right)^y$

We can find ordered pairs by choosing values for y and then computing values for x. Then we plot these points and connect them with a smooth curve.

For $y = 0$, $x = \left(\dfrac{1}{2}\right)^0 = 1$.

For $y = 1$, $x = \left(\dfrac{1}{2}\right)^1 = \dfrac{1}{2}$.

For $y = 2$, $x = \left(\dfrac{1}{2}\right)^2 = \dfrac{1}{4}$.

For $y = 3$, $x = \left(\dfrac{1}{2}\right)^3 = \dfrac{1}{8}$.

For $y = -1$, $x = \left(\dfrac{1}{2}\right)^{-1} = \dfrac{1}{\frac{1}{2}} = 2$.

For $y = -2$, $x = \left(\dfrac{1}{2}\right)^{-2} = \dfrac{1}{\frac{1}{4}} = 4$.

For $y = -3$, $x = \left(\dfrac{1}{2}\right)^{-3} = \dfrac{1}{\frac{1}{8}} = 8$.

x	y
1	0
$\dfrac{1}{2}$	1
$\dfrac{1}{4}$	2
$\dfrac{1}{8}$	3
2	-1
4	-2
8	-3

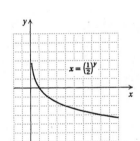

23. Graph: $x = 5^y$

We can find ordered pairs by choosing values for y and then computing values for x. Then we plot these points and connect them with a smooth curve.

For $y = 0$, $x = 5^0 = 1$.

For $y = 1$, $x = 5^1 = 5$.

For $y = 2$, $x = 5^2 = 25$.

For $y = -1$, $x = 5^{-1} = \dfrac{1}{5}$.

For $y = -2$, $x = 5^{-2} = \dfrac{1}{25}$.

x	y
1	0
5	1
25	2
$\dfrac{1}{5}$	-1
$\dfrac{1}{25}$	-2

25. Graph $y = 2^x$ (see Exercise 1) and $x = 2^y$ (see Exercise 19) using the same set of axes.

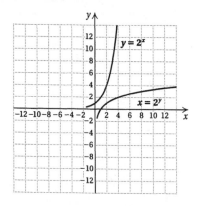

27. a) We substitute \$50,000 for P and 6%, or 0.06, for r in the formula $A = P(1+r)^t$:

$$A(t) = \$50,000(1 + 0.06)^t = \$50,000(1.06)^t$$

b) $A(0) = \$50,000(1.06)^0 = \$50,000$

$A(1) = \$50,000(1.06)^1 = \$53,000$

$A(2) = \$50,000(1.06)^2 = \$56,180$

$A(4) = \$50,000(1.06)^4 \approx \$63,123.85$

$A(8) = \$50,000(1.06)^8 \approx \$76,692.40$

$A(10) = \$50,000(1.06)^{10} \approx \$89,542.38$

$A(20) = \$50,000(1.06)^{20} \approx \$160,356.77$

c)

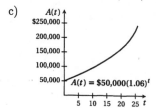

29. $V(t) = 4000(1.22)^t$

a) As the exercise states, $t = 0$ corresponds to 1958.
$V(0) = 4000(1.22)^0 = \$4000$

$1970 - 1958 = 12$, so $t = 12$ corresponds to 1970.
$V(12) = 4000(1.22)^{12} \approx \$43,489$

$1980 - 1958 = 22$, so $t = 22$ corresponds to 1980.
$V(22) = 4000(1.22)^{22} \approx \$317,670$

$1990 - 1958 = 32$, so $t = 32$ corresponds to 1990.
$V(32) = 4000(1.22)^{32} \approx \$2,320,463$

$1998 - 1958 = 40$, so $t = 40$ corresponds to 1998.
$V(40) = 4000(1.22)^{40} \approx \$11,388,151$

b) $1999 - 1958 = 41$, so $t = 41$ corresponds to 1999.
$V(41) = 4000(1.22)^{41} \approx \$13,893,544$

c) $2001 - 1958 = 43$, so $t = 43$ corresponds to 2001.
$V(43) = 4000(1.22)^{43} \approx \$20,679,151$

d)

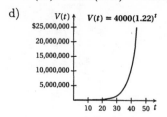

31. a) In 1930, $t = 1930 - 1900 = 30$.

$$P(t) = 150(0.960)^t$$
$$P(30) = 150(0.960)^{30}$$
$$\approx 44.079$$

In 1930, about 44.079 thousand, or 44,079, humpback whales were alive.
In 1960, $t = 1960 - 1900 = 60$.

$$P(t) = 150(0.960)^t$$
$$P(60) = 150(0.960)^{60}$$
$$\approx 12.953$$

In 1960, about 12.953 thousand, or 12,953, humpback whales were alive.

b) Plot the points found in part (a), $(30, 44,079)$ and $(60, 12,953)$ and additional points as needed and graph the function.

33. $N(t) = 3000(2)^{t/20}$

a) $N(10) = 3000(2)^{10/20} \approx 4243$

There will be approximately 4243 bacteria after 10 min.

$N(20) = 3000(2)^{20/20} = 6000$

There will be 6000 bacteria after 20 min.

$N(30) = 3000(2)^{30/20} \approx 8485$

There will be approximately 8485 bacteria after 30 min.

$N(40) = 3000(2)^{40/20} = 12,000$

There will be 12,000 bacteria after 40 min.

$N(60) = 3000(2)^{60/20} = 24,000$

There will be 24,000 bacteria after 60 min.

b) We use the function values computed in part (a) to draw the graph. Other values can also be computed if needed.

35. Discussion and Writing Exercise

37. $x^{-5} \cdot x^3 = x^{-5+3} = x^{-2} = \dfrac{1}{x^2}$

39. $9^0 = 1$ (For any nonzero number a, $a^0 = 1$.)

41. $\left(\dfrac{2}{3}\right)^1 = \dfrac{2}{3}$ (For any number a, $a^1 = a$.)

43. $\dfrac{x^{-3}}{x^4} = x^{-3-4} = x^{-7} = \dfrac{1}{x^7}$

45. $\dfrac{x}{x^0} = x^{1-0} = x^1 = x$

(This exercise could also be done as follows:
$\dfrac{x}{x^0} = \dfrac{x}{1} = x$.)

47. $(5^{\sqrt{2}})^{2\sqrt{2}} = 5^{\sqrt{2} \cdot 2\sqrt{2}} = 5^4$, or 625

49. Graph: $y = 2^x + 2^{-x}$

Construct a table of values, thinking of y as $f(x)$. Then plot these points and connect them with a curve.

$f(0) = 2^0 + 2^{-0} = 1 + 1 = 2$

$f(1) = 2^1 + 2^{-1} = 2 + \dfrac{1}{2} = 2\dfrac{1}{2}$

$f(2) = 2^2 + 2^{-2} = 4 + \dfrac{1}{4} = 4\dfrac{1}{4}$

$f(3) = 2^3 + 2^{-3} = 8 + \dfrac{1}{8} = 8\dfrac{1}{8}$

$f(-1) = 2^{-1} + 2^{-(-1)} = \dfrac{1}{2} + 2 = 2\dfrac{1}{2}$

$f(-2) = 2^{-2} + 2^{-(-2)} = \dfrac{1}{4} + 4 = 4\dfrac{1}{4}$

$f(-3) = 2^{-3} + 2^{-(-3)} = \dfrac{1}{8} + 8 = 8\dfrac{1}{8}$

x	y, or $f(x)$
0	2
1	$2\dfrac{1}{2}$
2	$4\dfrac{1}{4}$
3	$8\dfrac{1}{8}$
-1	$2\dfrac{1}{2}$
-2	$4\dfrac{1}{4}$
-3	$8\dfrac{1}{8}$

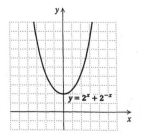

51. $y = \left|\left(\dfrac{1}{2}\right)^x - 1\right|$

Construct a table of values, thinking of y as $f(x)$. Then plot these points and connect them with a curve.

$f(-4) = \left|\left(\dfrac{1}{2}\right)^{-4} - 1\right| = |16 - 1| = |15| = 15$

$f(-2) = \left|\left(\dfrac{1}{2}\right)^{-2} - 1\right| = |4 - 1| = |3| = 3$

$f(-1) = \left|\left(\dfrac{1}{2}\right)^{-1} - 1\right| = |2 - 1| = |1| = 1$

$f(0) = \left|\left(\dfrac{1}{2}\right)^0 - 1\right| = |1 - 1| = |0| = 0$

$f(1) = \left|\left(\dfrac{1}{2}\right)^1 - 1\right| = \left|\dfrac{1}{2} - 1\right| = \left|-\dfrac{1}{2}\right| = \dfrac{1}{2}$

$f(2) = \left|\left(\dfrac{1}{2}\right)^2 - 1\right| = \left|\dfrac{1}{4} - 1\right| = \left|-\dfrac{3}{4}\right| = \dfrac{3}{4}$

$f(3) = \left|\left(\dfrac{1}{2}\right)^3 - 1\right| = \left|\dfrac{1}{8} - 1\right| = \left|-\dfrac{7}{8}\right| = \dfrac{7}{8}$

x	y, or $f(x)$
-4	15
-2	3
-1	1
0	0
1	$\dfrac{1}{2}$
2	$\dfrac{3}{4}$
3	$\dfrac{7}{8}$

53. Construct a table of values for each equation and then draw the graphs on the same set of axes.

For $y = 3^{-(x-1)}$:

x	y
-3	81
-2	27
-1	9
0	3
1	1
2	$\dfrac{1}{3}$
3	$\dfrac{1}{9}$
4	$\dfrac{1}{27}$

For $x = 3^{-(y-1)}$:

x	y
81	-3
27	-2
9	-1
3	0
1	1
$\dfrac{1}{3}$	2
$\dfrac{1}{9}$	3
$\dfrac{1}{27}$	4

55. Left to the student

Exercise Set 8.2

1. To find the inverse of the given relation we interchange the first and second coordinates of each ordered pair. The inverse of the relation is $\{(2,1),(-3,6),(-5,-3)\}$.

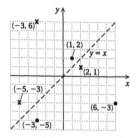

3. We interchange x and y to obtain an equation of the inverse of the relation. It is $x = 2y + 6$. The x-values in the first table become the y-values in the second table. We have

x	y
4	-1
6	0
8	1
10	2
12	3

We graph the original relation and its inverse. Since there is no horizontal line that crosses the graph more than once, the function is one-to-one.

5. The graph of $f(x) = x - 5$ is shown below. Since no horizontal line crosses the graph more than once, the function is one-to-one.

7. The graph of $f(x) = x^2 - 2$ is shown below. There are many horizontal lines that cross the graph more than once, so the function is not one-to-one.

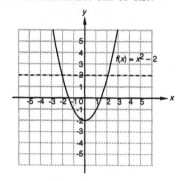

9. The graph of $g(x) = |x| - 3$ is shown below. There are many horizontal lines that cross the graph more than once, so the function is not one-to-one.

11. The graph of $g(x) = 3^x$ is shown below. Since no horizontal line crosses the graph more than once, the function is one-to-one.

13. The graph of $f(x) = 5x - 2$ is shown below. It passes the horizontal-line test, so it is one-to-one.

We find a formula for the inverse.

1. Replace $f(x)$ by y : $\quad y = 5x - 2$
2. Interchange x and y : $\quad x = 5y - 2$
3. Solve for y : $\quad x + 2 = 5y$
$$\frac{x+2}{5} = y$$
4. Replace y by $f^{-1}(x)$: $\quad f^{-1}(x) = \frac{x+2}{5}$

15. The graph of $f(x) = \dfrac{-2}{x}$ is shown below. It passes the horizontal-line test, so it is one-to-one.

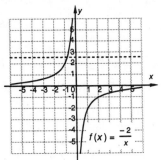

We find a formula for the inverse.

1. Replace $f(x)$ by y : $\quad y = \dfrac{-2}{x}$
2. Interchange x and y : $\quad x = \dfrac{-2}{y}$
3. Solve for y : $\quad y = \dfrac{-2}{x}$
4. Replace y by $f^{-1}(x)$: $\quad f^{-1}(x) = \dfrac{-2}{x}$

17. The graph of $f(x) = \dfrac{4}{3}x + 7$ is shown below. It passes the horizontal line test, so it is one-to-one.

We find a formula for the inverse.

1. Replace $f(x)$ by y: $\quad y = \dfrac{4}{3}x + 7$
2. Interchange x and y: $\quad x = \dfrac{4}{3}y + 7$
3. Solve for y: $\quad x - 7 = \dfrac{4}{3}y$
$$\frac{3}{4}(x - 7) = y$$
4. Replace y by $f^{(-1)}(x)$: $\quad f^{-1}(x) = \dfrac{3}{4}(x - 7)$

19. The graph of $f(x) = \dfrac{2}{x+5}$ is shown below. It passes the horizontal line test, so it is one-to-one.

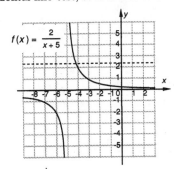

We find a formula for the inverse.

1. Replace $f(x)$ by y : $\quad y = \dfrac{2}{x+5}$
2. Interchange x and y : $\quad x = \dfrac{2}{y+5}$
3. Solve for y : $\quad x(y+5) = 2$
$$y + 5 = \frac{2}{x}$$
$$y = \frac{2}{x} - 5$$
4. Replace y by $f^{-1}(x)$: $\quad f^{-1}(x) = \dfrac{2}{x} - 5$

21. The graph of $f(x) = 5$ is shown below. The horizontal line $y = 5$ crosses the graph more than once, so the function is not one-to-one.

23. The graph of $f(x) = \dfrac{2x+1}{5x+3}$ is shown below. It passes the horizontal line test, so it is one-to-one.

We find a formula for the inverse.

1. Replace $f(x)$ by y: $y = \dfrac{2x+1}{5x+3}$

2. Interchange x and y: $x = \dfrac{2y+1}{5y+3}$

3. Solve for y: $5xy + 3x = 2y + 1$

$$5xy - 2y = 1 - 3x$$
$$y(5x - 2) = 1 - 3x$$
$$y = \dfrac{1 - 3x}{5x - 2}$$

4. Replace y by $f^{-1}(x)$: $f^{-1}(x) = \dfrac{1 - 3x}{5x - 2}$

25. The graph of $f(x) = x^3 - 1$ is shown below. It passes the horizontal line test, so it is one-to-one.

1. Replace $f(x)$ by y: $y = x^3 - 1$
2. Interchange x and y: $x = y^3 - 1$
3. Solve for y: $x + 1 = y^3$
$$\sqrt[3]{x+1} = y$$
4. Replace y by $f^{-1}(x)$: $f^{-1}(x) = \sqrt[3]{x+1}$

27. The graph of $f(x) = \sqrt[3]{x}$ is shown below. It passes the horizontal line test, so it is one-to-one.

1. Replace $f(x)$ by y: $y = \sqrt[3]{x}$
2. Interchange x and y: $x = \sqrt[3]{y}$
3. Solve for y: $x^3 = y$
4. Replace y by $f^{-1}(x)$: $f^{-1}(x) = x^3$

29. We first graph $f(x) = \dfrac{1}{2}x - 3$. The graph of f^{-1} can be obtained by reflecting the graph of f across the line $y = x$.

31. We first graph $f(x) = x^3$. The graph of f^{-1} can be obtained by reflecting the graph of f across the line $y = x$.

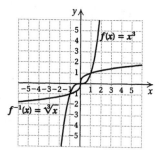

33. $f \circ g(x) = f(g(x)) = f(6 - 4x) = 2(6 - 4x) - 3 =$
$$12 - 8x - 3 = -8x + 9$$

$g \circ f(x) = g(f(x)) = g(2x - 3) = 6 - 4(2x - 3) =$
$$6 - 8x + 12 = -8x + 18$$

35. $f \circ g(x) = f(g(x)) = f(2x - 1) = 3(2x - 1)^2 + 2 =$
$$3(4x^2 - 4x + 1) + 2 = 12x^2 - 12x + 3 + 2 =$$
$$12x^2 - 12x + 5$$

$g \circ f(x) = g(f(x)) = g(3x^2 + 2) = 2(3x^2 + 2) - 1 =$
$$6x^2 + 4 - 1 = 6x^2 + 3$$

37. $f \circ g(x) = f(g(x)) = f\left(\dfrac{2}{x}\right) = 4\left(\dfrac{2}{x}\right)^2 - 1 =$

$$4\left(\dfrac{4}{x^2}\right) - 1 = \dfrac{16}{x^2} - 1$$

$$g \circ f(x) = g(f(x)) = g(4x^2 - 1) = \dfrac{2}{4x^2 - 1}$$

39. $f \circ g(x) = f(g(x)) = f(x^2 - 5) = (x^2 - 5)^2 + 5 =$

$$x^4 - 10x^2 + 25 + 5 = x^4 - 10x^2 + 30$$

$$g \circ f(x) = g(f(x)) = g(x^2 + 5) = (x^2 + 5)^2 - 5 =$$

$$x^4 + 10x^2 + 25 - 5 = x^4 + 10x^2 + 20$$

41. $h(x) = (5 - 3x)^2$

This is $5 - 3x$ raised to the second power, so the two most obvious functions are $f(x) = x^2$ and $g(x) = 5 - 3x$.

43. $h(x) = \sqrt{5x + 2}$

This is the square root of $5x + 2$, so the two most obvious functions are $f(x) = \sqrt{x}$ and $g(x) = 5x + 2$.

45. $h(x) = \dfrac{1}{x - 1}$

This is the reciprocal of $x - 1$, so the two most obvious functions are $f(x) = \dfrac{1}{x}$ and $g(x) = x - 1$.

47. $h(x) = \dfrac{1}{\sqrt{7x + 2}}$

This is the reciprocal of the square root of $7x + 2$. Two functions that can be used are $f(x) = \dfrac{1}{\sqrt{x}}$ and $g(x) = 7x + 2$.

49. $h(x) = (\sqrt{x} + 5)^4$

This is $\sqrt{x} + 5$ raised to the fourth power, so the two most obvious functions are $f(x) = x^4$ and $g(x) = \sqrt{x} + 5$.

51. We check to see that $f^{-1} \circ f(x) = x$ and $f \circ f^{-1}(x) = x$.

$$f^{-1} \circ f(x) = f^{-1}(f(x)) = f^{-1}\left(\dfrac{4}{5}x\right) =$$

$$\dfrac{5}{4} \cdot \dfrac{4}{5}x = x$$

$$f \circ f^{-1}(x) = f(f^{-1}(x)) = f\left(\dfrac{5}{4}x\right) =$$

$$\dfrac{4}{5} \cdot \dfrac{5}{4}x = x$$

53. We check to see that $f^{-1} \circ f(x) = x$ and $f \circ f^{-1}(x) = x$.

$$f^{-1} \circ f(x) = f^{-1}(f(x)) = f^{-1}\left(\dfrac{1 - x}{x}\right) =$$

$$\dfrac{1}{\dfrac{1 - x}{x} + 1} = \dfrac{1}{\dfrac{1 - x}{x} + 1} \cdot \dfrac{x}{x} = \dfrac{x}{1 - x + x} =$$

$$\dfrac{x}{1} = x$$

$$f \circ f^{-1}(x) = f(f^{-1}(x)) = f\left(\dfrac{1}{x + 1}\right) =$$

$$\dfrac{1 - \dfrac{1}{x + 1}}{\dfrac{1}{x + 1}} = \dfrac{1 - \dfrac{1}{x + 1}}{\dfrac{1}{x + 1}} \cdot \dfrac{x + 1}{x + 1} =$$

$$\dfrac{x + 1 - 1}{1} = \dfrac{x}{1} = x$$

55. The function $f(x) = 3x$ multiplies an input by 3, so the inverse would divide an input by 3. We have $f^{-1}(x) = \dfrac{x}{3}$.

Now we check to see that $f^{-1} \circ f(x) = x$ and $f \circ f^{-1}(x) = x$.

$$f^{-1} \circ f(x) = f^{-1}(f(x)) = f^{-1}(3x) = \dfrac{3x}{3} = x$$

$$f \circ f^{-1}(x) = f(f^{-1}(x)) = f\left(\dfrac{x}{3}\right) = 3 \cdot \dfrac{x}{3} = x$$

The inverse is correct.

57. The function $f(x) = -x$ takes the opposite of an input so the inverse would also take the opposite of an input. We have $f^{-1}(x) = -x$.

Now we check to see that $f^{-1} \circ f(x) = x$ and $f \circ f^{-1}(x) = x$.

$$f^{-1} \circ f(x) = f^{-1}(f(x)) = f^{-1}(-x) = -(-x) = x$$

$$f \circ f^{-1}(x) = f(f^{-1}(x)) = f(-x) = -(-x) = x$$

The inverse is correct.

59. The function $f(x) = \sqrt[3]{x - 5}$ subtracts 5 from an input and then takes the cube root of the difference, so the inverse would cube an input and then add 5. We have $f^{-1}(x) = x^3 + 5$.

Now we check to see that $f^{-1} \circ f(x) = x$ and $f \circ f^{-1}(x) = x$.

$$f^{-1} \circ f(x) = f^{-1}(f(x)) = f^{-1}(\sqrt[3]{x - 5}) = (\sqrt[3]{x - 5})^3 + 5 =$$

$$x - 5 + 5 = x$$

$$f \circ f^{-1}(x) = f(f^{-1}(x)) = f(x^3 + 5) = \sqrt[3]{x^3 + 5 - 5} = \sqrt[3]{x^3} = x$$

The inverse is correct.

61. a) $f(8) = 8 + 32 = 40$

Size 40 in France corresponds to size 8 in the U.S.

$f(10) = 10 + 32 = 42$

Size 42 in France corresponds to size 10 in the U.S.

$f(14) = 14 + 32 = 46$

Size 46 in France corresponds to size 14 in the U.S.

$f(18) = 18 + 32 = 50$

Size 50 in France corresponds to size 18 in the U.S.

b) The graph of $f(x) = x + 32$ is shown below. It passes the horizontal-line test, so the function is one-to-one and, hence, has an inverse that is a function.

We now find a formula for the inverse.

1. Replace $f(x)$ by y: $y = x + 32$
2. Interchange x and y: $x = y + 32$
3. Solve for y: $x - 32 = y$
4. Replace y by $f^{-1}(x)$: $f^{-1}(x) = x - 32$

c) $f^{-1}(40) = 40 - 32 = 8$

Size 8 in the U.S. corresponds to size 40 in France.

$f^{-1}(42) = 42 - 32 = 10$

Size 10 in the U.S. corresponds to size 42 in France.

$f^{-1}(46) = 46 - 32 = 14$

Size 14 in the U.S. corresponds to size 46 in France.

$f^{-1}(50) = 50 - 32 = 18$

Size 18 in the U.S. corresponds to size 50 in France.

63. Discussion and Writing Exercise

65. $\sqrt[6]{a^2} = a^{2/6} = a^{1/3} = \sqrt[3]{a}$

67. $\sqrt{a^4 b^6} = (a^4 b^6)^{1/2} = a^2 b^3$

69. $\sqrt[8]{81} = (3^4)^{1/8} = 3^{1/2} = \sqrt{3}$

71. $\sqrt[12]{64 x^6 y^6} = (2^6 x^6 y^6)^{1/12} = 2^{1/2} x^{1/2} y^{1/2} = (2xy)^{1/2} = \sqrt{2xy}$

73. $\sqrt[5]{32 a^{15} b^{40}} = (2^5 a^{15} b^{40})^{1/5} = 2 a^3 b^8$

75. $\sqrt[4]{81 a^8 b^8} = (3^4 a^8 b^8)^{1/4} = 3 a^2 b^2$

77. Graph the functions in a square window and determine whether one is a reflection of the other across the line $y = x$. The graphs show that these functions are not inverses of each other.

79. Graph the functions in a square window and determine whether one is a reflection of the other across the line $y = x$. The graphs show that these functions are inverses of each other.

81. (1) C; (2) A; (3) B; (4) D

83. Reflect the graph of f across the line $y = x$.

85. $f(x) = \dfrac{1}{2}x + 3$, $g(x) = 2x - 6$

Since $(f \circ g)(x) = x$ and $(g \circ f)(x) = x$, the functions are inverse.

Exercise Set 8.3

1. Graph: $f(x) = \log_2 x$

The equation $f(x) = y = \log_2 x$ is equivalent to $2^y = x$. We can find ordered pairs by choosing values for y and computing the corresponding x-values.

For $y = 0$, $x = 2^0 = 1$.

For $y = 1$, $x = 2^1 = 2$.

For $y = 2$, $x = 2^2 = 4$.

For $y = 3$, $x = 2^3 = 8$.

For $y = -1$, $x = 2^{-1} = \dfrac{1}{2}$.

For $y = -2$, $x = 2^{-2} = \dfrac{1}{4}$.

x, or 2^y	y
1	0
2	1
4	2
8	3
$\dfrac{1}{2}$	-1
$\dfrac{1}{4}$	-2
$\dfrac{1}{8}$	-3

└─ (1) Select y.

└─ (2) Compute x.

We plot the set of ordered pairs and connect the points with a smooth curve.

3. Graph: $f(x) = \log_{1/3} x$

The equation $f(x) = y = \log_{1/3} x$ is equivalent to $\left(\frac{1}{3}\right)^y = x$. We can find ordered pairs by choosing values for y and computing the corresponding x-values.

For $y = 0$, $x = \left(\frac{1}{3}\right)^0 = 1$.

For $y = 1$, $x = \left(\frac{1}{3}\right)^1 = \frac{1}{3}$.

For $y = 2$, $x = \left(\frac{1}{3}\right)^2 = \frac{1}{9}$.

For $y = -1$, $x = \left(\frac{1}{3}\right)^{-1} = 3$.

For $y = -2$, $x = \left(\frac{1}{3}\right)^{-2} = 9$.

x, or $\left(\frac{1}{3}\right)^y$	y
1	0
$\frac{1}{3}$	1
$\frac{1}{9}$	2
3	-1
9	-2

We plot the set of ordered pairs and connect the points with a smooth curve.

5. Graph $f(x) = 3^x$ (see Exercise Set 10.1, Exercise 2) and $f^{-1}(x) = \log_3 x$ on the same set of axes. We can obtain the graph of f^{-1} by reflecting the graph of f across the line $y = x$.

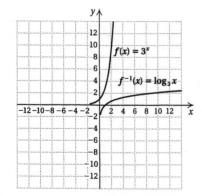

7.
The exponent is the logarithm.
$$10^3 = 1000 \Rightarrow 3 = \log_{10} 1000$$
The base remains the same.

9.
The exponent is the logarithm.
$$5^{-3} = \frac{1}{125} \Rightarrow -3 = \log_5 \frac{1}{125}$$
The base remains the same.

11. $8^{1/3} = 2 \Rightarrow \frac{1}{3} = \log_8 2$

13. $10^{0.3010} = 2 \Rightarrow 0.3010 = \log_{10} 2$

15. $e^2 = t \Rightarrow 2 = \log_e t$

17. $Q^t = x \Rightarrow t = \log_Q x$

19. $e^2 = 7.3891 \Rightarrow 2 = \log_e 7.3891$

21. $e^{-2} = 0.1353 \Rightarrow -2 = \log_e 0.1353$

23.
The logarithm is the exponent.
$$w = \log_4 10 \Rightarrow 4^w = 10$$
The base remains the same.

25.
The logarithm is the exponent.
$$\log_6 36 = 2 \Rightarrow 6^2 = 36$$
The base remains the same.

27. $\log_{10} 0.01 = -2 \Rightarrow 10^{-2} = 0.01$

29. $\log_{10} 8 = 0.9031 \Rightarrow 10^{0.9031} = 8$

31. $\log_e 100 = 4.6052 \Rightarrow e^{4.6052} = 100$

33. $\log_t Q = k \Rightarrow t^k = Q$

35. $\log_3 x = 2$

$3^2 = x$ Converting to an exponential equation

$9 = x$ Computing 3^2

37. $\log_x 16 = 2$

$x^2 = 16$ Converting to an exponential equation

$x = 4$ or $x = -4$ Principle of square roots

$\log_4 16 = 2$ because $4^2 = 16$. Thus, 4 is a solution. Since all logarithm bases must be positive, $\log_{-4} 16$ is not defined and -4 is not a solution.

39. $\log_2 16 = x$

$2^x = 16$ Converting to an exponential equation

$2^x = 2^4$

$x = 4$ The exponents are the same.

41. $\log_3 27 = x$

$3^x = 27$ Converting to an exponential equation

$3^x = 3^3$

$x = 3$ The exponents are the same.

43. $\log_x 25 = 1$

$x^1 = 25$ Converting to an exponential equation

$x = 25$

45. $\log_3 x = 0$

$\quad 3^0 = x$ Converting to an exponential equation

$\quad 1 = x$

47. $\log_2 x = -1$

$\quad 2^{-1} = x$ Converting to an exponential equation

$\quad \dfrac{1}{2} = x$ Simplifying

49. $\log_8 x = \dfrac{1}{3}$

$\quad 8^{1/3} = x$

$\quad 2 = x$

51. Let $\log_{10} 100 = x$. Then

$\quad 10^x = 100$

$\quad 10^x = 10^2$

$\quad x = 2$

Thus, $\log_{10} 100 = 2$.

53. Let $\log_{10} 0.1 = x$. Then

$\quad 10^x = 0.1 = \dfrac{1}{10}$

$\quad 10^x = 10^{-1}$

$\quad x = -1$

Thus, $\log_{10} 0.1 = -1$.

55. Let $\log_{10} 1 = x$. Then

$\quad 10^x = 1$

$\quad 10^x = 10^0$ $(10^0 = 1)$

$\quad x = 0$

Thus, $\log_{10} 1 = 0$.

57. Let $\log_5 625 = x$. Then

$\quad 5^x = 625$

$\quad 5^x = 5^4$

$\quad x = 4$

Thus, $\log_5 625 = 4$.

59. Think of the meaning of $\log_7 49$. It is the exponent to which you raise 7 to get 49. That exponent is 2. Therefore, $\log_7 49 = 2$.

61. Think of the meaning of $\log_2 8$. It is the exponent to which you raise 2 to get 8. That exponent is 3. Therefore, $\log_2 8 = 3$.

63. Let $\log_9 \dfrac{1}{81} = x$. Then

$\quad 9^x = \dfrac{1}{81}$

$\quad 9^x = 9^{-2}$

$\quad x = -2$

Thus, $\log_9 81 = -2$.

65. Let $\log_8 1 = x$. Then

$\quad 8^x = 1$

$\quad 8^x = 8^0$ $(8^0 = 1)$

$\quad x = 0$

Thus, $\log_8 1 = 0$.

67. Let $\log_e e = x$. Then

$\quad e^x = e$

$\quad e^x = e^1$

$\quad x = 1$

Thus, $\log_e e = 1$.

69. Let $\log_{27} 9 = x$. Then

$\quad 27^x = 9$

$\quad (3^3)^x = 3^2$

$\quad 3^{3x} = 3^2$

$\quad 3x = 2$

$\quad x = \dfrac{2}{3}$

Thus, $\log_{27} 9 = \dfrac{2}{3}$.

71. 4.8970

73. -0.1739

75. Does not exist

77. 0.9464

79. $6 = 10^{0.7782}$; $84 = 10^{1.9243}$; $987,606 = 10^{5.9946}$; $0.00987606 = 10^{-2.0054}$; $98,760.6 = 10^{4.9946}$; $70,000,000 = 10^{7.8451}$; $7000 = 10^{3.8451}$

81. Discussion and Writing Exercise

83. $f(x) = 4 - x^2$

a) The x-coordinate of the vertex is $-\dfrac{b}{2a} = -\dfrac{0}{-2} = 0$.

The y-coordinate is $f(0) = 4 - 0^2 = 4$.

The vertex is $(0, 4)$.

b) The line of symmetry is $x = 0$.

c) Since the coefficient of x^2 is negative, the graph opens down and, hence, has a maximum. The maximum value is 4.

d) We find some points on each side of the vertex and use them to draw the graph.

x	y
0	4
-1	3
1	3
-2	0
2	0
-3	-5
3	-5

85. $f(x) = -2(x-1)^2 - 3$

   a) The equation is in the form $f(x) = a(x-h)^2 + k$ so we know that the vertex is (h, k), or $(1, -3)$.

   b) The line of symmetry is $x = 1$.

   c) Since the coefficient of x^2 is negative, the graph opens down and, hence, has a maximum. The maximum value is -3.

   d) We find some points on each side of the vertex and use them to draw the graph.

x	y
0	-5
2	-5
-1	-11
3	-11

87.
$$E = mc^2$$
$$\frac{E}{m} = c^2 \qquad \text{Dividing by } m$$
$$\sqrt{\frac{E}{m}} = c \qquad \text{Taking the positive square root}$$

89.
$$A = \sqrt{3ab}$$
$$A^2 = (\sqrt{3ab})^2 \qquad \text{Squaring both sides}$$
$$A^2 = 3ab$$
$$\frac{A^2}{3a} = b \qquad \text{Dividing by } 3a$$

91. a) We substitute in the equation $y = ax^2 + bx + c$ and get a system of equations.

   $31 = a(20)^2 + b(20) + c$, or $31 = 400a + 20b + c$;

   $34 = a(24)^2 + b(24) + c$, or $34 = 576a + 24b + c$;

   $22 = a(34)^2 + b(34) + c$, or $22 = 1156a + 34b + c$

   The solution of the system of equation is

   $\left(-\dfrac{39}{280}, \dfrac{963}{140}, -\dfrac{356}{7}\right)$, so the quadratic function that fits the data is

   $f(x) = -\dfrac{39}{280}x^2 + \dfrac{963}{140}x - \dfrac{356}{7}$.

   b) $f(30) = -\dfrac{39}{280}(30)^2 + \dfrac{963}{140}(30) - \dfrac{356}{7} \approx 30$

   About 30% of drivers will be involved in accidents at age 30.

   $f(37) = -\dfrac{39}{280}(37)^2 + \dfrac{963}{140}(37) - \dfrac{356}{7} \approx 13$

   About 13% of drivers will be involved in accidents at age 37.

93. Graph: $f(x) = \log_3 |x+1|$

x	$f(x)$
0	0
2	1
8	2
-2	0
-4	1
-9	2

95. $\log_{125} x = \dfrac{2}{3}$

$$125^{2/3} = x$$
$$(5^3)^{2/3} = x$$
$$5^2 = x$$
$$25 = x$$

97. $\log_8(2x+1) = -1$

$$8^{-1} = 2x + 1$$
$$\frac{1}{8} = 2x + 1$$
$$1 = 16x + 8 \qquad \text{Multiplying by 8}$$
$$-7 = 16x$$
$$-\frac{7}{16} = x$$

99. Let $\log_{1/4} \dfrac{1}{64} = x$. Then

$$\left(\frac{1}{4}\right)^x = \frac{1}{64}$$
$$\left(\frac{1}{4}\right)^x = \left(\frac{1}{4}\right)^3$$
$$x = 3$$

Thus, $\log_{1/4} \dfrac{1}{64} = 3$.

101. $\log_{10}(\log_4(\log_3 81))$

$= \log_{10}(\log_4 4) \qquad (\log_3 81 = 4)$

$= \log_{10} 1 \qquad\qquad (\log_4 4 = 1)$

$= 0$

103. Let $\log_{1/5} 25 = x$. Then

$$\left(\frac{1}{5}\right)^x = 25$$
$$(5^{-1})^x = 25$$
$$5^{-x} = 5^2$$
$$-x = 2$$
$$x = -2$$

Thus, $\log_{1/5} 25 = -2$.

Exercise Set 8.4

1. $\log_2 (32 \cdot 8) = \log_2 32 + \log_2 8$ Property 1

3. $\log_4 (64 \cdot 16) = \log_4 64 + \log_4 16$ Property 1

5. $\log_a Qx = \log_a Q + \log_a x$ Property 1

7. $\log_b 3 + \log_b 84 = \log_b (3 \cdot 84)$ Property 1
$= \log_b 252$

9. $\log_c K + \log_c y = \log_c K \cdot y$ Property 1
$= \log_c Ky$

11. $\log_c y^4 = 4 \log_c y$ Property 2

13. $\log_b t^6 = 6 \log_b t$ Property 2

15. $\log_b C^{-3} = -3 \log_b C$ Property 2

17. $\log_a \dfrac{67}{5} = \log_a 67 - \log_a 5$ Property 3

19. $\log_b \dfrac{2}{5} = \log_b 2 - \log_b 5$ Property 3

21. $\log_c 22 - \log_c 3 = \log_c \dfrac{22}{3}$ Property 3

23. $\log_a x^2 y^3 z$
$= \log_a x^2 + \log_a y^3 + \log_b z$ Property 1
$= 2 \log_a x + 3 \log_a y + \log_a z$ Property 2

25. $\log_b \dfrac{xy^2}{z^3}$
$= \log_b xy^2 - \log_b z^3$ Property 3
$= \log_b x + \log_b y^2 - \log_b z^3$ Property 1
$= \log_b x + 2 \log_b y - 3 \log_b z$ Property 2

27. $\log_c \sqrt[3]{\dfrac{x^4}{y^3 z^2}}$
$= \log_c \left(\dfrac{x^4}{y^3 z^2} \right)^{1/3}$
$= \dfrac{1}{3} \log_c \dfrac{x^4}{y^3 z^2}$ Property 2
$= \dfrac{1}{3} (\log_c x^4 - \log_c y^3 z^2)$ Property 3
$= \dfrac{1}{3} [\log_c x^4 - (\log_c y^3 + \log_c z^2)]$ Property 1
$= \dfrac{1}{3} (\log_c x^4 - \log_c y^3 - \log_c z^2)$ Removing parentheses
$= \dfrac{1}{3} (4 \log_c x - 3 \log_c y - 2 \log_c z)$ Property 2
$= \dfrac{4}{3} \log_c x - \log_c y - \dfrac{2}{3} \log_c z$

29. $\log_a \sqrt[4]{\dfrac{m^8 n^{12}}{a^3 b^5}}$
$= \log_a \left(\dfrac{m^8 n^{12}}{a^3 b^5} \right)^{1/4}$
$= \dfrac{1}{4} \log_a \dfrac{m^8 n^{12}}{a^3 b^5}$ Property 2
$= \dfrac{1}{4} (\log_a m^8 n^{12} - \log_a a^3 b^5)$ Property 3
$= \dfrac{1}{4} [\log_a m^8 + \log_a n^{12} - (\log_a a^3 + \log_a b^5)]$ Property 1
$= \dfrac{1}{4} (\log_a m^8 + \log_a n^{12} - \log_a a^3 - \log_a b^5)$
Removing parentheses
$= \dfrac{1}{4} (\log_a m^8 + \log_a n^{12} - 3 - \log_a b^5)$ Property 4
$= \dfrac{1}{4} (8 \log_a m + 12 \log_a n - 3 - 5 \log_a b)$ Property 2
$= 2 \log_a m + 3 \log_a n - \dfrac{3}{4} - \dfrac{5}{4} \log_a b$

31. $\dfrac{2}{3} \log_a x - \dfrac{1}{2} \log_a y$
$= \log_a x^{2/3} - \log_a y^{1/2}$ Property 2
$= \log_a \dfrac{x^{2/3}}{y^{1/2}}$, or   Property 3
$\log_a \dfrac{\sqrt[3]{x^2}}{\sqrt{y}}$

33. $\log_a 2x + 3(\log_a x - \log_a y)$
$= \log_a 2x + 3 \log_a x - 3 \log_a y$
$= \log_a 2x + \log_a x^3 - \log_a y^3$ Property 2
$= \log_a 2x^4 - \log_a y^3$ Property 1
$= \log_a \dfrac{2x^4}{y^3}$ Property 3

35. $\log_a \dfrac{a}{\sqrt{x}} - \log_a \sqrt{ax}$
$= \log_a ax^{-1/2} - \log_a a^{1/2} x^{1/2}$
$= \log_a \dfrac{ax^{-1/2}}{a^{1/2} x^{1/2}}$ Property 3
$= \log_a \dfrac{a^{1/2}}{x}$, or
$\log_a \dfrac{\sqrt{a}}{x}$

37. $\log_b 15 = \log_b (3 \cdot 5)$
$= \log_b 3 + \log_b 5$ Property 1
$= 1.099 + 1.609$
$= 2.708$

39. $\log_b \dfrac{5}{3} = \log_b 5 - \log_b 3$ Property 3
$= 1.609 - 1.099$
$= 0.51$

41. $\log_b \dfrac{1}{5} = \log_b 1 - \log_b 5$ Property 3

$\qquad = 0 - 1.609 \qquad (\log_b 1 = 0)$

$\qquad = -1.609$

43. $\log_b \sqrt{b^3} = \log_b b^{3/2} = \dfrac{3}{2} \qquad$ Property 4

45. $\log_b 5b = \log_b 5 + \log_b b \qquad$ Property 1

$\qquad = 1.609 + 1 \qquad (\log_b b = 1)$

$\qquad = 2.609$

47. $\log_e e^t = t \qquad$ Property 4

49. $\log_p p^5 = 5 \qquad$ Property 4

51. $\log_2 2^7 = x$

$\qquad 7 = x \qquad$ Property 4

53. $\log_e e^x = -7$

$\qquad x = -7 \qquad$ Property 4

55. Discussion and Writing Exercise

57. $i^{29} = i^{28} \cdot i = (i^2)^{14} \cdot i = (-1)^{14} \cdot i = 1 \cdot i = i$

59. $(2+i)(2-i) = 4 - i^2 = 4 - (-1) = 4 + 1 = 5$

61. $(7 - 8i) - (-16 + 10i) = 7 - 8i + 16 - 10i = 23 - 18i$

63. $(8 + 3i)(-5 - 2i) = -40 - 16i - 15i - 6i^2 =$

$\qquad -40 - 16i - 15i + 6 = -34 - 31i$

65. Enter $y_1 = \log x^2$ and $y_2 = (\log x)(\log x)$ and show that the graphs are different and that the y-values in a table of values are not the same.

67. $\qquad \log_a (x^8 - y^8) - \log_a (x^2 + y^2)$

$= \log_a \dfrac{x^8 - y^8}{x^2 + y^2} \qquad$ Property 3

$= \log_a \dfrac{(x^4 + y^4)(x^2 + y^2)(x + y)(x - y)}{x^2 + y^2} \qquad$ Factoring

$= \log_a [(x^4 + y^4)(x + y)(x - y)] \qquad$ Simplifying

$= \log_a (x^6 - x^4 y^2 + x^2 y^4 - y^6) \qquad$ Multiplying

69. $\qquad \log_a \sqrt{1 - s^2}$

$= \log_a (1 - s^2)^{1/2}$

$= \dfrac{1}{2} \log_a (1 - s^2)$

$= \dfrac{1}{2} \log_a [(1 - s)(1 + s)]$

$= \dfrac{1}{2} \log_a (1 - s) + \dfrac{1}{2} \log_a (1 + s)$

71. False. For example, let $a = 10$, $P = 100$, and $Q = 10$.

$\dfrac{\log 100}{\log 10} = \dfrac{2}{1} = 2$, but

$\log \dfrac{100}{10} = \log 10 = 1.$

73. True, by Property 1

75. False. For example, let $a = 2$, $P = 1$, and $Q = 1$.

$\log_2 (1 + 1) = \log_2 2 = 1$, but

$\log_2 1 + \log_2 1 = 0 + 0 = 0.$

Exercise Set 8.5

1. 0.6931

3. 4.1271

5. 8.3814

7. -5.0832

9. -1.6094

11. Does not exist

13. -1.7455

15. 1

17. 15.0293

19. 0.0305

21. 109.9472

23. 5

25. We will use common logarithms for the conversion. Let $a = 10$, $b = 6$, and $M = 100$ and substitute in the change-of-base formula.

$$\log_b M = \frac{\log_a M}{\log_a b}$$

$$\log_6 100 = \frac{\log_{10} 100}{\log_{10} 6}$$

$$\approx \frac{2}{0.7782}$$

$$\approx 2.5702$$

27. We will use common logarithms for the conversion. Let $a = 10$, $b = 2$, and $M = 100$ and substitute in the change-of-base formula.

$$\log_2 100 = \frac{\log_{10} 100}{\log_{10} 2}$$

$$\approx \frac{2}{0.3010}$$

$$\approx 6.6439$$

29. We will use natural logarithms for the conversion. Let $a = e$, $b = 7$, and $M = 65$ and substitute in the change-of-base formula.

$$\log_7 65 = \frac{\ln 65}{\ln 7}$$

$$\approx \frac{4.1744}{1.9459}$$

$$\approx 2.1452$$

31. We will use natural logarithms for the conversion. Let $a = e$, $b = 0.5$, and $M = 5$ and substitute in the change-of-base formula.

$$\log_{0.5} 5 = \frac{\ln 5}{\ln 0.5}$$

$$\approx \frac{1.6094}{-0.6931}$$

$$\approx -2.3219$$

33. We will use common logarithms for the conversion. Let $a = 10$, $b = 2$, and $M = 0.2$ and substitute in the change-of-base formula.

$$\log_2 0.2 = \frac{\log_{10} 0.2}{\log_{10} 2}$$

$$\approx \frac{-0.6990}{0.3010}$$

$$\approx -2.3219$$

35. We will use natural logarithms for the conversion. Let $a = e$, $b = \pi$, and $M = 200$.

$$\log_\pi 200 = \frac{\ln 200}{\ln \pi}$$

$$\approx \frac{5.2983}{1.1447}$$

$$\approx 4.6285$$

If $\ln 200$ and $\ln \pi$ are not rounded before the division is performed, the result is 4.6284.

37. Graph: $f(x) = e^x$

We find some function values with a calculator. We use these values to plot points and draw the graph.

x	e^x
0	1
1	2.7
2	7.4
3	20.1
-1	0.4
-2	0.1
-3	0.05

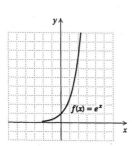

39. Graph: $f(x) = e^{-0.5x}$

We find some function values, plot points, and draw the graph.

x	$e^{-0.5x}$
0	1
1	0.61
2	0.37
-1	1.65
-2	2.72
-3	4.48
-4	7.39

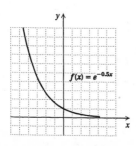

41. Graph: $f(x) = e^{x-1}$

We find some function values, plot points, and draw the graph.

x	e^{x-1}
0	0.4
1	1
2	2.7
3	7.4
4	20.1
-1	0.1
-2	0.05

43. Graph: $f(x) = e^{x+2}$

We find some function values, plot points, and draw the graph.

x	e^{x+2}
1	20.1
0	7.4
-2	1
-3	0.4
-4	0.1

45. Graph: $f(x) = e^x - 1$

We find some function values, plot points, and draw the graph.

x	$e^x - 1$
0	0
1	1.72
2	6.39
3	19.09
-1	-0.63
-2	-0.86
-4	-0.98

47. Graph: $f(x) = \ln(x + 2)$

We find some function values, plot points, and draw the graph.

x	$\ln(x + 2)$
0	0.69
1	1.10
2	1.39
3	1.61
-0.5	0.41
-1	0
-1.5	-0.69

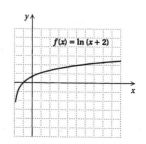

49. Graph: $f(x) = \ln(x - 3)$

We find some function values, plot points, and draw the graph.

x	$\ln(x - 3)$
3	Undefined
4	0
5	0.69
6	1.10
8	1.61
10	1.95

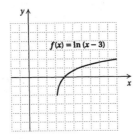

51. Graph: $f(x) = 2 \ln x$

x	$2 \ln x$
0.5	-1.4
1	0
2	1.4
3	2.2
4	2.8
5	3.2
6	3.6

53. Graph: $f(x) = \frac{1}{2} \ln x + 1$

x	$\frac{1}{2} \ln x + 1$
1	1
2	1.35
3	1.55
4	1.69
6	1.90

55. Graph: $f(x) = |\ln x|$

x	$\ln x$
$\frac{1}{4}$	1.4
$\frac{1}{2}$	0.7
1	0
3	1.1
5	1.6

57. Discussion and Writing Exercise

59. $x^{1/2} - 6x^{1/4} + 8 = 0$

Let $u = x^{1/4}$.

$u^2 - 6u + 8 = 0$ Substituting

$(u - 4)(u - 2) = 0$

$u = 4$ or $u = 2$

$x^{1/4} = 4$ or $x^{1/4} = 2$

$x = 256$ or $x = 16$ Raising both sides to the fourth power

Both numbers check. The solutions are 256 and 16.

61. $x - 18\sqrt{x} + 77 = 0$

Let $u = \sqrt{x}$.

$u^2 - 18u + 77 = 0$ Substituting

$(u - 7)(u - 11) = 0$

$u = 7$ or $u = 11$

$\sqrt{x} = 7$ or $\sqrt{x} = 11$

$x = 49$ or $x = 121$ Squaring both sides

Both numbers check. The solutions are 49 and 121.

63. Domain: $(-\infty, \infty)$, range: $[0, \infty)$

65. Domain: $(-\infty, \infty)$, range: $(-\infty, 100)$

67. $f(x)$ can be calculated for positive values of $2x - 5$. We have:

$2x - 5 > 0$

$2x > 5$

$x > \frac{5}{2}$

The domain is $\left\{ x \middle| x > \frac{5}{2} \right\}$, or $\left(\frac{5}{2}, \infty \right)$.

Exercise Set 8.6

1. $2^x = 8$

$2^x = 2^3$

$x = 3$ The exponents are the same.

3. $4^x = 256$

$4^x = 4^4$

$x = 4$ The exponents are the same.

5. $2^{2x} = 32$

$2^{2x} = 2^5$

$2x = 5$

$x = \frac{5}{2}$

7. $3^{5x} = 27$

$3^{5x} = 3^3$

$5x = 3$

$x = \frac{3}{5}$

9. $2^x = 11$

$\log 2^x = \log 11$ Taking the common logarithm on both sides

$x \log 2 = \log 11$ Property 2

$x = \dfrac{\log 11}{\log 2}$

$x \approx 3.4594$

11. $2^x = 43$

  $\log 2^x = \log 43$ Taking the common logarithm on both sides

  $x \log 2 = \log 43$ Property 2

  $x = \dfrac{\log 43}{\log 2}$

  $x \approx 5.4263$

13. $5^{4x-7} = 125$

  $5^{4x-7} = 5^3$

  $4x - 7 = 3$ The exponents are the same.

  $4x = 10$

  $x = \dfrac{10}{4}$, or $\dfrac{5}{2}$

15. $3^{x^2} \cdot 3^{4x} = \dfrac{1}{27}$

  $3^{x^2+4x} = 3^{-3}$

  $x^2 + 4x = -3$

  $x^2 + 4x + 3 = 0$

  $(x + 3)(x + 1) = 0$

  $x = -3 \ or \ x = -1$

17. $4^x = 8$

  $(2^2)^x = 2^3$

  $2^{2x} = 2^3$

  $2x = 3$ The exponents are the same.

  $x = \dfrac{3}{2}$

19. $e^t = 100$

  $\ln e^t = \ln 100$ Taking ln on both sides

  $t = \ln 100$ Property 4

  $t \approx 4.6052$ Using a calculator

21. $e^{-t} = 0.1$

  $\ln e^{-t} = \ln 0.1$ Taking ln on both sides

  $-t = \ln 0.1$ Property 4

  $-t \approx -2.3026$

  $t \approx 2.3026$

23. $e^{-0.02t} = 0.06$

  $\ln e^{-0.02t} = \ln 0.06$ Taking ln on both sides

  $-0.02t = \ln 0.06$ Property 4

  $t = \dfrac{\ln 0.06}{-0.02}$

  $t \approx \dfrac{-2.8134}{-0.02}$

  $t \approx 140.6705$

25. $2^x = 3^{x-1}$

  $\log 2^x = \log 3^{x-1}$

  $x \log 2 = (x - 1) \log 3$

  $x \log 2 = x \log 3 - \log 3$

  $\log 3 = x \log 3 - x \log 2$

  $\log 3 = x(\log 3 - \log 2)$

  $\dfrac{\log 3}{\log 3 - \log 2} = x$

  $\dfrac{0.4771}{0.4771 - 0.3010} \approx x$

  $2.7095 \approx x$

27. $(3.6)^x = 62$

  $\log (3.6)^x = \log 62$

  $x \log 3.6 = \log 62$

  $x = \dfrac{\log 62}{\log 3.6}$

  $x \approx 3.2220$

29. $\log_4 x = 4$

  $x = 4^4$ Writing an equivalent exponential equation

  $x = 256$

31. $\log_2 x = -5$

  $x = 2^{-5}$ Writing an equivalent exponential equation

  $x = \dfrac{1}{32}$

33. $\log x = 1$ The base is 10.

  $x = 10^1$

  $x = 10$

35. $\log x = -2$ The base is 10.

  $x = 10^{-2}$

  $x = \dfrac{1}{100}$

37. $\ln x = 2$

  $x = e^2 \approx 7.3891$

39. $\ln x = -1$

  $x = e^{-1}$

  $x = \dfrac{1}{e} \approx 0.3679$

41. $\log_3 (2x + 1) = 5$

  $2x + 1 = 3^5$ Writing an equivalent exponential equation

  $2x + 1 = 243$

  $2x = 242$

  $x = 121$

43. $\log x + \log (x - 9) = 1$ The base is 10.

$\log_{10} [x(x-9)] = 1$ Property 1

$x(x-9) = 10^1$

$x^2 - 9x = 10$

$x^2 - 9x - 10 = 0$

$(x-10)(x+1) = 0$

$x = 10 \ or \ x = -1$

Check: For 10:

$$\frac{\log x + \log (x-9) = 1}{\log 10 + \log (10-9) \ ? \ 1}$$
$$\log 10 + \log 1 \ \Big|$$
$$1 + 0$$
$$1 \ \Big| \qquad \text{TRUE}$$

For -1:

$$\frac{\log x + \log (x-9) = 1}{\log(-1) + \log (-1-9) \ ? \ 1} \qquad \text{FALSE}$$

The number -1 does not check, because negative numbers do not have logarithms. The solution is 10.

45. $\log x - \log (x+3) = -1$ The base is 10.

$\log_{10} \dfrac{x}{x+3} = -1$ Property 3

$\dfrac{x}{x+3} = 10^{-1}$

$\dfrac{x}{x+3} = \dfrac{1}{10}$

$10x = x + 3$

$9x = 3$

$x = \dfrac{1}{3}$

The answer checks. The solution is $\dfrac{1}{3}$.

47. $\log_2 (x+1) + \log_2 (x-1) = 3$

$\log_2[(x+1)(x-1)] = 3$ Property 1

$(x+1)(x-1) = 2^3$

$x^2 - 1 = 8$

$x^2 = 9$

$x = \pm 3$

The number 3 checks, but -3 does not. The solution is 3.

49. $\log_4 (x+6) - \log_4 x = 2$

$\log_4 \dfrac{x+6}{x} = 2$ Property 3

$\dfrac{x+6}{x} = 4^2$

$\dfrac{x+6}{x} = 16$

$x + 6 = 16x$

$6 = 15x$

$\dfrac{2}{5} = x$

The answer checks. The solution is $\dfrac{2}{5}$.

51. $\log_4 (x+3) + \log_4 (x-3) = 2$

$\log_4[(x+3)(x-3)] = 2$ Property 1

$(x+3)(x-3) = 4^2$

$x^2 - 9 = 16$

$x^2 = 25$

$x = \pm 5$

The number 5 checks, but -5 does not. The solution is 5.

53. $\log_3 (2x-6) - \log_3 (x+4) = 2$

$\log_3 \dfrac{2x-6}{x+4} = 2$ Property 3

$\dfrac{2x-6}{x+4} = 3^2$

$\dfrac{2x-6}{x+4} = 9$

$2x - 6 = 9x + 36$

       Multiplying by $(x+4)$

$-42 = 7x$

$-6 = x$

Check:

$$\frac{\log_3 (2x-6) - \log_3 (x+4) = 2}{\log_3 [2(-6) - 6] - \log_3 (-6+4) \ ? \ 2}$$
$$\log_3 (-18) - \log_3 (-2) \ \Big| \qquad \text{FALSE}$$

The number -6 does not check, because negative numbers do not have logarithms. There is no solution.

55. Discussion and Writing Exercise

57. $x^4 + 400 = 104x^2$

$x^4 - 104x^2 + 400 = 0$

Let $u = x^2$.

$u^2 - 104u + 400 = 0$

$(u-100)(u-4) = 0$

$u = 100 \ or \ u = 4$

$x^2 = 100 \ or \ x^2 = 4$ Replacing u with x^2

$x = \pm 10 \ or \ x = \pm 2$

The solutions are ± 10 and ± 2.

59.
$$(x^2 + 5x)^2 + 2(x^2 + 5x) = 24$$
$$(x^2 + 5x)^2 + 2(x^2 + 5x) - 24 = 0$$
Let $u = x^2 + 5x$.
$$u^2 + 2u - 24 = 0$$
$$(u + 6)(u - 4) = 0$$
$$u = -6 \quad or \quad u = 4$$
$$x^2 + 5x = 6 \quad or \quad x^2 + 5x = 4$$
Replacing u with $x^2 + 5x$
$$x^2 + 5x + 6 = 0 \quad or \ x^2 + 5x - 4 = 0$$
$$(x+3)(x+2) = 0 \quad or \qquad x =$$
$$\frac{-5 \pm \sqrt{5^2 - 4 \cdot 1(-4)}}{2 \cdot 1}$$
$$x = -3 \ or \ x = -2 \ or \qquad x = \frac{-5 \pm \sqrt{41}}{2}$$
The solutions are -3, -2, and $\dfrac{-5 \pm \sqrt{41}}{2}$.

61. $(125x^3 y^{-2} z^6)^{-2/3} =$
$$(5^3)^{-2/3} (x^3)^{-2/3} (y^{-2})^{-2/3} (z^6)^{-2/3} =$$
$$5^{-2} x^{-2} y^{4/3} z^{-4} = \frac{1}{25} x^{-2} y^{4/3} z^{-4}, \ or$$
$$\frac{y^{4/3}}{25 x^2 z^4}$$

63. Find the first coordinate of the point of intersection of $y_1 = \ln x$ and $y_2 = \log x$. The value of x for which the natural logarithm of x is the same as the common logarithm of x is 1.

65. a) 0.3770

   b) -1.9617

   c) 0.9036

   d) -1.5318

67.
$$2^{2x} + 128 = 24 \cdot 2^x$$
$$2^{2x} - 24 \cdot 2^x + 128 = 0$$
Let $u = 2^x$.
$$u^2 - 24u + 128 = 0$$
$$(u - 8)(u - 16) = 0$$
$$u = 8 \quad or \quad u = 16$$
$$2^x = 8 \quad or \ 2^x = 16 \quad \text{Replacing } u \text{ with } 2^x$$
$$2^x = 2^3 \ or \ 2^x = 2^4$$
$$x = 3 \quad or \quad x = 4$$
The solutions are 3 and 4.

69.
$$8^x = 16^{3x+9}$$
$$(2^3)^x = (2^4)^{3x+9}$$
$$2^{3x} = 2^{12x+36}$$
$$3x = 12x + 36$$
$$-36 = 9x$$
$$-4 = x$$

71.
$$\log_6 (\log_2 x) = 0$$
$$\log_2 x = 6^0$$
$$\log_2 x = 1$$
$$x = 2^1$$
$$x = 2$$

73.
$$\log_5 \sqrt{x^2 - 9} = 1$$
$$\sqrt{x^2 - 9} = 5^1$$
$$x^2 - 9 = 25 \qquad \text{Squaring both sides}$$
$$x^2 = 34$$
$$x = \pm\sqrt{34}$$
Both numbers check. The solutions are $\pm\sqrt{34}$.

75. $\log (\log x) = 5 \qquad$ The base is 10.
$$\log x = 10^5$$
$$\log x = 100,000$$
$$x = 10^{100,000}$$
The number checks. The solution is $10^{100,000}$

77.
$$\log x^2 = (\log x)^2$$
$$2 \log x = (\log x)^2$$
$$0 = (\log x)^2 - 2 \log x$$
Let $u = \log x$.
$$0 = u^2 - 2u$$
$$0 = u(u - 2)$$
$$u = 0 \quad or \quad u = 2$$
$$\log x = 0 \quad or \ \log x = 2$$
$$x = 10^0 \ or \qquad x = 10^2$$
$$x = 1 \quad or \qquad x = 100$$
Both numbers check. The solutions are 1 and 100.

79.
$$\log_a a^{x^2 + 4x} = 21$$
$$x^2 + 4x = 21 \qquad \text{Property 4}$$
$$x^2 + 4x - 21 = 0$$
$$(x + 7)(x - 3) = 0$$
$$x = -7 \ or \ x = 3$$
Both numbers check. The solutions are $= -7$ and 3.

81. $3^{2x} - 8 \cdot 3^x + 15 = 0$
Let $u = 3^x$ and substitute.
$$u^2 - 8u + 15 = 0$$
$$(u - 5)(u - 3) = 0$$
$$u = 5 \qquad or \quad u = 3$$
$$3^x = 5 \qquad or \ 3^x = 3 \quad \text{Substituting } 3^x \text{ for } u$$
$$\log 3^x = \log 5 \quad or \ 3^x = 3^1$$
$$x \log 3 = \log 5 \quad or \qquad x = 1$$
$$x = \frac{\log 5}{\log 3} \quad or \quad x = 1, \ or$$
$$x \approx 1.4650 \quad or \quad x = 1$$

Both numbers check. Note that we can also express $\dfrac{\log 5}{\log 3}$ as $\log_3 5$ using the change-of-base formula.

Exercise Set 8.7

1. $L = 10 \cdot \log \dfrac{I}{I_0}$

$= 10 \cdot \log \dfrac{3.2 \times 10^{-3}}{10^{-12}}$ Substituting

$= 10 \cdot \log(3.2 \times 10^9)$

$\approx 10(9.5)$

≈ 95

The sound level is about 95 dB.

3. $L = 10 \cdot \log \dfrac{I}{I_0}$

$105 = 10 \cdot \log \dfrac{I}{10^{-12}}$

$10.5 = \log \dfrac{I}{10^{-12}}$

$10.5 = \log I - \log 10^{-12}$ $(\log 10^a = a)$

$10.5 = \log I - (-12)$

$10.5 = \log I + 12$

$-1.5 = \log I$

$10^{-1.5} = I$ Converting to an exponential equation

$3.2 \times 10^{-2} \approx I$

The intensity of the sound is $10^{-1.5}$ W/m^2, or about 3.2×10^{-2} W/m^2.

5. $\text{pH} = -\log[H^+]$

$= -\log[1.6 \times 10^{-7}]$

$\approx -(-6.795880)$

≈ 6.8

The pH of milk is about 6.8.

7. $\text{pH} = -\log[H^+]$

$7.8 = -\log[H^+]$

$-7.8 = \log[H^+]$

$10^{-7.8} = [H^+]$

$1.58 \times 10^{-8} \approx [H^+]$

The hydrogen ion concentration is about 1.58×10^{-8} moles per liter.

9. $3,251,876 = 3251.876$ thousands

$w(P) = 0.37 \ln P + 0.05$

$w(3251.876) = 0.37 \ln 3251.876 + 0.05$

≈ 3.04 ft/sec

11. $311,121 = 311.121$ thousands

$w(P) = 0.37 \ln P + 0.05$

$w(311.121) = 0.37 \ln 311.121 + 0.05$

≈ 2.17 ft/sec

13. $N(t) = 3^t$

a) $N(5) = 3^5 = 243$ people

b) $\quad 6,200,000,000 = 3^t$

$\ln 6,200,000,000 = \ln 3^t$

$\ln 6,200,000,000 = t \ln 3$

$\dfrac{\ln 6,200,000,000}{\ln 3} = t$

$20.5 \approx t$

The acts of kindness will reach the entire world in about 20.5 months.

c) $\quad 2 = 3^t$

$\ln 2 = \ln 3^t$

$\ln 2 = t \ln 3$

$\dfrac{\ln 2}{\ln 3} = t$

$0.6 \approx t$

The doubling time is about 0.6 month.

15. a) In 2005, $t = 2005 - 2000$, or 5.

$C(5) = 11,054(1.06)^5 \approx \$14,793$

b) $\quad 21,000 = 11,054(1.06)^t$

$\dfrac{21,000}{11,054} = 1.06^t$

$\log \dfrac{21,000}{11,054} = \log 1.06^t$

$\log \dfrac{21,000}{11,054} = t \log 1.06$

$\dfrac{\log \dfrac{21,000}{11,054}}{\log 1.06} = t$

$11 \approx t$

The cost will be \$21,000 11 yr after 2000, or in 2011.

c) $\quad 22,108 = 11,054(1.06)^t$

$2 = (1.06)^t$

$\log 2 = \log(1.06)^t$

$\log 2 = t \log 1.06$

$\dfrac{\log 2}{\log 1.06} = t$

$11.9 \approx t$

The doubling time is about 11.9 years.

17. a) $P(t) = 6e^{0.015t}$, where $P(t)$ is in billions and t is the number of years after 1998.

b) In 2010, $t = 2010 - 1998$, or 12.

$P(12) = 6e^{0.015(12)} \approx 7.2$

In 2010, the population will be about 7.2 billion.

c)
$$10 = 6e^{0.015t}$$
$$\frac{5}{3} = e^{0.015t}$$
$$\ln\left(\frac{5}{3}\right) = \ln e^{0.015t}$$
$$\ln\left(\frac{5}{3}\right) = 0.015t$$
$$\frac{\ln\left(\frac{5}{3}\right)}{0.015} = t$$
$$34 \approx t$$

The population will be 10 billion 34 years after 1998, or in 2032.

d)
$$12 = 6e^{0.015t}$$
$$2 = e^{0.015t}$$
$$\ln 2 = \ln e^{0.015t}$$
$$\ln 2 = 0.015t$$
$$\frac{\ln 2}{0.015} = t$$
$$46.2 \approx t$$

The doubling time is about 46.2 yr.

19. a) $P(t) = P_0 \, e^{0.06t}$

b) To find the balance after one year, replace P_0 with 5000 and t with 1. We find $P(1)$:

$$P(1) = 5000 \, e^{0.06(1)} \approx \$5309.18$$

To find the balance after 2 years, replace P_0 with 5000 and t with 2. We find $P(2)$:

$$P(2) = 5000 \, e^{0.06(2)} \approx \$5637.48$$

To find the balance after 10 years, replace P_0 with 5000 and t with 10. We find $P(10)$: $P(10) = 5000e^{0.06(10)} \approx \$9110.59$

c) To find the doubling time, replace P_0 with 5000 and $P(t)$ with 10,000 and solve for t.

$$10{,}000 = 5000 \, e^{0.06t}$$
$$2 = e^{0.06t}$$
$$\ln 2 = \ln e^{0.06t} \quad \text{Taking the natural logarithm on both sides}$$
$$\ln 2 = 0.06t \quad \text{Finding the logarithm of the base to a power}$$
$$\frac{\ln 2}{0.06} = t$$
$$11.6 \approx t$$

The investment will double in about 11.6 years.

21. a)
$$P(t) = P_0 e^{kt}$$
$$1{,}563{,}282 = 852{,}737 e^{k \cdot 10}$$
$$\frac{1{,}563{,}282}{852{,}737} = e^{10k}$$
$$\ln \frac{1{,}563{,}282}{852{,}737} = \ln e^{10k}$$
$$\ln \frac{1{,}563{,}282}{852{,}737} = 10k$$
$$\frac{\ln \dfrac{1{,}563{,}282}{852{,}737}}{10} = k$$
$$0.061 \approx k$$

The exponential growth rate is 0.061, or 6.1%.

The exponential growth function is $P(t) = 852{,}737 e^{0.061t}$, where t is the number of years after 1990.

b) In 2010, $t = 2010 - 1990$, or 20.
$$P(20) = 852{,}737 e^{0.061(20)}$$
$$= 852{,}737 e^{1.22}$$
$$\approx 2{,}888{,}380$$

In 2010, the population of Las Vegas will be about 2,888,380.

c)
$$8{,}000{,}000 = 852{,}737 e^{0.061t}$$
$$\frac{8{,}000{,}000}{852{,}737} = e^{0.061t}$$
$$\ln \frac{8{,}000{,}000}{852{,}737} = \ln e^{0.061t}$$
$$\ln \frac{8{,}000{,}000}{852{,}737} = 0.061t$$
$$\frac{\ln \dfrac{8{,}000{,}000}{852{,}737}}{0.061} = t$$
$$37 \approx t$$

The population will reach 8,000,000 about 37 yr after 1990, or in 2027.

23. If the scrolls had lost 22.3% of their carbon-14 from an initial amount P_0, then 77.7%(P_0) is the amount present. To find the age t of the scrolls, we substitute 77.7%(P_0), or $0.777P_0$, for $P(t)$ in the carbon-14 decay function and solve for t.

$$P(t) = P_0 e^{-0.00012t}$$
$$0.777P_0 = P_0 e^{-0.00012t}$$
$$0.777 = e^{-0.00012t}$$
$$\ln 0.777 = \ln e^{-0.00012t}$$
$$-0.2523 \approx -0.00012t$$
$$t \approx \frac{-0.2523}{-0.00012} \approx 2103$$

The scrolls are about 2103 years old.

25. The function $P(t) = P_0\, e^{-kt}$, $k > 0$, can be used to model decay. For iodine-131, $k = 9.6\%$, or 0.096. To find the half-life we substitute 0.096 for k and $\frac{1}{2}\, P_0$ for $P(t)$, and solve for t.

$$\frac{1}{2}\, P_0 = P_0\, e^{-0.096t},\ \text{ or }\ \frac{1}{2} = e^{-0.096t}$$

$$\ln \frac{1}{2} = \ln e^{-0.096t} = -0.096t$$

$$t = \frac{\ln 0.5}{-0.096} \approx \frac{-0.6931}{-0.096} \approx 7.2 \text{ days}$$

27. The function $P(t) = P_0 e^{-kt}$, $k > 0$, can be used to model decay. We substitute $\frac{1}{2} P_0$ for $P(t)$ and 1 for t and solve for the decay rate k.

$$\frac{1}{2}P_0 = P_0 e^{-k \cdot 1}$$

$$\frac{1}{2} = e^{-k}$$

$$\ln \frac{1}{2} = \ln e^{-k}$$

$$-0.693 \approx -k$$

$$0.693 \approx k$$

The decay rate is 0.693, or 69.3% per year.

29. a) We use the exponential decay equation $W(t) = W_0 e^{-kt}$, where t is the number of years after 1996 and $W(t)$ is in millions of tons. In 1996, at $t = 0$, 17.5 million tons of yard waste were discarded. We substitute 17.5 for W_0.

$$W(t) = 17.5 e^{-kt}.$$

To find the exponential decay rate k, observe that 2 years after 1996, in 1998, 14.5 million tons of yard waste were discarded. We substitute 2 for t and 14.5 for $W(t)$.

$$14.5 = 17.5 e^{-k \cdot 2}$$

$$0.8286 \approx e^{-2k}$$

$$\ln 0.8286 \approx \ln e^{-2k}$$

$$\ln 0.8286 \approx -2k$$

$$\frac{\ln 0.8286}{-2} \approx k$$

$$0.094 \approx k$$

Then we have $W(t) = 17.5 e^{-0.094t}$, where t is the number of years after 1996 and $W(t)$ is in millions of tons.

b) In 2010, $t = 2010 - 1996 = 14$.

$$W(14) = 17.5 e^{-0.094(14)}$$

$$= 17.5 e^{-1.316}$$

$$\approx 4.7$$

In 2010, about 4.7 million tons of yard waste were discarded.

c) 1 ton is equivalent to 0.000001 million tons.

$$0.000001 = 17.5 e^{-0.094t}$$

$$5.71 \times 10^{-8} \approx e^{-0.094t}$$

$$\ln(5.71 \times 10^{-8}) \approx \ln e^{-0.094t}$$

$$\ln(5.71 \times 10^{-8}) \approx -0.094t$$

$$\frac{\ln(5.71 \times 10^{-8})}{-0.094} \approx t$$

$$177 \approx t$$

Only one ton of yard waste will be discarded about 177 years after 1996, or in 2173.

31. a) We start with the exponential growth equation

$$V(t) = V_0\, e^{kt},\ \text{where } t \text{ is the number}$$
of years after 1991.

Substituting 451,000 for V_0, we have

$$V(t) = 451,000\, e^{kt}.$$

To find the exponential growth rate k, observe that the card sold for $640,500 in 1996, or 5 years after 1991. We substitute and solve for k.

$$V(5) = 451,000\, e^{k \cdot 5}$$

$$640,500 = 451,000\, e^{5k}$$

$$1.42 = e^{5k}$$

$$\ln 1.42 = \ln e^{5k}$$

$$\ln 1.42 = 5k$$

$$\frac{\ln 1.42}{5} = k$$

$$0.07 \approx k$$

Thus the exponential growth function is $V(t) = 451,000\, e^{0.07t}$, where t is the number of years after 1991.

b) In 2005, $t = 2005 - 1991$, or 14.

$$V(14) = 451,000\, e^{0.07(14)} \approx 1,201,670$$

The card's value in 2005 will be about $1,201,670.

c) Substitute $902,000 for $V(t)$ and solve for t.

$$902,000 = 451,000\, e^{0.07t}$$

$$2 = e^{0.07t}$$

$$\ln 2 = \ln e^{0.07t}$$

$$\ln 2 = 0.07t$$

$$\frac{\ln 2}{0.07} = t$$

$$9.9 \approx t$$

The doubling time is about 9.9 years.

d) Substitute $1,000,000 for $V(t)$ and solve for t.

$$1,000,000 = 451,000\, e^{0.07t}$$

$$2.217 \approx e^{0.07t}$$

$$\ln 2.217 \approx \ln e^{0.07t}$$

$$\ln 2.217 \approx 0.07t$$

$$\frac{\ln 2.217}{0.07} \approx t$$

$$11.4 \approx t$$

The value of the card will be $1,000,000 in 1991+11, or 2002.

e) In 2001, $t = 2001 - 1991$, or 10.

$$V(10) = 451,000 e^{0.07(10)}$$

$$= 451,000 e^{0.7}$$

$$\approx 908,202$$

The function estimates that the card's value in 2001 would be about $908,202. According to this, the card would not be a good buy at $1.1 million.

33. a)
$$P(t) = P_0 e^{-kt}$$

$$2,242,798 = 2,394,811 e^{-k\cdot 10}$$

$$\frac{2,242,798}{2,394,811} = e^{-10k}$$

$$\ln \frac{2,242,798}{2,394,811} = \ln e^{-10k}$$

$$\ln \frac{2,242,798}{2,394,811} = -10k$$

$$\frac{\ln \dfrac{2,242,798}{2,394,811}}{-10} = k$$

$$0.007 \approx k$$

The exponential decay rate is 0.007, or 0.7%. The exponential decay function is $P(t) = 2,394,811 e^{-0.007t}$, where t is the number of years after 1990.

b) In 2010, $t = 2010 - 1990$, or 20.

$$P(20) = 2,394,811 e^{-0.007(20)}$$

$$= 2,394,811 e^{-0.14}$$

$$\approx 2,081,949$$

In 2010, the population of Pittsburgh will be about 2,081,949.

c)
$$1,000,000 = 2,394,811 e^{-0.007t}$$

$$\frac{1,000,000}{2,394,811} = e^{-0.007t}$$

$$\ln \frac{1,000,000}{2,394,811} = \ln e^{-0.007t}$$

$$\ln \frac{1,000,000}{2,394,811} = -0.007t$$

$$\frac{\ln \dfrac{1,000,000}{2,394,811}}{-0.007} = t$$

$$125 \approx t$$

The population will decline to 1 million about 125 yr after 1990, or in 2115.

35. Discussion and Writing Exercise

37. $i^{46} = (i^2)^{23} = (-1)^{23} = -1$

39. $i^{53} = (i^2)^{26} \cdot i = (-1)^{26} \cdot i = i$

41. $i^{14} + i^{15} = (i^2)^7 + (i^2)^7 \cdot i = (-1)^7 + (-1)^7 \cdot i = -1 - i$

43. $\dfrac{8-i}{8+i} = \dfrac{8-i}{8+i} \cdot \dfrac{8-i}{8-i}$

$$= \frac{64 - 16i + i^2}{64 - i^2}$$

$$= \frac{64 - 16i - 1}{64 - (-1)}$$

$$= \frac{63 - 16i}{65}$$

$$= \frac{63}{65} - \frac{16}{65}i$$

45. $(5 - 4i)(5 + 4i) = 25 - 16i^2 = 25 + 16 = 41$

47. $-0.937,\ 1.078,\ 58.770$

49. $-0.767,\ 2,\ 4$

51. We will use the exponential growth equation $V(t) = V_0 e^{kt}$, where t is the number of years after 2001 and $V(t)$ is in millions of dollars. We substitute 21 for $V(t)$, 0.05 for k, and 9 for t and solve for V_0.

$$21 = V_0 e^{0.05(9)}$$

$$21 = V_0 e^{0.45}$$

$$\frac{21}{e^{0.45}} = V_0$$

$$13.4 \approx V_0$$

George Steinbrenner needs to invest $13.4 million at 5% interest compounded continuously in order to have $21 million to pay Derek Jeter in 2010.

Chapter 9

Conic Sections

Exercise Set 9.1

1. Graph: $y = x^2$

The graph is a parabola. The vertex is $(0,0)$; the line of symmetry is $x = 0$. The curve opens upward. We choose some x-values on both sides of the vertex and compute the corresponding y-values. Then we plot the points and graph the parabola.

x	y
0	0
1	1
−1	1
2	4
−2	4

3. Graph: $x = y^2 + 4y + 1$

We complete the square.

$$x = (y^2 + 4y + 4 - 4) + 1$$
$$= (y^2 + 4y + 4) - 4 + 1$$
$$= (y + 2)^2 - 3, \text{ or}$$
$$= [y - (-2)]^2 + (-3)$$

The graph is a parabola. The vertex is $(-3, -2)$; the line of symmetry is $y = -2$. The curve opens to the right.

x	y
−3	−2
−2	−3
−2	−1
1	−4
1	0

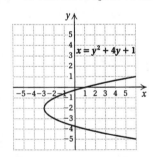

5. Graph: $y = -x^2 + 4x - 5$

We use the formula to find the first coordinate of the vertex:

$$x = -\frac{b}{2a} = -\frac{4}{2(-1)} = 2$$

Then $y = -x^2 + 4x - 5 = -(2)^2 + 4(2) - 5 = -1$.

The vertex is $(2, -1)$; the line of symmetry is $x = 2$. The curve opens downward.

x	y
2	−1
1	−2
3	−2
0	−5
4	−5

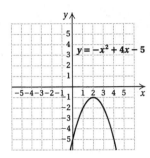

7. Graph: $x = -3y^2 - 6y - 1$

We complete the square.

$$x = -3(y^2 + 2y) - 1$$
$$= -3(y^2 + 2y + 1 - 1) - 1$$
$$= -3(y^2 + 2y + 1) + 3 - 1$$
$$= -3(y + 1)^2 + 2$$
$$= -3[y - (-1)]^2 + 2$$

The graph is a parabola. The vertex is $(2, -1)$; the line of symmetry is $y = -1$. The curve opens to the left.

x	y
2	−1
−1	−2
−1	0
−10	−3
−10	1

9.
$$d = \sqrt{(x_2 - x_1)^2 + (y_2 - y_1)^2}$$
$$d = \sqrt{(2 - 6)^2 + [-7 - (-4)]^2} \quad \text{Substituting}$$
$$= \sqrt{(-4)^2 + (-3)^2}$$
$$= \sqrt{25} = 5$$

11.
$$d = \sqrt{(x_2 - x_1)^2 + (y_2 - y_1)^2}$$
$$d = \sqrt{(5 - 0)^2 + [-6 - (-4)]^2}$$
$$= \sqrt{5^2 + (-2)^2}$$
$$= \sqrt{29} \approx 5.385$$

13.
$$d = \sqrt{(x_2 - x_1)^2 + (y_2 - y_1)^2}$$
$$d = \sqrt{(-9 - 9)^2 + (-9 - 9)^2}$$
$$= \sqrt{(-18)^2 + (-18)^2}$$
$$= \sqrt{648} = \sqrt{324 \cdot 2}$$
$$= 18\sqrt{2} \approx 25.456$$

15. $d = \sqrt{(x_2 - x_1)^2 + (y_2 - y_1)^2}$

$d = \sqrt{(-4.3 - 2.8)^2 + [-3.5 - (-3.5)]^2}$

$= \sqrt{(-7.1)^2 + 0^2} = \sqrt{(-7.1)^2}$

$= 7.1$

17. $d = \sqrt{(x_2 - x_1)^2 + (y_2 - y_1)^2}$

$d = \sqrt{\left(\dfrac{5}{7} - \dfrac{1}{7}\right)^2 + \left(\dfrac{1}{14} - \dfrac{11}{14}\right)^2}$

$= \sqrt{\left(\dfrac{4}{7}\right)^2 + \left(-\dfrac{5}{7}\right)^2}$

$= \sqrt{\dfrac{16}{49} + \dfrac{25}{49}}$

$= \sqrt{\dfrac{41}{49}}$

$= \dfrac{\sqrt{41}}{7} \approx 0.915$

19. $d = \sqrt{[56 - (-23)]^2 + (-17 - 10)^2}$

$= \sqrt{79^2 + (-27)^2} = \sqrt{6970} \approx 83.487$

21. $d = \sqrt{(a - 0)^2 + (b - 0)^2}$

$= \sqrt{a^2 + b^2}$

23. $d = \sqrt{(-\sqrt{7} - \sqrt{2})^2 + [\sqrt{5} - (-\sqrt{3})]^2}$

$= \sqrt{7 + 2\sqrt{14} + 2 + 5 + 2\sqrt{15} + 3}$

$= \sqrt{17 + 2\sqrt{14} + 2\sqrt{15}} \approx 5.677$

25. $d = \sqrt{[1000 - (-2000)]^2 + (-240 - 580)^2}$

$= \sqrt{3000^2 + (-820)^2}$

$= \sqrt{9,672,400} \approx 3110.048$

27. Using the midpoint formula $\left(\dfrac{x_1 + x_2}{2}, \dfrac{y_1 + y_2}{2}\right)$, we obtain

$\left(\dfrac{-1 + 4}{2}, \dfrac{9 + (-2)}{2}\right)$, or $\left(\dfrac{3}{2}, \dfrac{7}{2}\right)$.

29. Using the midpoint formula $\left(\dfrac{x_1 + x_2}{2}, \dfrac{y_1 + y_2}{2}\right)$, we obtain

$\left(\dfrac{3 + (-3)}{2}, \dfrac{5 + 6}{2}\right)$, or $\left(\dfrac{0}{2}, \dfrac{11}{2}\right)$, or $\left(0, \dfrac{11}{2}\right)$.

31. Using the midpoint formula $\left(\dfrac{x_1 + x_2}{2}, \dfrac{y_1 + y_2}{2}\right)$, we obtain

$\left(\dfrac{-10 + 8}{2}, \dfrac{-13 + (-4)}{2}\right)$, or $\left(\dfrac{-2}{2}, \dfrac{-17}{2}\right)$, or $\left(-1, -\dfrac{17}{2}\right)$.

33. Using the midpoint formula $\left(\dfrac{x_1 + x_2}{2}, \dfrac{y_1 + y_2}{2}\right)$, we obtain

$\left(\dfrac{-3.4 + 2.9}{2}, \dfrac{8.1 + (-8.7)}{2}\right)$, or $\left(\dfrac{-0.5}{2}, \dfrac{-0.6}{2}\right)$, or $(-0.25, -0.3)$.

35. Using the midpoint formula $\left(\dfrac{x_1 + x_2}{2}, \dfrac{y_1 + y_2}{2}\right)$, we obtain

$\left(\dfrac{\dfrac{1}{6} + \left(-\dfrac{1}{3}\right)}{2}, \dfrac{-\dfrac{3}{4} + \dfrac{5}{6}}{2}\right)$, or $\left(-\dfrac{1}{\dfrac{6}{2}}, \dfrac{\dfrac{1}{12}}{2}\right)$, or $\left(-\dfrac{1}{12}, \dfrac{1}{24}\right)$.

37. Using the midpoint formula $\left(\dfrac{x_1 + x_2}{2}, \dfrac{y_1 + y_2}{2}\right)$, we obtain

$\left(\dfrac{\sqrt{2} + \sqrt{3}}{2}, \dfrac{-1 + 4}{2}\right)$, or $\left(\dfrac{\sqrt{2} + \sqrt{3}}{2}, \dfrac{3}{2}\right)$.

39. $\quad (x + 1)^2 + (y + 3)^2 = 4$

$[x - (-1)]^2 + [y - (-3)]^2 = 2^2 \quad$ Standard form

The center is $(-1, -3)$, and the radius is 2.

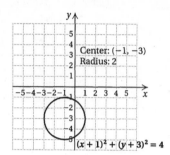

41. $\quad (x - 3)^2 + y^2 = 2$

$(x - 3)^2 + (y - 0)^2 = (\sqrt{2})^2 \quad$ Standard form

The center is $(3, 0)$, and the radius is $\sqrt{2}$.

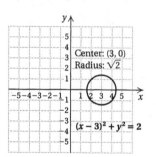

43. $\quad x^2 + y^2 = 25$

$(x - 0)^2 + (y - 0)^2 = 5^2 \quad$ Standard form

The center is $(0, 0)$, and the radius is 5.

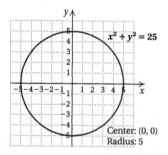

45. $(x - h)^2 + (y - k)^2 = r^2 \quad$ Standard form

$(x - 0)^2 + (y - 0)^2 = 7^2 \quad$ Substituting

$x^2 + y^2 = 49$

47. $(x - h)^2 + (y - k)^2 = r^2 \qquad$ Standard form

$[x - (-5)]^2 + (y - 3)^2 = (\sqrt{7})^2 \quad$ Substituting

$(x + 5)^2 + (y - 3)^2 = 7$

49.
$$x^2 + y^2 + 8x - 6y - 15 = 0$$
$$(x^2 + 8x) + (y^2 - 6y) - 15 = 0$$
Regrouping
$$(x^2 + 8x + 16 - 16) + (y^2 - 6y + 9 - 9) - 15 = 0$$
Completing the square twice
$$(x^2 + 8x + 16) + (y^2 - 6y + 9) - 16 - 9 - 15 = 0$$
$$(x + 4)^2 + (y - 3)^2 = 40$$
$$[x - (-4)]^2 + (y - 3)^2 = (\sqrt{40})^2$$
$$[x - (-4)]^2 + (y - 3)^2 = (2\sqrt{10})^2$$
The center is $(-4, 3)$, and the radius is $2\sqrt{10}$.

51.
$$x^2 + y^2 - 8x + 2y + 13 = 0$$
$$(x^2 - 8x) + (y^2 + 2y) + 13 = 0$$
Regrouping
$$(x^2 - 8x + 16 - 16) + (y^2 + 2y + 1 - 1) + 13 = 0$$
Completing the square twice
$$(x^2 - 8x + 16) + (y^2 + 2y + 1) - 16 - 1 + 13 = 0$$
$$(x - 4)^2 + (y + 1)^2 = 4$$
$$(x - 4)^2 + [y - (-1)]^2 = 2^2$$
The center is $(4, -1)$, and the radius is 2.

53.
$$x^2 + y^2 - 4x = 0$$
$$(x^2 - 4x) + y^2 = 0$$
$$(x^2 - 4x + 4 - 4) + y^2 = 0$$
$$(x^2 - 4x + 4) + y^2 - 4 = 0$$
$$(x - 2)^2 + y^2 = 4$$
$$(x - 2)^2 + (y - 0)^2 = 2^2$$
The center is $(2, 0)$, and the radius is 2.

55. Discussion and Writing Exercise

57. We use the elimination method.
$$\begin{array}{rl} x - y = 7 & (1) \\ x + y = 11 & (2) \\ \hline 2x \quad\;\; = 18 & \text{Adding} \\ x = 9 \end{array}$$
Substitute 9 for x in one of the original equations and solve for y.
$$x + y = 11 \quad (2)$$
$$9 + y = 11 \quad \text{Substituting}$$
$$y = 2$$
The solution is $(9, 2)$.

59. $y = 3x - 2,$ (1)
$2x - 4y = 50$ (2)

Substitute $3x - 2$ for y in Equation (2) and solve for y.
$$2x - 4(3x - 2) = 50$$
$$2x - 12x + 8 = 50$$
$$-10x = 42$$
$$x = -\frac{21}{5}$$

Substitute $-\dfrac{21}{5}$ for x in Equation (1) and compute y.
$$y = 3\left(-\frac{21}{5}\right) - 2 = -\frac{63}{5} - 2 = -\frac{73}{5}$$
The solution is $\left(-\dfrac{21}{5}, -\dfrac{73}{5}\right)$.

61. $-4x + 12y = -9,$ (1)
$\quad\; x - 3y = 2$ (2)

We use the elimination method.
$$\begin{array}{rl} -4x + 12y = -9 & (1) \\ -4x + 12y = -8 & \text{Multiplying (2) by } -4 \\ \hline 0 = -17 & \text{Adding} \end{array}$$
We get a false equation. The system of equations has no solution.

63. $x^2 - 16 = x^2 - 4^2 = (x + 4)(x - 4)$

65. $64p^2 - 81q^2 = (8p)^2 - (9q)^2 = (8p + 9q)(8p - 9q)$

67. We first find the length of the radius, which is the distance between $(0, 0)$ and $\left(\dfrac{1}{4}, \dfrac{\sqrt{31}}{4}\right)$.

$$\begin{aligned} r &= \sqrt{\left(\frac{1}{4} - 0\right)^2 + \left(\frac{\sqrt{31}}{4} - 0\right)^2} \\ &= \sqrt{\left(\frac{1}{4}\right)^2 + \left(\frac{\sqrt{31}}{4}\right)^2} \\ &= \sqrt{\frac{1}{16} + \frac{31}{16}} \\ &= \sqrt{\frac{32}{16}} \\ &= \sqrt{2} \end{aligned}$$

$$\begin{aligned} (x - h)^2 + (y - k)^2 &= r^2 \quad && \text{Standard form} \\ (x - 0)^2 + (y - 0)^2 &= (\sqrt{2})^2 \end{aligned}$$
Substituting $(0, 0)$ for the center
and $\sqrt{2}$ for the radius
$$x^2 + y^2 = 2$$

69.

The center is $(-3, -2)$ and the radius is 3.
$$\begin{aligned} (x - h)^2 + (y - k)^2 &= r^2 && \text{Standard form} \\ [x - (-3)]^2 + [y - (-2)]^2 &= 3^2 && \text{Substituting} \\ (x + 3)^2 + (y + 2)^2 &= 9 \end{aligned}$$

71. $d = \sqrt{(x_2 - x_1)^2 + (y_2 - y_1)^2}$

$d = \sqrt{(-1 - 6)^2 + (3k - 2k)^2}$ Substituting

$= \sqrt{(-7)^2 + (k)^2}$

$= \sqrt{49 + k^2}$

73. $d = \sqrt{(x_2 - x_1)^2 + (y_2 - y_1)^2}$

$d = \sqrt{[6m - (-2m)]^2 + (-7n - n)^2}$ Substituting

$= \sqrt{(8m)^2 + (-8n)^2}$

$= \sqrt{64m^2 + 64n^2}$

$= \sqrt{64(m^2 + n^2)}$

$= 8\sqrt{m^2 + n^2}$

75. The distance between $(-8, -5)$ and $(6, 1)$ is

$\sqrt{(-8 - 6)^2 + (-5 - 1)^2} = \sqrt{196 + 36} = \sqrt{232}$.

The distance between $(6, 1)$ and $(-4, 5)$ is

$\sqrt{[6 - (-4)]^2 + (1 - 5)^2} = \sqrt{100 + 16} = \sqrt{116}$.

The distance between $(-4, 5)$ and $(-8, -5)$ is

$\sqrt{[-4 - (-8)]^2 + [5 - (-5)]^2} = \sqrt{16 + 100} = \sqrt{116}$.

Since $(\sqrt{116})^2 + (\sqrt{116})^2 = (\sqrt{232})^2$, the points are vertices of a right triangle.

77. $\left(\dfrac{(2 - \sqrt{3}) + (2 + \sqrt{3})}{2}, \dfrac{5\sqrt{2} + 3\sqrt{2}}{2} \right)$, or $\left(\dfrac{4}{2}, \dfrac{8\sqrt{2}}{2} \right)$, or

$(2, 4\sqrt{2})$

79. a) Use the fact that the center of the circle $(0, k)$ is equidistant from the points $(-575, 0)$ and $(0, 19.5)$.

$\sqrt{(-575 - 0)^2 + (0 - k)^2} = \sqrt{(0 - 0)^2 + (19.5 - k)^2}$

$\sqrt{330,625 + k^2} = \sqrt{380.25 - 39k + k^2}$

$330,625 + k^2 = 380.25 - 39k + k^2$
                     Squaring both sides

$330,244.75 = -39k$

$-8467.8 \approx k$

Then the center of the circle is about $(0, -8467.8)$.

b) To find the radius we find the distance from the center, $(0, -8467.8)$ to any one of the points $(-575, 0)$, $(0, 19.5)$, or $(575, 0)$. We use $(0, 19.5)$.

$r = \sqrt{(0 - 0)^2 + [19.5 - (-8467.8)]^2} \approx$
8487.3 mm

Exercise Set 9.2

1. $\dfrac{x^2}{9} + \dfrac{y^2}{36} = 1$

$\dfrac{x^2}{3^2} + \dfrac{y^2}{6^2} = 1$

The x-intercepts are $(-3, 0)$ and $(3, 0)$, and the y-intercepts are $(0, -6)$ and $(0, 6)$. We plot these points and connect them with an oval-shaped curve.

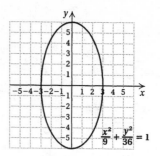

3. $\dfrac{x^2}{1} + \dfrac{y^2}{4} = 1$

$\dfrac{x^2}{1^2} + \dfrac{y^2}{2^2} = 1$

The x-intercepts are $(-1, 0)$ and $(1, 0)$, and the y-intercepts are $(0, -2)$ and $(0, 2)$. We plot these points and connect them with an oval-shaped curve.

5. $4x^2 + 9y^2 = 36$

$\dfrac{x^2}{9} + \dfrac{y^2}{4} = 1$ Dividing by 36

$\dfrac{x^2}{3^2} + \dfrac{y^2}{2^2} = 1$

The x-intercepts are $(-3, 0)$ and $(3, 0)$, and the y-intercepts are $(0, -2)$ and $(0, 2)$. We plot these points and connect them with an oval-shaped curve.

7. $x^2 + 4y^2 = 4$

$\dfrac{x^2}{4} + \dfrac{y^2}{1} = 1$ Dividing by 4

$\dfrac{x^2}{2^2} + \dfrac{y^2}{1^2} = 1$

The x-intercepts are $(-2, 0)$ and $(2, 0)$, and the y-intercepts are $(0, -1)$ and $(0, 1)$. We plot these points and connect them with an oval-shaped curve.

9. $2x^2 + 3y^2 = 6$

$$\frac{x^2}{3} + \frac{y^2}{2} = 1 \quad \text{Multiplying by } \frac{1}{6}$$

$$\frac{x^2}{(\sqrt{3})^2} + \frac{y^2}{(\sqrt{2})^2} = 1$$

The x-intercepts are $(\sqrt{3}, 0)$ and $(-\sqrt{3}, 0)$, and the y-intercepts are $(0, \sqrt{2})$ and $(0, -\sqrt{2})$. We plot these points and connect them with an oval-shaped curve.

11. $12x^2 + 5y^2 - 120 = 0$

$$12x^2 + 5y^2 = 120$$

$$\frac{x^2}{10} + \frac{y^2}{24} = 1 \quad \text{Multiplying by } \frac{1}{120}$$

$$\frac{x^2}{(\sqrt{10})^2} + \frac{y^2}{(\sqrt{24})^2} = 1$$

The x-intercepts are $(\sqrt{10}, 0)$ and $(-\sqrt{10}, 0)$, or about $(3.162, 0)$ and $(-3.162, 0)$. The y-intercepts are $(0, \sqrt{24})$ and $(0, -\sqrt{24})$, or about $(0, 4.899)$ and $(0, -4.899)$. We plot these points and connect them with an oval-shaped curve.

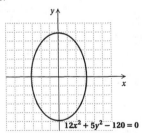

13. $\dfrac{(x-2)^2}{9} + \dfrac{(y-1)^2}{25} = 1$

$$\frac{(x-2)^2}{3^2} + \frac{(y-1)^2}{5^2} = 1$$

The center of the ellipse is $(2, 1)$. Note that $a = 3$ and $b = 5$. We locate the center and then plot the points $(2+3, 1)$ $(2-3, 1)$, $(2, 1+5)$, and $(2, 1-5)$, or $(5, 1)$,

$(-1, 1)$, $(2, 6)$, and $(2, -4)$. Connect these points with an oval-shaped curve.

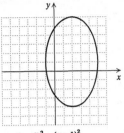

15. $\dfrac{(x+1)^2}{16} + \dfrac{(y+2)^2}{25} = 1$

$$\frac{[x-(-1)]^2}{4^2} + \frac{[y-(-2)]^2}{5^2} = 1$$

The center of the ellipse is $(-1, -2)$. Note that $a = 4$ and $b = 5$. We locate the center and then plot the points $(-1+4, -2)$, $(-1-4, -2)$, $(-1, -2+5)$, and $(-1, -2-5)$, or $(3, -2)$, $(-5, -2)$, $(-1, 3)$, and $(-1, -7)$. Connect these points with an oval-shaped curve.

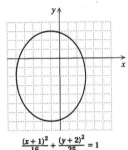

17. $12(x-1)^2 + 3(y+2)^2 = 48$

$$\frac{(x-1)^2}{4} + \frac{(y+2)^2}{16} = 1$$

$$\frac{(x-1)^2}{2^2} + \frac{(y-(-2))^2}{4^2} = 1$$

The center of the ellipse is $(1, -2)$. Note that $a = 2$ and $b = 4$. We locate the center and then plot the points $(1+2, -2)$, $(1-2, -2)$, $(1, -2+4)$, and $(1, -2-4)$, or $(3, -2)$, $(-1, -2)$, $(1, 2)$, and $(1, -6)$. Connect these points with an oval-shaped curve.

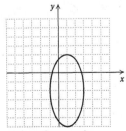

19. $\quad (x+3)^2 + 4(y+1)^2 - 10 = 6$

$\qquad (x+3)^2 + 4(y+1)^2 = 16$

$$\frac{(x+3)^2}{16} + \frac{(y+1)^2}{4} = 1$$

$$\frac{[x-(-3)]^2}{4^2} + \frac{[y-(-1)]^2}{2^2} = 1$$

The center of the ellipse is $(-3, -1)$. Note that $a = 4$ and $b = 2$. We locate the center and then plot the points $(-3+4, -1)$, $(-3-4, -1)$, $(-3, -1+2)$, and $(-3, -1-2)$, or $(1, -1)$, $(-7, -1)$, $(-3, 1)$, and $(-3, -3)$. Connect these points with an oval-shaped curve.

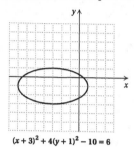

$(x+3)^2 + 4(y+1)^2 - 10 = 6$

21. Discussion and Writing Exercise

23. $\quad 3x^2 - 2x + 7 = 0$

$\qquad a = 3,\ b = -2,\ c = 7$

$$x = \frac{-b \pm \sqrt{b^2 - 4ac}}{2a}$$

$$x = \frac{-(-2) \pm \sqrt{(-2)^2 - 4 \cdot 3 \cdot 7}}{2 \cdot 3}$$

$$x = \frac{2 \pm \sqrt{4 - 84}}{6} = \frac{2 \pm \sqrt{-80}}{6}$$

$$x = \frac{2 \pm 4i\sqrt{5}}{6} = \frac{1 \pm 2i\sqrt{5}}{3}$$

The solutions are $\dfrac{1 + 2i\sqrt{5}}{3}$ and $\dfrac{1 - 2i\sqrt{5}}{3}$.

25. $\quad x^2 + 2x - 20 = 0$

$\qquad a = 1,\ b = 2,\ c = -20$

$$x = \frac{-b \pm \sqrt{b^2 - 4ac}}{2a}$$

$$x = \frac{-2 \pm \sqrt{2^2 - 4 \cdot 1 \cdot (-20)}}{2 \cdot 1}$$

$$x = \frac{-2 \pm \sqrt{4 + 80}}{2} = \frac{-2 \pm \sqrt{84}}{2}$$

$$x = \frac{-2 \pm 2\sqrt{21}}{2} = -1 \pm \sqrt{21}$$

The solutions are $-1 + \sqrt{21}$ and $-1 - \sqrt{21}$.

27. $\quad x^2 + x + 2 = 0$

$\qquad a = 1,\ b = 1,\ c = 2$

$$x = \frac{-b \pm \sqrt{b^2 - 4ac}}{2a}$$

$$x = \frac{-1 \pm \sqrt{1^2 - 4 \cdot 1 \cdot 2}}{2 \cdot 1}$$

$$x = \frac{-1 \pm \sqrt{1 - 8}}{2} = \frac{-1 \pm \sqrt{-7}}{2}$$

$$x = \frac{-1 \pm i\sqrt{7}}{2}$$

The solutions are $\dfrac{-1 + i\sqrt{7}}{2}$ and $\dfrac{-1 - i\sqrt{7}}{2}$.

29. $\quad x^2 + 2x - 17 = 0$

$\qquad a = 1,\ b = 2,\ c = -17$

$$x = \frac{-b \pm \sqrt{b^2 - 4ac}}{2a}$$

$$x = \frac{-2 \pm \sqrt{2^2 - 4 \cdot 1 \cdot (-17)}}{2 \cdot 1}$$

$$x = \frac{-2 \pm \sqrt{72}}{2} = \frac{-2 \pm 6\sqrt{2}}{2}$$

$$x = -1 \pm 3\sqrt{2}$$

The solutions are $-1 + 3\sqrt{2} \approx 3.2$ and $-1 - 3\sqrt{2} \approx -5.2$.

31. $\quad 3x^2 - 12x + 7 = 10 - x^2 + 5x$

$\qquad 4x^2 - 17x - 3 = 0$

$\qquad a = 4,\ b = -17,\ c = -3$

$$x = \frac{-b \pm \sqrt{b^2 - 4ac}}{2a}$$

$$x = \frac{-(-17) \pm \sqrt{(-17)^2 - 4 \cdot 4 \cdot (-3)}}{2 \cdot 4}$$

$$x = \frac{17 \pm \sqrt{337}}{8}$$

The solutions are $\dfrac{17 + \sqrt{337}}{8} \approx 4.4$ and $\dfrac{17 - \sqrt{337}}{8} \approx -0.2$.

33. Plot the given points.

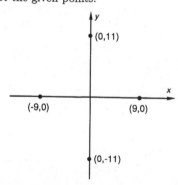

From the location of these points, we see that the ellipse that contains them is centered at the origin with $a = 9$ and $b = 11$. We write the equation of the ellipse:

$$\frac{x^2}{9^2} + \frac{y^2}{11^2} = 1$$

$$\frac{x^2}{81} + \frac{y^2}{121} = 1$$

35. Plot the given points.

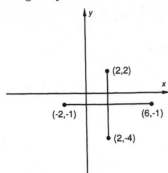

The midpoint of the segment from $(-2, -1)$ to $(6, -1)$ is $\left(\dfrac{-2+6}{2}, \dfrac{-1-1}{2}\right)$, or $(2, -1)$. The midpoint of the segment from $(2, -4)$ to $(2, 2)$ is $\left(\dfrac{2+2}{2}, \dfrac{-4+2}{2}\right)$, or $(2, -1)$. Thus, we can conclude that $(2, -1)$ is the center of the ellipse. The distance from $(-2, -1)$ to $(2, -1)$ is $\sqrt{[2-(-2)]^2 + [-1-(-1)]^2} = \sqrt{16} = 4$, so $a = 4$. The distance from $(2, 2)$ to $(2, -1)$ is $\sqrt{(2-2)^2 + (-1-2)^2} = \sqrt{9} = 3$, so $b = 3$. We write the equation of the ellipse.

$$\frac{(x-2)^2}{4^2} + \frac{(y-(-1))^2}{3^2} = 1$$

$$\frac{(x-2)^2}{16} + \frac{(y+1)^2}{9} = 1$$

37.
$$x^2 - 4x + 4y^2 + 8y - 8 = 0$$
$$x^2 - 4x + 4y^2 + 8y = 8$$
$$x^2 - 4x + 4(y^2 + 2y) = 8$$
$$(x^2 - 4x + 4 - 4) + 4(y^2 + 2y + 1 - 1) = 8$$
$$(x^2 - 4x + 4) + 4(y^2 + 2y + 1) = 8 + 4 + 4 \cdot 1$$
$$(x-2)^2 + 4(y+1)^2 = 16$$
$$\frac{(x-2)^2}{16} + \frac{(y+1)^2}{4} = 1$$
$$\frac{(x-2)^2}{4^2} + \frac{(y-(-1))^2}{2^2} = 1$$

39. Left to the student

Exercise Set 9.3

1. $\dfrac{y^2}{9} - \dfrac{x^2}{9} = 1$

$\dfrac{y^2}{3^2} - \dfrac{x^2}{3^2} = 1$

$a = 3$ and $b = 3$, so the asymptotes are $y = \dfrac{3}{3}x$ and $y = -\dfrac{3}{3}x$, or $y = x$ and $y = -x$. We sketch them.

Replacing x with 0 and solving for y, we get $y = \pm 3$, so the intercepts are $(0, 3)$ and $(0, -3)$.

We plot the intercepts and draw smooth curves through them that approach the asymptotes.

3. $\dfrac{x^2}{4} - \dfrac{y^2}{25} = 1$

$\dfrac{x^2}{2^2} - \dfrac{y^2}{5^2} = 1$

$a = 2$ and $b = 5$, so the asymptotes are $y = \dfrac{5}{2}x$ and $y = -\dfrac{5}{2}x$. We sketch them.

Replacing y with 0 and solving for x, we get $x = \pm 2$, so the intercepts are $(2, 0)$ and $(-2, 0)$.

We plot the intercepts and draw smooth curves through them that approach the asymptotes.

5. $\dfrac{y^2}{36} - \dfrac{x^2}{9} = 1$

$\dfrac{y^2}{6^2} - \dfrac{x^2}{3^2} = 1$

$a = 3$ and $b = 6$, so the asymptotes are $y = \dfrac{6}{3}x$ and $y = -\dfrac{6}{3}x$, or $y = 2x$ and $y = -2x$. We sketch them.

Replacing x with 0 and solving for y, we get $y = \pm 6$, so the intercepts are $(0, 6)$ and $(0, -6)$.

We plot the intercepts and draw smooth curves through them that approach the asymptotes.

7. $y^2 - x^2 = 25$

$$\frac{y^2}{25} - \frac{x^2}{25} = 1$$

$$\frac{y^2}{5^2} - \frac{x^2}{5^2} = 1$$

$a = 5$ and $b = 5$, so the asymptotes are $y = \frac{5}{5}x$ and $y = -\frac{5}{5}x$, or $y = x$ and $y = -x$. We sketch them.

Replacing x with 0 and solving for y, we get $y = \pm 5$, so the intercepts are $(0, 5)$ and $(0, -5)$.

We plot the intercepts and draw smooth curves through them that approach the asymptotes.

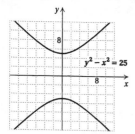

9. $x^2 = 1 + y^2$

$$x^2 - y^2 = 1$$

$$\frac{x^2}{1^2} - \frac{y^2}{1^2} = 1$$

$a = 1$ and $b = 1$, so the asymptotes are $y = \frac{1}{1}x$ and $y = -\frac{1}{1}x$, or $y = x$ and $y = -x$. We sketch them.

Replacing y with 0 and solving for x, we get $x = \pm 1$, so the intercepts are $(1, 0)$ and $(-1, 0)$.

We plot the intercepts and draw smooth curves through them that approach the asymptotes.

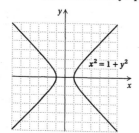

11. $25x^2 - 16y^2 = 400$

$$\frac{x^2}{16} - \frac{y^2}{25} = 1 \quad \text{Multiplying by } \frac{1}{400}$$

$$\frac{x^2}{4^2} - \frac{y^2}{5^2} = 1$$

$a = 4$ and $b = 5$, so the asymptotes are $y = \frac{5}{4}x$ and $y = -\frac{5}{4}x$. We sketch them.

Replacing y with 0 and solving for x, we get $x = \pm 4$, so the intercepts are $(4, 0)$ and $(-4, 0)$.

We plot the intercepts and draw smooth curves through them that approach the asymptotes.

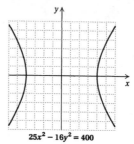

13. $xy = -4$

$$y = -\frac{4}{x} \quad \text{Solving for } y$$

We find some solutions, keeping the results in a table.

x	y
$\frac{1}{2}$	-8
1	-4
2	-2
4	-1
8	$-\frac{1}{2}$
$-\frac{1}{2}$	8
-1	4
-2	2
-8	$\frac{1}{2}$

Note that we cannot use 0 for x. The x-axis and the y-axis are the asymptotes.

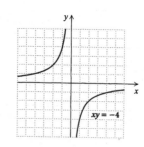

15. $xy = 3$

$y = \dfrac{3}{x}$ Solving for y

We find some solutions, keeping the results in a table.

x	y
$\dfrac{1}{3}$	9
$\dfrac{1}{2}$	6
1	3
3	1
6	$\dfrac{1}{2}$
9	$\dfrac{1}{3}$
$-\dfrac{1}{3}$	-9
$-\dfrac{1}{2}$	-6
-1	-3
-3	-1
-6	$-\dfrac{1}{2}$
-9	$-\dfrac{1}{3}$

Note that we cannot use 0 for x. The x-axis and the y-axis are the asymptotes.

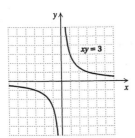

17. $xy = -2$

$y = -\dfrac{2}{x}$ Solving for y

x	y
$\dfrac{1}{2}$	-4
1	-2
2	-1
4	$-\dfrac{1}{2}$
$-\dfrac{1}{2}$	4
-1	2
-2	1
-4	$\dfrac{1}{2}$

Note that we cannot use 0 for x. The x-axis and the y-axis are the asymptotes.

19. $xy = \dfrac{1}{2}$

$y = \dfrac{1}{2x}$ Solving for y

x	y
$\dfrac{1}{8}$	4
$\dfrac{1}{4}$	2
$\dfrac{1}{2}$	1
1	$\dfrac{1}{2}$
2	$\dfrac{1}{4}$
$-\dfrac{1}{8}$	-4
$-\dfrac{1}{4}$	-2
$-\dfrac{1}{2}$	1
1	$\dfrac{1}{2}$
2	$\dfrac{1}{4}$

21. Discussion and Writing Exercise

23. $5^2 = 25 \Rightarrow 2 = \log_5 25$

25. $a^{-t} = b \Rightarrow -t = \log_a b$

27. $10^{2.3} = 199.53 \Rightarrow 2.3 = \log 199.53$

29. $a^{23.4} = 200 \Rightarrow 23.4 = \log_a 200$

31. $\ln 24 = 3.1781 \Rightarrow e^{3.1781} = 24$

33. $\log_a N = t \Rightarrow a^t = N$

35. $\log M = b \Rightarrow 10^b = M$

37. $\log 456 = 2.659 \Rightarrow 10^{2.659} = 456$

39. Left to the student

41.
$$x^2 + y^2 - 10x + 8y - 40 = 0$$
$$x^2 - 10x + y^2 + 8y = 40$$
$$(x^2 - 10x + 25) + (y^2 + 8y + 16) = 40 + 25 + 16$$
$$(x - 5)^2 + (y + 4)^2 = 81$$

The graph is a circle.

43.
$$1 - 3y = 2y^2 - x$$
$$x = 2y^2 + 3y - 1$$

The graph is a parabola.

45.
$$4x^2 + 25y^2 - 8x - 100y + 4 = 0$$
$$4x^2 - 8x + 25y^2 - 100y = -4$$
$$4(x^2 - 2x + 1) + 25(y^2 - 4y + 4) = -4 + 4 + 100$$
$$4(x-1)^2 + 25(y-2)^2 = 100$$
$$\frac{(x-1)^2}{25} + \frac{(y-2)^2}{4} = 1$$

The graph is an ellipse.

47. $x^2 + y^2 = 8$

The graph is a circle.

49. $x - \dfrac{3}{y} = 0$

$xy - 3 = 0$

$xy = 3$

The graph is a hyperbola.

51. $3x^2 + 5y^2 + x^2 = y^2 + 49$

$4x^2 + 4y^2 = 49$

$x^2 + y^2 = \dfrac{49}{4}$

The graph is a circle.

Exercise Set 9.4

1. $x^2 + y^2 = 100,$ (1)

$y - x = 2$ (2)

First solve Equation (2) for y.

$y = x + 2$ (3)

Then substitute $x + 2$ for y in Equation (1) and solve for x.
$$x^2 + y^2 = 100$$
$$x^2 + (x+2)^2 = 100$$
$$x^2 + x^2 + 4x + 4 = 100$$
$$2x^2 + 4x - 96 = 0$$
$$x^2 + 2x - 48 = 0 \qquad \text{Multiplying by } \tfrac{1}{2}$$
$$(x+8)(x-6) = 0$$

$x + 8 = 0$ or $x - 6 = 0$ Principle of zero products

$x = -8$ or $x = 6$

Now substitute these numbers into Equation (3) and solve for y.

$y = -8 + 2 = -6$

$y = 6 + 2 = 8$

The pairs $(-8, -6)$ and $(6, 8)$ check, so they are the solutions.

3. $9x^2 + 4y^2 = 36,$ (1)

$3x + 2y = 6$ (2)

First solve Equation (2) for x.

$3x = 6 - 2y$

$x = 2 - \dfrac{2}{3}y$ (3)

Then substitute $2 - \dfrac{2}{3}y$ for x in Equation (1) and solve for y.
$$9x^2 + 4y^2 = 36$$
$$9\left(2 - \frac{2}{3}y\right)^2 + 4y^2 = 36$$
$$9\left(4 - \frac{8}{3}y + \frac{4}{9}y^2\right) + 4y^2 = 36$$
$$36 - 24y + 4y^2 + 4y^2 = 36$$
$$8y^2 - 24y = 0$$
$$y^2 - 3y = 0$$
$$y(y-3) = 0$$

$y = 0$ or $y - 3 = 0$ Principle of zero products

$y = 0$ or $y = 3$

Now substitute these numbers into Equation (3) and solve for x.

$x = 2 - \dfrac{2}{3} \cdot 0 = 2$

$x = 2 - \dfrac{2}{3} \cdot 3 = 2 - 2 = 0$

The pairs $(2, 0)$ and $(0, 3)$ check, so they are the solutions.

5. $y^2 = x + 3,$ (1)

$2y = x + 4$ (2)

First solve Equation (2) for x.

$2y - 4 = x$ (3)

Then substitute $y - 4$ for x in Equation (1) and solve for y.
$$y^2 = x + 3$$
$$y^2 = (2y - 4) + 3$$
$$y^2 = 2y - 1$$
$$y^2 - 2y + 1 = 0$$
$$(y-1)(y-1) = 0$$

$y - 1 = 0$ or $y - 1 = 0$

$y = 1$ or $y = 1$

Now substitute 1 for y in Equation (3) and solve for x.

$2 \cdot 1 - 4 = x$

$-2 = x$

The pair $(-2, 1)$ checks. It is the solution.

7. $x^2 - xy + 3y^2 = 27,$ (1)

$x - y = 2$ (2)

First solve Equation (2) for y.

$x - 2 = y$ (3)

Then substitute $x - 2$ for y in Equation (1) and solve for x.

$$x^2 - xy + 3y^2 = 27$$
$$x^2 - x(x-2) + 3(x-2)^2 = 27$$
$$x^2 - x^2 + 2x + 3x^2 - 12x + 12 = 27$$
$$3x^2 - 10x - 15 = 0$$
$$x = \frac{-(-10) \pm \sqrt{(-10)^2 - 4(3)(-15)}}{2 \cdot 3}$$
$$x = \frac{10 \pm \sqrt{100 + 180}}{6} = \frac{10 \pm \sqrt{280}}{6}$$
$$x = \frac{10 \pm 2\sqrt{70}}{6} = \frac{5 \pm \sqrt{70}}{3}$$

Now substitute these numbers in Equation (3) and solve for y.

$$y = \frac{5 + \sqrt{70}}{3} - 2 = \frac{-1 + \sqrt{70}}{3}$$
$$y = \frac{5 - \sqrt{70}}{3} - 2 = \frac{-1 - \sqrt{70}}{3}$$

The pairs $\left(\dfrac{5 + \sqrt{70}}{3}, \dfrac{-1 + \sqrt{70}}{3}\right)$ and

$\left(\dfrac{5 - \sqrt{70}}{3}, \dfrac{-1 - \sqrt{70}}{3}\right)$ check, so they are the solutions.

9. $x^2 - xy + 3y^2 = 5,$ (1)

   $x - y = 2$ (2)

First solve Equation (2) for y.

   $x - 2 = y$ (3)

Then substitute $x - 2$ for y in Equation (1) and solve for x.

$$x^2 - xy + 3y^2 = 5$$
$$x^2 - x(x-2) + 3(x-2)^2 = 5$$
$$x^2 - x^2 + 2x + 3x^2 - 12x + 12 = 5$$
$$3x^2 - 10x + 7 = 0$$
$$(3x - 7)(x - 1) = 0$$
$$3x - 7 = 0 \quad or \quad x - 1 = 0$$
$$x = \frac{7}{3} \quad or \quad x = 1$$

Now substitute these numbers in Equation (3) and solve for y.

$$y = \frac{7}{3} - 2 = \frac{1}{3}$$
$$y = 1 - 2 = -1$$

The pairs $\left(\dfrac{7}{3}, \dfrac{1}{3}\right)$ and $(1, -1)$ check, so they are the solutions.

11. $a + b = -6,$ (1)

    $ab = -7$ (2)

First solve Equation (1) for a.

    $a = -b - 6$ (3)

Then substitute $-b - 6$ for a in Equation (2) and solve for b.

$$(-b - 6)b = -7$$
$$-b^2 - 6b = -7$$
$$0 = b^2 + 6b - 7$$
$$0 = (b + 7)(b - 1)$$
$$b + 7 = 0 \quad or \quad b - 1 = 0$$
$$b = -7 \quad or \quad b = 1$$

Now substitute these numbers in Equation (3) and solve for a.

$$a = -(-7) - 6 = 1$$
$$a = -1 - 6 = -7$$

The pairs $(-7, 1)$ and $(1, -7)$ check, so they are the solutions.

13. $2a + b = 1,$ (1)

    $b = 4 - a^2$ (2)

Equation (2) is already solved for b. Substitute $4 - a^2$ for b in Equation (1) and solve for a.

$$2a + 4 - a^2 = 1$$
$$0 = a^2 - 2a - 3$$
$$0 = (a - 3)(a + 1)$$
$$a - 3 = 0 \quad or \quad a + 1 = 0$$
$$a = 3 \quad or \quad a = -1$$

Substitute these numbers in Equation (2) and solve for b.

$$b = 4 - 3^2 = -5$$
$$b = 4 - (-1)^2 = 3$$

The pairs $(3, -5)$ and $(-1, 3)$ check.

15. $x^2 + y^2 = 5,$ (1)

    $x - y = 8$ (2)

First solve Equation (2) for x.

    $x = y + 8$ (3)

Then substitute $y + 8$ for x in Equation (1) and solve for y.

$$(y + 8)^2 + y^2 = 5$$
$$y^2 + 16y + 64 + y^2 = 5$$
$$2y^2 + 16y + 59 = 0$$
$$y = \frac{-16 \pm \sqrt{(16)^2 - 4(2)(59)}}{2 \cdot 2}$$
$$y = \frac{-16 \pm \sqrt{-216}}{4} = \frac{-16 \pm 6i\sqrt{6}}{4}$$
$$y = \frac{-8 \pm 3i\sqrt{6}}{2}, \text{ or } -4 \pm \frac{3}{2}i\sqrt{6}$$

Now substitute these numbers in Equation (3) and solve for x.

$$x = -4 + \frac{3}{2}i\sqrt{6} + 8 = 4 + \frac{3}{2}i\sqrt{6}, \text{ or } \frac{8 + 3i\sqrt{6}}{2}$$
$$x = -4 - \frac{3}{2}i\sqrt{6} + 8 = 4 - \frac{3}{2}i\sqrt{6}, \text{ or } \frac{8 - 3i\sqrt{6}}{2}$$

The pairs $\left(4 + \dfrac{3}{2}i\sqrt{6}, -4 + \dfrac{3}{2}i\sqrt{6}\right)$ and

$\left(4 - \frac{3}{2}i\sqrt{6}, -4 - \frac{3}{2}i\sqrt{6}\right)$, or $\left(\frac{8 + 3i\sqrt{6}}{2}, \frac{-8 + 3i\sqrt{6}}{2}\right)$ and $\left(\frac{8 - 3i\sqrt{6}}{2}, \frac{-8 - 3i\sqrt{6}}{2}\right)$ check.

17. $x^2 + y^2 = 25,$ (1)

     $y^2 = x + 5$ (2)

We substitute $x + 5$ for y^2 in Equation (1) and solve for x.

$$x^2 + y^2 = 25$$
$$x^2 + (x + 5) = 25$$
$$x^2 + x - 20 = 0$$
$$(x + 5)(x - 4) = 0$$
$$x + 5 = 0 \quad or \quad x - 4 = 0$$
$$x = -5 \quad or \qquad x = 4$$

We substitute these numbers for x in either Equation (1) or Equation (2) and solve for y. Here we use Equation (2).

$y^2 = -5 + 5 = 0$ and $y = 0$.

$y^2 = 4 + 5 = 9$ and $y = \pm 3$.

The pairs $(-5, 0)$, $(4, 3)$ and $(4, -3)$ check.

19. $x^2 + y^2 = 9,$ (1)

     $x^2 - y^2 = 9$ (2)

Here we use the elimination method.

$$
\begin{array}{rll}
x^2 + y^2 = & 9 & (1) \\
\underline{x^2 - y^2 = 9} & & (2) \\
2x^2 = & 18 & \text{Adding} \\
x^2 = & 9 & \\
x = & \pm 3 &
\end{array}
$$

If $x = 3$, $x^2 = 9$, and if $x = -3$, $x^2 = 9$, so substituting 3 or -3 in Equation (1) gives us

$$x^2 + y^2 = 9$$
$$9 + y^2 = 9$$
$$y^2 = 0$$
$$y = 0.$$

The pairs $(3, 0)$ and $(-3, 0)$ check.

21. $x^2 + y^2 = 20,$ (1)

     $xy = 8$ (2)

First we solve Equation (2) for y.

$$y = \frac{8}{x}$$

Then substitute $\frac{8}{x}$ for y in Equation (1) and solve for x.

$$x^2 + \left(\frac{8}{x}\right)^2 = 20$$
$$x^2 + \frac{64}{x^2} = 20$$
$$x^4 + 64 = 20x^2 \quad \text{Multiplying by } x^2$$
$$x^4 - 20x^2 + 64 = 0$$
$$u^2 - 20u + 64 = 0 \quad \text{Letting } u = x^2$$
$$(u - 4)(u - 16) = 0$$

$$u - 4 = 0 \quad or \quad u - 16 = 0$$
$$u = 4 \quad or \qquad u = 16$$

We now substitute x^2 for u and solve for x.

$$x^2 = 4 \quad or \quad x^2 = 16$$
$$x = \pm 2 \quad or \quad x = \pm 4$$

Since $y = \frac{8}{x}$, if $x = 2$, $y = 4$; if $x = -2$, $y = -4$; if $x = 4$, $y = 2$; if $x = -4$, $y = -2$. The pairs $(2, 4)$, $(-2, -4)$, $(4, 2)$, and $(-4, -2)$ check. They are the solutions.

23. $x^2 + y^2 = 13,$ (1)

     $xy = 6$ (2)

First we solve Equation (2) for y.

$$y = \frac{6}{x}$$

Then substitute $\frac{6}{x}$ for y in Equation (1) and solve for x.

$$x^2 + \left(\frac{6}{x}\right)^2 = 13$$
$$x^2 + \frac{36}{x^2} = 13$$
$$x^4 + 36 = 13x^2 \quad \text{Multiplying by } x^2$$
$$x^4 - 13x^2 + 36 = 0$$
$$u^2 - 13u + 36 = 0 \qquad \text{Letting } u = x^2$$
$$(u - 9)(u - 4) = 0$$
$$u - 9 = 0 \quad or \quad u - 4 = 0$$
$$u = 9 \quad or \qquad u = 4$$

We now substitute x^2 for u and solve for x.

$$x^2 = 9 \quad or \quad x^2 = 4$$
$$x = \pm 3 \quad or \quad x = \pm 2$$

Since $y = \frac{6}{x}$, if $x = 3$, $y = 2$; if $x = -3$, $y = -2$; if $x = 2$, $y = 3$; if $x = -2$, $y = -3$. The pairs $(3, 2)$, $(-3, -2)$, $(2, 3)$, and $(-2, -3)$ check. They are the solutions.

25. $2xy + 3y^2 = 7,$ (1)

     $3xy - 2y^2 = 4$ (2)

$$
\begin{array}{rll}
6xy + 9y^2 = & 21 & \text{Multiplying (1) by 3} \\
\underline{-6xy + 4y^2 = -8} & & \text{Multiplying (2) by } -2 \\
13y^2 = & 13 & \\
y^2 = & 1 & \\
y = & \pm 1 &
\end{array}
$$

Substitute for y in Equation (1) and solve for x.

When $y = 1$: $2 \cdot x \cdot 1 + 3 \cdot 1^2 = 7$

$$2x = 4$$
$$x = 2$$

When $y = -1$: $2 \cdot x \cdot (-1) + 3 \cdot (-1)^2 = 7$

$$-2x = 4$$
$$x = -2$$

The pairs $(2, 1)$ and $(-2, -1)$ check. They are the solutions.

27. $4a^2 - 25b^2 = 0,$ (1)

     $2a^2 - 10b^2 = 3b + 4$ (2)

$4a^2 - 25b^2 = 0$

$\underline{-4a^2 + 20b^2 = -6b - 8}$ Multiplying (2) by -2

$\quad\quad - 5b^2 = -6b - 8$

$\quad\quad 0 = 5b^2 - 6b - 8$

$\quad\quad 0 = (5b + 4)(b - 2)$

$5b + 4 = 0 \quad$ or $\quad b - 2 = 0$

$b = -\dfrac{4}{5} \quad$ or $\quad b = 2$

Substitute for b in Equation (1) and solve for a.

When $b = -\dfrac{4}{5}$: $4a^2 - 25\left(-\dfrac{4}{5}\right)^2 = 0$

$\quad\quad\quad\quad\quad\quad 4a^2 = 16$

$\quad\quad\quad\quad\quad\quad a^2 = 4$

$\quad\quad\quad\quad\quad\quad a = \pm 2$

When $b = 2$: $4a^2 - 25(2)^2 = 0$

$\quad\quad\quad\quad\quad 4a^2 = 100$

$\quad\quad\quad\quad\quad a^2 = 25$

$\quad\quad\quad\quad\quad a = \pm 5$

The pairs $\left(2, -\dfrac{4}{5}\right)$, $\left(-2, -\dfrac{4}{5}\right)$, $(5, 2)$ and $(-5, 2)$ check. They are the solutions.

29. $ab - b^2 = -4,$ (1)

     $ab - 2b^2 = -6$ (2)

$ab - b^2 = \quad -4$

$\underline{-ab + 2b^2 = \quad\quad 6}$ Multiplying (2) by -1

$\quad\quad b^2 = \quad\quad 2$

$\quad\quad b = \pm\sqrt{2}$

Substitute for b in Equation (1) and solve for a.

When $b = \sqrt{2}$: $a(\sqrt{2}) - (\sqrt{2})^2 = -4$

$\quad\quad\quad\quad\quad a\sqrt{2} = -2$

$\quad\quad\quad\quad\quad a = -\dfrac{2}{\sqrt{2}} = -\sqrt{2}$

When $b = -\sqrt{2}$: $a(-\sqrt{2}) - (-\sqrt{2})^2 = -4$

$\quad\quad\quad\quad\quad -a\sqrt{2} = -2$

$\quad\quad\quad\quad\quad a = \dfrac{2}{\sqrt{2}} = \sqrt{2}$

The pairs $(-\sqrt{2}, \sqrt{2})$ and $(\sqrt{2}, -\sqrt{2})$ check. They are the solutions.

31. $x^2 + y^2 = 25,$ (1)

     $9x^2 + 4y^2 = 36$ (2)

$-4x^2 - 4y^2 = -100 \quad$ Multiplying (1) by -4

$\underline{\ 9x^2 + 4y^2 = \quad 36}$

$\ 5x^2 \quad\quad = -64$

$x^2 = -\dfrac{64}{5}$

$x = \pm\sqrt{-\dfrac{64}{5}} = \pm\dfrac{8i}{\sqrt{5}}$

$x = \pm\dfrac{8i\sqrt{5}}{5} \quad$ Rationalizing the denominator

Substituting $\dfrac{8i\sqrt{5}}{5}$ or $-\dfrac{8i\sqrt{5}}{5}$ for x in Equation (1) and solving for y gives us

$-\dfrac{64}{5} + y^2 = 25$

$y^2 = \dfrac{189}{5}$

$y = \pm\sqrt{\dfrac{189}{5}} = \pm 3\sqrt{\dfrac{21}{5}}$

$y = \pm\dfrac{3\sqrt{105}}{5}.\quad$ Rationalizing the denominator

The pairs $\left(\dfrac{8i\sqrt{5}}{5}, \dfrac{3\sqrt{105}}{5}\right)$, $\left(-\dfrac{8i\sqrt{5}}{5}, \dfrac{3\sqrt{105}}{5}\right)$, $\left(\dfrac{8i\sqrt{5}}{5}, -\dfrac{3\sqrt{105}}{5}\right)$, and $\left(-\dfrac{8i\sqrt{5}}{5}, -\dfrac{3\sqrt{105}}{5}\right)$, check. They are the solutions.

33. *Familiarize*. Using the labels on the drawing in the text, we let $l =$ the length of the cargo area and $w =$ the width.

Translate. The area is 60 ft^2, so we have $lw = 60$. The length of a diagonal is 13 ft, so we use the Pythagorean equation to write another equation: $l^2 + w^2 = 13^2$, or $l^2 + w^2 = 169$.

Solve. We solve the system of equations.

$\quad lw = 60,$ (1)

$\quad l^2 + w^2 = 169$ (2)

First we solve Equation (1) for l.

$\quad l = \dfrac{60}{w}$

Then substitute $\dfrac{60}{w}$ for l in Equation (2) and solve for w.

$\quad l^2 + w^2 = 169$

$\quad \left(\dfrac{60}{w}\right)^2 + w^2 = 169$

$\quad \dfrac{3600}{w^2} + w^2 = 169$

$\quad 3600 + w^4 = 169w^2 \quad$ Multiplying by w^2

$w^4 - 169w^2 + 3600 = 0$

$u^2 - 169u + 3600 = 0 \quad\quad$ Letting $u = w^2$

$(u - 144)(u - 25) = 0$

$u = 144 \ or \ u = 25$

Now substitute w^2 for u and solve for x.

$$w^2 = 144 \quad or \quad w^2 = 25$$

$$w = \pm 12 \quad or \quad w = \pm 5$$

Check. The dimensions cannot be negative so -12 and -5 cannot be solutions. If $w = 12$, then $l = \dfrac{60}{12}$, or 5. If $w = 5$, then $l = \dfrac{60}{5}$, or 12. Since we usually consider length to be longer than width, we check $l = 12$ and $w = 5$. The area is $12 \cdot 5$, or 60 ft^2, and the length of a diagonal is $12^2 + 5^2 = 169 = 13^2$. The answer checks.

State. The dimensions are 12 ft by 5 ft.

35. Familiarize. We first make a drawing. We let $l =$ the length and $w =$ the width of the rectangle.

Translate.

Area: $lw = 14$

Perimeter: $2l + 2w = 18$, or $l + w = 9$

Solve. We solve the system.

Solve the second equation for l: $\quad l = 9 - w$

Substitute $9 - w$ for l in the first equation and solve for w.

$$(9 - w)w = 14$$

$$9w - w^2 = 14$$

$$0 = w^2 - 9w + 14$$

$$0 = (w - 7)(w - 2)$$

$$w - 7 = 0 \quad or \quad w - 2 = 0$$

$$w = 7 \quad or \quad w = 2$$

If $w = 7$, then $l = 9 - 7$, or 2. If $w = 2$, then $l = 9 - 2$, or 7. Since length is usually considered to be longer than the width, we have the solution $l = 7$ and $w = 2$, or $(7, 2)$.

Check. If $l = 7$ and $w = 2$, the area is $7 \cdot 2$, or 14. The perimeter is $2 \cdot 7 + 2 \cdot 2$, or 18. The numbers check.

State. The length is 7 in., and the width is 2 in.

37. Familiarize. Let $l =$ the length and $w =$ the width of the rectangle. Then the length of a diagonal is $\sqrt{l^2 + w^2}$.

Translate.

Solve. We solve the system of equations.

$$\sqrt{l^2 + w^2} = 1 + l, \qquad (1)$$

$$\sqrt{l^2 + w^2} = 3 + 2w \qquad (2)$$

We substitute $3 + 2w$ for $\sqrt{l^2 + w^2}$ in Equation (1) and solve for l.

$$3 + 2w = 1 + l$$

$$2 + 2w = l \qquad (3)$$

Now we substitute $2 + 2w$ for l in Equation (2).

$$\sqrt{(2 + 2w)^2 + w^2} = 3 + 2w$$

$$\sqrt{4 + 8w + 4w^2 + w^2} = 3 + 2w$$

$$\sqrt{5w^2 + 8w + 4} = 3 + 2w$$

$$(\sqrt{5w^2 + 8w + 4})^2 = (3 + 2w)^2$$

$$5w^2 + 8w + 4 = 9 + 12w + 4w^2$$

$$w^2 - 4w - 5 = 0$$

$$(w - 5)(w + 1) = 0$$

$$w - 5 = 0 \quad or \quad w + 1 = 0$$

$$w = 5 \quad or \qquad w = -1$$

Since the width cannot be negative, we consider only 5. We substitute 5 for w in Equation (3) and solve for l.

$$l = 2 + 2 \cdot 5 = 12$$

Check. The length of a diagonal of a 12 ft by 5 ft rectangle is $\sqrt{12^2 + 5^2} = \sqrt{169} = 13$. This is 1 ft longer than the length, 12, and 3 ft longer than twice the width, $2 \cdot 5$, or 10. The numbers check.

State. The length is 12 ft, and the width is 5 ft.

39. Familiarize. Let $l =$ the length and $h =$ the height, in cm.

Translate. Since the ratio of the length to the height is 4 to 3, we have one equation:

$$\frac{l}{h} = \frac{4}{3}$$

The Pythagorean equation gives us a second equation:

$$l^2 + h^2 = 31^2, \text{ or } l^2 + h^2 = 961$$

We have a system of equations.

$$\frac{l}{h} = \frac{4}{3}, \qquad (1)$$

$$l^2 + h^2 = 961 \quad (2)$$

Solve. We solve the system of equations. First we solve Eq. (1) for l:

$$\frac{l}{h} = \frac{4}{3}$$

$$l = \frac{4}{3}h \quad (3)$$

Now substitute $\dfrac{4}{3}h$ for w in Eq. (2) and solve for h.

$$l^2 + h^2 = 961$$

$$\left(\frac{4}{3}h\right)^2 + h^2 = 961$$

$$\frac{16}{9}h^2 + h^2 = 961$$

$$\frac{25}{9}h^2 = 961$$

$$h^2 = \frac{961 \cdot 9}{25} = \frac{8649}{25}$$

$$h = \frac{93}{5} \quad or \quad h = -\frac{93}{5}$$

Since the height cannot be negative, we consider only $\frac{93}{5}$.

Substitute $\frac{93}{5}$ for h in Eq. (3) and find l.

$$l = \frac{4}{3} \cdot \frac{93}{5} = \frac{124}{5}$$

Check. The ratio of $124/5$ to $93/5$ is $\frac{124/5}{93/5} =$

$\frac{124}{93} = \frac{4}{3}$. Also $\left(\frac{124}{5}\right)^2 + \left(\frac{93}{5}\right)^2 = 961 = 31^2$. The answer checks.

State. The length is $\frac{124}{5}$ cm, or 24.8 cm, and the height is $\frac{93}{5}$ cm, or 18.6 cm.

41. Familiarize. We let $x =$ the length of a side of one peanut bed and $y =$ the length of a side of the other peanut bed. Make a drawing.

Translate.

The sum of the areas is 832 ft^2.

$$x^2 + y^2 = 832$$

The difference of the areas is 320 ft^2.

$$x^2 - y^2 = 320$$

Solve. We solve the system of equations.

$$
\begin{array}{rl}
x^2 + y^2 = & 832 \\
x^2 - y^2 = & 320 \\
\hline
2x^2 \quad\;\; = & 1152 \quad \text{Adding} \\
x^2 = & 576 \\
x = & \pm 24
\end{array}
$$

Since length cannot be negative, we consider only $x = 24$. Substitute 24 for x in the first equation and solve for y.

$$24^2 + y^2 = 832$$
$$576 + y^2 = 832$$
$$y^2 = 256$$
$$y = \pm 16$$

Again, we consider only the positive value, 16. The possible solution is $(24, 16)$.

Check. The areas of the beds are 24^2, or 576, and 16^2, or 256. The sum of the areas is $576 + 256$, or 832. The difference of the areas is $576 - 256$, or 320. The values check.

State. The lengths of the beds are 24 ft and 16 ft.

43. Familiarize. We first make a drawing. We let $l =$ the length and $w =$ the width.

Translate.

Area: $\sqrt{2} = lw$ (1)

Using the Pythagorean equation: $l^2 + w^2 = (\sqrt{3})^2$, or

$$l^2 + w^2 = 3 \qquad (2)$$

Solve. We solve the system of equations. First we solve Equation (1) for w.

$$\frac{\sqrt{2}}{l} = w$$

Then we substitute $\frac{\sqrt{2}}{l}$ for w in Equation (2) and solve for l.

$$l^2 + \left(\frac{\sqrt{2}}{l}\right)^2 = 3$$
$$l^2 + \frac{2}{l^2} = 3$$
$$l^4 + 2 = 3l^2 \quad \text{Multiplying by } l^2$$
$$l^4 - 3l^2 + 2 = 0$$
$$u^2 - 3u + 2 = 0 \quad \text{Letting } u = l^2$$
$$(u - 2)(u - 1) = 0$$

$$
\begin{array}{lll}
u - 2 = 0 & or & u - 1 = 0 \\
u = 2 & or & u = 1 \\
l^2 = 2 & or & l^2 = 1 \quad \text{Substituting } l^2 \text{ for } u \\
l = \pm\sqrt{2} & or & l = \pm 1
\end{array}
$$

Length cannot be negative, we only need to consider $l = \sqrt{2}$ or $l = 1$. Since $w = \sqrt{2}/l$, if $l = \sqrt{2}$, $w = 1$ and if $l = 1$, $w = \sqrt{2}$. Length is usually considered to be longer than width, so we have the solution $l = \sqrt{2}$ and $w = 1$, or $(\sqrt{2}, 1)$.

Check. If $l = \sqrt{2}$ and $w = 1$, the area is $\sqrt{2} \cdot 1$, or $\sqrt{2}$. Also $(\sqrt{2})^2 + 1^2 = 2 + 1 = 3 = (\sqrt{3})^2$. The numbers check.

State. The length is $\sqrt{2}$ m, and the width is 1 m.

45. Discussion and Writing Exercise

47. $f(x) = 2x - 5$

The function passes the horizontal-line test, so it has an inverse.

1. Replace $f(x)$ by y: $y = 2x - 5$

2. Interchange x and y: $x = 2y - 5$

3. Solve for y: $x + 5 = 2y$

$$\frac{x + 5}{2} = y$$

4. Replace y by $f^{-1}(x)$: $f^{-1}(x) = \dfrac{x + 5}{2}$

49. $f(x) = \dfrac{x-2}{x+3}$

The function passes the horizontal-line test, so it has an inverse.

1. Replace $f(x)$ by y: $y = \dfrac{x-2}{x+3}$

2. Interchange x and y: $x = \dfrac{y-2}{y+3}$

3. Solve for y: $xy + 3x = y - 2$

$$3x + 2 = y - xy$$
$$3x + 2 = y(1-x)$$
$$\frac{3x+2}{1-x} = y$$

4. Replace y by $f^{-1}(x)$: $f^{-1}(x) = \dfrac{3x+2}{1-x}$

51. $f(x) = |x|$

Since a horizontal line can cross the graph more than once, the function is not one-to-one so it does not have an inverse.

53. $f(x) = 10^x$

The function passes the horizontal-line test, so it has an inverse.

1. Replace $f(x)$ by y: $y = 10^x$

2. Interchange x and y: $x = 10^y$

3. Solve for y: $\log x = \log 10^y$

$$\log x = y \log 10$$
$$\log x = y$$

4. Replace y by $f^{-1}(x)$: $f^{-1}(x) = \log x$

55. $f(x) = x^3 - 4$

The function passes the horizontal-line test, so it has an inverse.

1. Replace $f(x)$ by y: $y = x^3 - 4$

2. Interchange x and y: $x = y^3 - 4$

3. Solve for y: $\quad x + 4 = y^3$

$$\sqrt[3]{x+4} = y$$

4. Replace y by $f^{-1}(x)$: $f^{-1}(x) = \sqrt[3]{x+4}$

57. $f(x) = \ln x$

The function passes the horizontal-line test, so it has an inverse.

1. Replace $f(x)$ by y: $y = \ln x$

2. Interchange x and y: $x = \ln y$

3. Solve for y: $e^x = y$

4. Replace y by $f^{-1}(x)$: $f^{-1}(x) = e^x$

59. Left to the student

61. **Familiarize.** Let x = the length of the longer piece of wire and y = the length of the shorter piece. Then the lengths of the sides of the squares are $\dfrac{x}{4}$ and $\dfrac{y}{4}$.

Translate. The length of the wire is 100 cm, so we have $x + y = 100$. The area of one square is 144 cm^2 greater

than the area of the other, so we have a second equation:
$$\left(\frac{x}{4}\right)^2 + \left(\frac{y}{4}\right)^2 = 144.$$

Solve. The solution of the system of equations is $(61.52, 38.48)$.

Check. The sum of the lengths is $61.52 + 38.48$, or 100 cm. The length of a side of the larger square is $61.52/4$, or 15.38, and the area is $(15.38)^2$, or 236.5444 cm^2. The length of a side of the larger square is $38.48/4$, or 9.62, and the area is $(9.62)^2$, or 92.5444 cm^2. The larger area is 144 cm^2 greater than the smaller area. The answer checks.

State. The wire should be cut so that the length of one piece is 61.52, or $61\dfrac{13}{25}$ cm, and the other is 38.48, or $38\dfrac{12}{25}$ cm.

63.
$$R = C$$
$$100x + x^2 = 80x + 1500$$
$$x^2 + 20x - 1500 = 0$$
$$(x - 30)(x + 50) = 0$$
$$x = 30 \ or \ x = -50$$

Since the number of units cannot be negative, the solution of the problem is 30. Thus, 30 units must be sold in order to break even.

65. $\quad a + b = \dfrac{5}{6}, \qquad (1)$

$$\frac{a}{b} + \frac{b}{a} = \frac{13}{6} \qquad (2)$$

$$b = \frac{5}{6} - a = \frac{5-6a}{6} \qquad \text{Solving Eq. (1) for } b$$

$$\frac{a}{\dfrac{5-6a}{6}} + \frac{\dfrac{5-6a}{6}}{a} = \frac{13}{6} \qquad \begin{array}{l}\text{Substituting for } b \\ \text{in Eq. (2)}\end{array}$$

$$\frac{6a}{5-6a} + \frac{5-6a}{6a} = \frac{13}{6}$$

$$36a^2 + 25 - 60a + 36a^2 = 65a - 78a^2$$

$$150a^2 - 125a + 25 = 0$$

$$6a^2 - 5a + 1 = 0$$

$$(3a - 1)(2a - 1) = 0$$

$$a = \frac{1}{3} \ or \ a = \frac{1}{2}$$

Substitute for a and solve for b.

When $a = \dfrac{1}{3}$, $b = \dfrac{5 - 6\left(\dfrac{1}{3}\right)}{6} = \dfrac{1}{2}$.

When $a = \dfrac{1}{2}$, $b = \dfrac{5 - 6\left(\dfrac{1}{2}\right)}{6} = \dfrac{1}{3}$.

The pairs $\left(\dfrac{1}{3}, \dfrac{1}{2}\right)$ and $\left(\dfrac{1}{2}, \dfrac{1}{3}\right)$ check. They are the solutions.